THE GREATEST STORY
EVER TOLD

H H Osborn

Apologia Publications

ISBN   1 901566 01 3

Published in the UK by
Apologia Publications
5 St Matthew's Road,
Winchester   SO22
UK

Printed in UK by Redwood Books, Trowbridge, Wiltshire

Preface

THE GREATEST STORY EVER TOLD   is a compilation of biblical passages arranged so that a theme for each day is drawn from the Bible narrative in chronological order, as far as possible. The aim is to combine a teaching and a devotional role, particularly for readers in areas where there are few, if any, other aids to an understanding of the Bible. It was to meet this particular need that these readings were initially compiled. (See inside back cover.)

The introduction of the theme for each day is followed by quotations from the Bible relevant to the theme. The last paragraph, printed in italics, is of a devotional character. The wording of the quotations has been derived from consulting and reflecting on several translations of the Bible.

Further study of the daily themes is encouraged by lists of daily readings to be found on the inside back cover. These relate to wider themes or groups of themes. There is also, in the final pages, a comprehensive list of references.

The translation of 'YHWH' by 'Eternal-God'.

A significant departure from common practice has been the replacement of the title: "LORD" (in capital letters), by: "Eternal-God". Traditionally, and in most English translations, the name "YHWH" in the Hebrew text, is printed, 'LORD'. It is felt that the meaning of many passages of the Bible is made stronger when the original sense of 'Yahweh', the 'ETERNAL I AM' is maintained rather than by 'LORD', with its implications of a personal relationship. The nearest literal translation, "I AM", would not flow easily for common usage and 'Yahweh' or 'Jehovah' makes the meaning more distant. Many languages into which the Bible has been translated, appear to find a word which indicates the eternal nature of God, as conveyed by the original Hebrew. As an example of this, the familiar opening line of the 23rd Psalm: "The LORD is my shepherd," is rendered in these Bible Readings as "The Eternal-God is my shepherd." In French, this is: "L'Eternal est mon berger," and, in the language of the country in which the compiler served as a missionary (Rwanda): "Uwiteka ni we mwungeri wanjye". In both cases, 'L'Eternal' and 'Uwiteka' emphasise the eternal character of God. This usage should facilitate the translation of these readings into languages in which a translation of the Bible already exists.

The dangers of erroneous associations due to juxtaposing texts.

Two major factors have been faced in compiling these Bible readings. The first lies in the danger of conveying erroneous ideas through the selection and juxtaposition of biblical quotations. To minimise this danger, the use of square brackets has been adopted to insert a name or phrase to clarify the meaning where there could be a danger of misunderstanding.

(a) Where one passage follows another from two difference sources, this difference is indicated, where considered necessary, by a name which appears as [Moses:], [Jesus:], [Paul:]. Although the name may not appear in that place in the original text, the square brackets indicate that the name stated is the source of what follows - whether written or spoken. This should avoid imputing quotations to the wrong source.

(b) There is a danger that a quotation from a parable, allegory or vision may be misunderstood as being historical, and vice versa. Where, therefore, the context is not clear in the quotation cited, a phrase is inserted in square brackets to clarify its nature. An example of this occurs in Day 365:

[John:] I saw [in a vision] a new heaven and a new earth.

(c) God is ONE, in the sense that there is only ONE GOD. God is also a Family of Three who are each God - 'God the Father', 'God the Son' and 'God the Holy Spirit'. They are not three individual 'Gods' who act independently of each other. While the term 'gods' has meaning when, for instance, it refers to trinities of gods in other religions, the term 'Gods' is meaningless or false in biblical theology. The three God-Persons are each equally 'God', and they are also, together, 'God'. The Three God-Persons, who are each God, are bound to each other in a bond of 'perfect light' - everything (with one exception) is known to all three. The exception is that only 'God the Father' knew, according to Jesus, when He, 'God the Son', is coming to the earth again. And they are bound together in a bond of 'perfect love' - each always acts for the highest good of the others. In order to help in the understanding of passages where part of a title of God is given, the missing element is included in square brackets. As an illustration: "May the grace of our Lord Jesus Christ [God the Son], and the love of God [the Father] and the fellowship of [God] the Holy Spirit, be with you all."

The importance of the way these titles for God are written lies in maintaining both the biblical truths: (i) There is only ONE GOD - the God-Family of 'God the Father', 'God the Son' and 'God the Holy Spirit', and (ii) 'God the Father', 'God the Son' and 'God the Holy Spirit' are separately, individually God, who relate to each other in distinctive ways and are capable of acting independently, although they never have done so nor ever will do so.

In the introductions to the Daily Readings, the term 'God-Family' is used to refer to the ONE GOD who is 'God the Father', 'God the Son', and 'God the Holy Spirit'. Where reference is made to all those who have been given 'new birth' into the family of God, this appears as the 'God-family'.

In view of the way in which the term, 'Son of God' is given a very human and even degrading sense in some other religions, the title: 'God the Son' is used extensively in these readings to correspond with the titles of the other two members of the God-Family: 'God the Father' and 'God the Holy Spirit'. However, wherever the term 'Son of God' appears in the original of any quotation, that form is maintained.

Most modern English translations use the lower case: 'h', in printing the pronouns which refer to God. In deference to the wide preference for maintaining reverence and dignity in references to God, the capital 'H' is used in these Bible Readings for He, Him, His, Himself. To extend this further would be cumbersome.

Theological standpoints

The second factor which has been faced is that, in any translation of the Bible, although the aim is to convey as accurately as possible the sense of the original, the theological understanding of the translator is often a significant factor in the form of words used.

(a) The 'hiddenness' of God

For the compiler, the Christian faith only makes sense, when considered in the context of the physical universe as well as the spiritual domain. God brought all that exists into being in a particular way and hid Himself in it in the sense that He is not visibly or tangibly observable to the people He created. As indicated in Paul's speech to the Areopagus, in Athens, (see back cover), this was by design, so that every person would have to search for Him individually and would only find Him given certain conditions on the searcher's part.

An essential element in the 'hiddenness' of God is that He is not immediately observable either in the physical universe, in people or in the Bible. That is as He planned it to be. The question arises in acute form relative to the first 10 chapters of Genesis. Many Christians consider these to be myth or allegory. True history is often considered to have begun with Abraham. Science appears to confirm this. In the view of the compiler, it requires as, if not greater faith, to believe the scientific theories as that everything happened as the Bible records. Neither view can be proved scientifically; both are acts of faith. This is a consequence of the planned 'hiddenness' of God. In these Readings, quotations from the early chapters of Genesis are included as valid history in the same way as the rest of the Bible.

(b) Baptism

The practice of baptism varies worldwide. The complier's view is that the term 'baptism' refers primarily to the spiritual experience of conversion whereby the non-Christian, following repentance of sin and faith in Christ, is 'buried with Christ' spiritually, as far as life in the family of Satan is concerned, and rises with Christ spiritually into 'newness of life' in the family of God. The form of the outward ceremony may vary considerably but is most effective when it most faithfully represents in visible form the invisible spiritual experience. This view is reflected in references in these Readings to baptism. It is hoped that this interpretation will be acceptable to those whose beliefs about the outward rite may vary.

(c) Pain and evil

The existence of evil and suffering in the world is often considered as a problem. Here it is seen as following logically from the fact that God is hidden so that He is not observable in any visible or tangible sense. He also ensures that an equally real Satan is also hidden. Pain and evil entered the world through the sin of Adam and Eve and everybody is subject to the general effects of sin. Everyone born since then is born into the family of Satan. God's purpose in hiding Himself—and Satan—is to give them the opportunity to observe and compare in the world the effects of life in the family of Satan and life in the family of God. The former includes pain and suffering; the latter includes that which is of God, as observable in the universe, explained in His Word, the Bible, and illustrated by the life of Jesus Christ and His church. Everyone has the opportunity, either to do nothing about it and remain in the family of Satan for eternity, or to reject life in the family of Satan by repenting of sin and trusting in Christ's sacrifice for it, so allowing God to give the repentant sinner 'new birth' into His family and eternal life with Him, now and for ever.

'Brethren', 'brothers' and 'brothers and sisters'.

The use of the term 'brethren' in the New Testament sometimes refers only to men, but at other times it includes men and women. Some modern translations use the term 'brothers' to replace the now outdated 'brethren'. However, in common usage the term 'brothers' refers to men only. This is maintained in these Readings when the reference is only to men, as when, for instance, Joseph addressed his 'brethren'. He obviously meant only men as there were no women there. The term 'brothers' is, therefore a wholly appropriate translation. Where the term 'brethren' includes women, as, for instance when Paul wrote: "Finally, brethren, rejoice in the Lord," the inclusive term 'brothers and sisters' is used.

These Daily Readings are offered with the sincere prayer that, although many more passages could be quoted, these will encourage everyone to read the rest of the Bible, to come to know God in a personal way through being 'born again' into His family, to live their lives to the full, as Jesus promised, in the family of God and of His people worldwide, and for their individual stories to become part of THE GREATEST STORY EVER TOLD.

H H Osborn
Winchester
May 1998

Contents

Remember:

1 THE GREATEST STORY EVER TOLD is not a human invention. It is the story of the universe and of people as God, their Creator, has revealed it, and still reveals it, to people who genuinely want to know.

2 God is hidden in the Bible as He is in the whole of creation. He only reveals Himself to those who are genuine in their search for Him and honest in the way they act on the truth they know.

3 THE GREATEST STORY EVER TOLD is ONE story. It all goes together. Any one part of it must not be taken as the whole truth by itself. Everything it says is only true as it fits in with what all of it is saying.

4 THE GREATEST STORY EVER TOLD was written for a purpose which the Bible makes clear. God, who created people, wants everyone of those people to reject sin as the way of life in the 'family of Satan', into which they are born, and to desire and ask Him to give them 'new birth' into 'the family of God'. He will only do that if they really want it. This the story of the way that God is achieving that end.

6 The readings for each day give insights into the events which God has caused to happen. From these every one who reads them has the opportunity of coming to understand why they were created, what life is like in the 'family of Satan' and in the 'family of God', and how they can, if they want to, be 'born again' into the 'family of God' and live full lives in His family.

7 An important difference between this, THE GREATEST STORY EVER TOLD, and any other story, is that the Author, the Creator-God Himself, is present as people read it and will give understanding as He sees how genuine and honest the reader is. The human mind cannot on its own discover truth, even when it is stated clearly in the Bible. God Himself has promised to make the truth clear as He is Himself present to give understanding.

8. The last paragraph each day focuses on some aspects of the theme for the day for meditation, prayer and, possibly, action.

A prayer:
O God, as I (we) read your word, open my (our) understanding to your truth and help me (us) to be willing to be obedient to what you show me (us). Amen.

Day 1

God is the eternal 'Creator-God'. He was there at the beginning of time and He will be there at the end. Every thing and all life were created by Him. He made everything perfect at the beginning and He was very pleased with everything He had made. He created the universe and people for a great purpose. This was the first event in the greatest story the world has ever been told.

God created the heavens and the earth

In the beginning God created the universe: the heavens and the earth. ... Then God said, "Let there be light," and there was light. And God saw that the light was good ... Then God said, "Let the earth produce vegetation: plants yielding seed, and every kind of fruit with its seed." ... God saw that it was good. ... Then God said, "Let there be lights in the sky: the greater light to govern the day and the lesser light to govern the night." And it was so. ... God said, "Let the waters bring forth many living creatures, and the expanse of the sky teem with birds that fly in the air." So God created every living, moving thing in the waters, according to their kinds, and every bird according to its kind. ... Then God said, "Let the earth produce living creatures according to their kinds: wild animals and livestock, each according to its kind." God saw that it was good ... Then God said, "Let us make man like us and let them rule over the fish of the sea, the birds of the air, over all the wild animals and livestock. ... And it was so. God saw all that He had made and it was very good." [1]

The heavens were made by the word of the Eternal-God, the array of stars by His breath. ... Let all the world fear the Eternal-God; let all the people revere Him, for He spoke, and it was so; He commanded, and it stood firm. [2] It is by faith that we understand that the universe was created at God's command, so that what is visible cannot be explained by what is seen. [3]

[Paul:] "The God who made the world and everything in it is the Lord of the universe and does not live in temples made by human hands. ... He made every nation of people, from one single man, so that they should inhabit the whole earth. He determined the times when they would have life, and the exact places where they would live. God did this so that people would have to seek for Him, and perhaps reach out for Him and find Him, though He is near each one of us. 'For in Him we live and move and have our being.'" [4]

In the beginning you [God] laid the foundations of the earth, and the heavens are the work of your hands. They will disappear, but you remain; they will wear out like a garment. Like clothing they will be changed and discarded. But you never change, and your years will never come to an end. [5]

---

[1] Genesis 1:1,3,11,16,20,24,31   [2] Psalm 33:6,8-9   [3] Hebrews 11:3   [4] Acts 17:26-28   [5] Psalm 102:25-27

Day 2

God created people to be like Him. They are different from every other part of creation, including animals and birds. They alone were made 'in His image', that is, able to know good and evil and to think and act as God can, although in more limited ways. Only people are able to talk to God and to understand what He says to them. That people were made in the likeness of their Creator gives to each one of them a very great value. It also means that they have an ability and a responsibility to live their lives in the light of the truth that they are created beings.

God created Man in His own image

God said, "Let us make man like us, and let them rule over the fish of the sea, the birds of the air, over all the earth and over all the creatures that move on the earth." So God created man in His own image. ... He created them male and female.[1]

The Eternal God formed man from the ground and breathed into him the breath of life, and man became a living being.[2] When God created man, He made him in His own likeness.[3] Whoever sheds the blood of a man, by men shall his blood be shed; for every man bears the image of God who created him.[4]

The Eternal-God is merciful, He will not abandon or destroy you, nor will He forget the covenant He made with you. Ask about the days gone by, long before your time, ever since the day God created man on the earth.[5] "It was I who made the earth and created mankind upon it. It was my hands which spread out the heavens "[6]

This is what the Eternal-God says, He who created the heavens and spread them out, who shaped the earth and all that comes out of it, who gave breath to His people, and life to the creatures that move on it: "I, the Eternal-God, have called you in righteousness; I have held you by your hand."[7]

Worship the Eternal-God with gladness and come before Him with singing. Know that He is the Eternal-God. It is He who made us, and we belong to Him. We, His people, are the sheep of His pasture.[8]

With the tongue we praise the Lord and Father, and with it we curse people who were made in God's likeness. ... My brothers and sisters this should not be so.[9]

The heavens are yours and the earth is yours. You founded the world and all that is in it.[10] When I look at your heavens, made by your fingers, at the moon and the stars, which you set in place, what is man that you think of him, the son of man that you care for him?[11]

---

[1] Genesis 1:26-27 [2] Genesis 2:7 [3] Genesis 5:1 [4] Genesis 9:6 [5] Deuteronomy 4:32 [6] Isaiah 45:12
[7] Isaiah 42:5-6 [8] Psalm 100:2-3 [9] James 3:9-10 [10] Psalm 89:11 [11] Psalm 8:3-4

Day 3

God created the first person to be both man and woman. Then He made that one person into two separate people - male and female. Although different from each other, men and women are equal before God. Both have roles to play in life which are different but equally important. They are also very interdependent. They were created so that they would need each other to fulfil all that God planned for them.

God created man - male and female

The man gave names to all the livestock, the birds of the air and all the wild animals. But for Adam there was no suitable helper. So the Eternal-God caused the man to fall into a deep sleep. While he was asleep, He took one of the man's ribs from his side and closed up the place. Then the Eternal-God made a woman from the rib He had taken from the man, and He brought her to the man. The man said, "This is indeed bone of my bones and flesh of my flesh. She will be called 'woman', for she was taken out of man." [1]

This is the account of Adam's descendants. When God created man, He made him like Himself. He created them male and female and blessed them. When they were created, He called them "man". [2]

Jesus said, "Have you not read that, at the beginning, the Creator-God who made them, made them male and female." [3]

[Paul:] I want you to know that the head of every man is Christ, and the head of a woman is her husband, and the head of Christ [God the Son] is God [the Father]. ... However, in the Lord, 'woman' is not independent of 'man', nor is 'man' independent of 'woman'. For just as 'woman' came from 'man', so also 'man' is born of 'woman'. Both 'man and 'woman' come from God. [4]

In Christ Jesus, you are all sons of God through faith in Him, for all of you who were baptised into Christ have clothed yourselves with Him. As you are all one in Christ Jesus, there is neither Jew nor Greek, slave nor free, male nor female.[5]

This is what the Eternal-God, the Almighty, says: "Once again old men and women will sit in the streets of Jerusalem, each with a stick in hand, because of their old age. And boys and girls will be playing the city streets." [6]

At that time, I will pour out my Spirit on everyone. Your sons and daughters will prophesy, your old men will dream dreams, your young men will see visions. I will pour out my Spirit in those days even on slaves, both men and women. [7]

[1] Genesis 2:20-23 [2] Genesis 5:1-2 [3] Matthew 19:4 [4] 1 Corinthians 11:3,11 [5] Galatians 3:26-28
[6] Zechariah 8:4-5 [7] Joel 2:28-29

Day 4

God designed people to live in pairs—one man and one woman—as 'one body'. In a marriage relationship, a husband and wife commit themselves to each other—to love, support and submit to each other, and to make a home in which to bring up the children God gives them. A marriage is to last as long as both partners live. The relationship is so special that any wrong relationship between either marriage partner and any other men or women spoils the marriage.

God planned for marriage

God said, "It is not good that man should be alone. I will make a helper for him. ... Then the Eternal-God made a woman from the rib he had taken from the man, and He brought her to the man. ... That is why a man leaves his father and mother and becomes united to his wife, and they become one flesh. [1]

Some Pharisees came to Jesus and tested Him. They asked, "Is it lawful for a man to divorce his wife for any reason whatsoever?" He replied, "Have you not read that at the beginning the Creator made them male and female so that a man leaves his father and mother and becomes united to his wife, and they become one flesh? So they are no longer two, but one body. Do not let anyone divide what God has joined together." [2]

Marriage should be honoured by everyone, and the marriage bed kept holy, for God will judge adulterers and all who are sexually immoral. [3]

[Paul:] The body is meant not for sexual immorality but for the Lord, and the Lord for the body. ... Do you not know that your bodies are members of Christ. Can I take the members of Christ and join them with a prostitute. Never! Surely you know that anyone who unites his body with a prostitute becomes one body with her? For it is written, 'The two will become one flesh." [4]

Submit to each other for Christ's sake. Wives, submit to your husbands as to the Lord. ... Husbands, love your wives, as Christ loved the church and sacrificed Himself to make her holy, making her clean by washing her with water through the word, and presenting her to Himself as a glorious church ... holy and blameless. Similarly, husbands should love their wives as they love their own bodies. Whoever loves his wife loves himself. ... That is why a man leaves his father and mother and becomes united to his wife, and they become one flesh. [5]

As a young man marries a virgin so will your maker marry you. ... As a bridegroom rejoices in his bride, so your God will rejoice in you. [6]

[1] Genesis 2:18,22, 24   [2] Matthew 19:3-6   [3] Hebrews 13:4   [4] 1 Corinthians 6:13-16
[5] Ephesians 5:21-22, 25-31   [6] Isaiah 62:5

Day 5

Satan is the chief of all the angel spirits who were created by God to be good but who rebelled against Him and so became evil. Satan is God's enemy. He deceives people and falsely accuses them in order to keep them in his kingdom. God allows him and his evil companions to work so that people may have the possibility of seeing the effects of his rule in people, and then freely choosing either to continue to be in Satan's family or to reject that family and be 'born again' into God's family. At first there was no person through whom Satan could speak to people, so he used a snake.

Satan, the accuser

The serpent was more crafty than any other wild animal that the Eternal-God had made. He said to the woman, "Did God really say, 'You are not to eat from any tree in the garden'?" [1]

Jesus said to them, "If God were your Father, you would love me, for I came from God the Father and now here I am with you. I have not come on my own; it was He who sent me. Why are my words not clear to you? It is because you cannot hear what I am saying. You belong to your father, the devil, and it is natural for you to want to carry out his desires. He was a murderer from the beginning; he did not speak the truth because truth means nothing to him. When he lies, he behaves according to his nature. He is both a liar and the father of lies. [2]

[John:] He who habitually sins is a child of the devil. The devil has been sinning from the very beginning. The reason why the Son of God appeared was to destroy the work of the devil. No one who is born of God will continue to sin. God's seed remains in him. He cannot go on sinning because of his new life in God. [3]

[John] And I saw [in a vision] an angel coming down from heaven holding the keys to the abyss and grasping a great chain in his hand. He seized the dragon, that ancient serpent, who is the devil, or Satan, and put him in chains for a thousand years. He threw him into the Abyss, locked the entrance and sealed it to prevent him from deceiving the nations until the thousand years had ended. ... And the devil, who deceived them, was thrown into the lake of burning sulphur where the beast and the false prophet were, and they will be tormented day and night for ever and ever." [4]

[Peter:] Be disciplined and alert. Your enemy the devil is like a roaring lion prowling around, looking for someone to devour. Resist him, standing strong in the faith, knowing that your brothers throughout the world are having to endure the same kind of sufferings. [5]

[1] Genesis 3:1   [2] John 8:42-44   [3] 1 John 3:8   [4] Revelation 20: 1-3,10   [5] 1 Peter 5:8

Day 6

The first man and woman were sinless and in a close relationship with God, their Creator. At first they never did anything which was not pleasing to Him. Then they were given the opportunity of doing something which was not His will for them because to do it would bring them great harm: they would die physically—they would not live for ever, and they would die spiritually—they would be separated from God, their Creator. They, both Adam and Eve, listened to Satan's lies, disobeyed God and so rebelled against Him, and they died, spiritually at first, and then some years later, physically.

Sin enters through Adam and Eve

The Eternal-God planted a garden in Eden, in the east. There He put the man He had created. The Eternal-God made all kinds of trees to grow from the ground, trees that were pleasant to look at and good for food. In the centre of the garden were the 'tree of life' and the 'tree of the knowledge of good and evil'. ... The Eternal-God put the man in the Garden of Eden to dig it and look after it. He commanded the man, "You are free to eat from any tree in the garden except from the 'tree of the knowledge of good and evil', for when you eat its fruit you will surely die." [1]

Now the serpent was more crafty than any other of the wild animals the Eternal-God had made. He said to the woman, "Did God really say, 'You must not eat from any tree in the garden'?" The woman answered the serpent, "We may eat fruit from the trees in the garden, but God also said, 'You must not eat fruit from the tree that is in the middle of the garden. If you eat of its fruit you will die.'" The serpent said to the woman, "You will not surely die, God knows that when you eat its fruit your eyes will be opened, you will be like God Himself, and you too will know good and evil." When the woman understood that the fruit of the tree was good for food as well as pleasing to the sight and desirable for gaining knowledge, she took some and ate it. And she gave some to her husband who was with her, and he ate it." [2]

Sin came into the world through one man, and death through sin, and in this way death came to all men, because all have sinned. ... In fact, death reigned from the time of Adam to the time of Moses, even over those who did not sin by disobeying a command as Adam did. He was the pattern of the One to come. ... For if, by the trespass of one man [Adam], death reigned over everyone through that one man, how much more will those who receive God's unlimited grace and the free gift of right-eousness, reign in life through the one Man, Jesus Christ. [3]

As death came through a man, so the resurrection of the dead comes also through a Man. For as in Adam all are dead [spiritually], so in Christ all will be made alive. [4]

[1] Genesis 2:8-9,15-17   [2] Genesis 3:1-6   [3] Romans 5:12,14-17   [4] 1 Corinthians 15:21-22

Day 7

Before Adam and Eve sinned against God they were 'alive spiritually' and were 'one' with Him. They were members of His family. As soon as they sinned they 'died spiritually'. They could no longer be members of His family. They were separated from Him by their sin, although He was never very far from them. Satan welcomed Adam and Eve into his family. From then onwards all their children and their descendants have been born into the family of Satan, separated from God, and that includes people who are alive now.

Sin separates people from God

When the woman saw that the fruit of the tree was good for food, pleasing to the eyes and desirable for getting wisdom, she took some of it and ate it. And she gave some to her husband who was with her, and he, too, ate it. ... Then they heard the sound of the Eternal-God walking in the garden in the cool of the day, and they hid from Him among the trees of the garden. God called to the man, "Where are you?" He answered, "I heard your sound in the garden, and I was afraid. I was naked so I hid myself from you" The Eternal-God said, "Who told you that you were naked? Have you eaten from the tree that I commanded you not to touch?" The man said, "The woman you gave me to be with me, she gave me some fruit from the tree, and I ate it."

Then the Eternal-God said to the woman, "What have you done?" The woman said, "The serpent deceived me, and I ate." ... To the woman He said, "I will make childbearing much more painful for you; it will be with pain that you will give birth to children. Your desire will be for your husband, and he will be over you." To Adam he said, "Because you listened to your wife and ate from the tree from which I had forbidden you to eat, the ground is cursed because of you. By hard toil you will eat your food until you return to the ground from which you were taken. Dust you are and to dust you will return." ... So the Eternal-God drove him out of the Garden of Eden to work the ground from which he had been taken. And He placed an angel with a flaming sword to guard the way to the 'tree of life.' [1]

[Isaiah:] The arm of the Eternal-God is not too short to save, nor His ear too dull to hear. It is your iniquities which have separated you from your God and your sins which have hidden His face from you so that He does not hear. [2]

[Paul:] God is just. ... He will inflict retribution on those who do not know God and do not obey the gospel of our Lord Jesus Christ. They will suffer everlasting destruction and eternal separation from the presence of the Lord. [3]

For the wages of sin is death, but the free gift of God is eternal life in Christ Jesus our Lord. [4]

[1] Genesis 3:6-13,16-19, 23-24   [2] Isaiah 59:2   [3] 2 Thessalonians 1:6-9   [3] Romans 6:23

Day 8

Men and women were created with strong urges to unite sexually and so increase love for each other and bring children into the world. But this sexual urge has to be disciplined and expressed only in marriage, otherwise God's purposes in marriage are spoiled or destroyed. To make this possible, God ordered people to dress modestly, each according to his or her sex. To demonstrate this, He made the first clothes as a covering for both Adam and Eve.

God planned for the wearing of clothes

The Eternal-God made a woman from the rib He had taken out of the man, and He brought her to the man. ... Although the man and the woman, his wife, were both naked, they felt no shame. [1]

When the woman saw that the fruit of the tree was desirable ... she took some, ate it, and gave some to her husband, who was with her, and he ate it. Then their eyes were opened, and they realised that they were naked. They sewed together fig leaves to make coverings for themselves. The man and his wife heard the sound of the Eternal-God walking in the garden in the cool of the day, and they hid from Him among the trees of the garden. The Eternal-God called to the man, "Where are you?" He answered, "I heard you in the garden, and I was afraid. I was naked, so I hid." God said, "Who told you that you were naked? Have you eaten from the tree that I commanded you not to eat from?" The man said, "The woman you gave to be with me gave me some fruit from the tree and I ate it." ... The Eternal-God made garments of skin and clothed Adam and his wife with them. [2]

[Moses:] A woman must not wear men's clothes, nor a man wear women's clothes. To do this is detestable to the Eternal-God, your God. [3]

[Paul:] I want men everywhere to lift up holy hands in prayer, with no anger or disputing, and women to dress suitably with modesty and decency, not with braided hair or gold or jewellery or expensive clothes, but with actions that are good and appropriate for women who profess to worship God.[4]

[Peter:] Wives ... Your beauty should not be in the outward adorning of yourselves, such as braiding your hair and wearing gold, jewellery and fine clothes. Rather, it should come from your inner self, the unfading beauty of a gentle and quiet spirit."5

[Paul:] Let us put away the works of darkness and put on the armour of light. Let us live decently, as in the daylight, not in revelling and drunkenness, nor in sexual immorality and debauchery, nor in quarrelling and jealousy. Rather, clothe yourselves with the Lord Jesus Christ, and make no provision to gratify the desires of the sinful nature. [6]

[1] Genesis 2:22,25 [2] Genesis 3:6-12,21 [3] Deuteronomy 22:5 [4] 1 Timothy 2:8-9
[5] 1 Peter 3:1-4 [6] Romans 13:13-14

Day 9

Both Cain and Abel wanted to make offerings to God. They chose the best they knew: grain from Cain's crops and a young sheep from Abel's flock. God accepted Abel's offering but He rejected Cain's. God had something He wanted to teach them. Cain did not like what he was told and this questions his motives for making an offering at all. When shown his error he refused to repent, that is, to change his mind. He made things worse by killing His brother. God showed very clearly that we can only worship Him in ways He approves, and we are responsible to Him for the way we behave to each other.

Cain murders Abel

Some time later, Cain brought some of the produce of the soil as an offering to the Eternal-God. But Abel brought fat portions from the first-born of his flock. The Eternal-God looked with favour on Abel and his offering, but he was displeased with Cain and his offering. Cain was very angry, and his face was downcast. Then the Eternal-God said to Cain, "Why are you angry and why is your face downcast? If you do well, will you not be accepted? But if you do not do what is right, sin is lurking at your door. It desires to defeat you, but you must master it. Then Cain said to his brother Abel, "Let us go out to the field." While they were in the field, Cain attacked his brother Abel and killed him.

Then the Eternal-God said to Cain, "Where is your brother Abel?" He replied, "I do not know, am I my brother's keeper?" The Eternal-God said, "What have you done? Listen! Your brother's blood is crying out to me from the ground. ... Now you are cursed and driven from the ground which opened its mouth to receive your brother's blood from your hand. When you till the ground, it will no longer yield its strength for you. You will be a fugitive and wanderer on the earth."

Cain said to the Eternal-God, "My punishment is greater than I can bear. Today you are driving me from the land, and I will be hidden from you. I will be a restless wanderer on the earth, and whoever meets me will kill me." But the Eternal-God said to him, "Not so; if anyone kills Cain, he will suffer vengeance sevenfold." Then the Eternal-God put a mark on Cain so that no one who found him would kill him. Then Cain left the presence of the Eternal-God and lived in the land of Nod. [1]

[Jude:] Certain intruders whose condemnation was written about long ago have secretly slipped in among you. They are ungodly men, who change the grace of God into a licence for immorality. ... They go the way of Cain. [2]

[John:] Do not be like Cain, who was from the evil one and murdered his brother. And why did he murder him? Because his own actions were evil and his brothers were righteous. [3]

[1] Genesis 4:3-16   [2] Jude 4,11   [3] 1 John 3:12

Day 10

We do not know whether Cain and Abel knew what to do to please God before they decided to worship Him by giving Him gifts. Both chose to do what they thought was right. We are not told how, but God made it clear that what Abel did was acceptable to Him but what Cain did was not. God was teaching an important lesson: no one who was a sinner could worship Him without there being blood shed, that is, a life sacrificed, for his or her sin. At that time, the shedding of the blood of a sacrificial animal was a symbol of the blood Jesus would shed for sin centuries later.

God shows Cain and Abel how to worship Him

In the course of time, Cain brought some of the produce of the soil as an offering to the Eternal-God, but Abel brought fat portions from the first-born of his flock. The Eternal-God looked with favour on Abel and his offering, but He was displeased with Cain and his offering. [1]

Then [after the flood] Noah built an altar to the Eternal-God. He took some of all the clean animals and clean birds, and sacrificed them as burnt offerings on it. The Eternal-God smelled the pleasing aroma and said in His heart: "I will never again curse the ground because of man, even though every inclination of his heart is evil from childhood." [2] God blessed Noah and his sons, saying to them ... "Everything that lives and moves will be food for you ... but you must not eat meat that has its lifeblood still in it." [3] "For the life of the flesh is in the blood, and I have given it to you to make atonement for yourselves on the altar; it is the blood that makes atonement for one's life. ... You shall not eat the blood of any creature, because its life is in its blood." [4]

When Moses had given every commandment of the law, ... he took the blood of calves and goats, ... saying, "This is the blood of the covenant which God has commanded you to keep." ... In fact, the law demands that nearly everything be cleansed with blood, and without the shedding of blood there is no forgiveness of sins." [5]

By faith Abel offered God a better sacrifice than Cain did, and he was, therefore, commended as a righteous man. God approved of his offerings. By his faith he still speaks, even though he is dead.[6]

After supper He [Jesus] took the cup, saying, "This cup is the new covenant in my blood which is poured out for you." [7]

Every priest stands and performs his religious duties day after day. Again and again he offers the same sacrifices which can never take away sins. But when this priest [Jesus Christ] had offered one sacrifice for sins, once for all, He sat down at the right hand of God [the Father]. [8]

[1] Genesis 4:3-5   [2] Genesis 8:20-21   [3] Genesis 9:1,3-4   [4] Leviticus 17:11,14   [5] Hebrews 9:19-22
[6] Hebrews 11:4   [7] Luke 22:20   [8] Hebrews 10:11-12

Day 11

The first city ever built was called Enoch. Cities enable people to live near each other and enable them to work together. They have a special attraction for evil people. The greatest evil city was Babylon. Jerusalem was called the Holy City because God linked His name with it. Babylon was destroyed and all that it represented will also be destroyed. The last city, the 'New Jerusalem', that is, heaven, will last for ever.

The great cities of the world

Cain left the presence of the Eternal-God and lived in the land of Nod, east of Eden ... There Cain built a city and named it after his son, Enoch.[1]

Abram lived in the land of Canaan and Lot settled among the cities of the plain. He pitched his tents near Sodom. Now the people of Sodom were very wicked and were sinning greatly against the Eternal-God. [2] Then the Eternal-God rained down burning sulphur on Sodom and Gomorrah. ... And so He overthrew those cities and the entire plain, including all who lived there.[3]

[God said to Jonah:] "Should I not be concerned about the great city of Nineveh. It has more than a hundred and twenty thousand people in it who cannot tell their right hand from their left, and also many animals."[4]

Babylon, the jewel of the kingdoms, the glory and pride of the Babylonians, will be overthrown, as when God destroyed Sodom and Gomorrah. [5] ... "Fallen! Fallen is Babylon the Great, ... her sins are piled high up to heaven, and God has remembered her iniquities. ... The great city of Babylon will be thrown down with great violence, never to be found again. [6]

David captured the stronghold of Zion ... and called it the city of David. [7] The Eternal-God said to David, ... "In this temple and in Jerusalem, which I have chosen out of all the tribes of Israel, I will put my name for ever." [8] The Eternal-God loves the gates of Zion. ... Glorious things are said of you, O city of God. [9]

[John:] Then I saw [in a vision] a new heaven and a new earth, for the first heaven and the first earth had passed away, and there was no more sea. I saw the Holy City, the new Jerusalem, coming down out of heaven from God, prepared as a bride adorned for her husband. And I heard a loud voice from the throne saying, "Now God's dwelling is with men, and He will live with them." ... I saw no temple in the city, because the Lord God Almighty and the Lamb are its temple. The city needs no sun nor moon to shine on it, for the glory of God is its light, and the Lamb is its lamp. ... Nothing impure will enter it, nor will anyone who practises what is shameful or deceitful, but only those whose names are written in the Lamb's book of life. [10]

[1] Genesis 4:16-17 [2] Genesis 13:12-13 [3] Genesis 19:24-25 [4] Jonah 4:11 [5] Isaiah 13:19
[6] Revelation 18:2,5,21 [7] 2 Samuel 5:7,9 [8] 2 Kings 21:7 [9] Psalm 87:2-3 [10] Revelation 21:1-3, 22-23, 27

Day 12

Jabal was the first nomad or wanderer who is recorded as living from the meat of domesticated animals rather than by hunting wild animals. Abraham was the first nomad with a goal to aim for. That made him a 'pilgrim'. He was a pilgrim in a foreign land but he had God's promise that one day he and his descendants would live in that land. Jesus and all who follow Him are spiritual strangers in the world and pilgrims in this life. There is a goal to aim for: an eternal and secure City of God to which all Christians look forward with great anticipation.

Nomads and pilgrims

Lamech married two wives, one named Adah. ... Adah gave birth to Jabal. He was the father of those who live in tents and keep livestock. [1]

Jacob said to Pharaoh, "The years of my pilgrimage are one hundred and thirty. My years have been few and hard, and they are not equal to the years of the pilgrimage of my fathers." [2]

As they were going along the road, a man said to Him, "I will follow you wherever you go." Jesus replied, "Foxes have holes and birds of the air have nests, but the Son of Man has nowhere to lay his head." [3]

By faith Abraham, when called to set out for a place he would later receive as his inheritance, obeyed and went, even though he did not know where he was going. By faith he stayed in the promised land like a stranger in a foreign country. He lived in tents, as did Isaac and Jacob, who were heirs with him of the same promise. For he looked forward to the city that had foundations, whose architect and builder is God. ... All these died in faith. Although they did not receive the things promised, they saw them in the future and welcomed them from a distance. They admitted that they were foreigners and strangers on earth. Such people show that they are looking for a homeland of their own. If they had been thinking of the country they had left, they would have found an opportunity to return. Instead, they longed for a better country, a heavenly one. Therefore God is not ashamed to be called their God. It is for them He has prepared a city. [4]

[Paul:] Our citizenship is in heaven. It is from there that we eagerly await a Saviour, the Lord Jesus Christ. By the power that enables Him to bring everything under His control, He will transform our wretched bodies to be like His glorious body. [5]

[Peter:] Dear friends, I urge you as aliens and strangers in this world, to abstain from sinful desires which wage war against the soul. Live such honourable lives among the pagans that, although they may accuse you of doing evil, they may see your good deeds and glorify God on the day of His judgment. [6]

[1] Genesis 4:19-20 [2] Genesis 47:9 [3] Luke 9:57-58 [4] Hebrews 11: 8-10,13-16
[5] Philippians 3:20-22 [6] 1 Peter 2:11-12

Day 13

Jubal was the first of many men and women who have used music for good or evil purposes. Since his time, musical instruments have been used at celebrations, feasts, worship—true and false, in peace and war. They unite people in sounding out messages of joy, greetings, warnings or commands. Music can be an outward expression of an inward conviction or emotion. It can be a means of producing an inner sense of anger or peace. It can be a rallying call to violence or an encouragement to reconciliation.

The father of musicians

The name of the brother of Jabal was Jubal. He was the father of all who play the harp and flute.[1]

Then Miriam the prophetess, Aaron's sister, took a tambourine in her hand leading all the women. They followed her with tambourines and dancing. Miriam sang to them: "Sing to the Eternal-God, for He has triumphed marvellously." [2]

They set the ark of God on a new cart and brought it from the house of Abinadab. ... David and the whole house of Israel celebrated before the Eternal-God with all their might, with songs and with harps, lyres, tambourines, sistrums and cymbals.[3]

He [David] left Zadok the priest with his fellow priests ... to present burnt offerings to the Eternal-God. ... With them went Heman and Jeduthun and the rest of those selected and designated to give thanks to the Eternal-God, "For his love endures for ever." Heman and Jeduthun were responsible for sounding the trumpets and cymbals and for playing other instruments for the sacred songs.[4]

Woe to those who rise early in the morning looking for strong drinks, who stay up late at night to become inflamed with wine. At their feasts they have harps and lyres, tambourines and flutes, and wine, but they have no respect for the deeds of the Eternal-God, no consideration for the work of His hands.[5]

[John:] Then I looked, and there before me I saw [in a vision] the Lamb, standing on Mount Zion. ... And I heard a voice from heaven like the roar of rushing waters and like a loud peal of thunder. The voice I heard was like the sound of harpists playing their harps. And they sang a new song before the throne.[6]

Praise the Eternal-God! Praise God in His sanctuary; praise Him in His mighty universe! Praise Him for His powerful deeds; praise Him for His surpassing greatness! Praise Him with the sound of the trumpet! Praise Him with the harp and lyre! Praise Him with tambourine and dance! Praise Him with the strings and flute! Praise Him with the loud clang of cymbals! Praise Him with resounding clash of cymbals! Let everything that has breath praise the Eternal-God! Praise the Eternal-God! [7]

[1] Genesis 4:20-21 [2] Exodus 15:20-21 [3] 2 Samuel 6:3-5 [4] 1 Chronicles 16:39,41-42
[5] Isaiah 5.11-12 [6] Revelation 14.1-2 [7] Psalm 150:1-6

Day 14

Tubal-Cain was the first of many craftsmen in metals. Craftsmen made all the fine metal-work used in the Jewish worship of God. Metal craftsmen also made idols and shrines to false gods. God has given many people many skills. When used well and for His glory, they can make instruments for the true worship of God, and tools and machines to produce much of great and lasting value. When used wrongly those skills can make instruments of idolatry and immorality, and they can produce weapons of destruction.

The father of metal craftsmen

Lamech married two women, one named Adah and the other Zillah. ... Zillah had a son, Tubal-Cain, who forged all kinds of tools out of bronze and iron.[1]

The Eternal-God said to Moses, "I have chosen Bezalel ... and I have filled him with the Spirit of God, with skill, ability and knowledge in every kind of craft to make artistic designs for work in gold, silver and bronze, to cut and set stones, to work in wood and in all kinds of craftsmanship. ... I have also given skill to all the other craftsmen to make everything I have instructed you: the Tent of Meeting, the ark of the Testimony ... and all the other furnishings of the tent, the table and its utensils, the pure gold lampstand and all its accessories. [2]

Solomon sent this word to Hiram king of Tyre: "I am about to build a temple for the name of the Eternal-God, my God ... Send me, therefore, a man who is skilled to work in gold and silver, bronze and iron, in purple, crimson and blue yarn, and with skill in the art of engraving." ... Hiram king of Tyre replied by letter to Solomon: "I am sending you Huram-Abi, a man of great ability. ... He is skilled to work in gold and silver, bronze and iron. ... He is experienced in all kinds of engraving and is able to execute any design asked of him." [3]

About that time there arose a great disturbance concerning 'The Way'. A silver-smith named Demetrius, who made silver shrines of Artemis, brought in a lot of business for the craftsmen. He called them together with workmen in similar trades, and said, "Men, you know we earn a good income from this business. And you see and hear how this Paul has convinced and persuaded large numbers of people here in Ephesus and in practically the whole province of Asia, that gods made with hands are no gods at all. There is a great danger not only that our trade will lose its good name, but so will the temple of the great goddess Artemis." [4]

[Isaiah:] In the last days, ... many people will come and say, "Come, let us go up to the mountain of the Eternal-God. ... for the law will go out from Zion. ... They will beat their swords into ploughshares and their spears into pruning hooks. Nation will not take up sword against nation, nor will they learn war any more.[5]

[1] Genesis 4:19, 22 [2] Exodus 31:1-8 [3] 2 Chronicles 2:3-4, 7,11,13-14
[4] Acts 19:23-27 [5] Isaiah 2:2-4

Day 15

When people persist in doing what is wrong, they become increasingly corrupt. This happened a few centuries after God created Adam and Eve. More and more people became evil until, in His mercy, God saw fit to stop it by drastic action. God's severe condemnation was, at the same time, an offer of mercy, the offer of a new beginning. Only Noah and his family were willing to repent of the evil they saw around them, that is, to change their minds to think and act in God's ways rather than theirs. Only to those who repent of sin is God able to make a new beginning possible.

God's judgment on a wicked people

Now the earth was corrupt in God's sight and was filled with violence. ... The Eternal-God saw that the wickedness of people on the earth had become very great, and that their every thought was thoroughly corrupt all the time. The Eternal-God regretted that He had made man on the earth, and He was deeply grieved. So the Eternal-God said, "I will wipe mankind, whom I have created, from off the face of the earth - men and animals." So God said to Noah, "I am going to blot out all the people from the earth for they have filled it with violence. I am surely going to destroy both them and the earth. So make yourself an ark of cypress wood. Make rooms in it and coat it with pitch inside and out. ...

"I am going to bring a flood of waters on the earth. Everything on earth will perish. But I will establish my covenant with you, and you will enter the ark, you and your sons and your wife and your sons' wives with you. You are to bring into the ark two of all living creatures, male and female, to keep them alive with you." ... Noah did everything as God commanded him. [1]

By faith Noah, when warned about things not yet seen, felt a holy fear and built an ark to save his family. By his faith he condemned the world and became an heir of the righteousness that comes by faith. [2]

[Peter:] For if God did not spare angels when they sinned, but cast them into hell, ... and if He did not spare the ancient world by bringing the flood on its ungodly people, but protected Noah, a proclaimer of righteousness, and seven others, ... then the Lord knows how to rescue godly men from trials and to keep the unrighteous for the day of judgment. [3]

[Jesus said:] "As it was in the days of Noah, so it will be when the Son of Man comes. For, as in the days before the flood, people were eating and drinking, marrying and giving in marriage, until the day Noah entered the ark, and they knew nothing until the flood came and took them all away, so too will be the coming of the Son of Man. ... Keep alert, because you do not know on what day your Lord will come." [4]

[1] Genesis 6:11, 5-7,13-14,17-19, 22 [2] Hebrews 11:7 [3] 2 Peter 2:4-5, 9 [4] Matthew 24:37-39,42

Day 16

From the terrible judgment of the flood came God's first covenant with everybody. He promised never again to destroy all living creatures. But judgment on a wicked world will come again one day. Noah and his family were a picture of those who would be saved from that judgment in the ark of salvation', which is Jesus Christ. Until then, God's covenant is sure and the rainbow in the sky, when the sun and rain appear together, is His covenant sign.

God's covenant with Noah

The Eternal-God said to Noah, "Enter the ark, you and your whole family, because I have found you alone righteous in this generation. ... In the six hundredth year of Noah's life, on the seventeenth day of the second month ... all the fountains of the great deep burst forth and the windows of the heavens were opened. And rain fell on the earth forty days and forty nights. ... Every living thing on the face of the earth was blotted out; men and animals and every creature that moves along the ground and the birds of the air. Only Noah was left, and those with him in the ark. [1]

At the end of one hundred and fifty days the water had gone down, and on the seventeenth day of the seventh month the ark came to rest on the mountains of Ararat. ... By the first day of the first month of the year in which Noah was six hundred and one years of age, the water had dried up from the earth. [2]

Then Noah built an altar to the Eternal-God. ... The Eternal-God smelled the pleasing aroma and said to Himself: "Never again will I curse the ground because of man, even though his every thought is evil from childhood. Never again will I destroy every living creature, as I have done. As long as the earth exists, seed time and harvest, cold and heat, summer and winter, day and night, will never cease.

God said, "This is the sign of the covenant I am making between me, you and every living creature, a covenant for all future generations: I am setting my rainbow in the clouds, and that will be the sign of the covenant between me and the earth. Whenever I bring clouds over the earth and the bow appears in the clouds, I will remember my everlasting covenant between me and you and all living creatures. Never again will a flood destroy all life on the earth. [3]

[Isaiah:] "Though the mountains depart and the hills be removed, yet my steadfast love for you and my covenant of peace with you, will never be removed," says the Eternal-God, who has compassion on you. [4]

You, O God, are my king from of old, you have worked salvation on the earth. ... The day is yours and so is the night. You have established the stars and the sun. You who set all the boundaries of the earth, you made summer and winter. [5]

---

[1] Genesis 7:1,11-12, 23   [2] Genesis 8:3-4,13,   [3] Genesis 9:12-15   [4] Isaiah 54:10   [5] Psalm 74:12,17

Day 17

The more people there are, the greater is their strength when they are united. When this unity is bent on evil, its power is very destructive. At Babel, God made uniting more difficult by dividing people into language groups. Babel, later Babylon, became a symbol of the consequences of human pride, people seeking to build their own way to God. At Pentecost, God began to unite people again as those who listened to the disciples speaking in Hebrew heard them in their own languages.

The tower of Babel

Now the whole world had one language and used the same words. As people moved eastward, they settled in a plain in Shinar. ... Then they said to each other, "Let us build ourselves a city with a tower that reaches as high as the heavens." But the Eternal-God came down to see the city and the tower that they were building. He said, "If, united as one people and speaking the same language they begin to do this, then nothing they decide to do will be impossible for them. We will go down and confuse their language so they will not be able to understand each other." So the Eternal-God scattered them from there over all the face of the earth, and they ceased building the city. That place was called Babel because it was there that the Eternal-God confused the language of all the people. [1]

"I, Daniel, ... saw in my vision at night, One who looked like a Son of Man coming on the clouds of heaven. ... He was given dominion, glory and sovereign power, and all peoples, nations and men of every language worshipped Him." [2]

When the day of Pentecost came, they [the disciples] were all together in one place. Suddenly there came from heaven a sound like the rush of a violent wind which filled the whole house where they were sitting. ... All of them were filled with the Holy Spirit and began to speak in other languages as the Spirit gave them words to speak. Now there were staying in Jerusalem, God-fearing Jews from every nation under heaven. When they heard this sound, a crowd of them came together in bewilderment because each one of them heard the disciples speaking in his own language. In amazement, they asked, "Are not all these men who are speaking Galileans? How is it that each of us hears them in our own native language?" [3]

After this I saw another angel coming down from heaven. ... He shouted: "Fallen! Fallen is Babylon the Great! It has become a home for demons and a haunt for every evil spirit. ... Come out of her, my people, so that you do not share in her sins." [4]

[John:] I saw [in a vision] there before me a great multitude that no one could count, from every nation, tribe, people and language. ... They cried out in a loud voice: "Salvation belongs to our God, who is seated on the throne, and to the Lamb." [5]

[1] Genesis 11:1-9 [2] Daniel 7 : 2,13-14 [3] Acts 2:1-8,11 [4] Revelation 18:1-2,4 [5] Revelation 7:9-10

Day 18

Satan, the chief evil spirit whom God allows to test people, accused Job of following God for selfish reasons. God allowed Satan to test Job but not to destroy him. Satan's aim was defeated and Job learned a great deal about God through what he suffered. Job was never given the explanation for his suffering. The Bible tells us for our benefit. Job was tested to see if his faith in God was genuine. Satan was allowed to act according to his character, bringing pain and death. Job did not fall into the trap of blaming God for Satan's evil work. God works for our good, even in allowing pain and suffering.

Job is tested

There was a man in the land of Uz whose name was Job. ... The Eternal-God said to Satan, "Have you considered my servant Job? There is no one on earth like him. He is blameless and upright, he fears me and shuns evil." Satan replied, "Does Job fear God for nothing? Have you not put a fence around him and his household and everything he has? You have blessed the work of his hands and increased his flocks and herds throughout the land. But stretch out your hand and strike all that he has, and he will certainly curse you to your face." The Eternal-God said to Satan, "Very well, everything he has is in your hands, but do not lay a finger on him." Then Satan left the presence of the Eternal-God.

One day when Job's sons and daughters were feasting and drinking wine at the oldest brother's house, a messenger came to Job and said, "The oxen were ploughing and the donkeys were grazing nearby when the Sabeans attacked and carried them off. They killed the servants and I am the only one who has escaped to tell you!"

While he was still speaking, another messenger came and said, "The fire of God fell from the sky and burned up the sheep and the servants.".... Another messenger came and said, "The Chaldeans formed three raiding parties, swept down on your camels and carried them off.".... Yet another messenger came and said, "Your sons and daughters were feasting and drinking wine at the oldest brother's house, when suddenly a mighty wind swept in from the desert and struck the four corners of the house. It fell on them and they died, and I am the only one who has escaped to tell you!" At this, Job got up and tore his tunic, shaved his head, and fell to the ground in worship and said: "Naked I came from my mother's womb, and naked I shall return. The Eternal-God gave and He has taken away; may His name be praised." In all this, Job did not sin by accusing God with wrongdoing. [1] Job said: "Though He slay me, yet I will hope in Him." [2]

"I [Job] know that my Redeemer is alive, and that at the last He will stand upon the earth. After my skin has been destroyed, then in my flesh I will see God. I myself will see Him with my own eyes, on my side and not as a stranger." [3]

[1] Job 1:8-22   [2] Job 13:15   [3] Job 19:25-27

Day 19

Job's friends came to comfort him, but they did the opposite. They tried to find reasons why Job suffered so terribly. They tried to show that he deserved what he was suffering. They did not understand what was really happening. Job was suffering because God allowed him to be tested by Satan. Job remained true to what he knew about God and reflected His character in the way he prayed for his friends.

Job prays for his friends

The Eternal-God said to Job, "Shall he who argues with God not listen to what He has to say?' [1] Then Job said to the Eternal-God: "I know that you can do all things; no purpose of yours can be thwarted. ... Surely I spoke of things I did not understand, things that were too wonderful for me to know. ... I had heard of you but now my eyes have seen and I despise myself and repent in dust and ashes."

Then the Eternal-God said to Eliphaz the Temanite, "I am angry with you and your two friends, because you have not spoken of me what is right, as my servant Job has. Now take seven bulls and seven rams and go to my servant Job and offer a burnt offering for yourselves. My servant Job will pray for you, and I will accept his prayer and not deal with you according to your folly. "... So Eliphaz the Temanite, Bildad the Shuhite and Zophar the Naamathite did what the Eternal-God told them; and God accepted Job's prayer.

After Job had prayed for his friends, the Eternal-God prospered him again and gave him twice as much as he had before. All his brothers and sisters and everyone who had known him before came and ate bread with him in his house. They comforted and sympathised with him over all the trouble the Eternal-God had brought upon him, and each one gave him a piece of silver and a gold ring. The Eternal-God blessed the latter part of Job's life more than the first. He had fourteen thousand sheep, six thousand camels, a thousand yoke of oxen and a thousand donkeys. He also had seven sons and three daughters.[2]

[Peter:] Brothers and sisters, take the prophets who spoke in the name of the Lord as an example of patience in the face of suffering. Indeed, we consider blessed those who have endured. You have heard of Job's perseverance and have seen the end that the Eternal-God gave him. The Eternal-God is full of compassion and mercy. [3]

By his great mercy He [Jesus] has given us new birth into a living hope. ... In this you greatly rejoice, although for a little while you have had to suffer all kinds of trials so that your faith, of greater worth than perishable gold which is purified by fire, may be shown to be genuine and may result in praise, glory and honour when Jesus Christ is revealed. [4]

[1] Job 40:1 [2] Job 42:1-3,5,7-13 [3] James 5:10-1 [4] 1 Peter 1:3,6-7

Day 20

Abram was living a settled life in a great city when God called him to be a wanderer with only the promise that He would bless the world through his descendants. He was considered righteous by God for his faith before he did anything to show how genuine it was. His faith is an example of the faith that God wants everyone to have in Him.

God calls Abram and changes his name to Abraham

The Eternal-God said to Abram, "Leave your country, your people and your father's household and go to the land I will show you. I will make you into a great nation and I will bless you. I will make your name great, and you will be a blessing to others. I will bless those who bless you, and those who curse you I will curse. All peoples on earth will be blessed through you." Abram went as the Eternal-God had told him. [1]

They [Abram and his family] set out for the land of Canaan and arrived there. ... The Canaanites were the inhabitants of the land, but the Eternal-God appeared to Abram and said, "I will give this land to your descendants." Later, the word of the Eternal-God came to Abram in a vision: "Do not be afraid, Abram. I am your shield, your reward will be very great." But Abram said, "O Lord, Eternal-God, what can you give me since I am childless and a servant in my household will be my heir."

Then the word of the Eternal-God came to him: "This man will not be your heir. A son coming from your own body will be your heir." He took him outside and said, "Look at the heavens and count the stars if you can! So shall your descendants be." Abram believed the Eternal-God, and his faith was credited it to him as righteousness. [2]

When Abram was ninety-nine years old, the Eternal-God appeared to him. ... Abram fell face down, and God said to him, "As for me this is my covenant with you. ... No longer will you be called Abram, your name will be Abraham, for I have made you a father of many nations. [3]

By faith Abraham, when called to set out for a place he would later receive as an inheritance, obeyed and went, even though he did not know where he was going. By faith he stayed for a time in the promised land as a stranger in a foreign country. He lived in tents, as did Isaac and Jacob, who were heirs with him of the same promise. For he looked forward to the city with foundations, whose architect and builder is God. [4]

He is the Eternal-God, our God. His judgments are in all the earth. He remembers His covenant for ever ... the covenant that He made with Abraham. [5]

Without faith it is impossible to please God, because whoever comes to Him must believe that He exists and that He rewards those who seek Him. [6]

[1] Genesis 12:1-4   [2] Genesis 15:1-6   [3] Genesis 17:3-5   [4] Hebrews 11:8-10   [5] Psalm 105:7-9   [6] Hebrews 11:6

Day 21

Abraham's character and his faith in God are seen in the way he gave his nephew, Lot, the choice of where to live. Equally Lot's character and his lack of understanding of God's character are seen in his choice to live where the land was very fertile but near evil cities. There is no record of Lot asking God to show him where to live and he made a bad choice. Sodom and Gomorrah illustrate what the world is like without God.

Lot makes his choice

Lot travelled with Abram [his uncle], both had flocks, herds and tents. But the land could not support them when they were together. ... The herdsmen of Abram and Lot began to quarrel. So Abram said to Lot, "The whole land is before you. Let us separate. If you go to the left, I will go to the right; if you go to the right, I will go to the left. Lot surveyed the land and saw that the whole plain of the Jordan was well watered. ... So he chose the whole plain of the Jordan and set out eastwards. ... He settled among the cities of the plain and pitched his tents near Sodom. The men of Sodom were very wicked and sinned greatly against the Eternal-God. [1]

[Solomon:] "My son, if sinners entice you, do not yield to them. If they say, "Come along with us. Let us lie in wait to kill someone. Let us waylay some unsuspecting soul, ... do not go along with them, do not follow in their paths." [2] Do not envy wicked people, do not want to be in their company; for they plot violence in their hearts and their lips talk of mischief." [3]

[Paul:] I have written to you urging you not to associate with sexually immoral people, but I do not mean all the immoral people of this world, or the greedy or robbers, or idolaters. To do that you would have to leave this world. But I am writing to urge you not to associate with anyone who calls himself a brother and who is sexually immoral or greedy, an idolater or a slanderer, a drunkard or a robber. Do not even eat with such a person." [4]

Do not love the world or the things of the world. If anyone loves the world, he does not have the love of the Father in him. Everything in the world, the cravings of the sinful nature, the lust of the eyes and the boasting of possessions and accomplishments, come not from the Father but from the world. The world and its desires are passing, but those who do the will of God will live for ever. [5]

Once you were in darkness but now your are light in the Lord. Live as children of light. ... Take no part in the fruitless deeds of darkness. [6]

Blessed are those who do not follow the advice of the wicked or walk in the way of sinners or sit in the seat of scoffers. [7]

[1] Genesis 13:5-13   [2] Proverbs 1:10-11,15   [3] Proverbs 24:1-2   [4] 1 Corinthians 5:9-11
[5] 1 John 2:15-17   [6] Ephesians 5:8,11   [7] Psalm 1:1

Day 22

Abraham's faith in God was tested as time went by. He and his wife Sarai (later called Sarah) grew older and they had no children. They thought that they ought to help God keep His promises. So they tried to do His work for Him, but in their way. God overruled this 'mistake', blessed Ishmael, and forgave Abraham for his lack of faith. Then He fulfilled His promise in His own way by the birth of Isaac. Ishmael was born as a result of human contriving. Isaac was born as the fulfilment of God's promise.

The birth of Ishmael

Sarai, Abram's wife, had borne him no children. But she had an Egyptian slave-girl named Hagar. ... After Abram had lived in Canaan for ten years, Sarai took ... Hagar and gave her to her husband to be his wife. When Hagar realised that she was pregnant, she began to despise her mistress. Then Sarai said to Abram, "You are responsible for the wrong done to me. I put my servant in your arms and now that she knows she is pregnant, she treats me with contempt. May the Eternal-God judge between us." Abram replied, "Your servant is in your power. Do with her whatever you please."

Then Sarai treated Hagar harshly so that she fled from her. The angel of the Eternal-God found Hagar by a spring in the desert. ... He said to her, 'Return to your mistress and submit to her. ... I will so increase your descendants that they will be too numerous to count. ... Now you have conceived and you will have a son. You will name him Ishmael, for the Eternal-God has seen your misery." So Hagar bore Abram a son, and he gave him the name Ishmael. [1] The child grew and was weaned. On that day, Abraham held a great feast. Sarah saw that the son whom Hagar had borne to Abraham was playing with her son. She said to Abraham, "Get rid of that slave woman and her son, for the son of this slave woman will never share in the inheritance with my son Isaac." [2]

[Paul:] It is written that Abraham had two sons, the one by a slave woman was born 'according to the flesh'; but his son by the free woman was born 'according to a promise'. This is can be taken as an allegory, for the two women represent two covenants. One covenant is from Mount Sinai and bears children who are slaves, this is Hagar. ... But you, brothers and sisters, like Isaac, are 'children of the promise'. The son born 'according to the flesh' persecuted the son born according to the Spirit. It is the same now. What does the Scripture say? "Drive out the slave woman and her son, for the slave woman's son will never share the inheritance with the free woman's son." So then, brothers and sisters, we are not children of the slave woman, but of the free woman. [3]

It is for freedom that Christ has set us free. Stand firm, therefore, and do not submit again to a yoke of slavery. [4]

[1] Genesis 16:1, 3-11,15   [2] Genesis 21:8-10   [3] Galatians 4:22-24,28-31   [4] Galatians 5:1

Day 23

God speaks to people in many different ways. To Abraham He appeared as three Men. He wanted Abraham to understand what He was doing, and this included the good news that He had not forgotten His promise to him. He was going to keep that promise despite Sarah's disbelieving laugh. A son was to be born to them who would be the first of the many descendants God had promised Abraham. God always keeps His promises.

God fulfils His promise to give Abraham a son

The Eternal-God appeared to Abraham near the oak trees of Mamre as he sat at the entrance of his tent. ... Abraham looked up and saw three Men standing near him. He hurried from the entrance of his tent to meet them and bowed down to the ground. He said, "My Lord, if I find favour in your eyes, do not pass by your servant. Let a little water be brought to wash your feet, and rest yourselves under this tree. Let me bring some bread for you so you can be refreshed. Then you can go on your way." They answered, "Very well; do as you say." ...

He brought some curds, milk and the calf that he had prepared, and set them before them. While they ate, he stood near them under a tree. "Where is your wife Sarah?" they asked him. "There, in the tent," he said. Then the Eternal-God said, "I will surely return to you at the right time, and Sarah your wife will have a son."

Now Sarah was listening behind him at the entrance of the tent, ... and she laughed. Then the Eternal-God said, "Why did Sarah laugh and say, 'Now that I am old shall I indeed bear a child?' Is anything impossible for the Eternal-God? I will return to you at the set time next year and Sarah will have a son." [1]

The Eternal-God was gracious to Sarah and He did for Sarah what He had promised. She became pregnant and, at the very time God had promised, she bore Abraham a son in his old age. Abraham gave the name Isaac [meaning 'laughter'] to the son Sarah bore him. ... Abraham was a hundred years old when his son Isaac was born. Sarah said, "God has brought me laughter, and everyone who hears about this will laugh with me." [2]

When God made His promise to Abraham, because there was no one greater for Him to swear by, He swore by himself, saying, "I will surely bless you and multiply you." And so after having waited patiently, Abraham received what was promised. [3]

Although Abraham was old and Sarah barren, by faith Abraham was given power to become a father because he considered Him faithful who had promised. So from one man, and he as good as dead, came descendants who were more numerous than the stars in the sky or the grains of sand on the seashore. [4]

[1] Genesis 18:1-5,8-10,12-14   [2] Genesis 21:1-6   [3] Hebrews 6:13-15   [4] Hebrews 11:11-12

Day 24

Abraham knew that the people of Sodom were wicked but he wanted Lot, his family and servants to be kept safe. God in His mercy listened to his plea. He would not destroy the city if He found ten good people there. Abraham believed that there were more than ten righteous people in that city. In fact, there were only four. God saved those four people and then destroyed the wicked cities. God was gracious to Abraham in letting him know what He was about to do and giving him the opportunity to pray for Lot and his family, a prayer He answered by saving them in a miraculous way.

Abraham pleads for Lot

The three men rose to leave and set off in the direction of Sodom. Abraham walked with them to see them on their way. Then the Eternal-God said, "Shall I hide from Abraham what I am about to do?" ... "The outcry against Sodom and Gomorrah is so great and their sin so grievous that I must go down and see if what they are doing is as serious as the outcry that has come to me. If not I will know." The men turned away and went towards Sodom, but Abraham remained standing before the Eternal-God.

Then Abraham came near to Him and said, "Will you sweep away the righteous with the wicked? What if there are fifty righteous people in the city? Will you wipe it out and not spare it for the sake of the fifty righteous people who live there. Far be it from you to slay the righteous with the wicked! Will not the Judge of all the earth do right?" The Eternal-God said, "If I find fifty righteous people in Sodom I will spare the whole place for their sake." Then Abraham spoke again: "Now that I have taken upon myself to speak to the Eternal-God, though I am but dust and ashes, suppose the number of the righteous is forty-five? Will you destroy the whole city because of forty-five people?" He said, "If I find forty-five there, I will not destroy it." ... "I will not do it if I find thirty there."

Abraham said, "Now that I have been so bold as to speak to the Eternal-God, what if only twenty righteous people can be found there?" He said, "For the sake of twenty, I will not destroy it." Then Abraham said, "May the Eternal-God not be angry if I speak just once more. What if only ten can be found there?" He answered, "For the sake of ten, I will not destroy it." [1]

He who lives in the shelter of the Most High will stay in the shadow of the Almighty. I will say of the Eternal-God, "You are my refuge and my fortress, my God, in whom I trust." He will save you from the snare of the fowler and from the deadly pestilence. ... Because you make the Most High your refuge and the Eternal-God your dwellingplace, then no harm will come to you, no disaster will come near your tent. He will command His angels to guard you in all your ways. [2]

[1] Genesis 18:16,20-27, 30-32   [2] Psalm 91:1-3, 9-11

Day 25

Despite his unwise choice, Lot was a good man and he was very uncomfortable living near the open evil of Sodom and Gomorrah. Two facts about God are clear: He will not let unrepented sin go unpunished, and He knows how to save from the consequences of evil those who repent of their sin and trust in Him. The destruction of Sodom and Gomorrah became a symbol of the anger of God against evil, particularly when that evil was expressed in an open way by a community, family, city or nation.

Sodom and Gomorrah are destroyed

The two angels arrived at Sodom in the evening, and Lot was sitting in the gateway of the city. When he saw them, he got up to meet them, bowed to greet them and said, "My Lords, turn aside to the house of your servant and spend the night here" They answered, "No, we will spend the night in the square." But he insisted so strongly that they went with him and into his house. ... Before they lay down to sleep, men from every part of the city of Sodom surrounded the house. ... They called to Lot, "Where are the men who came to you tonight? Bring them out to us so that we may lie sexually with them." Lot went out to meet them, shut the door behind him and said, "No, my brothers I beg you, do not do this wicked thing." ... They replied, "Stand out of our way! ... This fellow came here as an alien and now he wants to be our judge! We will deal with you worse than them." Then the men inside reached out, pulled Lot back into the house and shut the door. ... At dawn, the angels urged Lot, saying, "Hurry! Take your wife and two daughters ... or you will be engulfed in the punishment of the city." When he lingered, the men grasped his hand ... and led them safely out of the city." Then the Eternal-God rained down fire and burning sulphur. ... So he overthrew those cities and the entire plain. [1]

These twelve disciples Jesus sent out with the instruction: ... "Whatever town or village you enter find out those who are worthy and stay there until you leave. ... If anyone will not accept you or listen to your words, shake the dust off your feet as you leave that house or town. ... I tell you the truth, it will be more tolerable for Sodom and Gomorrah on the day of judgement than for the inhabitants of that town." [2]

[Jude:] Sodom and Gomorrah ... indulged in sexual immorality and unnatural vice. They serve as examples of those who suffer the punishment of eternal fire. [3]

If He [God] condemned the cities of Sodom and Gomorrah to destruction by burning them to ashes, and made them an example of what is going to happen to the ungodly, and if He rescued Lot, a righteous man, who was greatly distressed by the immoral lives of lawless men, ... then the Lord knows how to rescue godly people from trials and hold the unrighteous for the day of judgment. [4]

[1] Genesis 19:1-10,15-16,24-25 [2] Matthew 10:5,11,14-15 [3] Jude 7 [4] 2 Peter 2:6-9

Day 26

Circumcision was the sign that God's chosen people, the Jews, were His by the Old Covenant. It was meant to be a physical sign with a spiritual meaning. It distinguished God's people from others. When Jesus Christ came as the reality which fulfilled the Old Testament signs and symbols, physical circumcision was no longer necessary. However, its spiritual meaning became even more important for those who were included in the New Covenant which Jesus made with His blood. As the Jews who bore this sign were different from members of every other nation, so Christians, of whatever nationality, who are baptised into Christ, are different from everyone else.

Circumcision - the sign of the covenant

When Abram was ninety-nine years old, the Eternal-God appeared to him and said, "I am God Almighty; walk before Me and be blameless. I will confirm my covenant with you and will greatly increase the number of your descendants. ... This is my covenant with you and your descendants after you: ... Every male among you shall be circumcised. ... It will be the sign of the covenant between me and you." [1]

Even though the universe and everything in it belongs to the Eternal-God, your God, yet He set His affection on your forefathers and loved them and He chose you, their descendants, out of all the nations, as it is today. Therefore, circumcise your hearts, and do not be stiff-necked any longer. [2] The Eternal-God, your God, will circumcise your hearts and the hearts of your descendants, so that you will love Him with all your heart and with all your soul, and so live. [3]

[Paul:] A man is not a Jew if he is only one outwardly, nor is circumcision merely an outward and physical sign. Rather, a man is a Jew if he is one inwardly; and true circumcision is circumcision of the heart, by the Spirit. [4]

It is for freedom that Christ has set us free. Stand firm, then, and do not let yourselves be bound again by a yoke of slavery. Note this! It is I, Paul [a Jew], who is telling you [Gentiles] that if you let yourselves be circumcised, Christ will be of no benefit to you at all. ... You, who want to be justified by the law, have been cut off from Christ ... for in Christ Jesus neither circumcision nor uncircumcision counts for anything. The only thing that matters is faith working through love.[5]

For in Him [Jesus Christ] all the fullness of God lives in bodily form, and you have been given that fullness in Christ. ... It was in Him that you were circumcised, by the putting off of the sinful nature, not with a circumcision done by human hands, but with the spiritual circumcision done by Christ. When you were buried with Him in baptism you were also raised with Him, through your faith in the power of God, who raised Him from the dead. [6]

[1] Genesis 17:1-2,10-11   [2] Deuteronomy 10:14-16   [3] Deuteronomy 30:6   [4] Romans 2:28-29
[5] Galatians 5:1-6   [6] Colossians 2:9-12

Day 27

Abraham's faith in God must have increased greatly when Isaac was born. His experience on Mount Moriah was a further test of his faith, but it was more: it was a picture of the way 'God the Father' was going to give His Son, Jesus Christ, to die on the same place [Mount Moriah] in Jerusalem for the sins of the world. Abraham had doubted God's word when Ishmael was born. Now his faith was firmer, and it became even stronger when God provided a sacrifice in the place of his son, Isaac.

Abraham is tested

The Eternal-God was gracious to Sarah and, as He had said, she bore a son to Abraham in his old age. [1] Some time later God tested Abraham. He said to him, "Take your son, your only son Isaac, whom you love, and go to the land of Moriah. There you are to offer him as a sacrifice, a burnt offering, on one of the mountains I will show you. Abraham rose early the next morning ... took with him two of his servants and his son Isaac. On the third day ... Abraham took the wood for the burnt offering and placed it on his son Isaac and he himself carried the fire and the knife. As they walked on together, Isaac asked, "Father! The fire and wood are here, but where is the lamb for the burnt offering?" Abraham answered, "God himself will provide the lamb for the burnt offering, my son."

When they reached the place that God had shown him, Abraham built an altar and arranged the wood on it. He bound his son Isaac and laid him on the wood on the altar. ... Then he reached out his hand and took the knife to kill his son. But the angel of the Eternal-God called out to him from heaven. "Abraham! Abraham! ... Do not touch the boy. Do not do anything to him. Now I know that you fear God, because you have not withheld from me your son, your only son." Abraham looked up and saw a ram caught by its horns in a thicket. He took the ram and sacrificed it as a burnt offering instead of his son. [2]

By faith Abraham, when God tested him, offered up Isaac as a sacrifice. He who had received the promises was prepared to sacrifice his one and only son, even though God had said to him, "It is through Isaac that your descendants will be reckoned." Abraham was convinced that God could raise the dead, and, metaphorically speaking, he did receive Isaac back from death. [3]

[Paul:] Consider Abraham: "He believed God, and it was credited to him as righteousness." It follows that those who believe are children of Abraham. ... And those who have faith are blessed with Abraham, the man of faith. [4]

For God [the Father] so loved the world that He gave His one and only [God the] Son, so that whoever believes in Him should not perish but have eternal life. [5]

[1] Genesis 21:1-2 [2] Genesis 22:1-13 [3] Hebrews 11:17-19 [4] Galatians 3:6,9 [5] John 3:16

Day 28

Since God made Eve to be a wife for Adam, He has guided people to the husband or wife of His choice, when they have wanted Him to do so. God guided Isaac to Rebecca in a remarkable way. Neither knew the other when the choice was made and they lived in different countries. Only God can bring two people together like that, and when He does, those two can love each other and fulfil His purposes in bringing them together.

God finds a wife for Isaac

Abraham was now old. The Eternal-God had blessed him in every way. Abraham said to the chief servant in his household, "Put your hand under my thigh. I want you to swear by the Eternal-God, the God of heaven and the God of earth, that you will not get a wife for my son from the daughters of the Canaanites, among whom I live but will go to my country and to my own relatives and get a wife for my son Isaac." ...

Then the servant left taking ten of his master's camels and all kinds of choice gifts from his master. He set out for Aram Naharaim and arrived at the town of Nahor. He made the camels kneel down near the well outside the town. It was towards evening, the time the women go out to draw water. Then he prayed, "O Eternal-God, God of my master Abraham, grant me success today, and show kindness to my master Abraham. See, I am standing here by this spring of water, and the daughters of the townspeople are coming out to draw water. Grant that when I say to a girl, 'Please, when you have drawn water, let me drink from your jar,' and she says, 'Drink, and I will give water to your camels too,' let her be the one you have chosen for your servant Isaac. By this I will be certain that you have shown kindness to my master."

Before he had finished praying, Rebekah came out with her jar on her shoulder. She was the daughter of Bethuel son of Milcah, wife of Abraham's brother Nahor. The girl was very beautiful and a virgin."

Now Isaac ... went out to the field to meditate one evening. As he looked up he saw camels approaching. Rebekah was also looking out and saw Isaac. She alighted from her camel and asked her servant, "Who is that man in the field walking to meet us?" The servant answered, "He is my master." So she covered herself with her veil. ... Isaac brought her into his mother Sarah's tent, and he married Rebekah. She became his wife and he loved her. [1]

[David:] Do not fret because of wicked men or be envious of wrongdoers. ... Take delight in the Eternal-God and He will give you the desires of your heart. Commit your way to the Eternal-God, trust in Him and He will act for you. He will make your righteousness shine like the noonday. ... Be still before the Eternal-God and wait patiently for Him. Do not fret because of those who ... carry out evil devices. [2]

[1] Genesis 24:1-5,10-16,62-67   [2] Psalm 37:1,4-7

Day 29

Because Esau was born first, his was the privilege of the special rights of being the firstborn. God knew that Esau was going to leave Him out of his life and He was going to give the birthright to Jacob. However, Jacob was wrong to gain the birthright by deception. Both were in the wrong. Esau's sin was the greater because he despised God.

Esau sells his birthright

Isaac prayed to the Eternal-God for his wife because she could not bear children. The Eternal-God answered his prayer, and Rebekah became pregnant. ... There were twin boys in her womb and when the time came for her to give birth, the first to come out was red, his whole body was like a hairy mantle, so they named him Esau. After this, his brother came out with his hand grasping Esau's heel. So he was named Jacob [meaning 'supplanter'] ... The boys grew up, and Esau became a skilful hunter. ...

One day, when Jacob was cooking some stew, Esau came in from the field, and he was very hungry. He said to Jacob, "Quick, let me have some of that red stew! I am famished." Jacob replied, "First sell me your birthright." Esau said, "I am about to die, what good is the birthright to me?" But Jacob said, "Swear to me first." So he swore on oath and sold his birthright to Jacob. [1]

When Isaac was old and his eyes were so weak that he could no longer see clearly, he called for his elder son Esau and said to him, "My son ... go out to the field to hunt for some wild game for me. Prepare me the kind of savoury food I like ... so that I may give you my blessing before I die."

Now Rebekah was listening as Isaac was speaking to his son Esau. ... She said to her son Jacob, "Look! I overheard your father say to your brother Esau. ... Now go to the flock and bring me two choice kids, so I can prepare some tasty food for your father ... so that he may give you his blessing before he dies."

So Jacob went out to get them and brought them to his mother. She prepared some savoury food, the way his father liked it. ... She put the skins of the kids on his hands and on his neck. ... So he went to his father and said, "My father, ... I am Esau."

Then Esau came in from hunting ... "I am ... your first born, Esau," ... Then he said, "He is rightly named Jacob? He has deceived me twice: He took my birthright and how he has taken my blessing!" ... Esau said to his father, "Do you have only one blessing, my father? Bless me too, my father!" Then Esau wept aloud. [2]

See that no one is ... godless like Esau, who for a single meal sold his birthright as the oldest son. Afterwards ... when he wanted to receive a blessing, he was rejected. He could not bring about any change of mind, though he sought the blessing with tears. [3]

---

[1] Genesis 25:21, 24-27, 29-33   [2] Genesis 27:1-6,9-10,14-18,30-32,38   [3] Hebrews 12:16-17

Day 30

Jacob tried to run away from Esau, but He could not run away from God. God knew Jacob better than he knew himself. The 'ladder reaching to heaven' showed Jacob that God was very near to Him even though he was running away from Esau in fear. God is near to everybody whether they are conscious of Him or not.

Jacob dreams of a ladder

Jacob left Beersheba ... He came to a certain place and there he stopped for the night. ... He took one of the stones that were there, put it under his head and lay down to sleep. In a dream, he saw a ladder set on the earth and reaching to heaven. On it the angels of God were ascending and descending. High above it stood the Eternal-God. He said, "I am the Eternal-God, the God of your father Abraham and the God of Isaac, ... I am going to give you the land on which you are lying and all peoples of the world will be blessed through you and your descendants. Know for sure that I am with you and will watch over you wherever you go. I will bring you back to this land. I will not leave you until I have done what I have promised you." Jacob awoke from sleep and said, "The Eternal-God is surely in this place and I did not know it." He was afraid and said, "How awesome is this place! This is none other than the house of God and this is the gate of heaven." ... He gave that place the name: Bethel. [1]

Then [over 20 years later] the Eternal-God said to Jacob, "Go back to the land of your fathers ... and I will be with you. ... I am the God of Bethel, where you anointed a stone and where you made a vow. Now leave this land at once and return to the land where you were born." [2]

That night Jacob took them [his family and servants] ... and sent them across the ford of the river Jabbok. ... So Jacob was left alone. A man wrestled with him till dawn. ... Then the man said, "Let me go for day is breaking." Jacob replied, "I will not let you go unless you bless me." The man asked him, "What is your name?" He answered, "Jacob." Then the man said, "Your name will no longer be Jacob, but Israel, because you have wrestled with God and with men and have prevailed." [3]

Then God said to Jacob, "Go to Bethel and settle there." ... So Jacob said to his household, "Let us go to Bethel; there I will build an altar to God who answered me when I was in distress and who has been with me wherever I have gone." [4]

The eyes of the Eternal-God are on those who fear Him and put their hope in His faithfulness to deliver them from death and keep them alive in famine. [5]

Blessed are those whose help is the God of Jacob, whose hope is in the Eternal-God, the Creator of heaven and earth, the sea and everything in them, who remains faithful for ever. [6]

---

[1] Genesis 28:10-19 [2] Genesis 31:3,13 [3] Genesis 32:22-28 [4] Genesis 35:1-3 [5] Psalm 33:18-19 [6] Psalm 146:5-6

Day 31

God chose Joseph to be the means of making Israel's family into a nation in Egypt. That did not prevent Joseph from being a proud young man at first. He trusted in God, however, and God did two things: He made Joseph into a gracious, responsible man, and He guided Israel to Egypt at a time of famine, and then to grow into a nation through whom He could achieve His purposes.

Joseph's dreams

Israel loved Joseph more than any other of his children. ... When his brothers saw that their father loved him more than any of them, they hated him and could not speak peaceably to him. Joseph had a dream, ... He said to his brothers, "We were binding our sheaves of corn in the field when my sheaf rose and stood upright, while your sheaves gathered round mine and bowed down to it." Then he had another dream. ... "Listen," he said, "I have had another dream. The sun, moon and eleven stars all bowed down to me." ... His father rebuked him, "Will your mother and I and your brothers really bow down to the ground before you?" His brothers were jealous of him but his father kept the things in mind.

His [Joseph's] brothers took their father's flocks to pasture near Shechem. Israel said to Joseph, "Go and see that all is well with your brothers and the flocks." So Joseph went in search of his brothers. ... They saw him a long way off. Before he reached them, they had plotted to kill him. "Here comes that dreamer!" they said to each other, "Let's kill him and throw his body into one of the pits here, and say that a wild animal has eaten him. Then we will see what will come of his dreams." ... So when Joseph came to his brothers, they stripped him of his robe ... and thew him into a pit. ... Judah said to his brothers, "We will gain nothing if we kill our brother and cover up his blood? Let us sell him to the Ishmaelites. Let us not lay our hands on him; he is, after all, our brother, our own flesh and blood." His brothers agreed.

So when the Midianite merchants were passing by, his brothers pulled Joseph up out of the pit and sold him to them for twenty shekels of silver. They took him to Egypt. ... Then Jacob tore his clothes, put on sackcloth and mourned for his son. ... Meanwhile, in Egypt, the Midianites sold Joseph to Potiphar, an official in Pharaoh's court, the captain of the guard. [1]

Jeremiah prayed: "I know, O Eternal-God, that a man's life is not his own. He cannot direct his own steps." [2]

Commit whatever you do to the Eternal-God, and your plans will work out right. The Eternal-God has His purposes for everything, even for the wicked in a day of disaster. ... A man plans what he will do, but the Eternal-God directs his steps.[3]

[1] Genesis 37:3-14,17-20,23-24,26-28, 34-36   [2] Jeremiah 10:23   [3] Proverbs 16:3-4,9

Day 32

Although a slave, Joseph did not forget God and God helped him. God allowed him to be severely tempted. He did not yield to temptation, and so he developed in character. Although put in prison, Joseph was becoming the kind of person to whom God could give great responsibilities. Pride when Joseph was young was being turned to humility in his manhood. In his early dreams he was the centre; now God was central in everything.

Joseph is tested at work and in prison

Joseph was taken to Egypt and sold to Potiphar, an Egyptian official of Pharaoh's court. The Eternal-God was with Joseph and he was successful in all that he did. He lived in the house of his Egyptian master. When his master saw that the Eternal-God was with him and gave him success in everything he did ... he put him in charge of his household. ... the Eternal-God blessed Potiphar's household because of Joseph.

Now Joseph was a well-built, handsome man. After a time his master's wife looked at Joseph and said, "Lie with me!" But he refused. He said to her, "I am in charge here. My master does not concern himself with anything in the running of this house, ... he has withheld nothing from me except you, and that is because you are his wife. How could I sin against God in doing such a wicked thing?" Though she pestered Joseph day after day, he refused to lie with her or even be near her.

One day he went into the house to attend to his work. None of the house servants was inside. She caught him by his cloak and said, "Come lie with me!" He ran out of the house leaving his cloak in her hands. ... She called her servants and said to them, "Look! He came in here to sleep with me but I cried out. When he heard me scream, he left his cloak here with me and ran out of the house."

When his master heard his wife's story ... he was very angry. He arrested him and put him in prison. ... While Joseph was there in the prison, the Eternal-God was with him ... and granted him favour in the sight of the chief jailor. [1]

My son, pay attention to my wise words. ... The lips of an adulteress drip honey. Her speech is smoother than oil. In the end she is bitter as wormwood, sharp as a double-edged sword. Her feet lead down to death; her steps to the grave. [2]

[Peter:] If, you do wrong and you suffer for it patiently, what credit is there in that? But if, when you do what is right and suffer for it unjustly, that is approved by God. It is to this that you have been called, for Christ suffered for you, leaving you an example to follow. [3]

Keep a clear conscience so that when people accuse you falsely as evildoers, they may see your good behaviour in Christ and be put to shame for their slander. It is better to suffer for doing good, when that is God's will, than for doing evil. [4]

[1] Genesis 39:1-15,19-21 [2] Proverbs 5: 1,3-5 [3] 1 Peter 2:20-21 [4] 1 Peter 3:17

Day 33

Joseph was in prison two years, forgotten by the men he had helped, but not forgotten by God. Then God gave Pharaoh dreams only He could explain. At last, the meaning of Joseph's dreams years before, was becoming clear. God was working out the next great move for Israel - to Egypt. And Joseph was His servant in bringing this about.

Joseph and Pharaoh's dreams

After two full years had passed [Joseph in prison], Pharaoh had a dream. He dreamed that he was standing by the river Nile when seven sleek and fat cows came out of the river and grazed among the reeds. After them, seven other ugly and gaunt cows came out of the Nile and stood beside the first cows on the river bank. The cows that were ugly and gaunt ate up the seven sleek, fat cows. Then Pharaoh woke up. He fell asleep again. In a second dream he saw seven heads of good, healthy corn growing on a single stalk. After them grew seven other heads of corn. These were thin and scorched by the east wind. The thin, scorched heads of corn swallowed up the seven full, healthy heads. Then Pharaoh woke up. He had been dreaming.

In the morning he was so troubled that he sent for all the magicians and wise men of Egypt. Pharaoh told them his dreams but no one was able to give him their meaning. Then the chief cup-bearer said to Pharaoh, "Once, Pharaoh was angry with his servants, and he put the chief baker and me in prison. ... Now a young Hebrew man was there with us, ... we told him our dreams, and he told us what they meant." ... So Pharaoh sent for Joseph. ... Pharaoh said to Joseph, "I had a dream, and no one can tell me what it means. I have heard that when you are told what a dream is, you can interpret it." Joseph said to Pharaoh, "I cannot do it myself, but God will give Pharaoh the answer he is asking for." Then Joseph said to Pharaoh, "The two dreams of Pharaoh are really one and the same. ... God has shown Pharaoh what he is going to do. ... Seven years of great plenty are coming throughout the land of Egypt, but then seven years of famine ... will bring desolation to the land.

Then Pharaoh said to Joseph, "Since God has revealed all this to you, there is no one else who is as discerning and wise as you are. I will put you in charge of my palace, and all my people are to submit to your orders." [1]

All of you, clothe yourselves with humility in dealing with one another, because, 'God opposes those who are proud but gives grace to the humble.' Humble yourselves, therefore, under God's mighty hand, that He may exalt you in due time. [2]

He [God] holds victory in store for the upright, ... for He guards the way of the just and preserves the way of those who are faithful to Him. [3]

---

[1] Genesis 41:1-16,25, 28-30,39-40 [2] 1 Peter 5:5-6 [3] Proverbs 2:7-8

Day 34

Joseph was very badly treated by his brothers, but God used what they did to him to take him to Egypt. As a slave he learned to be humble and God turned the injustices forced on him to prepare him for a great purpose. As God had been merciful to him, he was able to be merciful to his brothers. Joseph is a picture of Jesus Christ and the way He came to prepare a place in heaven for us.

Joseph meets his brothers again

When Jacob learned that there was corn in Egypt, he said to his sons, ... "Go down there and buy some grain for us that we may live and not die."... Now Joseph was the governor of Egypt and it was he who sold corn to all the people of the land. Joseph's brothers arrived there and they bowed down before him. ... As soon as Joseph saw them he recognised them. However, he acted as a stranger and spoke harshly to them. ... Joseph recognised his brothers, but they did not recognise him. ... After three days, Joseph said to them, "I fear God, so do this and you will live. If you are really honest men, leave one of your brothers here in prison while the rest of you go and take corn back for your famine stricken households. Then bring your youngest brother to me." They said to each another, "We are surely being punished for what we did to our brother. We saw his anguish when he pleaded with us for his life, but we would not listen; that's why this anguish has come upon us." ... Joseph spoke to his brothers through an interpreter, so they did not realise that he understood what they were saying to each other. [1]

The famine continued to be severe in Canaan. So when they [Israel and his family] had eaten all the corn, ... their father said to them, "Go back and buy us some more food." ... So the men took the gifts ... and they also took Benjamin with them. They hurried to Egypt and presented themselves before Joseph. [2] ...

Then Joseph could control himself no longer. He cried out to his attendants, "Send everyone out from here!" So Joseph was alone with his brothers when he made himself known to them. ... Joseph said to his brothers, "Come near to me. ... I am your brother Joseph. ... Do not be distressed nor angry with yourselves for selling me here. It was not you who sent me here, but God. [3] ... You wanted to harm me, but God intended it for good, to bring about the saving of many lives, and that is what is happening." [4] So Joseph settled his father and brothers in Egypt.[5]

[Jesus:] *" In my Father's house are many places. If that were not so, I would have told you. I am going to prepare a place for you. And if I go to prepare a place for you, I will surely come back for you so that you will be where I am."* [6]

[1] Genesis 42:1-2, 6-8,18-22 [2] Genesis 43:1-2,15 [3] Genesis 45:1,4-8 [4] Genesis 50:19-20
[5] Genesis 47:11 [6] John 14:1-3

Day 35

God fulfilled His promise to make Israel into a great nation but this was at the cost of making the Israelites a problem for the Egyptians. They feared the new growing nation among them. God used the oppression of the Israelites to get them out of Egypt, and as a picture of the much greater slavery of all people to sin. In saving them He gave a vivid picture of what He was going to do spiritually to save the world from sin.

Israel becomes a nation of slaves in Egypt

The generation of Joseph and his brothers died, but the Israelites continued to grow and they became very numerous, so that the land was filled with them. Then a new king, who did not know about Joseph, rose to power in Egypt. He said to the people, "Look, the Israelites have become far too numerous for us." ... So the Egyptians organised slave masters to oppress them with forced labour. ... However, the more they were oppressed, the more they increased in numbers. The Egyptians came to dread the Israelites and forced them ruthlessly to work as slaves. [1]

The Eternal-God said [to Moses], "I have seen the misery of my people in Egypt and I have heard their bitter cries because of their slave masters. I know the suffering they are enduring and I have come down to save them from the Egyptians and to bring them up out of that land into a good and spacious land which is flowing with milk and honey." [2]

[Stephen replied to the High Priest and Council] "God spoke to him [Abraham] in this way, 'Your descendants will be strangers in a strange country, and they will be made slaves and ill-treated for four hundred years. But I will judge the nation they serve as slaves.'" [3]

A man's ways are open to the Eternal-God and He examines all his ways. The evil deeds of a wicked man trap him; they hold him fast. [4]

[Paul:] You were dead in your trespasses and sins in which you lived when you followed the ways of this world ... the spirit who is now working in those who are disobedient. At one time, all of us also lived among them. We gratified the cravings of our sinful nature and followed the desires of our passions and senses. [5]

Jesus said to the Jews who believed Him, "If you continue in my teaching, you will be truly my disciples. You will know the truth, and the truth will set you free. They answered him, "We are Abraham's descendants and we have never been slaves of anyone. How can you say that we will be made free?" Jesus replied, "I tell you the truth, everyone who sins is a slave to sin. A slave has no permanent place in the household, but a son has a place in it for ever. So if the Son sets you free, you will be free indeed." [6]

[1] Exodus 1:7-13 [2] Exodus 3:7-8 [3] Acts 7: 6-7 [4] Proverbs 5:21-22 [5] Ephesians 2:1-3 [6] John 8:34-36

Day 36

God chose the children of Israel, made them into a nation and gave them a country to live in so that He could (a) reveal Himself and His purposes to the world through them, (b) prepare a people in whom Jesus Christ, God the Son, could be born, and (c) to work out what He was going to do to redeem people of all nations from the bondage of Satan. He chose Israel, not for their goodness, nor for their greatness, but because He loved them and He wanted to show through them that He loved all the people of the world.

God's chosen people

Hear, O Israel, "The Eternal-God, our God, is one ... [1] The Eternal-God your God has chosen you from all the peoples of the earth to be His people, His treasured possession. The Eternal-God did not set His heart on you and choose you because of your numbers, for you were the fewest of all peoples. It was because the Eternal-God loved you and kept the oath He swore to your forefathers that He brought you out with a mighty hand and redeemed you from the land of slavery and from the power of Pharaoh king of Egypt. Know therefore that the Eternal-God, your God, is God. He is the faithful God who keeps His covenant of love to a thousand generations of those who love and obey Him. [2]

I [Paul] speak the truth in Christ. ... I have great sorrow and unceasing anguish in my heart. For I could wish that I myself were cursed and cut off from Christ for the sake of my own people, the people of Israel. To them, the Israelites, belong the adoption as sons, the divine glory, the covenants, the receiving of the law, the worship and the promises. To them belong the patriarchs, and from them, humanly speaking, came Christ, who is God over all and for ever to be praised. Amen.

It is not that God's word failed, for not all who are descended from Israel truly belong to Israel. Nor are all Abraham's descendants, Abraham's children. It is only the children of the promise to Abraham who are Abraham's children. [3]

Brothers and sisters, my heart's desire and prayer to God is that the Israelites may be saved. I can testify that they have a zeal for God, but their zeal is not based on the true facts. Because they did not know the righteousness that comes from God and tried to establish their own, they did not submit to God's righteousness. Christ is the fulfilment of the law so that righteousness may be for everyone who believes. [4]

"I will take you [Israel] out of the nations; I will gather you from all the countries and bring you back into your own land. I will sprinkle you with clean water and you will be clean from all your uncleanness and I will cleanse you from all your idols. I will give you a new heart and put a new spirit in you. ... You will be my people and I will be your God." [5]

[1] Deuteronomy 6:4   [2] Deuteronomy 7:6-9   [3] Romans 9:1-8   [4] Romans 10:1-4   [5] Ezekiel 36:24-28

Day 37

Moses was prepared for leadership by God. It was God who guided Pharaoh's daughter to save him from death as a baby. In Pharaoh's court he was given the best education possible. God was directing Moses' life and, at the same time, working towards delivering the Israelites from their slavery in Egypt.

The birth of Moses

A king came to power in Egypt who did not know Joseph. He said to the people, "the Israelites have become far too numerous for us. ..." He also said to the Hebrew midwives, Shiphrah and Puah, "As you help the Hebrew women in childbirth, ... if a boy is born, kill him." [1]

A certain man of the house of Levi married a woman, also a Levite, and she gave birth to a son. She saw that he was a fine baby and she hid him for three months. When she could hide him no longer, she got a papyrus basket, plastered it with pitch, laid the baby in it and put it among the reeds on the bank of the Nile. His sister stood at a distance to see what would happen. Pharaoh's daughter went down to the Nile to bathe. There she saw the basket among the reeds and she sent her maid to get it. She opened it and saw the baby. He was crying, and she felt pity for him, "This is one of the Hebrew children," she said. Then Moses' sister said to Pharaoh's daughter, "Shall I go and get one of the Hebrew women to nurse the baby for you?" "Yes!" she answered. And the girl went and called the baby's mother. ... So the woman took the baby and nursed him. When the child grew up, she took him to Pharaoh's daughter and he became her son. She named him Moses, saying, "I drew him out of the water."

One day, after Moses had grown up, he went out to where his own people were being subjected to forced labour. He saw an Egyptian beating a Hebrew, one of his own people. He looked around him and saw no one in sight. Then he killed the Egyptian and hid his body in the sand. ... When Pharaoh heard of this, he set out to kill Moses, but Moses fled from Pharaoh and went to live in the land of Midian. [2]

By faith Moses' parents hid him for three months after he was born. They saw that he was a fine child, and they were not afraid of the king's edict. By faith Moses, when he had grown up, refused to be called a son of Pharaoh's daughter. He chose to be ill-treated along with the people of God rather than to enjoy for a while the pleasures of sin. He considered that to be ill-treated for the sake of Christ was of greater worth than all the treasures of Egypt. He was looking to the future, to his reward. By faith he left Egypt with no fear of the anger of the king. He had a purpose in mind which he pursued as seeing what was invisible. [3]

[1] Exodus 1:8,15   [2] Exodus 2:1-13,15   [3] Hebrews 11:23-26

Day 38

Although God had been directing his life from birth, Moses appears to have been unaware of it until God spoke to him when he was a man of about 40 years of age. Then He had to face some big questions: Was the God of his people, the Jews, really his God? Was he going to be obedient to the truth God showed him about himself? Was he prepared to let God fulfil His purposes for others through him? Reluctantly at first, then with greater confidence, Moses obeyed God's instructions, and in so doing, showed that his faith was truly in the God of his forefathers.

The call of Moses

Moses was tending the sheep of his father-in law Jethro, ... he came to Horeb, the mountain of God. There the angel of the Eternal-God appeared to him in the flame of a burning bush. Moses saw that, though the bush was on fire, it was not burning up. Moses thought, "I will go over and see this great sight, why the bush is not burning up." From within the bush, the voice of God spoke: "Moses, Moses!" Moses replied, "Here I am." God said, "Do not come any nearer. Take off your sandals. The place where you are standing is holy ground. ... I am the God of your father, the God of Abraham, the God of Isaac and the God of Jacob." Moses hid his face for he was afraid to look at God. The Eternal-God said to him, "I have seen the misery of my people in Egypt. I have heard their cries as they have suffered from their slave drivers. I know their suffering and I have come down to save them from the hand of the Egyptians. ... Go! I am sending you to Pharaoh to deliver my people out of Egypt. [1]

Moses said to God, "Who am I, that I should be the one to go to Pharaoh and deliver the Israelites out of Egypt?" God said, "I will be with you." Moses said , "O Eternal-God, I have never been an eloquent speaker, ... I am slow in speech." The Eternal-God said to him. "Who gives people the power to speak? Who makes a person deaf or mute? Who gives him sight or blindness. Is it not I, the Eternal-God? Now go! I will help you to speak and I will guide you in what to say." [2]

The word of the Eternal-God came to Jeremiah saying, "Before I formed you in the womb I knew you and before you were born I set you apart. I appointed you to be prophet to the nations." Then I said, "Ah, Sovereign Eternal-God, I do not know how to speak. I am only a child." But the Eternal-God said to me, "Do not say, 'I am only a child.' You are go to all to whom I send you and say everything I command you."[3]

[The word of the Eternal-God through Isaiah:] "From the beginning I have not spoken in secret. I am there when things happen." And now the Sovereign Eternal-God has sent me by His Spirit. This what He says: "I am the Eternal-God, your God, who teaches you what is good for you and who guides you in the way you should go."[4]

[1] Exodus 3:1-10 [2] Exodus 4:10-12 [3] Jeremiah 1:4-7 [4] Isaiah 48:16-17

Day 39

God's name for Himself was 'Yahweh'. In Hebrew, this sounds like: 'I AM'. The Jews felt that they could not say that most holy of names and so they used instead the word for 'Lord'. Usually 'I AM' is written as the 'LORD'. In these readings, the "I AM", is translated as the 'Eternal-God'. He is the eternal 'I AM' because He was, and is, and ever will be.

God's Name

Moses said to God, "If I go to the Israelites and say to them, 'The God of your fathers has sent me to you,' and they ask me, 'What is His name?' What shall I say?" God said to Moses, "I AM WHO I AM." This is what you are to say to the Israelites: "'I AM' has sent me to you." God also said to Moses, "Say to the Israelites, 'The 'I AM", the Eternal-God, the God of your fathers, the God of Abraham, the God of Isaac and the God of Jacob, has sent me to you.' This is My name by which I am to be remembered from generation to generation." [1]

God also said to Moses, "I am the Eternal-God. I appeared to Abraham, to Isaac and to Jacob as God Almighty (El Shaddai), but by my name, the Eternal-God (the I AM), I did not reveal myself to them. ... Say to the Israelites: 'I am the Eternal-God (the 'I AM'), and I will rescue you from the yoke of the Egyptians. I will free you from your slavery to them and I will redeem you with an outstretched arm and with mighty deeds of judgment. I will take you as my people and I will be your God. Then you will know that I am the Eternal-God, your God, who brought you out of Egypt, from under the yoke of the Egyptians.'" [2]

[Jesus:] "I am telling you the truth, if anyone keeps my word he will never suffer death." At this the Jews exclaimed, "Now we know that you are possessed by a demon! Abraham died and so did the prophets, yet you say that if a man keeps your word, he will never suffer death. Are you greater than our father Abraham?" ... Jesus replied, ... "Your father Abraham was overjoyed at the thought of seeing my day. He saw it and was glad." The Jews said to Him, "You are not yet fifty years old and you have seen Abraham!" Jesus answered them, "I tell you the truth, before Abraham was, I am!" [3]

O Eternal-God, you have been our secure dwelling-place through all generations. Before the mountains were brought forth or you formed the earth and the world, from everlasting to everlasting you are God. [4]

Let the name of the Eternal-God [the I AM] be praised, now and for ever. From the rising of the sun to the place of its going down, the name of the Eternal-God is to be praised. ... Who is like the Eternal-God, our God, who sits on His throne on high yet who comes down to look on the earth? [5]

---

[1] Exodus 3:13-15 [2] Exodus 6:2-3, 6-7 [3] John 8:51-53, 56-58 [4] Psalm 90:1-2 [5] Psalm 113:2-3,5

Day 40

The name 'God' is bound up with His character. He is a holy God who cannot live with sin. He is equally a compassionate, loving and faithful God towards those who repent of their sin and turn to Him for forgiveness. The Bible reveals God's character in words—He is just, loving, compassionate, gracious; and in actions—in the way He acted towards the rebellious Israelites, and particularly in the example and sacrifice of Jesus Christ, God the Son. To understand God, it is necessary to know about His character and about His actions. His actions illustrate His character as well as achieve His purposes.

God's character

Moses cut out two stone tablets like the first ones and went up Mount Sinai early in the morning. ... The Eternal-God came down in the cloud and stood with Moses. He proclaimed His name, the Eternal-God [the I AM]. And He passed before Moses proclaiming, "The Eternal-God, the Eternal-God, the compassionate and gracious God, slow to anger, abounding in steadfast love and faithfulness towards thousands, and forgiving wickedness, transgression and sin. Yet He by no means clears the guilty. He punishes the children and their children for the sins of their fathers to the third and fourth generation." [1]

"You came down on Mount Sinai; you spoke to them [the Israelites] from heaven. You gave them just regulations, righteous laws, decrees and commands that are good. ... But they, our forefathers, became proud and stiff-necked. They did not obey your commands. They refused to obey and failed to remember the wonders you performed among them. ... But you are a forgiving God. You are gracious and compassionate, slow to anger and abounding in love. Therefore you did not desert them ... and you did not abandon them in the desert." [2]

The Eternal-God is compassionate and gracious, slow to anger, abounding in love. He will not always accuse nor will He be angry for ever. He does not deal with us as we deserve or repay us according to our iniquities. As high as the heavens are above the earth, so great is His steadfast love towards those who fear Him. [3]

"Rend your heart and not your clothes. Return to the Eternal-God, your God, for He is gracious and compassionate, slow to anger and abounding in love." [4]

Bring joy to your servant, O Eternal-God, for to you I lift up my soul. You are forgiving and good, O Eternal-God, abounding in love to all who call to you. [5]

Jesus went through all the towns and villages, teaching in their synagogues, proclaiming the good news of the kingdom and healing every kind of disease and sickness. When He saw the crowds, He had compassion on them, because they were harassed and helpless, like sheep without a shepherd. [6]

---

[1] Exodus 34:4-7 [2] Nehemiah 9:13,16-19 [3] Psalm 103:8-11 [4] Joel 2:13 [5] Psalm 86:3-5 [6] Matthew 9:36

Day 41

God was going to deliver Israel from the Egyptians. It was important for everyone to see that it is not easy to escape from slavery, either that of Israel from Egypt or that of sinners from sin and Satan. It needed a powerful act of God to bring about the salvation of Israel. Pharaoh did not let the Israelites go into freedom easily, nor does Satan let sinners easily give up their sin for the freedom God offers.

The plagues on Egypt

The Eternal-God said to Moses, "You shall tell Pharaoh to let the Israelites go out of this country, ... he will not listen to you. ... The Egyptians will know that I am the Eternal-God when I act against Egypt and bring the Israelites out of it. ... By this you will know that I am the Eternal-God: ... The fish in the Nile will die, and the river will stink; [1] ... I will plague the whole country with frogs; ... dust will become gnats; ... I will send swarms of flies on you; [2] ... All the livestock of the Egyptians will die; ... festering boils broke out on men and animals, ... hail struck everything in the fields, [3] ... never before had there ever been such a severe plague of locusts, ... Egypt was in total darkness for three days.[4]

Then the Eternal-God said to Moses, "Go to Pharaoh, for I have hardened his heart and the hearts of his officials so that I may work these my miraculous signs among them. You will tell your children and your children's children how severely I dealt with the Egyptians and how I worked my signs among them. Then you will know that I am the Eternal-God." [5]

The Eternal-God said to Moses, "I will bring one more plague on Pharaoh and on Egypt. After that, he will let you go. When he does, he will drive you out for good." ... Moses said [to Pharaoh], "This is what the Eternal-God says: 'About midnight I will pass throughout the land of Egypt and every first-born son in it will die.'" [6] ... At midnight the Eternal-God struck down all the first-born in Egypt, from the first-born of Pharaoh, on the throne, to the first-born of the prisoner, in the dungeon. The Egyptians urged the people to go in haste from their country. [7]

[Paul:] Thanks be to God that, though you were slaves to sin, you wholeheartedly obeyed the teaching which was entrusted to you. You have been set free from sin and have become slaves to righteousness. ... For the wages of sin is death, but the gift of God is eternal life in Christ Jesus our Lord. [8]

To Him who loves us and has set us free from our sins by His blood, and has made us to be a kingdom, priests to serve His God and Father, to Him [Jesus] be glory and dominion for ever and ever! Amen. [9]

[1] Exodus 7:1-5,17-18   [2] Exodus 8:2,16, 21   [3] Exodus 9:6,10, 25   [4] Exodus 10:14, 22   [5] Exodus:10:1-2
[6] Exodus 11:1, 4   [7] Exodus 12:29,33   [8] Romans 6:17-18,23   [9] Revelation 1:5-6

Day 42

We do not understand how 'God hardened Pharaoh's heart' and, at the same time, 'Pharaoh hardened his heart'. We know that Pharaoh's hard heart, for which he was responsible, was part of God's plan to show the world how He could bring the Israelites out of the slavery of Egypt, and, later, sinners out of the slavery of sin.

Pharaoh's hardness of heart

The Eternal-God said to Moses, "When you return to Egypt, see that you perform before Pharaoh all the wonders I have given you the power to work. [1] I will harden Pharaoh's heart, and I will multiply my miraculous signs and wonders in Egypt, but he will not listen to you. ... The Egyptians will know that I am the Eternal-God when I stretch out my hand against Egypt and save the Israelites out of it."

Moses and Aaron went to Pharaoh and did as the Eternal-God had instructed them. ... Nevertheless, Pharaoh's heart became hardened and he would not listen to them. [2] ... When Pharaoh saw that there was some relief, he hardened his heart again and would not listen to Moses and Aaron. ... The flies left Pharaoh, his officials and his people until not a fly remained. Again Pharaoh hardened his heart and would not let the people go. [3] ... Pharaoh sent men to investigate and found that not even one of the Israelites' animals had died. Yet his heart was unyielding and he refused to let the people go. ... When Pharaoh saw that the rain, hail and thunder had ceased, he sinned again as he and his officials hardened their hearts. [4]

[Paul:] For the Scripture says to Pharaoh: "I raised you up for the very purpose of displaying my power in you, and that my name might be proclaimed in all the earth." God chooses on whom He will, and on whom He will not have mercy. ... What then, if God, in choosing to show His anger and make His power known, has endured with great patience those who are the objects of His anger ... in order to make known the riches of His glory to the objects of His mercy. ... That means us whom He has called, not only from the Jews but also from the Gentiles." [5]

Come, let us bow down and worship, let us kneel before the Eternal-God our Maker. He is our God and we are the people of His pasture, the sheep under His care. Today, if you hear His voice, do not harden your hearts as at Meribah, when your fathers tested me although they had seen my work. [6]

As the Holy Spirit says: 'Today, if you hear His voice, do not harden your hearts as you did when you rebelled in the desert. ... Rather encourage one another each day, as long as you have a 'Today', so that none of your hearts is hardened by the deceitfulness of sin. [7]

[1] Exodus 4:21   [2] Exodus 7:3-5,10,13   [3] Exodus 8:15,30   [4] Exodus 9:7,34   [5] Romans 9:17-18, 22-24
[6] Psalm 95:6-9   [7] Hebrews 3:7-8,13

Day 43

For the people of Israel, the Passover marked the greatest event in their history: their deliverance from Egypt. For the world, the fulfilment of the Passover in the death and resurrection of Jesus Christ, is the greatest event in all history. It was then that God made it possible for everyone to be delivered from Satan and from the guilt and power of sin. Those who are 'saved' have 'passed over' from death to life through Jesus Christ.

The Passover

The Eternal-God said to Moses and Aaron in Egypt, "This month is to be for you the first month of the year. Tell all the Israelites that on the tenth day of this month each man is to take a lamb for his family. ... The animals you choose must be males, a year old and without defect. They can be taken from the sheep or the goats. Tend them until the fourteenth day of the month. Then all the Israelites must slaughter them at twilight. They are to take some of the blood and sprinkle it on the sides and lintels of the door-frames of the houses where they eat the lambs. That same night they are to eat the meat roasted by fire together with bitter herbs, and bread made without yeast. ... On that night, I will pass through Egypt and strike down every first-born, both of men and of animals, and I will bring judgment on all the gods of Egypt, for I am the Eternal-God. The blood on the houses where you are will be a sign. When I see the blood, I will pass over you." [1]

Celebrate the Passover of the Eternal-God, your God, in the month of Abib, because in that month, He brought you out of Egypt by night. Sacrifice, as the Passover to the Eternal-God, your God, an animal from your flock or herd at the place the Eternal-God will choose as the dwellingplace for His name. [2]

The next day John [the Baptist] saw Jesus coming towards him. He said, "Look! There is the Lamb of God who takes away the sin of the world!" [3] Christ, our Passover Lamb, has been sacrificed. Therefore let us keep this Festival, not with the old yeast of malice and wickedness, but with the bread of sincerity and truth. [4]

[Peter:] You know that you were not redeemed from the empty way of life you inherited from your fathers, with perishable things like silver or gold, but with the precious blood of Christ, a Lamb without blemish or defect. [5]

[John:] Then I saw [in a vision] a Lamb standing in the centre of the throne looking as if it had been killed. Around it were the four living creatures and the elders. ... They sang a new song: "You [Jesus, the Lamb] are worthy to take the scroll and break its seals ... because you were slain, and with your blood you purchased men for God from every tribe, language, people and nation." [6]

[1] Exodus 12:1-8,12-13 [2] Deuteronomy 16:1-2 [3] John 1:29 [4] 1 Corinthians 5:7-8
[5] 1 Peter 1:18-19 [6] Revelation 5:6,9

Day 44

In crossing the Red Sea, Israel passed from slavery to liberty. The waters that parted for them to cross and that returned to destroy their enemies, are a picture of what Jesus Christ did when He died and rose again. He defeated Satan and sin and opened a path from spiritual slavery to freedom.

Israel is saved from Egypt

At midnight the Eternal-God struck down all the first-born in Egypt. ... That night Pharaoh summoned Moses and Aaron and said, "Go! Leave my people! ... Take your flocks and herds." ... The Israelites journeyed from Rameses to Succoth. [1]

When the king of Egypt heard that the people had fled, he and his officials changed their minds. ... As Pharaoh approached, the Israelites looked up and saw that the Egyptians were marching after them. They were terrified and cried out in fear to the Eternal-God. ... Moses said the people, "Do not be afraid. Stand firm and you will see the deliverance that the Eternal-God will give you today. ... The Eternal-God will fight for you, you have only to be still."

Then Moses stretched out his hand over the sea. All that night the Eternal-God pushed the sea back with a strong east wind and where there was sea there was now dry land. The waters were parted and the Israelites passed through on dry ground, with a wall of water on their right and on their left. All Pharaoh's horses, chariots and horsemen pursued them into the sea. ... At daybreak the sea returned to its place. As the Egyptians fled from it, the Eternal-God swept them into the sea. ... That day the Eternal-God rescued Israel from the hands of the Egyptians. ... When the Israelites saw the mighty power of the Eternal-God ... the people believed Him. They put their trust in Him and in His servant, Moses. [2]

[Joshua:] "For the Eternal-God, your God, did to the river Jordan as He had done to the Red Sea when He dried it up before us until we had crossed over. He did this so that all the peoples of the earth might know that the Eternal-God is powerful and that you might always fear the Eternal-God, your God. [3]

By faith the people passed through the Red Sea as on dry land but when the Egyptians tried to do the same, they were drowned. [4]

It was right that God, for whom and through whom everything exists, in bringing many children to glory, should make [Jesus] the Pioneer of their salvation perfect through suffering. ... Since the children are flesh and blood, He too shared in their humanity, so that through His death He might destroy him who holds the power of death, that is, the devil, and free those who live in the slavery of the fear of death.[5]

[1] Exodus 12:29, 31-33, 37   [2] Exodus 14:5,10,13, 21-23,27,30-31   [3] Joshua 4:23-24
[4] Hebrews 11:29   [5] Hebrews 2:10,14-15

Day 45

This is a song of God's triumph over His enemies. Egypt became an enemy of God when it oppressed His people. That oppression is a picture of the slavery of people by Satan and sin. God triumphed over the slavery of sin in Jesus Christ, 'the Lamb'. The Jews sang this song about their deliverance. All God's people will one day sing the Song of the Lamb and of the great deliverance Jesus won for them.

The Song of Moses

Then Moses and the Israelites sang this song to the Eternal-God:
"I will sing to the Eternal-God for He triumphed marvellously.
The horse and its rider He has thrown into the sea.
The Eternal-God, who is my strength and my song, has become my salvation.
He is my God, and I will praise him. He is my father's God, and I will exalt him. ...
Your right hand, O Eternal-God, was majestic in power.
Your right hand, O Eternal-God, shattered the enemy.
In the greatness of your majesty you overthrew those who opposed you. At the blast of your nostrils the waters piled up. ...
Who among the gods is like you, O Eternal-God, majestic in holiness, awesome in splendour and working wonders?
In your unfailing love you led the people you redeemed.
In your strength you will guide them to your holy dwellingplace.
The Eternal-God will reign for ever and ever. [1]
Great is the Eternal-God and greatly to be praised; His greatness is unsearchable. One generation will praise your works to another; they will tell of your mighty deeds and the glorious splendour of your majesty. And I will meditate on your wonderful works. ... The Eternal-God is gracious and compassionate, slow to anger and rich in unfailing love. [2]

[John:] I saw [in a vision] what appeared to be a sea of glass mixed with fire. By the sea, stood those who had been victorious over the beast and his image and over the number of his name. They held harps given to them by God and they sang the song of Moses the servant of God and the song of the Lamb: "Great and marvellous are your deeds, Eternal-God, God Almighty. Just and true are your ways, King of the nations. Who will not fear you, O Eternal-God, and bring glory to your name? For you alone are holy. All nations will come and worship before you, for your righteous acts have been revealed." [3]

[1] Exodus 15:1-2, 6-8,11-13,18 [2] Psalm 145:3-8 [3] Revelation 15:2-4

Day 46

When God delivered Israel by bringing them through the Red Sea, He did not leave them there on the edge of the desert. For forty years He gave them the visible sign of His presence in the pillar of cloud by day, which glowed as if on fire by night. A cloud over the special tent in which God met with Moses, showed that He was there with them in their camp. It was there that He spoke to Moses directly. That same presence, although not that sign, is with all His children, all the time, wherever they are .

The pillar of cloud and fire

The Eternal-God went ahead of the Israelites by day in a pillar of cloud to guide them on their way. By night a pillar of fire gave them light so that they could travel day or night. Neither the pillar of cloud by day nor the pillar of fire by night ever ceased to lead the people as they marched on. [1]

Moses used to pitch a tent some distance away from the camp. He called it the 'tent of meeting.' ... As Moses entered the tent, the cloud would come down and stay at the entrance while the Eternal-God spoke with Moses. Whenever the people saw the cloud at the entrance of the tent, they all stood, each at the entrance to his tent, and bowed down. [2]

On the day the tabernacle, the Tent of the Testimony, was set up, the cloud came down and covered it. From evening till morning the cloud above the tabernacle glowed like fire. [3]

In all the travels of the Israelites, whenever the cloud rose from above the tabernacle, the people would set out. If the cloud did not rise, they did not set out. ... During all their travels, the cloud of the Eternal-God remained day and night over the tabernacle in the sight of all Israel. At night it glowed as if from a fire within it. [4]

Even when the cloud remained over the tabernacle for a long time, the Israelites obeyed the orders of the Eternal-God and did not set out. ... Whether the cloud remained over the tabernacle for two days, a month or a year, the Israelites remained in the camp and did not set out. Only when it lifted did they set out. At the word of the Eternal-God they encamped, and at His command they set out. [5]

He [God] worked wonders in the sight of their fathers in the land of Egypt. ... He divided the sea and guided them through it. He made the water stand like a wall. He led them with the cloud by day and with fire all night. [6]

Who among the gods is like you, O Eternal-God? Who is like you majestic in holiness, awesome in splendour and working wonders? ... In your unfailing love you led the people you have redeemed. By your strength you guided them to your holy dwelling. [7]

[1] Exodus 13:21-22   [2] Exodus 33:7, 9-10   [3] Numbers 9:15-16   [4] Exodus 40:36-38
[5] Numbers 9:19,22-23   [6] Psalm 78:12-14   [7] Exodus 15:11-13

Day 47

For forty years, six days a week, God provided enough manna to keep every Israelite satisfied and healthy. On five days enough manna was given to them for each day. On the sixth day, enough was provided for two days. The manna is a picture of the 'spiritual bread' that everyone needs. Ordinary food is not enough. That spiritual bread is the life of Jesus Christ as He lives in people.

The manna in the wilderness

All the Israelites set out from Elim and came to the Desert of Sin. ... In the desert the people grumbled against Moses and Aaron, saying, ... "If only we had died by the hand of the Eternal-God in Egypt! There we used to sit round pots of meat and ate all that we wanted, but you have brought us out into the desert so that the entire assembly dies of hunger." Moses and Aaron said to all the Israelites, "This evening you will know that it was the Eternal-God who brought you out of Egypt ... when He gives you ... all the bread you need. ... In the morning there, on the ground, there was a layer of dew around the camp. When the dew had gone, thin flakes like frost appeared on the ground. When the Israelites saw it they said to each other, "What is it?" For they did not know what it was. Moses said to them, "It is the bread the Eternal-God has given you to eat. ... Each one is to gather as much as he needs. The people of Israel called the bread 'manna'. [1]

[Moses:] Remember how the Eternal-God, your God, has led you in the desert for forty years, to humble you and to test you in order to know what was in your heart. ... He humbled you by letting you be hungry and then feeding you with manna, which neither you nor your forefathers had known. This was to teach you that man does not live on bread alone but by every word that comes from the mouth of the Eternal-God. [2]

So they [the crowd of Jews] asked Jesus, "What miraculous sign will you give that we may see it and believe you? What will you do? Our forefathers ate manna in the desert, as it is written, 'He gave them bread from heaven to eat.'" Jesus said to them, "I tell you the truth, it was not Moses who gave you bread from heaven, but it is my Father who gives you the true bread from heaven. For the bread of God is the One who comes down from heaven and gives life to the world." "Sir," they said, "Give us this bread, now and for ever." [3]

Jesus answered them ... "I am the bread of life. Whoever comes to me will never be hungry, and whoever believes in me will never be thirsty. ... Your forefathers ate the manna in the desert and they died. But by this bread, which comes down from heaven, a man may live and not die. I am the living bread that has come down from heaven" [4]

---

[1] Exodus 16:1-3,6-8,13-15,31 [2] Deuteronomy 8:2-3 [3] John 6:30-34 [4] John 6:35,48-51

Day 48

The terrible sound of thousands of people wailing represented the rebellion of the people against God. They were receiving manna in a miraculous way, but they did not want to trust God for meat. God graciously satisfied their physical hunger, but they were spiritually poorer.

The wail and the quail

The people complained of their hardship in the presence of the Eternal-God. He heard them and He became very angry. Fire from the Eternal-God blazed among them and destroyed part of the camp. The people cried out to Moses. He prayed to the Eternal-God and the fire died down. ... The rabble among the people began to crave for other food, and all the Israelites began to wail. "If only we had meat to eat!" they cried, "We remember the fish we ate free in Egypt, and the cucumbers, melons, leeks, onions and garlic. Now we are wasting away. We eat nothing but this manna!"

Moses heard the wailing from the members of every family as they stood at the entrances to their tents. ... The Eternal-God said to Moses, ... "Say to the people: 'Consecrate yourselves for tomorrow, then you will eat meat. The Eternal-God heard you when you wailed: If only we had meat to eat! It was better for us in Egypt. Now the Eternal-God will give you meat, and you will eat it.'" ...

A wind from the Eternal-God drove quail in from the sea. They came down all around the camp to about a metre high and about a day's walk in any direction. All that day and night and all the next day the people gathered quail. No one gathered less that ten homers. Then they spread them out for themselves all around the camp. While the meat was still uneaten between their teeth, the anger of the Eternal-God burned against the people and He struck them with a great plague. The place was called Kibroth-Hattaavah because it was there that they buried the people who had craved for other food. [1]

He rebuked the Red Sea, and it dried up. He led them through the deep as through a desert. ... But they soon forgot His deeds and did not wait for His counsel. In the desert they gave in to their wanton craving. There they put God to the test. He gave them what they asked for, but a wasting disease came upon them. [2]

[Paul] These things happened as examples to keep us from setting our hearts on evil things as they [the Israelites] did. ... We should not put the Eternal-God to the test, as some of them did, so that twenty-three thousand of them died in one day. ... If you think that you are standing, be careful that you do not fall. [3]

[1] Numbers 11:1-6,10,16,18, 31-34   [2] Psalm 106:9,13-15   [3] 1 Corinthians 10:6,9,12

Day 49

The desert is not, normally, the place to find water. Yet it was there that the Israelites were given water from 'the rock'. It was God's provision for them. This world is a spiritual desert unless God gives the 'spiritual water' that all need. That 'water which springs up into eternal life' comes from the Rock, which is Jesus Christ.

Water from the rock

All the Israelites ... camped at Rephidim, but there was no water there for the people to drink. So they quarrelled with Moses and said, "Give us water to drink." Moses replied, "Why quarrel with me? Why do you put the Eternal-God to the test?"

Then Moses cried out to the Eternal-God, "What shall I do with these people? They are ready to stone me." The Eternal-God said to Moses, "Go on ahead of the people. Take some of the elders of Israel with you and take in your hand the rod with which you struck the Nile. I will stand there before you by the rock at Horeb. Strike the rock, and water will come out of it for the people to drink." Moses did as he was instructed in the sight of the elders of Israel. [1]

He [God] split the rocks in the desert and there poured out water as abundant as the seas. He made streams come out of rocks and water flow from them like rivers.[2]

[Nehemiah:] "It was because of your great compassion You did not abandon your people in the desert. ... You did not withhold your manna from them and you gave them water for their thirst. For forty years you sustained them in the desert and they lacked nothing." [3]

[The Eternal-God declares:] "Come, all you who are thirsty, come to the waters; you who have no money, come buy and eat! ... Why do you spend your money on what is not bread and your labour on what does not satisfy? [4]

[Paul] I do not want you to be unaware, my brothers and sisters, that our forefathers were all under the cloud and that they all passed through the sea. ... They all ate the same spiritual food and they drank the same spiritual drink, for they drank from the spiritual rock that followed them, and that rock was Christ. [5]

Jesus answered, "Everyone who drinks this water will be thirsty again, but whoever drinks the water I give him will never be thirsty again. The water that I give him will become in him a spring of water which wells up to eternal life." [6]

On the last and greatest day of the feast, Jesus stood and cried out, "If anyone is thirsty, let him come to me and drink. As the Scripture has said, streams of living water will flow from within whoever believes in me." By this He meant [God] the Holy Spirit, whom those who believed in Him would receive later. [7]

[1] Exodus 17:1-2,4-6   [2] Psalm 78:15-16   [3] Nehemiah 9:19-21   [4] Isaiah 55:1-2   [5] 1 Corinthians 10:1-4   [6] John 4:13-14   [7] John 7:37-39

Day 50

Mount Sinai was a frightening place for Israel. God came down to the mountain and no one, except Moses, was allowed to approach it. There God gave the Ten Commandments. The people were afraid to be near God, but Moses was not. This is a picture of the separation between people and God. The nearer God comes to people, the more terrible is the sin seen to be that separates them from Him. When that sin is dealt with, there is peace and joy in being near God. The awe is still there but the fear has gone.

The Covenant given on Mount Sinai

In the third month after the Israelites left Egypt ... they entered the Desert of Sinai. They camped in the desert before the mountain. Then Moses went up the mountain to God. There the Eternal-God called to him and said, ... "If you obey me fully and keep my covenant, then you, out of all the nations, will be my treasured possession. Although the whole earth is mine, you will be a kingdom of priests and a holy nation for me.'" ...

On the morning of the third day there was thunder and lightning. A thick cloud covered the mountain and there sounded a very loud trumpet blast. All the people trembled. Then Moses led the people of the camp to meet God. They stood at the foot of the mountain. Mount Sinai was wrapped in smoke because the Eternal-God descended on it in fire. Smoke went up from it like smoke from a furnace. The whole mountain shook violently and the sound of a trumpet grew louder and louder.

The Eternal-God descended to the top of Mount Sinai and called Moses to go to the top of the mountain. Moses went up and the Eternal-God said to him, "Go down and warn the people not to force their way through to look at the Eternal-God. If they do, many of them will perish." [1]

[Moses:] Remember the day you stood before the Eternal-God, your God, at Mount Horeb, when He said to me, "Assemble the people before me to hear my words that they may revere me as long as they live in the land, and may teach those words to their children. You approached and stood at the foot of the mountain while it blazed with fire, with black clouds and deep darkness. Then the Eternal-God spoke to you out of the fire " [2]

You have not come to a mountain that can be touched, to a blazing fire, to darkness, gloom and a storm, ... but you have come to Mount Zion, to the city of the living God, the heavenly Jerusalem. You have come to God, the judge of all men, to the spirits of righteous men made perfect, to Jesus the mediator of a new covenant, and to the sprinkled blood that speaks a better word than the blood of Abel. See to it that you do not refuse the One who speaks. [3]

[1] Exodus 19:1-6,16-21   [2] Deuteronomy 4:10-12   [3] Hebrews 12:18,22-25

Day 51

Despite all that they had seen God do for them, the children of Israel had not had a real 'change of heart'. They thought Moses had died on the mountain. He represented all they knew of God. They felt their need for a power greater than their own. They did not trust Moses' God, so they made a 'god' for themselves. Despite their words, Moses' God had not become truly their God. They rebelled against Him.

Israel and the golden calf

When the people saw that Moses was a long time in coming down from the mountain, they gathered round Aaron and said, "Come, make gods who will go before us. We do not know what has happened to this Moses who brought us out of Egypt." Then the people took off their gold earrings and brought them to Aaron. He took what they gave him and made it into an idol shaped like a calf. ... Then they cried, "These, O Israel, are your gods who brought you out of Egypt." ... The people rose early the next morning and sacrificed burnt offerings, ... they sat down to eat and drink and then got up to indulge in wild revelry.

Then the Eternal-God said to Moses, "Go down! Your people whom you brought up out of Egypt, have become corrupted. ... I have observed these people ... and they are indeed stiff-necked. Now leave me and I will destroy them in my great anger. In their stead, I will make you into a great nation. But Moses pleaded with the Eternal-God, his God, saying, "O Eternal-God, why are you so angry with your people, whom you brought out of Egypt with such great power? ... Then the Eternal-God changed His mind and did not bring about the disaster about which He had spoken ." [1]

[Stephen:] "The Eternal-God said to Moses: ... 'I am sending you to Egypt for I have come down to deliver Israel.' It was this same Moses whom Israel rejected, saying 'Who made you ruler and judge over us?' He was sent to be Israel's ruler and deliverer by God himself, who appeared to him in the burning bush. He worked wonders and miraculous signs in Egypt, then led them out of Egypt at the Red Sea and into the desert for forty years. ... But our forefathers refused to obey him. They rejected him and, in their hearts, returned to Egypt. They said to Aaron, 'Make gods who will go before us.' ... You stiff-necked people ... you are the same as your forefathers: You always oppose the Holy Spirit! Has there ever been a prophet your fathers did not persecute?" [2]

[Paul:] Formerly, when you did not know God, you were slaves to gods who did not exist. Now that you have come to know God, or rather are known by God, how is it that you can turn back to those weak and miserable principles? How can you want to be enslaved by them again. [3]

[1] Exodus 32:1-14   [2] Acts 7:33-36,39-40,51   [3] Galatians 4:8-9

Day 52

The Old Covenant was not a contract agreed to by God and the Israelites. It was a promise by God to guide and lead the Israelites so that they became established as a nation in the promised land and so be a blessing to the world. His promise depended on His character alone. The people accepted the Covenant but their acceptance was to be tested in the way they lived. The Covenant was sealed with the symbolic blood sacrifice of an animal. That Old Covenant would later be superseded by the New Covenant in the blood of Jesus Christ, God the Son.

The Old Covenant

God said to Moses, "Come up [Mount Sinai] to the Eternal-God, you, Aaron, ... and seventy of the elders of Israel. You are to worship at a distance, Moses alone is to come near the Eternal-God. ... Moses then wrote down everything the Eternal-God had said to him. He rose up early the next morning and built an altar at the foot of the mountain. He set up twelve stone pillars to represent the twelve tribes of Israel. ... There they offered burnt offerings and blood sacrifices of young bulls as fellowship offerings to the Eternal-God. Moses took half of the blood and put it in basins, and with the other half he sprinkled the altar. Then he took the 'book of the covenant' and read it to the people. They said, "All that the Eternal-God has commanded, we will obey." Then Moses took the blood, sprinkled it on the people and said, "This is the blood of the covenant that the Eternal-God has made with you according to all these words." [1]

Be careful not to forget the covenant the Eternal-God, your God, made with you; ... For the Eternal-God, your God, is a jealous God. He is like a consuming fire. [2]

Every high priest is appointed to offer gifts and sacrifices. ... The ministry Jesus received, however, is as far above theirs as the covenant, of which He is the mediator, is far superior to the old one. It is founded on better promises. If the first covenant had been sufficient, there would be no need for another. But God found fault with those people and said: "The time is coming ... when I will make a new covenant with Israel. ... This covenant will not be like the covenant I made with their forefathers. ... This is the covenant I will make with Israel, ... I will put my laws in their minds and write them on their hearts. I will be their God, and they will be my people.[3]

Jesus said to them, "I have earnestly desired to eat this Passover with you before I suffer. ... He took bread, gave thanks, then broke the bread and gave it to them, saying, "This is my body which is given for you. ..." In the same way, after supper, He took the cup saying, "This cup is the new covenant in my blood which is poured out for you." [4]

[1] Exodus 24:1-8 [2] Deuteronomy 4:23-24 [3] Hebrews 8:3,6-10 [4] Luke 22:15,19-20

Day 53

God gave the Ten Commandments as a sign of the Covenant between Him and Israel. They showed the way that God planned for people to live. It was by obeying these commandments that the Israelites would respond to the Covenant He had made with them. Through them, people could come to know what sin was, but keeping them could not take away sin. The death of Jesus Christ did what the law could not do.

The Ten Commandments

The Eternal-God spoke to you out of the fire. ... He declared to you His covenant, the Ten Commandments, which He commanded you to follow. Then He wrote them on two stone tablets. At that time, the Eternal-God instructed me to teach you the decrees and laws you are to observe in the land you are going to possess, when you have crossed the Jordan. [1]

The Eternal-God said to Moses, "Cut two stone tablets like the first ones, and I will write on them the same words that were on the first tablets ... for it is in accordance with these words that I have made a covenant with you and with Israel. He wrote on the tablets the words of the covenant, the Ten Commandments. [2]

One of the Pharisees, a lawyer, asked Jesus a question to test him: "Teacher, which is the greatest commandment?" Jesus replied: "'Love the Eternal-God, your God, with all your heart and with all your soul and with all your mind. This is the first and greatest commandment. The second is like it: 'Love your neighbour as yourself.' All the Law and the Prophets depend on these two commandments." [3]

[Paul:] Now we know that whatever the law says is addressed to those who are under the law, so that every mouth may be silenced and the whole world held accountable to God. No one will be declared righteous in God's sight by observing the law. It is, however, through the law that we become aware of sin. [4]

All who rely on keeping the law are under a curse, for it is written, "Cursed is every one who does not do, all the time, everything written in the Book of the Law." It is clear that no one is justified before God by the law, because, "Those who are righteous will live by faith." ... Is the law, therefore, opposed to the promises of God? Of course not! If there were a law that could give life, then righteousness would certainly have come by that law. But the Scripture declares that the whole world is in slavery to sin, so that what was promised might be given to those who believe. [5]

Christ redeemed us from the curse of the law by becoming a curse for us. It is written: "Cursed is everyone who is hung on a tree." He redeemed us in order that the blessing promised to Abraham might come to the Gentiles through Him. [6]

---

[1] Deuteronomy 4:12-14   [2] Exodus 34:1, 27-28   [3] Matthew 22:37-40   [4] Romans 3:19-20
[5] Galatians 3:10-11, 21-22   [6] Galatians 3:13-14

Day 54

There is only one God, the Creator-God. To worship other gods as if they existed and had the power and the knowledge that only He has, is to lower Him from His true and rightful place. It is also to act a lie. It is to behave as if what does not exist is really there. It is to steal from God the honour due to Him alone.

The Ten Commandments: You shall have no other gods

God spoke all these words: "I am the Eternal-God, your God. ... You shall have no other gods before me."[1] Do not call on the names of other gods. Do not let them be heard on your lips.[2] You shall have no strange god among you. You shall not bow down to a foreign God.[3] Take care that you are not enticed to turn away and worship other gods.[4] Do not worship any other god, for the Eternal-God, whose name is Jealous, is a jealous God.[5]

Jacob said to his household and to all who were with him, "Put away the foreign gods you have with you, purify yourselves and change your clothes. Then come, let us go up to Bethel, there I will build an altar to God. ... So they gave Jacob all the foreign gods and earrings they had and he buried them under the oak at Shechem. They set out, and the fear of God fell on the towns all around them so that no one pursued them.[6]

The Eternal-God said to me [Jeremiah], "There is a conspiracy among the inhabitants of Judah. ... They have turned back to the sins of their forefathers. ... They have gone after other gods to serve them." ... Therefore this is what the Eternal-God says, "I will bring a disaster on them which they will not be able to escape. Although they cry out to me, I will not listen to them."[7]

The heavens praise your wonders and your faithfulness, O Eternal-God, in the assembly of the holy ones. For who in the skies above can be compared with the Eternal-God? ... Who is like you, O Almighty Eternal-God? ... The heavens and the earth are yours; you founded the world and all that is in it.[8]

To the Eternal-God, your God, belong the heavens, ... the earth and all that is in it ... For the Eternal-God, your God, is God of gods and Lord of lords, the great God, mighty and awesome, who shows no partiality and takes no bribe.[9]

Formerly, when you did not know God, you were slaves to beings who by nature are not gods at all.[10]

[Isaiah:] They know nothing, those who pray to a god that cannot save. ... "There is no god apart from me. I am a righteous God and a Saviour. ... Turn to me and be saved, all you ends of the earth; for I am God and there is no other."[11]

---

[1] Exodus 20:3 [2] Exodus 23:13 [3] Psalm 81:9 [4] Deuteronomy 11:16 [5] Exodus 34:14 [6] Genesis 35:2-5 [7] Jeremiah 11:9-13 [8] Psalm 89:5-6,8,11 [9] Deuteronomy 10:14,17 [10] Galatians 4:8 [11] Isaiah 45:21-22

Day 55

God strictly forbade the making and worship of idols. He alone is to be worshipped. Idols are nothing in themselves, and the worship offered to them is taken to himself by Satan, the Devil. To worship an idol is both to worship Satan and it is to act a lie. To worship something that does not exist is to worship Satan. It is to act a lie because idols take the place of God, not only in worship, but in being the object of great value. Idol worship also deceives people into faith which is futile because it has no true foundation.

The Ten Commandments: You shall not make or worship idols

God spoke all these words: ... "You shall not make for yourself an idol in the form of anything in heaven above or on the earth beneath or in the waters below. You shall not bow down to them or worship them. I, the Eternal-God, your God, am a jealous God. I punish the children for the sins of their fathers to the third and fourth generation of those who rebel against me, but I show love to thousands who love me and keep my commandments. [1]

Do not make idols or set up carved images or pillars, and do not place in your land a stone, carved as a figure, to bow down to it. I am the Eternal-God, your God.[2]

[Micah:] "On that day," says the Eternal-God, "I will destroy your images and your carved stones. You will never again bow down to the work of your hands." [3]

[Isaiah:] Come and assemble together, you survivors from the nations. They know nothing, those who carry about idols of wood and pray to gods that cannot save. [4] All who make idols are nothing and the things they treasure are worth nothing. ... The carpenter ... cuts down a cedar, a cypress, or an oak tree, ... he takes part of it, lights a fire, warms himself and bakes bread. From the other part he carves a god and worships it ... he prays to it: "Save me! You are my god!" No one stops to ask ... 'Half of it I used to make a fire, ... how can I bow down to worship what is left? [5]

The wrath of God is revealed from heaven against all the godlessness and wickedness of men who suppress the truth by their wickedness. ... Although they knew God, they neither honoured Him as God nor gave thanks to Him, but their thinking became futile and their senseless minds were darkened. In claiming to be wise, they became fools. They exchanged the glory of the immortal God for images looking like people, birds, animals and reptiles. [6]

[John:] We know that the Son of God has come and has given us understanding so that we may know Him who is true. And we are in Him who is true. He is the true God and in Him is eternal life. Little children, keep yourselves from idols. [7]

[Isaiah:] This is what the Eternal-God says: ... "I am the Eternal-God, that is my name! I will give my glory to no one else nor my praise to idols." [8]

[1] Exodus 20:1,4-6   [2] Leviticus 26:1   [3] Micah 5:10,13   [4] Isaiah 45:20   [5] Isaiah 44:9,13,19
[6] Romans 1:18-23   [7] 1 John 5:21   [8] Isaiah 42:5, 8

Day 56

The 'name of God' represents God Himself. To use God's name in a dishonourable way is to dishonour Him. People profane God's name when they use it without reverence. It is also profaned when people, who are known to be 'people of God', behave in ways which do not honour Him. To misuse the name of God - 'God the Father', 'God the Son', and 'God the Holy Spirit' - is to dishonour Him as Creator and Redeemer.

The Ten Commandments: You shall not misuse the name of God

God spoke all these words: "You shall not misuse the name of the Eternal-God, your God, for He will hold anyone guilty who misuses His name." [1] "Do not swear falsely by my name for in doing so you profane the name of the Eternal-God, your God. I am the Eternal-God." [2]

The Eternal-God said to Moses, "Tell Aaron and his sons to handle with respect the sacred offerings the Israelites dedicate to me, so that they do not profane my holy name. I am the Eternal-God." [3] Do not sacrifice any of your children to the god, Molech. You must not profane the name of your God. I am the Eternal-God. [4]

Again the word of the Eternal-God came to me [Ezekiel] : "When the people of Israel lived in their own land, they defiled it by the way they behaved and acted. ... So I poured out my wrath on them. ... I scattered them among the nations. ... Wherever they went among the nations they profaned my name. It was said of them, 'These are the people of the Eternal-God, and they had to leave His land.' I was concerned for my holy name, which Israel profaned among the nations." ...

"This is what the Sovereign Eternal-God says: 'It is not for your sake, O house of Israel, that I am going to act. It is for the sake of my holy name, which you have profaned among the nations wherever you have gone. I will make holy my great name which has been profaned - which you have profaned - among the nations. The nations will know that I am the Eternal-God when I show myself to be holy through you before their eyes.'" [5]

This is what the Eternal-God says: "For three sins of Israel, and for four, I will not turn back my anger. ... They trample on the poor as upon the dust of the ground and deprive the oppressed of justice. Father and son use the same girl and so my holy name is profaned." [6] "From the rising to the setting of the sun, my name will be great among the nations... But you profane it by saying: 'The table of the Eternal-God is defiled', and of its food, 'It is contemptible.'" [7]

He [Jesus] said to them, "When you pray, say: 'Father, may your name be hallowed, your kingdom come.'" [8]

[1] Exodus 20:1,7   [2] Leviticus 19:12   [3] Leviticus 22:1-3   [4] Leviticus 18:21   [5] Ezekiel 36:16-23
[6] Amos 2:6-7   [7] Malachi 1:11-12   [8] Luke 11:2

Day 57

God's command, which reflects the way He made people, is that everyone should have one day's rest after six days of work. For the Jews, the 'day of rest' was called the Sabbath. After the resurrection of Jesus Christ on 'the first day of the week', this day was taken by the early Christians as the 'one day in seven' for rest and worship of God.

The Ten Commandments: Keep the day of rest

God spoke all these words: ... "Remember to keep the Sabbath holy. Six days you shall labour and do all your work, but the seventh day is a Sabbath to the Eternal-God, your God. On it neither you, nor your son or daughter, nor your manservant or maidservant, nor your animals, nor the strangers within your walls, shall do any work. For in six days the Eternal-God made the heavens and the earth, the sea, and all that is in it, but on the seventh day, He rested. In this way, the Eternal-God blessed the Sabbath day and set it apart to be holy. [1]

This is what the Eternal-God says: "Maintain justice and do what is right. ... Blessed is the man who does this steadfastly, keeps the Sabbath without desecrating it, and refrains from doing any evil." [2] "If you keep from breaking the Sabbath and from pleasing only yourself on my holy day. If you make the Sabbath a delight, and the holy day of the Eternal-God honourable, ... then you will delight in the Eternal-God, and you will ride on the heights of the earth and feast on the inheritance of your forefather Jacob." The mouth of the Eternal-God has said this.[3]

At that time Jesus walked through the cornfields on the Sabbath. His disciples were hungry and began to pick some ears of corn and eat them. When the Pharisees saw this, they said to Him, "Look! Your disciples are doing what it is unlawful to do on the Sabbath." He answered them, "Have you not read what David did when he and his companions were hungry? He entered the house of God, and ... ate the 'bread of the Presence' which was lawful for the priests to do, but not them. ... I tell you that there is One here who is greater than the temple." [4] Then He said to them, "The Sabbath was made for man, and not man for the Sabbath. So the 'Son of Man' is also 'Lord of the Sabbath'." [5]

Early on the first day of the week, ... Mary of Magdala went to the tomb and saw that the stone had been moved away from the entrance. ... On the evening of that first day of the week, while the disciples were together and the doors locked for fear of the Jews, Jesus came and stood among them and said, "Peace be with you!". [6]

On the first day of the week, when we [Luke, Paul and companions] met together to break bread, Paul went on talking with them until midnight. [7]

This is the day the Eternal-God has made; let us rejoice and be glad in it. [8]

[1] Exodus 20:1,8-11 [2] Isaiah 56:1-2 [3] Isaiah 58:13-14 [4] Matthew 12:1-6 [5] Mark 2:27
[6] John 20:1,19 [7] Acts 20:7 [8] Psalm 118:24

Day 58

God's plan is for children to honour their parents. This means to obey them and to respect them as those who, under God, have brought them into the world, and are there to love, teach and train them in preparation for adult life. Children who are disrespectful to their parents grow into adults who show no respect for God nor for those in authority over them. The way children are taught to respect and honour their parents is to be a preparation for the way in which, as adults, everyone respects and honours God, their 'heavenly' Father.

The Ten Commandments: Honour your father and mother

God spoke all these words: ... "Honour your father and your mother, so that you may live long in the land the Eternal-God, your God, is giving you." [1] "Each one of you shall respect his mother and father." [2] Listen to your father, who gave you life, and do not despise your mother in her old age.[3]

Every year His [Jesus'] parents went to Jerusalem for the Feast of the Passover. When He was twelve years old, they went to the Feast as usual. After the feast, while His parents were setting off for the journey home, they were unaware that the boy Jesus had stayed behind in Jerusalem. ... They began to look for Him among their relatives and friends. When they could not find Him, they returned to Jerusalem to look for Him there. After three days they found Him sitting among the teachers in the temple courts. He was listening to them and asking them questions ... When His parents saw Him, they were amazed. His mother said to Him, "Son, why have you behaved like this to us? Your father and I have been anxiously looking for you." "Why were you searching for me?" He asked, "did you not know that I must be in my Father's house?" ... Then He went to Nazareth with them and was obedient to them. ... Jesus grew in wisdom and years, in favour with both God and men. [4]

He [Jesus] said to them [the Pharisees]: "You have a fine way of putting aside the commands of God in order to keep your own traditions! Moses said, 'Honour your father and mother,' and, 'Anyone who speaks evil of his father or mother must be put to death.' But you say that if anyone says to his father or mother: 'Whatever help you might have received from me is Corban' (that is, a gift consecrated to God), then you refuse to let him do anything for his father or mother. Thus you make void the word of God by the tradition that you have had handed down to you." [5]

Children, obey your parents in the Lord, for this is right.[6] Children obey your parents in everything, for this is pleasing to the Lord. [7]

[Solomon:] My son, listen to your father's instruction and do not reject your mother's teaching.[8]

[1] Exodus 20:1,12 [2] Leviticus 19:3 [3] Proverbs 23:22 [4] Luke 2:41-52 [5] Mark 7:9-13 [6] Ephesians 6:1 [7] Colossians 3:20 [8] Proverbs 1:8

Day 59

The Bible distinguishes between (a) one person killing another when this is 'murder', that is, one person killing another for any reason, (b) accidental killing, when killing was not intended, and (c) the killing of a murderer by the ruling authorities in the cause of justice. God forbids murder very strongly. Men and women were made in the image of God. To kill someone is, therefore, symbolically to 'kill God' and so act against Him. He commands the killing of a proved murderer by those legally authorised to pursue justice. He also seeks to protect anyone who has killed someone by accident.

The Ten Commandments: You shall not murder

God spoke all these words: "You shall not murder." [1] "Do nothing that puts your neighbour's life in danger." [2] "Anyone who kills a human being must himself be killed." [3]

[God said to Noah:] "From an animal I will demand an account for human blood shed, ... also for a man I will require a reckoning for the life of his fellow man. Whoever sheds the blood of a man, by a man shall his blood be shed, for man was made in the image of God." [4]

"Bear no hatred in your heart for your brother. Tell your neighbour openly what is his offence, or you will share in his guilt. Do not seek vengeance or hold a grudge against any of your people. Love your neighbour as yourself." [5]

"Whoever strikes a man and so kills him shall be put to death. If he kills him accidentally, that is, God lets it happen, he is to flee to a place of safety which I will appoint. But if a man plans to kills another man deliberately, you are to take him away from my altar and put him to death." [6] "Whoever kills a person is to be put to death as a murderer on the evidence of witnesses, but no one is to be put to death on the testimony of one witness. [7]

Jesus said, "You have heard that it was said long ago, 'Do not murder, and anyone who murders will be liable to judgment.' I tell you that whoever is angry with his brother will be liable to judgment." [8] Whoever hates his brother is a murderer. You know that no murderer has eternal life. [9]

Where do disputes and quarrels among you come from? Do they not come from the cravings that are at war within you? You want something you do not have, so you kill. You covet what you do not have, because you do not ask God for it. [10]

[Jesus said:] "It is what comes out of a man that makes him 'unclean.' It is from within, out of men's hearts, that come evil thoughts, ... murder ... All these evils come from inside a man and make him 'unclean'." [11]

1 Exodus 20:1,13   2 Leviticus 19:16   3 Leviticus 24:17   4 Genesis 9:5-6   5 Leviticus 19:17-18
6 Exodus 21:12-13   7 Numbers 35:30   8 Matthew 5:21-22   9 1 John 3:15   10 James 4:1-3   11 Mark 7:20-23

Day 60

The sin of adultery lies in the way it weakens and destroys the God-ordained life-long relationship of marriage between a man and a woman. Physical union is part of spiritual union. To misuse one is to weaken or destroy the other. Adultery, as with any sexual action outside marriage, is a sin against God as well against a marriage-partner, because it is contrary to God's ordained union of love and trust in marriage.

The Ten Commandments: You shall not commit adultery

God spoke all these words: ..."You shall not commit adultery." [1] If a man commits adultery with the wife of his neighbour, both the adulterer and the adulteress shall be put to death. [2] Whoever keeps the whole law but fails in one point is guilty of breaking all of it, for He who said, you shall not commit adultery also said, you shall not kill. If you do not commit adultery but kill, your are guilty of breaking the law. [3]

[Jesus:] "You know that it was said, 'Do not commit adultery.' But I tell you than anyone who looks with lust at a woman has already committed adultery with her in his heart. [4] It is easier for heaven and earth to pass away than for the least stroke of a letter to be dropped from the Law. Anyone who divorces his wife and marries another woman commits adultery, and any man who marries a divorced woman commits adultery. [5]

The scribes and the Pharisees brought a woman caught in adultery and made her stand before them all. They said to Jesus, "Teacher, this woman was caught in the act of adultery. In the Law, Moses commanded us to stone such women. What do you say? ... Jesus bent down and started to write with His finger on the ground while they went on questioning Him. Then He straightened up and said to them, "Let any one of you who is without sin be the first to throw a stone at her." Again He stooped down and wrote on the ground. Seeing this, those who were there began to go away, one at a time, the elders first, until only Jesus was left. The woman still stood before Him there. Jesus straightened up and asked her, "Woman, where are they? Has no one condemned you?" She replied, "No one sir." Jesus said to her, "Then neither do I condemn you. Go and sin no more." [6]

Marriage should be honoured by all and the marriage bed kept undefiled, for God will judge fornicators and adulterers. [7]

[Paul:] Do you not know that sinners will not inherit the kingdom of God? Do not be deceived: Neither fornicators, nor idolaters, nor adulterers, sensual pleasure-seekers, nor homosexual offenders [sodomites], nor thieves, nor the greedy, nor drunkards, nor revilers, nor robbers will inherit the kingdom of God. [8]

[1] Exodus 20:1,14   [2] Leviticus 20:10   [3] James 2:10-11   [4] Matthew 5:27-28   [5] Luke 16:17-18
[6] John 8:3-11   [7] Hebrews 13:4   [8] 1 Corinthians 6:9-10

Day 61

God means people to own things. They are to hold them as a trust from Him. Everything really belongs to Him. To steal from someone else is to rob God. Stealing destroys the basis of a trusting fellowship in the life of a family or community. Stealing is an act of robbery—taking from someone what rightfully belongs to them, lying—saying that something which belongs to someone belongs to the one who steals, coveting—wrongly desiring what one should not have, and deceit—acting as though one possesses what one does not have.

The Ten Commandments: You shall not steal

God spoke all these words: ... "You shall not steal; you shall not deal falsely " [1] "You shall not defraud your neighbour or steal from him. You shall not hold back the wages of a labourer until the next day. [2]

If you go into your neighbour's vineyard, you may take all the grapes you can eat, but you may not put any in your basket. If you go into your neighbour's cornfield, you may pluck ears of corn with your hands, but you must not put a sickle to his standing corn.[3] If someone gives his neighbour silver or goods for safe keeping and they are stolen from the neighbour's house, the thief, if caught, must pay back double. [4] Do not rob the poor because they are poor and do not crush the needy in court, for the Eternal-God will plead their cause and will plunder those who plunder them.[5]

The word that came to Jeremiah from the Eternal-God, "Will you steal and murder, ... and then come and stand before me in my house, and say, 'We are safe!' - safe to do all these abominable things? Has this house, which bears my Name, become a den of robbers in your sight? Know this, that I have been watching!" declares the Eternal-God. [6]

Again the word of the Eternal-God came to me: [Ezekiel] ... "The people of the land have practised extortion and committed robbery. They have oppressed the poor and needy and ill-treated and denied justice to the alien. ... Therefore I have poured out my anger on them and consumed them with the fire of my wrath." [7] For I, the Eternal-God, love justice. I hate robbery and wickedness." [8]

[Paul:] You, then who teach others, will you not teach yourselves? You who preach against stealing, do you steal? [9] Whoever has been stealing must steal no longer, rather, he must work honestly with his own hands, so he will have something to share with those who are in need.[10]

Keep your lives free from the love of money and be content with what you have. God has said, "I will never leave you nor forsake you." [11]

[1] Exodus 20:1,15 [2] Leviticus 19:13 [3] Deuteronomy 23:24-25 [4] Exodus 22:7 [5] Proverbs 22:22-23
[6] Jeremiah 7:9-11 [7] Ezekiel 22:23,29,31 [8] Isaiah 61:8 [9] Romans 2:21 [10] Ephesians 4:28 [11] Hebrews 13:6

Day 62

Lying, giving false evidence and acting deceitfully are closely linked and are equally condemned by God. Lying—about oneself or about someone else—is contrary to God's character because lying destroys good relationships between people and between God and people. There can be no trust when there is lying and deceit. To be silent when one should speak out can be telling a lie.

The Ten Commandments: You shall not lie about your neighbour

God spoke all these words: ... "You shall not bear false testimony against your neighbour." [1] "Do not lie. Do not deceive one another." [2]

Do not spread a false report. Do not join hands with a wicked man by being a malicious witness. You shall not follow the crowd in evil doing nor pervert justice by siding with the majority when you give testimony in a lawsuit. Nor will you, in a court of law, show partiality to the poor. [3] A truthful witness gives honest evidence, but a false witness speaks deceitfully. ...[4] A false witness will be punished, but a liar will perish. ...[5] Do not be a witness against your neighbour without cause and do not deceive with your lips. [6]

[The word of the Eternal-God through Jeremiah:] "They [God's people] bend their tongues like bows to shoot lies. They have grown strong in the land by falsehood, not by truth. ... Beware of your neighbours. Do not trust your family. Every brother is a deceiver, and every neighbour a slanderer. Neighbours deceive neighbours. No one speaks the truth. ... You live in a deceitful world. In their deceit the people refuse to acknowledge me," declares the Eternal-God. [7]

This is what the Eternal-God says: ...The heart is deceitful above all things. Who can understand it? I, the Eternal-God, test the mind and search the heart, to reward a man according to his ways and according to what his deeds bring forth. [8]

Do not lie to one another, since you have put off your old self with its practices and have put on the new self, which is being renewed in knowledge in the image of its Creator. [9] You must all put off falsehood and speak truthfully to your neighbour, for we are all members one of another. [10]

[John] Then I saw [in a vision] a new heaven and a new earth. ... Nothing unclean will ever enter it, nor anyone who does what is shameful or false, but only those whose names are written in the Lamb's book of life.[11]

If we say that we have no sin, we deceive ourselves and the truth is not in us. If we confess our sins, God is faithful and just and will forgive us our sins and cleanse us from all unrighteousness." [12]

[1] Exodus 20:1,16 [2] Leviticus 19:11 [3] Exodus 23:1-2 [4] Proverbs 12:17 [5] Proverbs 19:9
[6] Proverbs 24:28 [7] Jeremiah 9:3-6 [8] Jeremiah 17:5,9-10 [9] Colossians 3:9-10
[10] Ephesians 4:25 [11] Revelation 21:1,27 [12] 1 John 1:8-9

Day 63

To covet is to desire what one should not have at that moment. Covetousness is closely linked to greed. Coveting is the sin in the heart that often leads to stealing. The remedy for covetousness is repentance, changing one's mind to see that God alone gives true contentment, because what He is and gives is fully satisfying.

The Ten Commandments: You shall not covet

God spoke all these words: ... "You shall not covet your neighbour's house. You shall not covet your neighbour's wife, or his male or female servant, his ox or donkey, or anything that belongs to your neighbour." [1]

Then Joshua said to Achan, "My son, give glory to the Eternal-God, the God of Israel, and confess to Him. Tell me what you have done; do not hide it from me." Achan replied, "It is true! I have sinned against the Eternal-God, the God of Israel. ... When I saw in the plunder a beautiful robe from Babylonia, two hundred shekels of silver and a wedge of gold weighing fifty shekels, I coveted them and took them. They lie hidden in the ground inside my tent, with the silver underneath." ... Joshua said, "Why have you brought this trouble on us? The Eternal-God will bring trouble on you today." [2]

Woe to those who devise iniquity and plot evil on their beds! ... They covet fields and seize them, and houses and take them. ... Therefore, the Eternal-God says: "I am planning to bring disaster on this people." [3]

Then the Eternal-God answered [Habakkuk]: "Look at those who are puffed up. Their spirit is not upright. But the righteous will live by faith. ... Woe to him who builds his wealth by unjust gain to set his nest on high, to escape the reach of harm! [4]

What shall we say, then? That the law is sin? Certainly not! I would not have known what sin was except through the Law. I would not have known what it was to covet if the law had not said, "Do not covet." But sin, seizing an opportunity in the commandment, produced every kind of covetous desire in me.[5]

Godliness with contentment is great gain. We brought nothing into the world, and we shall take nothing out of it. But if we have food and clothing, we will be content. Those who want to get rich fall into temptation and are trapped into many foolish and harmful desires that plunge men into ruin and destruction. For the love of money is a root of all kinds of evil. [6]

Then He [Jesus] said to them, "Take care! Be on your guard against all kinds of greed. A man's life does not consist in the abundance of his possessions." [7]

[1] Exodus 20:1,17 [2] Joshua 7:19-21,25 [3] Micah 2:1-3 [4] Habakkuk 2:2,4-5,9,14 [5] Romans 7:7-8
[6] 1 Timothy 6:6-10 [7] Luke 12:15

Day 64

Physical adultery is a picture of spiritual adultery. As physical adultery weakens or destroys the marriage relationship between a man and a woman, so a person's relationship with God is weakened or destroyed when idols or anything else take from Him the worship and obedience due to Him alone.

Idolatry is spiritual adultery

After that whole generation had died, another generation grew up, who knew neither the Eternal-God nor what He had done for Israel. Then the Israelites did what was evil in the eyes of the Eternal-God and served the Baals, ... they followed the gods of the peoples around them. In His anger against Israel the Eternal-God handed them over to raiders who plundered them. ... They would not listen to their judges but lusted after other gods and bowed down to them. [1]

They, the brave warriors, famous men and heads of their fathers' houses [of the half-tribe of Manasseh] were very numerous but they were unfaithful to the God of their fathers and prostituted themselves before the gods of the peoples of the land, peoples whom God had destroyed before them. [2]

[The word of the Eternal-God to Ezekiel:] "Those who escape the sword will remember me among the nations where they have been carried as captives, how I was grieved by their adulterous hearts, which have turned away from me, and by their eyes, which lusted after their idols. They will loathe themselves for the wickedness they have committed and for all their detestable practices. [3]

The Eternal-God said to me [Ezekiel], "Son of man ... declare to them their deeds. They have committed adultery and there is blood on their hands. They have committed adultery with their idols. They have sacrificed their children, whom they had borne to me, as food for those idols." [4]

He [Jesus] answered, "A wicked and adulterous generation asks for a sign! But no sign will be given it except the sign of the prophet Jonah" [5] "Whoever is ashamed of me and my words in this adulterous and sinful generation, of them the Son of Man will be ashamed when He comes in the glory of His father with the holy angels." [6]

[Paul:] Do not be yoked with unbelievers. What is there in common between light and darkness? What harmony is there between Christ and Belial? ... What agreement has the temple of God and idols? For we are the temple of the living God. ... Therefore "come out from them and be separate," says the Eternal-God, "do not touch any unclean thing and I will receive you." [7]

[1] Judges 2:10-17 [2] 1 Chronicles 5:24-25 [3] Ezekiel 6:9 [4] Ezekiel 23:36-37 [5] Matthew 12:39 [6] Mark 8:38 [7] 2 Corinthians 6:15-17

Day 65

The Tabernacle or the Tent of Meeting, and later, the Temple, were made according to God's pattern. It was a place where the Jews worshipped God and it was a picture of the way they could approach Him. Non-Jews were kept outside the courtyard which only Jews could enter. The priests could go into the Holy Place. God was in the Most Holy Place. Only the High Priest could go into the Most Holy Place. Now everyone can approach God directly because of what Jesus, the Great High Priest, has done for them.

The Tabernacle - The 'Tent of Meeting' with God

The Eternal-God said to Moses, "Tell the Israelites to bring me an offering from the people ... of gold, silver and bronze, blue, purple and scarlet yarn and fine linen, goat hair, ram skins dyed red. ... Then have them make for me a sanctuary where I will dwell among them. Make this tabernacle and all its furnishings exactly according to the pattern that I will show you." [1] So the tabernacle was set up. ... Then the cloud covered the Tent of Meeting, and the glory of the Eternal-God filled the tabernacle. [2]

They [the priests] serve in a sanctuary that is a picture and shadow of what is in heaven. That is why Moses was instructed: "Make sure that you make everything according to the pattern that was shown you on the mountain." [3]

In the first month of the first year of his reign, he [Hezekiah] opened the doors of the temple of the Eternal-God and repaired them. ... He said to the priests and Levites: "Listen to me, Levites! Sanctify yourselves and consecrate the temple of the Eternal-God, the God of your fathers. Remove all filth from the sanctuary. Our fathers were unfaithful. ... Therefore the anger of the Eternal-God has come on Judah and Jerusalem. [4]

The first covenant had regulations for worship and an earthly sanctuary. A tabernacle was built. In its first room were the lampstand, the table and the consecrated bread. This was called the Holy Place. Behind the second curtain was a room called the Most Holy Place. ... When all this had been completed, the priests entered regularly into the outer room to carry out their duties. ... By this, [God] the Holy Spirit showed that the way into the Most Holy Place had not yet been opened as long as the first tabernacle was still standing. ... When Christ came as High Priest of the good things that are now here, He entered through the greater and more perfect tabernacle that is not made by men's hands, that is to say, it is not a part of this creation. ... For Christ did not enter a man-made sanctuary that was a copy of the true one, but He entered into heaven itself, now to appear for us in the presence of God [the Father]. [5]

[In a vision, John:] And I heard a loud voice from the throne saying, "The dwelling of God is with men, He will live with them and they will be His people." [6]

[1] Exodus 25:1-8 [2] Exodus 40:17, 34 [3] Hebrews 8:5 [4] 2 Chronicles 29:3-6,8
[5] Hebrews 9:1-4, 6-9,11,24 [6] Revelation 21:3

Day 66

The courtyard of the tabernacle represented its limits. Only Jews could enter by the gate into the courtyard; non-Jews were forbidden entry. It represented the family or the kingdom of God. Only from the courtyard was there access to the presence of God. Only by becoming a member of God's family does a person enter the family of God. People are born outside that family but they can be 'born again' into it.

The Tabernacle: The courtyard

The Eternal-God said to Moses: "Make a courtyard for the tabernacle. The south side shall be made of curtains of finely twisted linen a hundred cubits long supported by twenty posts and twenty bronze bases and with silver hooks and bands on the posts. The north side is also to be a hundred cubits long. ... The west side of the courtyard is to be fifty cubits wide and have curtains, with ten posts and ten bases. On the east side, towards the sunrise, the courtyard shall also be fifty cubits wide. ... At the entrance to the courtyard, there is to be a curtain twenty cubits long, made of blue, purple and scarlet yarn. [1]

One of them [the sons of Aaron] shall take a handful [of the incense offering] ... and burn it on the altar as a fragrant memorial to the Eternal-God. Aaron and his sons shall eat the remainder, without yeast, in the courtyard of the Tent of Meeting. [2]

[God said to Jeremiah:] Stand in the courtyard of the house of the Eternal-God and speak to all the people of the cities of Judah who come to worship in the house of the Eternal-God and tell them all that I command you, do not leave out a word. [3]

How lovely is your dwelling-place, O Eternal-God, Almighty! My soul longs, even faints for the courts of the Eternal-God. ... A day in your courts is better than a thousand elsewhere. I would rather be a doorkeeper in the house of my God than live in the tents of the wicked. For the Eternal-God is a sun and shield. He bestows favour and honour. No good thing does He withhold from those who walk uprightly.[4]

The righteous flourish like a palm tree and grow like a cedar in Lebanon. They are planted in the house of the Eternal-God. They will flourish in the courts of our God. [5] Enter His gates with thanksgiving and His courts with praise. Give thanks to Him and praise His name. [6]

Ascribe to the Eternal-God the glory due to His name; bring an offering and come into His courts. Worship the Eternal-God in the splendour of His holiness; tremble before Him, all the earth.[7]

Blessed are those whom you choose and bring near to live in your courts! We shall be satisfied with the good things of your house, your holy temple. [8]

[1] Exodus 27:9-16   [2] Leviticus 6:15-16   [3] Jeremiah 26:2   [4] Psalm 84:1-2,10-11   [5] Psalm 92:12
[6] Psalm 100:4   [7] Psalm 96:8-9   [8] Psalm 65:4

Day 67

The Most Holy Place was a picture of where God lives. A curtain separated it from the Holy Place. Only the High Priest could pass through the curtain and go into the Most Holy Place where God was. The curtain represented the sin which separates people from God. Jesus Christ, the Great High Priest, offered Himself so that sinners need no longer be separated from God. At His death the separating curtain was torn from top to bottom - God did it. Sin need no longer separate the sinner from God.

The Tabernacle: The curtain

[The Eternal-God said to Moses:] "Make a curtain of blue, purple and scarlet and finely twisted linen, with cherubim skilfully worked into it. Hang it with gold hooks on four posts of acacia wood overlaid with gold and standing on four silver bases. Hang the curtain from the clasps. Place the ark of the Testimony behind the curtain. The curtain will separate the Holy Place from the Most Holy Place. [1]

The Eternal God said to Moses, "Tell your brother Aaron that he must not come whenever he chooses into the Most Holy Place beyond the curtain before the mercy seat, lest he die, for I appear in the cloud on the mercy seat." [2]

They came to a place called the 'Place of the Skull' [Hebrew: Golgotha; Greek: Calvary]. ... When they had crucified Jesus ... from the sixth hour [noon] until the ninth hour [3 pm] darkness came over all the land. About the ninth hour Jesus cried out in a loud voice ... "My God, my God, why have you forsaken me?" ... When Jesus had cried out again in a loud voice, He breathed His last breath. At that moment the curtain of the temple was torn in two from top to bottom." [3] "It was now about the sixth hour, the sun's light faded, darkness covered the land and the curtain of the temple was torn into two." [4]

We have this hope as a sure and secure anchor for the soul which enters the inner sanctuary behind the curtain, where Jesus, our forerunner, has entered on our behalf.[5]

[Paul:] Remember that at that time you [Gentiles] were separated from Christ, with no citizenship in Israel and strangers to the covenants of the promise, without hope and without God in the world. But now, in Christ Jesus, you who once were far away have been brought near by the blood of Christ. For He is our peace. By abolishing in His body the law with its commandments and regulations, He has made the two one, and has broken down the barrier, the dividing wall of hostility between us. [6]

My brothers and sisters, since we have confidence to enter the Most Holy Place by the blood of Jesus, by the new and living way opened for us through the curtain, that is, His body, ... let us draw near to God with a true heart and in full assurance of faith, with our hearts sprinkled to make them clean from a guilty conscience. [7]

[1] Exodus 26:31-33 [2] Leviticus 16:2 [3] Matthew 27:33,35,45-46,50-51 [4] Luke 23:45
[5] Hebrews 6:19 [6] Ephesians 2:11-15 [7] Hebrews 10:19-22

Day 68

The altar was a place of sacrifice. There an animal was killed and its blood poured out or sprinkled on the altar as an expression of repentance for sin against God. And the altar was the place where God accepted the sacrifice of an animal instead of the punishment due to a repentant sinner and he or she was forgiven. When the 'blood of Christ' was shed on the cross, the symbolic sacrifice of a lamb became a reality in the 'Lamb of God'. There was no further need for an altar.

The Tabernacle: The altar of sacrifice

[The Eternal-God said to Moses:] "Build an altar of acacia wood. ... Make horns, one at each of the four corners, so that the horns and the altar are of one piece. Overlay the altar with bronze. ...[1] Take the anointing oil, ... anoint the altar of burnt offering and all its utensils. Consecrate the altar, and it will be most holy. [2] The altar will be most holy and whatever touches it will be holy." [3]

Moses said to Aaron, "Draw near to the altar and offer your sin offering and your burnt offering and make atonement for yourself and for the people, as the Eternal-God has commanded. [4]

Moses and the elders of Israel commanded the people: ... When you have crossed the Jordan ... build there an altar of stones to the Eternal-God, your God. Do not use any iron tool on the stones. Build the altar of the Eternal-God, your God, with stones from the open field and offer burnt offerings on it to the Eternal-God, your God." [5]

When they came to the place God had told him about [Mount Moriah], Abraham built an altar and placed the wood on it. He bound his son Isaac and laid him on the wood on the altar. [6] [James:] Was not our forefather Abraham considered righteous when he offered his son Isaac on the altar? [7]

Then he said to me [Ezekiel], "Son of man, this is what the Sovereign Eternal-God says: These are the regulations for sacrificing burnt offerings and sprinkling blood upon the altar. ... At the end of these days ... the priests are to offer your burnt offerings on the altar. Then I will accept you, declares the Sovereign Eternal-God." [8]

So they took Jesus, carrying His own cross. Jesus went out to the Place of the Skull [Golgotha or Calvary, on Mount Moriah]. There they crucified Him, and with Him two others, one on either side and Jesus between them. [9]

[Isaiah:] Then one of the seraphs flew to me with a live coal which he had taken with tongs from the altar. He touched my mouth with it and said, "See, this has touched your lips; your guilt has been taken away and your sin has been blotted out." [10]

He [Jesus] Himself bore our sins in His body on the tree, so that we might die to sin and live for righteousness. [11]

---

[1] Exodus 27:1 [2] Exodus 40:9-10 [3] Exodus 29:37 [4] Leviticus 9:7 [5] Deuteronomy 27:2,4-6 [6] Genesis 22:9 [7] James 2:21 [8] Ezekiel 43:18,27 [9] John 19:17-18 [10] Isaiah 6:6-7 [11] 1 Peter 2:24

Day 69

Under the Law of Moses, there were many sacrifices depending on the nature of the sin committed and the wealth of the one who sinned. All meant the killing of an innocent, unblemished animal. This sacrificial animal was a picture of Jesus Christ, the Lamb of God, who offered Himself once for all as the perfect, sufficient sacrifice for all sin.

The sacrifice for sin

The Eternal-God said to Moses, "Say to the Israelites: 'When anyone sins unintentionally and breaks the commands of the Eternal-God. ...[1] When he becomes aware that he is guilty, he must confess his sin and bring to the Eternal-God a female lamb or goat from the flock as a sin-offering, a penalty for the sin he has committed. ...[2] The sin offering is to be killed before the Eternal-God ... and he will be forgiven for the sin of which he was guilty." [3]

When Christ came as high priest, ... He did not enter the Most Holy Place by the blood of goats and calves; but He entered there once for all by His own blood, by which He had obtained eternal redemption. ... Christ is, therefore, the mediator of a new covenant so that those who are called may receive the promised eternal inheritance. Christ died a death that was a ransom which sets them free from the sins committed according to the first covenant. Christ did not enter a sanctuary made with human hands that was only a copy of the real one, He entered heaven itself where He is now, appearing for us, in the presence of God [the Father]. Nor did He enter heaven in order to offer Himself again and again, as the high priest enters the Most Holy Place every year with blood that is not his own. If it had been like that, Christ would have had to suffer many times since the creation of the world. But now He has appeared once for all at the end of the age to put away sin by the sacrifice of Himself. ... Christ, who was sacrificed once to take away the sins of many, will come again" [4]

In subjecting everything to Jesus, God [the Father] left nothing outside His dominion. At present, however, we do not see everything subject to Him. But we see Jesus, who, for short time, was made a little lower than the angels, now crowned with glory and honour because ... by the grace of God He suffered death for everyone.[5]

He [Jesus Christ], gave Himself for us to redeem us from all wickedness and to purify for Himself a people that are His very own, zealous to do what is good. [6]

Christ loved us and gave Himself up for us as a fragrant offering and sacrifice to God [the Father]. [7] Grace and peace to you from God our Father and the Lord Jesus Christ, who gave Himself for our sins to set us free from the present evil age, according to the will of our God and Father, to whom be glory for ever and ever. Amen. [8]

[1] Leviticus 4:1 [2] Leviticus 5:5-6 [3] Leviticus 6:24,7 [4] Hebrews 9:11-12,15,24-28 [5] Hebrews 2:9
[6] Titus 2:13-14 [7] Ephesians 5:2 [8] Galatians 1:3-5

Day 70

In Bible language, 'breath' represented physical life. To cease to breathe is to die physically. 'Blood' represented spiritual life. The physical 'shedding of blood' of an animal or a person causes an unnatural physical death. It also represented symbolically a 'spiritual death'. The shed blood of a sacrificed animal represented symbolically what it was impossible for any animal to be. Its meaning became clear when Jesus Christ, God the Son, offered His own spiritual life to suffer, in His relationship with God the Father, the spiritual consequences of people's sin. The blood of a sacrificed animal was a picture of the real sacrifice of Jesus Christ. It is the 'Blood of Christ' which takes away sin.

The sprinkled blood

Aaron [the High Priest] is to offer the bull for his own sin to make atonement for himself and his household. ... He shall slaughter the goat for the sin offering for the people and take its blood inside the curtain. ... He shall sprinkle it on the mercy seat and in front of it. In this way he will make atonement for the Most Holy Place because of the uncleanness and rebellion of the Israelites, whatever their sins have been. ... He shall take some of the bull's blood and some of the goat's blood and put it on the horns of the altar. [1]

When Moses had proclaimed every commandment of the law to all the people, he took the blood of calves ... and sprinkled the scroll and all the people. He said, "This is the blood of the covenant which God has commanded you to keep." ... In fact, the law requires that nearly everything be cleansed with blood, and without the shedding of blood there is no forgiveness. It was necessary, then, for the copies of the heavenly things to be purified with these sacrifices, but the heavenly things themselves with better sacrifices than these. For Christ did not enter a man-made sanctuary ... the way the high priest enters the Most Holy Place every year, with blood that is not his own. ... But now He has appeared once for all at the end of the age to put away sin by the sacrifice of Himself. As man is destined to die once, and after that face judgment, so Christ was sacrificed once to take away the sin of many. He will appear a second time, not to suffer for sin, but to bring salvation to those who are waiting for Him. [2] The blood of goats and bulls ... sprinkled on those who are ceremonially unclean, cleanses them so that they are ceremonially clean. How much more will the blood of Christ, who offered Himself unblemished to God [the Father], through the eternal [Holy] Spirit, cleanse our consciences from dead works so that we may serve the living God. [3]

God [the Father] made Him [Jesus Christ, God the Son] to be a sin offering for us, so that in Him we might become the righteousness of God. [4]

[1] Leviticus 16:6,15-16,18   [2] Hebrews 9:19-28   [3] Hebrews 9:13-14   [4] 2 Corinthians 5:21

Day 71

Within the Tabernacle, in the Holy Place, stood the 'Table of the Presence', and on it was placed the 'Bread of the Presence'. This was a continual reminder to the Israelites of God's presence among them as the One who satisfies their spiritual needs. It was fulfilled with the coming of Jesus who was the true 'Bread of Life'. After the resurrection of Jesus Christ, the Table in the Tabernacle was replaced by the Lord's Table of the service of Holy Communion which Jesus instituted. That table can be anywhere.

The Tabernacle: The Table with the Bread of the Presence

[God said to Moses:] "Make a table of acacia wood. It is to be two cubits long, a cubit wide and a cubit and a half high. Overlay it with pure gold and make a gold moulding to go round it. ... Make four gold rings and fasten them to the four corners of the table. ... The rings are to be near to the rim to hold the poles to be used to carry the table. ... Place the bread of the Presence on this table. It is to be before me at all times." [1] "Take fine flour and bake twelve loaves of bread with it. ... Place them in two rows, six in each row, on the table of pure gold before the Eternal-God. Place in each row some pure frankincense to be a memorial with the bread and to be an offering made by fire to the Eternal-God. The bread is to be set out before the Eternal-God regularly, every Sabbath, as a lasting covenant on behalf of the Israelites." [2]

Then the Eternal-God said to Moses: "Set up the tabernacle, the Tent of Meeting. ... Bring in the table and arrange the bread on it. ... Moses placed the table in the Tent of Meeting on the north side of the tabernacle, outside the curtain, and set out in order the bread on it before the Eternal-God, as he had been commanded. [3]

The first covenant had regulations for worship. ... A tabernacle was set up. In the first room, the Holy Place, stood the lampstand, the table and the Bread of the Presence. ... This is an illustration for the time when gifts and sacrifices were offered which were not able to clear the conscience of the worshipper. ...[4] When Christ came into the world, He said, "Sacrifice and offering you did not desire, but a body you prepared for me." [5]

While they were eating, Jesus took some bread, gave thanks and broke it, and gave it to His disciples, saying, "Take, eat; this is my body." [6]

Then Jesus said to them, "I am the bread of life. Whoever comes to me will never be hungry, and whoever believes in me will never be thirsty. ... Everything that [God] the Father gives me will come to me, and whoever comes to me I will never drive away. For I have come down from heaven not to do my will but the will of Him who sent me. " [7]

[1] Exodus 25:23-30   [2] Leviticus 24:5-8   [3] Exodus 40:1-4,22-23   [4] Hebrews 9:1-2,9
[5] Hebrews 10:5   [6] Matthew 26:26   [7] John 6:35-38

Day 72

The Ark of the Covenant was a wooden box overlaid with gold. It was a picture of the presence and character of God as Redeemer. As the Ark was at the centre of Jewish life and worship, so it was a picture of the place Jesus Christ, God the Son, has, or should have, at the centre of the life of His people. It represented the place where God's mercy met the full demands of His justice and allowed sinful human beings, who repented of their sins, to be united with Him as members of His family.

The Tabernacle: The Ark of the Covenant

[God said to Moses:] "Make a chest of acacia wood. ... Overlay it with pure gold, inside and out, and make a gold moulding to go round it. Cast four gold rings and fasten them to its four feet. ... Make poles of acacia wood, overlay them with gold and insert them into the rings on the sides of the chest to carry it. Make a mercy-seat of pure gold. ... Make two cherubim of hammered gold and place them at the ends of the mercy-seat. ... The wings of the cherubim are to spread upward, overshadowing the mercy-seat. The cherubim are to face each other and turned towards the mercy-seat. Place the mercy-set on top of the ark. In the ark you shall put the Covenant which I will give you. There, above the mercy-seat, between the two cherubim, I will meet with you and give you all my commands for the Israelites. [1]

Moses turned and went down the mountain with the two tablets of the Covenant in his hands. They were inscribed on both sides, front and back. The tablets were the work of God and the writing was the writing of God, engraved on the tablets. [2]

When Moses entered the Tent of Meeting to speak with the Eternal-God, He heard the voice speaking to him from between the two cherubim above the mercy-seat on the ark of the Covenant. [3]

The ark of the covenant of the Eternal-God went before them. ... Whenever the ark set out, Moses said, "Rise up, O Eternal-God! Let your enemies be scattered and your foes flee from you. ... Whenever the ark came to rest, he said, "Return, O Eternal-God, to the ten thousand thousands of Israel." [4]

Then the temple of God in heaven was opened and the ark of the covenant was seen within it. [5]

"In those days ..." says the Eternal-God, "men will no longer say, 'The ark of the covenant of the Eternal-God.' It will never come to mind or be remembered. ... [6] *The time is coming ... when I will make a new covenant with the house of Israel and with the house of Judah. ... For I will forgive their iniquity and I will not remember their sins any more"* [7]

[1] Exodus 25:10-22   [2] Exodus 32:15-16   [3] Numbers 7:89   [4] Numbers 10:33-36
[5] Revelation 11:19   [6] Jeremiah 3:16   [7] Jeremiah 31:31,34

Day 73

The altar of incense was the place where the priests stood before God to pray for the people they represented. Only they had the right to offer incense to God and even they had to be purified first. Incense is a picture of prayer to God and the altar is a picture of Jesus Christ who gives everyone the right to pray to God in His Name.

The Tabernacle: The Altar of incense

[God said to Moses:] "Make an altar of acacia wood for burning incense. It is to be a cubit long, a cubit wide, and two cubits high. ... Overlay the top, the sides and the horns with pure gold, and make a moulding of gold to go round it. ... Take and blend fragrant spices, stacte, onycha and galbanum, in equal parts. ... Grind some of it into powder and place it in front of the Covenant in the Tent of Meeting where I will meet with you. It shall be most holy to you. ... Aaron is to offer fragrant incense on the altar every morning when he tends the lamps, and again when he lights the lamps in the evening, so that there will be a regular burning of incense before the Eternal-God throughout the generations to come." [1]

"If the anointed priest sins and so brings guilt on the people, he must bring to the Eternal-God a bull without defect as a sin offering for the sin he has committed. ... He is to lay his hand on the head of the bull and kill it before the Eternal-God. ... He shall then sprinkle some of the blood on the horns of the altar of fragrant incense that is in the Tent of Meeting and before the Eternal-God ." [2]

When Uzziah became powerful he became proud and this led to his downfall. He was unfaithful to the Eternal-God, his God. He entered the temple of the Eternal-God to burn incense on the altar of incense. Azariah the priest went in after him with eighty other priests. They withstood Uzziah and said to him, "It is not for you, Uzziah, to make offerings to the Eternal-God but for the priests only. ... Uzziah became very angry and, while holding a censer in his hand ready to burn incense and raging at the priests before the altar of incense in the temple of the Eternal-God, leprosy broke out on his forehead. [3]

At the time for the burning of incense, the assembly of worshippers were praying outside [the Temple]. An angel of the Lord appeared to him [Zechariah], standing at the right side of the altar of incense. ... He said: "Do not be afraid. Your prayer has been heard. Your wife Elizabeth will bear you a son and you will name him John." [4]

[John saw in a vision:] "Another angel, holding a golden censer, came and stood at the altar. ... The smoke of the incense, together with the prayers of the saints, went up to God from the angel's hand." [5]

[1] Exodus 30:1-3 ,34-36,7-8   [2] Leviticus 4:3-4,7   [3] 2 Chronicles 26:16-19
[4] Luke 1:10-13   [5] Revelation 8:3-4

Day 74

God had commanded that only incense which He approved could be used to represent the prayers of the people in the Tent of Meeting. Nadab and Abihu knew this and yet they disobeyed Him with terrible consequences for them. God has promised to answer prayer but only when certain conditions are fulfilled: Prayer must be genuine, not just a form of words. It must respect Him as holy and be according to His will.

The prayer that is not answered

Aaron's sons Nadab and Abihu put fire in their censers, laid incense on it and offered unholy fire before the Eternal-God which was not according to His commands. ... So fire came from the presence of the Eternal-God and consumed them. They died there before the Eternal-God. ... The Eternal-God said: 'Through those who approach me I will show myself holy; before all the people I will be honoured." [1]

"O, that one of you would shut the temple doors so that you do not kindle fire on my altar in vain! I am not pleased with you," says the Eternal-God, the Almighty, "and I will not accept any offering from you. ... In every place incense and pure offerings will be offered to my name, because my name is great among the nations."[2]

You rebelled against the command of the Eternal-God ... The Amorites who lived in those hills came out against you and pursued you like a swarm of bees. ... When you returned you wept before the Eternal-God, but He paid no attention to your weeping nor listened to your prayer. [3]

If anyone closes his ears to the cry of the poor, he will cry out and not be heard.[4] If a person pays no attention to the law, even his prayers become an abomination.[5]

The word of the Eternal-God came to Zechariah: "This is what the Eternal-God, the Almighty says: 'Administer true judgments, show mercy and compassion to one another. Do not oppress the widow, the orphan, the alien or the poor. Do not devise evil one against another.' But they refused to listen. Stubbornly they turned their backs and closed their ears so they could not hear. ... So the Eternal-God, the Almighty was very angry. "When I called, they did not listen," says the Eternal-God, the Almighty, "so when they called, I did not listen." [6]

[James:] Where do fights and quarrels among you come from? Do they not come from the desires that are at war within you? You want something you do not have, so you covet and kill. You do not have, because you do not ask. You ask, but you do not receive, because you ask wrongly, that you may spend what you have on pleasures.[7]

If I had cherished sin in my heart, the Eternal-God would not have listened; but truly God has listened and heard the words of my prayer.[8]

---

[1] Leviticus 10:1-3   [2] Malachi 1:10-11   [3] Deuteronomy 1:43-45   [4] Proverbs 21:13   [5] Proverbs 28:9
[6] Zechariah 7:8-13   [7] James 4:1-3   [8] Psalm 66:18

Day 75

The Golden lampstand in the Tent of Meeting supported seven lamps. The light from the lampstand lit the Holy Place where the priests performed their duties. It was a picture of Jesus Christ, the Light of the World. Later it came to include those people in whom the light of Christ shone out into the world.

The Tabernacle: The golden lampstand

[God said to Moses:] "Make a lampstand of pure gold. Hammer out of one piece its base, shaft and cups of flower-like buds and blossoms. Six branches are to go out from the side of the lampstand, three on one side and three on the other. Three cups, formed like almond flowers with buds and blossoms are to be on one branch, three on the next branch, and so on for all six branches going out from the lampstand. ... The buds and branches are to be hammered out of one piece of pure gold. Make its seven lamps and set them on the lampstand so that they light the space in front of it." [1]

The Eternal-God said to Moses, "Say to Aaron, 'Set up the seven lamps so that they give light in front of the lampstand.'" Aaron did so. He set up the lamps so that their light shone in front of the lampstand, exactly as the Eternal-God commanded Moses. [2]

[Zechariah:] The angel who talked with me woke me up. ... He said to me, "What do you see?" I answered, "I see a lampstand of solid gold with a bowl at the top and seven lamps on it, with seven channels to the lamps." ... I said to the angel who talked with me, "What are these, my Lord?" He answered, "This is the word of the Eternal-God to Zerubbabel: 'Not by might nor by power, but by my spirit'... These seven lamps are the eyes of the Eternal-God, which range through the whole earth." [3]

I, John, ... was on the island of Patmos because of the word of God and the testimony of Jesus. I was in the Spirit on the Lord's Day and I heard behind me a loud voice like a trumpet. ... I turned round to see whose voice it was that was speaking to me. I saw seven golden lampstands, and in the midst of the lampstands was someone like the 'Son of Man,' clothed in a robe reaching down to his feet. ... When I saw Him, I fell at His feet as though dead. Then He placed His right hand on me and said: "Do not be afraid. ... The mystery of the seven stars that you saw in my right hand and of the seven golden lampstands is this: the seven stars are the angels of the seven churches, and the seven lampstands are the seven churches." [4]

You, O Eternal-God, lit my lamp, you, my God, gives light in my darkness. [5]

Jesus spoke again to the people, saying, "I am the light of the world. Whoever follows me will never walk in darkness, but will have the light of life." [6]

[1] Exodus 25:31-32, 36-37 [2] Numbers 8:1-3 [3] Zechariah 4:1-6,10 [4] Revelation 1:9-10,12-13,17-20 [5] Psalm 18:28 [6] John 8:12

Day 76

The seven lamps on the golden lampstand gave their light only when there was oil in them. Oil is a picture of 'God the Holy Spirit'. Light is a picture of the truth God brings to people who live in the darkness of sin. It is also a picture of the good witness Christians show to others. That witness is only truly effective when a person is continually being 'filled with God the Holy Spirit'.

The Tabernacle: Oil for the lamps

[God said to Moses:] "Command the Israelites to bring you clear oil of pressed olives for the light so that the lamps may be kept burning. In the Tent of Meeting, outside the curtain that is before the Covenant, Aaron and his sons are to keep the lamps burning before the Eternal-God from evening till morning." [1] "He [Aaron] is to tend the lamps on the pure gold lampstand regularly before the Eternal-God." [2]

The Eternal-God is my light and my salvation, whom shall I fear? The Eternal-God is the stronghold of my life, of whom shall I be afraid? [3] Your word is a lamp to my feet and a light for my path. ... You are my hiding-place and my shield. I have put my hope in your word. [4]

[Jesus:] "The kingdom of heaven will be like ten bridesmaids who took their lamps and went to meet the bridegroom. Five of them were foolish and five were wise. The foolish ones took with them their lamps but no oil. ... While they were on their way to buy oil, the bridegroom arrived. The bridesmaids who were ready went in with him to the wedding banquet and the door was shut. Later the others also came saying, 'Lord! Lord! Open the door for us!' But he replied, 'I tell you the truth, I do not know you.' Keep alert, therefore, because you do not know the day or the hour."[5]

"This is the judgment: the light has come into the world, but men loved darkness rather than light because their deeds were evil. All who do evil hate the light and will not come to the light for fear that their deeds will be exposed. But those who live by the truth come to the light, so that it may be clearly seen that their deeds have been done through God" [6]

[John:] There will be no more night. There will be no need of the light of a lamp or the light of the sun, for the Lord God will give His people light. And they will reign for ever and ever.[7]

Jesus said, "You are the light of the world. A city set on a hill cannot be hidden. No one lights a lamp and then puts it under a bowl. Rather they put it on a stand, and it gives light to all in the house. In the same way, let your light so shine before others, that they may see your good deeds, and give glory to your Father in heaven.[8]

[1] Exodus 27:20-21 [2] Leviticus 24:4 [3] Psalm 27:1 [4] Psalm 119:105,114 [5] Matthew 25:1-3,10-13 [6] John 3:19-21 [7] Revelation 22:5 [8] Matthew 5:14-16

Day 77

To anoint someone or something is to set apart or appoint that person or thing for a special, holy use. Oil is a picture of 'God the Holy Spirit'. It is He who fulfils all the Old Testament ceremonies of anointing, and 'sets people apart' for any task He calls them to do. Then He works in them to do it.

The Tabernacle: The oil for anointing

The Eternal-God said to Moses, "Take these spices: liquid myrrh, fragrant cinnamon, fragrant cane and olive oil. Blend them into a sacred, fragrant anointing oil, the work of a perfumer. It is to be the sacred anointing oil. Use it to anoint the Tent of Meeting, the ark of the Testimony, the Table of the Presence and all its articles, the lampstand and its utensils, the altar of incense, the altar of burnt offering and all its utensils and the basin with its stand. You shall consecrate them so they will be most holy, and whatever touches them will be holy. Anoint Aaron and his sons and consecrate them in order that they may serve me as priests. ... This is to be my sacred anointing oil throughout your generations. Do not use it on the body and do not make any other oil in the same way. It is holy, and you are to keep it holy." [1]

Samuel took some oil and poured it on Saul's head and kissed him, saying, "The Eternal-God has anointed you ruler over His inheritance?" [2]

Jesse made seven of his sons pass before Samuel, and Samuel said, "The Eternal-God has not chosen any of these." He said to Jesse, "Are all your sons here?" Jesse answered, "There is still the youngest, but he is tending the sheep." Samuel said, "Send for him. We will not sit down until he comes." Jesse sent for him and had him brought in. ... Then the Eternal-God said to Samuel, "Rise and anoint him. He is the one." Samuel took the horn of oil and anointed David in the presence of his brothers. From that day the Spirit of the Eternal-God came upon David in power. [3]

How very good and pleasant it is when brothers live together in unity! It is like precious oil poured on the head, running down on to the beard, the beard of Aaron, on to the collar of his robes. It is like the dew of Hermon which falls on Mount Zion, for there the Eternal-God bestows His blessing, life for evermore. [4]

He [Jesus] came to Nazareth, where He had been brought up. On the Sabbath day He went to the Synagogue, as was His custom. He stood up to read. He was given the scroll of the prophet Isaiah. He unrolled the scroll and read where it was written: "The Spirit of the Lord is on me, because He has anointed me to preach good news to the poor. He has sent me to proclaim freedom for the captives and recovery of sight for the blind, to set free the oppressed and to proclaim the year of the Lord's favour." ... Then He said to them, "Today this scripture is fulfilled in your hearing." [5]

[1] Exodus 30:22-32   [2] 1 Samuel 10:1   [3] 1 Samuel 16:10-13   [4] Psalm 133:1-3   [5] Luke 4:16-21

Day 78

The basin of water in the Tent of Meeting was for the priests to wash their hands and feet. It was both a utensil and a symbol which spoke of the need for all those who belong to God, and especially those who serve Him, to be clean. The physical washing from dirt was a picture of the spiritual cleansing from sin. The 'blood of Jesus Christ' cleanses from sin as water washes away dirt.

The Tabernacle: The basin for washing

The Eternal-God said to Moses, "Make a bronze basin with a bronze stand for washing. ... Place it between the Tent of Meeting and the altar and put water in it. With the water Aaron and his sons are to wash their hands and feet. Whenever they enter the Tent of Meeting ... or come near to the altar to minister ... they shall wash their hands and feet so that they will not die." [1] "To purify them [the Levites] do this: sprinkle them with the water of cleansing. Make them shave their whole bodies and wash their clothes, and make themselves clean." [2] Moses took the anointing oil and anointed the tabernacle and everything in it, and so consecrated them. He sprinkled some of the oil ... on the basin with its stand, to consecrate them.[3]

Knowing that [God] the Father had put all things into His hands and that He had come from God [the Father] and was returning to God [the Father], Jesus rose from the meal, took off His outer clothing and wrapped a towel round Himself. He poured water into a basin and began to wash His disciples' feet, wiping them with the towel that was wrapped round Him. He came to Simon Peter who said to Him, "Lord, are you going to wash my feet?" Jesus said to him, "You do not understand now what I am doing, but later you will understand." Peter said, "You will never wash my feet." Jesus answered, "Unless I wash you, you have no part with me." Peter replied, "Lord, not my feet only but my hands and my head as well." Jesus answered, "He who has had a bath needs only to wash his feet. You are clean, though not all of you." [4]

Again the word of the Eternal-God came to me [Ezekiel:] "I will sprinkle clean water on you, and you will be clean from all your uncleanness and from all your idols. I will give you a new heart and put a new spirit within you. I will remove from you your heart of stone and give you a heart of flesh. I will put my [Holy] Spirit within you and you will follow my decrees and be careful to keep my laws." [5]

Therefore, brothers and sisters, since we have confidence to enter the Most Holy Place by the blood of Jesus, ... let us draw near to God with a true heart in full assurance of faith, with our hearts sprinkled to cleanse us from a guilty conscience and with our bodies washed with pure water. [6]

[1] Exodus 30:17-21   [2] Numbers 8:7   [3] Leviticus 8:10-11   [4] John 13:3-10
[5] Ezekiel 36:16,25-27   [6] Hebrews 10:19,22

Day 79

God ordained priests to act for Him towards people and to act for the people towards Him. When the people sinned, the priest accepted the sacrifice offered for sin, and God forgave the sin. The priest and the animal sacrifice are both pictures of Jesus Christ. He offered Himself as a sacrifice for sin to 'God the Father' once for all. After that there was no further need for a human priest. Now God forgives sin because of Jesus Christ.

The consecration of Priests

[God said to Moses:] "Call Aaron your brother with his sons to you from among the Israelites to serve me as priests. [1] "Take the Levites from among the Israelites and cleanse them. This is what you are to do to consecrate them ... taking seven days to ordain them. [2] When you bring the Levites before the Eternal-God, the Israelites will lay their hands on them. ... Then the Levites will stand before Aaron and his sons, and you will present them as a wave offering before the Eternal-God." [3]

"When you are guilty of any of these sins, you must confess the way in which you have sinned and, as a penalty for that sin, you must bring to the Eternal-God a female lamb or goat from the flock as a sin offering, and the priest will make atonement for your sin. ... You will be forgiven for any sin you have committed. [4] They [the priests] must be holy to their God and must not profane the name of their God, for they present the offerings made to the Eternal-God by fire. ... Therefore they are to be holy. [5] The lips of a priest must preserve knowledge. From his mouth men seek instruction. He is the messenger of the Eternal-God, the Almighty. [6]

Moses went up [Mount Sinai] to God, and the Eternal-God called to him: "Say this to the Israelites. ' If you obey my voice and keep my covenant, then you, out of all the nations, will be my own special people. The whole world is mine but you will be to me a kingdom of priests and a holy nation.'" [7]

Every priest stands, day after day, to perform his service; again and again he offers the same sacrifices, which can never take away sins. But when this priest, Jesus Christ, had offered one sacrifice for sins once for all time, He sat down at the right hand of God [the Father]. Since then He has been waiting for His enemies to be made a footstool for His feet. By one sacrifice He has made perfect for ever, those who are being sanctified. [8]

If God is for us, who can be against us? If God [the Father] did not withhold his own Son, but gave Him up for us all, will He not also, with Him, graciously give us all things? ... Who is there to condemn us? Christ Jesus, who died, yes, and who was raised to life again, is at the right hand of God [the Father] and is interceding for us. [9]

[1] Exodus 28:1-4   [2] Exodus 29:1,35   [3] Numbers 8:3,13   [4] Leviticus 5:5-6,13   [5] Leviticus 21:6
[6] Malachi 2:7   [7] Exodus 19:3-6   [8] Hebrews 10:11-14   [9] Romans 8:31-34

Day 80

The garments for the priests had two purposes: to give dignity to their office and to express in symbols what they did. The colours gold, blue, purple and scarlet had royal and priestly meanings. The gems with names engraved on them showed who they represented before God. The priests themselves were sinners but, when forgiven, they could act for God towards the people. Their priestly garments were a sign of that office.

The Tabernacle: The priest's garments

[The Eternal-God said to Moses:] "Make sacred garments for your brother Aaron, to adorn him with dignity and honour. ... These are the garments: a breastpiece, an ephod, a robe, a woven tunic, a turban and a sash. Make the ephod of gold, of blue, purple and scarlet yarn, and of finely twisted linen, the work of a craftsman. It is to have two shoulder pieces attached to two of its corners, so that it can be joined together. Take two onyx stones and engrave on them the names of the sons of Israel in order of their birth - six on one stone and six on the other. ... Then set the stones in gold filigree settings and fasten them on the shoulder pieces of the ephod as stones of remembrance for the sons of Israel. Aaron is to bear the names on his shoulders as a remembrance before the Eternal-God. Fashion a breastpiece of judgment. ... Then mount four rows of precious stones on it. ... There are to be twelve stones, one bearing the name of each of the sons of Israel.

Make all the robe beneath the ephod of blue cloth, with an opening for the head in the middle of it. ... Make pomegranates of blue, purple and scarlet yarn all round the hem of the robe with gold bells between them. ... The sound of the bells will be heard when the priest enters the Holy Place before the Eternal-God and when he comes out, so he will not die. Make a plate of pure gold and engrave on it as on a signet ring: HOLY TO THE ETERNAL-GOD. ... Fasten it on the front of the turban. It will be on Aaron's forehead, and he will bear any guilt there may be in the sacred gifts the Israelites offer to God. ... After you have put these clothes on your brother Aaron and his sons, anoint and ordain them. Consecrate them so they may serve me as priests.[1]

This is what the Eternal-God says: ... "Can a mother forget the baby at her breast and have no compassion for the child she has borne? Though she may forget, I will not forget you! I have engraved you on the palms of my hands." [2]

There have been many of those priests, since death prevented them from continuing in office. But He [Jesus] holds His priesthood for ever; He has a permanent priesthood. He is, therefore, able to save for all time those who come to God [the Father] through Him, since He always lives to intercede for them. [3]

[1] Exodus 28:1-4,6-12,15-21,31-41 [2] Isaiah 49:8,15-16 [3] Hebrews 7:23-25

Day 81

The priests acted on behalf of individual people; the High Priest acted for all the people. Only the High Priest could enter, once a year, the Most Holy Place. The sacrifice he offered was for the atonement, meaning 'covering', for the sins of all the people. This is a picture of the way Jesus Christ, the Great High Priest, entered the presence of 'God the Father' to offer a perfect sacrifice, once for all time, for all the people of the world.

The High Priest and the Day of Atonement

The High Priest is the priest who has been raised above his fellows and who has had the anointing oil poured on his head. ... He must not become unclean ... nor leave the sanctuary of his God and so desecrate it. [1]

The Eternal-God said to Moses, "Tell your brother Aaron not to enter the Most Holy Place whenever he pleases. If he does he will die because it is there above the mercy-seat that I appear in a cloud. [2] Once a year Aaron shall make atonement on the horns of the altar. This atonement must be made with the blood of the atoning sin-offering throughout your generations. It is most holy to the Eternal-God." [3]

Every high priest, chosen from among men, is appointed to act for them in matters related to God, in offering Him gifts and sacrifices for sins. He is able to deal gently with those who are ignorant and go astray, because he himself is subject to weakness. This is why he has to offer sacrifices for his own sins, as well as for the sins of the people he represents. No one presumes to take this honour upon himself; he must be called by God, as Aaron was. So Christ did not take on Himself the honour of becoming a High Priest, but God [the Father] said to Him, 'You are my Son, ... you are a Priest for ever.

During His life on earth, Jesus offered up prayers and supplications with loud cries and tears to the One who was able to save Him from death, and He was heard because of His reverent submission. Although He was a Son, He learned obedience through what He suffered and, when made perfect, He was designated by God [the Father] to be High Priest and the source of eternal salvation for all who obey Him. [4]

We have a High Priest, who has sat down at the right hand of the throne of the Majesty in heaven, and who ministers in the sanctuary, the true tabernacle that the Lord, not man, has set up. [5]

Since we have such a great High Priest, ... Jesus the Son of God, let us grasp firmly the faith we hold. For we do not have a high priest who is unable to sympathise with out weaknesses, but who has been tempted in every way as we are, yet without sinning. Let us therefore approach the throne of grace with confidence, so that we may receive mercy and find grace to help in our time of need. [6]

[1] Leviticus 21:10-12 [2] Leviticus 16:2 [3] Exodus 30:10 [4] Hebrews 5:1-10 [5] Hebrews 8:1-2 [6] Hebrews 4:14-15

Day 82

Under the Old Covenant, the priest stood between God and the people. God blessed people through the priest. When the priest blessed anyone, it was God blessing them. Since Jesus Christ came as the Great High Priest, God's blessing comes to people only through Him. There is no need for a human priest because every one can receive God's blessing directly from Him. That blessing can be in all circumstances.

The priest's blessing

The Eternal-God said to Moses, "Say to Aaron and his sons [the priests], 'This is how you are to bless the Israelites. Say to them: "The Eternal-God bless you and keep you; the Eternal-God make His face shine upon you and be gracious to you; the Eternal-God look with grace on you and give you peace."' So they will put my name on the Israelites and I will bless them." [1]

There was great joy in Jerusalem, for since the days of Solomon, son of David, king of Israel, nothing had happened to compare with this in Jerusalem. The priests and the Levites stood up to bless the people, and God heard them, for their prayer reached His holy dwelling place in heaven. [2]

There was a righteous and devout man in Jerusalem called Simeon. ... When the parents brought in the child Jesus to fulfil the requirements of the law ... Simeon blessed them and said to His mother Mary, : "This child is destined to bring about the falling and rising of many in Israel." [3]

People brought little children to Jesus. ... He took them in His arms, laid His hands on them and blessed them.[4]

He [Jesus] led them [His disciples] out as far as Bethany. He lifted up His hands and blessed them. While He was blessing them He was taken up into heaven, leaving them behind. [5]

May the God of peace who brought back from the dead our Lord Jesus, the great Shepherd of the sheep, through the blood of the eternal covenant, equip you with everything good to do His will, and may He work in us what pleases Him, through Jesus Christ, to whom be the glory for ever and ever. Amen. [6]

May the grace of the Lord Jesus Christ [God the Son], the love of God [the Father], and the fellowship of [God] the Holy Spirit be with all of you. [7]

To Him who is able to keep you from falling and to present you without blemish and with great joy in His glorious presence, to the only God our Saviour be glory, majesty, power and authority, through Jesus Christ our Lord, before all time, now and for evermore! Amen. [8]

---

[1] Numbers 6:22-27 [2] 2 Chronicles 30:26-27 [3] Luke 2:25,27, 34 [4] Mark 10:13,16
[5] Luke 24:50-51 [6] Hebrews 13:20-21 [7] 2 Corinthians 13:13 [8] Jude 24:25

Day 83

Moses instructed the Israelites to remember God's words 'in their hearts'. To help them do that he also said, 'Tie them to your hands and foreheads'. Jewish teachers took this literally and put written parts of the law in small leather boxes, called 'phylacteries', which they wore strapped to their hands and foreheads. Jesus showed that wearing these could be hypocrisy if there was no real remembering of God's words in the minds, hearts and deeds of those wearing them. Jesus did not condemn Moses' instructions to use phylacteries to help people remember what God had done. The symbol was to be an aid to remembering, not a substitute for it.

The Phylacteries

Moses said to the people, "When the Eternal-God has brought you into the land of the Canaanites and given it to you as He promised you and your forefathers on oath to do, give to the Eternal-God the first-born of every womb. ... Redeem every first-born son. ... In days to come when your son asks you, 'Why do you do this?' say to him, 'The Eternal-God brought us out of Egypt, the land of our slavery, with a mighty hand. ... This is why I sacrifice to the Eternal-God the first-born male of every womb and redeem each of my first-born sons.' It will serve as a sign on your hand and a symbol on your forehead, that it was by His mighty hand that God brought us out of Egypt."[1]

Put these words of mine in your hearts and minds; tie them as signs on your hands and bind them as symbols on your foreheads. Teach them to your children; talk about them when you sit at home, when you are walking, lying down or getting up. [2]

Keep in your hearts these commandments that I give you today. Tell them to your children. Talk about them when you are sitting at home, when you are walking, when you are lying down and when you get up. Bind them as symbols on your hands and your foreheads. Write them on the doorframes of your houses and on your gates.[3]

Jesus said to the crowds and to His disciples: "The scribes and the Pharisees sit in Moses' seat, therefore you must obey them and do what they tell you. But do not do what they do, because they do not practise what they preach. ... They make their phylacteries broad and the tassels of their prayer shawls long. They love the places of honour at banquets and the best seats in the synagogues." [4]

[Peter:] My loved ones, I am now writing my second letter to you, both of them to stir your minds by way of remembrance. I want you to remember the words spoken in the past by the holy prophets and the commandment given by the Lord and Saviour through the apostles. [5]

With all my heart I seek you; do not let me stray from your commands. I have hidden your word in my heart that I might not sin against you. [6]

---

[1] Exodus 13:11-16 [2] Deuteronomy 11:18-19 [3] Deuteronomy 6:6-9 [4] Matthew 23:1-7
[5] 2 Peter 3:1-2 [6] Psalm 119:10-11

Day 84

The laws of Moses required strict justice. It was important for the authorities to require an 'eye for an eye', but they could not go beyond that. The law was a protection as well as a judgment for offenders. Authorities had to be just and exercise their powers to execute judgment, but they were forbidden to be vindictive, cruel or oppressive. For people, acting towards each other, Jesus taught a better way.

The teaching of Moses: An eye for an eye

Moses said, "If anyone puts to death a human being, he must be put to death. Anyone who kills someone's animal must make restitution for it - a life for a life. If anyone injures his neighbour he must be made to suffer in the same way - fracture for fracture, eye for eye, tooth for tooth. As someone has injured another, so he is to be injured. Whoever kills an animal must make restitution, but whoever kills a man must be put to death. The same law is to apply for the alien and the native-born. I am the Eternal-God, your God." [1]

If a malicious witness accuses a man of a crime, both parties in the dispute must stand in the presence of the Eternal-God, before the priests and the judges who are in office then. The judges must make a thorough inquiry. If the witness is proved to be giving false testimony against his brother, then do to him as he intended to do to his brother. You must purge the evil from among you. The rest of the people will hear of this and be afraid, and such an evil thing will never be done among you again. Show no pity: life for life, eye for eye, tooth for tooth, hand for hand, foot for foot. [2]

"It is necessary to be subject to the authorities, not only because of the punishment they can exercise but also because of conscience. ... Give everyone what is owed to them: Pay taxes where taxes are due; revenue to whom it is due; respect to whom respect is due; honour to whom honour is due." [3]

Do not say, "I will pay back the evil that is done to me!" Wait for the Eternal-God and He will deliver you. [4] Do not take revenge, my friends, but allow God's anger to work, for it is written, "It is for me to avenge," says the Eternal-God, "I will repay." [5]

[Jesus said:] "You have heard that it was said in the past, 'An eye for an eye, and a tooth for a tooth.' But I tell you, do not resist an evil person. If someone strikes you on the right cheek, turn the other cheek to him as well. If someone wants to sue you in court and take your tunic, let him have your cloak as well. If someone forces you to go one mile, go with him a second mile. Give to whoever asks you, and do not turn away from anyone who wants to borrow from you." [6]

[1] Leviticus 24:17-22   [2] Deuteronomy 19:16-21   [3] Romans 13:5-7   [4] Proverbs 20:22
[5] Romans 12:19   [6] Matthew 5:38-42

Day 85

God's people are to be holy as He is holy. This holiness is to be seen in very practical ways. Double (different for different people) or false weights and measures are ways of stealing by deceiving. In a relationship of 'light' and 'love' there can be no such shameful, dishonest dealing. Christians are not to judge others by different standards. God's standards are the ultimate measures.

The teaching of Moses: Honest measures

The Eternal-God said to Moses, "Do not use dishonest measures for length, weight or quantity. Use honest scales and honest weights. I am the Eternal-God, your God." [1] "You shall not have two different weights in your bag, one heavy and one light. Do not have two different measures in your house, one large and one small. You must have full and honest weights and measures, so that you may live long in the land the Eternal-God, your God, is giving you. For the Eternal-God, your God, abhors anyone who does such things and deals dishonestly." [2]

The Eternal-God detests dishonest scales, but honest weights are His delight.[3] Honest scales and balances are from the Eternal-God; He makes all the weights. [4] The Eternal-God detests both differing weights and differing measures. [5]

Like the partridge that hatches eggs it did not lay, is the man who gains wealth by unjust means. When he has lived half his life they will go, and in the end they will leave him, and he will be seen to be a fool. [6]

This is what the Sovereign Eternal-God says, "Enough, O princes of Israel! Put away your violence and oppression and do what is just and right. ... You shall have honest scales, an honest ephah and an honest bath." [7]

Listen to what the Eternal-God says: ... "Can I forget, O wicked house, your ill-gotten gains and the scant measure which is accursed. Shall I tolerate a man with dishonest scales and a bag of false weights?" [8] The trader uses dishonest scales because he loves to defraud. ... But as for you, return to your God; hold fast to love and justice." [9]

If there was glory in the ministry that condemns injustice, how much more glorious is the ministry that brings about righteousness. ...[10] Therefore, since through God's mercy we are engaged in this ministry, we do not lose heart. Rather, we have renounced the shameful ways that hide the truth; we do not use deception, nor do we falsify the word of God. [11]

[1] Leviticus 19:35-36 [2] Deuteronomy 25:13-16 [3] Proverbs 11:1 [4] Proverbs 16:11 [5] Proverbs 20:10 [6] Jeremiah 17:11 [7] Ezekiel 45:9-10 [8] Micah 6:1,10-11 [9] Hosea 12:7 [10] 2 Corinthians 3:9 [11] 2 Corinthians 4:1-2

Day 86

One tenth of everything the Israelites earned as wages, grew as crops or gained as livestock, belonged to God. Their giving of this was a measure of their faithfulness to Him. When Jesus Christ came, the law was abolished as a legal requirement, but the principle was fulfilled in giving freely to God.

The teaching of Moses: the 'tithe' or the 'tenth'

Abram returned from defeating Kedorlaomer and the kings who were with him. ... Melchizedek, king of Salem and priest of the Most High God, brought out bread and wine. He blessed Abram ... and Abram gave him a tenth of everything.[1]

All tithes of everything from the land, whether grain from the ground or fruit from the trees, belong to the Eternal-God. They are holy to the Eternal-God .[2]

[Moses:] When you have finished setting aside the tithe of all your produce ... you shall give it to the Levite, the alien, the fatherless and the widow, so that they may eat and be satisfied in your towns.[3]

Jacob made a vow, saying, "If God will be with me and will keep me on this journey I am taking, and will give me food to eat and clothes to wear so that I return in peace to my house, then the Eternal-God will be my God and this stone that I have set up will be God's house, and of all that you give me I will give you a tenth." [4]

He [Melchizedek] met Abraham returning from the defeat of the kings and blessed him, and Abraham gave him a tenth of everything. Think how great he was. Even the patriarch Abraham gave him a tenth of the plunder. ... And this becomes even clearer when another priest [Jesus], like Melchizadek appears, one who has become a priest, not because of His human descent, but through the power of an indestructible life. It is stated of Him, 'Your are a Priest for ever, of the order of Melchizadek.' [5]

[Paul:] Let each one give as he has decided in his heart to give, not reluctantly or under pressure, for God loves a cheerful giver. [6]

The word of the Eternal-God to Israel through Malachi: [7] *"Ever since the time of your forefathers you have turned away from my laws and have not kept them. Return to me and I will return to you, says the Eternal-God, the Almighty. Will a man rob God? Yet you are robbing me. But you ask, 'How are we robbing you?' In your tithes and offerings. You, the whole nation of you, are under a curse because you are robbing me. Bring the full tithe into the storehouse, that there may be food in my house. 'Put me to the test in this,' says the Eternal-God, the Almighty, 'and see if I will not open the windows of heaven for you and pour you out so much blessing that you will not be able to contain it.'"* [8]

---

[1] Genesis 14:17,20   [2] Leviticus 27:30   [3] Deuteronomy 26:12   [4] Genesis 28:20-22
[5] Hebrews 7:2,7,15-16   [6] 2 Corinthians 9:7   [7] Malachi 1:1   [8] Malachi 3:7-10

Day 87

Every morning and evening the priests (a) sacrificed a lamb, (b) offered a mixture of cereal and oil, and (c) poured out some wine on the altar in the Tabernacle or Temple. This was a picture of the daily need for (a) cleansing from sin through Jesus Christ, (b) the filling of the whole person with God the Holy Spirit, (the cereal represents the body and the oil is a symbol of the Holy Spirit), and (c) the offering of one's daily work to God.

The teaching of Moses: The daily sacrifices

The Eternal-God said to Moses: ... "Give this command to the Israelites: At the appointed time, you are to present to the Eternal-God offerings made by fire with a pleasing aroma. Each day you are to offer, as a regular burnt offering, two lambs a year old without defect. Prepare one lamb in the morning. You shall also offer a grain offering of fine flour mixed with oil from pressed olives. With it is to be a drink offering of fermented drink. Pour out the drink offering to the Eternal-God in the sanctuary. Prepare the second lamb at twilight, together with the grain and drink offering, as in the morning. [1]

He [David] left Zadok the priest and his fellow priests before the tabernacle ... to offer burnt offerings to the Eternal-God on the altar of burnt offering regularly, morning and evening, in accordance with all that is written in the Law of Moses. [2] The duty of the Levites was ... to stand every morning and evening to thank and praise the Eternal-God. They were to do the same on Sabbaths and other appointed festivals. [3]

He [the angel] said, "Go your way, Daniel, because the words are to remain secret and sealed until the time of the end. Many will be purified, cleansed and refined, but the wicked will continue to be wicked. None of the wicked will understand, but those who are wise will understand. From the time that the daily sacrifice is abolished ... there will be 1290 days." [4]

The steadfast love of the Eternal-God never ceases, therefore we are not consumed. His compassion never fails, His mercies are new every morning; great is your faithfulness. [5] I will exalt you, my God and King. Every day I will praise you and lift high your name for ever and ever. [6]

Those who welcomed the message were baptised, and about three thousand were added to them that day. They devoted themselves to the apostles' teaching, to fellowship, and to the breaking of bread and to prayer. ... Every day they met together in the temple courts. They broke bread in their homes and ate their food together with glad and generous hearts. They praised God and enjoyed the goodwill of all the people. Every day God added to their number those who were being saved. [7]

[1] Numbers 28:1-8 [2] 1 Chronicles 16:39-40 [3] 1 Chronicles 23:28,30-31 [4] Daniel 12:9-11
[5] Lamentations 3:22-23 [6] Psalm 145:1-2 [7] Acts 2:41-47

Day 88

God made a distinction for the Jews between 'clean' animals which they could eat, and 'unclean' animals which they were forbidden to eat. This was a picture of the distinction God made between Jews and Gentiles, until the coming of Christ. That, in turn, was a picture of the distinction God makes between His children and those of Satan. Everyone is spiritually 'unclean' until made clean by the 'blood of Christ. There is then no distinction between Jew and Gentile, that is, between those of any race, colour or nation.

The teaching of Moses: Clean and unclean food

The Eternal-God said to Moses: ... "Say to the Israelites: You may eat any animal that has a completely split hoof and that chews the cud. ... Of all the creatures in the waters ... you may eat only those which have fins and scales ... you are not to eat these [carrion-eating] birds. ... Every creature that moves along the ground, on its belly or with many legs, is detestable. ... Do not defile yourselves by any of these creatures. [1]

At Caesarea there was a man named Cornelius, a centurion of the Italian Regiment. ... At about three one afternoon he had a vision. He saw clearly an angel of God coming to him and saying, "Cornelius ... send men to Joppa to bring back a man named Simon who is also called Peter." At about noon the next day ... Peter went up on the roof to pray. He became hungry and wanted something to eat. While a meal was being prepared, he fell into a trance. He saw heaven open and something like a large sheet was let down to earth by its four corners. In it were all kinds of four-footed animals, reptiles, and birds of the air. Then he heard a voice saying, "Get up, Peter. Kill and eat." Peter replied, "Certainly not, Lord! I have never eaten anything that is impure or unclean." ... The voice spoke to him a second time, "Do not call 'unclean' what God has made clean."

The following day he arrived in Caesarea. ... Peter went inside and found a large gathering of people. He said to them: "You know very well that it is against our law for a Jew to associate with a Gentile or to visit him. But God has shown me that I should not call any man impure or unclean. ... I understand now the truth that God shows no partiality but accepts men from every nation who fear Him and do what is right. All the prophets testify about Him [Jesus] ... that everyone who believes in Him receives forgiveness of sins through His name.[2]

[Paul:] Remember that at one time, you who are Gentiles by birth were without Christ, excluded from the commonwealth of Israel and strangers to the covenants of promise, without hope and without God in the world. But now in Christ Jesus you who once were far away have been brought near by the blood of Christ. [3] There is no longer Jew or Greek, slave or free, male or female, for you are all one in Christ Jesus.[4]

[1] Leviticus 11:1-3,9-10,13,41,43   [2] Acts 10:1,3-5,9-15,24-28,34,43   [3] Ephesians 2:11-13   [4] Galatians 3:28

Day 89

A person became ceremonially 'unclean' by touching a dead body. He became ceremonially 'clean' again by being washed in the 'cleansing water'. This was a picture of the true cleansing of the 'unclean heart' by the 'cleansing blood' of Jesus Christ, that is, His death which 'washes away' sin. Only a person who is 'clean' spiritually can enter God's presence.

The Tabernacle: The cleansing water

The Eternal-God said to Moses, "Tell the Israelites to bring you a red heifer without defect or blemish and which has never been under a yoke. Give it to Eleazar, the priest. It is to be taken outside the camp and slaughtered in his presence. Then Eleazar is to take some of its blood on his finger and sprinkle it seven times towards the front of the Tent of Meeting. While he watches, the heifer is to be burned. ... The priest is to take some cedar wood, hyssop and scarlet wool and throw them on to the fire which is burning the heifer. ... Someone who is clean is to gather up the ashes of the heifer and put them in a clean place outside the camp. They shall be kept by the Israelite community for use in the 'water of cleansing'.

"Whoever touches a dead body will be unclean for seven days. ... For the unclean person, put some ashes from the burned purification offering into a jar and pour fresh water over them. A man who is ceremonially clean is to take some hyssop, dip it in the water and sprinkle the tent [of the dead body], all its furnishings and the people who were there. The one being cleansed must wash his clothes and bathe with water. That evening he will be clean. [1]

When you stretch out your hands in prayer, I will hide my eyes from you; even if you offer many prayers I will not listen. Your hands are full of blood. Wash and make yourselves clean. Remove your evil deeds from my sight. [2]

Jesus called the crowd to Him again and said, "Listen to me, all of you, and understand this. There is nothing outside a man that can make him 'unclean' by going into him. It is what comes out of a man that makes him 'unclean'. ... It is from within, from men's hearts, that come evil thoughts, sexual immorality, theft, murder, adultery, greed, malice, deceit, lewdness, envy, slander, pride and folly. All these evil things come from within and make a man 'unclean'." [3]

Since we have these promises, dear friends, let us cleanse ourselves from everything that defiles body and spirit, perfecting holiness in the fear of God. [4]

We know that when He [Jesus] appears, we will be like Him, for we will see Him as He is. Everyone who has this hope in him purifies himself, just as He is pure. [5]

[1] Numbers 19:1-6,9,11-12,14-18,22 [2] Isaiah 1:15-16 [3] Mark 7:14-16,21-22
[4] 2 Corinthians 7:1 [5] 1 John 3:2-3

Day 90

The Nazirite vow was for people who wanted to be 'set apart to be holy' for God. They had to be separated from anything that would make them ceremonially 'unclean'. This was a picture of all members of God's family whom He was going to 'set apart to be holy' by His Holy Spirit.

The teaching of Moses: Setting apart to be holy for God

The Eternal-God said to Moses, "Speak to the Israelites and say to them: 'If a man or a woman wants to make a special vow, the vow of a 'Nazirite', to separate themselves to the Eternal-God, they must abstain from wine and other strong drink. ... No razor may be used on the head all the days of their nazirite vow. They must be holy until the period of separation to the Eternal-God is completed. The hair of the head must be allowed to grow long, ... they must not go near a dead body. Even if their father, mother, brother or sister dies, they must not make themselves ceremonially unclean because of them." [1]

Manoah ... had a wife who was sterile, having borne no children. The angel of the Eternal-God appeared to the woman and said, "You are sterile and childless, but you will conceive and have a son. Now be careful that you drink no wine or other strong drink and that you do not eat anything unclean, for you will conceive and give birth to a son. No razor is to be used on his head, because the boy is to be a Nazirite, to God from birth. [2]

[Jesus prayed:] "Father, ... I am coming to you now, but I say these things while I am still in the world, so that they may have my joy in all its fullness within them. I have given them your word and the world has hated them, for they are not of the world as I am not of the world. I pray, not that you take them out of the world, but that you protect them from the evil one. ... Sanctify them by the truth; your word is truth. As you sent me into the world so have I sent them into the world. For their sakes I sanctify myself, so that they too may be wholly sanctified." [3]

[Jesus said to Paul:] "I am sending you to them to open their eyes so they may turn from darkness to light, and from the power of Satan to God, so that they may receive forgiveness of sins and a place among those who are sanctified by me." [4]

[Peter:] Prepare your minds for action. Be disciplined. Set your hope fully on the grace that Jesus Christ will bring you when He is revealed. As obedient children, do not conform to the evil desires you used to have in your ignorance. As He who called you is holy, so be holy in all you do, as it is written, "Be holy, for I am holy." [5]

[1] Numbers 6:1-7 [2] Judges 13:2-5 [3] John 17:1,13-19 [4] Acts 26:17-18 [5] 1 Peter 1:13-16

Day 91

The Cities of Refuge protected unintentional murderers and the nation against the consequences of unjust bloodshed. Murder is a sin against God as well as against the victim and society. It was important for an intentional murderer to receive the full justice of the law. It was equally important that a person who killed accidentally should not be unjustly punished. The Cities of Refuge provided a means of avoiding such an injustice. The final refuge is in God. Heaven is the ultimate City of Refuge, where Jesus Christ is now.

The Cities of refuge

The Eternal-God said to Moses, "Command the Israelites to give the Levites towns to live in from the inheritance the Israelites will receive. ... Six of the towns you give the Levites will be cities of refuge where a person may flee who has killed someone without intent. ... They will be places of refuge from the avenger, so that a slayer may not die before he stands trial before the assembly."

"If anyone strikes someone else with an iron object so that he dies, ... or if anyone has a stone or a wooden object in his hand that could kill, and he hits someone so that he dies, ... if anyone with malice premeditatedly pushes another or throws something at him intentionally, ... or if he hits him with his fist so that he dies, that person shall be put to death; he is a murderer. The 'avenger of blood' shall put the murderer to death."

"But if someone suddenly pushes another without hostility or throws something at him unintentionally or, without seeing him, drops a stone on him that kills him, since he was not his enemy and he did not intend to harm him, the assembly must judge between him and the 'avenger of blood' according to these regulations. The assembly must rescue the one accused of murder from the 'avenger of blood' and send him back to the city of refuge to which he fled. He must stay there until the death of the high priest." [1] ... "Do this so that there will be no innocent blood shed in your land." [2]

Do not say, "I will repay this wrong!" Wait for the Eternal-God. He will deliver you. [3] Do not repay anyone evil for evil. ... Never avenge yourselves, my friends, but leave room for God's wrath, for it is written, "It is mine to avenge, I will repay," says the Eternal-God. "If your enemy is hungry, feed him; if he is thirsty, give him something to drink." Do not be overcome by evil, but overcome evil with good. [4]

In you, O Eternal-God, is my refuge: let me never be put to shame. Rescue me and deliver me in your righteousness; incline your ear to me and save me. Be to me a rock of refuge, a strong fortress to save me. [5]

[1] Numbers 35:1-2,6,11-12,16-25 [2] Deuteronomy 19:10 [3] Proverbs 20:22
[4] Romans 12:17,19-21 [5] Psalm 71:1-3

Day 92

God instructed the Jews to count every fiftieth year as a Jubilee. In it slaves were to be set free, debts were to be written off, and people were to return to the land God had given them. This was a picture of the setting free of people from sin and their return to God's family that Jesus Christ was going to make possible.

The year of Jubilee

The Eternal-God said to Moses, "Consecrate the fiftieth year and proclaim liberty throughout the land to all its inhabitants. It shall be a Jubilee for you. You are to return each to his family property and each to his own family. The fiftieth year shall be a jubilee for you. Do not sow; do not reap what grows of itself, or harvest the unpruned vines. ... You will eat only what the fields produce.

In this Year of Jubilee, ... when you sell land to one of your countrymen or buy land from him, do not take advantage of each other. You are to buy from your countryman counting only the number of years since the Jubilee. ... The land must not be sold permanently, for the land is mine and you are but aliens and tenants. ... If one of your countrymen becomes poor among you and sells himself to you, you shall not make him work as a slave, ... he will work for you until the year of Jubilee. Then he and his children are to be set free to go back to his own family and to the property inherited from his forefathers. [1]

If a man dedicates to the Eternal-God a field he has bought which is not part of his family land, the priest will work out its value up to the Year of Jubilee. The man must pay its value on that day as holy to the Eternal-God. In the year of Jubilee the field will return to the person from whom it was bought. [2]

He [Jesus] stood up to read: ... "The spirit of the Lord is on me, because He has anointed me to bring good news to the poor. He has sent me to proclaim freedom for the captives and recovery of sight for the blind, to free the oppressed and to proclaim the year of the Lord's favour." [The year of Jubilee] ... and He said to them, "Today this scripture is fulfilled in your hearing." [3]

Jesus said to the Jews who had believed in Him, "If you continue in my teaching, you are truly my disciples, and you will know the truth, and the truth will set you free." They answered Him, "We are descendants of Abraham and we have never been slaves to anyone. What do you mean when you say that we shall be set free?" Jesus replied, "I tell you the truth, everyone who sins is a slave to sin. Now a slave has no permanent place in the family, but a son has a place there for ever. So if the Son sets you free, you will be free indeed." [4]

[1] Leviticus 25:10-15,23,39-41 [2] Leviticus 27:22-24 [3] Luke 4:16-21 [4] John 8:31-36

Day 93

Moses was a great man, but only a man. The task of being the one person between God and the people was too much for him alone. More leaders were needed who would be fully in touch with God and with the people. To achieve this 'God the Holy Spirit' came to each of the elders to help them. Only when Jesus, 'God the Son', came was 'God the Holy Spirit' given to everyone who was made clean by Jesus' death.

The Holy Spirit rests on the Elders

Moses heard the wailing of every family as they stood at the entrances of their tents, The Eternal-God became angry and Moses was troubled. He said to the Eternal-God, "Why have you brought this great trouble on your servant? How have I displeased you that you put this burden of all the people on me? ... I am not able to carry all these people by myself; the burden is too heavy for me. If this is the way you are going to treat me ... put me to death right now."

The Eternal-God said to Moses: "Bring to me seventy of the elders of Israel who are known to be elders and officers among the people. Bring them to the Tent of Meeting and let them stand there with you. I will come down and talk with you there. I will take some of the Spirit that is on you and put it on them. They will share with you the burden of the people so that you will not have to carry it alone. So Moses ... brought together seventy of the elders and they stood around the tent. Then the Eternal-God came down in the cloud and spoke with him. He took some of the Spirit that was on Moses and put it on the seventy elders. When the Spirit rested on them, they prophesied. However, two men, Eldad and Medad, although listed among the elders, had remained in the camp and did not go out to the tent. Yet the Spirit also came on them, and they prophesied in the camp. A young man ran and told Moses, "Eldad and Medad are prophesying in the camp." Joshua, son of Nun, Moses' assistant, spoke up and said, "Moses, my lord, stop them!" But Moses replied, "Are you jealous for my sake? Would that all the people of the Eternal-God were prophets and that He would put His Spirit on them!" Then Moses and the elders of Israel returned to the camp. [1]

On the evening of that first day of the week, when the disciples were together and the doors of the house were locked for fear of the Jews, Jesus came and stood among them and said, "Peace be with you!" After He said this, He showed them His hands and His side. The disciples were filled with joy when they saw the Lord. Again Jesus said, "Peace be with you! As the Father has sent me so I am sending you." When He had said this He breathed on them and said, "Receive the Holy Spirit. If you forgive anyone his sins, they are forgiven; if you do not forgive them, they are not forgiven." [2]

[1] Numbers 11:10-17,24-27   [2] John 20:19-23

Day 94

The appointment of judges was a common sense action which arose from one man taking on too much responsibility. It needed someone from outside the situation to see how much it was needed. Then began the line of Jewish judges. These were a picture of God the righteous Judge of all the world. It was through the Judges that God ruled the Israelites until they were granted a king.

The Judges

Jethro, Moses' father-in-law, ... came to Moses in the desert. ... The next day Moses took his seat to judge the people. They stood around him from morning till evening. When his father-in-law saw all that Moses was doing for the people, he said, "What is this that you are doing for the people? Why do you sit alone as judge while all these people stand around you from morning till evening." Moses answered him, "Because the people come to know the will of God. Whenever they have a dispute, they come to me, and I decide between the disputing parties and make known to them God's decrees and laws." Moses' father-in-law said to him, "What you are doing is not good. ... Now listen to me. ... You must represent the people before God and bring their causes to Him, teach them the decrees and laws, and show them the way to live and the things they are to do. Now choose able men from all the people, men who fear God, are trustworthy and hate dishonest gain. ... Let them serve as judges for the people at all times, but let them bring important cases to you. ... Moses listened to his father-in-law and did everything he said. [1]

So I [Moses] took the leaders of your tribes, wise and respected men, and appointed them to be leaders to have authority over you. ... And I charged your judges at that time: Judge fairly between your brothers. ... Show no partiality in judging and hear both small and great alike. Do not be afraid of anyone, for judgment belongs to God. [2]

[God said to Moses:] You shall appoint judges throughout your tribes. ... Do not pervert justice, show partiality or accept a bribe, for bribes blind the eyes of the wise and undermine the cause of the righteous. Pursue justice and justice alone, so that you may live and possess the land the Eternal-God, your God, is giving you. [3]

Whenever Israel marched out to fight, the hand of the Eternal-God was against them to defeat them, just as He had warned them. They were in great distress. Then the Eternal-God raised up judges who delivered them from those who plundered them. Yet they did not listen to their judges. [4]

The Eternal-God reigns for ever. He has established His throne for judgment. He will judge the world in righteousness and the peoples with justice. [5]

[1] Exodus 18:5,13-26   [2] Deuteronomy 1:15-17   [3] Deuteronomy 16:18-20   [4] Judges 2:15-17   [5] Psalm 9:7-8

Day 95

Yeast is a picture of something from the past which is carried over to influence the future. For the Israelites, the Passover represented a complete break with the past and a new beginning with the God who had saved them from slavery. Everything to do with Egypt had to be left behind. Jesus, the Passover lamb, gives people who repent of their sin and trust in Him, a new start, free from the slavery of sin. All that was wrong in the old life is to be rejected and no trace to be brought into the new life in Christ.

The Feasts: The Passover

[God said to Moses:] "Three times a year you are to hold a festival to me. Celebrate the 'Feast of Unleavened Bread' and for seven days eat only bread made without yeast, as I commanded you. Do this in the month of Abib at the appointed time, for in that month you came out of Egypt. No one is to appear before me empty-handed." [1]

On the evening of the fourteenth day of the month, the Israelites camped at Gilgal and kept the Passover. ... On the day after the Passover, they ate some of the produce of the land, unleavened bread and roasted grain. The manna ceased the day after they ate food from the land, there was no longer manna for the Israelites to eat. From then on they ate of the produce of Canaan. [2]

Josiah removed and defiled all the shrines of the high places that the kings of Israel had built in the towns of Samaria which had provoked the Eternal-God to anger. ... The king commanded all the people: "Celebrate the Passover to the Eternal-God, your God, as it is written in this Book of the Covenant." Not since the days of the judges who led Israel, nor in the days of the kings of Israel and the kings of Judah, had a Passover been observed as this one was. [3]

On the first day of the 'Feast of Unleavened Bread', the disciples came to Jesus and said, "Where do you want us to make preparations for you to eat the Passover?" He replied, "Go into the city to a certain man and say to him, 'The Teacher says: My time is near. I am going to celebrate the Passover with my disciples at your house." So the disciples did as Jesus had instructed them and prepared the Passover. [4]

When the hour came, Jesus and His disciples took their places at the table. He said to them, "I have eagerly desired to eat this Passover with you before I suffer. I tell you, I will not eat it again until it is fulfilled in the kingdom of God." [5]

[Paul:] Get rid of the old yeast that you may be a new batch without yeast, unleavened as you really are. For Christ, our Passover Lamb, has been sacrificed. Therefore let us keep the festival, not with the old yeast, the yeast of malice and evil, but with unleavened bread, the bread of sincerity and truth. [6]

[1] Exodus 23:14-15 [2] Joshua 5:10-12 [3] 2 Kings 23:19-23 [4] Matthew 26:17-19
[5] Luke 22:14-15 [6] 1 Corinthians 5:7-8

Day 96

The 'Feast of Harvest' (or 'Weeks', or 'Pentecost') was held at the end of the barley harvest. It also commemorated the giving of the law through Moses. The offering of the 'first-fruits of the crops' expressed thankfulness to God who transforms seed dying in the ground to produce new life in harvest. This feast was fulfilled when 'God the Holy Spirit' came to live in, and give new life to believers through Jesus Christ and what He did on the Cross.

The Feasts: Pentecost

[God said to Moses:] "Observe the 'Feast of Harvest' with the first-fruits of what you sow in your field. [1] ... On the day of the first-fruits, when you offer to the Eternal-God an offering of new grain during the "Feast of Weeks", you are to hold a sacred assembly and do no normal work. Offer a burnt offering of two young bulls, one ram and seven male lambs a year old as an aroma pleasing to the Eternal-God. [2]

"Count seven weeks from the time you begin to put the sickle to the standing corn. Then keep the 'Feast of Weeks' to the Eternal-God, your God, by giving a free will offering in proportion to the blessing you have received from Him. Rejoice before the Eternal-God, your God, you and your sons and daughters, your slaves, the Levites in your towns, the orphans and widows and strangers, at the place the Eternal-God will choose as a dwelling for His Name. ... Remember that you were slaves in Egypt. Observe carefully these instructions." [3]

"When you enter the land I am going to give you and you reap its harvest, you are to bring to the priest a sheaf of the first-fruits of your harvest. He is to wave the sheaf before the Eternal-God so that it will be accepted for you. ... On the day you wave the sheaf, you are to offer to the Eternal-God, a lamb a year old without defect, together with a grain offering of fine flour mixed with oil, as a burnt-offering. Count off seven full weeks from the day after the Sabbath on which you brought the sheaf for the wave offering. Count off fifty days to the day after the seventh Sabbath, and then make an offering of new grain to the Eternal-God. ... On that same day you are to proclaim a holy assembly and do no normal work. This is to be a lasting ordinance for you, for all generations to come and wherever you live." [4]

When the day of Pentecost had come, they [the disciples] were all together in one place. Suddenly there came from heaven a sound like the rush of a violent wind and it filled the whole house where they were sitting. There appeared what looked like tongues of fire which came and rested on each of them. All of them were filled with [God] the Holy Spirit. [5]

---

[1] Exodus 23:16   [2] Numbers 28:26-27   [3] Deuteronomy 16:9-12   [4] Leviticus 23:10-13,15-21   [5] Acts 2:1-4

Day 97

The 'Feast of Tabernacles' or 'Feast of Booths' was a time of rejoicing and thanksgiving for harvest. Rain was recognised as a gift from God, necessary to produce good harvests. Many years later a ceremony of 'pouring out water' was included to represent rain. Jesus referred to this as a picture of Himself. He was the 'living water'.

The Feasts: Tabernacles or Booths

The Eternal-God said to Moses, "Say to the Israelites: 'On the fifteenth day of the seventh month there is to be the 'Feast of Tabernacles' to the Eternal-God for seven days." [1] You shall keep the 'Festival of Booths' for seven days after you have gathered the produce from your threshing-floor and your winepress. Be joyful at your Feast, you, your sons and daughters, your menservants and maidservants, and the Levites, the aliens, the fatherless and the widows who live in your towns. ... For the Eternal-God, your God, will bless you in all your harvest and in all the work of your hands, and you will be joyful. [2] "Live in booths for seven days. All native-born Israelites are to live in booths so that your children and their children will know that I made the Israelites live in booths when I brought them out of Egypt, and I am the Eternal-God, your God." [3]

A day of the Eternal-God is coming. ... Then all the survivors from all the nations that have come against Jerusalem will go up year after year to worship the King, the Eternal-God, the Almighty, and to keep the Feast of Tabernacles.[4]

On the second day of the month, the heads of all the families ... gathered round Ezra. ... They found written in the Law ... that the Israelites were to live in booths during the feast of the seventh month, and that they should proclaim this throughout all their towns and in Jerusalem. ... The whole company that had returned from exile built booths and lived in them. ... And there was very great joy. [5]

When the Jewish 'Feast of Booths' was near, the brothers of Jesus said to Him, "Leave here and go to Judea so that your disciples may see the miracles you do. No one who wants to become well-known acts in secret. As you are doing these things, show yourself to the world. ... Jesus said to them, "My time has not yet come but your time is always here. ... After His brothers had left for the Feast, He also went, not publicly but in secret.

On the last and greatest day of the Festival, Jesus stood and cried out in a loud voice, "If anyone is thirsty, and believes in me, let him come to me and drink. As the Scripture has said, "Out from him will flow streams of living water." By this He meant [God] the [Holy] Spirit, whom later, those who believed in Him were to receive.[6]

[1] Leviticus 23:33   [2] Deuteronomy 16:13-15   [3] Leviticus 23:42-43   [4] Zechariah 14:1,16
[5] Nehemiah 8:13-17   [6] John 7:2-4,10,37-39

Day 98

Moses could not see God, but he talked with Him as with someone he could see 'face to face'. It is not surprising that his face shone with a light that dazzled those who saw him after he had talked with God. Even more striking is the way God enlightens the minds of those who listen to Him speaking to them. Then, when those so enlightened tell others God's words to them, He enlightens those truths to them too.

Moses' shining face

As Moses came down from Mount Sinai with the two tablets of the Testimony in his hands, he did not know that his face was shining because he had been speaking with the Eternal-God. When Aaron and all the Israelites saw that the skin of Moses' face was shining, they were afraid to come near him. But Moses called them to him. ... When Moses had finished speaking to them, he put a veil over his face. Whenever he entered the presence of the Eternal-God to speak with Him, he removed the veil until he came out. When he came out and told the Israelites what he had been commanded, they saw that his face was shining. Then Moses would put the veil back over his face until he went to speak with the Eternal-God. [1]

Peter said to Jesus, 'You are the Messiah, the Son of the living God" [2] Six days later Jesus took with him Peter, James and his brother John, and led them up a high mountain by themselves. There He was transfigured before them. His face shone like the sun and His clothes became a dazzling white. ... A voice from the cloud said, "This is my beloved Son." [3]

If the ministry that brought death, which was engraved on stone tablets, came in glory so that the Israelites could not gaze at the face of Moses because of its glory, even though it was fading, how much more glorious will be the ministry of the Spirit? If the ministry that condemns brings glory, how much more will the ministry that makes people righteous bring greater glory! ... Since we have such a hope, we are very bold, not like Moses, who put a veil over his face to keep the Israelites from gazing at it while the glory was fading away. Their minds were hardened then and now the same veil is there when the old covenant is read. Only in Christ is it taken away. Indeed, to this day, a veil covers their minds when Moses is read. ... But whenever anyone turns to the Lord, the veil is taken away. Now the Lord is the Spirit and where the Spirit of the Lord is, there is freedom. And we, who with unveiled faces, reflect the glory of the Lord, are being transformed into His likeness, increasing from one degree of glory to another. This comes from the Lord, who is the Spirit. [4]

[David:] Those who look to the Lord are radiant; their faces are never covered with shame. ... The angel of the Eternal-God encamps around those who fear Him. [5]

[1] Exodus 34:29-35 [2] Matthew 16:16 [3] Matthew 17:1-2,5 [4] 2 Corinthians 3:7-18 [5] Psalm 34:5,7

Day 99

The way that God gave victory to the Israelites while Moses' hands were raised in prayer is a picture of the way God wants people to work together with Him in working out His purposes. God's people are meant to fight for truth and righteousness, at the same time, pray to Him, together and all the time, for strength and His victory.

Hands raised in prayer

The Amalekites came and fought the Israelites at Rephidim. Moses said to Joshua, "Choose some men and go out to fight for us against the Amalekites. Tomorrow I will stand on top of the hill with the staff of God in my hands." So Joshua fought the Amalekites as he had been ordered, and Moses, Aaron and Hur went to the top of the hill. As long as Moses held up his hands, the Israelites gained, but whenever he lowered his hands, the Amalekites gained. When Moses' hands grew weary, they took a stone and put it under him and he sat on it. Aaron and Hur held up his hands, one on one side, and the other on the other side, so that his hands remained steady till sunset. So Joshua defeated the Amalekite army with the sword. ... Moses built an altar and called it 'The Eternal-God is my Banner,' for, he said, "Hands were lifted up to the throne of the Eternal-God." [1]

Then Solomon stood before the altar of the Eternal-God and before the whole assembly of Israel. He spread out his hands towards heaven and said: "O Eternal-God, God of Israel, there is no God like you in heaven above or on earth below. You keep your covenant of steadfast love with your servants who continue wholeheartedly in your way. ... You promised with your mouth and this day you have fulfilled it with your hand." [2]

Praise is due to you, O God, in Zion. ... To you who answers prayer, all men will come. When we were overwhelmed by our sins, you forgave our transgressions. ... You answer us with awesome deeds, O God our Saviour. You are the hope of all the ends of the earth and of the farthest seas. [3]

To you, O Eternal-God, my Rock, I cry. ... Hear my plea for mercy as I call to you for help, as I lift up my hands towards your Most Holy Place. [4]

[Paul:] I urge, then, first of all, that requests, prayers, intercessions and thanksgiving be made for everyone, for kings and all those in positions of authority, that we may live peaceful and quiet lives in all godliness and holiness. ... I urge men everywhere to lift up holy hands in prayer, without anger or disputing. [5]

Be joyful always, pray continually, and give thanks in all circumstances, for this is the will of God for you in Christ Jesus. [6]

[1] Exodus 17:8-15 [2] 1 Kings 8:22-24 [3] Psalm 65:1-3,5 [4] Psalm 28:1-2
[5] 1 Timothy 2:1-2,8 [6] 1 Thessalonians 5:16

Day 100

The bronze snake that God told Moses to make was a picture of Jesus Christ. It was not, however, the bronze snake that healed people; it was God whom it represented who had the power to heal. And it was the faith of those who looked to it which enabled God to heal them. Even a good symbol can be misused. All the Israelites who had been bitten by snakes and who looked at the bronze snake 'lifted up on the pole', were healed: all who believe in Jesus Christ 'lifted up on the Cross' are saved from their sin.

The bronze snake

They [the Israelites] set out from Mount Hor. ... But the people became impatient on the way and they spoke against God and against Moses and said, "Why have you brought us up out of Egypt to die in the desert? There is no bread nor water here! And we hate this miserable food!" Then the Eternal-God sent poisonous snakes among them. They bit the people and many of them died. The people came to Moses and said, "We sinned by speaking against the Eternal-God and against you. Pray that the Eternal-God will take the snakes away from us." So Moses prayed for the people. The Eternal-God said to Moses, "Make a snake and set it on a pole. Everyone who is bitten and looks at it will live." So Moses made a bronze snake and set it up on a pole. Whoever was bitten by a snake and looked at the bronze snake lived. [1]

He [Hezekiah] removed the high places, broke down the sacred stones and smashed the Asherah poles. He broke in pieces the bronze snake Moses had made because the Israelites had called it Nehushtan and had burned incense to it. [2]

"Who are you?" the people asked. ... They did not understand that He was speaking to them about [God] His Father. So Jesus said, "When you have lifted up the Son of Man, then you will know who I am and that I do nothing on my own. I speak only what the Father has taught me." [3]

Jesus said, "The hour has come for the Son of Man to be glorified. ... Father, glorify your name!" Then a voice came from heaven. "I have glorified it, and I will glorify it again." ... Jesus said, "This voice was for your sake, not mine. Now is the time for judgment of this world. Now the ruler of this world will be driven out. But I, when I am lifted up from the earth, will draw all men to myself." He said this to indicate the kind of death He was going to die. [4]

Jesus said, "I have spoken to you about earthly things and you do not believe; how then will you believe if I speak of heavenly things? No one has ever ascended into heaven except the One who descended from heaven, the Son of Man. As Moses lifted up the snake in the wilderness, so the Son of Man must be lifted up so that whoever believes in Him may have eternal life." [5]

[1] Numbers 21:4-9 [2] 2 Kings 18:4 [3] John 8:25-28 [4] John 12:23, 28-33 [5] John 3:12-15

Day 101

Twelve spies went into Canaan. All saw the same things there. Ten of them brought back a discouraging report. Despite all that they had seen God do, they did not believe that His power was greater than that of the people of Canaan. Their unbelief was shared by the people. God could take them no further.

The ten spies in Canaan

The Eternal-God said to Moses, "Send some men to spy out the land of Canaan which I am giving to the Israelites, one man from each tribe. Moses sent them out as the Eternal-God had commanded. ... At the end of forty days they returned from spying out the land. They came back to Moses and Aaron and the whole Israelite community at Kadesh in the Desert of Paran. They gave a report to them and to the whole assembly and showed them the fruit of the land. They said: "We went into the land to which you sent us. It flows with milk and honey and here is some of its fruit. But the people who live there are powerful, and the cities are fortified and very large." ... Then Caleb quietened the people before Moses and said, "Let us go up and take possession of the land. We are well able to do it." But the men who had gone with him said, "We cannot attack those people; they are stronger than we are." And they spread a poor report among the Israelites about the land they had spied out. [1]

That night all the Israelites raised their voices and wept bitterly. They grumbled against Moses and Aaron ... and they threatened to stone them. Then the glory of the Eternal-God appeared to all the Israelites at the Tent of Meeting. The Eternal-God said to Moses, "How long will this people treat me with contempt? I will destroy them and make you into a nation greater and stronger than they. ... Moses said to the Eternal-God. "'The Eternal-God is slow to anger, abounding in love and forgiving sin and rebellion. By no means does He leave the guilty unpunished, He punishes the children with the sin of the fathers to the third and fourth generation. Forgive the sin of these people in accordance with your great love, as you have pardoned them from the time they left Egypt until now."

The Eternal-God replied, "I have forgiven them, as you have asked. Nevertheless, as surely as I live and as surely as the glory of the Eternal-God fills the whole earth, none of the men who have seen my glory and the miraculous signs I performed in Egypt and in the desert and who disobeyed me and tested me ten times, will enter the land I swore to give to your forefathers, except Caleb son of Jephunneh and Joshua son of Nun." [2]

Therefore, while the promise of entering his [God's] rest still stands, let us be careful that none of you falls short of reaching it. [3]

[1] Numbers 13:1-3,25-32 [2] Numbers 14:1-3,10,18-22,30 [3] Hebrews 4:1-2

Day 102

Balaam was a prophet who heard God speak to him but who was tempted by money to please those who did not like what God was saying. He let money rule his actions and he was silent when he knew what He should be saying in God's name. His love for things that were not God's will for him led him astray.

Balaam - the prophet who loved money

The Israelites set out and camped in the plains of Moab, along the Jordan and across from Jericho. The people of Moab were terrified because there were so many Israelites. Balak, son of Zippor, who was king of Moab at that time, saw all that Israel had done to the Amorites. He sent messengers to Balaam, son of Beor, at Pethor, which is on the river Euphrates, saying, "A people has come out of Egypt and they cover the face of the earth and have settled next to me. Now come and put a curse on these people, because they are too powerful for me. Perhaps I will be able to defeat them and drive them from the land. I know that those you bless are blessed, and those you curse are cursed." ... When they came to Balaam, they told him what Balak had said. "Stay here the night ," Balaam said to them, "and I will bring you back the word the Eternal-God gives me." So the Moabite princes stayed with him. God came to Balaam and asked, "Who are these men with you?" Balaam said to God, "Balak son of Zippor, king of Moab, sent me this message: 'A people that has come out of Egypt covers the face of the earth. Now come and put a curse on them for me. Perhaps I will be able to defeat them and drive them away.'" But God said to Balaam, "Do not go with them. You shall not put a curse on those people for they are blessed."
    The next morning Balaam rose and said to Balak's princes, "Go back to your own country, for the Eternal-God has refused to let me go with you." ... Then Balak sent other princes, more numerous and more distinguished than the first. They came to Balaam and said: "This is what Balak, son of Zippor, says: Do not let anything keep you from coming to me. I will reward you with great honour and do whatever you say. Come! Put a curse on these people for me." [1]
    [Moses:] Balaam rose in the morning, saddled his donkey, and went with the princes of Moab. ... The Eternal-God refused to listen to Balaam and turned the curse into a blessing for you, because the Eternal-God, your God, loves you." [2]

[Peter:] They [false prophets] rose among the people, as they will among you. ... They have left the straight way and gone astray to follow the way of Balaam, son of Beor, who loved the wages of wickedness. ... They promise freedom, while they themselves are slaves of depravity, for people are slaves to whatever masters him. [3]

[1] Numbers 22:1-17,21   [2] Deuteronomy 23:3-5   [3] 2 Peter 2:1,15-19

Day 103

Moses was the greatest of the Jewish prophets. He spoke of another prophet who would, like him, bring God's word directly to people. Many prophets spoke of the one who was to come. Without knowing it at the time, they were referring to Jesus Christ, 'God the Son', who came to bring God's word to everyone. He was the living 'Word of God'. As God gave the Old Covenant through Moses, He would, one day, give the New Covenant through Jesus Christ.

The teaching of Moses: Another prophet to come

[Moses:] "The nations you are about to dispossess give heed to those who practise sorcery and divination. As for you, the Eternal-God, your God, does not permit you to do so. The Eternal-God, your God, will raise up for you a prophet like me from among your own people, you will take heed of Him. For this is what you asked of the Eternal-God, your God, at Horeb on the day of the assembly when you said, "If we hear again the voice of the Eternal-God, our God, or see this great fire any more, we will die." The Eternal-God said to me: "What they say is right. I will raise up for them a prophet like you from among their own people. I will put my words in His mouth, and He will tell them everything I command Him. I myself will call to account anyone who does not listen to the words that He speaks in my name." [1]

This is what the Eternal-God, the Almighty, says: "In a little while I will once again shake the heavens and the earth, the sea and the dry land. I will shake all the nations, so that the One desired of all nations will come, and I will fill this house with glory. The silver is mine and the gold is mine, says the Eternal-God, the Almighty" [2]

"But you, O Bethlehem of Ephrathah, though you are small among the clans of Judah, out of you will come forth for me One who is to be ruler over Israel, whose origins are from of old, from ancient times." [3]

"See, I am sending my messenger to prepare the way before me. Suddenly, the Eternal-God whom you are seeking, the messenger of the covenant whom you desire, will come to His temple," says the Eternal-God, the Almighty. [4]

"Here is my servant, whom I uphold, my chosen one in whom I delight. I have put my Spirit on Him and He will bring justice to the nations. He will not shout or raise His voice in the streets. A bruised reed He will not break and a smouldering wick He will not snuff out. ... In faithfulness He will bring forth justice on the earth.[5]

In the past God [the Father] spoke to our forefathers through the prophets at many times and in various ways, but in these last days He has spoken to us by [God] the Son, whom He appointed heir of all things and through whom He created the universe.[6]

[1] Deuteronomy 18:14-19 [2] Haggai 2:6-7 [3] Micah 5:2 [4] Malachi 3:1 [5] Isaiah 42:1-2,3-4 [6] Hebrews 1:1-2

Day 104

The slavery of the Israelites in Egypt is a picture of the slavery of people to sin. Canaan, the Promised Land, is a picture of the freedom that is promised in God's family. As there were undefeated enemies in Canaan, so there are often undefeated sins in the lives of Christians. As God promised victory over their enemies for the Israelites, so God has promised victory for Christians, victory over the enemy of sin through Jesus Christ.

The undefeated enemies

[Moses said:] When the Eternal-God, your God, brings you into the land you are about to possess and drives out before you [many] nations ... you must destroy them totally. ... Do not intermarry with them ... for that will turn away your sons from following me to serve other gods. ... Break down their altars, smash their sacred stones, cut down their Asherah poles and burn their idols in the fire. For you are a people holy to the Eternal-God, your God. The Eternal-God, your God, will hand them over to you and throw them into great panic until they are destroyed. ... You are to burn in the fire the images of their gods. Do not covet their silver and their gold. Do not take it for yourselves or you will be ensnared by it. To do so is detestable to the Eternal-God, your God. [1] But if you do not drive out the inhabitants of the land, those you allow to remain will become barbs in your eyes and thorns in your sides. They will give you trouble in the land where you live. And then I will do to you what I plan to do to them" [2]

"If you turn back and join the remnants of the nations that remain among you, and if you intermarry with them, then know for certain that the Eternal-God, your God, will not continue to drive them out from before you. They will become snares and traps for you, whips on your backs, and thorns in your eyes, until you perish from the good land which the Eternal-God, your God, has given you." [3]

[Paul:] You, my brothers and sisters, were called to be free. So do not use your freedom as an opportunity to indulge your sinful nature. ... The deeds of the sinful nature are obvious: sexual immorality, impurity and licentiousness, idolatry and sorcery, hatred, discord, jealousy, anger, selfish ambition, dissensions, factions and envy, drunken orgies and the like. As I have already warned, those who live like that will not inherit the kingdom of God. [4]

Do not love the world or the things that are in the world. The love of the Father is not in anyone who loves the world. All that is in the world, the desires of sinful nature, the lust of the eyes and the pride in one's wealth, does not come from the Father but from the world. The world and its desires are passing, but whoever does the will of God lives for ever. [5]

[1] Deuteronomy 7:1-7,23-25   [2] Numbers 33:55   [3] Joshua 23:12-13   [4] Galatians 5:13,19-21   [5] 1 John 2:15-17

Day 105

When Moses sinned against God, it was a sad lapse for one of the greatest of Jewish leaders. It would not have been a great sin for an ordinary person, but for a leader whom God used to represent Him before the people, to act in such an 'ungodlike' way, was very serious. High position brings great responsibilities, especially when people's ideas of God are judged by the behaviour of the one holding the high position.

Moses' sin

In the first month, the Israelites came into the Desert of Zin. ... Now there was no water there for them, and the people gathered against Moses and Aaron. They quarrelled with Moses and said, "If only we had died with those who fell dead before the Eternal-God! Why have you brought the people of the Eternal-God into the desert so that we and our livestock should die here? Why have you brought us out of Egypt to this terrible place? Here there is no grain and there are no figs, grapes or pomegranates. And there is no water to drink." Moses and Aaron left the assembled people and went to the entrance to the Tent of Meeting and fell down on their faces. The glory of the Eternal-God appeared to them and He said to Moses, "Take the staff and you and your brother Aaron gather the people together. Command the rock before their eyes and it will pour out water. Thus you will bring water out of the rock for the people so that they and their livestock can drink."

So Moses took the staff from before the Eternal-God, and Aaron gathered the people together in front of the rock. Moses said to them, "Listen, you rebels, must we bring water for you out of this rock?" Then Moses raised his hand and struck the rock twice with his staff. Water gushed out and the people and their livestock drank. But the Eternal-God said to Moses and Aaron, "Because you did not trust in me to honour me as holy in the sight of the Israelites, you will not bring this people into the land I have given them." [1]

The Eternal-God said to Moses, "Go up this mountain ... and see the land I have given the Israelites. When you have seen it you will be gathered to your people ... because you disobeyed my command. You did not honour me as holy before them."[2]

Moses climbed Mount Nebo. ... There the Eternal-God showed him the whole land ... and He said to him, "I have let you see the land with your own eyes, but you will not cross over into it." [3]

So do not throw away your confidence; it will bring you a rich reward. You need to endure so that when you have done the will of God, you may receive what He has promised. ...We are not of those who shrink back and are lost but of those who have faith and are saved. [4]

[1] Numbers 20:1-12   [2] Numbers 27:12-14   [3] Deuteronomy 34:1,4   [4] Hebrews 10:35-39

Day 106

Canaan was meant to be a picture of the 'Kingdom of God'. As, in Canaan, God's people, the Jews, would enjoy peace, justice and all they needed, so in the Kingdom of God, His people, members of His family, enjoy peace of heart and mind, a right relationship with Him and all they need spiritually.

The promised land

[Moses:] "The Eternal-God, your God, is bringing you into a good land, a land flowing with streams, underground waters, pools of water and springs flowing in the valleys and hills, a land of wheat and barley, vines and fig trees, pomegranates, olive trees and honey; a land where bread will be plentiful and you will lack nothing; a land where the rocks are iron and you can mine copper out of the hills." [1]

"The land you are about to possess is not like the land of Egypt, from which you have come, where you sowed your seed and irrigated it by foot as a vegetable garden. The land you are crossing the Jordan to possess is a land of mountains and valleys watered by rain from heaven. It is a land the Eternal-God, your God, cares for. ... If you faithfully heed the commands I am giving you today, to love the Eternal-God, your God, and to serve Him with all your heart and with all your soul, then He will send rain on your land in its season, both early and late rains. You will gather in your grain, wine and oil and He will provide grass in the fields for your cattle, and you will eat and be satisfied." [2]

[The word of the Eternal-God to Ezekiel:] "I will take you out of the nations. I will gather you from all the countries and bring you back into your own land. I will sprinkle clean water on you, and you will be made clean from all your uncleanness and idols. ... You will live in the land I gave your forefathers. You will be my people and I will be your God. I will save you from all your uncleanness. I will call for the grain and make it plentiful and bring no famine on you again." [3]

[Peter:] Praise be to the God and Father of our Lord Jesus Christ! In His great mercy He has given us new birth into a living hope through the resurrection of Jesus Christ from the dead, and into an inheritance that can never perish, become defiled, spoiled, or fade away. This inheritance is being kept in heaven for you, who through faith, are shielded by the power of God until the coming of the salvation that is to be revealed in the last time. [4]

[Jesus:] *"Do not let your hearts be troubled. You trust in God, trust also in Me. In my Father's house there are many rooms. If that were not so would I have told you that I am going there to prepare a place for you? If I go and prepare a place for you, I will certainly come back for you so that where I am you too will be"* [5]

[1] Deuteronomy 8:7-9, [2] Deuteronomy 11:10-15 [3] Ezekiel 36:24-29 [4] 1 Peter 1:3-5 [5] John 14:1-3

Day 107

No people on earth has ever had the opportunity that the Israelites had of hearing God's word and seeing His powerful acts, but the effect of this was never so strong that they did not have the free choice to reject Him if they did not want to follow Him. That same choice has to be made by everybody today.

The choice of life or death

Moses summoned all the Israelites and said to them: "You have seen with your eyes all that the Eternal-God did in Egypt to Pharaoh. ... With your own eyes you saw those great trials, miraculous signs and great wonders. ... During the forty years that I have led you in the desert, your clothes have not worn out, nor the sandals on your feet. You have eaten no bread and drunk no wine or other strong drink. I did this so that you might know that I am the Eternal-God, your God."

"Make sure there is among you no man or woman, family or tribe, whose heart is turning away from the Eternal-God, our God, to serve the gods of those nations. Make sure there is no root among you that sprouts a bitter poison. ... The secret things belong to the Eternal-God, our God, but the things revealed to us and to our children are ours for ever, that we may observe all the words of this law." [1]

"Be sure that what I am commanding you today is not too difficult for you or too far away from you. It is not in heaven, so that you ask, 'Who will ascend into heaven to get it and tell us so that we may obey it?' Nor is it beyond the sea. ... No, the word is very near you: it is in your mouth and in your heart for you to obey. ... Today I call heaven and earth to witness against you that I have set before you life and death, blessings and curses. Now choose life so that you and your children may live and may love the Eternal-God, your God, hear His voice and hold fast to Him." [2]

[Joshua:] "Fear the Eternal-God and serve Him in sincerity and faithfulness and put away the gods which your forefathers served. ... But if you are unwilling to serve the Eternal-God, then choose for yourselves this day whom you will serve. ... As for me and my household, we will serve the Eternal-God." [3]

[Paul:] We have always to thank God for you, brothers and sisters, and rightly so, because your faith is growing, and the love every one of you has for each other is increasing. ... This shows that the judgment of God is right, so that you will be counted worthy of the kingdom of God. It is indeed just that God should repay with trouble those who trouble you, and to give relief to those who are troubled. ... He will punish those who do not know God and do not obey the gospel of our Lord Jesus. They will suffer the punishment of everlasting destruction and they will be shut out from the presence of the Lord and from the glory of His power. [4]

[1] Deuteronomy 29:2-6,18, 29 [2] Deuteronomy 30:11-14,19-20 [3] Joshua 24:14-15 [4] 2 Thessalonians 1:3,5-9

Day 108

Most of the Israelites could not read and write. God wanted them to remember Him and what He had done for them when they settled in the Promised Land, so He gave them another song to sing. It reminded them of Who He was, of what He had done for them and warned them of forgetting Him; He alone was God, their God.

The second Song of Moses

The Eternal-God said to Moses, "The time for you is near. Then this people will begin to prostitute themselves before the foreign gods of the land they are going to possess. ... Now, write down this song and teach it to the Israelites and make them sing it, so that it may be a witness for me against them when I have brought them into the land flowing with milk and honey. ... When they have eaten their fill and grown fat, they will turn to other gods, serve them and reject me and break my covenant. And when many disasters and troubles come upon them, this song will be a testimony against them." ... That day Moses wrote down this song and taught it to the Israelites.[1]

"O heavens! Listen and I will speak. O earth! H ear the words of my mouth.

"I will proclaim the name of the Eternal-God. I will praise the greatness of our God!

"He is the Rock, His works are perfect, and all His ways are just.

"Remember the days of old; consider the generations long past.

"Ask your father what happened and he will tell you, your elders and they will explain.

"For the portion of the Eternal-God is His people and Jacob His allotted inheritance.

"He found Israel in a desert land and sustained him in a barren and howling waste. He shielded him and cared for him. He guarded him as the apple of his eye.

"As an eagle stirs up its nest, hovers over its young and spreads its wings to catch them and carries them on its wings, so the Eternal-God alone led him.

"You deserted the Rock, who bore you; you forgot the God who gave you birth.

"See now that I alone am God, there is no god beside me." [2]

He led His people out like a flock. He led them like a shepherd through the desert. ... He brought them to the border of His holy land, to the mountain which His right hand had won. He drove out nations before them and allotted their land to them as a heritage. He settled the tribes of Israel in their tents. [3]

He was merciful to them and forgave their iniquities and did not destroy them. Many times He restrained His anger and did not stir up His full wrath. He remembered that they were but flesh, a breath of wind that passes and does not return. [4]

---

[1] Deuteronomy 31:16,19-22 [2] Deuteronomy 32:1-4,7,9-11,18,36-37,39 [3] Psalm 78:52-55 [4] Psalm 78:38-39

Day 109

Joshua had shown on many occasions that he was willing to be Moses' assistant. As God trained and used Moses to lead His people, so He trained Joshua to take over leadership from Moses. Having shown himself faithful in small duties he was now ready to take on greater responsibilities.

Joshua's commission

The Eternal-God said to Moses, "Go up this mountain of the Abarim range and see the land I have given the Israelites. When you have seen it, you will be gathered to your people. ... Moses said to the Eternal-God, "May the Eternal-God appoint a man over His people ... so that the people of the Eternal-God will not be like sheep without a shepherd." The Eternal-God said to Moses, "Take Joshua son of Nun, a man in whom is my Spirit and lay your hands on him. Let him stand before Eleazar the priest and the entire assembly and commission him in their presence. Give him some of your authority so that all the Israelites will obey him. ... Moses did as the Eternal-God commanded him. [1]

Moses said to all the people of Israel, "I am now a hundred and twenty years old and I am no longer able to lead you. The Eternal-God has said to me, 'You will not cross the Jordan.' The Eternal-God, your God, will Himself cross over before of you. He will destroy these nations before you, and you will take possession of their land. Joshua also will cross over before you. ... Then Moses summoned Joshua and said to him in the sight of all Israel, "Be strong and courageous, for you will go with this people into the land that the Eternal-God swore to their forefathers to give them, and you will divide it among them as their inheritance. The Eternal-God Himself goes before you and will be with you, He will never leave you nor forsake you. Do not be afraid and do not be dismayed." [2]

Joshua, son of Nun, was full of the spirit of wisdom because Moses had laid his hands on him. The Israelites listened to him and did what the Eternal-God had commanded Moses. [3]

I [Paul] am reminded of the sincere faith which both your [Timothy's] grandmother Lois and your mother Eunice had, and which I am sure you have now. That is why I remind you to fan into flame the gift of God which is in you. ... God did not give us a spirit of timidity, but a spirit of power, love and of self-discipline. [4]

"You then my son [Timothy], be strong in the grace that is in Christ Jesus. The things you have heard me say in the presence of many witnesses entrust to faithful men who will also be able to teach others." [5]

[1] Numbers 27:12-13,15-22   [2] Deuteronomy 31:1-3,7-8   [3] Deuteronomy 34:9
[4] 2 Timothy 1:5-7   [5] 2 Timothy 2:1-2

Day 110

The death of Moses marked the end of a most important period in the history of the Israelites. Through Moses, God taught people more about Himself and about the way He designed people to live than through anyone else except Jesus Christ. Jesus made it possible to live the way Moses taught.

The death of Moses

The Eternal-God appeared in a pillar of cloud which stood over the entrance to the Tent. The Eternal-God said to Moses: "Soon you will rest with your fathers, and these people will begin to prostitute themselves to the foreign gods of the land they are entering. They will forsake me and break the covenant I made with them." [1]

Moses came with Joshua son of Nun and recited all the words of this song in the hearing of the people. ... On that same day the Eternal-God spoke to Moses, "Go up into the Abarim Range to Mount Nebo, in the land of Moab, across from Jericho, and view the land of Canaan which I am giving the Israelites as their own possession. There you will die and be gathered to your people, just as your brother Aaron died on Mount Hor and was gathered to his people.[2]

Then Moses climbed Mount Nebo from the plains of Moab to the top of Pisgah, across from Jericho. There the Eternal-God showed him the whole land. ... Then the Eternal-God said to him, "This is the land I swore on oath to Abraham, Isaac and Jacob, saying, 'I will give it to your descendants. I have let you see it with your eyes, but you will not cross over there. Then Moses, the servant of the Eternal-God, died there in the land of Moab, as the Eternal-God had said. He buried him in Moab, in the valley opposite Beth Peor, but to this day no one knows where he was buried. Moses was a hundred and twenty years old when he died, yet his eyes were not weak nor had his strength gone. For thirty days the Israelites wept for Moses in the plains of Moab. ... Since then no prophet has risen in Israel like Moses whom the Eternal-God knew face to face. No one has ever shown the great power or performed the awesome wonders that Moses did before Pharaoh and in the sight of all Israel. [3]

Therefore, holy brothers, who share in the heavenly calling, fix your minds on Jesus, the apostle and high priest whom we confess. He was faithful to the one who appointed Him as Moses was faithful in all God's house. Yet Jesus is worthy of as greater honour than Moses, as the builder of a house has greater honour than the house itself. ... Moses was faithful as a servant in God's house, ... but Christ was faithful as a Son over God's house. And we are His house, if we hold firm to the confidence that comes from the hope we have in Him. [4]

---

[1] Deuteronomy 31:15-16,19 [2] Deuteronomy 32:44,48-50 [3] Deuteronomy 34:1,4-8,10-12
[4] Hebrews 3:1-3,5-6

Day 111

The names Joshua and Jesus mean the same thing - Saviour. Victory was promised to both but the nature of their fight was different. Joshua led the Israelites against evil nations to conquer a land for their inheritance. Jesus fought against Satan to gain a kingdom - the kingdom of God. Joshua's victory was visible, incomplete, and temporary. Jesus' victory is invisible but it is total and everlasting.

Joshua is made leader

After the death of Moses ... the Eternal-God said to Joshua son of Nun, Moses' assistant: "Moses my servant is dead. You and all these people are to get ready to cross the River Jordan into the land I am about to give to them. ... I have given you everywhere you set your feet, as I promised Moses. ... No one will be able to stand up against you all the days of your life. As I was with Moses, so I will be with you. I will never leave you nor forsake you. Be strong and courageous. You will lead these people to possess the land I swore to their forefathers to give them." ... Joshua commanded the officers of the people: "Go through the camp and tell the people: 'Get your provisions ready for in three days time you will cross the Jordan and go in and to take possession of the land the Eternal-God, your God, has given you to possess." They answered Joshua, "All you have commanded us we will do, and wherever you send us we will go. As we obeyed Moses in everything, so we will obey you. Only may the Eternal-God, your God, be with you as He was with Moses. Whoever rebels against your words and does not obey your commands will be put to death. Only be strong and courageous." [1]

Early in the morning Joshua and all the Israelites set out from Shittim and came to the Jordan, where they camped before crossing over. ... The Eternal-God said to Joshua, "Today I will begin to exalt you in the sight of all Israel so that they may know that I am with you as I was with Moses. It is you who will command the priests who carry the ark of the covenant." [2]

On that day the Eternal-God exalted Joshua in the sight of all the Israelites and they remained in awe of him, as they had been of Moses, all the days of his life. [3]

Let us fix our eyes on Jesus, the author and perfecter of our faith.[4] *He humbled Himself and became obedient to death, even to death on a cross! Therefore God [the Father] has exalted Him to the place of highest honour. He has given Him the name that is above every name, that at the name of Jesus every knee should bow, in heaven, on earth and under the earth, and every tongue confess that Jesus Christ is Lord, to the glory of God the Father.*[5]

[1] Joshua 1:1-3,5-7,10-11,16-18 [2] Joshua 3:1-7 [3] Joshua 4:14 [4] Hebrews 12:2 [5] Philippians 2:8-11

Day 112

The two spies that Joshua sent to Jericho found help in an unlikely place - the house of a prostitute. God had been speaking to Rahab, and in her heart she had responded. She acted towards the spies in faith. God honoured her faith. She and her family were saved. Then, even more remarkably, Rahab married a Jew named Salmon. One of his descendants was Joseph, the husband of Mary, the mother of Jesus.

Rahab

Joshua sent two spies secretly from Shittim, saying, "Go, spy out the land, especially Jericho." So they went and stayed at the house of a prostitute named Rahab. The king of Jericho was told about the spies and he sent a message to Rahab, "Bring out the men who came to you. They are spies." The woman took the two men and hid them. Then she said [to the messengers], "It is true, the men came to me, but I did not know where they had come from. At dusk, when it was time to close the city gate, the men left" ... She had taken the spies up to the roof and hidden them among stalks of flax. Before the spies lay down to sleep for the night, she went up on the roof and said to them, "I know that the Eternal-God has given this land to you and that a great dread of you has fallen on us. All the inhabitants of this land are melting in fear because of you. ... Since I have shown kindness to you, swear to me by the Eternal-God that you will show kindness to my family. Give me a sign that you will deal kindly with my father and mother, my brother and sisters, and all who belong to them, and that you will save us from death." The men said to her, "Our lives for yours! If you keep silent about what we are doing, we will deal kindly and faithfully with you when the Eternal-God gives us the land." Then she let them down by a rope through a window, for her house was on the outer side of the city wall. ... The men said to her, "The oath we have sworn will not be binding on us unless, when we enter the land, you have tied this scarlet cord in the window through which you let us down." [1] ... As the trumpet sounded, the people gave a loud shout and the wall collapsed. ... They burned the whole city and everything in it ... but Joshua spared Rahab the prostitute, her family and all who belonged to her. [2]

[James:] You see, a person is justified by his deeds and not by faith alone. Was not Rahab, the prostitute, justified by what she did when she gave lodging to the spies and sent them off in a different direction? As the body without the spirit is dead, so faith without works is dead. [3]

The genealogy of Jesus Christ ... Boaz whose mother was Rahab. [4]

By faith Rahab, the prostitute, was not killed with those who were disobedient because she received the spies. [5]

[1] Joshua 2:1,3,8-12,14-18   [2] Joshua 6:20,24-25   [3] James 2:24-26   [4] Matthew 1:1,5   [5] Hebrews 11:31

Day 113

Going 'into the water' and 'coming out again' on the other side is a picture of the 'baptism' of all God's children. It marks the end of one life and the beginning of another. For the Israelites, the new life meant Canaan: for the Christian, this is life in the 'family of God'. The stones were like the public rite of baptism - a testimony and a memorial.

The Israelites enter the promised land

Early in the morning Joshua and all the Israelites rose and set out from Shittim and came to the Jordan. They camped there before crossing over. ... Joshua said to the people, "Consecrate yourselves, for tomorrow the Eternal-God will perform wonders among you. To the priests he said, Take up the ark of the covenant of the Eternal-God and go ahead to the Jordan. ... When the feet of the priests who carry the ark of the covenant of the Eternal-God of all the earth touch the Jordan, the waters flowing downstream will be cut off and they will stand up in a heap."

The Jordan is in flood during the time of harvest, but, as soon as the priests who carried the ark reached the Jordan and their feet touched the water's edge, the water from upstream stopped and formed a heap at the city of Adam. ... So the people crossed over the Jordan opposite Jericho. The priests who carried the ark of the covenant of the Eternal-God stood still on dry ground in the middle of the river while the Israelites walked across, until the whole nation had crossed over on dry ground. [1]

When all the people had finished crossing the Jordan, the Eternal-God said to Joshua, "Choose twelve men from among the people, one from each tribe. Order them to take up and carry over with you, twelve stones from the middle of the Jordan, from the place where the priests stood, and set them down where you camp tonight." Joshua called together the twelve men he had appointed ... and said to them, "Go ahead before the ark of the Eternal-God, your God, into the middle of the Jordan. Each of you, according to the number of the tribes of the Israelites, is to take up a stone and carry it on his shoulder. It will serve as a sign for you. When your children ask you in the future, 'What do these stones mean?' you will tell them that the waters of the Jordan were cut off before the ark of the covenant of the Eternal-God. ... These stones are to be a memorial to the people of Israel forever."

"The Eternal-God, your God, did to the Jordan what he had done to the Red Sea. He dried it up ahead of us until we had crossed over. He did this so that all the peoples of the earth might know that the hand of the Eternal-God is mighty." [2]

Come and see what God has done, how awesome are His deeds among people! He turned the sea into dry land. They passed through the river on foot. We rejoiced in Him who rules by His great might for ever. [3]

[1] Joshua 3:1,5,11,15-17 [2] Joshua 4:1-8,23-24 [3] Psalm 66:5-7

Day 114

Jericho was protected by a strong wall that the Israelites could not have broken down on their own. God wanted His people to be quite sure that every victory He was going to give them would be from Him. To increase their faith in Him, He dried up the waters of the Jordan, and He caused Jericho to fall in a way which was clearly an act of God.

The fall of Jericho

Now Jericho was firmly shut up because of the Israelites. No one went out and no one went in. Then the Eternal-God said to Joshua, "See, I have delivered Jericho into your hands together with its king and its warriors. ... Joshua called the priests and said to them, "Take up the ark of the covenant of the Eternal-God and let seven priests carry trumpets in front of it." He commanded the people: "Go forward! March round the city. The armed men are to go in front of the ark of the Eternal-God."

As Joshua had commanded, the seven priests, carrying the seven trumpets before the Eternal-God, went forward, blowing their trumpets, and the ark of the covenant followed them. ... The trumpets were sounded continuously. But Joshua had commanded the people, "Do not cry out, do not raise your voices, do not say a word, until I tell you to shout. Then you will shout!" ... So the ark of the Eternal-God was carried right round the city once. ... They did this for six days.

On the seventh day, they rose at daybreak and marched around the city seven times as they had done before. ... At the seventh time around, when the priests had sounded the trumpets, Joshua commanded the people, "Shout! For the Eternal-God has given you this city! The city and all that is in it are to be devoted to the Eternal-God. Only Rahab the prostitute and all who are with her in her house are to be spared, because she hid the spies we sent. Keep away from the things which are to be destroyed, so that you will not bring about your destruction."

When the trumpets sounded, the people shouted. At the sound of the trumpet the people gave a loud shout. The wall collapsed and every man charged straight ahead into the city and they captured it. ... They burned the whole city and everything in it. The silver and gold and articles of bronze and iron they put into the treasury of the house of the Eternal-God. [1]

By faith the walls of Jericho fell, after the people had marched round them for seven days. [2]

[Paul:] We live in the world, but we do not fight as the world does. Our weapons are not the weapons of the world. Our weapons have the power of God to demolish strongholds, arguments and every power that sets itself up against the knowledge of God. [3]

---

[1] Joshua 6:1-2,6-11,14-18,20,24   [2] Hebrews 11:30   [3] 2 Corinthians 10:3-4

Day 115

In the defeat of the Israelites at Ai and the severe punishment of Achan, God showed that He is not only powerful, but also holy. The Israelites needed to learn this and God taught them in a severe way. God's mercy is great, but there is mercy only for those who repent of their sin. Later the sacrifice of Jesus Christ made it possible for Him to forgive where there is repentance, but that never diminishes His demand for holiness.

The sin of Achan

The Israelites acted unfaithfully in regard to the things to be destroyed. Achan son or Carmi ... took some of the forbidden things. The anger of the Eternal-God burned against Israel. Joshua sent men from Jericho to spy out Ai. When they returned to Joshua, they said, "Not all the people need to go up against Ai. Send two or three thousand men to take it for there are only a few men there." About three thousand men went up and they fled before the men of Ai. At this the hearts of the people melted and turned to water.

Joshua tore his clothes and fell face to the ground before the ark of the Eternal-God. "Ah, Sovereign, Eternal-God," he said, "Why did you bring this people across the Jordan to deliver us into the hands of the Amorites so as to destroy us?" The Eternal-God said to Joshua, "Stand up! Why have fallen down on your face? Israel has sinned. They have broken my covenant that I commanded them to keep. They have stolen some of the forbidden things, they have acted deceitfully. ... That is why the Israelites are unable stand against their enemies."

Joshua rose early the next morning and called Israel to come forward by tribes ... and Achan son of Carmi ... was taken. ... Achan replied, "It is true! I have sinned against the Eternal-God. ... When I saw a beautiful robe from Babylon ... silver... gold ... among the booty, I coveted them and took them. They are hidden in the ground inside my tent. ... Then all Israel stoned him. ... Therefore that place has been called the Valley of Achor ever since. [1]

The word of the Eternal-God that came to Hosea, "The Israelites will be like the sand on the seashore which cannot be measured or counted. Where it was said of them, 'You are not my people', they will be called sons of the living God' [2] I will give her back her vineyards, and I will turn the 'Valley of Achor' into a 'door of hope.'" [3]

Who is a God like you, who pardons iniquity and forgives the transgression of the remnant of His inheritance. You do not stay angry for ever but delight in showing mercy. You will again have compassion on us. You will tread our sins underfoot and cast all our sins into the depths of the sea. [4]

---

[1] Joshua 7:1,5-12,16-19,25-26 [2] Hosea 1:1,10 [3] Hosea 2:15 [4] Micah 7:18-19

Day 116

The Israelite's conquest of Canaan was not simply a matter of winning battles. They lost against Gibeon because they did not seek God's will. They won against the Amorites because God fought for them. The greatest fight for the Israelites was in keeping a right relationship with God, and that meant seeking His will for every action.

God fights for Israel

Joshua built an altar to the Eternal-God, the God of Israel, on Mount Ebal. ... They offered to the Eternal-God burnt offerings and sacrificed fellowship offerings on it. There, in the presence of the Israelites, Joshua wrote a copy of the law of Moses on stone. ... Afterwards, Joshua read all the words of the law, the blessing and the curses, as it is written in the Book of the Law. [1]

When all the kings west of the Jordan heard about these things ... they came together to make war against Joshua and Israel. ... However, when the people of Gibeon heard what Joshua had done to Jericho and Ai, they acted with cunning. They went to Joshua as a delegation ... "Your servants have come from a very distant country ..." they lied. The men of Israel ... did not enquire of the Eternal-God and Joshua made a treaty of peace with them. [2]

Adoni-Zedek, king of Jerusalem, heard how Joshua had destroyed Ai ... and Gideon had made peace with Israel; he and his people were very alarmed. ... Then the five kings of the Amorites ... took up positions against Gibeon and attacked it. The Gibeonites sent word to Joshua in the camp at Gilgal: "Do not abandon your servants. Come quickly and save us!"

So Joshua marched up from Gilgal with all his mighty warriors. The Eternal-God said to Joshua, "Do not be afraid of them for I have given them into your hand. Not one of them will be able to stand before you."

On the day the Eternal-God gave the Amorites over to the Israelites, Joshua said to the Eternal-God, in the presence of Israel: "Sun! Stand still over Gibeon, and moon, over the Valley of Aijalon." The sun stopped in the middle of the sky and did not go down about a whole day. There has never been a day like it before or since, when the Eternal-God listened to a man. Surely the Eternal-God fought for Israel! [3]

The Lord is my light and my salvation, whom shall I fear? The Lord is the stronghold of my life, of whom shall I be afraid? When evil men attack me to devour my flesh, when my enemies and my foes assail me, they will stumble and fall. ... In the day of trouble He will hide me in His dwelling-place; He will hide me in the shelter of His tabernacle and will set me high on a rock. [4]

[1] Joshua 8:30-34 [2] Joshua 9:1-4,15 [3] Joshua 10:1, 5, 7,12-14 [4] Psalm 27:1-3,5

Day 117

Canaan was subdued and the Israelites received their inheritance from God in the promised land. Joshua had been with the Israelites since they left Egypt. He recognised what God had done for them. He also knew how fickle the people could be. His testimony to God's goodness to the nation was clear and so were his warnings.

The death of Joshua

The Eternal-God gave Israel all the land He had sworn to give their forefathers. ... He gave them rest on every side. Not one of their enemies had withstood them for the Eternal-God had handed all their enemies over to them. Not one of all the good promises of the Eternal-God to the house of Israel failed. Every one was fulfilled. [1]

After a long time and the Eternal-God had given Israel rest from all the enemies around them, Joshua, by then old and well advance in years, summoned all Israel, elders, leaders, judges, and officials, and said to them: "I am old and well advanced in years. You have seen all that the Eternal-God, your God, has done to all these nations for your sake. It was the Eternal-God, your God, who fought for you. ... The Eternal-God has driven out great and powerful nations before you and, to this day, no one has been able to withstand you. One of you puts to flight a thousand because the Eternal-God, your God, fights for you, as He promised to do. So be very careful to love the Eternal-God, your God." [2]

"Now I am about to go the way of all the earth. You all know in your hearts and souls that not one of all the good promises the Eternal-God, your God, gave you has failed. ... But just as all the good promises of the Eternal-God, your God, have come to pass, so the Eternal-God will bring on you all the promises of evil, until He has destroyed you from this good land that He has given you. If you break the covenant of the Eternal-God, your God, ... and serve other gods, the anger of the Eternal-God will burn against you."

After these things, Joshua son of Nun, the servant of the Eternal-God, died at the age of a hundred and ten. And they buried him in his own inheritance. [3]

He drove out nations before them and allotted to them their land as an inheritance. ... But they put the Eternal-God to the test and rebelled against the Most High.[4]

So we see that they [the Israelites] were not able to enter [their rest] because of their unbelief. [5] *For if Joshua had given them rest, God would not have spoken later about another day. There remains, therefore, a Sabbath rest for the people of God. ... Let us, therefore, make every effort to enter that rest, so that no one falls short of it by following their disobedience.* [6]

[1] Joshua 21:43-45 [2] Joshua 23:1-3,9-11,14-16 [3] Joshua 24:29 [4] Psalm 78:51-56 [5] Hebrews 3:19 [6] Hebrews 4:8-11

Day 118

Without either Moses or Joshua, the Israelites had only the written Law of Moses to guide them. So shallow was their faith that, without a visible leader, they soon fell into idolatry and immorality. They never forgot, however, that, when in distress, they could turn to God for help, but that help would only be forthcoming if the people recognised their sin and turned from it to live according to His ways.

Disobedience leads to defeat

Joshua, son of Nun, the servant of the Eternal-God, died at the age of 110 years. ... That whole generation was gathered to their fathers and another generation grew up who did not know the Eternal-God nor what He had done for Israel. Then the Israelites did what was evil in the eyes of the Eternal-God and served the Baals. They forsook the Eternal-God, the God of their forefathers. This provoked the Eternal-God to great anger against Israel. ... Whenever Israel went out to fight, the hand of the Eternal-God was against them and they were defeated. ... Then the Eternal-God raised up judges, who saved them out of the hands of those who plundered them. Yet they would not listen to their judges but prostituted themselves to other gods and bowed down to them. ... Whenever the Eternal-God raised up a judge for them, He was with the judge and saved them out of the hands of their enemies all the days of the judge. ... But when the judge died, the people turned back to practices even more corrupt than those of their fathers. The Eternal-God was very angry with Israel and said, "Because this nation has broken my covenant with their forefathers and has not listened to me, I will no longer drive out before them any of the nations Joshua left when he died. I left them to test Israel, to see whether they would keep the way of the Eternal-God and walk in it as their forefathers did." [1]

They [the Israelites] did not destroy the nations of the land as the Eternal-God had commanded them, but they mingled with the nations and learned to do as they did. They worshipped their idols, which became a snare to them. ... Therefore the Eternal-God was angry with his people. ... He handed them over to the nations so that their foes ruled them. ... Nevertheless, for their sake He remembered His covenant and out of His great love He showed them compassion. [2]

Seek the Eternal-God while He may be found; call on Him while He is near. Let the wicked forsake his way and the evil man his thoughts. Let him turn to the Eternal-God and He will have mercy on Him, and to our God, for He will freely pardon. "For my thoughts are not your thoughts, neither are your ways my ways," declares the Eternal-God. "As the heavens are higher than the earth, so are my ways higher than your ways and my thoughts than your thoughts." [3]

[1] Judges 2:8,10-22 [2] Psalm 106:34-36,40-41,44-45 [3] Isaiah 55:6-9

Day 119

It took seven years of oppression by the Midianites for the Israelites to realise that they were suffering because of their sin. When they cried for help, God looked for someone through whom He could work to save His people. The man he found was of low standing, fearful and weak. His only strength was his faithfulness to God.

God calls Gideon

The Israelites did evil in the sight of the Eternal-God, and for seven years He gave them into the hands of the Midianites. ... Midian so impoverished them that they cried out to the Eternal-God to help them. The angel of the Eternal-God came and sat down under the oak that belonged to Joash the Abiezrite, in Ophrah. His son Gideon was threshing wheat in a winepress to hide it from the Midianites. The angel of the Eternal-God appeared to Gideon and said: "The Eternal-God is with you, you mighty warrior." Gideon answered, "But sir, if the Eternal-God is with us, why has all this happened to us?" ... The angel turned to him and said, "Go in the strength you have and deliver Israel from the hand of Midian. Am I not sending you?"

"But Sir," Gideon asked, "how can I save Israel? My clan is the weakest in Manasseh, and I am the least in my family." The Eternal-God answered, "I will be with you, and you will strike down all the Midianites." Gideon replied, "If I have found favour in your eyes, give me a sign that it is really you who is talking to me. Do not go away until I come back and bring my offering and set it before you." ... Gideon prepared a young goat ... he made bread without yeast ... he brought them out and set them before him under the oak. The angel of God said to him, "Take the meat and the unleavened bread, place them on this rock, and pour out the broth." Gideon did so. The angel of the Eternal-God touched the meat and the unleavened bread with the tip of the staff that was in his hand. Fire flared up from the rock and consumed the meat and the bread. Then the angel of the Eternal-God vanished out of sight. When Gideon realised that it was the angel of the Eternal-God, he said, "Help me, O Sovereign Eternal-God! for I have seen the angel of the Eternal-God face to face!" But the Eternal-God said to him, "Peace be with you! Do not be afraid. You will not die." [1]

What more shall I say? I do not have time to tell about Gideon, Barak, Samson, Jephthah, David, Samuel and the prophets, who through faith conquered kingdoms, administered justice and received what was promised. [2]

God has chosen the foolish things of the world to shame the wise. God has chosen the weak things of the world to shame the strong, so that no one can boast in His presence.[3]

---

[1] Judges 6:1-2,6,11-22   [2] Hebrews 11:32:33   [3]1 Corinthians 1:27,29

Day 120

The first thing God asked Gideon to do was to let others know where he stood with Him. He acted in a more bold way than anyone would expect from a quiet, unassuming man. His faith was strengthened. Although more sure of God, he was still not sure that he had understood God's instructions. He need not have been afraid to 'put out a fleece'. God wants people to be sure of Him provided they act honestly and sincerely.

God's victory through Gideon

Jerub-baal (that is, Gideon) and all his men camped at the spring of Harod. The Midianites were camped north of them in the valley near the hill of Moreh. The Eternal-God said to Gideon, "You have too many men for me to deliver the Midianites into your hands. The Israelites would boast that it was by their strength that they were saved. Say to your men, 'Let anyone who is trembling with fear go home.'" Twenty-two thousand men left and ten thousand remained. Then the Eternal-God, said to Gideon, "There are still too many men. Take them to the river and I will sift them out for you there. ... Gideon led the men down to the water. There the Eternal-God said to him, "Set on one side those who lap the water with their tongues like a dog, and on the other side, those who kneel down to drink." Three hundred men lapped water into their mouths with their hands. The remainder knelt down on their knees to drink. The Eternal-God said to Gideon, "With the three hundred men that lapped water with their hands, I will deliver the Midianites into your hands. Let all the other men return to their homes." So Gideon sent away the remainder of the Israelites to their tents. He kept the three hundred men and gave to them the provisions and the trumpets of those who had gone.

Gideon divided the three hundred men into three companies and put into their hands the trumpets and empty jars with torches inside. "Watch me," he said to them, "Follow me and when I get to the outskirts of the camp, do what I do. When I and those who are with me blow our trumpets, then you, from all round the camp, blow yours and shout, 'For the Eternal-God and for Gideon.'" ... When the three hundred trumpets sounded, the Eternal-God set each of the Midianites throughout the camp against each other with their swords. [1]

Jonathan said to his young armour-bearer, "Come, let's go over to the outpost of those uncircumcised men. It may be that the Eternal-God will act for us. Nothing can hinder the Eternal-God from saving by many or by few." [2]

The angel said to me [Zechariah], "This is the word of the Eternal-God to Zerubbabel: 'Not by might nor by power, but by my Spirit,' says the Eternal-God, the Almighty." [3]

[1] Judges 7:1-25   [2] 1 Samuel 14:6   [3] Zechariah 4:6

Day 121

Several men whom God used to serve Him were born to women who were, at first, unable to bear children. When He wanted to save His people Israel, who had again grievously sinned against Him, He chose such a woman, the wife of Manoah, to give birth to Samson. God promised great things for him, and with parents eager to do His will, no child has ever had a better start in life.

The birth of Samson

Again the Israelites did evil in the sight of the Eternal-God, so He delivered them into the hands of the Philistines for forty years. A certain man of Zorah, named Manoah ... had a wife who was sterile, she had no children. The angel of the Eternal-God appeared to her and said, "You are sterile and have no children, but you will conceive and have a son. Now make sure that you drink no wine or other fermented drink and that you eat nothing that is unclean. You will conceive and give birth to a son. No razor is to be used on his head for he is to be a Nazirite [set apart] to God from birth. He will begin to deliver Israel from the hands of the Philistines.

Manoah prayed earnestly to the Eternal-God: "O Eternal-God, let the man of God you sent to us come again to teach us what to do for the boy who is be born to us." God heard Manoah and the angel of God came again to the woman while she sat in the field. ... The woman ran to tell her husband. ... So Manoah asked him, "What is to be the rule for the boy's life and what is he to do?" The angel of the Eternal-God said to Manoah, "Your wife must take heed to do all that I have told her." ... Then Manoah said to the angel of the Eternal-God, "What is your name so that we may honour you when your words come true?" The angel replied, "Why do you ask me my name? It is beyond words." ... The woman gave birth to a boy and named him Samson. He grew and the Eternal-God blessed him. The Spirit of the Eternal-God began to stir him while he was in Mahaneh Dan, between Zorah and Eshtaol. [1]

[Paul:] When God, who set me apart before I was born and called me by His grace, was pleased to reveal His Son in me so that I might preach Him among the Gentiles, I did not consult anyone, nor did I go to Jerusalem to those who were Apostles before me, but I went away at once into Arabia. [2]

O Eternal-God, you have searched me and known me. ... You created my inmost being, you knit me together in my mother's womb. I praise you because I am fearfully and wonderfully made. Your works are wonderful, I know that very well. My frame was not hidden from you when I was made in secret. When I was woven together deep in the earth, your eyes saw my body, as yet unformed. All the days you ordained for me were written in your book before they came to be. [3]

[1] Judges 13:1-5,8-9,12-13,17-18,24   [2] Galatians 1:15-17   [3] Psalm 139:1,13-16

Day 122

Samson was privileged in knowing from childhood that God had made great promises about him. He was tempted to go his own way, as all men are, and he fell. Following the lust of his eyes, he chose to find his fulfilment and pleasure in enemy territory and he suffered the consequences. Samson's parent's question is one for everyone: "Must you go into the ungodly world to gain what God wants to give you - the best!"

Samson starts badly

Samson went down to Timnah and saw there a young Philistine woman. He returned and said to his father and mother, I have seen a Philistine woman in Timnah; now arrange for her to be my wife." His father and mother replied, "Is there no acceptable woman among your relatives or among all our people? Must you go to the uncircumcised Philistines to get a wife?" But Samson said to his father, "Get her for me. I want her."

Samson went down to Timnah with his father and mother. As they came near the vineyards of Timnah, suddenly a young lion roared at him. The Spirit of the Eternal-God came upon him in great power and he tore the lion apart with his bare hands as he might have torn a young goat. But he did not tell his father or his mother what he had done. Then he went down and talked with the woman, and he liked her. Some time later, he returned to marry her. He turned aside to look at the carcass of the lion. In it there was a swarm of bees and some honey. He scooped some of it out with his hands and ate it as he went along. When he came to his parents, he gave them some and they too ate it. But he did not tell them that he had taken the honey from the carcass of the lion. [1]

Do not love the world or the things that are in the world. The love of [God] the Father is not in anyone who loves the world. For all that is in the world, the cravings of the sinful nature, the lust of the eyes and the pride in wealth, comes not from the Father but from the world. The world and its desires will pass away, but those who do the will of God live for ever.[2]

[Paul] Live by the [Holy} Spirit, and you will not gratify the desires of the sinful nature. For the desires of the sinful nature are opposed to the [Holy] Spirit, and the [Holy] Spirit is opposed to the sinful nature. They are opposed to each other so that you do not do what you want to do. ... The deeds of the sinful nature are obvious: sexual immorality, impurity, debauchery, idolatry, sorcery, hatred, strife, orgies, ... I warn you, as I warned you before, that those who live like this will not inherit the kingdom of God. The fruit of the Spirit is love, joy, peace, patience, kindness, goodness, faithfulness, gentleness and self-discipline.[3]

[1] Judges 14:1-9   [2] 1 John 2:15-17   [3] Galatians 5:16-23

Day 123

Samson was judge in Israel for 20 years, but he never conquered his love for the world. This led to his downfall and a day came when he lost the sign—long, uncut hair—that God was with him, and he did not realise that God was no longer in him. But God had not rejected Him altogether. Even as a prisoner, his hair began to grow again and, in His grace and mercy, God gave him another chance to repent and turn to Him. While alive, it is never too late to seek God's forgiveness.

Samson and Delilah

Some time later, Samson fell in love a woman in the Valley of Sorek whose name was Delilah. The rulers of the Philistines went to her and said, "Lure him into telling you the secret of his great strength so that we may be able to overpower him. So Delilah said to Samson, "Tell me the secret of your great strength. How you could be bound and overpowered?" Samson said to her, "If someone binds me with seven fresh thongs that have not been dried, I will become weak like any other man." The rulers of the Philistines brought her seven fresh thongs that had not been dried and she bound him with them. While men were hidden in an inner room, she called to him, "Samson, the Philistines are upon you!" But he snapped the thongs as easily as a piece of string snaps when it touches a flame. ...

Then she said to him, "You have mocked me. How can you say. 'I love you,' when your heart is not with me. This is the third time you have mocked me and you have not told me the secret of your great strength." With such nagging she pestered him day after day until he was tired to death. So he told her everything. He said, "A razor has never been used on my head, I have been a Nazirite [set apart] to God since my birth. If my head were shaved I would lose all my strength." ... She let him fall asleep on her lap, then she called a man to shave off the seven locks of his hair, ... and his strength left him. ... When he awoke from sleep he thought, "I'll go out as before and shake myself free." He did not realise that the Eternal-God had left him. Then the Philistines seized him, gouged out his eyes and took him to Gaza where they bound him with bronze shackles and set him to grind at the mill in the prison.

But the hair on Samson's head began to grow again. ... The Philistine lords gathered to offer a great sacrifice to their god, Dagon. ... So they called Samson out of prison to perform for them. ... Then Samson cried, "O Eternal-God, remember me." ... Samson reached to grasp the two central pillars on which the temple stood. ... He pushed with all his strength and the temple fell on the rulers and all the people in it.[1]

Time would fail to tell of ... Samson ... who through faith ... saw their weakness turned to strength, became powerful in battle and routed foreign enemies.[2]

[1] Judges 16:1, 5-9,10-17,19-23, 25, 29   [2] Hebrews 11: 32,34

Day 124

The story of Naomi shows how God works His purposes out even in the apparently small and sometimes tragic events of life. Naomi and her husband left their home in Bethlehem and moved to Moab because of famine. To Naomi, Orpah and Ruth were foreign women who married her sons. When her sons died, her daughters-in-law behaved in very different ways. Naomi had left God's country but God had not forsaken her.

Ruth and Naomi

In the days when Israel was ruled by judges, there was a famine in the land, a man and his wife, named Elimelech and Naomi from Bethlehem in Judah, went to live in the country of Moab. Now Elimelech died and she was left with her two sons, Mahlon and Kilion. They married Moabite women, one named Orpah and the other Ruth. When they had lived there for about ten years, Naomi's sons both died and she was left without her two sons and her husband.

Then, while in Moab, Naomi heard that the Eternal-God had come to the aid of His people in Israel and had given them food. Naomi and her daughters-in-law ... set out on the road back to the land of Judah. Naomi said to her two daughters-in-law, "Go back, each of you, to your mother's home. May the Eternal-God deal kindly with you as you have done with your dead and with me. May the Eternal-God grant each of you rest in the home of another husband. She kissed them and they wept aloud and said to her, "No! We will go back with you to your people." Naomi replied, "Even if I thought that I could bear sons who would become your husbands, would you wait for them? God home, please! I am too old to have another husband."

At Naomi's words they wept again. Then Orpah kissed her mother-in-law to leave, but Ruth clung to her. "Look," said Naomi, "your sister-in-law is returning to her people and to her gods. You, too, go back with her." Ruth replied, "Do not press me to leave you or to turn back from going with you. Where you go I will go, and where you stay I will stay. Your people will be my people and your god my God. Where you die I will die, and there I will be buried. May the Eternal-God deal with me, however severely, if anything but death separates you and me.

So the two women went on their way until they arrived in Bethlehem. There, the whole town was stirred because of them and the women exclaimed, "Is this really Naomi?" "Don't call me Naomi," she said to them, "Call me Mara [meaning 'bitter'] ... I went away full, but the Eternal-God has brought me back empty." [1]

Where can I go where your Spirit is not? Where can I flee from your presence? ... If I fly with the wings of the dawn, or if I settle on the farthest side of the sea, even there your hand will guide me, your right hand will hold me fast." [2]

[1] Ruth 1:1-21   [2] Psalm 139:7-9

Day 125

Judah was a foreign and strange country for Ruth. Happenings which are unexpected to us are not unexpected to God. She set out to glean grain in the fields of some farmer and 'by chance' she found herself working in the field of Boaz, the son of Rahab, who had hidden the spies in Jericho. God was working out His purposes even in apparently chance happenings. Ruth joined her mother-in law Rahab, both foreign women, to become those of the line through whom Jesus, was descended.

Ruth and Boaz

Now Naomi had a relative on her husband Elimelech's side named Boaz. He was a man of standing in the community. Ruth said to Naomi, "Let me go to the fields and glean grain behind [the harvesters of] someone who is favourable to me, a Moabitess." Naomi said to her, "Go, my daughter." So she went out and began to glean in the fields behind the harvesters. It so happened that she found herself working in a field belonging to Boaz, a member of the Elimelech family. At that moment, Boaz arrived from Bethlehem and greeted the harvesters, "The Eternal-God be with you!" They replied. "The Eternal-God be with you!"

Boaz asked the head man of his harvesters, "To whom does this young woman belong?" The head man replied, "She is the Moabitess who returned from Moab with Naomi. She asked me, 'Please let me glean among the sheaves behind the harvesters'. She went into the field and has been working steadily from morning till now without resting." Boaz said to Ruth, "Listen to me, my daughter, do not go elsewhere to glean but stay here and keep close to the other young women who are working here." ... So Ruth gleaned in the field until evening. Her mother in law said to her, "Where did you glean today?" Ruth said to her mother-in-law, ... "The name of the man I worked with today is Boaz." Naomi said , "May the Eternal-God bless him," ... That man is a close relative of ours, he is one of our 'kinsman-redeemers'." [1]

So Boaz took Ruth and she became his wife. The Eternal-God enabled her to conceive and she gave birth to a son ... and they named him Obed. He was the father of Jesse, the father of David. [2]

The genealogy of Jesus Christ, ... Salmon, the father of Boaz, whose mother was Rahab; Boaz the father of Obed, whose mother was Ruth. Obed was the father of Jesse, and Jesse the father of King David. ... Jacob the father of Joseph, the husband of Mary, of whom was born Jesus, who is called Christ. [3]

[Solomon:] A person plans his way in his mind, but it is the Eternal-God who directs his steps. [4] *[Jeremiah:] I know, O Eternal-God, that a man cannot determine his own way himself. Instruct me, Eternal-God, with justice, not in anger.* [5]

[1] Ruth 2:1-8,17-20 [2] Ruth 4:13,17 [3] Matthew 1:1,5,16 [4] Proverbs 16:9 [5] Jeremiah 10:23-24

Day 126

Hannah had no children. This was not uncommon then or now. Hannah was driven to pray desperately that God would give her a child. With her prayer went her promise to give her son, if God granted one, back to God. That is always a good way to pray for something we desire. In God's gracious plan for Israel, the prophet who was to lead His people for many years, was the son God gave to Hannah.

The birth of Samuel

There was a man from Ramathaim ... whose name was Elkanah. He had two wives ... Peninnah had children, but Hannah had none. Year after year this man went from his town to worship and sacrifice to the Eternal-God, the Almighty, at Shiloh. Every year, on the day when Elkanah went to sacrifice, he would give portions of meat to his wife Peninnah, ... but to Hannah he gave a double portion because he loved her. But the Eternal-God had closed her womb.

Once when they had finished eating and drinking in Shiloh, Hannah rose and went to the temple. Eli the priest was sitting on a chair by the doorpost of the temple of the Eternal-God. There, Hannah wept bitterly and prayed to the Eternal-God. She made a vow saying, "O Eternal-God, the Almighty, if you will only look on the misery of your servant and remember me, and not forget me but give me a son, then I will give him to the Eternal-God for all his days until he dies. He will be a Nazirite [one set apart] before you and no razor will ever be used on his head."

As she was praying to the Eternal-God, Eli watched her mouth. Hannah was praying in her heart, her lips were moving but she made no sound. Eli thought she was drunk and said to her, "How long will you be drunk like this? Put away your wine." Hannah replied, "No! my lord, I am a woman who is deeply troubled. I have not drunk wine nor any strong drink, but I have been pouring out to God all that is in my heart." Eli answered, "Go in peace, and may the God of Israel grant you all that you have asked of him." Later, Hannah conceived and gave birth to a son. She named him Samuel, saying, "He is the answer to my prayer to the Eternal-God." [1]

Sons are a heritage from the Eternal-God and children a reward from Him. Like arrows in the hands of a warrior are sons born in one's youth. Blessed is the man who has his quiver full of them. [2]   Children's children are the crown of the aged [grandparents], and children are the pride of their parents. [3]

Delight yourself in the Eternal-God and He will give you the true desires of your heart. Commit your way to the Eternal-God; trust in Him and He will work it out: He will make your righteousness shine like the light of dawn and the justice of your cause like the noonday sun." [4]

[1] 1 Samuel 1:1-5,9-17,19 [2] Psalm 127:3-5 [3] Proverbs 17:6 [4] Psalms 37:4-6

Day 127

Samuel was only a boy when God first spoke to him. It came as a great surprise. God did not appear to be speaking to people very much at that time. We do not know why God did not speak directly to Eli, the High Priest, but to his boy servant Samuel. The great lesson that Samuel learned was to say to God, "Speak, Lord, for your servant is listening," and then to listen carefully and be obedient to what he learned.

God calls Samuel

The boy Samuel served the Eternal-God under Eli. In those days the word of the Eterenal-God was rarely heard and there were few visions. One night Eli, whose eyes were becoming so weak that he could hardly see, was lying down in his room. The lamp of God had not yet gone out, and Samuel was lying down in the temple of the Eternal-God, where the ark of God was. Then the Eternal-God called Samuel. Samuel answered, "Here I am." He ran to Eli and said, "Here I am! You called me." But Eli said, "I did not call you. Go back and lie down." So he went and lay down. Again the Eternal-God called, "Samuel!" And Samuel got up and went to Eli and said, "Here I am! You called me!" Eli said, "My son, I did not call. Lie down again."

Now Samuel did not yet know the Eternal-God, His word had not yet been revealed to him. The Eternal-God called Samuel for the third time. Samuel got up and went to Eli and said, "Here I am. You did call." Eli realised that it was the Eternal-God who was calling the boy. So Eli said to Samuel, "Go and lie down, and if He calls you, say, "Speak, Eternal-God, for your servant is listening."

Samuel went and lay down again. The Eternal-God came and stood there and called as He had done before, "Samuel! Samuel!" Samuel said, "Speak, for your servant is listening." Then the Eternal-God said to Samuel, "Look, I am about to do something in Israel that will make both ears of everyone who hears of it tingle. ..." Samuel lay there until morning and then opened the doors of the house of the Eternal-God. He was afraid to tell Eli the vision. But Eli called him and said, "Samuel, my son. ... What did He say to you?" Samuel told him everything, he hid nothing from him.

The Eternal-God was with Samuel as he grew up. Samuel took note of every word of the Eternal-God; not one did he let slip without attention.

All Israel ... knew that Samuel was a true prophet of the Eternal-God. [1]

[Isaiah:] The Sovereign Eternal-God has given me the tongue of a disciple so that I know the words that can sustain whose who are weary. He wakens me morning by morning so that I listen like a disciple, as one who wants to learn. The Sovereign Eternal-God has opened my ears, and I have not been rebellious nor turned back. [2]

[1] 1 Samuel 3:1-21   [2] Isaiah 50:4-5

Day 128

Since the Israelites became a nation, after their deliverance from Egypt, they had been led by God through judges and prophets: from Moses to Samuel. They differed from the nations around them, all of whom had kings. So they wanted a king too. God used the rebellious attitude of the Israelites to introduce them to the rule of a king. Eventually the great King would be Jesus Christ, the King of kings.

Israel asks for a king

When Samuel grew old, he appointed his sons to be judges in Israel. ... His sons did not follow his good ways. They turned from them to gain wealth dishonestly. They accepted bribes and perverted justice. All the elders of Israel gathered together and came to Samuel at Ramah and said to him, "You are old, and your sons do not walk in your good ways. Now then, appoint a king to govern us as kings govern all the other nations around us. When Samuel heard them say, "Give us a king to lead us," he was very displeased and he prayed to the Eternal-God. The Eternal-God said to him: "Listen to what the people are saying to you. It is not you they have rejected as their king, but me. ... Now listen to them and warn them solemnly. Show them what a king who reigns over them will do."

Samuel repeated all the words of the Eternal-God to the people who were asking for a king. He said, "This is what a king who reigns over you will do: He will take your sons and assign them to his chariots and horses. ... Some he will appoint to be commanders of thousands. ... He will take the best of your fields and vineyards. ... When that day comes you will cry out to be relieved of the king you have chosen. On that day the Eternal-God will not answer you." The people refused to listen to Samuel. "No!" they said, "We want a king over us so that we can be like all the other nations. We want a king to lead us, to go before us and fight our battles." [1]

Samuel said to all the Israelites, "When you saw Nahash king of the Ammonites was coming to attack you, you said to me, 'We want a king to rule over us', although the Eternal-God, your God, was your king. Now here is the king [Saul] you asked for. See, the Eternal-God has set a king over you. If both you and the king who reigns over you fear the Eternal-God, serve and obey Him and do not rebel against His commands all will be well. But if you do not obey the Eternal-God and you rebel against His commands, His hand will be against you and your king, as it was against your forefathers.[2]

Jesus said, "My kingdom is not of this world. If my kingdom were of this world, my servants would fight to keep me from being arrested by the Jews. As it is, my kingdom is not of this world." [3]

[1] 1 Samuel 8:1-20   [2] 1 Samuel 12:12-15   [3] John 18:36

Day 129

God chose Saul to be the first king of Israel. Saul failed so badly as king that people might wonder if God had made a mistake in choosing him. God never makes mistakes. Saul had all the physical and mental qualities needed to make a good king. What went wrong was not God's choice, but Saul's response to it. He did not continue to seek God to guide him in everything that he did.

Saul is made king

There was a wealthy Benjamite whose name was Kish. His son, named Saul, was a handsome young man who was taller and more impressive than anyone else. Now the donkeys belonging to Saul's father Kish had gone astray, and Kish said to his son Saul, "Take one of the men with you and go and search for the donkeys." Saul passed through the hill country of Ephraim and through the region of Shalisha, but they did not find the donkeys. ... When they reached the region of Zuph, Saul said to the man who was with him, "Let us go back, or my father will stop worrying about the donkeys and start to worry about us." The servant replied, "In this town there is a man of God who is held in honour and whatever he says comes true. Let us go to him there, perhaps he will guide us as to which way to go." ...

They went to the town, and as they were going up the hill into it, Samuel was coming towards them on his way to the sacred high place. The day before Saul came, the Eternal-God had revealed to Samuel that: "About this time tomorrow I will send to you a man from the land of Benjamin. You are to anoint him to be ruler over my people Israel. He will deliver my people from the hand of the Philistines, for the cry from the suffering of my people has reached me." When Samuel saw Saul, the Eternal-God said to him, "This is the man about whom I spoke to you, he will rule my people."

Saul approached Samuel at the gateway and said, "Please tell me where is the house of the seer?" Samuel replied, "I am the seer. Go on ahead of me to the sacred high place, for today you will eat with me and in the morning I will let you go." ... "As for the donkeys that were lost three days ago, do not worry about them. They have been found." ... They rose at dawn ... and Saul and Samuel went out into the road. As they were going down to the outskirts of the town, Samuel said to Saul, "Tell your man to go on ahead of us." [1]

Samuel took a flask of oil and poured it on Saul's head and kissed him. He said, "The Eternal-God has anointed you leader over His people. ... Then the Spirit of the Eternal-God will come upon you in power, and you will prophesy with the prophets, and you will be transformed into a different person." [2]

[1] 1 Samuel 9:1-6,10-20,26-27 [2] 1 Samuel 10:1,6

Day 130

Samuel served God all his life. As a young boy he had been given to God by his mother and father, now he was 'old and grey'. During all the years he had led the Israelites, he had been faithful to God, in both public and private life. Now he was handing over his leadership to a young king, offering him both his example and the assurance of his prayerful support. Samuel had lived the life God had planned for Him. There is nothing greater than living one's life for God.

Samuel's farewell speech

Samuel said to the Israelites, "I have listened to all that you said to me and have set a king over you. Now it is the king who leads you. As for me, I am old and grey, and my sons are here with you. I have led from my youth until this day. Here I am. Testify against me before the Eternal-God and before His anointed. Whose ox or whose donkey have I taken? Whom have I defrauded? Whom have I oppressed? From whose hand have I taken a bribe to make me not see? Testify against me if I have taken any of these things and I will restore it." They replied, "You have not defrauded or oppressed us, nor have you have taken anything from anyone's hand." Samuel said to them, "The Eternal-God is witness against you and His anointed one this day, that you have not found anything in my hand." They said, "He is our witness,"

Samuel said to the people, "It is the Eternal-God who appointed Moses and Aaron and brought your forefathers out of the land of Egypt. ... But they forgot the Eternal-God, their God, and He sold them into the hand of Sisera. ... They cried to the Eternal-God and said, 'We have sinned in forsaking the Eternal-God. ... Then the Eternal-God sent Jerubbaal, Barak, Jephthah and Samuel, and rescued you from the hands of your enemies who were on every side, so that you lived in safety.

"Now then, stand still and see this great thing that the Eternal-God will do before your eyes. It is the wheat harvest today, I will call on the Eternal-God to send thunder and rain and you will realise how great is your wickedness before God in demanding a king to rule over you. ... Then Samuel called upon the Eternal-God, and that day He sent thunder and rain so that all the people stood in fear and awe of the Eternal-God and of Samuel." [1]

O God, since my youth you have taught me, and to this day I proclaim your marvellous deeds. Even when I am old and grey, O God, do not forsake me, until I proclaim your power, your might and your righteousness to all the generations to come. Your power and righteousness reach to the heavens, O God, you who have done marvellous things. Who can be compared to you, O God? [2]

[1] 1 Samuel 12:1-11,16-18   [2] Psalm 71:17-19

Day 131

Saul was rejected by God who had chosen him to be king of Israel. The reason was not that Saul did not know what God's will for him was, but rather that he rebelled against it. It is not an easy thing for a strong person, especially one who is impatient, to acknowledge that God's way is best, even if it means waiting for it.

Saul is rejected

Saul reigned over Israel for forty-two years. The Philistines assembled to fight Israel. When the Israelites saw that they were in a perilous situation, they hid in caves, in holes in the ground, among the rocks, and in tombs and cisterns. Samuel remained at Gilgal, and all the troops with him trembled with fear. He waited for seven days, the time indicated by Samuel, but Samuel did not come to Gilgal, and Saul's men began to slip away from him. So Saul said "Bring me the burnt offering and the fellowship offerings." And he offered up the burnt offering.

As he finished offering the burnt-offering, Samuel arrived, and Saul went out to greet him. "What have you done?" asked Samuel. Saul replied, "When I saw that the men were slipping away, and that you did not come at the expected time, and that the Philistines were assembling at Michmash, I said, 'Now the Philistines will come against me at Gilgal, and I have not sought the will of the Eternal-God.' So I felt forced to offer the burnt offering." Samuel said, "You acted foolishly. You have not kept the command the Eternal-God, your God, gave you. The Eternal-God was about to establish your kingdom over Israel for all time. But now your kingdom will not endure. The Eternal-God has sought out a man after His own heart and has appointed him to be the ruler of His people, because you have not obeyed the command of the Eternal-God." [1]

Samuel said: "Does the Eternal-God take as much delight in burnt offerings and sacrifices as He does in obeying His voice? To obey is better than sacrifice, and to take heed is better than the fat of rams. For rebellion is sin like the sin of divination, and arrogance like the sin of idolatry. Because you have rejected the word of the Eternal-God, He has rejected you as king." ... As Samuel turned to leave, Saul caught hold of the hem of his robe, and it tore. Samuel said to him, "The Eternal-God has torn the kingdom of Israel from you today and has given it to your neighbour who is better than you. He who is the Glory of Israel does change His mind. He is not a man, that He should change His mind." [2]

The Eternal-God said to Samuel, "Do not consider his (Eliab's) appearance nor his height, for I have rejected him. ... Man looks at the outward appearance, but the Eternal-God looks at the heart." [3]

[1] 1 Samuel 13:1,5-14 [2] 1 Samuel 15:22-23,27-29 [3] 1 Samuel 16:7

Day 132

God has His reasons for choosing the people He calls to work for Him. Those reasons often differ from what people normally think. There are two reasons for this: the first is that God knows far better than people do what is needed in a person for any given task. Secondly, God sees far better than other people can, not only what people are but what they can become.

David is anointed king

The Eternal-God said to Samuel, "How long will you mourn for Saul for I have rejected him as king over Israel? Fill your horn with oil and set out; I am sending you to Jesse of Bethlehem because I have chosen a king from one of his sons." Samuel did what the Eternal-God had commanded. When he arrived at Bethlehem, the elders of the town came trembling to meet him. They said. "Do you come in peace?" Samuel replied, "Yes, I have come to sacrifice to the Eternal-God. Purify yourselves and come with me to the sacrifice." He consecrated Jesse and his sons and invited them to the sacrifice.

When they arrived, Samuel looked at Eliab and thought, "Surely this man standing before me is the anointed of the Eternal-God." But the Eternal-God said to Samuel, 'Do not judge him by his appearance or his height, for I have rejected him. The Eternal-God does not see as people do. People look at outward appearances but the Eternal-God looks at the heart." ... Jesse made seven of his sons pass before Samuel, but Samuel said to him, "The Eternal-God has not chosen any of these." He asked Jesse, "Are these all the sons you have?" Jesse answered, "There is still one left, he is the youngest, but he is looking after the sheep." Samuel said, "Send for him. We will not sit down to eat until he arrives." So Jesse sent for him and he came and stood before them. He had a ruddy appearance and handsome features. Then the Eternal-God said, "Rise and anoint him for he is the one." So Samuel took the horn of oil and anointed him with all his brothers present. From that day the Spirit of the Eternal-God came upon David in power. [1]

When He had removed Saul, God made David their king. Of him, He said: "I have found David, son of Jesse, a man after my own heart. He will do everything I desire of him." God has kept His promise and from this man's descendants He has raised up for Israel a Saviour, Jesus." [2]

[David:] "You have exalted me above my enemies; you have rescued me from violent men. Therefore I will exalt you among the nations, O Eternal-God, and I will sing praises to your name." He gives great victories to His king. He shows unfailing love to His anointed, to David and to His descendants for ever." [3]

[1] 1 Samuel 16:1,4-13   [2] Acts 13:22-23   [3] Psalm 18:48-50

Day 133

When David went out to meet Goliath, people thought that two men were facing each other: a weak stripling and a strong giant. In reality, God was with David while Goliath had a Philistine god who was, in fact, no god at all. God, in David, won that fight and David was quick to acknowledge that. David won the fight because He was on God's side. Goliath was not. When David fought for God, God fought for David.

David and Goliath

The Philistines assembled their forces for war at Socoh in Judah. ... Saul and the Israelites gathered and camped in the Valley of Elah and drew up their battle line to face the Philistines. The Philistines stood on one hill and the Israelites on another, with a valley between them. A champion named Goliath ... stepped out of the Philistine camp. He was over nine feet tall. He stood and shouted to the ranks of Israel, "Why have you come out and lined up for battle? ... Choose a man and let him come down to me. If he fights and kills me, we will become your subjects, but if I defeat him and kill him, you will become our subjects and be subject to us." ... On hearing these words, Saul and all the Israelites were dismayed and terrified.

Now Jesse had said to his son David, "Take ... these ten loaves of bread for your brothers and go quickly to their camp. ... David rose early in the morning and went to the camp as Jesse had commanded him. ... David asked the men standing near him, ... "Who is this Philistine that he should defy the armies of the living God?" ... David took his staff in his hand, chose five smooth stones from the stream and put them in his shepherd's bag and, with his sling in his hand, went to meet the Philistine. Goliath said to David, "Am I a dog, that you come to me with sticks? ..." David said to the Philistine, "You come to me with sword and spear and javelin, but I come to you in the name of the Eternal-God, the Almighty, the God of the armies of Israel, whom you have defied."

As the Philistine moved nearer to attack him, David ran towards the battle line to meet him. Reaching into his bag, he took out a stone, slung it and struck the Philistine on the forehead. The stone sank deep into his forehead and he fell face down on the ground. So David triumphed over the Philistine with a sling and a stone. [1]

"My trust is not in my bow. Victory is not mine through the sword. It is you who gives us victory over our enemies. It is you who puts our adversaries to shame. Our boast is in you, O God, we will praise your name for ever." [2]

Thanks be to God who, in Christ, shares His triumphal procession with us, and through us spreads everywhere the fragrance that comes from knowing Him. [3]

[1] 1 Samuel 17:1-11,17,22,26,40,43,48-50   [2] Psalm 44:6-9   [3] 2 Corinthians 2:14

Day 134

Jesus Christ is sometimes called the 'son of David'. Both Mary, the mother of Jesus, and Joseph, her husband, were descendents of David. 'King of the Jews' was the title of David, the greatest of the Jewish kings. That was also the title nailed on the wooden cross on which Jesus was crucified. As David was king of the 'Kingdom of Israel', so Jesus is King of the 'Kingdom of God'.

David is made king over Israel

All the tribes of Israel came to David at Hebron and said, "See, we are your own flesh and blood. While Saul was king over us, it was you who led Israel's armies. The Eternal-God said to you, 'You will be the shepherd of my people Israel, and you will be their ruler.'" ... David made a covenant with them at Hebron before the Eternal-God and they anointed him king over Israel. [1]

King David sat before the Eternal-God and said: "Who am I, O Sovereign Eternal-God, and what is my family, that you have brought me as far as this? And as if this were not enough in your sight, O Sovereign Eternal-God, you have spoken of the your servant's descendants for a great while to come. What more can David say to you, O Sovereign Eternal-God? ... Now, Eternal-God, keep the promise you have made concerning your servant and his house for ever. Do as you have promised so that your name will be magnified for ever. Then people will say, 'The Eternal-God, the Almighty, is the God of Israel!' And the house of your servant David will be established before you."

"O Sovereign Eternal-God, you are God! Your words are true and you have promised these good things to your servant. Now may it please you to bless the house of your servant, so that it may continue for ever before you, for you, O Sovereign Eternal-God, have spoken, and, because you have blessed it, the house of your servant will be blessed for ever." [2]

David reigned over all Israel. He administered the law and judged all his people with justice. [3]

[Isaiah:] To us a child is born; to us a son is given. The authority will rest on His shoulders. He will be named: Wonderful Counsellor, Mighty God, Everlasting Father, Prince of Peace. Of the increase of His government and of peace there will be no end. He will reign on the throne of David and His kingdom will be established. He will uphold it with justice and righteousness from that time on and for evermore. The zeal of the Eternal-God, the Almighty, will accomplish this. [4]

[1] 2 Samuel 5:1-3; 27 [2] 2 Samuel 7:18-19, 25-26, 28-29 [3] 2 Samuel 8:15 [4] Isaiah 9:6-8

Day 135

The Bible tells of many people who sinned against God. What was special about David was that he repented of his sin. He recognised that his sin against Bathsheba and Uriah was sin against God. He repented of his sin with great sorrow. God forgives that kind of repentance, however great the sin.

David and Bathsheba

In the spring, when kings go to war, David sent Joab with his officers and the whole army of Israel. ... David remained in Jerusalem. Towards evening one day, David got up from his couch and walked around on the palace roof. From there, he saw a woman bathing. The woman was very beautiful. David sent someone to inquire about her. He was told that she was Bathsheba, the daughter of Eliam and the wife of Uriah the Hittite. Then David sent messengers to bring her to him and he slept with her. ... Then she returned to her house.

The woman conceived and sent word to David, "I am pregnant." David sent this message to Joab: "Send me Uriah the Hittite." ... Then David said to Uriah, "Go down to your house and wash your feet." ... However Uriah slept at the palace entrance with all his master's guards and did not go down to his house. ...

In the morning, David wrote a letter to Joab and sent it by the hand of Uriah. In it he wrote, "Put Uriah in the forefront of the fiercest fighting. Then draw back from him so that he will be struck down and die." While Joab was besieging the city, he put Uriah where he knew the most powerful defenders were. ... Some of the men in David's army were killed and so was Uriah the Hittite. [1]

The Eternal-God was displeased with what David had done and He sent Nathan to him. Nathan said to David, "There were two men in a certain city, one was rich and the other poor. The rich man had very many sheep and cattle but the poor man had nothing except one little ewe lamb. ... Now a traveller came to the rich man but he did not want to take one of his flock or herd, so he took the ewe lamb that belonged to the poor man and prepared it for the guest who had come to him. David's anger flared up against the rich man and he said to Nathan. "As surely as the Eternal-God lives, the man who did this deserves to die. He must restore the lamb fourfold for doing such a thing without any pity" Then Nathan said to David, "You are the man!" [2]

[David:] Have mercy on me, O God, according to your great love. Blot out my transgressions according to your great mercy. Wash me clean from my guilt and cleanse me from my sin. I know my transgressions and my sin is constantly before me. Against you, you only, have I sinned and done this evil in your sight. ... Create a clean heart in me, O God, and put a new spirit within me. [3]

---

[1] 2 Samuel 11:1-9,14-16   [2] 2 Samuel 12:1-7   [3] Psalm 51:1-4,7

Day 136

Many people have enemies. The worst enemies are those of one's own family. David had many enemies at different times but the one who most nearly succeeded in destroying him was his own son, Absalom. Despite his son's rebellion against him, David loved him to the end. In this David's love was a picture of God's love for sinners. David loved Absalom despite his rebellion against Him. God loves people while hating their sinful rebellion.

Absalom conspires against his father David

Absalom had a chariot, horses and fifty men who ran ahead of him. He would rise early and stand by the side of the road leading to the gate of the city. Whenever anyone came with a case for the king to judge, Absalom would call out ... "Look, your claims are good and proper, but the king has given no one the authority to hear you. If I were judge in this land then everyone who came with a complaint would receive justice. ... So he stole the hearts of the people of Israel. [1]

A messenger came to David and said, "The hearts of the people of Israel are now with Absalom." Then David said to the officers who were with him in Jerusalem, "We must flee at once or none of us will escape from Absalom. We must leave immediately or he will overtake us and bring disaster upon us and put the city to the sword." The king set out and his entire household went with him. [2]

David assembled the men who were with him. ... He sent the troops out saying, "Deal gently with the young man Absalom for my sake." ... The army of Israel was defeated by David's men, and the slaughter that day was great. ... David was sitting between the two gates. ... The lookout saw another man running. ... Then the Cushite came and said, "It is good news, my Lord. The Eternal-God has delivered you today from all who rebelled against you." The king asked him, "Is all well with the young man Absalom?" The Cushite replied, "May the enemies of my lord the king and all who rebel against you be as that young man is." The king was deeply shaken. He went up to the room over the gate and wept bitterly. As he went, he cried: "O my son Absalom! My son, my son Absalom! Would that I had died instead of you, O Absalom, my son, my son!" [3]

At the right time, when we were still helpless, Christ died for the ungodly. It is rare for one man to die for a righteous man, though for a good man someone might dare to die. But God [the Father] shows His own love for us in that while we were still sinners, Christ [God the Son] died for us. ... If, when we were enemies of God [the Father], we were reconciled to Him through the death of His Son, how much more, having been reconciled, shall we be saved through His risen life! [4]

[1] 2 Samuel 15:1-6 [2] 2 Samuel 15:13-16 [3] 2 Samuel 18:1-7; 25,32-33 [4] Romans 5:6-10

Day 137

Solomon was the son of David and Bathsheba. He was God's choice to follow David as King. He inherited not only a great kingdom, but peace with the countries around. His was the glory and honour which his father had won. Nations near and far came to see that glory. He began well but later he allowed things and people into his life which led him away from God.

Solomon is made king

King David said, "Call Bathsheba to come to me." So she came and stood before him. The king then swore by an oath: "As the Eternal-God lives, who has saved me from every diversity, I will fulfil today what I swore to you by the Eternal-God, the God of Israel: your son Solomon will be king after me, and he will sit in my place on my throne." Bathsheba bowed with her face to the ground and knelt before the king. She said, "May my lord King David live for ever!" [1]

As the time drew near for David to die, he gave a charge to Solomon, his son: "I am about to go the way of all the earth, so be strong, be courageous, and obey all that the Eternal-God, your God, commands. Walk in His ways, keep His decrees and commandments, His laws and precepts, as written in the Law of Moses, so that you may prosper in all you do and wherever you are, that the Eternal-God may keep His promise to me: 'If your descendants take heed to how they live, and if they walk faithfully before me with all their heart and soul, there will never fail to be a successor of yours on the throne of Israel. ... Then David slept with his fathers and was buried in the City of David. ... So Solomon sat on the throne of his father David, and his reign was firmly established. [2]

King Solomon, however, loved many foreign women including Pharaoh's daughter. ... They came from nations about which the Eternal-God had said to the Israelites, "You shall not enter into marriage relationships with them, because they will surely turn your hearts to follow after their gods." But Solomon clung to them in love. ... As Solomon grew old, his wives turned his heart to follow after other gods, and his heart was not wholly true to the Eternal-God, his God, as was the heart of David his father. ... Solomon did what was evil in the eyes of the Eternal-God. He did not follow the Eternal-God wholeheartedly as David his father had done. [3]

[Paul:] Those who live according to the sinful nature set their minds on its desires; but those who live according to [God] the [Holy] Spirit set their minds on what the Spirit desires. To set the mind to follow the sinful nature leads to death, but to set the mind on the Spirit leads to life and peace. [4]

---

[1] 1 Kings 1:28-31   [2] 1 Kings 2:1-4,10,12   [3] 1 Kings 11:1-6   [4] Romans 8:5-6

Day 138

Solomon was a great king. The greatest thing he ever did was to ask God for wisdom to rule his nation. The wisest thing he ever said was, "The fear of the Lord is the beginning of wisdom."[1] The most foolish thing he did was to forsake the 'fear of the Lord' and go his own way, particularly in desiring wrong things.

Solomon asks for wisdom

At Gibeon the Eternal-God appeared to Solomon in a dream at night. God said to him, "Ask for whatever you would like me to give you." Solomon answered, "You showed great kindness to your servant my father David. ... Now, O Eternal-God, my God, you have made your servant king in the place of my father David. I am only a little child, I do not know how to rule as king. ... Give your servant, therefore, an understanding mind to govern your people and to discern between right and wrong. For who is able to govern this your people which is so great?"

The Eternal-God was pleased that Solomon had asked for this. So God said to him, "Since you have asked for this and not for long life or riches for yourself, nor for the death of your enemies, but for understanding and discerning what is right, I will do as you have asked. I will give you a wise and discerning mind, so that there will be no one like you in the past, nor will there ever be in the future. More than that, I will give you what you have not asked for, both riches and honour, so that in your lifetime there will be no king who will compare with you." Then Solomon awoke: it had been a dream.[2]

God gave Solomon great wisdom. ... His wisdom was greater than that of all the men of the East; it surpassed all the wisdom of Egypt. ... His fame spread to all the nations around.[3]

[Jesus:] "The Queen of the South will rise at the judgment of this generation and condemn it. She came from the ends of the earth to hear Solomon's wisdom, and now there is One here who is greater than Solomon."[4]

[Paul:] Think, my brothers and sisters, of your call [to be Christians]. Not many of you were wise by human standards; not many of you were powerful; not many of you were of noble birth. But God chose what is foolish to the world to shame what, to the world, is wisdom; He chose what is weak, to the world, to shame what, to the world, is strong; He chose what is lowly and despised to the world and the things which, to the world, are nothing, to reduce to nothing, the things which, to the world, are something, so that no one may boast before Him. It is through Him that you are in Christ Jesus, who is, for us, our wisdom, our righteousness, our holiness and our redemption.[5]

---

[1] Proverbs 9:10 [2] 1 Kings 3:5-15 [3] 1 Kings 4:29-31,34 [4] Matthew 12:42 [5] 1 Corinthians 1:26-30

Day 139

The Temple built by Solomon followed the pattern of the 'Tent of Meeting' or Tabernacle, which was designed by God who gave His instructions to Moses. It was more magnificent than the Tabernacle, but its plan and purposes remained the same: it was where ordinary people, through the Priests and High Priest, could approach God and worship Him. It taught the way in which God, who is holy, could accept sinful people.

The Temple is built and consecrated

Hiram, king of Tyre, heard that Solomon had been anointed to be king in the place of his father David, so he sent his envoys to Solomon, for Hiram had always been a friend of David. ... Solomon replied with this message to Hiram. "You know that my father, David, could not build a temple for the name of the Eternal-God, his God, because he was at war with his enemies until the Eternal-God put them under his feet. Now that the Eternal-God, my God, has given me rest on all sides and there is no enemy or disaster, I intend to build a temple for the name of the Eternal-God as He had directed my father David when He said, 'your son, whom I will set on the throne in your place, will build the house for my name." [1]

The word of the Eternal-God came to Solomon: "This house you are building: if you follow my statutes and obey my commands, I will fulfil through you the promise I made to David, your father. I will live among the children of Israel and will not forsake my people Israel. Solomon built the temple and finished it. [2]

King Solomon called to him all the elders of Israel, at Jerusalem. ... All the men of Israel assembled and came to King Solomon at the time of the feast. ... When all the elders of Israel had arrived, ... the priests brought the ark of the covenant of the Eternal-God to its place in the inner sanctuary of the temple, the Most holy Place, and placed it beneath the wings of the cherubim. ... There was nothing in the ark except the two tablets of stone that Moses had placed there at Horeb, when the Eternal-God made a covenant with the Israelites, after they came out of the land of Egypt. When the priests came out from the Holy Place, a cloud filled the temple of the Eternal-God. The priests could not perform their duties because of the cloud, for the glory of the Eternal-God filled His house. [3]

Do you not know that your body is a temple of [God] the Holy Spirit, who is within you, whom you have received from God [the Father]? You are not your own, you have been bought with a price. Therefore honour God in your body. [4]

I [John in a vision] saw no temple in the city [the new Jerusalem]. The temple is the Lord God, the Almighty and the Lamb. The city needs no sun or moon, for the glory of God is its light and the Lamb is its lamp. [5]

[1] 1 Kings 5:1-5 [2] 1 Kings 6:11-14 [3] 1 Kings 8:1, 6-11 [4] 1 Corinthians 6:19-20 [5] Revelation 21:22-23

Day 140

Solomon's fame reached the ends of the then-known world, including Ethiopia. The Queen of Sheba came from Ethiopia to see the glory of Solomon's court and buildings, and to hear his wisdom. She was deeply impressed. She was even more impressed with Solomon's God who had given him all the glory at which she marvelled. Solomon was true to God at this time and gave Him all the credit for what He had achieved through him. It was later in his life that he turned away from the true God to other gods.

The visit of the Queen of Sheba

When the queen of Sheba heard of the fame of Solomon, a fame which came from the name of the Eternal-God, she came to test him with hard questions. She came to Jerusalem with a very great caravan of camels carrying spices, great quantities of gold and precious stones. She talked to Solomon about all that she had on her mind. Solomon answered all her questions; there was nothing which was too difficult for him to explain to her. When the queen of Sheba saw all the wisdom of Solomon, the palace he had built, the food of his table, the seating of his officials, the attendance of his servants, his cupbearers, and the burnt offerings he offered at the temple of the Eternal-God, she was overcome with wonder. She said to the king, "All that I was told in my own country about you, your achievements and your wisdom is true. I did not believe all that I heard until I came and saw it with my own eyes; even so, not even half was told me. Your wisdom and wealth far exceed all that I heard. ... Happy are your servants, who serve you all the time and who hear your wisdom!" ... In wealth and wisdom, Solomon was greater than all the other kings of the earth. The whole world wanted to meet Solomon and hear the wisdom God had given him. [1]

However, King Solomon loved many foreign women. ... As he grew old, his wives turned his heart to follow other gods and his heart was not wholly true to the Eternal-God, his God, as the heart of David his father had been. [2]

[Jesus said:] Why do you worry about clothes? Consider the lilies of the field and the way they grow. They neither labour nor spin. I tell you, not even Solomon in all his magnificent splendour was arrayed like one of these. If God clothes like that the grass of the field, which is here today and tomorrow is tossed into the fire, will He not much more surely clothe you, O you of little faith? So do not be anxious, saying, 'What are we going to eat?' or 'What are we going to drink?' or "What are we going we wear?'. It is the heathen who strive after all these things. Your heavenly Father knows that you need them. If you seek first of all His kingdom and His righteousness, all these other things will be given to you as well. [3]

[1] 1 Kings 10:1-9,23-24   [2] 1 Kings 11:1,4   [3] Matthew 6:28-34

Day 141

As Solomon grew old, so his children grew up. His son, Rehoboam, had memories of his father as an idolater. No wonder he went about ruling the kingdom he had inherited according to his own ideas and those of his young advisors, rather than according to the commands of God who had made his father great. Sin always bring division where there should be unity. That is what happened to the kingdom of Israel.

The kingdom of Israel is divided

Rehoboam went to Shechem, for all Israel had gone there to make him king. When Jeroboam, son of Nebat, heard this, ... he returned from Egypt. So they sent for him. He and the whole assembly of Israel went to Rehoboam and said to him: "Your father laid a heavy yoke on us. Now, therefore, lighten the hard labour and the heavy yoke he put on us, and we will serve you." Rehoboam answered, "Go away now! In three days come back to me." So the people went away.

King Rehoboam consulted the old men who had served his father, Solomon, while he was alive. "What answer would you advise me to give to these people?" he asked. They replied, "If you want to be a servant to these people and serve them, give them a favourable answer today, and they will be your servants for ever." But Rehoboam rejected the advice of the old men, and consulted the young men who had grown up with him and served him then.

On the third day, the day appointed by the king, all the people returned to Rehoboam. ... The king answered the people roughly. He rejected the advice given him by the old men and followed the advice of the young men. He said to them, "My father made your yoke heavy but I will make it heavier. My father scourged you with whips but I will scourge you with scorpions." So the king paid no attention to the people. ... When the Israelites saw that the king did not listen to them, they said to him: "What part do we have in David? What do we inherit from Jesse's son? To your tents, O Israel!" Israel rebelled against the house of David, from that day to this." [1]

Since an overseer is God's steward, he must be blameless, not self-willed, overbearing, quick-tempered, given to strong drink, violent, nor greedy for dishonest gain. Rather he must be hospitable, love what is good, be sober-minded, upright, holy and disciplined. [2]

Jesus said to them, "You know that the rulers of the Gentiles lord it over their people, and their leaders hold them in subjection. It shall not be so with you. Whoever wants to be great among you must be your servant, and whoever wants to be first must be your slave. The Son of Man did not come to be served, but to serve, and to give His life as a ransom for many. [3]

[1] 1 Kings 12:1-16,19   [2] Titus 1:7-8   [3] Matthew 20:25-28

Day 142

The miraculous feeding of Elijah by ravens demonstrated that God's word, spoken by His prophet, was the truth. The prophet Elijah was sent to a woman in Sidon rather than to someone in Israel at this time of famine. God was showing that His word was not limited to the country or the people of Israel. Both these miracles happened 'according to the word of God'. To ignore God's word is to ignore God. To trust His word is to trust Him.

Elijah is fed by ravens and a widow

Elijah the Tishbite, from Tishbe in Gilead, said to [King] Ahab, "As the Eternal-God, the God of Israel, lives, before whom I stand, there will be no dew nor rain in the coming years unless I give my word." Then the word of the Eternal-God came to Elijah: "Go from here, turn eastward and hide yourself by the brook Kerith that is east of the Jordan. You will drink from the brook, and I have commanded the ravens to feed to you there." So he did what the Eternal-God had commanded him. ... The ravens brought him bread and meat in the morning and in the evening, and he drank from the brook.

After a while the brook dried up because there was no rain in the land. Then the word of the Eternal-God came to him: "Go now to Zarephath of Sidon and stay there." He went to Zarephaph. ... A widow was there gathering sticks. He called to her, "Bring me a little water in a jar so I may drink?" As she was going to get it, he called to her, "And bring me a piece of bread." She replied, "As surely as the Eternal-God, your God, lives, I have no bread, only a handful of flour in a jar and a little oil in a bottle. I am gathering a few sticks to take home, bake it for me and my son, that we may eat it, and die." Elijah said to her, "Do not be afraid. Do as you have said. But first bake a small cake of bread for me and then prepare something for yourself and your son. This is what the Eternal-God, the God of Israel, says: 'The jar of flour will not be used up nor will the jug of oil run dry until the day the Eternal-God gives rain on the land.'" ... The flour was not used up and the jar of oil did not run dry, according to the word of the Eternal-God. [1]

He [Jesus] said to His disciples: "I tell you, do not anxious about your life, what you will eat, or about your body, what you will wear. Life is more than food, and the body is more than clothes. Consider the ravens! They neither sow nor reap. They have no storehouse or barn. Yet God feeds them. And you are worth much more than the birds. [2]

Sing to the Eternal-God with thanksgiving. ... He provides for animals the food they need, and for young ravens what they cry out for. ... The Eternal-God takes pleasure in those who fear Him, who put their hope in His lovingkindness. [3]

[1] 1 Kings 17:1-16　[2] Luke 12:22-24　[3] Psalm 147:7,9,11

Day 143

From time to time God acts in a dramatic way and presents His people with a clear choice: either to turn to Him and serve Him, or to turn away from Him, to serve their false gods. God acted in this way through Elijah. The choice before the people was clear. How genuine were they in saying, "The Eternal-God, He is God"? Later events showed that for many, this was a temporary return to God. It is not difficult to react to a situation and for that reaction to be far from a genuine expression of the will.

Elijah and the prophets of Baal

After a long time, the word of the Eternal-God came to Elijah: "Go! Present yourself to Ahab, and I will send rain on the earth." Elijah set off to present himself to Ahab. When he [Ahab] saw Elijah, he said to him, "There you are! You troubler of Israel?" "I have not caused trouble for Israel," Elijah replied. "But you have and so has your father's house. You have forsaken the commandments of the Eternal-God and have followed the Baals. Now assemble all the people from all over Israel and meet me on Mount Carmel. Bring the four hundred and fifty prophets of Baal and the four hundred prophets of the Asherah, who eat at Jezebel's table.

So Ahab sent word to all the Israelites and assembled the prophets on Mount Carmel. Elijah approached the people and said, "How long will you limp from one leg to the other? If the Eternal-God is God, follow Him, but if Baal is God, follow him." The people said nothing. Then Elijah said to them, "I alone am left of the prophets of the Eternal-God, but Baal has four hundred and fifty prophets. Bring here two bulls for us. Let them [the prophets] choose one for themselves, cut it into pieces, put it on the wood but do not set fire to it. I will prepare the other bull and put it on the wood but I will not set fire to it. Then you call on the name of your god, and I will call on the name of the Eternal-God. The one who answers by fire, He is God."

So they [the prophets of Baal] took the bull, prepared it, then they called on the name of Baal from morning till noon. ... Then Elijah said to all the people, "Come near to me." They came to him. He began by repairing the altar of the Eternal-God which was in ruins. He took twelve stones, ... with them he built an altar in the name of the Eternal-God, and he dug a trench round it. ... Then he said, "Fill four jars with water and pour it on the burnt offering and on the wood." ... Then the fire of the Eternal-God fell and burned up the sacrifice, the wood, the stones and the earth, and licked up the water in the trench. When all the people saw this, they fell down on their faces and cried, "The Eternal-God, He is God! The Eternal-God, He is God." [1]

[Moses:] "This day I call heaven and earth to witness against you, that I have set before you life and death, the blessing and the curse. Now choose life." [2]

[1] 1 Kings 18:1-2,16-24,30-33,36-39   [2] Deuteronomy 30:19

Day 144

Elijah was one of the few people who went to heaven without dying. God had a special place for him. Jesus linked Elijah with John the Baptist. When Jesus was transfigured before His disciples, it was Moses and Elijah who appeared with Him.

Elijah is taken up to heaven in a chariot of fire

When the Eternal-God was about to take Elijah up to heaven in a whirlwind, Elijah and Elisha were going from Gilgal. Elijah said to Elisha, "Wait here! The Eternal-God has sent me to Bethel." Elisha said, "As surely as the Eternal-God lives and as you live, I will not leave you." So they went on to Bethel. The 'sons of the prophets' at Bethel came to Elisha and said, "Do you know that the Eternal-God will take your master from you today?" Elisha replied, "Yes, I know, but keep quiet about it."

Fifty men of the 'sons of the prophets' went and stood watching at a distance from the place where Elijah and Elisha stood by the Jordan. Elijah took his mantle, rolled it up and struck the water with it. The water parted to the right and to the left, and the two of them crossed over on dry ground. When they had crossed over, Elijah said to Elisha, "Ask what you would have me do for you before I am taken from you" Elisha replied, "Let a double portion of your spirit be on me," Elijah said, "You have asked a hard thing, but if you see me when I am taken from you, it will be as you ask, otherwise not."

As they walked and talked together, a chariot of fire and horses of fire appeared and parted the two of them. Elijah went up to heaven in a whirlwind. Elisha saw this and cried, "My father! My father! The chariots of Israel and its horsemen!" And Elisha saw him no more.[1]

[The Eternal-God, the Almighty says:] "Look, I will send you the prophet Elijah before the great and dreadful day of the Eternal-God comes. He will reconcile the hearts of the fathers to their children, and the hearts of the children to their fathers; lest I come and strike the land with a curse." [2]

From the days of John the Baptist until now, the kingdom of heaven has been forcefully advancing and forceful men lay hold of it. For all the prophets and the Law prophesied until John. And if you are willing to accept it, he is the Elijah who was to come. He who has ears to hear, let him hear. [3]

About eight days after Jesus had said these things, He took Peter, John and James and went up on to a mountain to pray. As He was praying, the appearance of His face changed, His clothes became as dazzlingly brilliant as a flash of lightning, and He talked to two men, Moses and Elijah, whose appearance was equally dazzling.[4]

[1] 2 Kings 2:1-3,7-12   [2] Malachi 4:5-6   [3] Matthew 11:12-14   [4] Luke 9:28-30

Day 145

The son of the Shunammite woman was one of the few people in the Bible who were restored to life from the dead. God worked this miracle because He had promised a son to the old couple. He kept His promise: He gave the woman a son - twice, through a miraculous birth and through an equally miraculous restoration to life from the dead.

Elisha and the Shunammite woman

One day Elisha went to Shunem. A rich woman was there who insisted on him staying for a meal. After that, whenever he passed by, he stopped there for a meal. She said to her husband, "I am sure that this man, who often passes our way, is a holy man of God. Let us make a small room on the housetop and put in it a bed, a table, a chair and a lamp for him. Then he can rest there whenever he comes to us."

One day Elisha came and went up to his room and lay down there. He said to his servant Gehazi, "Call this Shunammite." He asked the woman through Gehazi, "What would you wish to be done for you?" She replied, "I live among my people and that is enough." ... Gehazi said, "She has no son and her husband is old." Elisha said to the woman, "About this time next year you will hold a son in your arms.".... The woman became pregnant, and the next year about the same time she gave birth to a son."

The child grew up. One day he went to his father, who was with the reapers. "My head! My head!" he cried. His father said to a servant, "Carry him to his mother." ... The boy sat on her lap until noon and then died. The woman set out and came to the man of God at Mount Carmel. ... She said to him, "Did I ask you for a son, my lord? Did I not say to you, 'Do not deceive me'?"

When Elisha reached the house, the boy lay there dead on his couch. He went in, shut the door on the two of them and prayed to the Eternal-God. Then he lay on the boy, mouth to mouth, eyes to eyes and hands to hands. ... As he stretched himself out on him, the boy's body grew warm. ... The boy sneezed seven times and opened his eyes. Elisha called Gehazi and said, "Call the Shunammite woman." When she came, he said to her, "Take your son." She came and fell at his feet and bowed herself to the ground. Then she took her son and went out. [1]

And what more shall I say? I do not have time to tell about Gideon, Barak, Samson, Jephthah, David, Samuel and the prophets, who through faith conquered kingdoms ... Women received their dead raised back to life again. [2]

May the God of peace, who, through the blood that sealed the eternal covenant, brought back from the dead our Lord Jesus, the great Shepherd of the sheep, equip you with everything good that you may carry out His will, and may He work in you what pleases Him, through Jesus Christ, to whom be glory for ever and ever. Amen. [3]

[1] 2 Kings 4:8-20, 25, 28, 32-37 [2] Hebrews 11:32-33,35 [3] Hebrews 13:20-21

Day 146

At the time of Elisha, the disease of leprosy was incurable and meant that sufferers were separated from the rest of the people. It was a good picture then of sin and the separation from God which it brings about. Naaman learned that only God could cure leprosy and that did not depend on his greatness, riches or power. He needed only to be washed, in God's way, and he would be clean. So it is with sin. The river Jordon is a picture of the 'Blood of Christ'. All who are washed in it become clean in God's sight.

Naaman is healed of leprosy

Naaman was commander of the army of the king of Syria. He was a great man in the sight of his master and highly respected because it had been through him that God had given victory to Syria. ... He was a valiant soldier but he had leprosy.

Now raiding bands from Syria had taken captive a young girl from Israel, and she waited on Naaman's wife. She said to her mistress. "If only my master would see the prophet who is in Samaria, he would heal him of his leprosy." Naaman went to his master and told him what the slave-girl from Israel had said. The king replied, "Go, and I will send a letter to the king of Israel." So Naaman left, taking with him ten talents of silver, six thousand shekels of gold and ten changes of clothes. When the king of Israel read the letter, he tore his robes and said, "Am I God to kill and bring back to life again? Why has this man sent someone to me to be cured of his leprosy? He is trying to start a quarrel with me!"

When Elisha, the man of God, heard that the king of Israel had torn his clothes, he sent this message to him: "Why have you torn your clothes? Let the man come to me and he will know that there is a prophet in Israel." Naaman went with his horses and chariots and stopped at the door of Elisha's house. Elisha sent a messenger to say to him, "Go and wash seven times in the Jordan, and your flesh will be restored and you will be clean." Naaman was very angry and said, "I thought that he would surely come out to me and stand and call on the name of the Eternal-God, his God, wave his hand over the place and heal me of my leprosy. ... So he turned and went off in a rage.

Naaman's servants came to him and said, "My father, if the prophet had told you to do some great thing, would you not have done it? How much more, then, when he says to you, 'Wash and be clean?" So Naaman went down and dipped himself in the Jordan seven times, as the man of God had told him, and his flesh was restored like that of a little child and he was clean. [1]

Come now, let us reason together, says the Eternal-God, though your sins are like scarlet, they shall be as white as snow, though they are red as crimson, they shall be as wool. [2]

[1] 2 Kings 5:1-14   [2] Isaiah 1:18

Day 147

With our human eyes we cannot see God nor the many angels that protect us. God gave Elisha's servant the rare privilege of having a glimpse of the mighty army of angels that surrounded Elisha and His people. God still protects His people even though they cannot see the angels He has commanded to watch over them.

Elisha sees God's army

The king of Syria was at war with Israel. After conferring with his servants, he said, "I will pitch my camp in such and such a place." The man of God sent word to the king of Israel, saying, "Beware that you do not pass that place for the Syrians have camped there." The king of Israel sent men to the place indicated by the man of God. Several times Elisha warned the king so that he was able to save himself from running into danger. The king of Syria was enraged. He called together his servants and said to them, "Tell me, which of us is betraying us to the king of Israel?" One of his men said, "None of us, my lord the king, it is Elisha, the prophet who is in Israel who tells the king of Israel the words you speak in your bedroom." The king replied "Go and find out where he is, so that I can send men to capture him." The king was told: "He is in Dothan."

Then he sent a large force of horses and chariots. They reached there during the night and surrounded the city. The next day, Elisha rose early and there, surrounding the town, was an army of horses and chariots. His servant said to him, "Oh, my lord, what are we to do?" The prophet answered, "Do not be afraid. Those who are with us are more than those who are with them." Elisha prayed, "O Eternal-God, open his eyes that he may see." Then the Eternal-God opened the servant's eyes. He looked up and saw the mountain covered with horses and chariots of fire surrounding Elisha.

When the Syrians came down towards him, Elisha prayed to the Eternal-God, "Lord, smite these people with blindness." God struck them with blindness as Elisha had prayed. ... He led them to Samaria. When they had entered the city, Elisha said, "Lord, open the eyes of these men that they may see." Then the Eternal-God opened their eyes and they saw that they were inside Samaria. ... So he [the king] prepared a great feast for them. When they had finished eating and drinking, he sent them away, and they returned to their master. The Syrian bands ceased raiding the land of Israel.[1]

The chariots of God are twenty-thousand, even thousands of thousands. ... Our God is a God who saves; from the Eternal-God comes escape from death. [2]

If you make the Most High your dwelling and the Eternal-God your refuge, then no evil will befall you and no disaster will come near your tent. For He will command His angels to guard you in all your ways. [3]

---

[1] 2 Kings 6:8-23 [2] Psalm 68:17,20 [3] Psalm 91:9-11

Day 148

Like Josiah, Uzziah was made king while he was still a boy. Also like Josiah, he obeyed God's word and was well instructed by the prophet Zechariah. While he was obedient to God all went well. Then, as king, he grew strong and pride crept in and he thought he could do what God had not planned for anyone to do, except a priest. God spoke to the Prophet Isaiah through the tragic death of Uzziah.

King Uzziah and the prophet Isaiah

The people of Judah took Uzziah, who was sixteen years old, and made him king in the place of his father Amaziah. ... He did what was right in the sight of the Eternal-God. ... As long as he sought the Eternal-God, God made him prosper. ... Then Uzziah became powerful and his pride led to his downfall. He sinned against the Eternal-God, his God, and entered the temple of the Eternal-God to burn incense on the altar of incense. Azariah the priest together with eighty other courageous priests of the Eternal-God, followed him in [to the temple]. They faced him and said, "It is not for you, Uzziah, to burn incense to the Eternal-God; that is for the Priests ..." Uzziah, was holding a censer in his hand ready to burn incense and he became very angry. As he stood beside the altar of incense in the temple of the Eternal-God and raged at the priests, leprosy broke out on his forehead. ... King Uzziah had leprosy until the day of his death. [1]

In the year that King Uzziah died, I [Isaiah] saw the Eternal-God seated on a throne, high and lifted up, and the skirts of His robe filled the temple. Above Him stood the seraphs, each with six wings. One cried to another: "Holy, holy, holy is the Eternal-God, the Almighty. The whole earth is full of his glory." At the sound of their voices the foundations shook and the temple was filled with smoke. "Woe is me!" I cried. "I am ruined! I am a man of unclean lips, and I live among a people of unclean lips and my eyes have seen the King, the Eternal-God, the Almighty."

One of the seraphim [angels] flew to me with a live coal in his hand, which he had taken off the altar with tongs. He touched my mouth with it and said, "Look, this has touched your lips; your guilt is taken away and your sin is forgiven." Then I heard the voice of the Eternal-God saying, "Whom shall I send and who will go for us?" Then I said, "Here am I. Send me!" He said, "Go! Tell this people: 'Hear! but do not understand. Look! but do not see. Make dull the heart of this people, ... lest they see with their eyes, hear with their ears, understand with their hearts, then turn and be healed." [2]

[Jesus prayed:] "Father ... As you sent me into the world, so am I sending them [the disciples] into the world. ... protect them from the evil one." [3]

[1] 2 Chronicles 26:1,4-5,16-19, 21   [2] Isaiah 6:1-10   [3] John 17:18,15

Day 149

For many years the two kingdoms of Judah (2 tribes) and Israel (10 tribes) had turned away from God and had not followed His laws. Almost all the kings did not do "what was right in God's sight". There were few exceptions. Josiah was one of them. The discovery of the Book of Moses in the temple and the king's obedience to its commands, brought about a great change in the country. God's word was again being obeyed by the country's leaders. Changes happen in a person's life when God's word is known and obeyed.

King Josiah finds the book of the Law

Josiah was eight years old when he became king. He reigned for thirty-one years in Jerusalem. He did what was right in the eyes of the Eternal-God and walked in the ways of his father David. In the eighth year of his reign, he began to purge Judah and Jerusalem of the high places, sacred stones and carved images. ... In the eighteenth year of Josiah's reign, and in order to purify the land and the temple, he sent Shaphan, son of Azaliah, Maaseiah, the governor of the city, with Joah, son of Joahaz, the recorder, to repair the house of the Eternal-God, his God. ... As they were bringing out the money that had been brought into the temple of the Eternal-God, Hilkiah the priest found the Book of the Law of the Eternal-God which had been given through Moses. Shaphan took the book to the king ... and Shaphan read it to the king.

When King Josiah heard the words of the Law, he tore his clothes. He commanded Hilkiah, "Go and inquire of the Eternal-God for me and for those who are left in Israel and Judah, about the words of this book that has been found. Great is the anger of the Eternal-God that is poured out on us ..."

Hilkiah ... went to the prophetess Huldah. ... She said to them, "This is what the Eternal-God, the God of Israel, says, ... I am going to bring disaster on this land and on its people. ... They have forsaken me and burned incense to other gods; they have provoked me to anger by all that they have done. ... But, because your heart was penitent and you humbled yourself before God when you heard His words against this place and its people, and because you humbled yourself before me and tore your robes and wept in my presence, I have heard you, declares the Eternal-God. Now you will die and you will be buried in peace. Your will not see all the disaster I will bring on this place and on those who live here." ... Josiah removed all the abominable idols from all the land belonging to the Israelites; and he made all who lived in Israel serve the Eternal-God, their God. [1]

Blessed are they whose ways are upright, who live according to the law of the Eternal-God. Blessed are they who keep His commands and seek Him wholeheartedly. ... I have hidden your words in my heart that I might not sin against you. [2]

[1] 2 Chronicles 34:1-2,8,14-28, 33 [2] Psalm 119:1-2,11

Day 150

There are many records in the Old Testament of God telling His people, through the prophets, that a Messiah would come one day to save Israel and the world. The Jews expected this Messiah to be a conquering king. They did not understand the meaning of the prophecies until Jesus was born exactly as foretold. And then it was only slowly that they, first the disciples, then others of that time, learned the full truth of what had been foretold centuries before. Many Jews still do not understand today.

A Saviour is promised

[Isaiah:] This is what the Eternal-God says: "The Eternal-God will Himself give you a sign: A virgin will conceive and will give birth to a son, and will name him Immanuel [meaning 'God with us']. [1] For to us a Child is born, to us a Son is given, and the government will be on His shoulder, and He will be called Wonderful Counsellor, Mighty God, Everlasting Father, Prince of Peace. Of the increase of His government and of peace there will be no end. He will reign on the throne of David and will establish His kingdom. He will uphold it with justice and righteousness from that time forth and for evermore. The zeal of the Eternal-God, the Almighty, will bring this to pass. [2]

And there will come forth a shoot from the stock of Jesse, and a Branch from his roots will grow and bear fruit. The spirit of the Eternal-God will rest on Him, the Spirit of wisdom and understanding, the Spirit of counsel and might, the Spirit of knowledge and of the fear of the Eternal-God. He will not judge by what He sees with His eyes nor by what He hears with his ears; but He will judge the poor with justice and the downtrodden of the earth with fairness. [3]

[Micah:] You, Bethlehem Ephrathah, you are little among the clans of Judah, but out of you will come forth for me one who will be ruler in Israel, whose origins are from of old, from ancient times. [4]

[Malachi:] Look, I send my messenger and he will prepare the way before me. And the Lord you are seeking will come suddenly to His temple: the angel of the covenant, whom you desire, will come," says the Eternal-God, Almighty. [5]

"Praise be to the Eternal-God, the God of Israel, because He has come to us and has brought deliverance to His people. He has raised up a 'Horn [a powerful source] of Salvation' for us in the house of His servant David. Through His holy prophets long ago, He promised salvation from our enemies, deliverance from those who hate us, mercy to our forefathers, to remember His holy covenant which He swore on oath to our forefather Abraham, to save us from the hands of our enemies, so that we may serve Him without fear in holiness and righteousness all the days of our lives." [6]

[1] Isaiah 7:7,14 [2] Isaiah 9:6-7 [3] Isaiah 11:1-4 [4] Micah 5:1 [5] Malachi 3:1-2 [6] Luke 1:68-75

Day 151

God called Jeremiah to do a special task for Him and Jeremiah was afraid. He felt very unworthy and unqualified to be God's spokesman. He had yet to learn what Moses and others, men and women, have discovered: God always enables people to do what He calls them to do.

The call of Jeremiah

The words of Jeremiah, son of Hilkiah, a priest in Anathoth in the land of Benjamin, which came to him in the days of Josiah, king of Judah. ... The word of the Eternal-God came to me, saying, "Before I formed you in the womb I knew you, before you were born I set you apart and I appointed you to be a prophet to the nations." Then I said, "Ah, Sovereign Eternal-God, I cannot speak for I am only a child." But the Eternal-God said to me, "Do not say, 'I am only a child,' for you will go to everyone to whom I send you and say whatever I command you. Do not be afraid of them, for I am with you and will deliver you from them."

Then the Eternal-God put out His hand and touched my mouth and said to me. "See! I have put my words in your mouth. Today I have appointed you to be over nations and kingdoms, to root out and pull down, to destroy and overthrow, to build and to plant." [1]

[Paul:] Then I said, "Who are you, Lord?" And He said, "I am Jesus, whom you are persecuting. Now get up and stand on your feet. I have appeared to you for this purpose, to appoint you as a servant and as a witness of what you have seen of me now and of what I have yet to show you. I will deliver you from your own people and from the Gentiles to whom I am sending you, to open their eyes so that they may turn from darkness to light, and from the dominion of Satan to God, and, through faith in me, receive forgiveness of sins and an inheritance among those who are sanctified by me." [2]

Then he [Ananias] said [to Paul]: "The God of our forefathers has chosen you to know His will and to see the Righteous One [Jesus Christ] and to hear from His mouth. You will be His witness to all men of all that you have seen and heard. And now what are you waiting for? Get up, be baptised, and by calling on His name have your sins washed away.' [3]

Moses said to the Eternal-God, "O Eternal-God, I have never been eloquent, neither before nor since you have spoken to your servant. I am a man slow of speech and of few words." The Eternal-God said to him, "Who gave man his mouth? Who makes him deaf or dumb? Who gives him sight or makes him blind? Is it not I, the Eternal-God? Go, therefore, I will help you to speak and tell you what to say." [4]

[1] Jeremiah 1:1,4-10 [2] Acts 26:15-18 [3] Acts 22:14-16 [4] Exodus 4:10-12

Day 152

Despite all the promises God had given to Israel, the people sinned against Him. They were like a pot which a potter had designed to be a perfect vase, but it had become spoilt. Sin deforms and destroys. With God there is always hope. His word to Israel, is the same word to all whose lives have been spoiled by sin.

God is like a potter

This is the word that came to Jeremiah from the Eternal-God: "Go to the potter's house, and there I will speak to you." So I went to the potter's house and I saw him working at the potter's wheel. The pot he was making from the clay was spoiled in his hands; so the potter reworked it into another pot, shaping it as seemed good to him. The word of the Eternal-God came to me: "O house of Israel, cannot I do with you as this potter has done? Like clay in the hands of the potter, so are you in my hands, O house of Israel. If I say about a nation or kingdom that it is to be uprooted, broken down and destroyed, and if the nation I have warned repents of its evil, then I will relent and not bring on it the disaster I had planned. If, at another time, I say that a nation or kingdom is to be built and planted, and it does evil in my sight and does not obey me, then I will not do the good I had intended. Say, therefore, to the people of Judah and the inhabitants of Jerusalem, 'This is what the Eternal-God says: Look! I am planning a disaster for you and devising a plan against you. Turn from your evil ways, every one of you and change your ways and your actions.'" [1]

Woe to those who try to hide their plans from the Eternal-God, who work in darkness and say, "Who sees us? Who knows what we are doing? You turn things upside down and think that the clay is more important than the potter. Shall what is made say to its maker, "He did not make me"? Can the pot say of the potter, "He does not understand"? [2]

Woe to him who quarrels with his Maker. Can a piece of broken pottery, lying on the ground among other pieces of broken pottery, say to the potter, 'What do you think you are you making?' Can it say, 'Your are not skilled enough.' [3]

[Paul:] You will say to me: "Why does God find fault with us? Who can resist his will?" Who are you, a mere man, to answer back to God? Shall what is formed say to Him who formed it, 'Why have you made me like this?' Does not the potter have the right to make out of the same lump of clay one piece of pottery for a noble purpose and another for ordinary use? [4]

[Isaiah:] O Eternal-God, you are our Father and we are the clay. You are the potter and we are all the work of your hand. Do not be over angry with us, O Eternal-God. Do not remember our sins for ever, for we are all your people. [5]

---

[1] Jeremiah 18:1-11   [2] Isaiah 29:15-16   [3] Isaiah 45:9   [4] Romans 9:19-21   [5] Isaiah 64:8-9

Day 153

Jeremiah's message from God was that the Jewish people should not resist the Babylonian invaders. That was to be His punishment for their sin. The message was not received. Some leaders claimed that Jeremiah was a traitor because his words discouraged the people. He was not a traitor, but God's word can be discouraging to those who will not repentant. Jeremiah suffered for his courageous stand.

Jeremiah is thrown into a cistern

Shephatiah, son of Mattan, Gedaliah, son of Pashhur, Jehudal, son of Shelemiah, and Pashhur, son of Malkijah heard the words of Jeremiah to the people when he said, "This is what the Eternal-God says: 'Whoever remains in this city will die by the sword, by famine or by plague, but whoever goes over to the Babylonians will escape with his life; he will live.' And this is what the Eternal-God says: 'This city will surely be handed over to the army of the king of Babylon and he will capture it.'"

The officials said to the king, "This man should be put to death. By talking like this he is discouraging the soldiers who have stayed in this city, as well as all the people. This man is not seeking the good of this people but their ruin." Zedekiah the king answered. "He is in your hand. The king cannot stop you."

They took Jeremiah and put him into the cistern of Malkijah, the king's son, which was in the court of the guard. They let Jeremiah down by ropes into the cistern. There was no water in it, only mud, and Jeremiah sank down into the mire. Now Ebed-Melech, an Ethiopian, an official in the king's palace, heard that they had put Jeremiah into the cistern. While the king was sitting at the Benjamin Gate, Ebed-Melech went out of the king's palace and said to him, "My lord the king, these men have done evil in all they have done to Jeremiah the prophet. They have thrown him into a cistern. He will starve to death for there is no more bread in the city."

Then the king commanded Ebed-Melech, "Take thirty men from here with you and raise Jeremiah the prophet out of the cistern before he dies. So Ebed-Melech took the men with him and went to a room in the palace which was under the treasury. He took some old rags and worn-out clothes from there and let them down by ropes to Jeremiah in the cistern. Ebed-Melech, the Ethiopian, said to Jeremiah, "Put these old rags and worn-out clothes under your arms and under the ropes." Jeremiah did so, and they pulled him up with the ropes and lifted him out of the cistern.[1]

[David sang:] I waited patiently for the Eternal-God. He stooped down to me and heard my cry. He lifted me out of the horrible pit, out of the miry clay. He set my feet on a rock and steadied me on my feet. He put a new song in my mouth, a song of praise to our God. Many will see and fear and put their trust in the Eternal-God.[2]

---

[1] Jeremiah 38:1-13 [2] Psalm 40:1-3

Day 154

God's amazing love and grace to His people is shown in the way He promises to restore them to their own land and make a new covenant with them, even before He punishes them by sending them into captivity. God's covenants are wholly on His side. People can either accept or reject them. The Old Covenant was sealed with the blood of an animal sacrifice in the desert at Mount Sinai. The New Covenant was sealed by the 'blood of Christ' shed on the Cross.

God promises Israel restoration and a New Covenant

[Jeremiah:] This is what the Eternal-God, the Almighty, the God of Israel, says: "When I bring my people back from exile, those who are in the land of Judah will once again say: 'The Eternal-God bless you, O righteous home of justice, O holy mountain.'"

"The days are coming," says the Eternal-God, "when I will sow the house of Israel and the house of Judah with the offspring of men and of animals. As I watched over them to pluck up and tear down, to overthrow, destroy and bring disaster, so I will watch over them to build and to plant. In those days people will no longer say, 'The fathers have eaten sour grapes, and the children's teeth are set on edge.' Instead, everyone will die for his own sin. Whoever eats sour grapes will have his own teeth set on edge. The time is coming when I will make a new covenant with the house of Israel and with the house of Judah. It will not be like the covenant I made with their forefathers when I took them by the hand to bring them out of Egypt, the covenant which they broke although I was a husband to them."

"This will be the covenant that I will make with the house of Israel. After those days," declares the Eternal-God, "I will write my law in their minds and in their hearts. I will be their God, and they will be my people. No longer will a man teach his neighbour nor a man his brother, saying, 'Know the Eternal-God,' for they will all know me from the least of them to the greatest," says the Eternal-God. "For I will forgive their wickedness and I will remember their sins no more." [1]

When God speaks of a new covenant, He thereby makes the first one out of date; and what is out of date because of age is ready to disappear. [2] You have come to ... the living God, ... to the judge of all men, to the spirits of righteous men who have been made perfect, to Jesus the mediator of a new covenant, and to the sprinkled blood which pleads more effectively than the blood of Abel. [3]

While they were eating, Jesus took the bread, gave thanks and broke it, and gave it to the disciples, saying, "Take eat; this is my body." Then He took a cup, gave thanks and gave it to them, saying, "Drink of it, all of you. This is my blood of the new covenant, which is poured out for many for the forgiveness of sins." [4]

[1] Jeremiah 31:23,27-34   [2] Hebrews 8:13   [3] Hebrews 12:22-24   [4] Matthew 26:26-28

Day 155

Israel reached its heights as a people of God during the reign of King David. Towards the end of King Solomon's life, he and the people began to reject God and they followed other gods and their detestable practices. In the end, God could do nothing but reject them temporarily, let them be conquered and suffer the consequences of their actions in order to bring them back to Him.

The fall of Jerusalem

In the ninth year of Zedekiah, king of Judah, in the tenth month, Nebuchadnezzar king of Babylon with his whole army came against Jerusalem and laid siege to it. On the ninth day of the fourth month of the eleventh year of Zedekiah's reign, they broke through the city wall. ... When Zedekiah king of Judah and all the men of war saw them, they fled. ... The Babylonian army pursued them and overtook Zedekiah in the plains of Jericho. ... They set fire to the royal palace and the houses of the people and broke down the walls of Jerusalem. Nebuzaradan, commander of the guard carried captive to Babylon all the people who remained in the city with those who had deserted to him.[1]

After Nebuzaradan, commander of the guard, had released him [Jeremiah] at Ramah, the word from the Eternal-God came to Jeremiah. He [Nebuzaradan] had found Jeremiah bound in chains among all the captives from Jerusalem and Judah who were being carried into exile in Babylon. When the commander of the guard found Jeremiah, he said him, "The Eternal-God, your God, decreed this disaster for this place. Now the Eternal-God has brought it about. He has done as he said He would because you sinned against the Eternal-God and you did not obey Him. Now I am setting you free. If it seems good to you, come with me to Babylon and I will look after you." [2]

The Eternal-God, the Almighty says, "This whole land will be a desolate wasteland and these nations will serve the king of Babylon for seventy years. ... When seventy years are completed, I will punish the king of Babylon and make the land of the Babylonians a desolate wasteland for ever." [3] "The days are coming," says the Eternal-God, "when I will restore the fortunes of my people and I will bring them back to the land I gave to their forefathers as a possession." [4]

"I know the plans that I have for you," says the Eternal-God, "plans for your welfare and not to harm you, plans to give you hope for the future. Then you will call on me and come and pray to me and I will hear you. You will seek me and find me when you seek me with all your heart. I will be found by you," says the Eternal-God, "and I will bring you back from your captivity." [5]

---

[1] Jeremiah 39:1-5,8-10 [2] Jeremiah 40:1-3 [3] Jeremiah 25:8,11 [4] Jeremiah 30:3 [5] Jeremiah 29:11-13

Day 156

Ezekiel's vision left him in no doubt that God was calling him to a very difficult task: to take God's message to the people of Israel who had rebelled against Him. Despite their rebellion, God still loved them, not because of what they were or had done to earn that love. He loved Israel when the nation was like a baby thrown out on to the hillside to die. He loves us while we are still sinners in rebellion against Him.

The call of Ezekiel

In the thirtieth year, on the fifth day of the fourth month, I [Ezekiel] was among the exiles by the Kebar River, when the heavens were opened and I saw visions of God. ... When I saw it, I fell face down and I heard the voice of someone speaking. [1]

He said to me, "Son of man, stand up on your feet and I will speak to you." As He spoke, the Spirit came into me and lifted me to my feet, and I heard Him saying to me: "Son of man, I am sending you to the children of Israel. They are a nation of rebels that have rebelled against me. They and their forefathers have been in revolt against me even to this day. ... Whether they listen or refuse to listen, for they are a rebellious people, they will know that a prophet has been among them. And you, son of man, do not be afraid of them or their words. Though briers and thorns are all around and you sit among scorpions, do not be afraid. ... Speak my words to them, whether they listen or refuse to listen, for they are rebellious people. And you, son of man, listen to what I say to you and do not rebel against me like that rebellious house. Open your mouth and eat what I give you." [2]

The word of the Eternal-God came to me: "Son of man, make known to Jerusalem her abominable practices and say, 'This is what the Sovereign Eternal-God says to Jerusalem: By your origin and birth you belong to the land of the Canaanites. Your [spiritual] father was an Amorite and your [spiritual] mother was a Hittite. On the day you were born your navel cord was not cut, and you were not washed with water to make you clean, nor were you rubbed with salt or wrapped in napkins. No one pitied you nor had compassion to do any of these things for you. On the day you were born you were unloved and you were thrown out into the open field. Then I passed by and saw you rolling about in your blood, and as you lay there in your blood I said to you "Live!" And I caused you to increase as a bud which grows in the field until you reached maturity." [3]

[Paul:] At the right time, when we were powerless, Christ died for the ungodly. It is rare for anyone to die for a righteous man, though for a good man someone might dare to die. But God shows His love for us in that while we were still sinners, Christ died for us. [4]

[1] Ezekiel 1:1,28   [2] Ezekiel 2:1-8   [3] Ezekiel 16:1-7   [4] Romans 5:6-8

Day 157

The Israelites were in captivity because of their sin. But God had not rejected His people for ever. His covenants with Abraham and David had yet to be fulfilled. So God gives the prophet Ezekiel a picture of what God had in store for them, His people, the Jews, but also for the world through Jesus Christ and through God the Holy Spirit.

Ezekiel and the valley of dry bones

The hand of the Eternal-God was upon me, ... He set me in the middle of a valley which was full of bones. He led me up and down among them, and I saw very many bones on the floor of the valley. The bones were very dry. He said me, "Son of man, can these bones live?" I answered, "O Sovereign Eternal-God, only you know." Then He said to me, "Prophesy to these bones and say to them: 'Dry bones, hear the word of the Eternal-God! This is what the Sovereign Eternal-God says to these bones: I will cause breath to enter you, and you will live. I will put sinews on you and make flesh come upon you and cover you with skin. I will put breath into you, and you will live. Then you will know that I am the Eternal-God."

So I prophesied as I was commanded. As I was prophesying, there was a loud noise, a shaking, rattling sound, and the bones came together, bone to bone. I looked, and sinews came on the bones, then flesh appeared on them and skin covered them, but there was no breath in them. Then He said to me, "Prophesy to the breath: 'This is what the Sovereign Eternal-God says: Come from the four winds, O breath, and breathe into these who have been slain, that they may live.'" I prophesied as He commanded me, and breath came into them and they came alive and stood up on their feet, a vast army.

Then He said to me: "Son of man, these bones are the whole house of Israel. They say, 'Our bones are dried up and our hope is gone and we have no hope.' Therefore prophesy and say to them: This is what the Sovereign Eternal-God says: 'O my people, I am going to open your graves and cause you to rise from them. I will put my spirit in you and you will live, and I will bring you back to your own land. Then you will know that I the Eternal-God has spoken and I have done it.'" [1]

[Paul:] If anyone is in Christ Jesus, he is a new creation; the old has passed away, the new has come. All this is from God, who has reconciled us to Himself through Christ and has given us the ministry of reconciliation. [2]

[This is what the Eternal-God says:] I will pour water on whoever is thirsty and floods on the dry ground. I will pour my Spirit on your offspring and my blessing on your descendants. They will spring up like grass or willows by running streams. [3]

---

[1] Ezekiel 37:1-14 [2] 2 Corinthians 5:17-19 [3] Isaiah 44:3-4

Day 158

Daniel and his three friends faced a great future by being chosen to be trained for the king's service. It meant, however, 'defiling' themselves with what they knew was wrong for them in God' sight. They decided to put God first. Through trial and triumph, they saw God working for them in their country of exile. Because of Daniel's faithfulness to God in the smaller things, like food and drink, God was able to use him to tell His people Israel of many things which would happen in the future.

Daniel and his friends made rulers in Babylon

In the third year of the reign of Jehoikim king of Judah, Nebuchadnezzar king of Babylon came to Jerusalem and besieged it. The Eternal-God delivered Jehoikim king of Judah into his hand. ... The king ordered Ashpenaz, his chief officer, to bring in some of the children of the Israelites from the royal family and from the nobility, youths without any physical defect, handsome, and showing aptitude for learning, well informed, quick to understand, and able to serve in the king's palace. He was to educate them in the language and literature of the Babylonians. The king assigned them a daily ration of food and wine from the king's table. They were to be trained for three years and then they were to serve the king.

Among these were Daniel, Hananiah, Mishael and Azariah, from Judah. ... But Daniel determined not to defile himself with food and wine from the royal table. He asked the chief official to spare him from defilement in this way. Now God had made the chief officer favourable and sympathetic to Daniel. However, he said to Daniel, "I am afraid lest my lord the king, who has assigned your food and drink, should see you looking worse than the other youths of your age? Then my head would be in danger from the king because of you." Daniel said to the guard, "Give your servants a trial for ten days. Give us nothing but vegetables to eat and water to drink. Then compare our appearance with that of the youths who eat the royal food and deal with us according to what you see." He agreed and gave them a ten day trial. At the end of the ten days the youths looked healthier and better nourished than any of the other youths who ate the royal food. ... To these four young men God gave skill and understanding in all kinds of literature and learning. ... In all matters of wisdom and understanding about which the king questioned them, he found them ten times better informed than any of the magicians and enchanters in his entire kingdom. [1]

[Jesus:] "Blessed are those who hunger and thirst for righteousness, for they will be satisfied. Blessed are the pure in heart, for they will see God. Blessed are the merciful for they will obtain mercy. Blessed are those who are persecuted for righteousness' sake, for theirs is the kingdom of heaven." [2]

[1] Daniel 1:1-20   [2] Matthew 5:6, 8,10

Day 159

Nebuchadnezzar was a very powerful king. At his word people were raised to places of honour or killed. God used Nebuchadnezzar to speak to the world by giving him a vision which even the cleverest Babylonian wise men could not understand or interpret. But God gave that knowledge to Daniel who, although only a captive slave of the king, knew God. Nebuchadnezzar did not.

Daniel interprets Nebuchadnezzar's dream

In the second year of his reign, Nebuchadnezzar had dreams which caused him to be deeply troubled and he could not sleep. He summoned the magicians, enchanters, sorcerers and astrologers and commanded them to tell him what he had dreamed. ... The astrologers answered the king in Aramaic, "O king, live for ever! Tell your servants the dream and we will interpret it for you." The king answered the astrologers, "The dream has gone from me. And I have made a firm decision: If you do not make known to me what my dream was and interpret it for me, I will have you cut into pieces and your houses razed to the ground. If, however, you tell me what I dreamed and give me its interpretation, you will receive gifts, rewards and great honour. Now tell me the dream and interpret it for me." ... The astrologers answered the king, "There is not a man in the world who can do what the king is asking!" ...

Arioch, the commander of the king's guard, set out to put to death the wise men of Babylon. Daniel, who was among them, spoke to him with great wisdom and tact. He said to Arioch, "Why all this urgency about this harsh decree?" Arioch explained the situation to Daniel. At this, Daniel went to the king and asked for time after which he would interpret the dream for him.

Daniel returned to his house and explained the situation to his friends Hananiah, Mishael and Azariah and asked them to seek earnestly for mercy from the God of heaven concerning this mystery, so that he and his friends might not perish with the rest of the wise men of Babylon. That night the mystery was revealed to Daniel in a vision. Daniel praised the God of heaven and said:

Blessed be to the name of God for ever and ever. Wisdom and might are His. He changes the times and the seasons. He sets up kings and removes them. He gives wisdom to the wise and knowledge to the discerning. He reveals the deep and hidden things. He knows what lies in the darkness, and light dwells with Him. I thank and praise you, O God of my fathers, for you have given me wisdom and might, and you have made known to me what we asked of you, you have revealed to us what was troubling the king." [1]

---

[1] Daniel 2:1-23

Day 160

Shadrach, Meshach and Abednego were friends of Daniel. They had all suffered at the hands of their Babylonian conquerors. Their stand for their God whom they knew to be the only true God, was vindicated in a way which has inspired thousands of people when persecuted for their faith. They trusted God whatever happened, if He saved them from the fiery furnace, or if He did not.

The fiery furnace

Nebuchadnezzar, the king, made an image of gold, ninety feet high and nine feet wide. ... He then summoned ... all the officers of his kingdom to come to the dedication of the image he had set up. ... The herald cried out, " O peoples, nations and men of every language: As soon as you hear the sound of the horn, flute, zither, lyre, harp, pipes and all kinds of music, you are commanded to fall down and worship the image of gold that King Nebuchadnezzar has set up. Whoever does not fall down and worship will be thrown into a burning fiery furnace."

Some Chaldeans came forward and maliciously accused the Jews. They said to King Nebuchadnezzar, "There are some Jews ... who pay no attention to you O king." ... In a rage, Nebuchadnezzar summoned Shadrach, Meshach and Abednego ... and said to them, "Is it true ... that you do not serve my gods or worship the golden image I have set up?"

They replied: "O Nebuchadnezzar, it is not necessary for us to defend ourselves before you in this matter. If we are thrown into the blazing furnace, our God, whom we serve, is able to save us from it and to rescue us from your hand. But even if He does not, know this, O king, we will not serve your gods or worship the golden image you have set up."

Nebuchadnezzar was furious and his attitude changed towards Shadrach, Meshach and Abednego. He commanded that the furnace be heated seven times hotter than usual. Then he commanded the strongest men in his army to tie up Shadrach, Meshach and Abednego and throw them into the blazing furnace. ... Then King Nebuchadnezzar leaped to his feet in amazement and said his counsellors, "Were there not three men tied up and thrown into the fire?" They replied, "True, O king." He said: "Look! I see four men walking in the midst of the fire, they are loose and unharmed, and the fourth is like a son of the gods."

Then Nebuchadnezzar said, "Blessed be to the God of Shadrach, Meshach and Abednego, who has sent His angel and delivered His servants who trusted in Him." They defied the king's command and yielded their bodies rather serve or worship any god except their own God. [1]

[1] Daniel 3:1-28

Day 161

Nebuchadnezzar was one of the most powerful kings who ever lived. Everyone obeyed him. They dared not do otherwise. He had the power over people of life or death. He was supreme in his kingdom and he thought that he was supreme in the world! Nebuchadnezzar had to learn that he, like everyone else, is a created being and God alone is supreme in the world of people and in the universe.

Nebuchadnezzar is given an animal's mind

"I, Nebuchadnezzar, was at rest in my house, content and prosperous. I had a dream that made me afraid. ... So I made a decree that all the wise men of Babylon be brought before me to interpret the dream for me. ... I told them the dream, but they could not interpret it for me. At last, Daniel came in before me ... and I told him the dream: ... I looked, and there stood a tree in the midst of the land. Its height was great and it continued to grow large and strong and it reached the sky and was visible to the ends of the earth. ... The animals of the field found shelter under it and the birds of the air nested in its branches. ... I looked, and there before me was a 'watcher', a holy one, coming down from heaven. He cried in a loud voice: 'Hew down the tree and cut off its branches, shake off its leaves and scatter its fruit. Let the animals flee from under it and birds from its branches. But let the stump and its roots be bound with a band of iron and bronze, and let it be drenched with the dew of heaven and let it share with the animals the grass of the field.'

Belteshazzar [Daniel] answered, ... "It is you, O king, who has become strong, your greatness reaches to the heavens. ... You will be driven away from people and you will live with wild animals. You will eat grass like oxen and you will be drenched with the dew of heaven. Seven times will pass until you acknowledge that the Most High is sovereign over the kingdoms of men and gives them to whoever He wills."

Twelve months later, ... all this was fulfilled. Nebuchadnezzar was driven away from people and he ate grass as oxen do and his body was drenched with the dew of heaven, his hair grew like the feathers of an eagle and his nails became like the claws of a bird.

"At the end of that time, I, Nebuchadnezzar, raised my eyes towards heaven and my understanding and the use of my mind was restored to me.

Then I praised the Most High and I honoured and gave glory to Him who lives for ever, whose dominion is an eternal dominion and His kingdom endures from generation to generation. All the people of the earth are as nothing to Him and He does what He pleases among the galaxies of the sky and among the peoples of the earth. No one can limit His power or say to Him: "What are you doing?" [1]

[1] Daniel 4:4-16,19,24-26,28-35

Day 162

When Daniel prayed openly every day, God blessed him. Some people respected him, but others hated him for his integrity and success. They tried to attack him, but God foiled their plan. Faithfulness to God always brings respect from those who respect God. It also brings ridicule and opposition from those who reject Him. God honours those who honour Him, but that does not always mean they avoid danger, as Daniel found.

Daniel is thrown into a den of lions

It pleased [King] Darius to set over his kingdom 120 satraps and over them three presidents, one of whom was Daniel. ... Daniel so distinguished himself by his exceptional spirit that the king planned to set him over the whole realm. Because of this, the satraps and presidents looked for grounds for accusations against Daniel in affairs of state, but they were unable to do so. ... At last they said, "We will never find any grounds for charges against Daniel unless it has something to do with the law of his God. So they went as a body to the king and said: "O King Darius, we have all agreed that the king should issue and enforce a royal edict that anyone who asks anything of any god or man during the next thirty days, except you, O king, shall be thrown into the den of lions." ... King Darius put the decree in writing and signed it.

When Daniel learned that the decree had been signed, he went into his house and upstairs to a room where the windows opened towards Jerusalem. Three times a day he knelt to pray and give thanks to his God, as he had always done. ... Then these men went to the king and said to him, ... "Daniel, one of the exiles from Judah, pays no attention to you, O king, or the decree that you have signed. He still prays three times a day." On hearing this the king was greatly distressed and set his mind on seeking to save him until sunset. ... So the king gave the order, and Daniel was brought and thrown into the den of lions. The king said to Daniel, "May your God, whom you serve continually, rescue you!" ...

Very early in the morning, the king rose and hurried to the den of lions, ... and cried in anguish, ... "Daniel, servant of the living God, has your God, whom you serve continually, been able to deliver you from the lions?" Daniel answered, "O king, live for ever! My God has sent His angel, and has shut the mouths of the lions. ... The king was overjoyed and gave orders to lift Daniel out of the den. ... Then King Darius wrote to all peoples, nations and languages in his kingdom:

"In all my dominion, men are to fear the God of Daniel, for He is the living God. His kingdom will never be destroyed, His dominion will never end. He is a saviour and a deliverer who performs wonders in the heavens and on the earth. He has rescued Daniel from the power of the lions." [1]

---

[1] Daniel 6:1-27

Day 163

God spoke to His people through Daniel, not only about their situation then, but also about events which would happen many years in the future. As God was 'in the beginning', so He will be 'in the end. Even today, we do not understand all that God said through Daniel because there are some events which have yet to be fulfilled.

God tells Daniel about the future

In the third year of Cyrus king of Persia, a word was revealed to Daniel. ... "On the twenty-fourth day of the first month, as I was standing on the bank of the great river Tigris, I looked up and there before me was a man dressed in linen, and wearing a belt of pure gold round his waist. ... A hand touched me and set me trembling on my knees. He said, 'Daniel, you are a man who is greatly loved, listen carefully to the words I am about to speak to you. Stand up, for I have been sent to you. Do not be afraid.'[1]

In those days, ... there will be a time of distress such as has never been since there were nations until then. But at that time every one of your people whose names are found written in the book will be delivered. Multitudes who sleep in the dust of the earth will awake: some to everlasting life and others to everlasting shame and contempt. Those who are wise will shine like the brightness of the sky, and those who turn many to righteousness, like the stars for ever and ever. ...

Then the angel said, "Go your way, Daniel, for the words are shut up and sealed until the time of the end. Many will be purified, made spotlessly white and refined, but the wicked will continue to be wicked. None of the wicked will understand, but those who are wise will understand. ... As for you, go your way till the end. You will rest and then, at the end of the days, you will rise to receive your allotted inheritance.[2]

[Jesus said:] "You will hear of wars and rumours of wars, but do not be alarmed. These things will happen, but the end is not yet. ... There will be great distress, such as has not been since the beginning of the world until now, and never will be again. If those days had not been shortened, no one would survive, but for the sake of God's chosen ones those days will be shortened. ... Then the sign of the Son of Man will appear in the sky and all the nations of the earth will cry in anguish. They will see the Son of Man coming on the clouds of the sky, with power and great glory. ... And His angels will gather His chosen ones from the four corners of the earth.

I tell you the truth, this generation will not pass away until all these things have taken place. Heaven and earth will pass away, but my words will never pass away. Of that day and hour no one knows, not even the angels of heaven, only [God] the Father. Therefore keep watch, for you do not know on what day your Lord will come.[3]

[1] Daniel 10:1,4-12   [2] Daniel 12:1-4, 9-10,13   [3] Matthew 24:6, 21,30-31,34-35,42

Day 164

The prophet Jonah did not want to warn the people of Nineveh of God's condemnation for their sin. That was strange. It could not have been because he was afraid. He had already boldly taken a message of God's judgment to King Amaziah. That King had repented and God was merciful to him. Was it that Jonah knew that Nineveh would also repent and he, Jonah, would feel foolish to have delivered such a message of judgment, then see God act graciously to them? God rescued Jonah from the big fish in order that he could take His message to the people of Nineveh, and also that His deliverance should be a sign of the 'three days and three nights' which Jesus would spend in the grave before He was resurrected to take the message of salvation to the world.

Jonah disobeys God

The word of the Eternal-God came to Jonah, son of Amittai. "Go to the great city of Nineveh and cry out against it, because the wickedness of its people has come up before me." But Jonah set out to flee from the Eternal-God to Tarshish. He went down to Joppa and found a ship going to Tarshish. He paid the fare and went aboard to go to Tarshish, away from the presence of the Eternal-God.

But the Eternal-God sent a great wind on the sea, and there was such a violent storm that the ship was about to break up. The sailors were afraid and each man cried out to his god. They threw the cargo into the sea to lighten the ship. Now Jonah had gone below deck where he lay fast sleep. The captain went to him and said, "What do you mean by sleeping now? Get up and call on your God! Perhaps He will take notice of us so that we do not perish." The sailors said to each other, "Let us cast lots that we may know who is responsible for this evil." They cast lots and the lot fell on Jonah. So they said to him, "Tell us, who is responsible for bringing all this trouble on us? What do you do and where do you come from?" ... They knew Jonah was fleeing from the presence of the Eternal-God because he had already told them so. ... "Take me up and throw me into the sea," he said to them, "and the sea will become calm. I know that it is because of me that this great storm has come upon you." ... Then they took Jonah and threw him into the sea, and the sea grew calm." ... Now the Eternal-God provided a great fish to swallow Jonah, and he was inside the fish for three days and three nights. [1]

From inside the fish Jonah prayed to the Eternal-God, his God: "In my distress I called to the Eternal-God and He answered me. From the belly of the grave I cried for help and you heard me. ... As my life was ebbing away, I remembered the Eternal-God, and my prayer came to you in your holy temple. Those who cling to vain idols forfeit the grace of God. As for me I will sacrifice to you with thanksgiving." [2]

[1] Jonah:1:1-17   [2] Jonah 2:1-2, 7-9

Day 165

Jonah was right! He knew that God was gracious and longsuffering. The people of Nineveh repented of their sin and God forgave them. Instead of being joyful at the repentance of the people to whom he had proclaimed God's mercy, Jonah was angry. What he had warned the people would happen to them if they did not repent, did not happen, because they repented. Only from God's point of view were there grounds for rejoicing. It hurt Jonah's pride. He would have to repent of that.

God has mercy on Nineveh

The Eternal-God spoke to the fish and it vomited Jonah on to dry land. [1] Then the word of the Lord came to Jonah a second time: "Go to Nineveh, that great city, and proclaim to it the message that I give you." Jonah set out according to the word of the Eternal-God and came to Nineveh. ... He proclaimed: "In forty days Nineveh will be overthrown." The people of Nineveh believed God. They proclaimed a fast, and they all, from the greatest to the least, put on sackcloth. The word reached the king of Nineveh. He rose from his throne, took off his royal robes, covered himself with sackcloth and sat in ashes. ... When God saw what they did and how they turned from their evil way, He changed His mind and did not destroy them as He had said He would. [2]

Jonah was greatly displeased and he became very angry. He prayed to the Eternal-God, "O Eternal-God, is this not what I said would happen when I was still in my own country? That is why I fled to Tarshish. I knew that you are a gracious and compassionate God, slow to anger and abounding in love, a God who changes His mind about bringing disaster on people. Now, O Eternal-God, take my life from me, for it is better for me to die than to live." But the Eternal-God replied, "Is it right for you to be angry? ... In Nineveh there are more than a hundred and twenty thousand people who do not yet know their right hand from their left, and there are many cattle as well." [3]

[God said to Ezekiel] Say to them [the Israelites:] "As I live, says the Sovereign Eternal-God, I take no pleasure in the death of the wicked, but rather that the wicked turn from their ways and live. Turn back! Turn back from your evil ways! Why will you die, O house of Israel?'" [4]

"And you, my child, [Jesus] will be called a prophet of the Most High; for you will go on before the face of the Lord to prepare the way for Him, to bring the knowledge of salvation to His people through the forgiveness of their sins, by the tender mercy of our God ." [5]

---

[1] Jonah 2:10 [2] Jonah 3:1-6,10 [3] Jonah 4:1-4,10-11 [4] Ezekiel 33:11 [5] Luke 1:76-79

Day 166

Esther was a Jewish captive in Babylon. The disobedience of the Babylonian Queen Vashti led to King Xerxes looking for another queen. Because of her beauty, Esther was considered for this position. In ignorance of her Jewish nationality she was made queen. Unknown to anybody, God was working out a way of defeating the intentions of the high official Haman to eliminate the Jews. Esther obeyed God's call to her through Mordecai and she became the right person in the right place at the right time to bring about God's intention to save the Jews from their evil enemy.

Esther rises to the day of opportunity

There was a Jew of the tribe of Benjamin, named Mordecai, in the citadel of Susa ... who had been carried into exile from Jerusalem by Nebuchadnezzar king of Babylon. ... Mordecai had brought up a cousin named Hadassah, a daughter of his uncle who had been orphaned. Hadassah, also known as Esther, was lovely in face and figure. ... When the king's command and decree had been proclaimed, many girls were brought to the citadel of Susa and put in the care of Hegai, the keeper of the women. ... She [Esther] pleased him and gained his favour. With no delay he provided her with her beauty treatment and her special food.

Esther had not revealed her nationality or family background because Mordecai had forbidden her to do so. ... When the turn came for Esther to go to the king ... he liked her more than any of the other women. She won his favour and approval more than any of the other girls so he set a royal crown on her head and made her queen instead of Vashti. [1]

When Haman saw that Mordecai did not bow down to him or pay him honour, he was very angry ... he looked for a way to destroy Mordecai and all the Jews. ... [2]

When they had told Mordecai what Esther had said, he sent her this answer: "Do not think that you alone of all the Jews will escape because you are in the king's palace. If you remain silent at this time, relief and deliverance for the Jews will come from elsewhere, but you and your father's family will perish. And who knows but that you have come to the throne for such a time as this?" [3]

Esther spoke again to the king, falling at his feet and weeping. She pleaded with him to put an end to the evil plan of Haman, the Agagite, which he had devised against the Jews. Then the king extended the golden sceptre to Esther and she arose and stood before him. [4] On the very day when the enemies of the Jews planned to massacre them, the opposite happened; it was the Jews who crushed their enemies. [5]

That which exalts a man does not come from the east or the west or from the wilderness. God is the judge. One He brings down, another He lifts up. [6]

[1] Esther 2:5-10,15-17 [2] Esther 3:5-6 [3] Esther 4:12-14 [4] Esther 8:3-4 [5] Esther 9:1 [6] Psalm 75:6

Day 167

The story of the Old Testament was nearing its end. God was going to do something new to complete His purposes for the world He had created. Through His prophets He foretold that a Messiah, a Saviour, was coming, to be born in the Jewish nation, and yet who would be older than that nation. God was going to live among the people He had created, but they would not understand how that was to be until He came.

Micah is told about the coming of Jesus

The word of the Eternal-God that came to Micah: ... "Look! The Eternal-God is coming from His holy place. He will come down and tread on the high places of the earth.[1]   But you, Bethlehem Ephrathah, though you are small among the clans of Judah, from you will come for me One who will rule over Israel, whose origins are in the distant past, from ancient times." Israel will be abandoned until the time comes when she who is in labour gives birth. ... He will stand and feed His flock in the strength of the Eternal-God and in the majesty of the name of the Eternal-God, His God. They will live securely, for His greatness will reach to the ends of the earth. [2]

[Isaiah:] "Hear, O house of David! It is a small thing to try the patience of men; will you try the patience of my God also? Therefore the Eternal-God Himself will give you a sign: The virgin will conceive and give birth to a Son, and will call Him Immanuel (God with us)."[3]

[Solomon:] "Will God really dwell on earth? The highest heavens cannot contain you. How much less this temple I have built!"[4]

[Isaiah:] "Heaven is my throne, and the earth is my footstool. What kind of house would you will build for me? Where could be my resting place? My hand made all these things, and brought them into being?" declares the Eternal-God.[5]

The Eternal-God is high over all the nations and His glory above the heavens. Who is like the Eternal-God, our God, who sits enthroned on high yet stoops down to look on the heavens and the earth? [6]   This is what the high and lofty One says, He who is eternal, whose name is holy: "I live in the high and holy place but also with him who is contrite and humble in spirit." [7]

When the time had fully come, God sent His Son, born of a woman, born subject to the law, to redeem those who are under the law, that we might be adopted as sons. Because you are sons, God [the Father] has sent the Spirit of His Son into our hearts, and we cry, "Abba," that is, "Father". You are, therefore, no longer slaves, but sons; and as sons you are also heirs. [8]

[1] Micah 1:3 [2] Micah 5:2-4 [3] Isaiah 7:13-14 [4] 1 Kings 8:27 [5] Isaiah 66:1-2 [6] Psalm 113:4-6 [7] Isaiah 57:15 [8] Galatians 4:4-7

Day 168

The Old Testament ends with a curse - a warning of the terrible consequences of rejecting God. With the warning there is, however, a gracious offer of mercy. The New Testament is the story of how that offer of mercy became a reality in Jesus Christ. The curse of eternal separation from God that sin brings was borne by Jesus Christ on the Cross, for all who repent of their sin and put their trust in Him.

Malachi and the day of judgement

The word of the Eternal-God to Israel through Malachi: "'I have loved you,' says the Eternal-God, But you ask, 'How have you loved us?' [1] ... 'I, the Eternal-God, do not change. That is why you, O sons of Jacob, are not destroyed. From the time of your forefathers you have turned away from my decrees and have not kept them. Return to me, and I will return to you,' says the Eternal-God, the Almighty. But you ask, 'How shall we return?' Will a man rob God? Yet you rob me.' You ask, 'How do we rob you?' 'You are robbing me in tithes and offerings, therefore, you are under a curse. Bring all the tithes into the storehouse. ... Prove me,' says the Eternal-God, the Almighty, 'and see if I will not open the floodgates of heaven and pour out so much blessing that you will not have room enough to receive it.'" [2]

"The day is coming which will burn like a furnace. On that day, all who are proud and all who do wickedly will be like stubble which is set on fire," says the Eternal-God, the Almighty. "They will be left with neither root nor branch. But for you who revere my name, the sun of righteousness will rise with healing in its wings, and you will go out and leap for joy like calves released from the stall. See, I will send you the prophet Elijah before that great and dreadful day of the Eternal-God comes. He will turn the hearts of the fathers to their children, and the hearts of the children to their fathers; lest I will come and strike the land with a curse." [3]

[Paul:] Since we are God's offspring, we should not think that God is like gold or silver or stone, an image made by human art and skill. In the past God overlooked such ignorance, but now he commands everyone everywhere to repent. He has set a day when He will judge the world with justice by the man He has appointed for that task. He has given evidence of this to everyone by raising Him from the dead." [4]

If we go on deliberately sinning after we have received the knowledge of the truth, there is no longer any sacrifice left to atone for sin. There is only a fearful looking forward to judgment and the fury of burning anger that will consume all those who oppose God. [5]

There is now no condemnation for those who are in Christ Jesus. The law of the Spirit of life in Christ Jesus has set you free from the law of sin and death.[6]

[1] Malachi1:1 [2] Malachi 3:6-10 [3] Malachi 4:1-2,5-6 [4] Acts 17:29-31 [5] Hebrews 10:26-29 [6] Romans 8:1

Day 169

John was a special child. The prophets had spoken of someone who would prepare the people for the coming of the 'most special' person, Jesus Christ. God worked a miracle to enable Zechariah and Elizabeth to have the baby, John. God was with him in a special way right from his birth.

John the Baptist prepares the way for Jesus

When Herod was king of Judea, there was a priest of the priestly division of Abijah, named Zechariah. He and his wife Elizabeth were descendants of Aaron. Both of them observed blamelessly all the commandments and regulations of the Eternal-God, but they had no children, for Elizabeth was barren and they were both well advanced in years.

Once when Zechariah's division was on duty and he was serving as priest before God, ... there appeared to him an angel of the Eternal-God. ... When Zechariah saw him, he was terrified. But the angel said to him, "Do not be afraid, Zechariah; your prayer has been heard. Your wife Elizabeth will bear you a son, and you are to name him John. You will have joy and gladness, and many will rejoice because of his birth, for he will be great in the sight of the Lord. He must never drink wine or other strong drink, and he will be filled with the Holy Spirit even from birth. ... Zechariah said to the angel, "How can I be sure of this? I am an old man and my wife is well advanced in years." The angel answered, "I am Gabriel. I stand in the presence of God and I was sent to bring you this good news. Now you will be silent and unable to speak until the day this is fulfilled, because you did not believe my words. My words will be fulfilled at the right time." ...

The time for Elizabeth to have her baby came and she gave birth to a son. ... On the eighth day they came to circumcise the child. They were going to name him after his father Zechariah, but his mother said, "No! He is to be called John." ... Then they made signs to his father to find out what he wanted to name the child. He asked for a writing tablet and wrote, "His name is John." They were all astonished. At once his mouth was opened and his tongue was loosed, and he began to speak, praising God. Fear came on all their neighbours. People talked about what had happened throughout the hill country of Judea. All who heard about him wondered and asked the question "What is this child going to be?" For the hand of the Eternal-God was with him. [1]

This is he who was spoken of by the prophet Isaiah: "The voice of one crying in the wilderness, 'Prepare the way for the Lord, make His paths straight.'" [2]

[1] Luke 1:5-8,11-15,18-20,57-66   [2] Matthew 3:3

Day 170

God is a family of three Persons. It was now time to reveal clearly one of the three - 'God the Son', Jesus Christ. From then on, the name 'God', used on its own usually referred to 'God the Father'. 'God the Holy Spirit' had yet to be revealed clearly. When 'God the Son' was born in the likeness of an ordinary human baby, He came as the One who would reveal in human form what the God Persons were like.

Jesus Christ, 'God the Son', becomes Man

In the beginning was the Word, and the Word was with God, and the Word was God. He was with God in the beginning. Through him all things were made; nothing was made without him. ... The Word became flesh and lived among us. We have seen His glory, the glory that He alone receives from [God] the Father, full of grace and truth.[1]

At various times in the past and in different ways, God spoke to our forefathers through the prophets, but in these last days He has spoken to us by [God] the Son, whom He [God the Father] appointed heir of all things, and through whom He created the universe. The Son alone expresses the full glory of God [the Father] and He is the exact image of His being, sustaining all things by His mighty power. [2]

[Paul:] He is the exact visible likeness of the invisible God, the first-born of all creation. By him all things in heaven and on earth were created: both visible and invisible, whether thrones, dominions, rulers or authorities. All things were created by Him and for Him. He was before all things and He is the one in whom all things are held together. The church is His body and He is its head. He is the beginning, the first-born from the dead, so that in everything He might have the highest place. God [the Father] was pleased that in Him should be all that is 'God'. [3] For in Christ all that is 'God' lives in bodily form, and you too have all that is 'God' living in you, He is the head over every ruler and authority. [4]

The people who walked in darkness have seen a great light. ... For to us a Child is born, to us a Son is given, and the government will be on His shoulders, and His name will be Wonderful Counsellor, Mighty God, Everlasting Father, Prince of Peace. Of the increase of His government and of peace there will be no end. [5]

All this took place to fulfil what the Eternal-God had spoken through the prophet: "The virgin will be with child and will give birth to a Son, and they will call Him Immanuel", which means: "God with us." [6]

No one has ever seen God, but the one and only [God the] Son, who is near to the heart of [God] the Father, has made Him known.[7]

[1] John 1:1-3,14   [2] Hebrews 1:1-3   [3] Colossians 1:15-19   [4] Colossians 2:9-10   [5] Isaiah 9:2,6-7
[6] Matthew 1:22-23   [7] John 1:18

Day 171

God sent an angel to both Joseph and Mary separately. Mary was to be the mother of the baby, Jesus, and Joseph was to act as His father. Jesus had no need of a human father because He was 'God the Son'. It was 'God the Holy Spirit' who enabled the conception in Mary to take place. The conception of Jesus was unique. In no other conception has the spirit of a baby been alive before the conception took place. Jesus Christ was there at the creation of the world ... and He will be there at its end.

The conception of Jesus Christ

The birth of Jesus Christ came about like this. His mother Mary was pledged to be married to Joseph, but before they came together [in sexual union], she was found to be with child through the Holy Spirit. Her husband was a righteous man and, because he was unwilling to expose her to public disgrace, he made up his mind to divorce her quietly. As he was thinking about this, an angel of the Eternal-God appeared to him in a dream and said, "Joseph, son of David, do not be afraid to take Mary as your wife because what is conceived in her is from [God] the Holy Spirit. She will give birth to a Son." ... When Joseph awoke, he did what the angel of the Lord had commanded him. He took Mary to be his wife, but he had no [sexual] union with her until she had given birth to a Son. To Him he gave the name 'Jesus'. [1]

Six months [after John was conceived in Elizabeth], God sent the angel Gabriel to Nazareth, a town of Galilee, to a virgin, named Mary, who was pledged to be married to a man named Joseph, a descendant of David. The angel went to her and said, "Hail, you who are highly favoured! The Lord is with you." Mary was greatly troubled at these words and wondered what the greeting could mean. But the angel said to her, "Do not be afraid, Mary, you have found favour with God. Listen! You will conceive and give birth to a son, and you are to name him 'Jesus'. He will be great and will be called the Son of the Most High. The Eternal-God will give Him the throne of His forefather David, and He will reign over the house of Jacob for ever; His reign will never end. Mary said to the angel, "How can this be since I am a virgin?" The angel said to her, "[God] the Holy Spirit will come upon you, and the power of the Most High will overshadow you and the holy One who will be born will be called 'Son of God'." ... "I am the handmaid of the Eternal-God," Mary answered, "May it be to me according to what you have said." Then the angel left her. [2]

"But you, Bethlehem Ephrathah, ... out of you will come for me one who will be ruler over Israel, whose origins are from past ages, from ancient times." [3]

[The angel said to Joseph:] "You are to give Him the name 'Jesus' [meaning 'Saviour'], because He will save His people from their sins." [4]

[1] Matthew 1:18-21,24-25 [2] Luke 1:26-35,38 [3] Micah 5:2 [4] Matthew 1:21

Day 172

The conception of Jesus was different from that of every other baby, but His birth was like that of every one born to a human mother. Mary was specially chosen by God to be the mother of Jesus. That means she deserves our greatest respect, but not our worship because she was not God. The birth of Jesus was as painful to Mary as giving birth is to any mother.

The birth of Jesus Christ

In those days Caesar Augustus issued a decree that there should be a register of the entire Roman world. ... Everyone went to register in his home town. So Joseph went from the town of Nazareth in Galilee, to Bethlehem in Judea, the town of David. He went to register there with Mary, who was pledged to be his wife and expecting to give birth to a child. While they were there, the time came for the baby to be born, and she gave birth to her firstborn, a Son. She wrapped him in swaddling clothes and laid Him in a manger, because there was no room for them in the inn.

There were shepherds in the fields near there who were keeping watch over the their flocks at night. An angel of the Lord appeared to them, and the glory of the Eternal-God shone round them. They were terrified. But the angel said to them, "Do not be afraid. I bring you good news of great joy for all the world. Today, in the town of David, a Saviour has been born: He is Christ [Messiah] the Lord. This is be a sign for you [to recognize him]: You will find a baby wrapped in swaddling cloths and lying in a manger.

Suddenly there appeared with the angel, a great company of the heavenly host praising God and saying, "Glory to God in the highest heaven and on earth peace among people of good will with whom He is pleased."... So they set off in haste and found Mary, Joseph, and the baby, who was lying in a manger. When they saw Him, they made known what they had been told about this Child. All who heard it were amazed at what the shepherds told them. But Mary treasured all these things in her heart and pondered over them. The shepherds returned, glorifying and praising God for all the things they had heard and seen; it was exactly as they had been told. [1]

Christ Jesus, who in His being was God, did not regard equality with God [the Father] something to be grasped, but emptied Himself to take on the nature of 'man'. [2]

Mary said: "My soul magnifies the Lord and my spirit rejoices in God, my Saviour, for He has looked with favour on the humble state of His servant. From now on all generations will call me blessed, for He who is the Mighty One has done great things for me, and holy is His name. His mercy is on those who fear Him from generation to generation." [3]

[1] Luke 2:1-20   [2] Philippians 2:5-7   [3] Luke 1:46-49

Day 173

For the Wise Men from the east, it was the star that pointed to Jesus as Israel's Messiah. For the Jews it was their Scriptures that spoke of Him. His birth and where that would take place were clearly foretold. The Wise Men were Gentiles. The Baby that they came to worship was to be the Saviour not only of the Jews, but of everyone in the world who would accept Him as their Saviour and King.

The visit of the wise men

After Jesus was born in Bethlehem in Judea, during the reign of King Herod, Magi [Wise Men] came from the east to Jerusalem and asked, "Where is the One who has been born king of the Jews? We have seen His star in the east and we have come to worship Him."

When King Herod heard this he was troubled, and all Jerusalem with him. So he called together all the chief priests and scribes and asked them where the Christ was to be born. They replied, "In Bethlehem of Judea, for the prophet wrote: 'But you, Bethlehem, in the land of Judah, are in no way least among the cities of Judah, for out of you will come a ruler who will be the shepherd of my people Israel.'"

Then Herod called for the Magi secretly and learned from them the time when the star appeared. Then he sent them to Bethlehem and said, "Go and make a thorough search for the child and when you find Him, let me know so that I too may go and worship Him."

When they had heard the words of the king, they went on their way. The star they had seen rising in the east went ahead of them until it stopped and stood over the place where the child was. When they saw that the star had stopped, they were over-joyed. Going into the house, they saw the Child with Mary, His mother, and they bowed down and worshipped Him. Then they opened their treasures and presented to Him gifts of gold, frankincense and myrrh. They were warned in a dream not to go back to Herod, so they returned to their country by a different way. [1]

There is none like you, O Eternal-God, among the gods. No other deeds can compare with yours. All the nations that you have made will come and worship before you, O Eternal-God, they will glorify your name. For you are great and work wonders; you alone are God. [2]

"From the rising to the setting of the sun, my name will be great among the nations. In every place incense and pure offerings will be offered to my name, because my name will be great among the Nations," says the Eternal-God, the Almighty. [3]

[1] Matthew 2:1-12 [2] Psalm 86:8-10 [3] Malachi 1:11

Day 174

Jesus was a refugee from the authorities which wanted to destroy Him. After giving birth to Jesus in a place which was far from their home, Mary and Joseph had to pack their things and move to another country. Joseph's life had been changed completely following a message from an angel of God telling him he was to act as father to a Child who was greater than he knew. Now he was told to flee to Egypt. Joseph had learned to trust God whose protection and salvation would go beyond the boundaries of Palestine and reach the world.

The flight to Egypt

When they [the Wise Men] had gone, an angel of the Eternal-God appeared to Joseph in a dream and said "Get up! Take the young child and His mother and flee to Egypt. Stay there until I tell you, for Herod is about to search for the child in order to kill Him." So he got up, took the child and His mother and left during the night for Egypt. He stayed until the death of Herod. This fulfilled what the Eternal-God had said through the prophet: "Out of Egypt I have called my Son."

When Herod realised that he had been misled by the Magi, he was furious and gave orders to put to death all the male children in Bethlehem and its vicinity who were two years old and under. He reckoned the time from what he had learned from the wise men. Then was fulfilled what was spoken through the prophet Jeremiah: "A voice was heard in Ramah, wailing with loud lamentations: Rachel weeping for her children and refusing to be comforted, because they were no more."

After Herod died, an angel of the Eternal-God appeared to Joseph in a dream while he was in Egypt and said, "Get up, take the child and His mother and go to the land of Israel, for those who were seeking to take the child's life are dead." Then he awoke, got up, took the child and his mother and came to the land of Israel. When he heard that Archelaus was reigning over Judea in the place of his father Herod, he was afraid to go there. After being warned in a dream, he withdrew to the region of Galilee. There he went and lived in a town called Nazareth. This fulfilled what was spoken through the prophets: "He will be called a Nazarene." [1]

When Jesus entered Jerusalem the whole city was in a turmoil and people asked, "Who is this?" The crowds answered, "This is Jesus, the Prophet from Nazareth in Galilee." [2]

Philip found Nathanael and said to him, "We have found the One about whom Moses wrote in the Law and about whom the prophets also wrote: Jesus of Nazareth, son of Joseph. Nathanael said to him, "Can any good thing come out of Nazareth? Philip said to him, "Come and see!" [3]

[1] Matthew 2:13-23   [2] Matthew 21: 10-11   [3] John 1:45-46

Day 175

Although Jesus Christ was 'God the Son', He humbled Himself to be born into a poor human family and to be brought up as one of several brothers and sisters. He was obedient to His parents, even when they did not understand why He did some things. In outward appearance He was like any other good boy.

The boy Jesus in the temple

When they [Joseph and Mary] had done everything [for the baby, Jesus] required by the Law of the Eternal-God, they returned to Galilee to their own town of Nazareth. The child grew and became strong and filled with wisdom and the grace of God was upon Him. Every year His parents went to Jerusalem for the Feast of the Passover. When He was twelve years old, they went to the Feast, as was their custom.

When the Feast was over and as His parents were returning home, the boy Jesus stayed behind in Jerusalem. His parents were unaware of this. They travelled for a day supposing Him to be in the caravan. Then they began looking for Him among their relatives and friends. When they failed to find Him, they returned to Jerusalem to look for Him.

After three days they found Him in the courts of the temple, sitting among the teachers, listening to them and asking them questions. All who heard Him were amazed at His understanding and His answers. When His parents saw Him, they were astonished. His mother said to Him, "Son, why have you treated us like this? Your father and I have been searching for you anxiously." He asked them, "Why is it that you were searching for me? Did you not know that I had to be about my Father's house?" They did not understand what He was saying to them, but He went to Nazareth with them and was obedient to them. His mother guarded all these things in her heart. Jesus grew in wisdom and stature, and in favour with God and men. [1]

Although He [Jesus] was a Son, He learned obedience through what He suffered and, being made perfect, He became the source of eternal salvation to all who obey Him. [2]

Christ Jesus: Who, in His being was God, did not consider equality with God [the Father] something to be grasped, but made Himself nothing and took on the very nature of a slave, being made as a 'man'. And being found in the form of a man, He humbled Himself and became obedient to death, even death on a cross. Therefore God [the Father] has highly exalted Him and given Him a name that is above every other name, so that at the name of 'Jesus' every knee in heaven and on earth will bow, and every tongue will confess that Jesus Christ is Lord, to the glory of God the Father. [3]

[1] Luke 2:39-52 [2] Hebrews 5:8-9 [3] Philippians 2:5-8

Day 176

The task God gave John the Baptist was to announce the coming of Jesus Christ and the Kingdom of God. He recognised that he was only a 'voice in the wilderness' but his message was a very important one. He fulfilled his task and Jesus Christ spoke of him as the greatest of the prophets.

John the Baptist starts his work

The word of God came to John [the Baptist] and he went into all the country around the Jordan, preaching a baptism of repentance for the forgiveness of sins. As it is written in the book of Isaiah the prophet: "The voice of one crying in the wilderness, 'Prepare the way for the Eternal-God, make His paths straight paths. Every valley will be filled in, every mountain and hill made low. The crooked paths will be made straight, and rough ways smooth. And all mankind will see the salvation of God.'"

John said to the crowds coming out to be baptised by him, "You brood of vipers! Who has warned you to flee from the wrath that is coming? Bear fruit that goes with repentance, and do not say to yourselves, 'We have Abraham as our father.' I tell you that from these stones God can raise up children for Abraham. Even now the axe is laid to the root of the trees, and every tree that does not bear good fruit will be cut down and thrown into the fire." The crowd asked him, "What shall we do then?" He answered, "He who has two tunics share with him who has none, similarly for whoever has food." ... A sense of expectation grew among the people as they wondered if John might be the Christ [the Messiah]." [1]

"Who are you?" the people asked. He replied with the words of the prophet Isaiah, "I am the voice of one crying in the desert, 'Prepare the way of the Eternal-God.'" Some men who had been sent by the Pharisees questioned him, "Why are you baptising people if you are not the Christ, nor Elijah, nor the Prophet?" [2] He answered them, "I baptise you with water. But One who is more powerful than I am is coming, the straps of whose sandals I am not worthy to untie. He will baptise you with [God] the Holy Spirit and with fire." [3]

"A man can receive nothing except what is given him from heaven. You are my witnesses that I said, 'I am not the Christ but I have been sent ahead of Him.' The bride belongs to the bridegroom. The friend of the bridegroom is full of joy when he hears the bridegroom's voice. That joy is mine and it is complete. He must increase, but I must decrease." [4]

[Jesus said:] "I tell you the truth, among those born of women there has not risen anyone greater than John the Baptist. Nevertheless, he who is least in the kingdom of heaven is greater that he.[5]

[1] Luke 3:1-11,15 [2] John 1:23-24 [3] Luke 3:16 [4] John 3:27-30 [5] Matthew 11:11

Day 177

The Baptism of John is sometimes called the 'Baptism of Repentance'. Jesus never did anything of which He needed to repent. Jesus let John the Baptist baptise Him to show that He was about to begin His life's work and so that 'God the Father' could let the world know that Jesus Christ, the Messiah, was 'God the Son'.

The baptism of Jesus

Jesus came from Galilee to the Jordan to be baptised by John. John tried to persuade Him not to be baptised, saying, "It is I who needs to be baptised by you, not you by me?" Jesus replied, "Let it be so now. It is fitting to do this to fulfil all that righteousness requires." Then John agreed. On being baptised, Jesus went up out of the water. At that moment, suddenly the heavens opened, and John saw the Spirit of God descending like a dove and lighting on Him [Jesus]. And a voice from heaven said, "This is my Son, my Beloved, with whom I am well pleased." [1]

The next day John [the Baptist] saw Jesus coming towards him and said, "Look! There is the Lamb of God who takes away the sin of the world! This is He of whom I said, 'After me a man is coming, One who is greater than I am and who was before me.' I did not know Him myself, but the reason I came baptising with water was that He might be revealed to Israel."

Then John gave this testimony: "I saw the Spirit come down from heaven as a dove and rest on Him. I did not know who He was, but the One who sent me to baptise with water said to me, 'He on whom you see the Spirit come down and rest is He who will baptise with [God] the Holy Spirit.' I have seen and I testify that this is the Son of God." [2]

When all the people were baptised and when Jesus too was baptised and was praying, heaven opened and the Holy Spirit descended on Him in bodily form like a dove. A voice came from heaven: "You are my Son, my Beloved, with you I am well pleased."

Jesus, being, as was supposed, the son of Joseph, the son of Heli, was about thirty years old when He began His work. [3] [Jesus said:] "Do not think that I have come to abolish the Law or the Prophets. I have not come to abolish them but to fulfil them."[4]

[Peter:] We were not following cleverly devised stories when we made known to you the power and coming of our Lord Jesus Christ [the Messiah], but we were eyewitnesses of His majesty. For He received honour and glory from 'God the Father' when the voice came to Him from the Majestic Glory, saying, "This is my Son, my Beloved, with Him I am well pleased." [5]

[1] Matthew 3:13-17 [2] John 1:29-34 [3] Luke 3:21-23 [4] Matthew 5:17 [5] 2 Peter 1:16-17

Day 178

Although Jesus Christ was 'God the Son', He could have yielded to Satan's temptation, joined him, and set up an evil kingdom which would have included everyone except 'God the Father', 'God the Holy Spirit', and their angels. No one could have escaped from that evil kingdom. But, because Jesus did not yield to Satan, and later died in their place, everyone who trusts Him is freed from Satan's kingdom, and 'God the Father' has raised Jesus Christ, 'God the Son' to the place of highest honour.

The temptation of Jesus by Satan

Jesus, full of the Holy Spirit, returned from the Jordan and was led by the Spirit into the wilderness, where He was tempted by the devil for forty days. He ate nothing during those days, and when they were over, He was hungry. The devil [Satan] said to Him, "If you are the Son of God, command these stones to become bread." Jesus answered, "It is written: 'Man does not live by bread alone.'"

The devil led Him up to a height and showed Him all the kingdoms of the world in a moment of time. And he said to Him, "All the authority and glory of these kingdoms has been given to me, and I can give it to anyone I please. If you worship me, it will all be yours." Jesus answered, "It is written: 'Worship the Eternal-God, your God, and serve Him alone.'"

The devil took Him to Jerusalem and set Him on the highest point of the temple. "If you are the Son of God," he said, "throw yourself down from here. For it is written: 'He will command His angels to guard you carefully and they will bear you up in their hands lest you strike your foot against a stone.'" Jesus answered, "It is written: 'Do not put the Eternal-God, your God, to the test.'" When the devil had ended tempting Jesus, he left Him until a another suitable time. [1]

Since we have a great high priest who has passed through the heavens, Jesus, the Son of God, let us hold firmly to the faith we confess. For we do not have a High Priest who is unable to sympathise with our weaknesses, but we have One who has been tempted in every respect as we are, but without sin. Let us then approach the throne of grace with confidence, so that we may receive mercy and find grace to help in time of need. [2] Because He Himself suffered temptation, He is able to help those who are being tempted. [3]

[Paul:] If you think that you are standing firm, be careful that you do not fall! No temptation has overtaken you that is not common to man. God is faithful. He will not let you be tempted beyond what you can bear, but will, with the temptation, provide a way out so that you will be able to bear it. [4]

[1] Luke 4:1-13   [2] Hebrews 4:14-16   [3] Hebrews 2:18   [4] 1 Corinthians 10:12-13

Day 179

Jesus chose simple men to be His followers. They all responded willingly. He forced no one to be His disciple. He could see in them far more than they could see themselves. He called Simon, a 'waverer', and made him into Cephas, a 'rock'. That happened to them all, except Judas who did not go on to become an apostle like the others, not because Jesus made a bad choice, but because he refused to repent of his sin.

Jesus chooses His disciples

The next day, as John [the Baptist] was standing there with two of his disciples, he saw Jesus passing by and said, "Look! There is the Lamb of God!" When the two disciples heard him say this, they followed Jesus. One of the two who heard what John said and followed Jesus, was Andrew, the brother of Simon Peter. Andrew immediately found his brother Simon and said to him, "We have found the Messiah!" (that is, the Christ). And he brought him to Jesus. Jesus looked at him and said, "You are Simon, the son of John. You will be called Cephas" (which, when translated, is Peter. [a stone]). [1]

As Jesus was walking by the Sea of Galilee, He saw two brothers, Simon, who is called Peter, and his brother Andrew. They were casting a net into the lake, for they were fishermen. "Come! Follow me," Jesus said to them, "and I will make you fishers of men." At once they left their nets and followed Him. As He went from there, He saw two other brothers, James, the son of Zebedee, and his brother John who were in a boat with their father Zebedee, mending their nets. Jesus called them and immediately they left the boat and their father and followed Him. [2]

The next day Jesus decided to go to Galilee. There, He found Philip and said to him, "Follow me." Philip was from Bethsaida, the city of Andrew and Peter. Philip found Nathanael and said to him, "We have found the one Moses wrote about in the Law, and about whom the prophets also wrote, Jesus of Nazareth, the son of Joseph." ... When Jesus saw Nathanael coming to Him, He said of him, "Here is an Israelite indeed, in whom there is nothing false." "How do you know me?" Nathanael asked. Jesus answered, " Before Philip called you, while you were still under the fig-tree, I saw you." [3]

Jesus said to them [his disciples]: "Did I not choose you, the Twelve? And one of you is a devil!" He was speaking of Judas, the son of Simon Iscariot, who, although one of the twelve, was later to betray him. [4]

[Jesus said to His disciples], "You did not choose me, but I chose you and appointed you to go and bear fruit, fruit that will last." [5]

[1] John 1:35-37,40-42   [2] Matthew 4:18-21   [3] John 1:43-48   [4] John 6:70-71   [5] John 15:16

Day 180

Tax collectors collected not only taxes for the roman rulers, but often they took more than was required of them and kept the extra for themselves. They were, therefore, hated and despised by the people. Matthew was a tax collector and yet Jesus chose him to be one of His disciples. He could see in Matthew, not only what he was, but also what he would like to be and what Jesus could make him.

The call of Matthew

As Jesus was walking along, He saw a man named Matthew sitting at the tax collector's booth. He said to him, "Follow me." He got up and followed Him. [1] Even tax collectors came [to John the Baptist] to be baptised. "Teacher," they asked, "what ought we to do?" "Collect no more than you are required to," he said to them. [2]

[Jesus said to the chief priests and elders of the people:] "What do you think? There was a man who had two sons. He went to the first and said, 'Son, go and work today in the vineyard.' 'I will not,' he answered, but later he changed his mind and went. Then the man went to the second son and said the same thing. He answered, 'I will, sir,' but he did not go. Which of the two did the will of his father?" "The first one," they answered. Jesus said to them, "I tell you the truth, the tax collectors and the prostitutes will enter the kingdom of God before you. For John [the Baptist] came to you as an example of the way of righteousness, and you did not believe him, but the tax collectors and the prostitutes did believe him. And you, even when you saw this, you did not change your minds and believe him." [3]

All the people who heard the words of Jesus, even the tax-collectors, acknowledged, by being baptised by John [the Baptist], that God's way was just. But the Pharisees and experts in the law, by refusing to be baptised by John, rejected God's purpose for them. ...

[Jesus:] "To what shall I compare this generation. ... John the Baptist came neither eating bread nor drinking wine, and you say, 'He has a demon.' The Son of Man has come eating and drinking, and you say, 'He is a glutton and a drunkard, a friend of tax-collectors and 'sinners'. But wisdom is proved right by her children." [4]

Matthew prepared a great banquet for Jesus in his house. Many tax collectors and 'sinners' came and ate with Him and His disciples. When the Pharisees and the scribes saw this, they said to His disciples, "Why do you eat and drink with tax collectors and 'sinners'?"

Jesus answered them, "It is not the healthy who need a doctor, but those who are sick. I have not come to call the righteous but sinners to repentance." [5]

[1] Matthew 9:9   [2] Luke 3:12-13   [3] Matthew 21:28-32   [4] Luke 7:29-35   [5] Luke 5:29-32

Day 181

The ministry of Jesus was different from anything the people of that time had ever seen or heard about. Jesus spoke with great authority, although everyone knew He had not been highly educated in the way the Pharisees were. He performed remarkable miracles, yet did not want people to believe in Him because of them. His ministry was to change people through the way they thought, that is, through repentance.

Jesus announces the beginning of His ministry

Jesus returned [from the Jordan] in the power of [God] the [Holy] Spirit and went into Galilee. News about him spread through the whole region. He taught in their synagogues and was praised by everyone. He came to Nazareth, where He had been brought up, and He went into the synagogue, as was His custom on the Sabbath day, and He stood up to read. There was handed to Him the scroll of the prophet Isaiah. He unrolled it and found the place where it is written: "The Spirit of the Eternal-God is on me, because He has anointed me to preach the good news to the poor. He has sent me to proclaim release for the captives, and recovery of sight for the blind, to deliver the oppressed, and to proclaim the acceptable year of the Eternal-God." Then He rolled up the scroll, gave it back to the attendant and sat down. The eyes of everyone in the synagogue were fixed on Him. He began by saying to them: "Today this scripture is fulfilled in your hearing." All spoke well of Him and were amazed at the gracious words that came from His mouth.

Then He said to them, "You will quote this proverb to me: 'Physician, heal yourself! Do here in your home town what you did in Capernaum. I tell you the truth, no prophet is accepted in his own country." ... He went down to Capernaum, and there He continued to teach the people on the Sabbath. The people were astonished at His teaching because He spoke with authority." [1]

After John had been arrested, Jesus went into Galilee preaching the good news of God. He said, "The time has come. The kingdom of God is near at hand. Repent and believe the good news." [2] From that time on Jesus began to preach, "Repent, for the kingdom of heaven is near." [3]

At daybreak Jesus left [Peter's house] and went out to an isolated place. The people looked for Him and when they found where He was, they tried to prevent Him from leaving them. But He said to them, "I must preach the good news of the kingdom of God to the other cities also, because that is the purpose for which I was sent." So He continued preaching in the synagogues of Judea. [4]

This is a trustworthy saying and worthy of full acceptance: Christ Jesus came into the world to save sinners. [5]

[1] Luke 4:14-24,31-32   [2] Mark 1:14-15   [3] Matthew 4:17   [4] Luke 4:42-44   [5] 1 Timothy 3:1

Day 182

When Jesus spoke in the synagogue of His home town, Nazareth, some of those listening were full of praise, others were angry. That often happens when people hear God's gracious words to them and then go on to understand what they really mean. Approval of words is not repentance of sin. As soon as He began to announce His mission to fulfil the prophecies about a Messiah who would save people from the slavery of sin, He met opposition, not least from those who were most learned in their Jewish faith.

Jesus is rejected in His home town

He [Jesus] came to Nazareth, where He had been brought up. On the Sabbath day He went into the synagogue, as was His custom. ... All spoke well of Him and were amazed at the gracious words that came from His mouth. ... Then He continued, "I tell you the truth, no prophet is accepted in his home town. In truth, there were many widows in Israel in the days of Elijah, when the heavens were shut for three years and six months and there was a severe famine throughout the land. Yet Elijah was not sent to any of them, but to a widow of Zarephath, in the region of Sidon. And there were many in Israel with leprosy in the time of Elisha the prophet, yet none of them was cleansed, except Naaman, the Syrian." When they heard this, the people in the synagogue were filled with rage. They got up and drove Jesus out of the town, and led Him to the brow of the hill on which the town was built, in order to throw Him down headlong. But He passed through the crowd and went on His way. [1]

[Jesus said to His disciples:] You have not chosen me, but I have chosen you. ... If the world hates you, you know that it hated me before it hated you. ... If you belonged to the world, the world would love you as one of its own, but, because you are not of the world, the world hates you. Remember what I said to you: 'A servant is not greater than his master.' If they persecute me, they will also persecute you. If they obey my teaching they will also obey yours. They will do this to you because of my name, for they do not know the One who sent me. Whoever hates me, hates my Father also. If I had not done among them what no one else has ever done, they would not be guilty of sin. But now they have seen and hated both me and my Father. The word written in their law has been fulfilled: "They hated me without a cause." [2]

They [the High Priest and the Jewish leaders] called the apostles before them and had them flogged. They ordered them not to speak in the name of Jesus and let them go. They left the council, rejoicing that they had been counted worthy of suffering for the Name. They did not cease, every day, to proclaim the good news of Jesus. [3]

[1] Luke 4:16-21,28 [2] John 15:18-25 [3] Acts 5:40-41

Day 183

The Jews knew from their prophets that the Messiah, when He came, would show His power and authority by performing miracles. Even when Jesus worked these before their eyes, many did not accept His authority. Miracles, by themselves, do not convince anybody. They only help those to believe who want to believe.

The first of Jesus' miracles

On the third day there was a wedding at Cana in Galilee and the mother of Jesus was there. Jesus also and His disciples were invited to the wedding. When the wine was all gone, Jesus' mother said to Him, "They have no more wine." Jesus said to her, "Woman, what concern is that to you and me? My time has not yet come." His mother said to the servants, "Whatever He tells you to do, do it!"

Nearby there were six stone water jars ... each holding from twenty to thirty gallons. Jesus said to them [the servants], "Fill the water jars with water". So they filled them to the brim. Then He said to them, "Now draw some out and take it to the chief steward of the feast." They did so, and the chief steward of the feast tasted the water that had been turned into wine. He did not know where it had come from, though the servants who had drawn the water knew. He called the bridegroom and said to him, "Everyone serves the best wine first and then that which is not so good after the guests have drunk freely, but you have kept the best wine till now."

This was the first of the miraculous signs Jesus performed in Cana of Galilee, in which He revealed His glory, and His disciples believed in Him. After this He went down to Capernaum with His mother and brothers and His disciples and stayed there for only a few days. ...

While He was in Jerusalem at the Feast of the Passover, many people saw the miraculous signs He performed and believed in His name. But Jesus did not trust himself to them, for He knew all men. He did not need anyone to tell him about people; He knew very well what was in a man. [1]

Jesus came again to Cana in Galilee, where he had turned the water into wine. There was a royal official there whose son was lying ill at Capernaum. When he heard that Jesus had come back from Judea into Galilee, he went to meet Him and begged Him to come and heal his son, who was lying at the point of death. Jesus said to him, "Unless you see miraculous signs and wonders, you will never believe." The royal official said, "Sir, come down now before my child dies." Jesus said to him, "Go in peace! Your son will live."... His servants met him and said, "Your son is alive." [2]

[Peter said to the people:] "Jesus of Nazareth was a man attested by God to you by miraculous signs and wonders, which God did among you through Him." [3]

[1] John 2:1-13,23-25 [2] John 4:46-51 [3] Acts 2:22

Day 184

Nicodemus was a well-known Pharisee of high standing, afraid of public opinion, but sincere. Jesus answered his questions in simple words which had deep meanings. As each person is 'born of the flesh', that is, born naturally, into the family of people, so God wants everyone to be 'born of the spirit' into His family.

Jesus and Nicodemus

There was a leader among the Jews, a Pharisee named Nicodemus. He came to Jesus at night and said, "Rabbi, we know that you are a teacher who has come from God. No one can work the miraculous signs you are performing if God is not with him." Jesus answered him, "I tell you the truth, unless a man is born again he cannot see the kingdom of God ." Nicodemus said to Him, "How can a man be born again when he is old? Can he enter his mother's womb a second time and be born?" Jesus answered, "I tell you the truth, unless a man is born of water and the Spirit he cannot enter the kingdom of God. That which is born of the flesh is flesh, and that which is born of the Spirit is spirit. Do not be surprised at my saying, 'You must be born again.' The wind blows where it pleases. You hear its sound, but you cannot tell where it comes from or where it is going. So it is with every one who is born of the Spirit."

"How can this be?" Nicodemus asked. "You are a teacher of Israel and you not understand these things?" said Jesus, " I tell you the truth, we speak of what we know, and we testify to what we have seen, yet you do not accept our testimony. If you do not believe me when I have spoken to you of earthly things, how can you believe me if I speak of heavenly things? No one has ever gone up to heaven, except the One who came down from heaven, the Son of Man. As Moses lifted up the snake in the desert, so the Son of Man must be lifted up, so that everyone who believes in Him may have eternal life.

God [the Father] so loved the world that He gave His only [God the] Son, that whoever believes in Him shall not perish but have eternal life. For God [the Father] did not send [God] the Son into the world to condemn the world but that the world might be saved through Him. Whoever believes in Him is not condemned, but whoever does not believe in Him is condemned already, because He refuses to believe in the name of the only Son of God. ... Whoever believes in the Son has eternal life, but whoever refuses to believe in the Son will never see life, for the wrath of God remains on him." [1]

[Peter:] You know that you were not redeemed from the empty ways of life that you inherited from your forefathers with perishable things such as silver or gold, but with the precious blood of Christ, who was a 'lamb without blemish or defect'. [2]

[1] John 3:1-18,36   [2] 1 Peter 1:18

Day 185

Jesus, who was Man as well as God, knew what it was to be tired and thirsty. He asked the Samaritan woman for water - ordinary water to quench His thirst. Then He used the word 'water' to describe 'God the Holy Spirit'. The promise of Jesus to 'give living water' is the same as His later promise to 'give God the Holy Spirit'. The woman needed both in her fruitless search for happiness.

Jesus and the Samaritan woman

He [Jesus] left Judea to return to Galilee and so He had to go through Samaria. He came to a town in Samaria called Sychar. ... Jacob's well was there. Jesus, tired from the journey, sat down by the well. ... A Samaritan woman came to draw water and Jesus said to her, "Give me a drink?" ... The Samaritan woman said to Him, "How is it that you, a Jew, ask me, a Samaritan woman, for a drink?" (Jews have nothing to do with Samaritans.) Jesus answered her, "If you knew the gift of God and who it is that is saying to you, "Give me a drink," you would have asked Him and He would have given you living water." She said to Him, "Sir , you have nothing to draw with and the well is deep. Where do you get this living water? ... Jesus answered her, "All who drinks this water will be thirsty again, but whoever drinks the water I give him will never thirst. The water that I give him will become in him a spring of water welling up to eternal life." The woman said to Him, "Sir, give me this water so that I will never get thirsty and have to come here to draw water."

Jesus said to her, "Go, call your husband and come back here." She replied, "I have no husband," Jesus said to her, "You have spoken the truth when you say you have no husband. You have had five husbands, and the man you are now living with is not your husband. What you have said is true." "Sir," the woman said, "I see that you are a prophet. Our forefathers worshipped on this mountain, but you [Jews] say that Jerusalem is the place where we must worship."

Jesus said, "Woman, believe me, a time is coming when you will worship the Father neither on this mountain nor in Jerusalem. You [Samaritans] do not know what you worship. We [Jews] know what we worship, for salvation is from the Jews. A time is coming, indeed it is already here, when true worshippers will worship [God the] Father in spirit and in truth. It is such as these that [God] the Father seeks. God is spirit, and those who worship Him must worship Him in spirit and in truth." [1]

On the final and greatest day of the feast, Jesus stood up and cried in a loud voice, "If anyone is thirsty, let him come to me and drink. Whoever believes in me, as the Scripture says: From him will flow streams of living water." He said this about [God] the [Holy] Spirit, whom those who believed in Him were later to receive. [2]

[1] John 4:1-24 [2] John 7:37-39

Day 186

John the Baptist was a fearless preacher of the truth and this brought him into conflict with King Herod. In prison, he must have been discouraged at what was happening to him. He wondered what had become of the Messiah He had been called of God to announce. But Jesus' kingdom was not of this world, and John had fulfilled his ministry.

John the Baptist in prison

Herod had John [the Baptist] arrested, bound and put in prison on account of Herodias, his brother Philip's wife. John had said to him: "It is not lawful for you to have her." Herod wanted to kill John, but he was afraid of the people, because they regarded him as a prophet. [1]

When John heard in prison what Christ was doing, he sent a message to Him by his disciples, asking "Are you He who was to come, or should we expect someone else?" Jesus replied, "Go back and report to John what you hear and see: the blind receive their sight, the lame walk, those who have leprosy are healed, the deaf hear, the dead are raised up again, and the good news is preached to the poor. Blessed is the man who is not offended on account of me.

As the disciples of John were leaving, Jesus began to speak to the crowd about John. "What did you go out into the desert to see? A reed swayed by the wind? ... A man dressed in fine clothes? Those who wear find clothes are in the palaces of kings. ... Then what did you go out to see? A prophet? Yes, I tell you, and more than a prophet. ... I tell you the truth, among those born of women there has not risen anyone greater than John the Baptist; yet he who is least in the kingdom of heaven is greater than he." [2]

[Malachi:] You have wearied the Eternal-God with your words. Yet you say, "How have we wearied him?" By saying, "Everyone who does evil is good in the sight of the Eternal-God, and He is pleased with them" or "Where is the God of justice?" ... "See, I send my messenger, who will prepare the way before me. Suddenly, the Lord you are seeking will come to His temple. The messenger of the covenant, whom you desire, will come," says the Eternal-God, the Almighty. Who will be able to endure the day of his coming? Who will stand when he appears? [3]

[Isaiah:] "A voice said, "Cry out!". And I said, "What shall I cry?" "Everybody is like grass, as frail as the flower of the field. The grass withers and the flowers fade when the breath of the Eternal-God blows on them. ... The grass withers and the flowers fade, but the word of our God will stand for ever. You who bring good news to Zion, go up to the high mountain. ... Lift up your voice with strength ... say to the cities of Judah, "Here is your God." [4]

[1] Matthew 14:3-5   [2] Matthew 11:2-9,11   [3] Malachi 2:17 -3:1-2   [4] Isaiah 40:6-9

Day 187

Peter was a fisherman. He knew when it was a good time to cast nets for fish. Although he knew it was not the right moment, he obeyed Jesus and, to his great surprise, he drew in a great catch. In a similar way, obeying Jesus was going to mean for him a life of 'catching' people for God's kingdom.

The great catch of fish

As Jesus was standing by the Lake of Gennesaret, with people crowding round Him and listening to the word of God, He saw, at the water's edge, two boats drawn up on the lake shore. They had been left there by fishermen who were washing their nets. He got into one of the boats, the one belonging to Simon, and asked him to pull away from the shore a little. Then He sat down and taught the crowd from the boat.

When He had finished speaking, He said to Simon, "Put out into the deep, and let down your nets for a catch." Simon answered, "Master, we have worked all night and caught nothing. But, because you say so, I will let down the nets." When they had done this, they caught so many fish that their nets began to break. They signalled to their partners in the other boat to come and help them. They came and they filled both boats so that they began to sink.

When Simon Peter saw this, he fell down at Jesus' knees and said, "Go away from me, O Lord, for I am a sinful man!" He and all who were with him were amazed at the catch of fish that they had taken, so were James and John, the sons of Zebedee, who were partners of Simon. Then Jesus said to Simon, "Do not be afraid. From now on you will be catching men." They brought their boats on to the shore, left everything and followed Him." [1]

Jesus came to them [the disciples] and said: "All authority in heaven and on earth has been given to me. Go, therefore, and make disciples of all nations, baptize them in the name of [God the] Father, and of [God the] Son and of [God the] Holy Spirit, and teach them to observe everything that I have commanded you. And I will surely be with you always, right to the end of the age." [2]

[Jesus, God the Son, prayed to God the Father:] "I have brought glory to you on earth by completing the work that you gave me to do. Now Father, glorify me with the glory that I had with you before the world was created. I have made known your name to those you have given me from the world [the disciples]. ... They are not of the world as I am not of the world. Sanctify them in the truth; your word is truth. As you sent me into the world, so I am sending them into the world." [3]

[1] Luke 5:1-11   [2] Matthew 28:18-20   [3] John 17:4-6,16-18

Day 188

Satan and his evil spirits have great power, but they are only allowed to have that power by God, so that people, born into the family of Satan, can see the effects of Satan's domination. They then have the choice of either staying in Satan's family or rejecting Satan and allowing God to give them 'new birth' into His family. God is more powerful than Satan and any evil spirits, and He offers full protection to those who trust in Him.

Jesus drives out evil spirits

They went to Capernaum, and immediately, on the Sabbath, Jesus went into the synagogue and began to teach. The people were amazed at His teaching, because He taught them as one who had authority, not as the scribes. There was in the synagogue a man who was possessed by an evil spirit. He cried out, "What have you to do with us, Jesus of Nazareth? Have you come to destroy us? I know who you are, the Holy One of God!" Jesus rebuked him saying, "Shut up and come out of him!" The evil spirit threw the man into convulsions and with a loud cry came out of him.

The people were amazed and asked each other, "What is this? What new teaching can this be which has such authority! With authority, He orders evil spirits and they obey him." His fame spread quickly throughout the whole region of Galilee.[1]

Jesus appointed another seventy and sent them ahead of Him, two by two, into every town where He intended to go. ... The seventy returned with joy and said, "Lord, even the demons submit to us in your name." He said to them, "I saw Satan fall like lightning from heaven. See, I have given you authority to trample on snakes and scorpions and strength to overcome all the power of the enemy. Nothing will harm you. Nevertheless, do not rejoice in this, that the spirits submit to you, but rejoice that your names are written in heaven."

Then Jesus, full of joy through [God] the Holy Spirit, said, "I thank you, Father, Lord of heaven and earth, because you have hidden these things from the wise and learned, and revealed them to little children. Yes, Father, for such was your gracious will." ... Then He turned to His disciples in private and said, "Blessed are those whose eyes see what you see. I tell you that many prophets and kings have desired to see what you see but did not see it, and to hear what you hear but did not hear it."[2]

[Paul:] Finally, be strong in the Lord and in the might of His power. Put on the full armour of God so that you may be able to stand against the wiles of the devil. Our struggle is not against enemies of flesh and blood, but against the authorities and the powers of this dark world and against the spirit forces of evil in the heavenly realms. Therefore, put on the full armour of God, so that you may be able to stand your ground when the day of evil comes, and after having done all this, to stand firm.[3]

[1] Mark 1:21-28 [2] Luke 10:1,17-23 [3] Ephesians 6:10-13

Day 189

It is a terrible experience to be under the control of evil spirits. Some people put themselves under demonic powers; some are given to Satan in childhood. But God is greater than any demonic power and He sets free, in the name of Jesus, those so possessed who trust in Him. He then wants them to tell others of His saving power.

Jesus heals a demon-possessed man

They [Jesus and His disciples] went across the lake to the country of the Gerasenes. As Jesus got out of the boat, there came to meet Him a man with an evil spirit. He came from the tombs where he lived. No one could restrain him, not even with a chain. Often he had been chained hand and foot, but he wrenched them apart and broke the iron shackles on his feet. No one was strong enough to restrain him. Night and day among the tombs and on the hills he cried out and cut himself with stones. He saw Jesus from a distance, ran and fell on his knees before Him. He shouted with a loud voice, "What have you to do with me, Jesus, Son of the Most High God? Swear by God that you will not torture me!" For Jesus had said to him, "Come out of the man, you evil spirit!" Then Jesus asked him, "What is your name?" He replied, "My name is Legion, for we are many." He begged Jesus not to send them [himself and the demons] out of the region. On the hillside near there, a large herd of pigs were feeding. The demons begged Jesus, "Send us to the pigs, let us to go into them." He gave them permission. The evil spirits came out of the man and went into the pigs. The herd, numbering about two thousand, rushed down the steep slope into the water and were drowned. ...

As Jesus was getting into the boat, the man who had been possessed by the evil spirits begged to go with Him. Jesus refused him and said, "Go home to your family and tell them how much the Lord in His mercy has done for you." So the man went away and began to tell in the Decapolis how much Jesus had done for him. And every one was amazed. [1]

More and more men and women believed in the Lord and joined their number. People brought the sick into the streets and laid them on beds and sleeping-mats, so that Peter's shadow might fall on some of them as he passed by. A great number also gathered from the towns around Jerusalem, bringing those who were sick and those who were tormented by evil spirits, and they were all healed. [2]

When evening came, they brought to Him many who were under the power of demons. With a word He drove out the demons and healed all who were sick. And so He fulfilled the words of the prophet Isaiah, "He took on Himself our infirmities and bore out diseases." [3]

[1] Mark 5:1-20   [2] Acts 5:14-16   [3] Matthew 8:16-17

Day 190

Jesus demonstrated clearly that He was the Messiah by showing His power over Satan, evil spirits, sickness and disease. He enabled His disciples to share in His power. This could only happen when there was faith in Jesus and in His power over evil spirits. Because they were human, the disciples did not always fulfil the conditions for that power to be used rightly. Jesus, being God, as well as human, never failed to set people free from evil domination.

Faith in Jesus defeats the power of evil spirits

While they [Jesus and His disciples] were leaving [Capernaum], a man who was dumb and possessed by an evil spirit was brought to Jesus. When the demon had been driven out, the man who had been dumb spoke. The crowd was amazed and said, "Never before has anything like this been seen in Israel." But the Pharisees said, "He drives out demons by the prince of demons." [1]

When they came to the crowd, a man came to Jesus and kneeling before Him said: "Lord, have mercy on my son; he has epilepsy and suffers greatly. He often falls into the fire or into the water. I brought him to your disciples, but they could not heal him." Jesus said, "O faithless and perverse generation, how long shall I be with you? How long shall I bear with you? Bring him here to me." Jesus rebuked the demon, and it came out of the boy. From that moment he was healed .

Then the disciples came to Jesus privately and asked, "Why could not we drive it out?" He said to them, "Because of your little faith. I tell you the truth, if you have faith as small as a grain of mustard seed, you will say to this mountain, 'Move from here to there' and it will move. Nothing will be impossible for you." [2]

I tell you the truth, anyone who believes in me will be able to do what I have been doing, and he will be able to do even greater things than these, because I am going to [God] the Father. I will do whatever you ask in my name, so that [God] the Father may be glorified in [God] the Son. You may ask me for anything in my name, and I will do it. [3]

[God the Holy] Spirit has expressly declared that in later times, some will abandon the faith and follow deceitful spirits and the teaching of demons. [4]

[Jesus said to His disciples:] "Go into all the world and preach the good news to everyone. Whoever believes and is baptized will be saved. ... And these signs will accompany those who believe; in my name they will drive out demons. [5]

Since the children have flesh and blood, He too shared in their humanity so that by His death He might destroy him who holds the power of death, that is, the devil, and free those who all their lives were held in slavery by their fear of death.[6]

[1] Matthew 9:32-34 [2] Matthew 17:14-21 [3] John 14:12-15 [4] 1 Timothy 4:1 [5] Mark 16:15-17 [6] Hebrews 2:14-15

Day 191

Satan, or the Devil, is called by many names in different religions. Beelzebub was the name of a Philistine god which the Jews later used to refer to Satan. Whatever his name, his character never changes. The only sin which God cannot forgive is that of calling Jesus the devil. Many religious people can cast out devils and appear to leave the one possessed 'swept clean'. Only when Jesus enters that life can evil spirits find it impossible to return. When Jesus is not allowed to enter that life, the evil spirit can return and bring other evil spirits with him.

Jesus and Beelzebub

Jesus drove out a demon from a man who was dumb. When the demon left, the man who had been dumb spoke. The crowd was amazed, but some of them said, "He drives out demons by Beelzebub, the prince of demons." Others asked Him, as a test, for a sign from heaven. Jesus knew what they were thinking and said to them: "A kingdom which is divided against itself will perish and a house which is divided against itself will fall. You say that I drive out demons by Beelzebub, but if Satan is divided against himself, how can his kingdom stand? If I drive out demons by Beelzebub, by whom do those who drive out demons among you drive them out? They will be the judges of what you say. But if I drive out demons by the finger of God, then the kingdom of God has come to you.

"When a strong, fully armed man, guards his house, his property is safe. But when someone stronger than he is, attacks and overpowers him, he removes the armour in which the man trusts and divides up his goods. He who is not with me is against me, and he who does not gather with me, scatters.

"When an evil spirit leaves a man, it roams through waterless places seeking rest. When it does not find it, it says, 'I will go back to the house I left.' When it arrives, it finds the house swept clean and put in order. Then it brings seven other spirits more wicked than itself, and they go in and live there. The final condition of that man is worse than the first." [1]

"Truly I tell you, all sins and blasphemies of men will be forgiven them. But whoever blasphemes against [God] the Holy Spirit will never be forgiven for that is an eternal sin. Jesus said this because they were saying, "He has an evil spirit." [2]

[James:] Be disciplined and alert. Your enemy the devil prowls around like a roaring lion looking for someone to devour. Withstand him, standing firm in the faith. [3] Submit yourselves to God. Resist the devil, and he will flee from you. [4]

[John:] Little children, you are from God and you have overcome them [evil spirits], for the One who is in you is greater than the one who is in the world. [5]

---

[1] Luke 11:14-26 [2] Mark 3:28-30 [3] 1 Peter 5:8-9 [4] James 4:7 [5] 1 John 4:4

Day 192

Jesus knew that sometimes people only wanted to see miracles being performed; they did not want to accept the One who was working them. The Roman centurion knew that action was the true sign of faith. He believed in Jesus and in the power of His word and was not just amazed at the miracles He performed. As a soldier he knew what it meant both to give and obey orders. His action was a sign of his faith.

Jesus responds to the faith of a soldier

As Jesus entered Capernaum a centurion came to Him and said, "Lord, my servant is lying at home paralysed and in terrible pain." Jesus said to him, "I will come and heal him." The centurion replied, "Lord, I am not worthy for you to come under my roof. Speak the word only, and my servant will be healed. I am myself a man under authority, with soldiers under me. I say to this one, 'Go!' and he goes, to that one, 'Come!' and he comes, and to my servant, 'Do this!' and he does it."

When Jesus heard this, He was amazed and said to those who followed Him, "I tell you the truth, I have not found such great faith in anyone in Israel. I tell you that many will come from the east and from the west, and will sit at the table with Abraham, Isaac and Jacob in the kingdom of heaven, while the heirs of the kingdom will be driven outside into the darkness where there will be weeping and gnashing of teeth." Then Jesus said to the centurion, "Go! It will be done for you as you have believed." At that very hour his servant was healed. [1]

Take Abraham as an example: "He believed God, and it was reckoned to him as righteousness." It follows, then, that it is those who believe [God] who are children of Abraham. Therefore, those who believe [God], receive the same blessing as Abraham, the man of faith. [2]

When a man works, he does not receive his wages as a gift, but as a debt which he is owed. To the man who does not work, however, but trusts God who justifies the ungodly, it is his faith which is credited to him as righteousness. [3]

Without faith it is impossible to please God, because whoever comes to Him must believe that He exists and that He rewards those who earnestly seek for Him. [4]

[Jesus said:] "I tell you the truth, whoever hears my words and believes in Him who sent me, has eternal life and will not be condemned. He has already passed from death to life." [5]

[James:] Faith by itself, if it is not expressed in action, is dead. But someone will say, "You have faith but I have good deeds." You show me your faith without deeds, and I will show you my faith by my deeds. You believe that God is one. Good! The demons believe that too, and shudder. [6]

---

[1] Matthew 8:5-13   [2] Galatians 3:6,9   [3] Romans 4:4-5   [4] Hebrews 11:6   [5] John 5:24   [6] James 2:17-19

Day 193

Jesus came to seek and to save those who were lost. Sometimes in seeking for people He healed their sickness, but this was only in order that He might save them from being lost, as far as God was concerned. Here Jesus shows He has power to do both - to save and to heal. He also shows that to have sins forgiven is more important than to have a whole body.

Jesus heals a man suffering from paralysis

When Jesus again entered Capernaum, the news spread rapidly that He was home. So many gathered that there was not enough room for them, even around the door, and He preached the word to them. Four men came carrying a paralysed man. They could not get him near to Jesus because of the crowd, so they made a hole in the roof above Him, then lowered the mat the paralysed man was lying on. When Jesus saw their faith, He said to the paralysed man, "Son, your sins are forgiven."

Now some scribes were sitting there and they thought to themselves, "Why does this man talk like that? He is blaspheming! Who can forgive sins but God alone?" Jesus knew in His spirit what they were thinking to themselves, and He said to them, "Why are you thinking as you are? Which is easier: to say to the paralysed man, 'Your sins are forgiven,' or to say, 'Get up, take your mat and walk'? So that you may know that the Son of Man has authority on earth to forgive sins. ... " He said to the paralysed man, "I say to you, get up, take your mat and go home." He got up, picked up his mat and walked out in front of them all. Everyone was amazed and praised God, saying, "We have never ever seen anything like this!" [1]

Praise the Eternal-God, O my soul, and do not forget all His benefits. He who forgives all your sins, who heals all your diseases, who redeems your life from the pit and crowns you with steadfast love and compassion, who satisfies you with good things so that your youth is renewed like the eagle's. The Eternal-God executes righteousness and justice for the oppressed. He made known His ways to Moses and His deeds to the people of Israel. The Eternal-God is merciful and gracious, slow to be angry and abounding in loving-kindness. ... For as the heavens are high above the earth, so great is His loving-kindness towards those who fear Him. As far as the east is from the west, so far has He removed our transgressions from us. As a father has compassion on his children, so the Eternal-God has compassion on those who fear Him. He knows our frame. He remembers that we are dust. [2]

"I, even I, am He who blots out your transgressions, for my own sake. I will never again remember your sins." [3] *[John:] If we confess our sins, He is faithful and just and will forgive us our sins and cleanse us from all unrighteousness.* [4]

[1] Mark 2:1-12 [2] Psalm 103:2-14 [3] Isaiah 43:25 [4] 1 John 1:9

Day 194

The meanness of sinful human nature is seen in the refusal of the Jewish religious leaders to rejoice in the good that others receive. Instead of praising God for a notable deliverance, they criticised Jesus for 'working' on the Sabbath. They would have saved a donkey which had fallen into a pit on the Sabbath day, but they would not agree to a much greater 'saving' of a sick man. This was very far from the spirit of Jesus.

The healing at the pool of Bethesda

Jesus went to Jerusalem for a feast of the Jews. There, near the Sheep Gate, is a pool, which is called, in Hebrew, 'Bethesda'. It consists of five covered colonnades where a great number of sick people, the blind, the lame, and the paralysed, used to lie. One man who was there had been paralysed for thirty-eight years. Jesus saw him lying there helpless. Knowing that he had been like that for a long time, He asked him, "Do you want to be well?" "Sir," the sick man replied, "I have no one to help me into the pool when the water is being stirred up. While I am on my way to get in, someone else goes down ahead of me." Then Jesus said to him, "Get up! Pick up your mat and walk." Instantly the man was healed. He picked up his mat and walked.

The day on which this happened was a Sabbath. The Jews said to the man who had been healed. "It is the Sabbath. It is not lawful for you to carry your mat." He replied, "The man who healed me said to me, 'Pick up your mat and walk.'" Then they asked him, "Who is this man who said to you 'Pick up your mat and walk.'?" The man who was healed did not know who it was, for Jesus had quietly disappeared into the crowd that was there. Later Jesus found him in the temple and said to him, "Look, you are well now. Stop sinning or something worse may happen to you." The man went away and told the Jews that it was Jesus who had healed him." [1]

The Pharisees said to Jesus, "Why are they [His disciples] doing what it is not lawful to do on the Sabbath. ... Jesus said to them, "The Sabbath was made for man, not man for the Sabbath. The Son of Man is Lord even of the Sabbath." [2]

You, who were dead in your sins and in the uncircumcision of your sinful nature, God [the Father] has made alive with Christ [God the Son]. By nailing to the cross the record of accusations held against us, He has blotted it out and has forgiven all our sins. Then, having disarmed the rulers and authorities ranged against us, He made a public spectacle of them in triumphing over them in the cross. Therefore do not let anyone sit in judgment on you in matters of food and drink, nor with regard to the observance of a religious festival, a New Moon celebration or a Sabbath day. Such things are a picture of the things that were to come. The reality is to be found in Christ. [3]

[1] John 5:1-15   [2] Mark 2:24,27-28   [3] Colossians 2:13-17

Day 195

Unlike the Jews of those days, Jesus held women in very high esteem. Whenever one came to Him for help or healing, He always treated her with the greatest respect and responded to the faith shown. The way Jesus addressed women, including His mother, showed His respect for them as persons. As women were part of the human family of Jesus, so they are part of the family of God's people.

Jesus heals two women and a girl

Jesus left the synagogue and went to the house of Simon. Now Simon's mother-in-law was suffering from a high fever, and they asked Jesus to help her. Standing over her, He rebuked the fever, and it left her. At once she got up and began to serve them.[1]

While He was talking, a ruler of the synagogue entered, knelt down and said, "My daughter has just died, but come, lay your hands on her and she will live." Jesus got up to go with him when a woman who had suffered from haemorrhages for twelve years came up behind Him and touched the fringe of His cloak. She said to herself, "If I only touch His cloak, I will be healed." Jesus turned, saw her and said, "Courage, my daughter, your faith has made you well." Instantly the woman was healed. Then Jesus entered the ruler's house and, seeing the crowd, said, "Go away! The girl is not dead but is sleeping. ... He went in, took the girl by the hand, and she stood up.[2]

Jesus was teaching in one of the synagogues on a Sabbath, and a woman was there with an evil spirit which had crippled her for eighteen years. She was bent over and unable to stand up straight. When Jesus saw her, He called her and said to her, "Woman, you are set free from your infirmity." He laid His hands on her, and immediately she straightened up and praised God. The ruler of the synagogue was indignant because Jesus had healed on the Sabbath. He said to the people, "There are six days in which to work. Come on those days and be healed, but not on the Sabbath." The Lord answered him, "You hypocrites! Do you not, every one of you, untie his ox or donkey from the stall and lead it out to give it water on the Sabbath? Then should not this woman, a daughter of Abraham, whom Satan has bound for eighteen years, be set free from her bondage on the Sabbath day?" When He said this, all his opponents were put to shame, but the people rejoiced over all the wonderful things He was doing.[3]

Jesus' mother and brothers arrived and stood outside. A crowd was sitting around Him and they said to Him, "Your mother and brothers are outside looking for you." "Who are my mother and my brothers?" He asked. Then He looked at those seated in a circle around Him and said, "Here are my mother and my brothers! Whoever does the will of God is my brother and sister and mother." [4]

[1] Luke 4:38-39 [2] Matthew 9:20-25 [3] Luke 13:10-17 [4] Mark 3:31-35

Day 196

Leprosy was a particularly terrible disease because those who suffered from it were not allowed to live with their families. When Jesus healed people of leprosy, He not only cured their disease, but He reunited them with their relatives and friends. So, when Jesus makes people clean from their sins, He unites them with Himself and with the great family of God's people. The more such people know of what Jesus has done for them, the more they want to praise Him and witness to Him among their people.

Jesus heals a man suffering from leprosy

When He [Jesus] came down from the mountain, large crowds followed Him. A man suffering from leprosy came forward, knelt before Him and said, "Lord, if you will, you can make me clean." Jesus stretched out His hand, touched the man and said, "I am willing, be clean!" Immediately he was healed of his leprosy. Then Jesus said to him, "Say nothing about this to anyone. Go, show yourself to the priest and present the offering commanded by Moses, as a testimony to the people." [1] Nevertheless, the news about Jesus spread all the more, so that large crowds of people came to hear Him and to be healed of their diseases. [2]

On His way to Jerusalem, Jesus passed through the region between Samaria and Galilee. As He was going into a village, He was met by ten men who had leprosy. Standing at a distance they called out in a loud voice, "Jesus, Master, have mercy on us!" When He saw them, He said, "Go! Show yourselves to the priests." As they were going along, they were healed. One of them, when he saw that he was healed, came back and praised God in a loud voice. He threw himself down at Jesus' feet and thanked him. He was a Samaritan. Jesus asked him, "Were not all ten of you made clean? Where are the other nine? Was there not even one of them who gave thanks to God, except this foreigner?" Then He said to him, "Get up and go on your way; your faith has made you well." [3]

"I tell you the truth," Jesus said, "no prophet is ever accepted in his home town. The truth is that there were many widows in Israel in the time of Elijah, when the heavens were shut for three and a half years and there was a severe famine throughout the land. Yet Elijah was sent to none of them, but to a widow in Zarephath in the region of Sidon. And there were many in Israel with leprosy in the time of Elisha the prophet. Not one of them was cleansed, except Naaman, and he was a Syrian." [4]

[Paul:] I am speaking to you who are Gentiles. ... If the rejection of them [the Jews] led to the reconciliation of the world to God, what will their acceptance mean but life from the dead? ... Consider, therefore, the kindness and the severity of God: severity to those who have fallen, but kindness to you. [5]

[1] Matthew 8:1-4 [2] Luke 5:15-16 [3] Luke 17:11-18 [4] Luke 4:24-27 [5] Romans 11:13-15,22

Day 197

The man whom Jesus healed had a shrivelled hand. He could not stretch it out to do what hands are meant to do. There are lives like that too. They are shrivelled and cannot be or do what God planned for them. Whether shrivelled because they are like the branch which becomes detached from the vine or like the seed which did not grow because it was sown on rocky places, Jesus can heal and make to flourish.

Jesus heals a man with a withered hand

Going on from there, He [Jesus] went into their synagogue where there was a man with a withered hand. Looking for some reason to accuse Jesus, they [the leaders of the Synagogue] asked Him, "Is it lawful to heal on the Sabbath?" He said to them, "If one of you has only one sheep and it falls into a pit on the Sabbath, will you not take hold of it and lift it out? Of how much greater value is a man than a sheep! Therefore it is lawful to do good on the Sabbath. Then He said to the man, "Stretch out your hand." He stretched it out and it was completely restored, as sound as the other hand."[1]

[Jesus:] "I am the vine, you are the branches. Whoever remains in me and I in him will bear much fruit. Apart from me you can do nothing. If anyone does not remain in me, he is like a branch that is thrown away and withers. Such branches are gathered up, thrown into the fire and burned." [2]

"Listen! A sower went out to sow his seed. As he was sowing the seed, some fell on a path and birds came and ate it up. Some fell on ground full of rocks where it did not have much soil. Because the soil was shallow, the seeds sprang up quickly. When the sun came up, they [the young plants] were scorched and they withered because they had not taken root." [3]

Blessed is the man who does not walk in the counsel of the ungodly nor stands in the path of sinners nor sits in the seat of the scornful. But his delight is in the law of the Eternal-God, and on this he meditates day and night. He is like a tree planted by streams of water, which yields its fruit in season and whose leaf does not wither. Everything he does prospers. Not so the wicked! They are like chaff which the wind drives away. Therefore the wicked will not stand in the judgment, nor sinners in the assembly of the righteous. For the Eternal-God watches over the ways of the righteous, but ways of the wicked will perish. [4]

The righteous will flourish like the palm tree, they will grow like the cedar in Lebanon. For they are planted in the house of the Eternal-God. They will flourish in the courts of our God. They will still bring forth fruit in old age, they will stay green and full of sap." [5]

[1] Matthew 12:9-13   [2] John 15:5-6   [3] Mark 4:3-6   [4] Psalm 1:1-6   [5] Psalms 92:12-15

Day 198

When Jesus healed blind people, it was not only to give them back their physical sight so they could see things around them, it was also to give them spiritual sight so that they could see, that is, understand the even more real and lasting things of the Kingdom of God. Physical sight is a picture of spiritual understanding.

Jesus heals blind people

As Jesus was walking, two blind men followed Him, shouting loudly, "Have mercy on us, Son of David!" He entered a house and the blind men came to Him. He said to them, "Do you believe that I am able to do this?" "Yes, Lord," they replied. Then He touched their eyes, saying, "According to your faith let it be done to you". And their eyes were opened. Jesus ordered them sternly, "See that you let no one know about this." But they went out and spread the news about Him all over that region.[1]

As Jesus came near to Jericho, there was a blind man sitting by the roadside begging. As he heard the crowd going by, he asked what was happening. They told him, "Jesus of Nazareth is passing by." Then he shouted, "Jesus, Son of David, have mercy on me!" Those who were in front told him keep quiet, but he cried out all the more, "Son of David, have mercy on me!" Jesus stood still and ordered that the man be brought to Him. When he came near, Jesus asked him, "What do you want me to do for you?" He replied, "Lord, that I might receive my sight." Jesus said to him, "Receive your sight; your faith has healed you." Immediately he received his sight and followed Jesus, praising God. All the people who saw it, also praised God.[2]

The disciples of John [the Baptist] told him about all these happenings. He called two of them and he sent them to the Lord. ... The men came to Jesus and said to him, "John the Baptist sent us to you to ask you, 'Are you the one who was to come, or are we to expect someone else?" At that time Jesus healed many who had diseases, plagues and evil spirits, and to those who were blind He gave sight.[3]

Jesus went into the temple and drove out all who were buying and selling there. He overturned the tables of the money-changers and the seats of those who were selling doves. He said to them, "It is written, 'My house will be called a house of prayer', but you have made it a 'den of robbers'." The blind and the lame came to Him in the temple, and He healed them.[4]

[Jesus said:] "The Spirit of the Lord is on me, because He has anointed me to preach good news to the poor. He has sent me to announce release for the prisoners and recovery of sight for the blind, to set free the oppressed, to proclaim the year of the Lord's favour." [5]

[1] Matthew 9:27-29   [2] Luke 18:35-43   [3] Luke 7:18-21   [4] Matthew 21:12-14   [5] Luke 4:18-19

Day 199

In the healing of the man who was blind from birth, Jesus made it clear that 'physical blindness' was a picture of 'spiritual blindness'. One of the most important reasons for His coming to earth was that men and women, born spiritual blind in their sin, should have their spiritual sight restored so that they could see right from wrong, and would understand that if they continued in the ways of the world, they would end eternally separated from God, and that He, Jesus, was the only way to eternal life with God.

Jesus heals a man who was blind from birth

As He was walking along, He saw a man who had been blind from birth. His disciples asked Him, "Rabbi, who sinned, this man or his parents, that he was born blind?" Jesus answered, "Neither this man nor his parents sinned, he was born blind to reveal through him the way God works. We must do the work of Him who sent me while as it is day. Night is coming when no one can work. As long as I am in the world, I am the light of the world." When He had said this, He spat on the ground, made some mud with the saliva, spread it on the man's eyes, and said, "Go! Wash in the Pool of Siloam". The man went and washed and came back seeing.

His neighbours and those who knew him by sight as a beggar, asked, "Is this not the same man who used to sit and beg?" Some said, "It is he." Others said, "No! But he looks like him." But he said, "Yes! I am the man." They asked him "How were your eyes opened?" He replied, "The man they call Jesus made some mud and spread it on my eyes. He said to me, "Go to Siloam and wash. So I went and washed, and I received my sight." ...

However, the Jews did not believe that he had been blind and had received his sight until they called for the man's parents and asked them, "Is this your son whom you say was born blind? How is it that now he sees?" The parents answered, "We know this is our son, and that he was born blind, but how he has now come to see, or who opened his eyes, we do not know. He is of age, ask him. Let him speak for himself." Again they called the man who had been blind. "Give glory to God," they said. "This man [Jesus] is a sinner." He replied, "Whether He is a sinner or not, I do not know. But one thing I do know. Once I was blind but now I see!"

Jesus found him and said, "Do you believe in the Son of Man?" The man said, "Who is He, sir, that I may believe in Him." Jesus said to him, "You have seen Him. He is talking to you now. Then the man said, "Lord, I believe," and he worshipped Him.

Jesus said, "I have come into this world for judgment, so that the blind, who do not see, may see, and that those who [think they can] see, may become blind." [1]

[1] John 9:1-11,18-21,24-25,35-39

Day 200

'Physical life' is used in the Bible as a picture of 'spiritual life'. As the body is joined to the spirit to form physical life, so a man or woman who is united with God has 'spiritual life'. 'Physical life' ends at 'physical death'. 'Spiritual life' and 'spiritual death' go on for ever. Everyone is born 'spiritually dead', that is, separated from God, in Satan's family. 'Spiritual life', that is, eternal life with God, is given by Him only through Jesus Christ.

The teaching of Jesus: Life through 'God the Son'

Jesus said to them [the Jewish leaders]: "My Father has been working to this very day, and I, too, am working." This made them even more determined to kill Him, He was not only breaking the Sabbath, but He was calling God His own Father, so making Himself equal with God. Jesus answered them: "I tell you the truth, the Son can do nothing by Himself. He is only able to do what He sees His Father doing. Whatever the Father does, so does the Son. For the Father loves the Son and shows him all that He does. Yes, He will show Him even greater things than these which will amaze you. As [God] the Father raises up the dead and gives them life, so [God] the Son also gives life to whom He wills. In fact, the Father does not judge anyone, but has given all judgment to the Son, so that all may honour the Son, as they honour the Father. He who does not honour the Son, does not honour the Father who sent Him.

"I tell you the truth, whoever hears my word and believes Him who sent me has eternal life and will not come into judgment. He has passed from death to life. Believe me when I say that a time is coming and is now here, when the dead will hear the voice of the Son of God and those who hear will live. As [God] the Father has life in Himself, so He has granted [God] the Son to have life in Himself. And He has given Him authority to judge because He is the Son of Man." [1]

Thomas said to Him [Jesus], "Lord, we do not know where you are going, so how can we know the way?" Jesus said to him, "I am the way and the truth and the life. No one comes to the Father except through me." [2]

Martha answered, "I know he (Lazarus) will rise again in the resurrection at the last day." Jesus said to her, "I am the resurrection and the life. He who believes in me will live, even though he dies, and whoever lives and believes in me will never die. Do you believe this?" [3]

Jesus said to him [Thomas], "Because you have seen me, you believe. Blessed are those who have not seen me and yet have believed. Jesus did many other miraculous signs in the presence of His disciples, which are not written in this book. But these are written so that you may believe that Jesus is the Christ [the Messiah], the Son of God, and that by believing you may have life in His name.[4]

[1] John 5:16-30 [2] John 14:5-6 [3] John 11:24-25 [4] John 20:29-31

Day 201

God ordained one day's rest in seven as right and necessary for everyone. However, it was not to be such a hard law that obeying it meant breaking other, equally important laws. It was the principle that was important. To neglect that principle was harmful. To keep it and in so doing break other laws was hypocrisy. To honour God's day of rest is to honour God who is Lord of that day.

The teaching of Jesus: Lord of the Sabbath

One Sabbath Jesus and His disciples were walking through cornfields. The disciples began to pluck ears of corn. The Pharisees said to Him, "Look, why are they doing what is not lawful on the Sabbath?" He said to them, "Have you never read what David did when he and those who were with him were hungry and in need of food; how, in the days of Abiathar the high priest, he went into the house of God and ate the sacred bread, which it is lawful for the priests alone to eat, and gave some to those who were with him? The Sabbath was made for man, not man for the Sabbath. The Son of Man is, therefore, also Lord of the Sabbath." [1]

On another Sabbath Jesus went into the synagogue and taught. There was a man there whose right hand was withered. The Pharisees and the teachers of the law ... watched Him closely to see if He would heal on the Sabbath. But Jesus knew what they were thinking ... He said to them, "I ask you, is it lawful on the Sabbath to do good or to do evil, to save life or to destroy it? He looked round at them then He said to the man, "Stretch out your hand!" He did so and it was completely restored" [2]

They brought the man who had been blind to the Pharisees. Now the day on which Jesus had mixed the mud and opened the mans' eyes was a Sabbath. ... Some of the Pharisees said, "This man is not from God, for He does not keep the Sabbath." But others said, "How can a man who is a sinner perform such miracles?" So there was a difference of opinion among them. [3]

On the Sabbath we [Paul, Luke and their companions] went outside the city to the river where we expected to find a place of prayer. We sat down and spoke to the women who had gathered there. [4] Every Sabbath, he [Paul] would reason with, and seek to convince, both Jews and Greeks. [5]

[Isaiah:] "If you refrain from trampling the Sabbath under foot, and from doing as you please on my holy day; if you call the Sabbath a delight and the holy day of the Eternal-God honourable, and if you honour it by not going your own ways and not serving your own interests or speaking idle words, then you will find your joy in the Eternal-God, and I will make you ride on the heights of the land and I will feed you on the inheritance of your father Jacob." The mouth of the Eternal-God has spoken.[6]

---

[1] Mark 2:23-28   [2] Luke 6:6-9   [3] John 9:13-16   [4] Acts 16:13   [5] Acts 18:4   [6] Isaiah 58:13-14

Day 202

True happiness comes from being blessed by God. He makes very clear the kind of people that He will bless. Those people who are rich, powerful, of high birth or for whom everything seems to go well are not necessarily happy. Often their happiness comes from the material things they have, and those are not lasting. True happiness comes from what God gives to those with whom He is pleased to live and whom He blesses.

The teaching of Jesus: Those who are blessed

When Jesus saw the crowds, He went up a hill and sat down. His disciples came to Him and He taught them, saying:

Blessed are the poor in spirit, for theirs is the kingdom of heaven.

Blessed are those who mourn, for they will be comforted.

Blessed are the meek, for they will inherit the earth.

Blessed are those who hunger and thirst for righteousness, for they will be filled.

Blessed are the merciful, for they will receive mercy.

Blessed are the pure in heart, for they will see God.

Blessed are the peacemakers, for they will be called sons of God.

Blessed are those who are persecuted because of righteousness, for theirs is the kingdom of heaven.

Blessed are you when people revile you, and persecute you and say all kinds of evil things against you falsely because of me. Rejoice and be glad, for great is your reward in heaven. They persecuted the prophets who were before you in the same way ." [1]

Blessed is the man who fears the Eternal-God and finds great delight in His commands. ... Light dawns in the darkness for the upright, gracious, compassionate and righteous man. It is well with the man who deals generously, lends freely and conducts his affairs with justice. A righteous man will never be shaken and he will be remembered for ever. He will not fear bad news; his heart is secure, trusting in the Eternal-God. [2]

Who will ascend the hill of the Eternal-God? Who will stand in His holy place? He who has clean hands and a pure heart, who does not trust in falsehood or swear by what is false. He will receive blessing from the Eternal-God and righteousness from God his Saviour. [3]

Blessed be the God and Father of our Lord Jesus Christ, who has blessed us with every spiritual blessing of the heavenly realms in Christ. For He chose us in Christ before the foundation of the world, to be holy and blameless before Him in love. He destined us to be adopted as His sons through Jesus Christ. [4]

[1] Matthew 5.1-12   [2] Psalms 112:1,4,5-7   [3] Psalm 24:3-5   [4] Ephesians 1:3

Day 203

Salt gives food its attractive and savoury taste. It is also an antiseptic useful in maintaining hygiene. In the Old Testament it symbolised hospitality. Salt is a picture of the way Christians live which makes the Christian faith attractive and wholesome. Christians who do not live in a truly Christian way harm the cause of Christ. Their testimony spoils the proclamation of the Gospel like salt which has a bad flavour when it is added to good food.

The teaching of Jesus: The salt of the earth

[Jesus said to His disciples:] You are the salt of the earth. If salt loses its salty flavour, what can make it salty again? It is no longer good for anything, except to be thrown out and trampled under foot by men. [1] It is fit neither for the soil nor for the manure heap but to be thrown away. [2] Have salt in yourselves, and be at peace with one another. [3]

The Eternal-God said to Aaron, ... "All the holy offerings that the Israelites present to the Eternal-God I give to you and your sons and daughters as being due to you. It is a covenant of salt before the Eternal-God for ever for both you and your descendants." [4] "No grain offering that you bring to the Eternal-God is to be made with yeast ... All your grain offerings are to be seasoned with salt. Do not leave the 'salt of the covenant' of your God out of any of your grain offerings. Salt is to be added to all your offerings." [5]

[Paul:] Be wise in the way you behave towards those of the outside world [non-Christians]. Make the most of every opportunity. Let your conversation be gracious at all times, seasoned with salt, so that you may know how to answer everyone of them. [6]

[Peter:] No one can tame the tongue. ... With it we praise the Lord and Father, and with it we curse men, who were made in God's likeness. Out of the same mouth come blessing and cursing. My brothers, it ought not to be like that. Can the same spring bring forth both fresh water and salt water? Can a fig tree bear olives, or a grapevine figs? Neither can a salty spring provide fresh water. [7]

The day of the Lord will come like a thief. The heavens will pass away with a loud noise. The elements will be dissolved by fire, and the earth and everything in it will be burned up. Since everything is going to be destroyed in this way, what kind of people ought you to be, as you live holy and godly lives, looking forward to the day of God and hastening its coming? For in that day, when it comes, the heavens will be dissolved by fire, and the elements will be melted in the heat. [8]

[1] Matthew 5:13   [2] Luke 14:35   [2] Mark 9:50   [4] Numbers 18:8,19   [5] Leviticus 2:11-13
[6] Colossians 4:5-6   [7] James 3:9-12   [8] 2 Peter 3:10-12

Day 204

Some of the Jewish leaders thought that Jesus was teaching a different way of serving God other than by obeying the Ten Commandments given to them through Moses. He showed them that, in fact, He was teaching exactly the same truths but at a much deeper level. It was not sufficient not to do wrong. It was equally important to have the right thoughts and intentions to go with the right actions.

The teaching of Jesus: The demands of the Law of Moses

[Jesus said:] "Do not think that I have come to abolish the Law or the Prophets. I have not come to abolish them but to fulfil them. I tell you the truth, until heaven and earth pass away, not even the smallest stroke of a single letter, will disappear from the Law until everything has been accomplished. Whoever breaks one of the least of these commandments and teaches others to do the same will be called least in the kingdom of heaven, but whoever practises them and teaches them will be called great in the kingdom of heaven. I am telling you the truth when I say that unless your righteousness is greater than that of the Pharisees and the scribes, you will never enter the kingdom of heaven.

"You have heard that it was said to the people in the past, 'Do not murder', and 'whoever murders will be liable to judgment.' But I say to you that anyone who is angry with his brother will be subject to judgment. Anyone who insults his brother is answerable to the council [Sanhedrin], but anyone who says, 'Raca' (that is, 'You fool!') will be in danger of the fire of hell. ... You have heard that it was said, 'Do not commit adultery.' But I say to you that anyone who looks at a woman lustfully has already committed adultery with her in his heart.

If your right eye causes you to sin, pluck it out and throw it away. It is better for you to lose one member of your body than for your whole body to be thrown into hell. And if your right hand causes you to sin, cut it off and throw it away. It is better for you to lose one of the members of your body than for your whole body to go to hell. [1]

[Paul:] No one will be judged righteous in God's sight by observing the law. However, it is through the law that we become conscious of sin. But now the righteousness that comes from God, which is apart from the law, has been revealed and to this the Law and the Prophets testify. This righteousness from God comes through faith in Jesus Christ to all who believe. There is no distinction, for all have sinned and fall short of the glory of God, and all are justified freely by His grace through the redemption that is in Christ Jesus. For God [the Father] presented Him [Jesus Christ, God the Son] as a sacrifice of atonement by His blood, received through faith. [2]

[1] Matthew 5:17-22,27-30,43-48   [2] Romans 3:20-25

Day 205

To swear by an oath is the strongest possible kind of promise. The oath binds those who swear by something that is greater than they are. It is right for a Christian to do this when the promise being made is before God, as, for instance, in marriage. Then God is the witness and He is greater than all. This happens too in some courts of law. In ordinary life, it should not be necessary for a Christian to promise by swearing by anyone or anything. A simple promise indicating "Yes! I will," or "No, I will not" is sufficient.

The teaching of Jesus: Taking oaths

[Jesus said:] "Again, you have heard that it was said to the people in times past, 'Do not swear falsely, but keep the oaths that you have made to the Eternal-God.' But I tell you, do not swear at all: either by heaven, for it is God's throne, or by the earth, for it is His footstool, or by Jerusalem, for it is the city of the Great King. Do not swear by your head, for you cannot make one hair white or black. Let your 'Yes' be 'Yes', and your 'No' be 'No'. Anything more than that comes from the evil one." [1]

"Woe to you, blind guides! You say, 'If anyone swears by the sanctuary [Temple], it is nothing; but if anyone swears by the gold of the sanctuary, he is bound by his oath.' You blind fools! Which is greater: the gold, or the sanctuary that has made the gold sacred? You also say, 'If anyone swears by the altar, it means nothing; but if anyone swears by the offering on the altar, he is bound by his oath.' You blind men! Which is greater: the offering, or the altar which makes the gift sacred? Whoever swears by the altar swears by it and by everything on it. And he who swears by the sanctuary swears by it and by the one who dwells in it. Whoever swears by heaven swears by God's throne and by Him who sits on it. [2]

The Eternal-God said to Moses, "Speak to the assembly of Israel and say to them: "Be holy for I, the Eternal-God, your God, am holy. ... Do not swear by my name falsely and so profane the name of your God. I am the Eternal-God. [3]

[James:] Above all, my brothers and sisters, do not swear, either by heaven or by earth or by anything else. Let your "Yes" be 'yes', and your "No" be 'no'. Otherwise you will make yourselves liable to be condemned. [4]

Men indeed swear by something greater than themselves, and the confirmation by an oath of what is said puts an end to all argument. Similarly, God wanted to show clearly the unchangable nature of His purpose to the heirs of what He promised, and so He confirmed it with an oath. God did this so that, by two unchangeable things [His promise and His oath], in which it is impossible for Him to lie, we who have fled for refuge in the hope offered to us, may be greatly encouraged. This hope is a firm and secure anchor for the soul.[5]

[1] Matthew 5:33-37 [2] Matthew 23:16-22 [3] Leviticus 19:1-2,12 [4] James 5:12 [5] Hebrews 6:16-20

Day 206

Love for God or for any person is an attitude of heart and mind which always wants and works for the best for God or for that person. God's commandments are not meant to be kept only because of fear of Him, but out of love for Him. Fear of God is usually the first step. Then God becomes a Friend rather than an enemy. Only those who break His laws need fear Him. Only when we love God can we really love other people, even our enemies.

The teaching of Jesus: Love your enemies

[Jesus said:] "You have heard that it was said, 'An eye for an eye, and a tooth for a tooth.' But I tell you, do not resist an evil doer. If anyone strikes you on the right cheek, turn the other one to him also. And if someone wants to sue you and take your tunic, let him have your cloak as well. If someone forces you to go one mile, go with him the second mile. Give to anyone who begs from you, and do not refuse whoever wants to borrow from you.

"You have heard that it was said, 'You shall love your neighbour and hate your enemy.' But I say to you: love your enemies, pray for those who persecute you, so you may be sons of your Father who is in heaven. He makes His sun to rise on the evil and the good, and sends rain to fall on the righteous and the unrighteous. What reward do you have if you love only those who love you? Do not even the tax collectors do that? And if you greet only your brothers, what are you doing more than anyone else? Even pagans do that? Be perfect, therefore, as your heavenly Father is perfect." [1]

"Who among you, if his son asks for bread, will give him a stone? Or if he asks for a fish, will give him a snake? If you, then, who are evil, know how to give good gifts to your children, how much more will your Father who is in heaven give good things to those who ask Him! In everything, always do to others what you would have them do to you, for this sums up the Law and the Prophets." [2]

"I give you a new commandment: Love one another. As I have loved you, so you are to love one another. Everyone will know that you are my disciples by the way you love one another." [3]

[John:] God is love and whoever lives in God lives in the love of God. Love has been made perfect among us ... because as He is, so are we in the world. There is no fear in love, for fear is driven out by love. We love because He first loved us. If anyone says, "I love God," and hates his brother, he is a liar. Whoever does not love his brother, whom he has seen, cannot love God, whom he has not seen. This is the command we have from Him: Whoever loves God will also love his brother. [4]

[1] Matthew 5:38-48 [2] Matthew 7:9-12 [3] John 13:34-35 [4] 1 John 4:16-21

Day 207

"Let your light shine," said Jesus, and by that He meant that what people said and did should show that they were Christians. He also made it clear that He hated an outward show of religious acts. Actions in public can very easily be hypocritical. Christians are to let their *purity be seen* - honesty, purity, kindness, but to let their *piety be hidden* - prayer, giving, worship.

The teaching of Jesus: Purity and piety

[Jesus said], "Take care not to do your acts of piety before men, in order to be seen by them, for you will then have no reward from your Father in heaven. When you give to the poor, do not sound a trumpet before you, as the hypocrites do in the synagogues and in the streets, so that they may be honoured by men. I tell you the truth, they have their reward in full. When you give to the poor, do not let your left hand know what your right hand is doing. Your Father, who sees what is done in secret, will reward you. When you pray, do not be like the hypocrites, for they love to pray, standing in public places that they may be seen. [1]

Then Jesus said to the crowds and to His disciples: "The scribes and the Pharisees sit in Moses' seat. So obey them and do what they tell you to do. But do not do what they do, for they do not practise what they preach. They tie up heavy loads and place them on people's shoulders, but they themselves are not willing to lift a finger to help them bear them. Everything they do is done for show; they make their phylacteries wide and the tassels on their garments long. They love the places of honour at banquets and the best seats in the synagogues. They love to be greeted with honour in the marketplaces and to have people call them 'Rabbi'. But you are not to be called 'Rabbi', for you have only one teacher [rabbi] and you are all brothers and sisters. Do not call anyone on earth 'father', for you have one Father, and He is in heaven. You are not to be called 'master', for you have one Master, the Christ. He who is greatest among you will be your servant. For whoever exalts himself will be humbled, and whoever humbles himself will be exalted." [2]

Beware of the teachers of the law [scribes] who like to walk around in long robes and love to be greeted in the marketplaces and have the best seats in the synagogues and the places of honour at banquets. They devour widow's houses and make lengthy prayers for show. They will receive the greater condemnation. [3]

[Peter:] Clothe yourselves with humility in your relationships with one another, for God opposes the proud but gives grace to the humble. Humble yourselves under the mighty hand of God, so that He may raise you up at the right time. [4]

[1] Matthew 6:1-4 [2] Matthew 23:1-12 [3] Luke 20:46-47 [4] 1 Peter 5:6

Day 208

God looks after His own people. That does not mean that they do not have to work for a living, plan for the future or keep out of danger. But they know that He is in control and they need not worry or be anxious in the wrong way. If a person puts first being right with God and seeking His will, God will look after the rest.

The teaching of Jesus: Worry and anxiety

[Jesus said:] "Do not worry about your life, what you will eat or what you will drink, or about your body, what you will wear. Does not life mean more than food, and the body more than clothes? Look at the birds of the air; they do not sow or reap or gather food into barns, and yet your heavenly Father feeds them. Are you not worth more than they? Which of you by worrying can add a single hour to the length of your life? And why do you worry about clothes? Consider how the lilies of the field grow; they neither toil nor spin. Yet I tell you, not even Solomon in all his glory was arrayed like one of these. If God clothes the grass of the field like that, grass which is here today and tomorrow is thrown into the fire, will He not much more clothe you, O you of little faith? So do not worry, saying, 'What shall we eat?' or 'What shall we drink?' or 'What shall we wear?' It is the pagans [non-Christians] who chase after all these things. Your heavenly Father knows what you need. Seek first His kingdom and His righteousness, and all these things will be given to you as well. So do not worry about tomorrow, for tomorrow will take care of itself. Each day has enough trouble of its own.[1]

When you are accused before synagogues, magistrates and authorities, do not be anxious about how to defend yourselves and what you will say, for [God] the Holy Spirit will teach you at that moment what to say. ... Do not be afraid, little flock, for it pleases [God] your Father to give you the kingdom. Sell what you possess and give to the poor. Make for yourselves purses which will not wear out and put your treasure in heaven where no thief comes near nor moth destroys. For where your treasure is, there your heart will be also." [2]

[Paul:] Do not be anxious about anything, but in everything, by prayer and supplication, with thanksgiving, let your requests be known to God. And the peace of God, which passes all understanding, will guard your hearts and minds in Christ Jesus.[3]

[Peter:] Unload all your anxiety on Him because He cares for you.[4]

Delight yourself in the Eternal-God and He will give you the desires of your heart. Commit your way to the Eternal-God, trust in Him and He will bring it to pass. He will make your uprightness shine like the dawn and the justice of your cause like the sun at noonday. [5]

[1] Matthew 6:25-34   [2] Luke 12:11-12,32,34   [3] Philippians 4:6-7   [4] 1 Peter 5:7   [5] Psalm 37:4-6

Day 209

Only God knows what someone else is thinking. He alone can judge why other people do what they do. Christians can and must judge whether other peoples' actions appear to be right or wrong. Sometimes they can help those who are blind or indifferent to their wrong actions. However, no one has the right to condemn anyone else when their knowledge of that person is so imperfect.

The teaching of Jesus: Judging others

[Jesus said:] "Do not judge, so that you will not be judged. As you judge others, so you will be judged. You will be measured by the measure with which you measure others. Why do you stare at the speck of dust in your brother's eye, and take no notice of the beam of wood in your own eye? How can you say to your brother, 'Let me take the speck out of your eye,' while there is a wooden beam in your own eye? You hypocrite, first take the wooden beam out of your own eye, and then you will see clearly to take the speck from your brother's eye." [1]

"Do not judge, and you will not be judged. Do not condemn, and you will not be condemned. Forgive, and you will be forgiven. Give, and it will be given to you. A good measure, pressed down, shaken together and running over, will be put into your lap. For the measure you use in giving will be the measure with which you receive."[2]

Brothers and sisters, do not speak evil of each other. Whoever speaks evil against his brother or judges him, speaks against the law and passes judgment on it. When you judge the law, you do not keep it, but you sit in judgment on it. There is only one Lawgiver and Judge who is able to save and to destroy. Who are you, then, to judge your neighbour? [3]

[James:] Judge nothing before the appointed time when the Lord comes. He will bring to light the things that are hidden in darkness and He will bring to light the motives of men's hearts. Then every one will receive from God the praise due to him.[4]

[Paul:] Christ died and rose again for this purpose, that He might be the Lord of both the dead and the living. Then why do you judge your brother or look down on him? We will all stand before the judgment seat of God. It is written: "'As surely as I live,' says the Eternal-God, 'Every knee will bow before me and every tongue will acknowledge God.'" Each one of us will give an account of himself to God. Therefore let us cease passing judgment on each other. Instead, let us resolve never to put any stumbling-block or obstacle in the way of a brother. ... Blessed is the man who has no reason to judge himself condemned in doing what he believes to be right. [5]

[1] Matthew 7:1-5 [2] Luke 6:37-38 [3] James 4:11-12 [4] 1 Corinthians 4:5 [5] Romans 14:9-12

Day 210

From time to time, Jesus took his disciples to some quiet place to pray. They watched and listened while He prayed. They saw the difference between this way of praying and the formal, often lifeless way they saw their religious leaders praying. They wanted to be able to pray like Jesus did. He showed them that praying was talking to His Father— 'God the Father', who had become their Father too.

The teaching of Jesus: How to pray

Once, when Jesus had finished praying, one of His disciples said to Him, "Lord, teach us to pray, as John [the Baptist] taught his disciples." He said to them, "When you pray, say:

Father, hallowed be your name, your kingdom come.

Give us each day our daily bread.

Forgive us our sins, for we ourselves forgive everyone who sins against us.

Lead us not into temptation."

Then He said to them, "Suppose one of you has a friend, and you go to him at midnight and say, 'Friend, lend me three loaves of bread, for a friend of mine who is on a journey has just arrived, and I have nothing to set before him.' And the friend answers from inside [his house], 'Don't disturb me. The door is locked, and my children are with me in bed. I cannot get up and give you anything.' I tell you, although he will not get up and give him the bread because he is his friend, yet because of the man persistence, he will get up and give him as much as he needs.

"So I say to you: Ask and it will be given to you, seek and you will find; knock and the door will be opened to you. For he who asks receives, he who seeks finds, and to him who knocks, the door will be opened." [1]

[The word of God through Isaiah:] I will create new heavens and a new earth. ... Before they call, I will answer and while they are speaking I will hear. [2]

Praise is due to you in Zion, O God, to you shall our vows be performed. O you who hears prayer, to you all people will come. When our sins overwhelmed us, you forgave our transgressions. ... You answer us by awesome deeds of deliverance, O God our Saviour, the hope of all the ends of the earth and those on the farthest seas. [3]

[God] the [Holy] Spirit helps us in our weakness for we do not know what we ought to pray for, but [God] the [Holy] Spirit himself intercedes for us with sighs that speak of yearnings which words cannot express. And He who searches the hearts of people knows the mind of [God] the [Holy] Spirit, because He intercedes for the saints in accordance with the will of God. [4] *[Jesus said:] "If you remain in me and my words remain in you, whatever you ask for will be given you."* [5]

[1] Luke 11:1-8 [2] Isaiah 65:17,24 [3] Psalm 65:1-3,5 [4] Romans 8:26-27 [5] John 15:7

Day 211

During their lifetime, God gives people a choice: to stay in the kingdom of Satan in which they are born, or to repent of their sin, trust in Jesus Christ and be 'born again' into the kingdom of God. Jesus pictured that choice as between going through a wide gate, which was easy to pass through, in the family of Satan, or to enter by a narrow gate, to the family of God.

The teaching of Jesus: The few who will be in heaven

[Jesus said:] "Enter through the narrow gate, for wide is the gate and broad is the way that leads to destruction, and many go along that road. But narrow is the gate that leads to life and the road is hard, and those who find it are few. [1]

Jesus went through the towns and villages teaching as He made His way to Jerusalem. Someone asked Him, "Lord, will there be only a few people saved?" He said to them, "Make every effort to enter through the narrow gate, because many, I tell you, will try to enter and will not be able to. When the owner of the house gets up and closes the door, and you are outside knocking and saying, 'Lord, open the door for us,' He will answer, 'I do not know you or where you come from.' Then you will say, 'We ate and drank with you, and you taught in our streets.' Then He will say, 'I do not know you or where you come from. Go away from me, all you evildoers!' There will be weeping and gnashing of teeth when you see Abraham, Isaac and Jacob and all the prophets in the kingdom of God, but you yourselves driven out. People will come from east and west and from north and south, and will sit down in their places at the feast in the kingdom of God. Indeed, there are some who are last now, but who will be first then, and some who are first now, who will be last then." [2]

Jesus told them a parable. The kingdom of heaven is like a king who gave a wedding banquet for his son. ... When the king came in to see his guests he saw a man who was not wearing wedding clothes. ... The king said to the attendants, "Tie him hand and foot and throw him out into the darkness outside ... for many are called but few are chosen." [3]

"I tell you the truth, the man who does not enter the sheep pen by the gate, but climbs in by some other way, is a thief and a robber. The man who enters by the gate is the shepherd of his sheep." Jesus said again, "I tell you the truth, I am the gate for the sheep. All who ever came before me were thieves and robbers, but the sheep did not listen to them. I am the gate; whoever enters through me will be saved. He will come in and go out, and find pasture. The thief comes only to steal and kill and destroy; I have come that they may have life, and have it to the full." [4]

[1] Matthew 7:13-14 [2] Luke 13:22-30 [3] Matthew 22:1- 5,11-14 [4] John 10:1,7-10

Day 212

A tree is known by its fruit. So men and women are known by God and recognised by people according to the way they live. Good deeds are the fruit of good and honest hearts. When God makes the heart clean and lives within a person, that shows itself in good actions. Such actions count for eternity because they come from God. Evil actions can only come from an evil heart. True followers of Jesus show that fact by the character of their actions.

The teaching of Jesus: True and false followers

[Jesus said:] "Beware of false prophets, who come to you appearing to be sheep, but inwardly they are ferocious wolves. You will recognise them by their fruits. Do people pick grapes from thorn-bushes or figs from thistles? A good tree bears good fruit, but a bad tree bears bad fruit. A good tree cannot bear bad fruit and a bad tree cannot bear good fruit. Every tree that does not bear good fruit is cut down and thrown into the fire. It is by their fruit that you will know them.

"Not everyone who says to me, 'Lord, Lord, will enter the kingdom of heaven, but only those who do the will of my Father who is in heaven. Many will say to me on that day, 'Lord, Lord, did we not prophesy, drive out demons and perform many miracles in your name?' Then I will say to them, 'I never knew you. Go away from me, you evildoers.'" [1]

[Solomon:] He who ploughs evil will reap it, and the rod of his anger will fall on himself. A generous man will be blessed, for he shares his food with the poor. [2]

[Paul:] Do not be deceived. God is not mocked. You reap what you sow. If you sow to please your sinful nature, from that sinful nature you will reap corruption, but if you sow to please [God] the [Holy] Spirit, from [God] the [Holy] Spirit you will reap eternal life. [3] For once you were darkness, but now you are light in the Lord. Live as children of light, for the fruit of the light is expressed in all goodness, righteousness and truth. Seek to find out what pleases the Lord. Take no part in the unfruitful deeds of darkness, but rather expose them. [4]

The deeds of the sinful nature are obvious to all: fornication, impurity, debauchery, sorcery, hatred, jealousy, anger, selfish ambition, dissensions, factions, envy, drunkenness, orgies, and the like. I warn you again, as I have already done, that those who live like this will not inherit the kingdom of God. But the fruit of [God] the [Holy] Spirit is love, joy, peace, patience, kindness, goodness, faithfulness, gentleness and self-discipline. Against such things there is no law. Those who belong to Christ Jesus have crucified the sinful nature with its passions and desires. We live by [God] the [Holy] Spirit; let us then be guided by Him. [5]

---

[1] Matthew 7:15-23 [2] Proverbs 22:8-9 [3] Galatians 6:7-8 [4] Ephesians 5:8-11 [5] Galatians 5:19-23

Day 213

The security of every building depends on its foundations. The greatest foolishness is to live as if the foundations for one's life did not matter. The beginning of wisdom to build one's life on the only true foundation: God and the truth He has revealed in Jesus Christ. He is the only foundation which will survive death and lead to eternal security.

The teaching of Jesus: The wise and the foolish builders

[Jesus said:] "Everyone who hears these my words and acts on them is like a wise man who built his house on the rock. The rain came down, the floods rose, and the winds blew and beat against that house, yet it did not fall, because it was built on rock. Everyone who hears these my words and does not act on them is like a foolish man who built his house on sand. The rain came down, the floods rose, and the winds blew and beat against that house, and it fell and great was its fall." [1]

[Job:] Can a man, who is mortal, be more righteous than God? Can he be more pure than his Maker? If God does not trust His angels and finds fault with them, how can those stand before Him who live in houses of clay, whose foundations are dust and who are more easily crushed than a moth? [2]

As for God, His way is perfect. The word of the Eternal-God is faultless. He is a shield for all who take refuge in Him. For who is God besides the Eternal-God? And who is a Rock except our God? [3]

This is what the Sovereign Eternal-God says: "See, I am laying a stone in Zion, a tested stone, a precious cornerstone, a sure foundation. Whoever trusts in Him will never be shaken.[4] God's foundation stands secure, sealed with this inscription: "The Lord knows those who are His," and, "Let everyone who confesses the name of the Lord turn away from wickedness." [5]

[Paul to Timothy:] Instruct those who are rich in this world not to be proud or to put their trust in uncertain wealth. Tell them to do good and to be rich in good deeds, to be generous and ready to share what they have. In this way they will store up riches for themselves which will be a firm foundation for the age to come." [6]

[Paul:] No other foundation can anyone lay than that which is already laid, which is Jesus Christ. If any man builds on this foundation with gold, silver, precious stones, wood, hay or straw, his work will be revealed for, when the day comes, it will be brought to light. It will be revealed by fire which will test the worth of each man's work. If what he has done survives, he will received his reward. If it is burned up, he will suffer loss but he himself will be saved, but only as one who escapes through burning flames. [7]

---

[1] Matthew 7:24-27   [2] Job 4:17-19   [3] Psalms 18:30-31   [4] Isaiah 28:16   [5] 2 Timothy 2:19
[6] 1 Timothy 6:17-19   [7] 1 Corinthians 3:11-15

Day 214

Jesus Christ could raise people from the dead because He is the source of life. He is the only person who has died, been raised from the dead, and has not then died again. He is alive for evermore. When He died on the Cross and rose again from the grave, He not only showed that He was alive physically, but that He was still alive spiritually and could make alive all those who believe in Him.

Jesus raises to life a widow's son.

Jesus went to a town called Nain. His disciples and a large crowd went along with Him. As He came near to the town gate, the body of a man who had died was being carried out. He was the only son of his mother, and she was a widow. A large crowd from the town accompanied her. When the Lord saw her, He had compassion on her and said, "Do not weep." Then He went forward and touched the coffin, and those who were carrying it stood still. He said, "Young man, I say to you, get up!" The dead man sat up and began to speak. Jesus gave him to his mother. They were all seized with fear and praised God, saying, "A great prophet has appeared among us, God has come to help His people." This word about Jesus spread throughout Judea and the surrounding country. [1]

When Jesus had cried out again in a loud voice, He gave up His spirit. At that moment the curtain of the temple was torn in two from top to bottom. The earth shook and the rocks split. The tombs were opened and the bodies of many holy people who had died were raised to life. They came out of the tombs and, after the resurrection of Jesus, they went into the holy city and appeared to many people. [2]

"I tell you the truth, whoever hears my word and believes Him who sent me has eternal life. He will not be condemned because He has passed from death to life. I tell you the truth, a time is coming and is now here, when the dead will hear the voice of the Son of God and those who hear it will live. For, as [God] the Father has life in himself, so He has granted to [God] the Son to have life in Himself." [3]

"And this is the will of Him who sent me, that I should not lose any of all that He has given me, but that I should raise them up at the last day. It is the will of [God] my Father that everyone who looks to [God] the Son and believes in Him should have eternal life, and I will raise him up at the last day." [4]

Jesus said to her, "Your brother will rise again." Martha replied, "I know he will rise again in the resurrection at the last day." Jesus said to her, "I am the resurrection and the life. Whoever believes in me, though he dies, he will live. Whoever lives and believes in me will never die. Do you believe this?" [5]

---

[1] Luke 7:11-17 [2] Matthew 27:50-53 [3] John 5:24-26 [4] John 6:39-40 [5] John 11:23-26

Day 215

God is merciful but His mercy never extends to those who do not repent of their sin, that is, change their minds about that sin, and hence, their actions. God is also all-knowing and He knows how people would have responded if they had heard His Good News in Jesus Christ. It is on this principle that the cities of Sodom and Gomorrah were less guilty before God than the cities of Korazin and Bethsaida. The greater the knowledge the greater is the responsibility for living according to that knowledge.

Jesus rebukes unrepentant cities

Jesus began to denounce the cities in which He had performed most of His miracles because they did not repent. "Woe to you, Korazin!" He said, "Woe to you, Bethsaida! If the miracles that were performed in you had been performed in Tyre and Sidon, they would have repented in sackcloth and ashes a long time ago. But I tell you, it will be more bearable for Tyre and Sidon on the day of judgment than for you. And you, Capernaum, will you be exalted up to the heavens? No, you will be brought down to Hades [the place of the dead]. If the miracles that were performed in you had been performed in Sodom, it would be here to this day. But I tell you, it will be more bearable for Sodom on the day of Judgment than for you." [1]

The men of Nineveh will stand up with this generation at the judgment and condemn it for they repented at the preaching of Jonah, and here there is One who is greater than Jonah. The Queen of the South will stand up with this generation at the judgment and condemn it. She came from the ends of the earth to listen to the wisdom of Solomon, and here there is One who is greater than Solomon. [2]

Jesus sent out these twelve [disciples], saying, "Do not go among the Gentiles and do not enter any town of the Samaritans. Go rather to the lost sheep of the house Israel. ... If anyone will not welcome you or listen to your words, as you leave that home or town, shake the dust of it from your feet. I tell you the truth, it will be more bearable for the land of Sodom and Gomorrah on the day of judgment than for that town." [3]

[Jesus said:] "Not everyone who says to me, 'Lord, Lord,' will enter the kingdom of heaven, but only He who does the will of my Father who is in heaven. Many will say to me on that day, 'Lord, Lord, have we not prophesied in your name, and in your name driven out demons and performed many miracles?' Then I will say to them plainly, 'I never knew you. Depart from me, you evildoers!'" [4]

[James:] Be doers of the word and not merely listeners, so deceiving yourselves. Whoever listens to the word but does not obey it, is like a man who looks in a mirror, sees what he looks like, then goes away and forgets the kind of person he is. [5]

[1] Matthew 11:20-24   [2] Matthew 12:41-42   [3] Matthew 10:5-6,14-15   [4] Matthew 7:21-23   [5] James 1:22-24

Day 216

The depth of our love for God depends on how much we are aware of God's love for us. The sinful woman whom Jesus forgave, loved Jesus greatly because she knew the depth of the sin which Jesus had forgiven and the kind of life from which He had saved her. The Pharisees who were watching what Jesus was doing, were not conscious of any sin. They did not, therefore, have any love for Him who could have forgiven them their sin.

Jesus is anointed by a sinful woman

One of the Pharisees asked Jesus to have dinner with him, so He went into his house and reclined at the table. A woman who was a sinner in that town learned that Jesus was eating at the Pharisee's house. She brought an alabaster jar of perfume and, standing behind Him, she wept and began to wet His feet with her tears. Then she wiped them with her hair, kissed them and poured the perfume on them.

When the Pharisee who had invited Him saw this, he said to himself, "If this man were a prophet, He would know what kind of woman was touching Him for she is a sinner." Jesus answered him, "Simon, I have something to say to you." "Go on, teacher, speak!" He said, "A certain moneylender had two debtors. One owed him five hundred denarii, and the other fifty. Neither of them had the means to pay him back, so he freely forgave them both. Now which of them will love him more?" Simon replied, "I suppose it was the one who was forgiven most." "You are quite right," Jesus said. Then He turned towards the woman and said to Simon, "Do you see this woman? When I came into your house, you did not give me any water for my feet, but she has wet my feet with her tears and wiped them with her hair. You gave me no kiss, but this woman, from the time I came in has not stopped kissing my feet. You did not put oil on my head, but she has poured perfume on my feet. Therefore, I tell you, her sins are forgiven because she loved much. He who is forgiven little loves little." Then Jesus said to her, "Your sins are forgiven." The other guests began to say among themselves, "Who is this who even forgives sins?" Jesus said to the woman, "Your faith has saved you, go in peace." [1]

He [God] chose us in Him [Jesus] before the foundation of the world to be holy and blameless in His sight. In love He planned for us to be adopted as His sons through Jesus Christ, in accordance with His pleasure and will so that we might be to the praise of His glorious grace, which He has freely given us in His [the Father's] Beloved. In him we have redemption through His blood, the forgiveness of sins, in accordance with the riches of grace, which He has lavished on us with all wisdom and understanding. [2]

[1] Luke 7:36-50   [2] Ephesians 1:4-8

Day 217

The Jews were looking for a great Messiah to save them from their conquerors, the Romans. They found it hard to understand why 'death' should have to come to their Messiah before there could be 'life'. Jesus showed His disciples that He was the Messiah and unless they understood what 'death' was going to be for Him, they could never understand what the 'life' that He was going to give them meant. The 'sign of Jonah', as applied to Jesus, indicated that He would, like Jonah who spent three nights in the "belly of a big fish', spend three nights in the 'belly of death', then rise to life again.

The teaching of Jesus: The sign of Jonah

Some of the scribes and Pharisees said to Him [Jesus], "Teacher, we would like to see you perform a miracle." He answered them, "An evil and adulterous generation asks for a miraculous sign. No sign will be given it except the sign of the prophet Jonah. For as Jonah was three days and three nights in the belly of a sea monster, so the Son of Man will be three days and three nights in the heart of the earth. The men of Nineveh will stand up with this generation at the judgment and condemn it; for they repented at the preaching of Jonah, and now there is here One who is greater than Jonah. [1]

From that time on Jesus began to show His disciples that He must go to Jerusalem and suffer many things at the hands of the elders, chief priests and scribes, and that He must be killed and on the third day be raised to life. Peter took Him aside and began to rebuke Him. He said, "God forbid, Lord, that this should ever happen to you!" Jesus turned away from Peter and said, "Get behind me, Satan! You are a stumbling-block to me for you are concerned not with the things of God, but with the things of men." Then Jesus said to His disciples, "If anyone will follow me, he must deny himself and take up his cross and follow me. For whoever wants to save his life will lose it, but whoever loses his life for my sake will find it." [2]

They [the women] found the stone rolled away from the tomb. ... While they were perplexed about this, suddenly two men in dazzling clothes stood beside them. The women were terrified and bowed down with their faces to the ground, but the men said to them, "Why do you look for the living among the dead? He is not here. He has risen! Remember how He told you, while He was with you in Galilee: 'The Son of Man must be delivered into the hands of sinful men and be crucified, and on the third day rise again." Then they remembered His words. [3]

Jesus answered them, "The hour has come for the Son of Man to be glorified. I tell you the truth, unless a grain of wheat falls to the earth and dies, it remains a single seed. But if it dies, it yields a rich harvest" [4]

---

[1] Matthew 12:38-41 [2] Matthew 16:21-26 [3] Luke 24:2-8 [4] John 12:23-24

Day 218

The mother and father, brothers and sisters of Jesus in the home at Nazareth were ordinary people. It took them a long time to realise that one of their family was unlike any of them or anyone else. Neighbours were even more perplexed. Jesus explained that His heavenly family was a much greater one than His human one.

Jesus' mother and brothers

Coming to His home town, He [Jesus] taught in the synagogue there, and they were amazed and said, "Where did this man get this wisdom and these miraculous powers? Is this not the carpenter's son? Is not His mother called Mary, and are not His brothers James, Joseph, Simon and Judas? Are not all His sisters with us here? Where then did this man get all this?" And they would not accept Him." [1]

While Jesus was talking to the crowd, His mother and brothers stood outside, wanting to speak to Him. Someone said to Him, "Your mother and brothers are standing outside, wanting to speak to you." He replied, "Who is my mother, and who are my brothers?" Stretching out his hand to point to His disciples, He said, "Here are my mother and my brothers. For whoever does the will of my Father in heaven is my brother and my sister and my mother." [2] "My mother and brothers are those who listen to the word of God and do it." [3]

On the third day there was a wedding at Cana in Galilee. Jesus' mother was there, and Jesus and His disciples had also been invited to the wedding. ... After this He went to Capernaum with His mother and brothers and His disciples. There they stayed for a few days. [4]

The Jewish Feast of Tabernacles was near so the brothers of Jesus said to Him, "Leave here and go to Judea, so that your disciples may see the miracles you do. No one who wants to be known acts in secret. As you are doing these things, show yourself to the world." Even His own brothers did not believe in Him. [5]

All these [disciples] joined together constantly in prayer, together with the women and Mary the mother of Jesus, and His brothers. [6]

"I tell you the truth," Jesus said, "everyone who has left home or brothers or sisters or mother or father or children or fields for my sake and for the sake of the gospel will receive a hundred times as much in this age - homes, brothers, sisters, mothers, children and fields - and with them, persecutions, and in the age to come, eternal life." [7]

[1] Matthew 13:54-57 [2] Matthew 12:46-50 [3] Luke 8:21 [4] John 2:1,12 [5] John 7:2-5
[6] Acts 1:14 [7] Mark 10:29-30

Day 219

It is very easy to think that, because no one else knows our thoughts, then neither does God. Not only is nothing hidden from Him now, but all will be revealed to everyone when Jesus comes to earth again. Then 'God the Father' will judge everyone openly. Christians do not fear that judgment because they have not tried to hide anything from Him in this life. As they have repented of their sin and trusted in Jesus for forgiveness, there will be nothing to condemn.

The teaching of Jesus: Nothing is hidden from God

A crowd gathered which was so large that people were trampling on one another, Jesus spoke first to His disciples, saying: "Be on your guard against the yeast of the Pharisees which is hypocrisy. There is nothing covered up which will not be uncovered. What you have said in the dark will be heard in the light, and what you have whispered in someone's ear behind closed doors will be proclaimed from the housetops." [1]

"No one lights a lamp and then hides it in a jar or puts it under a bed, but he puts it on a stand, so that those who come in can see the light. For there is nothing hidden that will not be disclosed, and there is nothing secret which will not be made known and brought out into the open. Be careful, therefore, how you listen, for to him who has, more will be given, and to him who does not have, even what he thinks he has will be taken from him." [2]

"Do not be afraid of them [those who persecute you]. There is nothing covered up which that will not be uncovered, there is nothing hidden that will not be made known. What I say to you in the dark, speak in the light; what is whispered in your ear, proclaim from the housetops." [3]

From heaven the Eternal-God looks down on all mankind. From his dwelling-place, He who forms the hearts of all men and considers all their doings, watches over all the inhabitants of the earth. [4] For a man's ways are in full view of the Eternal-God, and He examines all that He does. [5]

Do not make judgments before the appointed time when the Lord comes. He will bring to light what is hidden in darkness and will expose the motives of the heart. Then everyone will receive whatever praise is due to them from God. [6]

The word of God is living and active. It is sharper than any two-edged sword. It pierces even between soul and spirit, and between joints and marrow, and it judges the thoughts and attitudes of the heart. There is nothing in all creation which is hidden from God's sight; everything is open and laid bare before the eyes of Him to whom we must give an account of ourselves. [7]

[1] Luke 12:1-3   [2] Luke 8:16-18   [3] Matthew 10:26-27   [4] Psalm 33:13-15   [5] Proverbs 5:21
[6] 1 Corinthian 4:5-6   [7] Hebrews 4:12-13

Day 220

The Bible calls a person a fool who acts foolishly in the light of what he or she knows. The greatest folly is to live as if God does not exist and to act as if He will not require an account of each person's life. What this world calls riches can be of little or great worth depending on how God sees them and the way they are used.

The teaching of Jesus: Warnings about riches

Someone in the crowd said to Him, "Teacher, tell my brother to divide the family inheritance with me." Jesus replied, "Man, who has made me a judge over you?" Then He said to them, " Take care! Be on your guard against all kinds of greed. The life of a man does not consist in the abundance of his possessions."

Then He told them this parable: "The ground of a rich man yielded a good crop. He thought to himself, 'What shall I do? I do not have enough room to store my harvest." Then he said, 'This is what I will do. I will pull down my storehouses and build bigger ones, and there I will store all my grain and my goods. And I will say to myself, 'You have plenty of good things laid up for many years. Take it easy: eat, drink and be merry.' But God said to Him, 'You fool! This very night your life will be required of you. Now who will get all the things which you have prepared for yourself!' So it will be with all who store up things for themselves but are not rich towards God." [1]

The man who gains riches by unjust means is like a partridge that hatches eggs it did not lay. When his days are half gone, his riches will desert him, and in the end he will be shown to be a fool. [2] Do not wear yourself out to get rich; be wise enough to show restraint. Take a look at riches, and they are gone. They make wings for themselves and fly off into the sky like an eagle. [3] Man goes to and fro like a shadow. He rushes about heaping riches, but only in vain for he does not know who will get them.[4] If riches increase, do not set your heart on them.[5] It is fitting and good for a man to eat and to drink and to find enjoyment in his work during the brief life God has given him. Furthermore, when God gives him riches and possessions and enables him to enjoy them, this is God's gift to him. [6]

[Jesus:] No one can serve two masters. Either he will hate one and love the other, or he will be devoted to one and despise the other. You cannot serve both God and money. [7]

[Jesus said:] Make purses for yourselves that will not wear out, an inexhaustible treasure in heaven, where no thief comes near and no moth destroys. For where your treasure is, there will your heart be also. [8]

[1] Luke 12:13-21   [2] Jeremiah 17:11   [3] Proverbs 23:4-5   [4] Psalms 39:6   [5] Psalms 62:10
[6] Ecclesiastes 5:18-19   [7] Matthew 6:24   [8] Luke 12:33-34

Day 221

No one knows when Jesus will come again. That fact should keep Christians alert so that they will be ready should He come soon. Even if His coming is delayed, however, we may be called by death to meet Him at any time. We should, therefore, always be watchful so that we may be ready to meet Him either at death on when He comes again.

The teaching of Jesus: His coming to earth again

[Jesus said:] "Be dressed ready for action and keep your lamps alight. Be like men waiting for their master to return from a wedding feast, so that when he comes and knocks, they will be ready to open the door to him. Blessed are the servants whose master finds them watching when he comes. I tell you the truth, he will have them sitting at the table to eat while he serves them. Blessed are those servants if, at whatever time he comes, he finds them ready for him. ... But know this: if the owner of a house had known at what time a thief was coming, he would not have allowed his house to be broken into. You also must be ready, because the Son of Man will come at a time when you do not expect him.

Peter said to Him, "Lord, are telling this parable for us, or for everyone?" The Lord said, "Work out for yourselves the kind of steward who is faithful and wise, whom a master puts in charge of his servants to give them their allowance of food at the proper time? Happy will be that steward when the master finds him so doing when he returns. I tell you the truth, he will put him over all his possessions. But suppose that steward says to himself, 'My master is delayed in coming,' and he begins to beat the menservants and maidservants, and to eat and drink and get drunk. The master of that steward will come on a day when he does not expect him and at an hour that he does not know. He will cut him off and assign him a place with those who are unfaithful. [1]

[Paul:] But you, brothers and sisters, are not in darkness for that day to overtake you by surprise like a thief. You are all sons of light and sons of the day. We do not belong either to the night or to darkness. So then, let us not sleep, as others do, but let us be alert and self-disciplined. [2]

[Jesus:] "I tell you the truth, this generation will certainly not pass away until all these things have taken place. Heaven and earth will pass away, but my words will never pass away. Watch, therefore, or your hearts will be weighed down with self-indulgence, drunkenness and the anxieties of life, and that day will come on you unexpectedly like a trap. For it will come upon all who live on the face of the whole earth. Be always alert, and pray that you may have the strength to endure all that is to take place, and then stand before the Son of Man." [3]

---

[1] Luke 12:35-46   [2] 1 Thessalonians 5:4-6   [3] Luke 21:32-36

Day 222

The power of evil is such that it will destroy families if at all possible. When a man or woman stands up for what is right and true, those who oppose him or her the strongest may well be the members of that person's own family. Only a strong sense of belonging to God and to His family will keep a person true to Him when that happens.

The teaching of Jesus: Not peace but division

[Jesus said to His disciples] "I am sending you out like sheep in the midst of wolves. Be as wise as serpents and as innocent as doves. Be on your guard against men who will hand you over to the local councils and flog you in their synagogues. You will be brought before governors and kings for my sake, to bear witness to them and to the Gentiles. When they arrest you, do not worry about what you will say or how you will say it. You will be given what to say at that time, for it will not be you speaking, but the [Holy] Spirit of [God] your Father speaking through you. Brother will betray brother to death, and a father his child. Children will rise against their parents and have them put to death. You will be hated by all men because of me, but he who stands firm to the end will be saved. When they persecute you in one place, flee to another. I tell you the truth, you will not have gone through all the cities of Israel before the Son of Man comes. ...

"Do not think that I have come to bring peace to the earth. I have not come to bring peace, but a sword. For I have come to set a man against his father, a daughter against her mother, a daughter-in-law against her mother-in-law. A man's enemies will be the members of his own household." [1]

"Brother will betray brother to death, and a father his child. Children will rise up against their parents and have them put to death. You will be hated by everybody for my Names' sake. But he who stands firm to the end will be saved. [2]

"I have come to bring fire on the earth. I sincerely wish it were already kindled! But I have a baptism with which to be baptized and I am distressed until it is completed. Do you think that I have come to bring peace on earth? No, I say to you, but rather division. From now on there will be five in one family who will be divided, three against two and two against three. ... When you see a cloud rising in the west you say it is going to rain ... you know how to interpret the face of the sky, ... How is it that you do not know how to interpret the present times." [3]

[Micah:] Do not trust a neighbour nor put confidence in a friend. Guard your mouth, even with her whom you embrace. For ... a man's enemies are the members of his own household. [4]

[1] Matthew 10:17-23,34-36   [2] Mark 13:12-13   [3] Luke 12:49-56   [4] Micah 7:5-6

Day 223

There is a great deal of pain and suffering in the world caused by accidents, hatred and greed. God allows this so that we may see what life is like under the rule of Satan. God offers everyone now the opportunity to repent and be saved into His kingdom where, one day in the future, in His heaven, nothing like that will ever happen. 'Repent now!' means changing one's mind now from the world's way of thinking to God's.

The teaching of Jesus: Pain and suffering

Some people came to Jesus and told Him about the Galileans whose blood Pilate had mixed with their sacrifices. Jesus said to them, "Do you think that those Galileans were greater sinners than all the other Galileans because they suffered this way? I tell you, No! But unless you repent, you too will all perish. Or those eighteen who were killed when the tower in Siloam fell on them; do you think that they were more guilty than everyone else living in Jerusalem? I tell you, No! But unless you repent, you too will all perish.

Then he told them this parable: "A man had a fig-tree planted in his vineyard. He went to it looking for fruit but he did not find any. So he said to the vinedresser, 'For three years now I have come looking for fruit on this fig-tree and I have not found any. Cut it down! Why should it go on taking up ground?' 'Sir,' the man replied, 'leave it alone for one more year. I will dig round it and put manure on it. Perhaps it will bear fruit next year. If not, it can be cut down.'" [1]

Jesus saw a man who had been blind from birth. His disciples asked him, "Rabbi, who sinned, this man or his parents, that he was born blind?" Jesus answered, "Neither this man nor his parents sinned, he was born blind to reveal through him the way God works. [2]

[The word of God through Ezekiel:] "Repent and turn away from all your transgressions so that sin will not be your downfall. ... Why will you die, O house of Israel? I take no pleasure in the death of anyone, declares the Eternal-God. Repent and live!" [3]

When the people heard this, they were cut to the heart and said to Peter and the other apostles, "Brothers, what shall we do?" Peter said to them, "Repent and be baptised, every one of you, in the name of Jesus Christ for the forgiveness of your sins, and you will receive the gift of [God] the Holy Spirit." [4]

In the past, God overlooked the times of man's ignorance, but now He commands all people everywhere to repent. For He has set a day when He will judge the world in righteousness by the man [Jesus] He has appointed. He has confirmed this to all men by raising Him from the dead. [5]

[1] Luke 13:1-8   [2] John 9:1-3   [3] Ezekiel 18:30-32   [4] Acts 2:37-39   [5] Acts 17:30-31

Day 224

This parable is about both sowing the seed and the soil in which the seed is planted. The seed sown is the same but it falls on different kinds of soil. The soils represent different people. The difference between the 'soils' in the parable and people, is that people are responsible for the kind of soil they are. How a person responds to the word of God, depends on the will as well as on the understanding, on the heart as well as the mind.

The teaching of Jesus: The sower and the soils

When a big crowd had gathered, He [Jesus] told this parable: "A sower went out to sow His seed. Some seed fell along the path and it was trampled under foot, and the birds of the air ate it up. Some seed fell on rocky soil. When it came up, the plants withered because they had no moisture. Other seed fell among thorns, and the thorns grew with it and choked the plants. Still other seed fell on to good soil. It grew up and yielded a crop which was a hundred times more than was sown." When He had said this, He called out, "Let him hear who has ears to hear."

Then His disciples asked Him the meaning of this parable. He said, "To you it has been given to know the secrets of the kingdom of God, but for others I speak in parables so that 'looking they may not perceive, and hearing they may not understand.' Now this is the meaning of the parable. The seed is the word of God. The path is those people who receive it, and then the devil comes and takes away the word from their hearts so that they do not believe and be saved. The rock is those who, when they hear the word, receive it with joy but they have no root; they believe for a while, but in a time of testing, they fall away. The soil where the seed fell among thorns is those who hear, but as they go on their way they are choked by life's cares, riches and pleasures, and they do not grow to maturity. The good soil is those who hear the word with a noble and good heart, retain it, and by patient endurance yield a good crop. [1]

[Hosea:] Sow righteousness for yourselves and reap unfailing love. Break up your uncultivated ground for it is time to seek the Eternal-God. ... Because you have trusted in your own strength, you have planted wickedness, and you have reaped injustice." [2] "They sow the wind and they will reap the whirlwind." [3]

[Haggai:] This is what the Eternal-God, the Almighty, says: "Give careful thought to your ways. You have sown much, but you have reaped little. You eat, but you never have enough. You drink but never have your fill. You clothe yourselves, but you are not warm. You earn wages to put them in a bag with holes." [4]

[Paul:] Let us not become weary in doing what is good, for in due time we will reap a harvest, if we do not give up. [5]

[1] Luke 8:4-8,9,11-15 [2] Hosea 10:12-13 [3] Hosea 8:7 [4] Haggai 1:5-6 [5] Galatians 6:9

Day 225

Jesus explains who are represented by the wheat and the weeds. He also explains who sows the wheat and who sows the weeds. God and Satan are both active. While they are growing, wheat and weeds look very much alike. The day of reaping is yet to come, when the wheat and the weeds will be separated. For most people, it is difficult to tell who are Christians and who are not. But the day is coming when God will separate them for eternal life with Him or for eternal separation from Him.

The teaching of Jesus: The wheat and the weeds

Jesus told them another parable: "The kingdom of heaven is like a man who sowed good seed in his field. But while everyone was asleep, his enemy came and sowed weeds among the wheat, and then went away. When the wheat sprouted then the weeds also appeared. The servants of the owner came to him and said, 'Sir, did you not you sow good seed in your field? Then where did the weeds come from?' 'An enemy has done this,' he replied. The servants said to him, 'Do you want us to go and pull up the weeds?' 'No,' he answered, 'while you are pulling up the weeds, you may pull up the wheat as well. Let both grow together until the harvest when I will say to the harvesters: First gather the weeds and tie them in bundles to be burned, then gather the wheat and put it into my barn.'" ...

Then He left the crowd and went into the house. His disciples came to Him and said, "Explain to us the parable of the weeds in the field." He answered, "The one who sowed the good seed is the Son of Man. The field is the world, and the good seed is the sons of the kingdom. The weeds are the sons of the evil one, and the enemy who sowed them is the devil. The harvest is the end of the age, and the reapers are angels. As the weeds are pulled up and burned with the fire, so it will be at the end of the age. The Son of Man will send out His angels, and they will gather out of His kingdom everything that causes sin and all evildoers. They will throw them into the fiery furnace where there will be weeping and gnashing of teeth. Then the righteous will shine like the sun in the kingdom of their Father. Let him who has ears hear." [1]

[The angel said to Daniel] "At that time every one of your people whose name is written in the book will be delivered. Many who sleep in the dust of the earth will awake, some to everlasting life and some to shame and everlasting contempt." [2]

[John the Baptist:] "I baptise you with water for repentance, but He who is coming after me is more powerful than I am. I am not worthy to carry His sandals. He will baptise you with [God] the Holy Spirit and with fire. His winnowing-fork is in His hand, and He will clear out His threshing-floor and gather His wheat into the barn; but He will burn up the chaff with unquenchable fire." [3]

[1] Matthew 13:24-30,36-43   [2] Daniel 12:1-2   [3] Matthew 3:11-12

Day 226

The seed of the mustard tree is one of smallest there is. It is difficult to believe that from such a small seed grows such a large tree. Jesus taught that it is not so much how much faith we have that is important, but how real is the little faith we have and in whom we put that faith. When our small faith is in the great God, then actions that seem like moving mountains become possible. The growth of God's kingdom depends not on our little faith, but in the greatness of God in whom we put our faith.

The teaching of Jesus: The kingdom of God is like a mustard seed

He [Jesus] told them another parable: "The kingdom of heaven is like a mustard seed which someone took and planted in his field. It is the smallest of all the seeds, yet when it has grown, it becomes a tree, the largest of garden plants, so that the birds of the air come and shelter in its branches." [1]

When they came to the crowd, a man came to Jesus and knelt before Him saying. "Lord, have mercy on my son, he has epilepsy and suffers greatly. He frequently falls into the fire or into the water. I brought him to your disciples, but they were not able to heal him." Jesus said , "O unbelieving and perverse generation, how long shall I be with you? How long shall I bear with you? Bring the boy here to me." Jesus rebuked the demon. It came out of the boy and he was healed instantly. Then the disciples came to Jesus privately and asked, "Why could we not drive it out? He said to them, "Because of the smallness of your faith. I tell you the truth, if you have faith as small as a mustard seed, you will say to this mountain, 'Move from here to there' and it will move. Nothing will be impossible for you." [2]

The apostles said to the Lord, "Increase our faith!" He replied, "If you had faith the size of a mustard seed, you would say to this mulberry tree, 'Be uprooted and planted in the sea', and it would obey you." [3]

[Habukkuk:] The earth will be filled with the knowledge of the Eternal-God as the waters cover the sea.. [4] Every day they [the disciples] met together in the courts of the temple and they broke bread in their homes and ate together with glad and generous hearts ... and the Lord added daily to their number those who were being saved. [5] The word of God spread and the number of disciples increased greatly in Jerusalem and a large number of priests were obedient to the faith. [6]

I will declare the decree of the Eternal-God: He said to me, "You are my Son; today I have become your Father. Ask of me, and I will make the nations your inheritance, the ends of the earth your possession. You will break them with an iron rod; you will dash them to pieces like pottery." [7]

[1] Matthew 13:31-32 [2] Matthew 17:14-20 [3] Luke 17:5-6 [4] Habukkuk 2:14 [5] Acts 2:46-47
[6] Acts 6:7 [7] Psalms 2:7-9

Day 227

Yeast has two important qualities. It is part of the old dough which is carried into the new, and a little yeast affects a lot of dough. It was for the first quality that the Israelites were forbidden to put yeast from Egypt into their Passover bread. Here, however, Jesus speaks of the way in which a very little yeast can work its way through a large amount of dough.

The teaching of Jesus: Good and bad yeast

Jesus said, "What is the kingdom of God like? It is like yeast which a woman took and mixed with three measures of flour until it was leavened all through." [1]

When the disciples reached the other side of the lake, they found that they had forgotten to take any bread. "Be careful," Jesus said to them. "Be on your guard against the yeast of the Pharisees and Sadducees." They said to one another, "He said this because we did not bring any bread." Jesus, aware of what they were saying, said, "You of little faith, why are you talking among yourselves about having no bread? Do you still not understand? Do you not remember the five loaves for the five thousand, and how many basketfuls you gathered? Or the seven loaves for the four thousand, and how many basketfuls you gathered? How is it that you fail to understand that I was not talking to you about bread? But be on your guard against the yeast of the Pharisees and Sadducees. Then they understood that He was not telling them to beware of the yeast used in bread, but of the teaching of the Pharisees and Sadducees. [2]

The Eternal-God said to Moses and Aaron: "This day [the Passover] shall be for you a day of remembrance. ... For seven days you are to eat unleavened bread. On the first day, put away the yeast from your houses, for whoever eats anything with yeast in it, from the first until the seventh day shall be cut off from Israel. ... Observe the Feast of Unleavened Bread, because it was on this very day that I brought your people out of Egypt. ... For seven days no yeast is to be found in your houses." [3]

[Paul to the Galatians:] You were running a good race. Who hindered you from obeying the truth? That kind of persuasion does not come from Him who called you. A little yeast leavens through the whole batch of dough. [4]

Your boasting is not good. Do you not know that a little yeast works through the whole batch of dough? Clean out the old yeast that you may be a new batch untouched by yeast, as you really are. For Christ, our Passover [Lamb], has been sacrificed. Therefore let us keep the Feast, not with the old yeast, the yeast of malice and wickedness, but with the unleavened bread of sincerity and truth. [5]

[1] Luke 13:20-21 [2] Matthew 16:5-12 [3] Exodus 12:1,14-15,17-19 [4] Galatians 5:7-9 [5] 1 Corinthians 5:6-8

Day 228

These parables of the kingdom of heaven can be understood in two ways. Either, people are the treasure which Jesus found in a field (the world) and then paid a great price in order to get them. Or, Jesus is the treasure, and when we find Him we give up everything in order to follow Him. In both interpretations, the treasure is so valuable that it is worth giving everything that one possesses in order to gain it. Jesus gave up His glory in heaven and died a cruel death for us, His treasure. We can do no less than give everything we have and are, to gain Him as our treasure.

The teaching of Jesus: The hidden treasure and the pearl

[Jesus said:] "The kingdom of heaven is like treasure hidden in a field, which a man finds, then hides it again. In his joy he goes and sells all that he has and buys that field. Again, the kingdom of heaven is like a merchant in search of fine pearls. When he finds one of great value, he goes away and sells everything he has and buys it." [1]

By faith Moses, when he was grown up, refused to be known as the son of Pharaoh's daughter. He chose rather to share the oppression of the people of God rather than enjoy the fleeting pleasures of sin. He considered the contempt suffered for the sake of Christ as greater wealth than all the treasures of Egypt, because he was looking to the future for his reward. [2]

[Paul:] It is we who belong to Christ, who worship God by His Spirit and put no confidence in the flesh [human grounds for pride]. ... I have more grounds for putting my confidence in the flesh than anyone else. I was circumcised [as a Jew] on the eighth day, of the people of Israel, of the tribe of Benjamin, a Hebrew son of Hebrews; as to the law [of Moses], I was a Pharisee; as for zeal, I was a persecutor of the church; as for righteousness according to the law [of Moses], I was blameless. But whatever I had that could be counted as gain, I now consider as loss for the sake of Christ. What is more, I count everything as loss compared to the surpassing greatness of knowing Christ Jesus my Lord, for whose sake I have suffered the loss of all things. I consider them refuse, that I may gain Christ and be found in Him, not having a righteousness of my own that comes from obedience of the law, but that which is through faith in Christ, the righteousness that comes from God by faith. I want to know Christ and the power of His resurrection and the fellowship of His suffering by becoming like Him in His death, that if possible I may attain to the resurrection from the dead. [3]

You guide me with your counsel, and afterwards you will receive me into glory. Whom have I in heaven but you? And I desire nothing on earth besides you. My flesh and my heart may fail, but God is the strength of my heart and my portion for ever. [4]

[1] Matthew 13:44-45   [2] Hebrews 11:24-26   [3] Philippians 3:4-11   [4] Psalm 73:24-26

Day 229

Fishing was an occupation the Jews knew very well. Sorting out the good, edible, fishes from those they could not eat was something they could understand easily. It happened every day on the shores of Lake Galilee. It was not so easy for them to accept that one day God is going to sort out those who have been made good in Jesus Christ from those who are 'bad' because they have rejected Him and His offer of mercy.

The teaching of Jesus: The fish net

[Jesus said] "The kingdom of heaven is like a net that was thrown into the lake and caught all kinds of fish. When it was full, the fishermen dragged it up on the shore. Then they sat down and sorted them out, putting the good fish into baskets and throwing the worthless ones away. So it will be at the end of the age. The angels will come and separate the wicked from the righteous and throw them into the furnace of fire, where there will be weeping and gnashing of teeth. [1]

"When the Son of Man comes in His glory, and all the angels with Him, He will sit on the throne of His glory. All the nations will be gathered before Him, and He will separate people one from another as a shepherd separates the sheep from the goats. He will put the sheep on His right hand and the goats on His left." [2]

We give thanks for you, brothers and sisters, because your faith is growing greater and your love for one another is increasing. This is evidence that God's judgment is right and you will be counted worthy of the kingdom of God, for which you are suffering. God is indeed just to repay with trouble those who trouble you and give relief to you who are troubled, as well as to us, when the Lord Jesus is revealed from heaven in blazing fire, with His powerful angels. He will inflict His judgment on those who do not know God and do not obey the gospel of our Lord Jesus. They will be punished with everlasting destruction and separated from the presence of the Lord and from the glory of His power when He comes to be glorified in His holy people and to be marvelled at among all those who have believed, including yourselves, because you believed our testimony to you. [3]

[John] I saw [in a vision] the dead, great and small, standing there before the throne ... and another book was opened which is the book of life. ... Anyone whose name was not found written in the book of life, was thrown into the lake of fire. [4]

[Jesus said:] "He [God the Father] has given Him [Jesus Christ, God the Son] authority to execute judgment because He is the Son of Man. Do not be surprised at this, for a time is coming when all who are in their graves will hear His voice and come out: those who have done good will come out to the resurrection to life, and those have done evil will come out to face their judgment. [5]

[1] Matthew 13:47-50 [2] Matthew 25:31-33 [3] 2 Thessalonians 1:5-10 [4] Revelation 20:11-15 [5] John 5:26-29

Day 230

Jesus showed His power on many occasions but never as dramatically as when He calmed a raging sea while His disciples feared for their lives in a small boat. Jesus was master of every situation, even the most frightening storm. He had created the wind and the water. Calming the sea was easy for Him compared with what He did on the Cross to gain our reconciliation with Him. Calming our guilty consciences was very costly for Him, but He had the power to do that too.

Jesus calms the storm

One day He [Jesus] said to His disciples, "Let us go across to the other side of the lake." So they set out. As they were sailing, He fell asleep. A squall came down on the lake and the boat was filling with water. They were in great danger. The disciples came to Him and woke Him, saying, "Master, Master, we are going to perish!" He woke up and rebuked the wind and the raging waves. The storm abated and there was a calm. He said to them, "Where is your faith?" They were afraid and in their amazement asked one another, "Who is this that He commands even the winds and the water and they obey Him." [1]

O give thanks to the Eternal-God for He is good. ... Some go down to the sea in ships and do business in great mighty waters. These see the works of the Eternal-God and His wonders in the deep. For He gives His command and raises the stormy wind. They [those in ships] mount up to the heavens and go down again to the depths. In their peril their courage melts away. They reel and stagger like drunken men at their wits' end. Then they cry out to the Eternal-God in their trouble, and He brings them to their desired haven. He stills the storm to a whisper, He hushes the waves of the sea. Then they were glad when it grew calm, and He guided them to their desired haven. O that men would praise the Eternal-God for His goodness. [2]

By awesome deeds of righteousness, you answer us by delivering us, O God, our Saviour. You who are the hope of all the ends of the earth and of the farthest seas. You, who are of great might, formed the mountains by your power. You still the roaring of the seas and of their waves, and you still the turmoil of nations. [3]

[The word of God by Jeremiah] Listen to this, you foolish and senseless people. "Do you not fear me?" says the Eternal-God. "Do you not tremble in my presence? I made the sand to be a boundary for the sea, and an everlasting barrier which it cannot cross. The waves of the sea may toss and roar, but they cannot pass over it. [4]

[Paul:] Now to Him who, by His power that is at work within us, is able to do immeasurably more than all we ask or imagine, to Him be glory in the church and in Christ Jesus throughout all generations, for ever and ever! Amen. [5]

[1] Luke 8:22-25   [2] Psalms 107:23-31   [3] Psalm 65:5-7   [4] Jeremiah 5:21-22   [5] Ephesians 3:20-21

Day 231

Whenever Jesus raised someone from physical death to life the miracle vindicated who He was - God. No one else could do such things. It demonstrated that He had defeated 'physical death'. Equally, it demonstrated that He had the power to defeat 'spiritual death' that is, spiritual separation from God His Father, for Himself and for all who trust in Him. That was the victory He won by His death on the Cross.

Jesus raises a dead girl to life

Jesus again crossed over by boat to the other side of the lake. A large crowd gathered round Him there by the shore of the lake. One of the rulers of the synagogue, named Jairus, came to Jesus, fell at His feet and earnestly pleaded with Him, saying, "My little daughter is dying. Come and lay your hands on Her so that she will be healed and live." So Jesus went with him. ...

While Jesus was still speaking [to the woman whom He had just healed of a haemorrhage], some men came from the house of Jairus, the ruler of the synagogue, saying, "Your daughter is dead. Why trouble the teacher any more?" Jesus overheard what they were saying but ignored it and said to the ruler of the synagogue, "Do not be afraid; only believe." He let no one follow Him except Peter, James and John the brother of James. When they came to the home of the ruler of the synagogue, Jesus saw a commotion of people crying and wailing loudly. He went in and said to them, "Why all this commotion and wailing? The little girl is not dead but asleep." And they laughed at Him. Then He put them all out, and, with the child's father and mother and the disciples who were Him, went in where the child was. He took her by the hand and said to her, "Talitha cumi!" (which means, 'Little girl, I say to you, get up!') Immediately the girl stood up and walked around (she was twelve years old). At this they were utterly amazed. [1]

[Paul to Timothy] Do not be ashamed to testify about our Lord ... who has saved us and called us to be holy, not according to what we have done but because of His own purpose and grace. This grace was given us in Christ Jesus before the world was created, but it has now been made known through the appearing of our Saviour, Christ Jesus, who has destroyed death and has brought life and immortality to light through the gospel. ... I am not ashamed, for I know whom I have believed, and am convinced that He is able to guard what I have committed to Him until that day. [2]

Christ has indeed been raised from the dead, the first-fruits of those who have fallen asleep. Since it was through a man that death came, so it is that through a Man comes the resurrection of the dead. For as in Adam all die, so in Christ all will be made alive. [3]

[1] Mark 5:21-43 [2] 2 Timothy 1:8-10,12 [3] 1 Corinthians 15:20-22

Day 232

Jesus did not fit into people's ideas of what a great man should be. They reasoned that someone special could not be an ordinary person, as they were. Jesus was the most truly ordinary person there has ever been, ordinary in the sense that He was what God planned everyone to be. Because He was perfect, He was also the most extraordinary Person there has ever been. Everybody else has been spoiled by sin and it is natural for them to reject perfection when it shows up their imperfection.

Jesus is rejected again

Coming to His home town, He [Jesus] taught the people in their synagogue, and they were amazed. "Where did this man get this wisdom and these miraculous powers?"... And they took offence at him. But Jesus said to them, "a prophet is not without honour except in his home town and in his own house," And He did not do many miracles there because of their lack of faith.[1]

[Isaiah:] He [the Servant of God] grew up before Him like a tender plant and like a root out of dry ground. He had no form or majesty that would attract us to Him, there was nothing in His appearance that we should desire Him. He was despised and rejected by men, a man of sorrows, and acquainted with grief. Like one from whom men hide their faces He was despised, and we thought nothing of him. We saw him as stricken, smitten and afflicted by God, but surely He bore our infirmities and carried our sorrows. He was wounded for our transgressions, He was bruised for our iniquities. The punishment that brings us peace was upon Him and by His stripes we are healed.[2]

[Nehemiah prayed before the people:] "They, our forefathers, became arrogant and stiff-necked and paid no heed to your commands. They refused to listen and did not remember the miracles you performed among them. But you are a God who is forgiving, gracious and merciful, slow to anger and of great love. ...They were disobedient and rebelled against you; they put your law behind their backs."[3]

To the wicked God says: "You hate my instruction and cast my words behind you. Then what right have you to recite my laws or take my covenant on your lips? ... You give your mouth to evil and harness your tongue to deceit. ... These things you have done and I kept silent. You thought that I was altogether like you."[4]

He [Jesus] came into the world, and though the world was made through Him, the world did not recognise Him. He came to His own, but His own did not receive Him. Yet to as many as received Him and believed in His name, He gave the right to become children of God, born not of blood, nor of the will of the flesh, nor of the will of man, but of God.[5]

---

[1] Matthew 13:54-58 [2] Isaiah 53:2-5 [3] Nehemiah 9:16-17,26 [4] Psalm 50:16-17,19,21 [5] John 1:10-13

Day 233

The message that Jesus came to proclaim was for the world, not only for the Jews. So He began by sending out His disciples first to the people around them. Later He was to send them out much further afield. "Go into all the world ..." was one of His last commands. This 'sending out' of His disciples was a lesson to prepare them for what was to come.

Jesus sends out the twelve disciples

He [Jesus] called His twelve disciples to Him and gave them authority to drive out unclean spirits and to heal every disease and every sickness. ... Jesus sent out these twelve with these instructions: "Do not go among the Gentiles and do not enter any town of the Samaritans. Go rather to the lost sheep of the house of Israel. As you go, preach saying: 'The kingdom of heaven is near.' Heal the sick, raise the dead, cleanse those who have leprosy, drive out demons. You have received freely, give freely. Do not take any gold, silver or copper in your purses. Take no provisions for the journey, or extra tunic, nor sandals, nor a staff, for the worker deserves his food. Whatever town or village you enter, look for some worthy person and stay at his house until you leave. As you enter the house, give it your greetings. If the home is deserving, let your peace rest on it; if it is not, let your peace return to you. If anyone will not welcome you or listen to your words, shake off the dust from your feet as you leave that house or town. I tell you, it will be more tolerable for Sodom and Gomorrah in the day of judgment than for that town. I am sending you out as sheep among wolves. Therefore be as wise as snakes and as innocent as doves. [1] They went out and preached that men should repent. They drove out many demons and anointed with oil many sick people and healed them. [2]

The apostles gathered round Jesus and reported to Him all they had done and taught. Then, because so many people were coming and going that they did not even have a chance to eat, He said to them, "Come with me by yourselves to a quiet place and get some rest." [3] Then He took them on their own and withdrew to a city called Bethsaida. [4]

[Jesus prayed to God, His Father] "Now I am coming to you, but I say these things while I am still in the world, so that my joy may be made complete in them. I have given them your word and the world has hated them, for they are not of the world as I am not of the world. I do not ask you to take them out of the world but that you protect them from the evil one. They are not of the world, as I am not of the world. Sanctify them by the truth. Your word is truth. As you sent me into the world, so I have sent them into the world. [5]

[1] Matthew 10:1-16 [2] Mark 6:12-13 [3] Mark 6:30-31 [4] Luke 9:10 [5] John 17:13-18

Day 234

Sheep need a shepherd. So people, who are lost in this world on their own, need a Shepherd to guide them. Jesus not only had compassion on people when He saw them confused and wandering about aimlessly but He came to be their Good Shepherd. God intended everyone to live a full and joyous life as one of His sheep. People are blind who do not recognise that Jesus is the only true Shepherd.

Jesus has compassion on the crowds

Jesus went through all the towns and villages, teaching in their synagogues, preaching the good news of the kingdom and healing every disease and every sickness. When He saw the crowds, He had compassion on them, because they were harassed and helpless, like sheep without a shepherd. Then He said to His disciples, "The harvest is plentiful but the workers are few. Therefore pray the Lord of the harvest to thrust out workers into his harvest." [1]

[The word of the Eternal-God through Zechariah:] The teraphim [idols] speak nonsense and the diviners see visions that are lies. Those who dream tell dreams that are false, they comfort in vain. Therefore the people wander like sheep; they suffer for lack of a shepherd. [2]

"This is what the Sovereign Eternal-God says: [through the prophet Ezekiel] I myself will search for my sheep and seek them out. As a shepherd seeks out his sheep when the flock is scattered, so will I seek out my sheep. I will rescue them from all the places where they have been scattered in the day of clouds and darkness. I will bring them out from the nations and gather them from the far countries, and I will bring them into their own land. I will feed them on the mountains of Israel, by the water-courses and in all the inhabited places in the land. I will feed them with good pasture and their grazing land will be the high mountains of Israel. There they will lie down in good grazing land, and there they will feed on rich pasture on the mountains of Israel. I myself will feed my sheep and make them lie down," declares the Sovereign Eternal-God. "I will search for the lost and I will bring back those who have strayed. I will bind up the injured and strengthen the weak. But the fat and the strong I will feed with justice." [3]

We all, like sheep, have gone astray. Every one of us has turned to his own way, and the Eternal-God has laid on Him the iniquity of us all. [4]

May the God of peace, who brought back from the dead our Lord Jesus, that great Shepherd of the sheep, make you complete through the blood of the eternal covenant, and equip you with every good thing to do His will, and may He work in you what pleases Him, through Jesus Christ, to whom be glory for ever and ever. Amen. [5]

[1] Matthew 9:35-38   [2] Zechariah 10:2   [3] Ezekiel 34:11   [4] Isaiah 53:6   [5] Hebrews 13:20-21

Day 235

John the Baptist was the last of the Old Testament prophets who suffered for their stand for God and for the truth. He needed great courage to condemn the sin of someone in a high government position. John fulfilled the mission for which God had brought him into the world and prepared him. That is all God desires of every man and woman.

The death of John the Baptist

At that time Herod the Tetrarch heard the reports about Jesus. He said to his attendants, "This is John the Baptist. He has been raised from the dead! That is why miraculous powers are at work in him." Now Herod had arrested John, bound him and put him in prison because of Herodias, his brother Philip's wife. John had said to him: "It is not lawful for you to have her." Although Herod wanted to kill John, he was afraid of the people, because they regarded him as a prophet.

On Herod's birthday, the daughter of Herodias danced for them and pleased Herod so much that he promised on oath to give her whatever she asked. She, prompted by her mother, said, "Give me the head of John the Baptist here on a platter." The king was distressed, but because of his oaths and his guests, he ordered that her request be granted and John was beheaded in the prison. His head was brought in on a platter and given to the girl, who brought it to her mother. John's disciples came, took his body and buried it. Then they went and told Jesus. [1]

And what more shall I say? Time would fail me to tell of Gideon, Barak, Samson, Jephthah, David, Samuel and the prophets, who through faith conquered kingdoms, administered justice. ... Others were tortured and refused to be released, so that they might gain a better resurrection. Some were mocked and flogged, while others were chained and put in prison. They were stoned to death; they were sawn in two; they were slaughtered by the sword. They went about in sheepskins and goatskins, destitute, persecuted and cruelly treated. The world was not worthy of them. They roamed in deserts and mountains, and in caves and holes in the ground. These were all commended for their faith, yet none of them received the fulfilment of what had been promised. [2]

[John saw in his vision:] When He [the Lamb] broke open the fifth seal, I saw at the foot of the altar, the souls of those who had been slain for the word of God and for their testimony. ... Each of them was given a white robe and they were told to rest a little longer until the number of those who would be killed was complete. [3]

Therefore, since we are surrounded by so great a cloud of witnesses, let us lay aside everything that hinders us and the sin that so easily entangles us, and let us run with perseverance the race that is set before us. [4]

[1] Matthew 14:1-12 [2] Hebrews 11:32-39 [3] Revelation 6:9,11 [4] Hebrews 12:1

Day 236

The miracles of Jesus were not simply a way of demonstrating His power as God, but they had meanings which His hearers did not find it easy to understand. Ordinary bread satisfies a person's physical hunger. There is another hunger which ordinary bread can never satisfy. That is, a spiritual hunger for a meaning for life, for power to live in a sinful world and for a hope after death. Jesus can and does satisfy that hunger.

Jesus feeds five thousand people

Later, Jesus crossed to the far shore of the Sea of Galilee (that is, the Sea of Tiberias), A great crowd of people followed Him because they saw the miraculous signs which He performed on the sick. Jesus went up the side of a mountain and sat down there with His disciples. Now the Passover, a Jewish Feast, was near. Jesus looked up and saw a great crowd coming towards Him. He said to Philip, "Where are we to buy bread for all these people to eat?" He said this to test him, for He knew what he was going to do. Philip answered Him, "Two hundred denarii would not be enough to buy enough bread for each one to have a little!" Another of His disciples, Andrew, Simon Peter's brother, said to him, "There is a boy here with five small barley loaves and two small fish, but what are they among so many?" Jesus said, "Make all the people sit down."

There was plenty of grass in that place, and the men sat down, about five thousand of them. Jesus took the loaves and when He had given thanks, He distributed them to those who were seated. He did the same with the fish. Everyone had as much as they wanted. When they had all had enough, He said to His disciples, "Gather up the fragments which are left over so that nothing is wasted." So they gathered them up and from the five barley loaves left over by those who had eaten, they filled twelve baskets. When the people saw the miraculous sign that Jesus did, they said, "Surely this is the Prophet who is to come into the world." Jesus, knowing that they intended to seize Him and make Him king by force, withdrew again to a mountain by Himself. ... So the people, finding that neither Jesus nor His disciples were there, got into small boats and went to Capernaum looking for Jesus. ... They said to Jesus, "What miraculous sign will you give us that we may see it and believe you? ... Our forefathers ate the manna in the desert. It is written: 'He gave them bread from heaven to eat.'" Jesus said to them, "I tell you the truth, it was not Moses who gave you the bread from heaven, but it is my Father who gives you the true bread from heaven. For the Bread of God is He who comes down from heaven and gives life to the world."

Jesus said to them, "I am the Bread of Life. He who comes to me will never be hungry and he who believes in me will never be thirsty." [1]

[1] John 6:1-15,24,30-35

Day 237

On several occasions Jesus showed that He was Lord of the universe. He was there when it was created. He still had the power to control it. It was a power that amazed the disciples. They had yet to learn that His was the even greater power to forgive their sins and transfer them from the kingdom of Satan to the Kingdom of God.

Jesus calms the sea again

Jesus made the disciples get into the boat and go ahead of Him to the other side, while He sent the crowd away. After He had dismissed them, He went up the mountain to pray by Himself. When evening came, He was there alone but the boat was already well away from the land and was being buffeted by the waves because the wind was against it. During the fourth watch of the night Jesus came to them walking on the lake. When the disciples saw Him walking on the sea, they were terrified and cried out in fear, "It is a ghost," Immediately Jesus said to them: "Take courage! It is I. Do not be afraid." Peter answered Him, "Lord, if it is you, command me to come to you on the water." "Come," He said. Peter got out of the boat, walked on the water and came to Jesus. But when he saw the strong wind, he was afraid and, beginning to sink, cried out, "Lord, save me!" Immediately Jesus reached out His hand and caught him, and said, "O you of little faith, why did you doubt?" When they got into the boat, the wind died down. Then those who were in the boat knelt down and worshipped Him, saying, "Truly you are the Son of God." [1]

Let the heavens praise your wonders, O Lord, your faithfulness in the assembly of the holy angels, for who in the heavens can be compared with you. Who in the heavens can be compared with the Eternal-God. ... You rule the raging of the sea; when the waves mount up, you still them. ... The heavens and the earth are yours, so is the world and all that is in it. [2]

[Isaiah:] Was it not you who dried up the sea, the waters of the great deep, who made a way in the depths of the sea so that the redeemed might cross over? ... "I am the Eternal-God, your God, who stirs up the seas so that its waves roar." [3]

Then the Eternal-God answered Job out of the storm. ... "Where were you when I laid the foundations of the earth? Who determined its dimensions or who stretched a measuring line across it. ... Who shut up the sea behind doors when it burst out from the womb, when I made the clouds its garment and thick darkness its swaddling bands, when I fixed boundaries for it and set its doors and bars in place, when I said, 'Thus far you may come and no farther; here is where your proud waves are stopped?' ... Have you explored the springs of the sea, or walked in the recesses of the deep? [4]

[1] Matthew 14:22-42 [2] Psalm 89:5-6, 9-11 [3] Isaiah 51:10,15 [4] Job 38:1,4-5, 8-11,16

Day 238

When we eat bread it is to satisfy our physical hunger. Jesus uses this picture of bread to show us that only through His life can men and women be spiritually satisfied. To eat the 'Bread of life' and to 'feed spiritually' means to believe in Jesus Christ and to experience Him and the meaning He gives to life.

Jesus - the Bread of Life

When they [the crowds] found Him [Jesus] on the other side of the lake, they asked Him, "Rabbi, when did you get here?" Jesus answered, "I tell you the truth, you are looking for me, not because you saw miraculous signs but because you were fed with the loaves and were satisfied. Do not work for food that perishes, but for food that endures to eternal life which the Son of Man will give you. It is on Him that God the Father has set His seal of approval." Then they said to Him, "What must we do to do the works of God?" Jesus answered, "This is the work of God which He asks of you: to believe in the One whom He has sent. ... I am the bread of life. He who comes to me will never go hungry, and he who believes in me will never be thirsty. ... Your forefathers ate the manna in the wilderness and they died. This is the bread that comes from heaven which anyone may eat and not die. I am the living bread which came down from heaven. ... The bread that I will give for the life of the world is my flesh. Then the Jews argued among themselves, one saying to another, "How can this man give us His flesh to eat? Jesus said to them, "I tell you the truth, you can have no [spiritual] life in you unless you eat the flesh of the Son of Man and drink His blood. Whoever eats my flesh and drinks my blood has eternal life and I will raise him up at the last day. ... [God] the [Holy] Spirit gives life, there is no profit in the flesh. It is the words that I have been speaking to you which are spirit and life. [1]

[Isaiah:] "Come, every one who is thirsty; come to the waters. You who have no money, come, buy and eat! Come, buy wine and milk without money and without price. Why do you spend money on that which is not bread and work for that which does not satisfy? Listen carefully to me and eat what is good, and let your soul delight in the richest of food." [2]

[Paul:] I received from the Lord [Jesus] what I have passed on to you, that the Lord Jesus, on the night when He was betrayed, took bread. When He had given thanks He broke it and said, " This is my body which is for you. Do this in r emembrance of me." In the same way, when supper was ended, He took the cup saying, "This cup is the new covenant in my blood. Do this, as often as you drink it, in remembrance of me." As often as you eat this bread and drink this cup, you proclaim the Lord's death until He comes. [3]

[1] John 6:25-29,35,52-53,63 [2] Isaiah 55:1-2 [3] 1 Corinthians 11:23-26

Day 239

Some people rejected Jesus because they did not understand what He was talking about. Others rejected Him because they understood what He meant but would not accept it. God knows what is in people's minds and to those who do not understand but want to, He has promised to open their understanding. But those who do not want to accept His words will be left in their blindness.

Some disciples leave Jesus

Jesus said: "As [God the] Father who sent me is living, and I live because of Him, so whoever feeds on me will live because of me. ... Your forefathers ate manna and died, but He who feeds on this bread will live for ever." He said these things while teaching in a synagogue in Capernaum. When His disciples heard it they said, "This is a hard teaching. Who can accept it?" Jesus knew that His disciples were grumbling about this and said to them, "Does this offend you? What if you see the Son of Man ascend to where He was before! It is [God] the [Holy] Spirit who gives life; the flesh does nothing. The words I have spoken to you are spirit and they are life. But there are some of you who do not believe." For Jesus knew from the beginning which of them did not believe and who would betray Him. He said, "This is why I told you that no one can come to me unless the Father lets him."

After this, many of His disciples turned back and no longer followed Him. Jesus said to the Twelve. "Will you also go away,?" Simon Peter answered Him, "Lord, to whom shall we go? You have the words of eternal life. We believe and know that you are the Holy One, the Son of the living God." Then Jesus answered them, "Have I not chosen you, the Twelve? And one of you is a devil!" He was speaking of Judas, the son of Simon Iscariot, who, although one of the Twelve, was about to betray Him.1

As they were going along the road, a man said to Him, "I will follow you wherever you go." Jesus replied, "Foxes have holes and birds of the air have nests, but the Son of Man has nowhere to lay His head." He said to another man, "Follow me." But he said, "Lord, first let me go and bury my father." Jesus said to him, "Let the dead bury their own dead, but as for you, go and proclaim the kingdom of God." Still another said, "I will follow you, Lord, but first let me go and say goodbye to those at my home." Jesus replied, "No one who puts his hand to the plough and looks back is fit for service in the kingdom of God." [2]

[John:] Then I saw [in a vision] a new heaven and a new earth, for the first heaven and the first earth had passed away. ... He who sat on the throne said to me, "It is done. I am the Alpha and the Omega, the beginning and the end. ... He who overcomes will inherit all these things. I will be his God and he will be my son.[3]

[1] John 6:57-71   [2] Luke 9:57-62   [3] Revelation 21:1,5-7

Day 240

People make rules to suit themselves. God's rules are the best for everybody. Jesus spoke very strongly about people who twisted God's rules to suit themselves and then went on to teach others that what they said was God's word. Tradition can be a good thing when it preserves the good. It can be bad when it twists the truth.

The teaching of Jesus: The tradition of the Pharisees

Some Pharisees and scribes came to Jesus from Jerusalem and asked, "Why do your disciples break the tradition of the elders? They do not wash their hands before they eat!" Jesus replied, "Why do you break the command of God for the sake of your tradition? God said, 'Honour your father and mother' and 'Whoever speaks evil of his father or mother must be put to death.' But you say that whoever says to his father or mother, 'Whatever help you might receive from me is a gift devoted to God,' that person need not honour his father [or his mother]' with it. For the sake of your tradition, you set aside the word of God. You hypocrites! Isaiah was right when he prophesied about you: "'These people honour me with their lips, but their hearts are far from me. They worship me in vain for they teach their rules as if they were commands from God. [1]

[Paul:] When you were dead in your trespasses and in the uncircumcision [indiscipline] of your sinful nature, God made you alive with Christ. He forgave us all our trespasses, blotted out the record of what was against us and took it away nailing it to the cross. ... Therefore do not let anyone judge you in matters of food and drink, or with regard to feast days, a New Moon celebration or a Sabbath day. Such things were symbols of the things that were to come; the reality is in Christ. ... Since, with Christ you died to the material principles of this world, why, as though you still belonged to it, do you submit to its rules: "Do not handle! Do not taste! Do not touch!"? All these relate to things which will perish with use, because they are based on human commands and teachings. Indeed, such have the appearance of wisdom, with their self-imposed piety, their false humility and their harsh treatment of the body, but they do nothing to restrain self-indulgence. [2]

The Pharisees and scribes asked Jesus, "Why do your disciples not live according to the tradition of the elders; they eat their food with unclean hands? He replied, "Isaiah was right when he prophesied about you hypocrites. ... You have abandoned the commands of God and are following the traditions of men." [3]

[Paul:] Since you have been raised with Christ, set your hearts on things above, where Christ is seated at the right hand of God. Set your minds on heavenly things, not on earthly things. For you have died, and your life is hidden with Christ in God.[4]

[1] Matthew 15:1-9   [2] Colossians 2:13-17,20-23   [3] Mark 7:5-8   [4] Colossians 3:1-3

Day 241

God revealed Himself first to the Jews, but His concern was not only for them. His promise to Abraham was that all nations would be blessed as a result of what He was going to do through his descendants. He was going to reach the world with His Good News through them, supremely through Jesus, 'God the Son', who, as a Man, was a Jew. It was after His resurrection and ascension into heaven, on the day of Pentecost, that God sent out His messengers with a Gospel for the whole world.

The faith of the Canaanite woman

Jesus went to the region of Tyre and Sidon. A Canaanite woman from that region came to Him, crying out, "O Lord, Son of David, have mercy on me! My daughter is being tormented terribly by a demon." Jesus did not answer her a word. His disciples came to Him and urged Him, "Send her away, for she keeps shouting out after us." He answered, "I was sent only to the lost sheep of the house of Israel." The woman came and knelt before Him saying, "Lord, help me!" He replied, "It is not right to take the children's bread and throw it to their dogs." "Yes, Lord," she said, "but even the dogs eat the crumbs that fall from their masters' table." Then Jesus answered, "Woman, great is your faith! Let it be done for you as you have asked." At that moment, her daughter was healed. [1]

[Jesus said:] I am the good shepherd. I know my own and my own know me, just as [God] the Father knows me and I know Him. I am laying down my life for the sheep. I have other sheep that are not of this fold, I must bring them also. They too will listen to my voice, and there will be one flock and one shepherd. [2]

Then Peter began to speak [to the household of Cornelius]: "I now understand how true it is that God shows no favouritism but accepts from every nation those who fear Him and do what is right." [3]

[Paul:] What advantage, then, has the Jew, or what value is there in circumcision? Much in every way. In the first place, they [the Jews] have been entrusted with the spoken words of God. ... What then? Are we [Jews] better than they [the Gentiles]? Not at all! We have already stated that Jews and Gentiles are all alike under sin. ... As it is written, No one is righteous, no, not one. No one understands; no one seeks God. ... there is no difference, for all have sinned and fall short of the glory of God. All are justified freely by His grace through the redemption that is in Christ Jesus. [4]

[Jesus said:] People will come from east and west and from north and south, and will sit down at the feast in the kingdom of God. Indeed there are some who are last who will be first, and there are some who are first who will be last." [5]

---

[1] Matthew 15:21-28 [2] John 10:14-16 [3] Acts 10:34-35 [4] Romans 3:1-2,9-11,22-24 [5] Luke 13:29-30

Day 242

For a second time Jesus fed a multitude of people from a very little. The disciples were amazed at the miracle, but they did not understand the One who performed the miracle and He was even more amazing. He had come to give Himself, an apparently weak and much criticized Man, so that millions of people could have the food which most mattered, spiritual food, that of eternal life through Him.

Jesus feeds four thousand people

In those days another large crowd gathered and they had nothing to eat. Jesus called His disciples to Him and said, "I have compassion for these people for they have been with me three days now and have nothing to eat. If I send them home hungry they will faint on the way. Some of them have come a long way." His disciples answered, "How can anyone get enough bread to feed these people here in this desolate place?" He asked them, "How many loaves do you have?" "Seven," they replied.

He ordered the crowd to sit down on the ground. He took the seven loaves, gave thanks, broke them and gave them to His disciples to set before the people, and they did so. They also had a few small fish and, when He had given thanks for them, He ordered the disciples to distribute them too. The people ate and were satisfied. Then the disciples picked up seven basketfuls of broken pieces that were left over. There were about four thousand men present. He dismissed them and got into the boat with His disciples and went to the region of Dalmanutha. ... Again He left them, got into the boat and crossed to the other side. Now the disciples had forgotten to bring bread ... Jesus said to them: "Why are you talking about having no bread? Do you still not see or understand? Are your hearts hardened? Do you have eyes but do not see, and ears but do not hear? Do you not remember? When I broke the five loaves for the five thousand, how many basketfuls of broken pieces did you pick up?" They said to him, "Twelve." "And the seven loaves for the four thousand, how many basketfuls of broken pieces did you pick up?" They answered, "Seven." He said to them, "Do you still not understand?" [1]

A man came bringing the man of God [Elisha] twenty barley loaves ... "Give it to the men to eat," Elisha said. "How can I set this before a hundred men?" his servant asked. Elisha answered, "Give it to the men to eat, for this is what the Eternal-God says. 'They will be fed and have some left over.'" Then he set it before them. They ate and some was left over, according to the word of the Eternal-God. [2]

[Paul:] I am well supplied now that I have received from Epaphroditus the gifts you sent me. ... My God will meet fully your every need according to His riches in glory in Christ Jesus. [3]

[1] Mark 8:1-10,13-21 [2] 2 Kings 4:42-44 [3] Philippians 4:18-19

Day 243

Jesus performed many signs and wonders but He knew that such things did not convince people who did not want to believe. The greatest of all signs was that of Jesus Himself who, as 'God the Son', became a Man, in many ways like us. Only those understand that sign who accept what Jesus taught, and believe what He said and did.

The people demand a miraculous sign from Jesus

The Pharisees and Sadducees came to Jesus and, to test who He was, they asked Him to work a miraculous a sign from heaven. He replied, "When it is evening you say, 'It will be fair weather, for the sky is red,' and in the morning, 'It will be stormy today, for the sky is red and overcast.' You know how to interpret the appearance of the sky, but you cannot interpret the signs of the times." [1]

Then some of the Scribes and Pharisees said to him, "Teacher, we would like to see a miraculous sign from you." He answered, "An evil and adulterous generation asks for a sign, but no sign will be given it except the sign of the prophet Jonah. For as Jonah was three days and three nights in the belly of a large fish, so the Son of Man will be three days and three nights in the heart of the earth. The men of Nineveh will stand up at the judgment with this generation and condemn it; for they repented at the preaching of Jonah, and now One greater than Jonah is here. The Queen of the South will rise at the judgment with this generation and condemn it, for she came from the ends of the earth to listen to the wisdom of Solomon, and here there is One who is greater than Solomon." [2]

[Paul:] For the message of the cross is foolishness to those who are perishing, but to us who are being saved it is the power of God. For it is written: "I will destroy the learning of the learned and the philosophy of the philosophers I will frustrate." Where is the wise man? Where is the scholar? Where is the philosopher of this age? Has not God shown the wisdom of the world to be foolish? For since, in the wisdom of God, the world through its wisdom did not know Him, God was pleased through the foolishness of preaching to save those who have believed. Jews look for miraculous signs and Greeks look for wisdom, but we preach the crucified Christ, who, to the Jews, is a stumbling block, and to the Greeks, foolishness, but to those whom God has called, both Jews and Greeks, Christ the power of God and the wisdom of God.[3]

While He was in Jerusalem, during the Feast of Passover, many people saw the miraculous signs He was doing and believed in His name. But Jesus would not trust Himself to them, for He knew ... what was in a man. [4]

---

[1] Matthew 16:1-4   [2] Matthew 12:38-45   [3] 1 Corinthians 1:18-24   [4] John 2:23-25

Day 244

Peter did not recognise who Jesus was because he was clever or well educated. God the Father saw something in Peter's attitude to Jesus which enabled Him to open his understanding. Peter followed his confession to Jesus: "You are the Christ!" with the proclamation "He is the Christ!" to others. That too was God working in him.

Peter's confession of Christ

When Jesus came to the region of Caesarea Philippi, He asked His disciples, "Who do people say that the Son of Man is?" They replied, "Some say John the Baptist; others say Elijah, and still others, Jeremiah or one of the prophets." Then He said to them, "But who do you say that I am?" Simon Peter answered, "You are the Christ [Messiah], the Son of the living God." Jesus said to him, "Blessed are you, Simon Bar-Jonah, for flesh and blood has not revealed this [truth] to you, but my Father in heaven. I tell you that you are Peter [*Petros*, a 'rock'], and on this rock [*Petra*, a 'huge rock' (the truth)] I will build my church, and the gates of Hades will not prevail against it." I will give you the keys of the kingdom of heaven. Whatever you bind on earth will be bound in heaven, and whatever you loose on earth will be loosed in heaven." Then He warned His disciples not to tell anyone that He was the Christ. [1]

He said to them, "The Son of Man must suffer many things and be rejected by the elders, chief priests and scribes, and He will be killed and on the third day be raised." Then He said to them all: "If anyone will come after me, let him deny himself and take up his cross daily and follow me. For whoever wants to save his life will lose it, but whoever loses his life for my sake will save it. What profit is it for a man to gain the whole world, and yet lose or forfeit himself? Whoever is ashamed of me and my words, of him will the Son of Man will be ashamed when He comes in His glory and in the glory of [God] the Father and of the holy angels. I tell you the truth, there are some who are standing here who will not taste death before they see the kingdom of God." [2]

"I tell you, whoever acknowledges me before men, him will the Son of Man acknowledge before the angels of God. But he who disowns me before men will be disowned before the angels of God." [3]

Who is a liar but he who denies that Jesus is the Christ? He is antichrist because he denies [God] the Father and [God] the Son. No one who denies [God] the Son has [God] the Father; whoever confesses [God] the Son has [God] the Father also. [4]

[Jesus said:] "Every one who acknowledges me before men, I will also acknowledge him before my Father who is in heaven. But whoever disowns me before men, I will disown him before my Father in heaven." [5]

[1] Matthew 16:13-20 [2] Luke 9:21-27 [3] Luke 12:8-9 [4] 1 John 2:23 [5] Matthew 10:32-33

Day 245

When Peter, James and John saw Jesus in the glory of His transfiguration it made such a big impression on them that they never forgot it. That impression gave a strong ring of truth to the way they spoke about Him. They really had been with Jesus. That experience transformed their lives and added great conviction to what they said about Jesus. Being with Jesus always changes lives.

The transfiguration of Jesus

Jesus took with Him Peter, James and John the brother of James, and led them up a high mountain by themselves. There He was transfigured before them. His face shone like the sun, and His clothes became as white as the light. Then Moses and Elijah appeared to them, talking with Jesus. Peter said to Jesus, "Lord, it is good for us to be here. If you wish, I will put up three booths, one for you, one for Moses and one for Elijah." While he was speaking, a bright cloud covered them, and a voice from the cloud said, "This is my Son, my Beloved; with Him I am well pleased. Listen to Him!" When the disciples heard this, they were terrified and fell on their faces to the ground. But Jesus came and touched them and said, "Get up! Do not be afraid." When they looked up, they saw no one but Jesus only. As they were coming down the mountain, Jesus commanded them, "Do not tell anyone what you have seen, until the Son of Man has been raised from the dead." [1]

[Peter:] We did not follow cleverly devised stories when we made known to you the power and coming of our Lord Jesus Christ, but we were eyewitnesses of His majesty. For He received honour and glory from God the Father when the voice came to Him from the Majestic Glory, saying, "This is my Son, my Beloved, with Him I am well pleased." We ourselves heard this voice come from heaven for we were with Him on the holy mountain. This gave even firmer confirmation to the words of the prophets, to which you will do well to pay close attention as to a light shining in a dark place, until the day breaks and the morning star rises in your hearts. It is of first importance that you understand that no prophecy ever came because of man's will, but men spoke from God [the Father] moved by [God the] Holy Spirit. [2]

[John:] That which was from the beginning, concerning the word of life, which we have heard, which we have seen with our eyes, which we have looked at and touched with our hands, this we declare to you. The life was revealed and we saw it and we testify to you that the eternal life, which was with [God] the Father was revealed to us. We declare to you what we have seen and heard, so that you too may have fellowship with us, for our fellowship is truly with [God] the Father and with [God] His Son, Jesus Christ. [3]

[1] Matthew 17:1-10   [2] 2 Peter 1:16-19   [3] 1 John 1:1-3

Day 246

Everyone has a duty to respect the authorities over them. In some countries, where there is injustice and corruption, this is difficult. Where, however, the government is just and respects people's rights, it acts in God's place to maintain law and order. To owe money to a government is just as wrong as to owe it to a person.

Peter and the temple tax

When they [Jesus and His disciples] arrived in Capernaum, the collectors of the half-shekel tax came to Peter and asked, "Does your teacher not pay the half-shekel tax?" "Yes, he does," he replied. He came into the house but before he could say anything, Jesus said to him, "What do you think, Simon? From whom do the kings of the earth collect duty or tributes, from their own sons or from others?" Peter answered, "From others," Jesus said to him, "Then the sons are exempt. However, so that we do not offend them, go to the sea and throw out your line. Take the first fish that comes up, open its mouth and you will find a shekel. Take it and give it to them to pay for my tax and yours." [1]

Let every person be subject to the governing authorities, for there is no authority except from God and the authorities that exist are there by God's appointment. Consequently, he who sets himself against the authorities rebels against what God has instituted, and those who do so will bring down judgment on themselves. For rulers are no terror for those who do right, but for those who do wrong. Would you be free from fear of those in authority? Then do what is right and you will be commended. For the one in authority is God's servant for your good. But if you do wrong, be afraid, for he does not bear the sword for nothing. He is God's servant, to execute his punishment on the wrongdoer. Therefore, one must submit to the authorities, not only for fear of punishment but for the sake of conscience. For the same reason you pay taxes, for the authorities are servants who, under God, devote themselves to this service. Give to all men what is due to them. Pay taxes to whom taxes are due, revenue to whom revenue is due, respect to whom respect is due and honour to whom honour is due honour. [2] [Paul to Titus:] Remind people to be subject to rulers and authorities; to be obedient and ready to do any good work, to speak evil of no one, to avoid being quarrelsome, but to be considerate and gentle towards everybody. [3]

They [the scribes and chief priests] sent spies to question Him [Jesus] ... "Is it lawful for us to pay taxes to Caesar or not?" they asked. He saw their craftiness and said to them, "Show me a denarius. Whose image and inscription does it bear?" "Caesar's," they replied. He said to them "Then give to Caesar what is Caesar's, and to God what is God's." [4]

[1] Matthew 17:24-27   [2] Romans 13:1-7   [3] Titus:3:1-2   [4] Luke 20:21-25

Day 247

In God's kingdom, the order of greatness is the opposite to that in the world. In the world, the wealthiest and highest in social position come first and the poor and lowly come last. With God, a person who is humble is of far greater worth than are the proud and mighty. Jesus, who is 'God the Son', is also the greatest Man who ever lived. He gave the clearest example of who was great in His kingdom by becoming a servant!

The teaching of Jesus: The greatest in the kingdom of heaven

They [Jesus and His disciples] came to Capernaum. When He was in the house, He asked them, "What were you arguing about on the road?" But they kept quiet because on the way they had been arguing with one another about who was the greatest. Jesus sat down, called the Twelve and said to them, "If one of you wants to be first, he must be the last of all and the servant of all." [1]

An argument arose among them as to which of them was the greatest. Jesus, knowing their thoughts, took a little child and drew him to stand beside Him. Then He said to them, "Whoever receives this child in my name receives me; and whoever receives me receives the One who sent me. For he who is least among you all is the greatest." [2] Jesus said to them, "The kings of the Gentiles lord it over them; and those who exercise authority over them are called benefactors. But it is not to be like that with you. On the contrary, let him who is the greatest among you be like the least, and he who is chief among you be as one who serves. For who is greater, the one who sits at the table or the one who serves? Is it not he who sits at the table? But I am among you as One who serves. [3]

Jesus called a little child to Him and put him in the middle of them. He said, "I tell you the truth, unless you repent and become like little children, you will never enter the kingdom of heaven. Whoever humbles himself therefore and becomes like this little child is the greatest in the kingdom of heaven. [4]

Pride goes before destruction and a haughty spirit before a fall. It is better to be humble in spirit and among the meek than to divide the spoil with the proud. [5] The reward for humility and the fear of the Eternal-God, is wealth and honour and life. [6] For everyone who exalts himself will be humbled and he who humbles himself will be exalted [7] He [God] gives us more grace. That is why it is written: "God opposes the proud but gives grace to the humble." Therefore submit yourselves to God. [8]

[Micah:] Listen to what the Eternal-God says: ... "He has showed you, O man, what is good. And what does the Eternal-God require of you but to act justly, to love mercy and to walk humbly with your God." [9]

[1] Mark 9:33-35   [2] Luke 9:46-48   [3] Luke 22:25-27   [4] Matthew 18:3-4   [5] Proverbs 16:18-19
[6] Proverbs 22:4   [7] Luke 14:11   [8] James 4:6-7   [9] Micah 6:1, 8

Day 248

God cannot forgive those who sin against Him if they do not repent of their sin. A sure sign of the genuineness of that repentance is the way they forgive those who sin against them. Not to forgive others is clear evidence that there is no real repentance for the sins committed against God. 'Repentance' means to change one's mind about some action. The unmerciful servant was forgiven for his sin, but he had not 'changed his mind' about it and his plea for mercy was wholly selfish and unacceptable.

The teaching of Jesus: How to forgive

Peter came to Jesus and asked, "Lord, how many times must I forgive my brother if he sins against me? As many as seven times?" Jesus answered, "I tell you, not seven times, but seventy times seven. The kingdom of heaven is like a king who wanted to settle accounts with his servants. As he began the accounting, a man was brought to him who owed him ten thousand talents. He was not able to pay, so the master ordered that he together with his wife and children and all that he had be sold to repay the debt. The servant fell on his knees and begged him, 'Be patient with me and I will pay you everything.' The heart of the servant's master was moved with compassion and he cancelled the debt and let him go. But when that servant went out, he found one of his fellow-servants who owed him a hundred denarii. He grabbed him by the throat and said, 'Pay what you owe me!' His fellow-servant fell to his knees and begged him, 'Have patience with me, and I will pay you back.' But he refused. He went off and had the man put in prison until he had paid the debt.

When his fellow-servants saw what had happened, they were greatly distressed and went and told their master everything that had happened. Then the master called the servant in and said to him, 'You wicked servant, I cancelled all that debt of yours because you begged me to. Should you not have had mercy on your fellow-servant as I had on you?' In anger his master turned him over to the jailers until he should pay back all he owed. This is how my heavenly Father will deal with you unless you forgive your brother from your heart." [1]

He said to them, "When you pray, say: 'Our Father in heaven, hallowed be your name, your kingdom come. Your will be done on earth as it is in heaven. Give us each day our daily bread. Forgive us our sins, for we also forgive everyone who sins against us.'" [2]

[Jesus said:] "I tell you, whatever you ask for in prayer, believe that it has been granted to you, and it will be yours. When you stand praying, if you have anything against any one, forgive him, so that your Father, who is in heaven may forgive you your sins." [3]

[1] Matthew 18:21-35 [2] Luke 11:2,4 [3] Mark 11:24-25

Day 249

A second time Jesus sent His disciples into the region around. This time there were seventy of them. They were to do 'His work' in His Name. When they saw the amazing results of God working, their joy was great. It was the joy of knowing that, as God was so clearly working in and through them, that meant that they were eternally in His family, their names were written in the 'Lamb's book of life'.

Jesus sends out seventy disciples

The Lord appointed seventy others and sent them out, two by two, ahead of Him to every town and place where He was about to go. He said to them, "The harvest is plentiful, but the workers are few. Therefore pray the Lord of the harvest to send out workers into His harvest. Go! I send you out like lambs into the midst of wolves. Carry no purse or provisions or sandals and do not greet anyone on the way. Whatever house you enter, first say, 'Peace to this house.' If a man of peace is there, your peace will come upon him; if not, it will come back to you. Stay in the same house, eating and drinking whatever they give you, for the worker is worthy of his wages. Do not move from house to house.

"When you enter a town and they receive you, eat what is set before you. Heal the sick who are there and say to them, 'The kingdom of God has come near you.' But when you enter a town and you are not welcomed, go out into its streets and say, 'Even the dust of your town that clings to our feet we wipe off against you. ... I tell you, it will be more tolerable on that day for Sodom than for that town.

"Woe to you, Korazin! Woe to you, Bethsaida! For if the miracles that were performed in you had been performed in Tyre and Sidon, they would have repented long ago, sitting in sackcloth and ashes. It will be more tolerable for Tyre and Sidon at the judgment than for you. And you, Capernaum, will you be lifted up to the skies? No, you will be brought down to the depths. Whoever listens to you listens to me and whoever rejects you rejects me, and he who rejects me rejects Him who sent me." The seventy returned with joy saying, "Lord, even the demons submit to us in your name."

He said to them, "I saw Satan falling like lightning from heaven. See, I have given you authority to trample on snakes and scorpions and over all the power of the enemy. Nothing will harm you. However, do not rejoice at this, that the spirits are subject to you, but rejoice that your names are written in heaven." [1]

Nothing impure will ever enter it [heaven], nor will anyone who does anything that is an abomination or deceitful, but only those whose names are written in the Lamb's book of life. [2]

[1] Luke 10:1-20   [2] Revelation 21:27

Day 250

When Jesus went to Jerusalem for the Feast of Tabernacles, He knew that many people were talking about Him. They whispered so that He could not hear them but He knew what was in their minds. There was a division between the Jewish leaders and the ordinary people. There is always that kind of division where Jesus is. Happy are those who recognise that only God can speak as Jesus did.

The teaching of Jesus: At the Feast of Tabernacles

After His brothers had left for the Feast, Jesus went also, not publicly, but in secret. Now at the Feast, the Jews were watching for Him and asking, "Where is that man?" Among the crowds there was widespread whispering about Him. Some said, "He is a good man." Others replied, "No, He deceives the people." But no one would say anything publicly about Him for fear of the Jews. Not until halfway through the Feast did Jesus go up to the temple courts and begin to teach. The Jews were amazed and asked, "How did this Man get such learning without having been taught?" The Pharisees heard the crowd whispering such things about Him. Then the chief priests and the Pharisees sent temple guards to arrest Him. Jesus said, "I am with you for only a short time, and then I go to the One who sent me. You will look for me, but you will not find me; and where I am, you cannot come."

The Jews said to one another, "Where does this Man intend to go that we cannot find Him? Will He go where our people live scattered among the Greeks, and teach the Greeks? What did He mean when He said, 'You will look for me, but you will not find me,' and 'Where I am, you cannot come'?" On hearing His words, some of the people said, "Surely this man is the Prophet." Others said, "He is the Christ." Still others asked, "How can the Christ come from Galilee? Does not the Scripture say that the Christ will come from David's family and from Bethlehem, the town where David lived?" Thus the people were divided because of Jesus. Some wanted to seize Him, but no one laid a hand on Him.

Finally the temple guards went back to the chief priests and Pharisees who asked them, "Why did you not bring Him in?" The guards declared, "No one ever spoke the way this Man does," [1] When Jesus had finished saying these things, the crowds were amazed at His teaching, because He taught as One who had authority, and not as their teachers of the law. [2]

(Jesus said:) "Whoever rejects me and does not accept my words will, on the last day, be judged by what He has heard me say, for I have not spoken of my own accord, but [God] the Father who sent me commanded me what to say and how to say it." [3]

[1] John 7:10-15,32-36,40-46 [2] Matthew 7:28 [3] John 12:48

Day 251

God hates the sin but He loves the sinner. Nevertheless the sinner can never be reconciled to God while he or she loves the sin. When the sinner repents of the sin, God forgives and accepts the sinner in Jesus' Name. The woman caught in adultery found that forgiveness. The man, whoever he was, who was equally guilty with her, did not.

Jesus, the woman caught in adultery and her accusers

They went each to his own home, but Jesus went to the Mount of Olives. At dawn He appeared again in the temple court, where crowds of people gathered round Him, and He sat down and taught them. The Scribes and Pharisees brought a woman caught in adultery and they made her stand before the group. They said to Jesus, "Teacher, this woman was caught in the very act of adultery. In the Law, Moses commanded us to stone such women to death. Now what do you say?" They asked this question as a trap in order to find some charge to bring against Him. Jesus stooped down and wrote on the ground with His finger. When they persisted in their questioning, He straightened up and said to them, "Let whoever among you is without sin be the first to throw a stone at her." Again He stooped down and wrote on the ground. When they heard this they began to go away, one at a time, the oldest ones first, then down to the last one, until only Jesus was left. The woman alone stood before Him in the middle of the court. Jesus straightened up and said to her, "Woman, where are they? Has no-one condemned you?" She answered. "No one, sir." Jesus said to her, "Then neither do I condemn you. Go on your way and sin no more." [1]

[Paul:] The death He [Jesus] died, He died to sin once for all, and the life he lives, He lives to God [the Father]. So, you too, count yourselves dead to sin but alive to God in Christ Jesus. Do not let sin reign in your mortal body so that you obey its cravings. Do not offer the members of your body to sin, as instruments of wickedness, but rather offer yourselves to God, as those who have been raised to life from the dead. Offer the members of your body to Him as instruments of righteousness. For sin shall not have dominion over you, since you are not under law but under grace. [2]

God [the Father] did not send [God] the Son into the world to condemn the world, but that the world might be saved through Him. Whoever believes in Him is not condemned, but whoever does not believe is condemned already because He has not believed in the name of the one and only Son of God. [3]

[Jesus said] "I tell you the truth, whoever hears my word and believes Him [God the Father] who sent me has eternal life and does not come under condemnation. He has passed out of death into life." [4]

[1] John 7:53-8:11   [2] Romans 6:10-14   [3] John 3:17-18   [4] John 5:24

Day 252

Some people find the idea of God being a God-Family of three God-Persons difficult to understand. The most important point to grasp is that they are not three, independent gods, each doing whatever they like for their own separate reasons. The THREE Persons are each GOD - 'God the Father', Jesus Christ 'God the Son', and 'God the Holy Spirit'. Together, as a God-Family they are ONE GOD, not three Gods. The members of the God-Family are held together by a bond of 'light'—everything open to the others with nothing hidden, and 'love'—each always seeks the best for the others. The most amazing thing about the God-Family is that they love those of us who are their children, as much as they love each other and they desire that we who are in the God-family, live in the 'light' and 'love' which binds them in their God-Family.

The teaching of Jesus: About God the Father, His Father

Jesus said, "Even if I testify on my own behalf, my testimony is true, for I know where I came from and where I am going. But you do not know where I came from or where I am going. You judge by human standards. I pass judgment on no one. Yet if I judge, my judgment is true, because I am not alone but I with [God] the Father, who sent me. In your own Law it is written that the testimony of two persons is valid. I [God the Son] am One who testifies for myself. [God] my Father who sent me, also witnesses to me" Then they said to Him, "Where is your father?" Jesus replied, "You do not know me nor do you know my Father. If you knew me, you would know my Father also." [1]

They [the Pharisees] asked Jesus, "Who are you?" He replied, "I am what I have told you from the beginning. ... He who sent me is true. I tell the world only what I have heard from Him. They did not understand that He was speaking to them about [God] the Father. Jesus went on to say, "When you have lifted up the Son of Man, then you will know that I am He [the one I claim to be], and that I do nothing on my own but speak what [God] the Father has taught me. The One who sent me is with me, He has not left me alone, for I always do what pleases Him." [2]

Jesus said [to Thomas], "I am the way and the truth and the life. No one comes to [God] the Father except through me. If you knew me, you would also know my Father. From now on, you know Him and have seen Him" Philip said to Him, "Lord, show us [God] the Father and we will be satisfied." Jesus answered him: "Have I been with you for so long and you do not you know me, Philip? Anyone who has seen me has seen [God] the Father. [3]

[Jesus said:] "All things have been entrusted to me by my Father. No one knows [God] the Son except [God] the Father, and no one knows [God] the Father except [God] the Son and those to whom [God] the Son chooses to reveal Him." [4]

[1] John 8:14-20 [2] John 8:25-30 [3] John 14:6-9 [4] Matthew 11:27

Day 253

The people of the time when Jesus lived in Palestine knew all about slavery. They did not know so much about the slavery of sin. Jesus showed them that, as ordinary slaves could be set free by a change of master, so could those who were slaves to sin. It depended on who was the master - Satan or God.

The teaching of Jesus: Sin and slavery

Jesus said to the Jews who believed in Him, "If you hold fast to my teaching, you are truly my disciples; you will know the truth, and the truth will set you free." They answered Him, "We are Abraham's descendants and have never been slaves of anyone. What do you mean by saying that we shall be set free?" Jesus answered them, "I tell you the truth, whoever sins is a slave to sin. A slave has no permanent place in the household, but a son has a place there for ever. So if [God] the Son sets you free, you will be free indeed. I know you are descendants of Abraham, yet you are planning to kill me, because my word has no place in you. I tell you what I have seen in the presence of [God] the Father, and you do what you have heard from your father [the devil]." They answered. "Abraham is our father." Jesus said, "If you were Abraham's children, you would do what Abraham did. ... You are of your father, the devil, and it is your will to carry out your father's desire. He was a murderer from the beginning, not keeping to the truth for there is no truth in him. When he lies, he speaks what is natural to him, for he is a liar and the father of lies. Yet when I tell the truth, you do not believe me! Which of you can convict me of sin? If I speak the truth, why do you not believe me? Whoever is [a child] of God listens to the words of God. The reason you do not hear them is that you are not [children] of God." [1]

[Paul:] Do you not know that if you surrender yourselves to someone to do his will, you are slaves of the one you obey, whether that is to sin, which leads to death, or to obedience [to God] which leads to righteousness? Thanks be to God that you, who once were slaves to sin, have become obedient with all your heart, to the teaching to which you were entrusted and now, having been set free from sin, you have become slaves of righteousness. [2]

So then, with my mind I am a slave to the law of God, but with my flesh I am a slave to the law of sin. There is, therefore, now no condemnation for those who are in Christ Jesus for, through Christ Jesus, the law of the Spirit of life has set me free from the law of sin and death. For God has done what obedience to the law could not do. By sending His own Son ... He condemned sin in sinful man in order that the righteous requirements of the law might be fully met in us. [3]

[1] John 8:31-39,42-47   [2] Romans 6:16-18   [3] Romans 7:26-8:1-3

Day 254

The two most important commands of the 'Law of God' are: 'Love God' and 'Love your neighbour'. The Bible says a great deal about loving God. Here Jesus makes it clear who is our neighbour. A neighbour is anyone we come into contact with, the person living near us, with whom we work or with whom we have any contact, particularly anyone who has a need which we can meet in Jesus' name, even someone with whom we would not be expected to associate, like the Samaritan for the Jews.

The teaching of Jesus: Who is one's neighbour?

On one occasion a lawyer stood up and, to test Jesus, asked Him, "Teacher, what must I do to inherit eternal life?" Jesus said to him, "What is written in the Law? How do you read it?" He answered: "'You shall love the Lord your God with all your heart, with all your soul, with all your strength and with all your mind' and, 'Love your neighbour as yourself.'" Jesus answered him, "You have answered correctly. Do this and you will live." The man was anxious to justify himself, so he said to Jesus, "And who is my neighbour?"

Jesus replied: "A man was going down from Jerusalem to Jericho. He fell into the hands of robbers who stripped him of his clothes, beat him and went away, leaving him half dead. By chance a priest was going down that road. When he saw the man, he passed by on the other side. In the same way, a Levite came to the place, saw the man and passed by on the other side. But a Samaritan, as he travelled, came near to where the man was. When he saw him, he took pity on him. He went to him and dressed his wounds with oil and wine. Then he set the man on his own donkey, brought him to an inn and took care of him. The next day he took out two denarii and gave them to the innkeeper, saying, 'Look after him, and when I return, I will repay you for whatever more you may spend.' Which of these three do you think was a neighbour to the man who fell into the hands of robbers?" The lawyer replied, "The one who showed mercy to him." Jesus said to him, "Go and do likewise." [1]

[James:] If indeed you keep the royal law in accordance with the Scripture, "Love your neighbour as yourself," you do well. [2] [Paul:] Love does no wrong to a neighbour. Therefore to love is to fulfil the law. [3] We who are strong ought to bear with the failings of the weak and not to please ourselves. Let each of us please his neighbour for his good, to build him up. [4]

You, my brothers, were called to freedom. But do not use your freedom to indulge the sinful nature, but serve one another in love. The whole law is summed up in a single command: "Love your neighbour as yourself." [5]

[1] Luke 10:25-37 [2] James 2:8 [3] Romans 13:10 [4] Romans 15:1-2 [5] Galatians 5:13-14

Day 255

God gives us many things to enjoy and share with others. There are, however, priorities and doing some things or simply sitting and listening, have to be given their rightful time and place. Doing a good thing at the wrong moment, can take the place of doing something more important. Mary and Martha had different personalities and did things differently. Jesus had a place for both of them, provided they put their priorities in the right order.

Jesus at home with Martha and Mary

Jesus and His disciples came to a village where a woman, named Martha, received Jesus into her home. She had a sister named Mary who seated herself at the Lord's feet listening to what He said. But Martha was distracted by her many household tasks. She came to Him and said, "Lord, is it nothing to you that my sister has left me to do all the work by myself? Tell her to help me!" The Lord answered, "Martha, Martha, you are worried and troubled about many things. There is need of only one thing and Mary has chosen the better part. It will not be taken away from her." [1]

Six days before the Passover, Jesus came to Bethany, where Lazarus lived, whom Jesus had raised from the dead. They prepared supper for Him and Martha served, while Lazarus was one of those at the table with Him. Then Mary took about a pint of pure liquid nard, which was a very expensive perfume. She poured it on Jesus' feet and wiped them with her hair. And the whole house was filled with the fragrance of the perfume. [2]

[Peter:] Above all, love each other sincerely, for love covers a multitude of sins. Be hospitable to one another without grumbling. Serve one another with whatever gift God has given you, as faithful stewards of God's grace in its various forms. [3]

Love each other as brothers and sisters. Do not forget to give hospitality to strangers. By doing so some people have entertained angels without knowing it. [4]

One thing I ask of the Lord, this is what I seek: that I may dwell in the house of the Eternal-God all the days of my life, to gaze upon the beauty of the Eternal-God and to seek Him in His temple. ... Wait for the Lord. Be strong and take heart and wait for the Lord. [5]

God is our refuge and strength, a very present help in trouble. ... The nations are in uproar and kingdoms totter. He speaks and the earth melts. The Eternal-God, the Almighty, is with us, the God of Jacob is our refuge. Come! See the works of the Eternal-God. See what desolations He has brought on the earth. He makes wars to cease to the ends of the earth. He breaks the bow and shatters the spear. He burns the shields with fire. Be still and know that I am God. [6]

[1] Luke 10:38-42 [2] John 12:1-3 [3] 1 Peter 4:8-10 [4] Hebrews 13:1-2 [5] Psalm 27:4,14 [6] Psalm 46:1,6-10

Day 256

When God promises something He always keeps His word. He has promised to hear the prayers of all who call on Him. However, He does not always answer immediately and only He knows the reasons for this. Jesus encouraged His disciples to pray, and to go on praying. To do so was not a sign of lack of faith; rather it was a sign of faith - faith that God would answer in the best way possible at the best time for everyone.

The teaching of Jesus: Persisting in prayer

He [Jesus] said to them, "Suppose one of you has a friend, and you go to him at midnight and say, 'Friend, lend me three loaves of bread, for a friend of mine, who is on a journey, has arrived and I have nothing to set before him.' Then he from within answers, 'Do not disturb me. The door is already locked and my children are with me in bed. I cannot get up and give you anything.' I tell you, although he will not get up and give him anything because he is his friend, yet because of his persistence he will get up and give him as much as he needs. So I say to you: Ask and it will be given to you; seek and you will find; knock and the door will be opened to you. For he who asks receives; he who seeks finds; and to him who knocks, the door will be opened.

"What father among you, if his son asks for bread, will give him a stone? Or if he asks for a fish, will give him a snake? Or if he asks for an egg, will give him a scorpion? If you then, who are evil, know how to give good gifts to your children, how much more will [God the] Father in heaven give [God] the Holy Spirit to those who ask Him!" [1]

[The word of God through Isaiah:] I am about to create new heavens and a new earth. The former things will not be remembered nor be brought to mind. ... They [Israel] will not work in vain nor bear children doomed for disaster, for they and their descendants will be a people blessed by the Eternal-God. Before they call, I will answer, and while they are speaking, I will hear. The wolf and the lamb will feed together, the lion will eat straw like an ox, and dust will be the food of the serpent. They will not hurt or destroy on all my holy mountain. [2]

"Is this not the fast that I have chosen: to loose the chains of injustice and undo the bands of the yoke, to set the oppressed free and to break every yoke? ... Then you will call, and the Eternal-God will answer; you will cry for help, and He will say: Here am I. [3]

[The word of God through Jeremiah:] "I know the plans I have for you," says the Eternal-God, "plans for your welfare and not for evil, plans to give you hope in the future. Then you will call upon me. You will come and pray to me, and I will hear you. You will seek for me and find me, when you seek for me with all your heart." [4]

[1] Luke 11:5-13 [2] Isaiah 65:17,23-25 [3] Isaiah 58:6,9 [4] Jeremiah 29:11-13

Day 257

Jesus said, "I am the Light of the world" and He spoke of those who, like Him, "loved the light". In the light nothing is hidden. There is no deceit, no sham, no hidden motives. To pretend to be 'in the light' when one is behaving deceitfully is hypocrisy. Not only did Jesus hate hypocrisy, but no hypocrite is acceptable in His kingdom.

The teaching of Jesus: The sin of hypocrisy

While Jesus was speaking, a Pharisee invited Him to dine with him, so He went in and sat at the table. The Pharisee noticed that Jesus did not wash before the meal and was surprised. The Lord said to him, "You Pharisees clean the outside of the cup and the plate, but inside you are full of greed and wickedness. You foolish people! Did not he who made the outside make the inside also? But give to the poor what is within and everything will be clean for you.

"Woe to you, Pharisees! You give God a tenth of your mint, rue and all kinds of herbs, but you neglect justice and the love of God. These you should practise without leaving the others undone. Woe to you Pharisees! You love to have the best seats in the synagogues and be greeted in the market-places. Woe to you, because you are like graves which are unmarked so that men walk over them without knowing it."

One of the experts in the Law [of Moses] answered Him, "Teacher, when you say these things, you insult us." Jesus replied, "Woe to you, lawyers also! You load people down with burdens that are hard to bear, but you yourselves will not lift one finger to help them. Woe to you! You rebuild the tombs of the prophets whom your forefathers killed, and so you show by these monuments, that you consent to what they did. ...

"Woe to you, lawyers, for you have taken away the key to knowledge. You yourselves do not enter [into that knowledge], and you hinder those who are entering." As Jesus left there, the scribes and the Pharisees were very angry with Him and set out to oppose Him fiercely and to attack Him with questions, trying to catch Him out in something He might say." [1]

[Peter:] Rid yourselves of all malice, deceit, hypocrisy, envy, and evil speaking. Like newborn babies, crave for pure spiritual milk, so that you may grow to maturity in your salvation, now that you have tasted that the Lord is good. [2]

[Jesus said:] "Why do you see the speck in your brother's eye and pay no attention to the beam in your own eye? How can you say to your brother, 'Brother, let me take the speck out of your eye,' when you yourself do not to see the beam in your own eye? You hypocrite, first take the beam out of your eye, and then you will see clearly to take out the speck from your brother's eye." [3]

---

[1] Luke 11:37-46,52-53   [2] 1 Peter 2:1-3   [3] Luke 6:41-42

Day 258

In the days when Jesus lived in Palestine, there were good and bad shepherds. Everyone knew the difference. The bad shepherd put the safety and welfare of himself before that of his sheep. The good shepherd walked ahead of his flock and guided them along narrow and dangerous paths. He protected them from wild animals and robbers. The first care of the good shepherd was the wellbeing of his sheep. Jesus is the Good Shepherd because He knows individually, guides and protects every one of His sheep.

The teaching of Jesus: The Good Shepherd

[Jesus said:] "I tell you the truth, whoever does not enter the sheepfold by the gate, but climbs in some other way, is a thief and a robber. But he who enters by the gate is the shepherd of his sheep. For this man, the watchman opens the gate, and to his voice, the sheep listen. He calls his own sheep by name and leads them out. When he has brought out his own sheep, he goes on ahead of them, and his sheep follow him because they know his voice. They will never follow a stranger, because they do not recognise the voice of a stranger but they will run away from him." Jesus used this figure of speech, but they did not understand what He was saying to them. So Jesus spoke to them again. He said, "I tell you the truth. I am myself the good shepherd. ... The good shepherd lays down his life for the sheep. The hired servant is not the shepherd and he does not own the sheep. So when he sees the wolf coming, he leaves the sheep and runs away. Then the wolf snatches the flock and scatters it. The hired servant runs away because he serves for wages and cares nothing for the sheep.

"I am the good Shepherd. I know my sheep and my sheep know me, in the same way that [God] the Father knows me and I [God the Son] know the Father. I lay down my life for the sheep. I have other sheep that are not of this fold, them also I must lead. They too will listen to my voice, and there will be one flock and one Shepherd. The reason [God] my Father loves me is that I lay down my life in order to take it up again. No one takes it from me, but I lay it down of my own accord. I have power to lay it down and power to take it up again. This is the command I received from [God] my Father." [1]

"But you, Bethlehem Ephrathah ... out of you will come forth for me one who will be ruler over Israel. ... He will stand and shepherd His flock in the strength and majesty of the name of the Eternal-God, His God. And they will live securely, for His greatness will reach to the ends so the earth, for He will be their peace. [2]

[David:] The Eternal-God is my shepherd, I shall not want. He makes me lie down in green pastures, He leads me beside still waters, He restores my soul, He leads me in the paths of righteousness for His name's sake. [3]

[1] John 10:1-6,11-18   [2] Micah 5:2,4-5   [3] Psalms 23:1-3

Day 259

The problem with the Jewish leaders of the time when Jesus lived among them was not that they could not believe the truth He was telling them, but that they did not want to believe it. The leaders preferred to believe what would give them power and prestige over the people, not the humble service and trust in God which Jesus talked about. God does not reveal Himself to people unless they are genuine in their search and are honest in handling what they know to be true.

Jesus faces unbelieving Jews

At the time of the Feast of Dedication at Jerusalem, it was winter, and Jesus was walking in Solomon's Colonnade in the court of the temple. The Jews gathered round Him, saying, "How long are you going to keep us in suspense? If you are the Christ, tell us plainly." Jesus answered them, "I have told you, but you do not believe me. The miracles that I do in the name of [God] my Father witness to me, but you do not believe because you are not of my sheepfold. The sheep that are mine listen to my voice. I know them, and they follow me. I give them eternal life, and they will never perish. No one is able to snatch them out of my hand. My Father, who has given them to me, is greater than all. No one can snatch them out of my Father's hand. I [God the Son] and [God] the Father are one."

The Jews picked up stones to stone Him, but Jesus said to them, "My Father has given me power to perform many great miracles among you. For which of these do you stone me?" The Jews replied, "We are not going to stone you for any good deed, but for blasphemy; because you, a mere man, make yourself God." Jesus answered them, "Is it not written in your Law, 'I said you are gods'? If those to whom the word of God came were called 'gods', and the Scripture cannot be broken, what about me, the One whom [God] the Father set apart as His very own and sent into the world? Why do you accuse me of blasphemy because I said, 'I am the Son of God'? If I am not doing the works of God, then do not believe me, if I do them, even though you do not believe me, believe them, so that you may know and understand that [God] the Father is in me, and I [God the Son] am in the Father." Again they tried to arrest Him, but He escaped from their hands. [1]

Jesus looked towards heaven and prayed: "Father, the hour has come. Glorify your Son, that your Son may glorify you. You granted Him authority over all people that He may give eternal life to all those you have given Him. This is eternal life: to know you, the only true God [the Father], and Jesus Christ [God the Son] whom you have sent. ... The words that you gave me, I have given them, and they have received them ... and they have believed that you sent me." [2]

[1] John 10:22-39   [2] John 17:1-3,8

Day 260

The raising of Lazarus from the dead was a great miracle. But Jesus wanted people to know that, even more than the ability to bring people to 'physical life' again, He was able to give people new 'spiritual life'. In this way He could raise people from the 'spiritual death' of eternal separation from God, to the 'spiritual life' of eternal union with Him. Jesus was, therefore, Himself, the 'resurrection and the life.'

Jesus raises Lazarus from the dead

A man named Lazarus was sick. ... When He heard this, Jesus said, "This sickness will not end in death, but it is for God's glory so the Son of God may be glorified through it." ... When Jesus arrived, He found that Lazarus had already been in the tomb for four days. Bethany was about two miles from Jerusalem, and many Jews had gone to Martha and Mary to comfort them over the death of their brother.

When Martha heard that Jesus was coming, she went to meet Him, but Mary stayed at home. Martha said to Jesus, "Lord, if you had been here, my brother would not have died. But even now I know that God will grant you whatever you ask." Jesus said to her, "Your brother will rise again." Martha answered, "I know that he will rise again at the resurrection in the last day." Jesus said to her, "I am the resurrection and the life. Whoever believes in me, even though he dies, yet will he live, and whoever lives and believes in me will never die. Do you believe this?" She said to him, "Yes, Lord, I believe that you are the Messiah, the Son of God, the One who was to come into the world."

Jesus again sighed deeply and came to the tomb. It was a cave with a stone lying across the entrance. He said, "Take away the stone." Martha, the sister of the dead man, exclaimed, "But Lord, by this time there will be a bad smell. He has been dead for four days." Jesus said, "Did I not tell you that if you believed you would see the glory of God?" So they took away the stone. Jesus looked up and said, "Father, I thank you that you have heard me. I know that you always hear me, but I said this for the benefit of the people standing here, so that they may believe that you sent me." When He had said this, Jesus cried in a loud voice, "Lazarus, come out!" The dead man came out, his hands and feet wrapped in burial clothes and a cloth around his face. Jesus said to them, "Free him from the grave clothes and let him go." [1]

[Isaiah:] On this mountain He will destroy the shroud that is cast over all peoples, the sheet that covers all nations. He will swallow up death for ever. Then the Sovereign Eternal-God will wipe away the tears from all faces. [2]

[Jesus said:] I will not leave you orphans, I will come to you. In a little while the world will see me no more, but you will see me. Because I live, you also will live. [3]

[1] John 11:1,3,17-25,38-44 [2] Isaiah 25:7-8 [3] John 14:18-19

Day 261

Caiaphas was a Jewish leader who saw that Jesus was no ordinary man. It seems that God had shown him that, not only was Jesus going to die, but He was going to die for others. That did not prevent the Jewish leaders plotting to kill Jesus. Those leaders may have thought they were doing something new in seeking a way to kill Jesus, but God had worked it all out long ago. He knew what both they and He were going to do.

The Jewish leaders plot to kill Jesus

Many of the Jews who had come to visit Mary, and saw what Jesus did [in raising Lazarus from the dead], put their faith in Him. But some of them went to the Pharisees and told them what Jesus had done. Then the chief priests and the Pharisees called a meeting of the Sanhedrin. "What are we to do?" they asked. "This man is performing many miraculous signs. If we let Him go on like this, everyone will believe in Him, and then the Romans will come and destroy both our holy place and our nation."

One of them, named Caiaphas, who was the high priest that year, said to them, "You know nothing at all! You do not understand that it is better that one man die for the people than that the whole nation should perish." He did not say this on his own, but being the high priest that year, he prophesied that Jesus was to die for the [Jewish] nation, but also to bring together and make one the scattered children of God. From that day on they plotted together how they might put Him to death. For that reason Jesus no longer appeared publicly among the Jews but left there and withdrew to a region on the edge of the wilderness, to a village called Ephraim. There He stayed with His disciples.

The Jewish Passover was near and many from the country went up to Jerusalem to purify themselves before the Passover. They looked for Jesus and, as they stood in the temple, they asked each other, "What do you think? Will he come to the feast or not?" [1]

When they [the apostles] were released, they went to their people and told them all that the priests and elders had said. When they heard this, they raised their voices together to God saying, "Sovereign Lord, you made the heaven and the earth and everything in them, and you spoke by the mouth of your servant, our forefather, David: 'Why do the nations rage and the peoples plot in vain? The kings of the earth took their stand and the rulers gathered together against the Eternal-God and against His Anointed One.' In this city, Herod and Pontius Pilate, with the Gentiles and the people of Israel, joined together to conspire against your holy servant Jesus, whom you anointed to carry out all that your hand and your purpose had planned to happen. [2]

[1] John 11:45-56   [2] Acts 4:23-28

Day 262

In the world, important men and women are given seats of honour. God does the same thing, but His idea of what makes people important and great is not that of the world. We are to take our places in the world based on what we know to be important to God. The lowest place at a feast of the world may well be an important one in God's eyes.

Jesus is invited to the house of a Pharisee

One Sabbath day, Jesus went for a meal in the house of one of the ruling Pharisees. He was watched closely. ... Jesus noticed how the guests chose the places of honour at the table, so He told them this parable: "When you are invited by someone to a wedding banquet, do not take the place of honour, for someone more distinguished than you are may have been invited, and the host will come and say to you, 'Give this man your place.' Then you will be humiliated and have to take the lowest place. But when you are invited, go to the lowest place and sit there so that when your host comes, he will say to you, 'Friend, move up higher.' Then you will be honoured in the presence of all who sit at table with you. For every one who exalts himself will be humbled, and he who humbles himself will be exalted."

Jesus also said to His host, "When you give a luncheon or dinner, do not invite your friends, your brothers or relatives, or your wealthy neighbours, lest they invite you back and you are repaid. But when you give a banquet, invite the poor, the crippled, the lame, the blind. You will be blessed because they cannot repay you, and you will receive your recompense at the resurrection of the righteous." [1]

[Solomon:] Do not put yourself forward in the presence of a king, and do not stand in the place of great men. It is better for you to be told, 'Come up here,' than for you to be placed lower in the presence of a prince. [2]

Though the Eternal-God is high, He regards those who are lowly. The proud He recognises from a distance. [3] A man's pride will bring him low, but a man of humble spirit gains honour. [4]

"The pride of your heart has deceived you, you who live in the clefts of the rocks and make your home on the heights, you who say in your hearts, 'Who can bring me down to the ground?' Though you mount on high like the eagle and make your nest among the stars, I will bring you down from there," declares the Eternal-God. [5]

[Jesus said:] "There will be weeping there and gnashing of teeth, when you see Abraham, Isaac and Jacob and all the prophets in the kingdom of God, but you your-selves thrown out. People will come from east and west, and from north and south, and will sit down at the feast in the kingdom of God. Indeed, there are some who are last who will be first, and there are some who are first, who will be last." [6]

[1] Luke 14:1,7-14 [2] Proverbs 25:6-7 [3] Psalm 138:6 [4] Proverbs 29:23 [5] Obadiah 3-4 [6] Luke 13:28-30

Day 263

When Jesus comes again for all those who have received Him as Saviour and Lord, it will be like a banquet to which many guests are invited. Some of those who are invited will not be there because they have not responded to His invitation and some will try to get in not properly dressed, that is, clothed in their own good works. Some will be those you would least expect to be there.

The teaching of Jesus: The banquet for the king's son

One of those who sat at the table said to Jesus, "Blessed is he who will eat bread in the kingdom of God." Jesus said to him, "A man was preparing a great banquet and he invited many guests. At the time for the banquet he sent his servant to say to those who had been invited, 'Come, for everything is now ready.' But they all alike began to make excuses. The first said, 'I have just bought a piece of land and I must go and see it. Please excuse me.' Another said, 'I have bought five yoke of oxen, and I am going to try them out. Please excuse me.' Still another said, 'I have married a wife and so I am unable to come.'

The servant returned and reported this to his master. Then the master of the house became angry and said to his servant, 'Go quickly into the streets and lanes of the city and bring in the poor, the crippled, the blind and the lame.' The servant said, 'Sir! What you commanded has been done and there is still room.' Then the master said to his servant, 'Go out to the highways and country lanes and urge them to come in, so that my house will be full. I tell you, not one of those who were invited will have a taste of my banquet.' [1]

"When the king came in to see the guests, he noticed a man there who was not wearing a wedding robe. He said to him, 'Friend, how did you get in here without a wedding robe?' The man was speechless. Then the king said to the attendants, 'Tie him hand and foot, and throw him into the darkness outside where there will be weeping and gnashing of teeth.' For many are called, but few are chosen." [2]

[Solomon:] In his shade I delight to sit and his fruit is sweet to my taste. He brought me to the banquet house, and his banner over me is love. [3]

[John saw in his vision of heaven:] From the throne there came a voice saying, "Praise our God, all you His servants, all who fear Him, both small and great. Then I heard what sounded like the voice of a great multitude ... crying out, Hallelujah, for the Lord out God, the omnipotent reigns. Let us rejoice and be glad and give Him the glory! For the marriage of the Lamb has come and His bride has made herself ready. ... Then the angel said to me, "Write: 'Blessed are those who are invited to the wedding supper of the Lamb!'" [4]

---

[1] Luke 14:15-24 [2] Matthew 22:11-14 [3] Song of Songs 2:3-4 [4] Revelation 19:5-9

Day 264

We pay for something according to its worth. The most valuable thing anyone possesses is life - physical and spiritual. Jesus showed how easy it was to lose one's life, especially one's spiritual life, if we follow our own ideas rather than God's. He values each of our lives very highly indeed. Jesus gave Himself that we might be in His family. The more we see how much we mean to God, the more we are willing to pay the cost of being a disciple of Jesus.

The teaching of Jesus: The cost of following Him

Large crowds were travelling with Jesus. He turned to them and said: "If anyone comes to me and does not hate his father and mother, his wife and children, his brothers and sisters, even his own life, he cannot be my disciple. And anyone who does not carry his cross and follow me cannot be my disciple.

"Which of you who wants to build a tower, will not first sit down and count the cost to see if he has the means to complete it? Otherwise, when he has laid the foundation and is not able to finish it, everyone who sees it will ridicule him, saying, 'This man began to build but was not able to finish.' Or what king, who is about to go to war against another king, will not first sit down and consider whether he is able with ten thousand men to meet the one coming against him with twenty thousand? If he cannot, he will send a delegation and ask for terms of peace while the other is still a long way off. In the same way, whoever of you does not give up everything he has cannot be my disciple." [1]

"Whoever loves his father or mother more than me is not worthy of me; whoever loves his son or daughter more than me is not worthy of me; and anyone who does not take his cross and follow me is not worthy of me. Whoever finds his life will lose it, and whoever loses his life on my account will find it." [2]

Peter said to Him [Jesus], "We [the disciples] have left all we had to follow you!" Jesus said to them, "I tell you the truth, there is no one who has left home or wife or brothers or parents or children for the sake of the kingdom of God, who will not receive in return, many times more in this age, and, in the age to come, eternal life."[3]

[Paul wrote:] Whatever I had in the past which were gains to me, I have come to consider as loss for the sake of Christ. Furthermore, I count everything as loss compared to the surpassing gain of knowing Christ Jesus my Lord, for whose sake I have lost everything. I consider them as refuse, that I may gain Christ and be found in Him, not having a righteousness of my own that comes from obeying the law, but that which is through faith in Christ, the righteousness from God that comes by faith.[4]

[1] Luke 14:25-33 [2] Matthew 10:37-39 [3] Luke 18:28-30 [4] Philippians 3:7-9

Day 265

Everyone begins life as one of God's lost sheep. As he or she grows older, he or she strays further and further from Him, but He never ceases to look for His lost sheep. When the 'lost sheep' repents of his or her sin and trusts in Jesus Christ, there is great rejoicing in heaven because the lost sheep has been found. Even the angels sing for joy when we cease to stray from God and allow Him to find us and bring us into His fold.

The parables of Jesus: The lost sheep

The tax collectors and sinners came to listen to Jesus. The Pharisees and the scribes muttered, "This man welcomes sinners and eats with them." So Jesus told them this parable: "What man among you who has a hundred sheep and loses one of them, will not leave the ninety-nine in the wilderness and go after the lost sheep until he finds it? When he finds it, he lays it on his shoulders and goes home with great joy. When he arrives home, he gathers together his friends and neighbours and says, 'Rejoice with me for I have found my sheep which was lost.' I tell you, there will be more rejoicing in heaven over one sinner who repents than over ninety-nine righteous persons who have no need of repentance." [1]

"What do you think? If a man has a hundred sheep, and one of them goes astray, will he not leave the ninety-nine on the mountain and go to look for the one that is lost? I tell you the truth, if he finds it, he will be happier about that one sheep than about the ninety-nine that did not go astray. It is not the will of my Father in heaven that any of these little ones should be lost." [2]

"In those days and at that time," says the Eternal-God [through Jeremiah], "the people of Israel and people of Judah will go weeping together to seek the Eternal-God, their God. ... My people have been lost sheep, their shepherds have led them astray and caused them to roam on the mountains. They have gone from one mountain or hill to another, and they have forgotten their own resting place. Whoever found them devoured them and their enemies said, 'We are not guilty because they have sinned against the Eternal-God, their true pasture, the Eternal-God, the hope of their forefathers.'" [3]

[The word of God through Isaiah:] The Sovereign Eternal-God will come with power ... He will feed his flock like a shepherd. He will gather the lambs in his arms and carry them close to His bosom. He will gently lead those that have young. [4]

For this is what the Sovereign Eternal-God says [through Ezekiel]: "I myself will search for my sheep and seek them out. As a shepherd who is with his sheep, seeks out those which are scattered, so will I seek after my sheep and I will rescue them from every place where they were scattered in the day of clouds and darkness." [5]

1 Luke 15:1-7 2 Matthew 18:12-14 3 Jeremiah 50:4-7 4 Isaiah 40:10-11 5 Ezekiel 34:11-12

Day 266

Sheep stray foolishly from their shepherds. Coins are lost through no fault of their own. For whatever reason people are outside God's sheepfold, He searches for them not wanting one to be lost. Some people are like the lost coin which did nothing to be lost. Such people live in places or in families where the Good News of Jesus is not known. Finding them means going to where they are in their ignorance. Telling the Good News and showing what it means in our lives, is God's way of seeking for them.

The teaching of Jesus: The lost coin

[Jesus said:] "What woman who has ten silver coins and loses one, will not light a lamp, sweep the house and search carefully until she finds it? And when she has found it, she will call her friends and neighbours together and say, 'Rejoice with me! I have found the silver coin which I had lost.' I tell you, there is joy in the presence of the angels of God over one sinner who repents." [1]

Jesus saw Nathanael coming towards Him and said about him, "See, here is a true Israelite, in whom there is guile." Nathanael said to Jesus, "How is it that you know that about me?" Jesus answered, "Before Philip called you, while you were still under the fig-tree, I saw you." Then Nathanael said, "Teacher, you are the Son of God! You are the King of Israel!" [2]

"Am I a God near at hand," says the Eternal-God [through Jeremiah], "and not a God far off? Can anyone hide in secret places so that I cannot see him?" says the Eternal-God, "Do I not fill heaven and earth?" [3]

[God said through Isaiah:] "I was ready to reveal myself to those who did not ask for me, and to be found by those who did not seek for me. To a nation that did not call on my name, I said, 'Here am I, here I AM'. I have held out my hands all day long to a rebellious people who walk in a way that is not good, who pursue their own thoughts and who continually provoke me to my face." [4]

[Peter:] The Lord is not slow in keeping His promises, as some understand slowness, but He is patient with you, not wanting anyone to perish, but that all come to repentance. [5]

[David:] Where can I go from your Spirit? Where can I flee from your presence? If I ascend into heaven, you are there. If I make my bed in Sheol [the place of the dead], you are there. If I rise on the wings of the morning and settle on the farthest limits of the sea, even there your hand will lead me, your right hand will hold me fast. If I say, "Surely the darkness will hide me and the light around me become night," even the darkness hides nothing from you, and the night shines like the day, for darkness and light are alike to you. [6]

---

[1] Luke 15:8-10   [2] John 1:47-49   [3] Jeremiah 23:23-24   [4] Isaiah 65:1-3   [5] 2 Peter 3:9   [6] Psalms 139:7-12

Day 267

The son in this story represents every man and woman who has deliberately rebelled against God. The world without God looks very attractive, promises a lot but never keeps those promises. God waits, like the father in the story, for His rebellious and wayward children to return to Him, seek His forgiveness and restoration into His family.

The teaching of Jesus: The wayward son

Jesus said [to the 'sinners', Pharisees and scribes:] "There was a man who had two sons. The younger of them said to his father, 'Father give me the share of the property that will come to me.' So he divided his property between them. Soon after that, the younger son got together all that he had, set off for a distant country and there squandered his wealth in reckless living. When he had spent all that he had, there was a severe famine in that country, and he began to be in need. So he hired himself out to a citizen of that country who sent him into his fields to feed pigs. He would gladly have filled his stomach with the pods that the pigs were eating, but no one gave him anything. When he came to himself, he said, 'How many hired servants of my father have enough food to spare, and here I am dying of hunger! I will go back to my father and say to him: 'Father, I have sinned against heaven and against you. I am no longer worthy to be called your son; make me as one of your hired servants.' So he got up and went to his father.

"While he was still a long way off, his father saw him and was filled with compassion for him. He ran to his son, threw his arms round him and kissed him. The son said to him, 'Father, I have sinned against heaven and against you. I am no longer worthy to be called your son. Make me as one of your hired servants.' But the father said to his servants, 'Bring quickly the best robe and put it on him. Give him a ring for his finger and sandals for his feet. Bring the fatted calf and kill it. Let us have a feast and celebrate, for this my son was dead and is alive again; he was lost and is found.' So they began to celebrate. Now the older son was in the field. ... 'My son,' the father said, 'you are always with me, and all that I have is yours. We had to celebrate and rejoice, because this your brother was dead and is alive again; he was lost and is found.'" [1]

The word of the Eternal-God came to Jeremiah: "My people have exchanged their God, their glory for that which does not profit. ... My people have committed two sins: They have forsaken me, the fountain of living water, and they have dug cisterns for themselves, broken cisterns which cannot hold water." [2]

[David:] You, O Eternal-God, are a God who is merciful and gracious, slow to anger, abounding in love and faithfulness. Turn to me and be gracious to me.[3]

---

[1] Luke 15:11-25,31   [2] Jeremiah 2:12-13   [3] Psalm 86:15-16

Day 268

God is just. He shows mercy to all who repent of their sin and turn in faith to Him. Then He gives them work to do for Him, to live for His praise and honour. He asks from them faithfulness to Him, and an honest handling of all that He entrusts to them. He will reward those who serve Him, according to their faithfulness.

The teaching of Jesus: The unjust steward

Jesus said to His disciples: "There was a rich man who had a manager of his estate. The manager was accused of squandering the rich man's possessions. He called him and said to him, 'What is this I hear about you? Give an account of your management, because you cannot be manager any longer.' The manager of the estate said to himself, 'What shall I do now that my master is taking away my job. I am not strong enough to dig, and I am ashamed to beg. I know what to do so that, when I lose my job, people will welcome me into their houses.'

"He called in his master's debtors one by one. He asked the first, 'How much do you owe my master?' He said, 'One hundred measures of olive oil.' The manager said to him, 'Take your bill, sit down quickly, and write down fifty measures'. Then he asked another, 'And how much do you owe?' He said, 'One hundred measures of wheat.' He said to him, 'Take your bill and write eighty.' The master praised the dishonest manager because he had acted shrewdly. For the people of this world are more shrewd in dealing with their own generation than are the people of light. I tell you, make friends for yourselves by means of riches, so that when they have gone, you will be welcomed for ever into the homes of your friends.

"Whoever can be trusted with little things can be trusted with much, and whoever is dishonest with very little will also be dishonest with much. If, therefore, you have not been faithful in handling worldly wealth, who will trust you with true riches? If you have not been trustworthy with that which belongs to another, how can you be trusted with property of your own? No servant can serve two masters. Either he will hate one and love the other, or he will be devoted to one and despise the other. You cannot serve both God and wealth."

The Pharisees, who loved money, heard all this and ridiculed Him. He said to them, "You justify yourselves in the eyes of men, but God knows your hearts. What is highly valued among men is detestable in God's sight. ... It is easier for heaven and earth to pass away than for one jot of the law to become void. "[1]

"Every one to whom much is given, of him will much be required, and of him to whom much is entrusted, much more will be demanded." [2]

[1] Luke 16:1-15 [2] Luke 12:48

Day 269

Today, while we are alive is the time of opportunity to turn to God and live as He would have us live. After we die there will a great abyss or barrier between those in God's family and those in Satan's. We shall then acknowledge how just and merciful God has been in keeping His word. We shall not, then, be able to cross that abyss. We cannot even imagine what the two worlds separated by that abyss will be like, but in this story Jesus gives us very important information and a warning about that situation.

The teaching of Jesus: The rich man and Lazarus

[Jesus said:] "There was a rich man who was dressed in purple and fine linen and feasted every day. At his gate there was laid a destitute man named Lazarus who was covered with sores and longed to fill himself with what fell from the rich man's table. Even the dogs came and licked his sores. The time came when the poor man died and the angels carried him to be with Abraham. The rich man also died and was buried. In Hades [the place of the dead], he was in torment. He looked up and saw Abraham far away, with Lazarus by his side. So he cried out and said, 'Father Abraham, have pity on me and send Lazarus to dip the tip of his finger in water and cool my tongue, because I am in agony in this flame.' But Abraham said, 'Child, remember that you in your lifetime received your good things while Lazarus received bad things. Now he is comforted here and you are in agony. And besides all this, between us and you a great chasm has been fixed, so that those who want to pass from here to you cannot, nor can anyone pass over from there to us.' He answered, 'Then I beg you, father, send him to my father's house, for I have five brothers, so that he may warn them, lest they too come to this place of torment.' Abraham said, 'They have Moses and the Prophets. Let them listen to them.' He said, 'No, father Abraham, but if someone from the dead goes to them, they will repent.' He said to him, 'If they do not listen to Moses and the Prophets, neither will they be convinced even if someone should rise from the dead.'" [1]

[Paul:] This is evidence of God's righteous judgment so that you may be counted worthy of the kingdom of God for which you are suffering. ... He will punish those who do not know God and who do not obey the gospel of our Lord Jesus. They will suffer the punishment of everlasting destruction and banishment from the presence of the Lord and from the glory of His might on the day He comes to be glorified in His holy people, and all those who have believed in Him will marvel at Him. [2]

As it is appointed for men to die once, and after that to face judgment, so Christ, having been offered to take on Himself the sins of many people, will appear a second time, not to bear sin, but to bring full salvation to those who await Him. [3]

[1] Luke 16:19-31   [2] 2 Thessalonians 1:9-10   [3] Hebrews 9:27-28

Day 270

Faith is putting our trust in what we cannot see or touch. But we are not to put our faith in anything. God asks us to use our minds to understand who He is and what He has done. He then opens our minds to see that what He has said and done is right and true. We have faith in a living God who speaks to us through His word.

The teaching of Jesus: Faith

The apostles said to the Lord, "Increase our faith!" He replied, "If you have faith the size of a mustard seed, you could say to this mulberry tree, 'Be uprooted and be planted in the sea,' and it would obey you. [1] "I say to you, if you have faith like a mustard seed, you could say to this mountain, 'Move from here to there' and it will move. Nothing will be impossible for you." [2]

Early in the morning, as He [Jesus] was coming back to the city, he was hungry. He saw a fig-tree by the road, went up to it but found nothing on it except leaves. Then He said to it, "Never again will you bear fruit!" At once the tree withered. When the disciples saw this, they were amazed and they asked, "How is it that the fig-tree withered so quickly?" Jesus replied, "I tell you the truth, if you have faith and do not doubt, you will do not only what was done to the fig-tree, but even if you say to this mountain, 'Get up! Throw yourself into the sea,' it will be done. Whatever you ask for in prayer, with faith, you will receive." [3]

When they found Him [Jesus] on the other side of the lake, they said to Him, "Rabbi, when did you come here?" Jesus answered them, "I tell you the truth, you are looking for me, not because you saw the miracles but because you ate your fill. Do not work for the food that perishes, but work for the food that endures into eternal life. Then they said to Him, "What must we do to do the works of God?" Jesus answered, "This is the work of God, that you believe in the One He has sent." [4]

Faith is the assurance of things we hope for and the conviction of things we do not see. It was for faith that our forefathers were commended. By faith we understand that the universe was created by the word of God, so that what we see was not made out of things that are visible. ... Without faith it is impossible to please God, for whoever would come near to God must believe that He exists and that He rewards those who earnestly seek Him. [5]

[Jesus:] *"Whoever believes in me [Jesus Christ, God the Son] does not believe in me alone, but in the One [God the Father] who sent me. Whoever sees me, sees the One who sent me. I have come as a light into the world so that whoever believes in me should not live in darkness." [6]*

[1] Luke 17:5-6 [2] Matthew 17:20-21 [3] Matthew 21:18-22 [4] John 6:25,28-29
[5] Hebrews 11:1-2,6 [6] John 12:44-46

Day 271

Christians have been 'saved' from the 'family of Satan' to become members of the 'family of God' through faith in what Jesus Christ did for them on the Cross. That faith brings not only privileges but responsibilities. Our faith in God changes the way we look at everything and the way we behave. We owe it to God to serve Him with all our minds and strength because of all that He has done for us in creating us and saving us from the slavery of sin.

The teaching of Jesus: Faith and duty

Jesus said to His disciples: "Stumbling blocks are bound to come, but woe to those through whom they come. It would be better for him if he was thrown into the sea with a millstone tied round his neck than for him to cause one of these little ones to sin. So be on your guard. If your brother sins, rebuke him, and if he repents, forgive him. Even if he sins against you seven times in a day, and seven times turns to you and says, 'I repent,' forgive him."

"Would any one of you who had a servant ploughing or looking after the sheep, say to him when he comes in from the field, 'Come now and take your place at the table'? Would he not rather say, 'Get my supper ready and wait on me while I eat and drink and after that you may eat and drink'? Would he thank the servant for doing what he was commanded to do? So you also, when you have done everything you have been commanded, should say, 'We are unworthy servants; we have only done what it was our duty to do.'" [1]

[Jeremiah:] The word of the Eternal-God has meant insult and derision all day long for me. If I say, 'I will not mention Him or speak any more in His name,' there is within me as if a burning fire were shut up in my bones, and I am weary of holding it in. Indeed, I cannot. [2]

[The word of the Eternal-God through Amos:] Surely the Sovereign Eternal-God does nothing without revealing His secret to His servants the prophets. The lion has roared: who will not fear? The Sovereign Eternal-God has spoken: who can but prophesy? [3]

[Paul] When I preach the gospel, that gives me no grounds for boasting. I feel compelled to preach. Woe to me if I do not preach the gospel! If I do this of my own free will, then I have my reward, but if under compulsion, I am discharging the commission entrusted to me. [4]

So then, think of us [Apostles] as servants of Christ and trustees of the secret things of God. Moreover, it is required of stewards that they prove themselves faithful. ... I do not judge myself ... It is the Lord who judges me. [5]

[1] Luke 17:1-3,7-10   [2] Jeremiah 20:8-9   [3] Amos 3:7-8   [4] 1 Corinthians 9:16-17   [5] 1 Corinthians 4:1-4

Day 272

As Jesus left this earth to ascend into heaven in the sight of His disciples, so He will come again and then every eye will see Him. Most people will not believe that and will be surprised when He comes. Not so those believers who trust His word and are looking for His coming.

The teaching of Jesus: The coming of God's kingdom

The Pharisees asked Jesus when the kingdom of God would come. He replied, "The kingdom of God does not come with signs that you can see, nor will people say, 'Here it is,' or 'There it is,' because the kingdom of God is within you." Then He said to the disciples, "The time is coming when you will long to see one of the days of the Son of Man, and you will not see it. They will say to you, 'Look, there He is!' or 'Look, here He is!' Do not go running after them. For as the lightning, which flashes and lights up the sky from one end to the other, so will be the day of the Son of Man. But first he must suffer many things and be rejected by this generation.

"As it was in the days of Noah, so it will it be in the days of the Son of Man. They were eating, drinking, marrying and being given in marriage right up to the day when Noah entered the ark. Then the flood came and destroyed them all. ... I tell you, on that night there will be two people in one bed; one will be taken and the other will be left. There will be two women grinding grain together; one will be taken and the other will be left. There will be two men in the field; one will be taken and the other will be left." [1]

[Daniel said to Nebuchadnezzar:] "In the days of those kings, the God of heaven will set up a kingdom that will never be destroyed, nor will it ever be left to another people. It will crush all those kingdoms and bring them to an end, but it will endure for ever." [2]

[John:] To Him [Jesus] who loves us and has freed us from our sins by His blood, and has made us to be a kingdom and priests to serve His God and Father, to Him be the glory and the power for ever and ever! Amen. Look, He is coming with the clouds. Every eye will see Him, even those who pierced Him; and all the peoples of the earth will mourn because of Him. Even so shall it be! Amen. [3]

[Jesus said:] "At that time the sign of the Son of Man will appear in the sky, and all the tribes of the earth will mourn. They will see the Son of Man coming on the clouds of the heavens with power and great glory. He will send out His angels with a loud trumpet call, and they will gather His elect from the four winds, from one end of the heavens to the other." [4]

---

[1] Luke 17:20-27,34-37   [2] Daniel 2:44   [3] Revelation 1:5-7   [4] Matthew 24:30-31

Day 273

Some people ask, 'If God knows everything, why do we need to go on praying for the same things?' (a) It is God who knows everything who urges us to persevere; (b) He is working things out for the good of many, not for ours alone. (c) His knowledge of the right time to do things is greater than ours. We trust God to act to vindicate His justice, to fulfil His world-wide eternal purposes and to work out the best for each one of us.

The teaching of Jesus: The persistent widow

Jesus said: "In a certain town there was a judge who neither feared God nor respected men. There was a widow in that town who kept coming to him and saying, 'Grant me justice against my adversary.' For a time he refused, but later he said to himself, 'Even though I have no respect for God or for men, because this widow keeps bothering me, I will see that justice is done lest she wears me out with her continual coming!'" The Lord said, "Listen to what the unjust judge says. And will not God bring about justice for His chosen ones, who cry out to Him day and night? Will He delay in helping them? I tell you, He will see that they get justice, and speedily. However, when the Son of Man comes, will He find faith on the earth?" [1]

[Paul:] Finally, be strong in the Lord and in His strength. ... Take the helmet of salvation and the sword of the Spirit, which is the word of God. Pray on all occasions in the Spirit with all kinds of prayer and requests, so that you keep alert and persevere in praying for all the saints. [2] Be joyful always; pray continually; give thanks in all circumstances, for this is God's will for you in Christ Jesus.[3]

[Jesus:] "Be on your guard lest your hearts be overburdened with self-indulgence and that day come on you suddenly, as it will come on all who live on the face of the whole earth. Be always alert and pray that you may be able to escape all these things that will take place and stand in the presence of the Son of Man. [4]

[John:] Beloved, if our hearts do not condemn us, we have confidence before God and receive from Him whatever we ask because we obey His commands and do what pleases Him. [5] I write this to you who believe in the name of the Son of God so that you may know that you have eternal life. And we have this assurance that if we ask anything according to His will, He hears us. And knowing, as we do, that He hears us, we also know that He will grant us whatever we ask of Him.[6]

[Peter:] Dear brothers and sisters, do not forget that, with the Lord, one day is as a thousand years, and a thousand years as one day. The Lord is not slow in keeping His promises, according some people's ideas of slowness, but is patient with you, not wanting that anyone should perish, but that everyone should come to repentance. [7]

[1] Luke 18:1-8   [2] Ephesians 6:10,17-18   [3] 1 Thessalonians 5:16-17   [4] Luke 21:34-36
[5] 1 John 3:21-22   [6] 1 John 5:13-15   [7] 2 Peter 3:8-9

Jesus came to seek and to save people from the kingdom of Satan and to give them 'new birth' into the kingdom of God. But only those who are good can enter that kingdom - 'good' as God means that word. Those who think they are good, but are not, He will reject. Those who recognise that they are sinful but want to be good in God's eyes, He will make fit for His kingdom.

The teaching of Jesus: Selfrighteousness

Jesus told this parable to people who trusted in their own goodness and despised everyone else: "Two men went to the temple to pray, one was a Pharisee and the other a tax collector. The Pharisee stood up and prayed to himself: 'God, I thank you that I am not like other men, thieves, evildoers, adulterers, or even like this tax collector. I fast twice a week and I give a tenth of all I earn.' But the tax collector, standing at a distance, would not even look up to heaven, but beat his breast saying, 'O God, be merciful to me, a sinner.' I tell you, this man went home justified before God, rather than the other, for everyone who exalts himself will be humbled, but he who humbles himself will be exalted." [1] Woe to you, scribes and Pharisees, you hypocrites! You shut the kingdom of heaven in men's faces. You neither enter yourselves nor do you let those enter who are about to do so. ... You swallow up widows' houses and then cover it up by making long prayers. You will receive the greater condemnation" [2]

Jesus answered them, "It is not those who are healthy who need a doctor, but those who are sick. I have not come to call the righteous, but sinners to repentance. ... No one sews a patch from a new garment on to an old one. If he does, the new one will be torn, and the patch from the new one will not match the old one. No one pours new wine into old wineskins. If he does, the new wine will burst the skins, the wine will be spilled, and the wineskins will be ruined. New wine must be put into new wineskins.[3]

[Paul:] The wrath of God is revealed from heaven against all ungodliness and unrighteousness of men, who, in their wickedness suppress the truth, for what can be known of God has been made plain for them to see. Since the creation of the world God's eternal power and His divine nature, although invisible, have been made clearly understandable by what is visible, so that everyone is without excuse. Although they knew God they neither honoured Him as God, nor gave thanks to Him and so they became darkened in their thinking and futile in their reasoning.[4] You, therefore, are without excuse, for in passing judgment on another you condemn yourself. [5]

This righteousness from God comes through believing in Jesus Christ for all who believe. There is no difference, for all have sinned and fall short of the glory of God.[6]

[1] Luke 18:9-14   [2] Matthew 23:13-14   [3] Luke 5:31-32,36-38   [4] Romans 1:18-21   [5] Romans 2:1   [6] Romans 3:22-23

Day 275

God's plan for people is always the best. He designed men and women to live in a life-long marriage bond. That is the best way for them, for their children and for society. When things go wrong and God allows a different plan, that never replaces His original plan. God is gracious and He restores those who have sinned against Him.

The teaching of Jesus: Marriage and divorce

Some Pharisees came to test Jesus. They asked Him, "Is it lawful for a man to divorce his wife?" He answered them, "What did Moses command you?" They said, "Moses permitted a man to write a 'bill of divorce' and send her away." Jesus said to them, "It was because of your hardness of heart that Moses wrote this precept in your law. But from the beginning of creation God made them male and female. For this reason a man will leave his father and mother and be joined to his wife. The two will so become one flesh that they are no longer two, but one. Therefore what God has joined together, let man not separate." When they were in the house again, the disciples questioned Jesus about this. He said to them, "Whoever divorces his wife and marries another woman commits adultery against her. And if a woman divorces her husband and marries another man, she commits adultery." [1]

"It was also said, 'Whoever divorces his wife must give her a certificate of divorce,' but I tell you that anyone who divorces his wife, except on the grounds of marital unfaithfulness, causes her to commit adultery, and whoever marries a woman who has been divorced commits adultery." [2]

The disciples said to Him, "If this is the case between a husband and his wife, it is better not to marry." Jesus said to them, "Not everyone can accept what I have said, but only those to whom it has been given. There are eunuchs who have born that way, others have been made eunuchs by men, and others have made themselves eunuchs for the sake of the kingdom of heaven. Let anyone who can accept this do so" [3]

To those who are married, I [Paul] give this command (not I, but the Lord): A wife is not to separate from her husband. But if she does, let her remain unmarried or else be reconciled to her husband. A husband must not divorce his wife. To the rest I say this (I, not the Lord): If a brother [believer] has a wife who is not a believer and she agrees to live with him, he must not divorce her. And if a woman has a husband who is not a believer and he agrees to live with her, she must not divorce him. ... Whatever may be the situation, let each of you lead the life which God assigned to you when God called you. [4]

Let marriage be honoured by all, and the marriage bed kept pure, for fornicators and adulterers will come under God's judgment. [5]

---

[1] Mark 10:2-12   [2] Matthew 5:31-32   [3] Matthew 19:10-12   [4] 1 Corinthians 7:10-13   [5] Hebrews 13:4

Day 276

Jesus loved little children as well as grown-up men and women. He understood the simple way in which their minds worked. Children have a very simple trust in their parents. Jesus wants the faith of adults in God to be as simple and whole-hearted as the faith of a child in its parents.

Jesus blesses little children

Jesus sat down, called the twelve to Him and said, "If anyone wants to be first, he must be the last of all and the servant of all." He took a little child, put him in the midst of them, and, taking him in His arms, said to them, "Whoever receives a child like this in my name, receives me; and whoever receives me like this does not receive me but the One who sent me." [1]

People brought little children to Jesus so that He might touch them, but the disciples rebuked them. When Jesus saw this, He was indignant and said to them, "Let the little children come to me, and do not stop them, for the kingdom of God belongs to such as these. I tell you the truth, whoever will not receive the kingdom of God like a little child will not enter it at all." He took the children in His arms, laid His hands on them and blessed them.[2]

[Nehemiah:] At the dedication of the wall of Jerusalem, they sought out the Levites from where they lived and brought them to Jerusalem to celebrate joyfully the dedication with gladness and thanksgiving and with singing and with the music of cymbals, harps and lyres. ... On that day they offered great sacrifices and were glad because God had made then rejoice with great joy. The women and children also rejoiced. The sound of joy in Jerusalem was heard far away. [3]

[The word of the Eternal-God through Isaiah:] He [God] feeds His flock like a shepherd. He gathers the lambs in His arms and carries them close to Himself. He gently leads those that have young. [4]

When they had eaten, Jesus said to Simon Peter, "Simon, son of John, do you love me more than these?" He said to Him, "Yes, Lord. You know that I do." Jesus said to him, "Feed my lambs." [5]

The disciples came to Jesus and asked Him, "Who is the greatest in the kingdom of heaven?" He called a little child and put him in the midst of them. Then He said: "I tell you the truth, unless you repent and become like little children, you will never enter the kingdom of heaven. Therefore, whoever humbles himself and becomes as this little child is the greatest in the kingdom of heaven. And whoever receives a little child like this in my name receives me." [6]

---

[1] Mark 9:35-37 [2] Mark 10:13-16 [3] Nehemiah 12:27,43 [4] Isaiah 40:11 [5] John 21:15 [6] Matthew 18:1-5

Day 277

Most people would like to be rich in this world, and there is nothing wrong with riches rightly gained and used. But this world's riches only last while people are alive to enjoy them. God promises much greater and more lasting riches to those who give themselves to Him and use all they have as in trust from Him, to be used to honour Him and in ways which are pleasing to him. We cannot take our riches with us when we die, but we can use them to lay up spiritual treasure to be there for us after we die.

Jesus and the rich young man

As Jesus was setting out on a journey, a man ran up to Him and fell on his knees before Him and said, "Good Teacher, what must I do to inherit eternal life?" Jesus said to him, "Why do you call me good? No one is good except God. You know the commandments: 'You shall not murder. You shall not commit adultery. You shall not steal. You shall not bear false testimony. You shall not steal. Honour your father and mother.'" He replied, "Teacher, all these I have kept from my youth." Jesus looked at him and loved him and said to him, "One thing you lack: go and sell everything you have and give to the poor, and you will have treasure in heaven, then come, follow me."

On hearing this the man's face fell and he went sorrowfully away, because he had great possessions. Jesus looked around and said to His disciples, "How hard it is for the rich to enter the kingdom of God!" The disciples were amazed at His words, but Jesus said to them again, "Children, it is hard to enter the kingdom of God! It is easier for a camel to go through the eye of a needle than for a rich man to enter the kingdom of God." The disciples were even more astonished and said to each other, "Who then can be saved?" Jesus looked at them and said, "With man this is impossible, but not with God, for all things are possible with God." [1]

"Do not store up for yourselves treasures on earth, where moth and rust destroy, and where thieves break in and steal. Store up for yourselves treasures in heaven, where neither moth nor rust destroy, and where thieves do not break in and steal. For where your treasure is, there will your heart be also. ... No one can serve two masters. Either he will hate the one and love the other, or he will be devoted to the one and despise the other. You cannot serve God and wealth. [2]

[Paul:] Godliness with contentment is a source of great gain. We brought nothing into the world, and we will take nothing out of it. But if we have food and clothing, we will be content with them. Those who want to get rich fall into temptation and are trapped into many foolish and harmful desires that plunge men into ruin and destruction. For the love of money is the root of all kinds of evil. [3]

[1] Mark 10:17-27   [2] Matthew 6:19-21,24   [3] 1 Timothy 6:6-10

Day 278

When people repent of their sin and turn to God, He gives them what they need and not what they deserve. All the workers in the vineyard received the wages they had earned. Some received more, but that was because of the grace of the landowner and the amount was not based on the amount of work they had done. God's grace to sinners is like that. The forgiveness they receive is unearned and undeserved and is not related to the good works they do.

The teaching of Jesus: The workmen in the vineyard

[Jesus said:] "The kingdom of heaven is like a landowner who went out early in the morning to hire workmen for his vineyard. He agreed to pay some workers a denarius for the day and sent them into his vineyard. About the third hour [9 am] he went out and saw others standing idle in the market-place. He said to them, 'You also go and work in my vineyard, and I will pay you whatever is right.' So they went. He went out again about the sixth hour [noon] and about the ninth hour [3 pm] and did the same thing. About the eleventh hour [5 pm] he went out and found others still standing around. He said to them, 'Why are you standing here idle all day?' They answered him, 'Because no one has hired us.' He said to them, 'You also go into my vineyard.'

"When evening came, the owner of the vineyard said to his manager, 'Call the workmen and pay them their wages, beginning with the last ones hired and ending with the first.' The workmen who were hired about the eleventh hour [5 pm] came and each one received a denarius. When the first came, they expected to receive more, but each one of them also received a denarius. On receiving this, they grumbled against the landowner saying, 'These who came last have worked only one hour, and you have made them equal to us who have borne the burden of the work during the heat of the day.' He answered one of them, 'Friend, I am not being unjust to you. Did you not agree with me to work for a denarius? Take what you have earned and go. I have chosen to give the man who was hired last the same as I gave you. Do I not have the right to do what I choose with my own money? Or are you envious because I am generous?' So the last will be first, and the first will be last." [1]

[Paul:] When a man works, his wages are not credited to him as a gift, but as an obligation. But to the man who does not work but trusts in Him [God] who justifies the ungodly, his faith is credited to him as righteousness. [2]

It is by grace you have been saved, through faith. This is not of your own doing, it is the gift of God. It is not because of works, so that no one can boast. [3]

1 Matthew 20:1-16 2 Romans 4:4-5 3 Ephesians 2:8-9

Day 279

The disciples were with Jesus for three years and often heard Him teaching people about God, His Father, but they found it very difficult to understand what He was planning to do. How could the Messiah they were hoping Jesus was, suffer ridicule and death? Only when Jesus rose again from the dead did they understood.

Jesus foretells His suffering

Jesus and His disciples went on to the villages of Caesarea Philippi. On the way He asked them, "Who do people say that I am?" They answered him, "Some say John the Baptist; others say Elijah; and still others, one of the prophets." He asked them, "But what about you? Who do you say that I am?" Peter answered, "You are the Christ [the Messiah]." Jesus charged them to tell no one about Him. He then began to teach them that the Son of Man must undergo much suffering and be rejected by the elders, the chief priests and the scribes, and that He must be put to death and after three days rise again. [1]

They [the disciples] were on the road up to Jerusalem, with Jesus walking in front of them. The disciples, who were following, were astonished and afraid. Again He took the twelve aside and began to tell them what was about to happen to Him. He said, "See, we are going up to Jerusalem, and the Son of Man will be handed over to the chief priests and scribes. They will condemn Him to death and will hand Him over to the Gentiles, who will mock Him and spit on Him, flog Him and kill Him. After three days He will rise." [2]

When the time approached for Jesus to be taken up, He set his face to go to Jerusalem, and He sent messengers on ahead of Him. They went into a Samaritan village to get things ready for Him, but the people there did not receive Him because His face was set for Jerusalem. When the disciples James and John saw this, they said, "Lord, do you want us to command fire to come down from heaven to consume them?" Jesus turned and rebuked them saying, "You do not know what kind of spirit you are showing, for the Son of Man did not come to destroy men's lives, but to save them." Then they went on to another village. [3]

[Paul:] Now, brothers and sisters, let me remind you of the gospel I preached to you, which you received, on which your faith stands and by which you are saved, that is, if you have held firmly to what I preached to you. Otherwise, you believed in vain. I passed on to you what I received. First of all, that Christ died for our sins according to the Scriptures, that He was buried and that He rose from the dead on the third day according to the Scriptures. [4]

[1] Mark 8:27-31 [2] Mark 10:32-34 [3] Luke 9:51-56 [4] 1 Corinthians 4:1-4

Day 280

People are born with a nature which makes them always want to put themselves first. It is natural for us to seek the place of the greatest benefit and of the greatest honour. Jesus came to teach that the wrong kind of ambition only leads to discord. Putting others first is His way, and only when His way is followed is there perfect harmony among people. Those who will be considered great in the kingdom of God will be those who have worked to serve others in the lowest, humblest situations.

The teaching of Jesus: Ambition

James and John, the sons of Zebedee, came to Him [Jesus] and said to Him, "Teacher! Will you please do for us whatever we ask." He asked them, "What do you want me to do for you?" They replied, "Grant that we may sit, one on you right and one on your left, in your glory." Jesus said to them, "You do not know what you are asking," "Are you able to drink the cup that I drink or be baptised with the baptism with which I am baptised?" They answered, "We are able." Jesus said to them, " The cup which I drink, you will drink and you will be baptised with the baptism with which I am baptised, but to sit at my right hand or at my left hand is not for me to grant. These places are for those for whom they have been prepared."

When the ten heard about this, they were indignant with James and John. Jesus called them together and said to them, "You know that those who are recognized as rulers of the Gentiles lord it over them, and their great men exercise authority over them. It must not be so with you. Instead, whoever desires to become great among you must be your servant, and whoever wants to be first among you must be the slave of all. For even the Son of Man did not come to be served, but to serve, and to give His life as a ransom for many." [1]

Peter said to Him, "We have left everything and followed you! What then will we receive? Jesus said to them, "I tell you the truth, in the new age when the Son of Man sits down on the throne of His glory, you who have followed me will also sit on twelve thrones and judge the twelve tribes of Israel. [2]

[Paul:] I am determined to know Christ and the power of His resurrection; to share in His sufferings by becoming like Him in His death so that, somehow, I might attain to the resurrection from the dead. Not that I have already attained this, nor that I have already been made perfect, but I press on to grasp and make my own, that for which Christ Jesus grasped me to make me His own. I do not consider, brothers and sisters, that I have yet grasped it, but this one thing I do, forgetting what lies in the past, I press on towards the goal of winning the heavenly prize to which God in Christ Jesus calls me. [3]

[1] Mark 10:35-45   [2] Matthew 19:27-29   [3] Philippians 3:10-14

Day 281

Jesus, as the Light of the world, shows people what they should be doing at any time in order to fulfil the purpose of their creation. Here is His warning to us to use every moment we have of life, first of all to be right with God, and then to fulfil His purposes for us. When we appear before Him at the judgment it will be too late.

The teaching of Jesus: A right time for everything

[Jesus said to the Pharisees and Sadducees:] "In the evening you say, 'It will be fair weather for the sky is red'. And in the morning you say, 'It will be stormy today, for the sky is red.' You know how to interpret the appearance of the sky, but you cannot interpret the signs of the times. [1] He also said to the crowds, "When you see a cloud rising in the west, you say, "It is going to rain," and it does. When the wind blows from the south, you say, "It is going to be hot," and it is. You hypocrites, you know how to interpret the signs of the earth and sky but you do not know how to interpret the present time. Why do not you not judge for yourselves what is right for this moment? Then, as you are going with your accuser to the magistrate, make every effort to be reconciled to him while you are on the way, lest he drag you to the judge, and the judge turn you over to the officer, and the officer put you into prison. I tell you the truth, you will not get out until you have paid the last penny." [2]

These were the men who came to David at Ziklag, ... men of Issachar, who understood the times and knew what Israel should do, 200 chiefs. [3]

[Solomon:] For everything, there is a season and for every activity under heaven there is a time: a time to be born and a time to die, ... a time to tear down and a time to build, a time to weep and a time to laugh, a time to mourn and a time to dance, a time to scatter stones and a time to gather them, a time to embrace and a time to refrain, a time to search and a time to give up, a time to keep and a time to throw away, a time to tear and a time to mend, a time to be silent and a time to speak, a time to love and a time to hate, a time for war and a time for peace. ... He has made everything beautiful in its time. He has also set eternity in the hearts of men; yet they cannot fathom what God has done from beginning to end. [4]

[Solomon:] Remember your Creator in the days of your youth, before the evil days come and the years approach when you will say, "I find no enjoyment in them."[5]

[David:] I trust in you, O Eternal-God. I say, "You are my God. My times are in your hands." [6] Every day that you ordained for me was written in your book before there were any of them. [7]

Teach us to number our days aright, that we may gain a heart of wisdom.[8]

[1] Matthew 16:1-3 [2] Luke 12:54-59 [3] 1 Chronicles 12:1,32 [4] Ecclesiastes 3:1-11 [5] Ecclesiastes 12:1 [6] Psalm 31:1-3,15 [7] Psalm 139:16 [8] Psalm 90:12

Day 282

Many people think that good people mix with good people and bad with bad. For a good man to mix with bad people surely means that the 'good man' is really bad! Not so with Jesus. He could mix with bad people because He could make them good. We can do the same thing if Jesus is with us, and that is what He wants us to do for Him.

Zacchaeus meets Jesus

He [Jesus] entered Jericho and was passing through it. There was a man there named Zacchaeus. He was a chief tax collector and was rich. He tried to see who Jesus was, but he could not because of the crowd, for he was short in stature. So he ran ahead and climbed up into a sycamore tree in order to see Him, for Jesus was about to pass that way. When Jesus reached the place, He looked up and said to Him, "Zacchaeus, hurry, come down for I must stay at your house today." So He hurried down and received him joyfully. When the people saw this they muttered among themselves, saying "He has gone to be the guest of a 'sinner'." But Zacchaeus stood up and said to the Lord, "See, Lord! I give now half of my possessions to the poor, and if I have cheated anyone out of anything, I will pay him back four times the amount." Jesus said to him, "Today salvation has come to this house, because this man too, is a son of Abraham. For the Son of Man came to seek and to save the lost." [1]

Tax collectors also came [to John the Baptist] to be baptised and they said to him, "Teacher, what should we do?" He said to them, "Do not collect more than the amount fixed for you," Some soldiers asked Him, "And what shall we do?" He replied, "Do not extort money by threats and do not accuse people falsely. Be satisfied with your pay." [2]

Jesus went out again by the shore of the lake. A large crowd came to Him, and He taught them. As He walked along, He saw Levi son of Alphaeus sitting at the tax collector's booth. Jesus said to Him, "Follow me." He got up and followed Him. As Jesus was sitting at table in Levi's house, many tax collectors and "sinners" were also eating with Him and His disciples, for there were many who followed Him. When the scribes of the Pharisees saw Him eating with the "sinners" and tax collectors, they asked His disciples: "Why does He eat with tax collectors and 'sinners'?" When Jesus heard this, He said to them, "Those who are well do not need a doctor, but only those who are sick. I have not come to call the righteous, but sinners." [3]

"To what shall I compare this generation? ... John came neither eating nor drinking, and they say, 'He has a demon.' The Son of Man came eating and drinking, and they say, 'He is a glutton and a drunkard, a friend of tax collectors and 'sinners.' Yet wisdom is vindicated by her actions. [4]

[1] Luke 19:1-10 [2] Luke 3:12-14 [3] Mark 2:13-17 [4] Matthew 11:16,18-19

Day 283

This parable is for Christians. To each one God entrusts life, time, possibly money and different abilities. One day each person will have to give an account of what God has entrusted to him or her. The measure will not be the amount of profit gained but faithfulness in the use of whatever God has entrusted to them.

The teaching of Jesus: The employer, the servants and the talents

[Jesus said of the kingdom of heaven:] "It is like a man who was about to go on a journey. He called his servants together and entrusted his property to them. To one he gave five talents, to another two talents, and to another one talent, each according to his ability. Then he went on his journey. ... After a long time the master of those servants returned and settled his accounts with them. He who had received the five talents came and brought him five more, saying, 'Master, you entrusted me with five talents. See, I have gained five more.' His master said to him, 'Well done, good and faithful servant! You have been faithful with a few things; I will put you in charge of many things. Come and share your master's happiness!'

"The man with the two talents also came. ... His master replied, 'Well done, good and faithful servant! You have been faithful over little; I will put you in charge of much. ... Then the man who had received one talent came saying, 'Master, I knew you to be a hard man, reaping where you did not sow and gathering where you have not scattered seed. I was afraid and so I went and hid your talent in the ground. Here you have what is yours.' His master answered him, 'You wicked and lazy servant! ... 'Take the talent away from him and give it to the one who has the ten talents. For to everyone who has, more will be given, and he will have an abundance. But from those who have nothing, even what they have will be taken from them. And throw that worthless servant into the outer darkness where there will be weeping and gnashing of teeth.'" [1]

[Paul wrote to servants:] Serve wholeheartedly, as to the Lord and not to men, for you know that whatever good anyone does, he will receive his reward from the Lord, whether he is a slave or free. [2]

[Paul:] No other foundation can any one lay other than that which is already laid, which is Jesus Christ. If any one builds on this foundation using gold, silver, precious stones, wood, hay or straw, his work will be shown to be what it is, because the Day will reveal it. It will be revealed with fire, for fire will test the worth of each man's work. If what he has built on the foundation survives, he will receive his reward. If it is burned up, he will suffer loss. He himself will be saved, but only as one who has escaped through flames. [3]

[1] Matthew 25:14-16,19-30   [2] Ephesians 6:7-8   [3] 1 Corinthians 3:11-15

Day 284

The perfume which Mary poured on Jesus' feet was a measure of her respect for Him. The impression Jesus gave to people who knew Him and accepted Him was like that of a sweet smelling scent. To those who rejected Him, He was like the 'scent of death'. To those who accepted Him, He was like the 'scent of life'. So it is with the impression true Christians give to others.

Jesus is anointing with perfume

Six days before the Passover, Jesus came to Bethany, where Lazarus lived, whom Jesus had raised from the dead. There they prepared a supper for Him. Martha served, while Lazarus was among those who sat at the table with Him. Mary took about a pint of pure nard, an expensive perfume and she poured it on Jesus' feet and wiped them with her hair. The house was filled with the fragrance of the perfume. But one of His disciples, Judas Iscariot, who was about to betray Him, said, "Why was this perfume not sold for three hundred denarii and given to the poor." He did not say this because he cared for the poor but because he was a thief and he held the bag of money; he took for himself what was put into it. Jesus said, "Leave her alone. She bought it so that she might have if for the day of my burial. You always have the poor with you, but you will not always have me." [1] "She has done what she could. She has anointed my body for the burial. I tell you the truth, wherever the gospel is preached throughout the world, what she has done will be told, in remembrance of her." [2]

"Your throne, O God, is for ever and ever. The sceptre of righteousness is the sceptre of your kingdom. You love righteousness and hate wickedness, therefore God, your God, has anointed you with the oil of joy above your fellows. All your robes are fragrant with myrrh, aloes and cassia. From ivory palaces the music of stringed instruments makes you glad. [3]

Then Noah built an altar to the Lord. He took of every clean animal and clean bird and sacrificed them as burnt offerings on the altar. When the Eternal-God smelled the pleasing aroma He said in His heart: "I will never again curse the ground because of man, for every inclination of his heart is evil from his youth, nor will I ever again destroy all living creatures, as I have done." [4]

[Paul:] Thanks be to God, who always leads us in triumphal procession in Christ and through us spreads everywhere the fragrance of the knowledge of God. For we are to God [the Father] the aroma of Christ [God the Son] among both those who are being saved and those who are perishing. To the latter we are the smell of death; to the former, the fragrance of life. Who is qualified for this ministry? Unlike many, we do not peddle God's word for profit. We speak like men sent from God. [5]

[1] John 12:2-8　[2] Mark 14:9　[3] Psalm 45: 6-8　[4] Genesis 8:20-21　[5] 2 Corinthians 2:14-17

Day 285

The people who thronged around Jesus as He rode on a donkey into Jerusalem did not realise that what was happening then had been foretold centuries before in their Scriptures, our Old Testament. Everything said about Him there was fulfilled. This was a moment of triumph for Jesus which would not be repeated until He came to earth again to lead His people into the New Jerusalem.

Jesus enters Jerusalem in triumph

Jesus went on ahead of them [His disciples], on His way to Jerusalem. As He came near Bethphage and Bethany, at the hill called the Mount of Olives, He sent two of His disciples, saying to them, "Go into the village ahead of you, and as you enter it, you will find a colt tied there, which no one has ever ridden. Untie it and bring it here. If anyone asks you, 'Why are you untying it?' say this, 'The Lord has need of it.'" Those who were sent ahead went and found it as He had told them. As they were untying the colt, its owners said to them, "Why are you untying the colt?" They said, "The Lord has need of it." They brought it to Jesus, threw their cloaks over the colt and set Jesus on it. As He rode along, people spread their cloaks on the road.

When He came near where the road goes down the Mount of Olives, the whole crowd of disciples began to rejoice and loudly to praise God for all the miracles they had seen, crying: "Blessed is the king who comes in the name of the Lord!" and "Peace in heaven and glory in the highest heaven!" Some of the Pharisees in the crowd said to Jesus, "Teacher, restrain your disciples!" He replied, "I tell you that if these kept quiet, the stones would cry out."

As He approached the city He looked at it and wept over it, saying, "O that you knew in this your day what would bring you peace! But now it is hidden from your eyes. The time is coming upon you when your enemies will build fortifications against you and shut you in on every side. They will dash you to the ground, you and the children within you. They will not leave one stone upon another, because you did not recognise the time when God was visiting you." [1]

This took place to fulfil what was spoken through the prophet [Zechariah]: [2] "Rejoice greatly, O Daughter of Zion! Shout aloud, O daughter of Jerusalem. See, your king comes to you, triumphant and victorious, gentle, and riding on a donkey, on a colt, the foal of a donkey." [3]

"Do not be afraid, O Daughter of Zion; see, your king is coming, sitting on a colt, the foal of a donkey." His disciples did not understand these things at first, but when Jesus was glorified they remembered that these things which had been written about Him, had happened to Him. [4]

[1] Luke 19:28-44   [2] Matthew 21:4   [3] Zechariah 9:9   [4] John 12:15-16

Day 286

Good crops of figs on many fig trees was a symbol of prosperity for Israel. The loss of a crop was a symbol of national disaster. A fig-tree without figs was a picture of failure. The fig-tree is, therefore, a picture of people who fail to fulfil the purpose for which God created them. God is gracious and gives them time to repent and turn to Him.

The teaching of Jesus: The unfruitful fig-tree

He [Jesus] told them this parable: "A man had a fig-tree planted in his vineyard. When he went to look for fruit on it he did not find any. So he said to the vinedresser, 'For three years now I have been coming to look for fruit on this fig-tree and have found none. Cut it down! Why should it take up the ground?' The man answered him, 'Sir, leave it alone for one more year, and I will dig round it and put manure on it. Perhaps it will bear fruit next year, but if not, cut it down'" [1]

As they were leaving Bethany, Jesus was hungry. Seeing in the distance a fig-tree in leaf, He went to see if there was any fruit on it. When He came to it, He found nothing but leaves, because it was not yet the season for figs. Then He said to the tree, "May no one ever eat fruit from you again." His disciples heard Him say this. ... In the morning, as they were passing it, they saw the fig-tree withered from the roots. Peter remembered and said to Jesus, "Rabbi, look! The fig-tree you cursed has withered!" Jesus answered, "Have faith in God. ... I tell you, whatever you ask for in prayer, believe that you have received it and it will be yours."" [2]

When he [John the Baptist] saw many of the pharisees and Sadducees coming to be baptised, he said to them, " You brood of vipers! Who warned you to flee from the wrath to come. Bear fruit that is in keeping with repentance. Do not think that you can presume to say to yourselves, 'We have Abraham as our forefather.' I tell you that God is able from these stones to raise up children to Abraham. The axe is already laid to the roots of the trees and every tree that does not yield good fruit will be cut down and thrown into the fire. [3]

[The word of God through Isaiah:] Come near you nations and listen, give heed, you peoples! ... For the Eternal-God is angry with all nations, His wrath is on all their armies. ... All the stars of the heavens will be dissolved and the sky will be rolled up like a scroll. The multitudes of stars will drop from the skies like withered leaves from a vine, like shrivelled figs from a fig-tree. [4]

[The prayer of the prophet Habakkuk:] Though the fig-tree does not blossom and there is no fruit on the vines, though the olive crop fails and the fields yield no food, though there are no sheep in the pen and no cattle in the stalls, yet I will rejoice in the Eternal-God. I will be joyful in the God of my salvation. [5]

[1] Luke 13:6-9 [2] Mark 11:12-14,20-21,24 [3] Matthew 3:7-10 [4] Isaiah 34:1-4 [5] Habakkuk 3:17-18

Day 287

The Temple was the Holy place where God met His people and where they could offer sacrifices for their sins. When people did things which were detestable to God in the temple, He had either to clear out the evil or cease to live there.

Jesus cleans up the temple

When Jesus entered Jerusalem [riding on a donkey] the city was in turmoil and some people asked, "Who is this?" Others said, "This is the prophet, Jesus from Nazareth of Galilee." Jesus went into the temple and drove out all who bought and sold there. He overturned the tables of the money changers and the seats of those who sold doves. He said to them, "It is written, 'My house will be called a house of prayer,' but you have made it a 'den of robbers'." The blind and the lame came to Him in the temple and He healed them. When the chief priests and the scribes saw the wonderful things He did and heard the children crying out in the temple, "Hosanna to the Son of David," they were indignant. They said to Him. "Do you hear what these are saying?" Jesus replied, "Yes! Have you never read, 'Out of the mouths of children and infants comes praise to you.'?" [1]

Every day He taught in the temple. The chief priests, scribes and the leading men among the people were seeking to put Him to death, but they could not find any way to do so, because all the people hung on His words. [2]

The word that came to Jeremiah from the Eternal-God: Stand at the gate of the Lord's house and proclaim this word: Hear the word of the Eternal-God, all you people of Judah who enter by these gates to worship the Lord. This is what the Eternal-God, the Almighty, the God of Israel, says: Mend your ways and your actions, and I will remain with you in this place. Do not trust in deceptive words and say, "This is the temple of the Eternal-God, the temple of the Eternal-God, the temple of the Eternal-God!" If you truly mend your ways and your actions and deal justly with each other; if you do not oppress the alien, the fatherless or the widow and do not shed innocent blood in this place, and if you do not follow after other gods to your own harm, then I will live with you in this place, in the land I gave to your forefathers for ever." [3]

Guard your steps when you go to the house of God. Draw near and listen rather than offer the sacrifice of fools, who do not know that they are doing evil. Do not be rash in what you say; do not be hasty in your heart to utter a word before God. God is in heaven and you are on earth, therefore let your words be few. [4]

[Peter:] The time has come for judgment to begin with the family of God. If it begins with us, what will the end be for those who do not obey the gospel of God? [5]

[1] Matthew 21:10-16 [2] Luke 19:47-48 [3] Jeremiah 7:2-7 [4] Ecclesiastes 5:1-2,15 [5] 1 Peter 4:17

Day 288

Jesus performed many miracles. The signs and wonders that He did were demonstrations of His authority. But He never flaunted His authority. People recognised it when their hearts were right. If their attitude to Him was wrong, they could only criticise what He did. One day, every one will bow in worship to Jesus - some unwillingly as they recognise the One they rejected. True Christians will do so willingly and with great joy.

Jesus' authority is questioned

While Jesus was walking about in the temple, the chief priests, the scribes and the elders came to Him and said, "By what authority are you doing these things? And who gave you authority to do these things?" Jesus replied, "I will ask you a question; answer me, and I will tell you by what authority I am doing these things. The baptism of John [the Baptist]: Was it from heaven, or from men? Tell me!" They discussed it among themselves and argued like this: "If we say, 'From heaven', He will say, 'Then why did you not believe him?' But can we say, 'From men'? for they were afraid of the people, for everyone held that John really was a prophet. So they replied, "We do not know." Jesus said to them, "Neither will I tell you by what authority I am doing these things." [1]

There was a man in their synagogue [at Capernaum] who was possessed by an evil spirit. He cried out, "What have you to do with us, Jesus of Nazareth? Have you come to destroy us? I know who you are: the Holy One of God!" Jesus rebuked him saying, "Be quiet! Come out of him!" The evil spirit threw the man into convulsions and, with a loud cry, came out of him. The people were all so amazed that they asked each other, "What is this? What new teaching is this? What authority is this? He commands evil spirits and they obey him." [2]

[Daniel:] "In my vision at night I saw before me One like a Son of Man, coming with the clouds of heaven. He approached the Ancient of Days and was led into His presence. To Him was given authority, glory and kingship, so that all peoples, nations and those of every language worship Him. His dominion will never pass away, and His kingdom will never be destroyed." [3]

[Paul:] I pray that the eyes of your heart may be opened so that may know ... what is the immeasurable greatness of His [God the Father's] power ... which He exerted in Christ when He raised Him from the dead and seated Him at His right hand in the heavenly places, far above all rule and authority and power and dominion and every name, not only in the present age but also in the one to come. God [the Father] has put all things under His feet and has appointed Him to be head over all things for the church. [4]

---

[1] Mark 11:27-33   [2] Mark 1:23-27   [3] Daniel 7:13-14   [4] Ephesians 1:18-22

Day 289

Although those who heard Jesus tell this parable did not understand that the son in the story represented Him, they would have been in no doubt as to whom Jesus was referring when He spoke of the tenants. The Jewish leaders had ill-treated many of God's servants, the prophets. It was not till after the death and resurrection of Jesus that some would have understood the full meaning of this story.

The teaching of Jesus: The wicked husbandman

[Jesus said:] "Listen to another parable: There was a landowner who planted a vineyard, put a hedge around it, dug a winepress in it and built a watchtower. Then he rented the vineyard to some tenants and went to another country. When the harvest time came, he sent his servants to the tenants to collect his fruit. The tenants seized his servants, beat one, killed another, and stoned yet another. Then he sent other servants to them, more than the first time, and the tenants treated them in the same way. Finally, he sent his son to them, saying. 'They will respect my son.' But when the tenants saw the son, they said to themselves, 'This is the heir. Come, let us kill him and take his inheritance.' So they took him, threw him out of the vineyard and killed him. Now, when the owner of the vineyard returns, what will he do to those tenants? They said to him, 'He will put those evil tenants to a wretched death, and he will rent the vineyard to other tenants, who will give him his fruit at harvest time.'"

Jesus said to them, "Have you never read in the Scriptures: 'The stone which the builders rejected has become the cornerstone; this was the Lord's doing, and it is marvellous in our eyes'? I tell you, the kingdom of God will be taken away from you and given to a people who will produce the fruit of the kingdom. Whoever falls on this stone will be broken to pieces, but he on whom it falls will be crushed." [1]

[Paul:] Think of us as servants of Christ and stewards of the secret things of God. Moreover, it is required of stewards that they should be found faithful. It matters little to me that I should be judged by you or by any human court for I do not even judge myself. I am not conscious of anything against myself, but that does not make me innocent. It is the Lord who judges me. Therefore do not judge anything before the time when the Lord comes who will bring to light what is hidden in darkness and will reveal the motives of men's hearts. Then every one will receive his commendation from God. [2]

[Peter:] In Scripture it says: "See, I am laying in Zion a chosen and precious cornerstone. Whoever believes in Him will never be put to shame." To you, then, who believe, this stone is precious, but to those who do not believe, 'The stone that the builders rejected has become the cornerstone that causes people to stumble." [3]

[1] Matthew 21:33-44   [2] 1 Corinthians 4:1-5   [3] 1 Peter 2:4-7

Day 290

The Bible can open people's minds to the great truths of why God created the universe and particularly people, why He allowed sin to enter the world and how He has made it possible for people to see their sin, reject it and turn to Him to become members of His eternal family. However, God only opens the minds of those people who reject sin, handle truth they see with honesty and act genuinely.

The teaching of Jesus: Seeing and hearing

Although Jesus had done all these miraculous signs before their eyes, they still would not believe in Him. So was fulfilled the word of Isaiah the prophet: "Eternal-God, who has believed our message and to whom has the arm of the Eternal-God been revealed?" They could not believe, because, as Isaiah also said: "He has blinded their eyes and hardened their hearts, so they cannot see with their eyes, nor understand with their hearts, nor turn to me and I would heal them." [1]

[Isaiah:] Then I said, "Woe to me! I am ruined, because I am a man of unclean lips, and I live among a people of unclean lips, and my eyes have seen the King, the Eternal-God, the Almighty." Then one of the seraphs flew to me with a live coal in his hand, which he had taken with tongs from the altar, and with it he touched my mouth and said, "See, this has touched your lips; your guilt is taken away and your sin forgiven." Then I heard the voice of the Eternal-God saying, "Whom shall I send and who will go for us?" And I said, "Here am I. Send me!" He said, "Go and tell this people: 'Go on hearing, but never understanding. Go on seeing, but never understanding.' Make the heart of this people fat; make their ears dull and shut their eyes, lest they see with their eyes, hear with their ears, understand with their hearts, and turn and be healed." [2]

The disciples came to Him [Jesus] and asked Him what was the meaning of the parable. He replied, "To you it has been given to know the secrets of the kingdom of heaven but not for others. I speak to them in parables so that 'seeing, they do not perceive and hearing, they do not understand." [3] ... But blessed are your eyes because they see, and your ears because they hear. [4]

[Paul:] The God who made the world and everything in it is Lord of heaven and earth and does not live in temples made by hands, nor is He is served by human hands, as if He needed anything, for He himself gives all people life and breath and everything else. From one man He made every nation to inhabit the whole earth. He determined the times for them to live, and the places which they would inhabit. God did this so that people would have to seek for Him, reach out and grope for Him, and perhaps find Him, though He is not far from each one of us. [5]

[1] John 12:37-46   [2] Isaiah 6:5-10   [3] Luke 8:9-10   [4] Matthew 13:16   [5] Acts 17:24-27

Day 291

Jesus had already shown His answer to whether or not people should pay taxes when He provided the temple tax for Peter and Himself. Now He is asked a similar question in order to trap Him. In answer He lays down an important principle of the Kingdom of God. Everyone has responsibilities, to God, as Creator, and to the authorities who have been placed over us by God. These responsibilities should not be in conflict. Obedience to God includes obedience to the authorities over us where these are not in direct conflict.

The teaching of Jesus: Paying taxes

The Pharisees plotted among themselves how they might trap Jesus in what He said. They sent their disciples to Him along with the Herodians, saying "Teacher, we know that you are sincere and that you teach the way of God in accordance with the truth, without partiality towards anyone. Tell us then, what do you think? Is it right to pay taxes to Caesar or not?" Jesus, aware of their malicious intentions, said, "You hypocrites, why are you trying to trap me? Show me a coin used for paying the tax." They brought him a denarius. Jesus said to them, "Whose head is this and whose inscription?" They said, "Caesar's," Then He said to them, "Give to Caesar what is Caesar's, and to God what is God's." When they heard this, they were amazed and left Him and went away. [1]

[Solomon:] I counsel you to obey the king's command because you took an oath before God. ... The word of a king is powerful, who can say to him, "What are you doing?" Whoever obeys his command will not come to any harm, and the wise will know what to do and when to do it. There is a right time and process for every matter although the misery of people may weigh heavily upon them. [2]

[Paul:] These things you should teach, urge and rebuke with all authority. Do not let anyone despise you. Remind people to be subject to rulers and authorities, to be obedient, to be ready for every good work, to slander no one, to be peaceable and show courtesy and true humility towards everybody. [3]

[Peter:] Submit yourselves to the authorities of every human institution for the sake of the Lord: whether to the emperor, as supreme, or to governors, who are sent by Him to punish those who do wrong and to commend those who do right. For it is God's will that by doing what is right, you should silence the ignorant accusations of foolish people. Live as those who are free, but do not use your freedom as an excuse for evil. Live as servants of God. Show respect for everyone. Love the fellowship of believers, fear God, honour the emperor. [4]

There is wisdom in the heart of the discerning but in the heart of fools, wisdom is not known. Righteousness exalts a nation, but sin is a reproach to any people. [5]

[1] Matthew 22:15-22   [2] Ecclesiastes 8:2-6   [3] Titus 2:15 - 3:2   [4] 1 Peter 2:13-17   [5] Proverbs 14:34

Day 292

What will it be like in heaven? Jesus gave us some facts. We shall not have the physical bodies we have here on earth. Our new bodies will be eternal. No more children will be born and there will, therefore, be no more sexual differences between people. The loving fellowship there between everyone will be greater than the deepest fellowship here between a man and his wife.

The teaching of Jesus: Marriage at the resurrection

Some of the Sadducees, who say there is no resurrection, came to Jesus and asked Him a question: "Teacher, Moses gave us a law that if a man's brother dies and leaves a wife but no children, the man shall marry the woman and have children for his brother. Now there were seven brothers. The first one took a wife and died without having any children. The second and the third married her, and similarly all the seven married her and died leaving no children. Last of all, the woman died. Now then, in the resurrection, whose wife will the woman be, since all seven were married to her?" Jesus said to them, "The people of this age marry and are given in marriage. But those who are considered worthy of a place in the age to come and in the resurrection from the dead will neither marry nor be given in marriage, for they cannot die but are like the angels and, as children of God, they are children of the resurrection." [1]

[Paul:] But someone will ask, "How can the dead be raised? With what kind of body will they come?" These are foolish questions! Whenever you plant seed, what you sow does not come to life unless it first dies. Nor is the seed that you sow the plant that it will be; it is only a seed, perhaps of wheat or of something else. But God gives it a body which He has determined, and to each kind of seed He gives its own body. ... So it is with the resurrection of the dead. What is sown is perishable, what is raised is imperishable. It is sown in dishonour, it is raised in glory. It is sown in weakness, it is raised in power. It is sown a natural body, it is raised a spiritual body. As there is a natural body, so there is also a spiritual body. ... The first man [Adam] was of the dust of the earth, the second man [Jesus] is from heaven. As was the first 'man from dust', so are those who are of the earth, and as is the 'man from heaven', so are those who are of heaven. As we have borne the likeness of the 'man from dust', so shall we bear the likeness of the 'man from heaven'. [2]

[John:] See how great is the love the Father has lavished on us, that we should be called children of God. And so we are! The reason that the world does not know us is that it does not know Him. Beloved, we are now children of God, and what we will be has yet to be made known, but we know that when He is revealed, we shall be like Him, for we shall see Him as He is. [3]

[1] Luke 20:27-36   [2] 1 Corinthians 15:35-38,42-44,47-48   [3] 1 John 3:1-2

Day 293

God's two great commandments: "Love God," and "love your neighbour," cannot be obeyed perfectly without His help. That is why the Law, by itself, condemns, because it is impossible to obey it fully always. The first purpose of God's laws is to indicate that people are sinners who cannot by themselves obey those laws. Only those who have been 'born again' into God's family can fully love Him and love their neighbours.

The teaching of Jesus: The great Commandments

One of the scribes came and heard them [Jesus and the disciples] disputing with one another, and noting that Jesus had answered them well, he asked Him, "Which commandment is the most important?" Jesus answered, "The most important one is this: 'Hear, O Israel, the Eternal-God, our God, is one Eternal-God. You shall love the Eternal-God, your God, with all your heart and with all your soul and with all your mind and with all your strength.' The second is this: 'You shall love your neighbour as yourself.' There is no commandment greater than these." The scribe said to Him, "Teacher! You are right when you say that God is one and there is no other but He. To love Him with all one's heart, with all one's understanding and with all one's strength, and to love one's neighbour as oneself, is more important than all burnt offerings and sacrifices." When Jesus saw that he had answered wisely, He said to him, "You are not far from the kingdom of God." After that no one dared to ask Him any more questions. [1]

[Paul:] Owe no one anything, except to love one another, for he who loves his neighbour has fulfilled the law. The commandments, 'You shall not commit adultery, you shall not murder, you shall not steal, you shall not covet,' and any other commandment, are summed up in this one commandment: 'Love your neighbour as yourself.' Love does no wrong to one's neighbour. Therefore love is the fulfilling of the law. [2]

[John:] Everyone who believes that Jesus [God the Son] is the Christ is born of God [the Father], and everyone who loves the Father loves His Child. This is how we know that we love the children of God, when we love God and obey His commands, for to love God is to obey His commands. His commands are not burdensome, for whatever is born of God, is victorious over the world. This is the victory that has conquered the world, even our faith. Who is it who is victorious over the world but he who believes that Jesus is the Son of God. [3]

[Paul:] You, my brethren, were called to be free, but do not use your freedom to indulge the sinful nature, rather, by love serve one another. The whole law is summed up in one command: "Love your neighbour as yourself." [4]

[1] Mark 12:28-34 [2] Romans 13:8-10 [3] 1 John 5:1-5 [4] Galatians 5:13-14

Day 294

The Jews found it difficult to understand who Jesus was because He spoke of Himself as more than a prophet. Even His own disciples took a long time to learn that He, to them a man, was also God. Jesus taught them slowly that He was 'God the Son', the Messiah, and that His Father, was 'God the Father'. Later they would learn that they, 'God the Father' and 'God the Son', with 'God the Holy Spirit', were One God.

The teaching of Jesus: About Himself

Jesus said to them [His disciples], "How can people say that the Christ [the Messiah] is the Son of David? David himself says: 'The Eternal-God said to my Lord: Sit at my right hand until I make your enemies your footstool.' So David calls him 'Lord'. How then can He be his son?" While all the people were listening, He said to His disciples, "Beware of the scribes. They like to walk around in flowing robes and they love to be greeted in the market-places and to have the most important seats in the synagogues and the places of honour at banquets. They devour widows' houses and for show make long prayers. They will receive the greater condemnation." [1]

Jesus said to them [Jewish leaders], "My Father has been working to this day, and I, too, am working." This made the Jews even more determined to kill Him for He was not only breaking the Sabbath, but He was calling God His own Father, so making himself equal with God. Jesus said to them, "I tell you the truth, the Son can do nothing of His own accord, He can do only what He sees His Father doing. Whatever the Father does, so the Son does also. The Father loves the Son and shows Him all that He is doing, and He will show Him even greater things than these so that you will be amazed. As the Father raises the dead to life, so the Son gives life to whom He pleases. The Father judges no one but has given all judgment to the Son, so that all may honour [God] the Son as they honour [God] the Father. He who does not honour the Son, does not honour the Father who sent Him." [2]

Philip said to Him [Jesus], "Lord, show us the Father and we will be satisfied. Jesus answered Him, "Have I been with you so long, Philip, and you do not yet know me. Any one who has seen me has seen the Father." [3]

Paul, a servant of Jesus Christ, called to be an apostle and set apart for the gospel of God [the Father], which he promised beforehand through His prophets in the holy Scriptures, concerning his Son [Jesus]. As to His human nature, He was descended from David, and, according to the Spirit of holiness, He was declared with power to be the Son of God by His resurrection from the dead, even Jesus Christ our Lord. [4]

[Paul:] If you confess with your mouth that Jesus is Lord and believe in your heart that God raised Him from the dead, you will be saved. [5]

[1] Luke 20:41-47   [2] John 5:17-23   [3] John 14:8-9   [4] Romans 1:1-4   [5] Romans 13:9

Day 295

The measure of giving to God is not the amount of the gift, but how much is left after the gift is made. The only genuine gift God desires of people is all of themselves. The amount given is a measure of that willingness for Him to have all that we are and have. We are to use all that we have in ways which honour Him.

The teaching of Jesus: The widow's mite

Jesus sat down opposite the treasury [where people placed their offerings] and watched the crowd putting their money into it. Many rich people put in large sums. A poor widow came and put in two mites [the smallest coins], worth a very little. He called His disciples to Him and said to them, "I tell you the truth, this poor widow has put in more than all the others who have made offerings to the treasury. They all gave out of their abundance, but she, out of her poverty, put in everything she had to live on." [1]

[Paul:] In all that I have done, I have shown you that by working hard we must support the weak, remembering the words of the Lord Jesus, "It is more blessed to give than to receive." [2]

Remember this: Whoever sows grudgingly will reap sparingly, and whoever sows generously will reap bountifully. Let each of you give what he has decided in his heart to give, not reluctantly or under compulsion, for God loves a cheerful giver. God is able to make all grace yours in abundance, so that you may at all times and in all circumstances, have all you need, and so be able to share in every good work. As it is written: "He scatters abroad His gifts to the poor and His righteousness endures for ever." Now He who provides seed for sowing and bread for eating, will also supply and increase your store of seed for sowing and will enlarge the harvest of your righteousness. You will be made rich in every way so that you can be generous, and through us your generosity will result in thanksgiving to God. [3]

Honour the Eternal-God with your wealth and with the first-fruits of all that you gain; then your barns will be filled to overflowing, and your vats will overflow with new wine. [4]

[Paul:] We urged Titus ... to complete this generous undertaking ... I am not giving you a command, but to show your sincerity by pointing out the zeal of others. For you know the grace of our Lord Jesus Christ; though He was rich, yet for your sakes He became poor, so that, through His poverty, you might become rich. This is what I advise as best for you in this matter. Last year you were the first not only to give but even to have the desire to do so. ... For if the willingness is there, the gift is acceptable according to what one has, not according to what one does not have. [5]

[1] Mark 12:41-44 [2] Acts 20:35 [3] 2 Corinthians 9:6-11 [4] Proverbs 3:9-10 [5] 2 Corinthians 8:9-12

Day 296

Among the Jews who worshipped God in Jerusalem were some from other nations who were attracted by the God of the Jews. He was very different from the many gods they worshipped. Some of the Greek visitors were particularly interested in the Jesus of whom they had heard. They, and many others, who have sought to know about Him, found that 'knowing Him' meant 'following Him'.

The visit of the Greeks

Among those who went up [to Jerusalem] to worship at the Feast, were some Greeks. They came to Philip ... with a request. They said, "Sir, we would like to see Jesus." Philip went and told Andrew, then Andrew and Philip together told Jesus. Jesus answered them, "The hour has come for the Son of Man to be glorified. I tell you the truth, unless a grain of wheat falls into the ground and dies, it remains only a single grain. But if it dies, it yields a rich harvest. Whoever loves his life will lose it, but whoever does not regard his life for himself in this world, will keep it for ever. Whoever serves me must follow me, and where I am, there will my servant be also. My Father will honour whoever serves me.

"Now my soul is troubled, and what shall I say? 'Father, save me from this hour'? No, it is for this very reason I have came to this hour. Father, glorify your name!" Then there came a voice from heaven, "I have glorified it, and I will glorify it again." The crowd that was standing there heard it and said it had thundered; others said, "An angel had spoken to Him." Jesus said, "This voice was not for my sake, but for yours. Now is the judgment on this world. Now the prince of this world will be driven out. And I, when I am lifted up from the earth, will draw all men to myself." He said this to show the kind of death He was going to die. Hearing this, the people said to Him, "We have learned from the Law [of Moses] that the Christ [Messiah] will live for ever. How then can you say that the Son of man must be lifted up? Who is this Son of man?" Jesus said to them, You will have the light for a little longer. ... Put your faith in the light while you have it, so that you may become children of light.[1]

Everything that [God] the Father has given me will come to me, and whoever comes to me I will never drive away. I have come down from heaven, not to do my will, but to do the will of Him who sent me. And this is the will of Him who sent me, that I should not lose any of all that He has given me, but that I should raise them up at the last day. It is my Father's will that every one who looks to the Son and believes in Him should have eternal life, and I will raise them up at the last day. [2]

[1] John 12:20-36 [2] John 6:37-40

Day 297

When Jesus came to earth the first time, it was in humility to do something that no one else could do, that is, suffer for the sin of everyone who would repent of their sin and trust in Him. He is coming again but then it will be with great glory. He warns His disciples of many great events and troubles which will take place on earth before then.

The teaching of Jesus: His coming to earth again

Jesus left the temple and was going away when His disciples came up to Him and drew His attention to the temple buildings. Jesus said to them, "Do you see all these? I tell you the truth, there will not be left here one stone upon another; every one will be thrown down." As He was sitting on the Mount of Olives, the disciples came to Him privately and said, "Tell us, when will this take place, and what will be the sign of your coming and of the end of the age?" Jesus answered: "Take care that no one deceives you. Many will come in my name, saying, 'I am the Christ [the Messiah],' and they will lead many astray. You will hear of wars and rumours of wars, make sure that you are not alarmed. These things must happen, but the end is not yet. Nation will rise against nation, and kingdom against kingdom. There will be famines and earthquakes in various places. All this is only the beginning of the birth pangs.

"Then you will be handed over to be tortured and put to death, and you will be hated by all nations for my name's sake. Then many will turn away from the faith and they will betray and hate each other, and many false prophets will appear and lead many people astray. Because of the increase of lawlessness, the love of many people will grow cold, but he who endures to the end will be saved. This gospel of the kingdom will be preached throughout the whole world as a testimony to all nations, and then the end will come. ... If anyone says to you then, 'Look, here is the Christ!' or, 'There he is!' do not believe it. For false Christs and false prophets will arise and work great signs and wonders to lead astray even the elect, if that is possible. ... Then the sign of the Son of man will appear in the sky and all the nations of the earth will mourn. They will see the Son of man coming on the clouds of heaven with power and great glory." [1]

[John:] The day of the Lord will come like a thief. The heavens will vanish with a roar. The elements will be dissolved with fire, and the earth and everything in it will be burned up. Since everything will be dissolved in this way, what kind of persons ought you to be? You ought to be living holy and godly lives as you wait for the day of God and hasten its coming, the day on which the heavens will be dissolved with fire and the elements melt in the heat. But, in accordance with His promise, we are looking forward to a new heaven and a new earth, the home of righteousness. [2]

[1] Matthew 24:1-14,23-24,30 [2] 2 Peter 3:10-13

Day 298

No one knows the hour or the day when Jesus will come again, but He warned us very strongly to be ready for His coming, whenever it will be. This parable emphasises that warning. In the Bible, 'oil' is often used as a picture of 'God, the Holy Spirit'. The best way to be ready to meet Jesus is to be kept clean by the 'blood of Jesus' so that the Holy Spirit may live in us and prepare us for that great day.

The teaching of Jesus: The wise and foolish virgins

[Jesus said:] "At that time the kingdom of heaven will be like ten virgins who took their lamps and went to meet the bridegroom. Five of them were foolish and five were wise. When the foolish ones took their lamps they did not take any oil with them, but the wise took flasks of oil for their lamps. As the bridegroom was delayed in coming, they all became drowsy and fell asleep. At midnight there was a shout: 'Look, the bridegroom is here! Come to meet him!' Then all the virgins woke up and trimmed their lamps. The foolish ones said to the wise, 'Give us some of your oil for our lamps are going out.' But the wise replied, 'No, there will not be enough for us and for you. Instead, go to the dealers and buy some for yourselves.' While they had gone away to buy oil, the bridegroom arrived and those who were ready went in with him to the wedding banquet and the door was shut. Later the other virgins also came and said, 'Lord, Lord, open the door to us!' He replied, 'I tell you the truth, I do not know you.' Keep watch, therefore, because you do not know either the day or the hour." [1]

[Paul:] Brothers and sisters, we do not want you to be ignorant about those who fall asleep, so that you may not grieve as others do who have no hope. Since we believe that Jesus died and rose again, we also believe that God will bring with Him those who have fallen asleep in Him. This we declare to you by the word of the Lord, that we who are alive and remain till the coming of the Lord, will certainly not precede those who have fallen asleep. For the Lord Himself will come down from heaven, with a loud cry of command, with the voice of the archangel and with the trumpet call of God, and the dead in Christ will rise first. Then we who are still alive and remain will be caught up together with them in the clouds to meet the Lord in the air, and so we will be with the Lord for ever. [2]

[Jesus:] Be dressed ready for action and with your lamps burning, like those who are waiting for their master to return from a wedding banquet, so that when He comes and knocks, they will be able to open the door for Him immediately. [3]

[1] Matthew 25:1-13 [2] 1 Thessalonians 4:13-18 [3] Luke 12:35-36

Day 299

God has fixed a day when He will pronounce judgment on everyone who has ever lived. For those who have trusted in Jesus Christ to be their righteousness, the judgment will have already been made. They have passed from death to life already. For them, there remains the rewards that God will give to all who have lived faithfully for Him. For those who have rejected Him there remains only a judgment of eternal separation from Him.

The teaching of Jesus: The day of judgment

[Jesus said:] "When the Son of Man comes in His glory, and all the angels with Him, He will sit on His throne of glory. All the nations will be gathered before Him, and He will separate the people one from another as a shepherd separates the sheep from the goats. He will put the sheep on His right side and the goats on His left. Then the King will say to those on His right, 'Come, you who are blessed by my Father; receive the kingdom prepared for you since the creation of the world. For I was hungry and you gave me food, I was thirsty and you gave me something to drink, I was a stranger and you welcomed me, I was naked and you clothed me, I was sick and you took care of me, I was in prison and you visited me.'

"Then the righteous will answer him, 'Lord, when did we see you hungry and gave you food, or thirsty and give you something to drink? When did we see you a stranger and welcomed you, or naked and clothed you? When did we see you sick or in prison and visited you?' The King will reply, 'I tell you the truth, as you did this for one of the least of these my brethren, you did for me.' Then He will say to those on His left, 'Depart from me, you who are cursed, into the eternal fire prepared for the devil and his angels. For I was hungry and you gave me no food, I was thirsty and you gave me nothing to drink, I was a stranger and you did not welcome me in, I was naked and you did not clothe me, I was sick and in prison and you did not visit me.' Then they will answer, Lord, when did we see you hungry or thirsty or a stranger or naked or in prison and did not minister to you. He will reply, 'I tell you the truth, as you did not do these things to the least of these my brethren, you did not do them to me.' These will go away to eternal punishment, but the righteous to eternal life." [1]

If we keep on sinning deliberately after we have received the knowledge of the truth, there is no longer any sacrifice left to atone for our sin, but only a fearful prospect of judgment and of burning anger that will consume the enemies of God.[2]

[Paul:] In the past, God overlooked people's ignorance, but now He commands all people everywhere to repent. For He has set a day when He will judge the world in righteousness, by the man [Jesus Christ] whom He has appointed. [3]

[1] Matthew 25:31-43, 45-46   [2] Hebrews 10:26-27   [3] Acts 17:30-31

Day 300

God speaks to people through His word, the Bible. He also speaks through symbols. When Jesus instituted the Holy Communion He gave very special meanings to two symbolic acts: To 'breaking and eating the bread', He gave the special meaning of representing His body which was cruelly broken on the Cross. To 'drinking the wine', He gave the special meaning of representing the 'blood of Christ shed for sin'. The power of the Lord's Supper lies in the reality of the meaning of these symbols and symbolic acts to those taking part. Given no meaning or wrong meanings, 'The Lord's Supper' can be meaningless or even harmful, if it opens the door to evil powers.

Jesus institutes 'The Lord's Supper'

On the first day of the Feast of Unleavened Bread, the disciples came to Jesus and said to Him, "Where do you want us to make the preparations for you to eat the Passover?" He said, "Go into the city to a certain man and say to him, 'The Teacher says: My time is near. I will keep the Passover at your house with my disciples .'" The disciples did as Jesus had said to them and they prepared the Passover supper. When it was evening, Jesus sat at the table with the Twelve. While they were eating, He said, "I tell you the truth, one of you will betray me." They were very distressed and said to Him one after the other, "Surely not I, Lord?" He replied, "He who has dipped his hand into the bowl with me will betray me. The Son of Man will go as it is written of Him, but woe to that man by whom the Son of Man is betrayed! It would have been better for him if he had not been born." Then Judas, the one who would betray Him, said, "Surely not I, Rabbi?" He answered, "Yes, it is as you have said."

As they were eating, Jesus took bread, gave thanks and broke it, and gave it to His disciples and said, "Take, eat; this is my body." Then He took a cup, gave thanks and gave it to them, saying, "Drink from it, all of you, for this is my blood of the new covenant, which is poured out for many for the forgiveness of sins. I tell you, I will not drink of this fruit of the vine until that day when I drink it new with you in my Father's kingdom." When they had sung a hymn, they went out to the Mount of Olives." [1]

[Paul:] I received from the Lord what I have passed on to you, that the Lord Jesus, on the night when He was betrayed, took bread, and when He had given thanks, He broke it and said, "This is my body which is for you; do this in remembrance of me." In the same way, after supper, He took the cup, saying, "This cup is the new covenant in my blood. Do this, every time you drink it, in remembrance of me. For whenever you eat this bread and drink this cup, you proclaim the Lord's death until He comes. [2]

[1] Matthew 26:17-30   [2] 1 Corinthians 11:23-26

Day 301

It was the custom at the time of Jesus, for visitors to have their weary and dusty feet washed before they were offered food and drink. It was the task of the lowest person, a child or a servant, to wash visitor's feet. Jesus humbled Himself to perform the task of the lowest servant. By that He gave a perfect demonstration of what He meant by saying that only the humble and meek would inherit the kingdom of God.

Jesus washes His disciples feet

Before the Passover Feast, Jesus knew that the time had come for Him to leave this world and go to [God] the Father. ... During supper, Satan having already prompted Judas Iscariot, son of Simon, to betray Him, Jesus, knowing that the Father had put all things into His hands, and that He had come from God and was returning to God, got up from the meal, took off His outer robe, and, taking a towel, tied it round His waist. Then He poured water into a basin and began to wash His disciples' feet and to dry them with the towel that was wrapped round Him. He came to Simon Peter who said to Him, "Lord, are you going to wash my feet?" Jesus said to him, "You do not understand now what I am doing, but later you will understand." Peter said to Him, "You will never wash my feet." Jesus answered him, "Unless I wash you, you have no part with me." Simon Peter said to Him, "Lord, not only my feet but my hands and my head as well!" Jesus answered, "Anyone who has bathed needs only to wash his feet for his whole body is clean. And you are clean, though not every one of you." For He knew who was going to betray Him. ... When He had finished washing their feet, and had put on His robe and sat down again, He said to them, "Do you understand what I have done to you? You call me 'Teacher' and 'Lord', and you are right to do so, for that is what I am. If I, your Lord and Teacher, have washed your feet, you also should wash one another's feet. I have given you an example so that you should do as I have done to you. I tell you the truth, a servant is not greater than his master, and no messenger is greater than the one who sent him. Now that you know these things, you will be blessed if you do them." [1]

"Whoever wants to be great among you must be your servant, and whoever wants to be first must be your slave, in the same way that the Son of Man did not come to be served but to serve, and to give His life a ransom for any. [2]

[Paul:] Let the same mind be in you which was in Christ Jesus, who, although in very nature God, did not regard equality with God as something to be grasped, but emptied Himself and, being born as a man, He took the form of a servant. Then, being found as a Man, He humbled Himself and became obedient, even to death on a cross! [3]

[1] John 13:1-17   [2] Matthew 20:26-28   [3] Philippians 2:5-8

Day 302

Although Jesus told His disciples that He was going to leave them, they did not understand what He was talking about. That made it difficult for them to understand what He meant when He said that someone called the 'Counsellor', another One like Him, would come. After the death and resurrection of Jesus and the coming of 'God the Holy Spirit', on the day of Pentecost, the words of Jesus became clear. He, Jesus Christ, 'God the Son', was going to leave them, but not for ever. He was going ahead of them to prepare an eternal home for them. 'God the Holy Spirit' would make that clear later.

Jesus prepares His disciples for His going away

[Jesus said:] "Do not let your hearts be troubled. Trust in God [the Father], trust also in me. In my Father's house there are many rooms. If it were not so, I would have told you, for I am going to prepare a place for you. And if I go and prepare a place for you, I will come back again and take you to be with me, so that where I am, you may be also. You know the way to where I am going." Thomas said to Him, "Lord, we do not know where you are going, so how can we know the way?" Jesus said to him, "I am the way and the truth and the life. No one comes to the Father except through me. If you knew me, you would also know my Father. ...

"I tell you the truth, whoever has faith in me will do what I have been doing, and he will do even greater things than these, because I am going to the Father. And I will do whatever you ask in my name, so that [God] the Father may be glorified in [God the] Son. If you ask for anything in my name I will do it. ...

"I have said these things to you while I am with you. But the Counsellor, [God] the Holy Spirit, whom [God] the Father will send in my name, will teach you all things and will remind you of everything I have said to you. Peace I leave with you; my peace I give you. I do not give to you as the world gives. Do not let your hearts be troubled and do not be afraid. You heard me say to you, I am going away and I am coming back to you. If you loved me you would rejoice that I am going to the Father, for the Father is greater than I am. I have told you now before it happens so that when it does happen, you will believe. I will not talk with you much longer for the ruler of this world is coming. He has no power over me, but I do as the Father has commanded me, so that the world may know that I love the Father." [1]

"Now I am going to Him who sent me, yet not one of you asks me, 'Where are you going?' Because I have said these things, your hearts are filled with sorrow. I tell you the truth, it is for your good that I am going away, because if I do not go away, the Counsellor will not come to you, but if I go, I will send Him to you. ... I have many things to say to you. When the Spirit of truth comes, He will guide you into all truth"[2]

[1] John 14:1-7,12-13,25-27 [2] John 16:5-7,12-13

Day 303

One of the great truths of the Bible is that when we repent of our sin and are made clean by the 'blood of Jesus' shed on the Cross, God the Father, God the Son and God the Holy Spirit live within us in a way which was until then impossible. Jesus described this relationship as being like that of a branch—we who believe, growing from a vine—Jesus. When the branch is separated from the vine, it dies. The meaning for us is clear. We must 'live in Jesus' if we are to keep spiritually alive.

The teaching of Jesus: The true vine

[Jesus:] "I am the true vine, and my Father is the vinedresser. Every branch that bears no fruit He cuts off and every branch that bears fruit He prunes so that it will be even more fruitful. You have been made clean by the word I have spoken to you. Remain in me, and I will remain in you. As no branch can bear fruit by itself unless it remains in the vine, so you cannot bear fruit unless you remain in me.

"I am the vine, you are the branches. Whoever lives in me and I in him, bears much fruit. Apart from me you can do nothing. Whoever does not live in me is thrown away like a branch and withers. Such branches are gathered up, thrown into the fire and burned. If you live in me and my words remain in you, ask whatever you will, and it will be done for you. When you bear much fruit, my Father is glorified, and you show yourselves to be my disciples. As the Father has loved me, so I have loved you. Now remain in my love. If you obey my commandments you will remain in my love, just as I have obeyed my Father's commandments and remain in His love. I have told you these things so that my joy may be in you and that your joy may be complete. This is my commandment, that you love one another as I have loved you. No one has greater love than this, that he lay down his life for his friends. You are my friends if you do what I command. I do not call you servants, for the servant does not know what his master is doing, but I have called you friends because I have made known to you everything that I have heard from my Father. You did not choose me, but I chose you and appointed you to go and bear fruit, fruit that will last." [1]

"If anyone loves me, he will obey my teaching; my Father will love him, and We will come to him and make our home with him." [2]

Everyone who sins is guilty of lawlessness, for sin is lawlessness. You know that He [Jesus] appeared so that He might take away sin. In Him there is no sin. No one who lives in Him keeps on sinning. [3]

[Paul:] *I have been crucified with Christ. It is no longer I who live, but Christ who lives in me. The life I live in the body, I live by faith in the Son of God, who loved me and gave Himself for me."* [4]

[1] John 15:1-16   [2] John 14:23   [3] 1 John 3:4-6   [4] Galatians 2:20

Day 304

Some of the things which Jesus said to His disciples were very difficult to understand. How could He say, "I am with you always," and also "I am going away"? For people who had always believed that God was 'one Person' it was hard for them to understand how Jesus could claim to be God and also speak of God, His Father. At first He seemed to make it more difficult still in speaking of Another One who was coming to be with them. It took time for them understand that God is the God-Family of God the Father, God the Son and God the Holy Spirit. Each One is God, but they are so bound together that they cannot be called three Gods. The three of them together are one God.

Jesus promises the coming of God the Holy Spirit

[Jesus:] "If you love me, you will obey my commands, and I will ask [God] the Father and He will give you another Comforter ['The One alongside'; God the Holy Spirit] to be with you for ever. He is the 'Spirit of Truth' whom the world cannot receive because it neither sees Him nor knows Him. You know Him because He lives with you and will be in you." [1]

"I tell you the truth: It is for your good that I am going away, because if I do not go away, the Comforter [God the Holy Spirit] will not come to you, but if I go, I will send Him to you. When He comes, He will convict the world of sin and righteousness and judgment: of sin, because people do not believe in me; of righteousness, because I am going to my Father and you will no longer see me; of judgment, because the prince of this world already stands condemned. I still have many things to say to you, but you are unable to bear them now. When He, the Spirit of Truth, comes, He will guide you into all truth. He will not speak on His own account; He will speak only what He hears. He will declare to you things that are yet to come. He will bring glory to me because He will take what is mine and reveal it to you. All that the Father has is mine." [2]

After His suffering, He showed Himself to His disciples with many convincing proofs that He was alive. While He was eating with them, He commanded them not to leave Jerusalem, but to wait for the promise of [God] the Father, of whom, He said, "you have heard me speak. John baptised with water, but not many days from now you will be baptised with [God] the Holy Spirit." When they met together, they asked Him, "Lord, is this the time when you are going to restore the kingdom to Israel?

He said to them: "It is not for you to know the times or dates that [God] the Father has set by His own authority. But you will receive power when [God] the Holy Spirit has come on you, and you will be my witnesses in Jerusalem, in all Judea and Samaria, and to the ends of the earth." [3]

[1] John 14:15-17   [2] John 16:7-15   [3] Acts 1:4-8

Day 305

Jesus, 'God the Son', often prayed to 'God the Father', His Father. On a few occasions we are told what Jesus prayed. These prayers teach us a great deal about the relationship between Jesus [God the Son] and [God] His Father and about their concern for those who become members of God's family. While still in the world, Christians are not of the world, but they share some very great promises for now and for the future.

Jesus prays for His disciples

He [Jesus] looked up to heaven and prayed: "Father, the hour has come. Glorify your Son so that your Son may glorify you. ... I have made known your name to those whom you gave me out of the world. They were yours, you gave them to me and they have obeyed your word. Now they know that everything you have given me comes from you. I gave them the words you gave me and they have accepted them. They know with certainty that I came from you, and they have believed that you sent me. I am praying for them. I am not praying for the world, but for those you have given me because they are yours. ... All that is mine is yours, and all you have is mine and I have been glorified in them. Now I am no longer in the world, but they are still in the world, and I am coming to you. Holy Father, keep in your name those you have given me so that they may be one as we are one. While I was with them, I kept them in your name. Not one has been lost except the one destined to be lost. ...

"My prayer is not that you take them out of the world but that you protect them from the evil one. They are not of the world, even as I am not of it. Sanctify them by the truth; your word is truth. As you sent me into the world so I have sent them into the world. ... I pray not only for these but also for those who will believe in me through their word, that they all may be one, as you, Father are in me and I in you, and that they also may be one in us, so that the world may believe that you have sent me. I have given them the glory that you gave me, that they may be one as we are one, I in them and you in me, so that they be brought to complete unity, that the world may know that you sent me and have loved them even as you have loved me. Father, I desire that those you have given me may be with me where I am, so that they may see my glory which you gave me because you loved me before the creation of the world."[1]

[John] I looked and there before me [in a vision of heaven] was a great multitude which no one could count, from every nation, tribe, people and language, standing before the throne and before the Lamb, robed in white and with palm branches in their hands and they cried in a loud voice, "Salvation belongs to our God who sits on the throne, and to the Lamb." [2]

[1] John 17:1,6-12,20-24   [2] Revelation 7:9-10

Day 306

Because He was God as well as Man, Jesus knew from before the creation of the world that one day He would suffer physical and spiritual death. He spoke of what He would go through to His disciples, but they did not understand. On the evening before He was crucified, He knew that the greatest event in history was about to take place and He knew the suffering that awaited Him. Even at that moment, He could have changed His mind. He did not do so. He said to His Father, "Not my will but yours be done." Millions of people give thanks and praise to God for that decision.

The crucifixion of Jesus: The agony in the garden

Jesus went with them [His disciples] to a place called Gethsemane. He said to them, "Sit here while I go over there and pray." He took with him Peter and the two sons of Zebedee, and He began to be sorrowful and distressed. Then He said to them, "My soul is overwhelmed with grief, even to the point of death. Wait here and keep watch with me." Going a little farther, He fell with His face to the ground and prayed, "My Father, if it is possible, let this cup pass from me, nevertheless, not my will but yours be done."

He came to His disciples and found them sleeping. He said to Peter. "Could you men not stay awake with me for one hour? Watch and pray so that you do not fall into temptation. The spirit indeed is willing, but the flesh is weak." A second time He went away and prayed, "My Father, if this cup cannot be taken away unless I drink it, your will be done." Again He came and found them sleeping, because their eyes were heavy. So He left them and went away again and prayed the third time, saying the same words. Then He returned to the disciples and said to them, "Are you still sleeping and taking your rest? Look, the hour is near, and the Son of Man is betrayed into the hands of sinners. Rise, let us be going! My betrayer is at hand!"

While He was speaking, Judas, one of the Twelve, arrived and with him was a large crowd with swords and clubs, sent from the chief priests and the elders of the people. Now the betrayer had given them a sign, saying: "The one I kiss is the man. Arrest Him." Going straight to Jesus, Judas said, "Greetings, Rabbi!" and kissed Him. Jesus said to him, "Friend, do what you came here to do." [1] Jesus, knowing all that was going to happen to Him, went forward and asked them, "Who are you looking for?" They answered Him, "Jesus of Nazareth." Jesus answered, "I am He!" ... So the soldiers, the captain and the guards arrested Jesus and bound Him." [2]

Let us keep our eyes on Jesus, the source and perfecter of our faith, who for the joy that was set before Him endured the cross, disregarded its shame, and is now seated at the right hand of the throne of God. [3]

[1] Matthew 26:36-48   [2] John 18:4-5,12   [3] Hebrews 12:2

Day 307

It was the Roman soldiers who actually killed Jesus, but it was the Jewish leaders who brought about His condemnation. They were very jealous of the influence He was having on the ordinary people. They believed that His teaching was contrary to their Jewish faith. Jesus did not prevent them from condemning Him because He knew that through their terrible action, God's purposes for redeeming the world would be fulfilled.

The crucifixion of Jesus: Jesus before the High Priest

They [the soldiers] brought Him [Jesus] first before Annas, ... who questioned Him about His teaching. Jesus said, "I have spoken openly to the world. ... I have said nothing in secret. Why question me. Ask those who heard me. ... An attendant struck Jesus on the face saying, "Is that how you answer the high priest?" Jesus said, "If I have said something wrong, tell me. But if I spoke rightly, why do you strike me."

Then Annas sent Him bound to Caiaphas the high priest,[1] ... where the scribes and the elders had assembled. ... The chief priests and the whole Sanhedrin looked for false witnesses to testify against Jesus so that they might put Him to death, but they did not find any, though many witnesses came forward. At last, two came forward who said, "This fellow said, 'I am able to destroy the temple of God and build it again in three days.'"

The high priest stood up and said to Jesus, "Have you no answer? What about this that these men testify against you?" But Jesus remained silent. The high priest said to Him, "I call upon you to answer under oath before the living God: Say if you are the Christ, the Son of God." Jesus said to them, "It is as you say. Moreover, I tell you, in the future you will see the Son of Man seated at the right hand of God Almighty and coming on the clouds of heaven."

The high priest tore his clothes and said, "He has blasphemed! What need do we have of any more witnesses? Now you have heard His blasphemy. Now what do you think?" They answered, "He deserves to be put to death." Then some spat in His face and struck Him with their fists while others slapped Him on the face and said, "Prophesy to us, you Christ. Who was it that struck you?" [1] When it was morning all the chief priests and the elders of the people decided together to put Jesus to death. They bound Him, led Him away, and handed Him over to Pilate, the governor" [2]

[Stephen:] "You stiff-necked people with godless hearts and ears! You always resist [God] the Holy Spirit as did your forefathers! Which of the prophets did your forefathers not persecute? They even killed those who prophesied the coming of the Righteous One, whom you have now betrayed and murdered." [3]

[1] Matthew 26:57-68   [2] Matthew 27:1   [3] Acts 7:51-53

Day 308

It seemed unthinkable to Peter that he could deny his Lord and Master. But he did! He was afraid of what might be done to him if he was seen to be a friend of Jesus. When he had denied Jesus, He could have behaved as Judas did later, by hanging himself. Instead he repented—changed his mind—about what he had done. God forgave him and gave him a position of leadership in the new church that was born in Jerusalem. With God, failure—where there is repentance and faith in Jesus—is never final.

The crucifixion of Jesus: Peter denies Jesus

Jesus said to His disciples, "This very night you will all fall away on account of me, for it is written: "I will strike the shepherd, and the sheep of the flock will be scattered.' But after I am raised up, I will go ahead of you into Galilee." Peter said to Him, "Even if all desert you, I will never do so." Jesus said to Him, "I tell you the truth, this very night, before the cock crows, you will deny me three times." Peter said to Him, "Even if I have to die with you, I will never deny you." And all the other disciples said the same thing. [1]

Simon Peter and another disciple followed Jesus. That disciple was known to the high priest so he went with Jesus into the court of the palace of the high priest, but Peter stood outside at the door. The other disciple, who was known to the high priest, went out and spoke to the woman on duty at the door and brought Peter in. The woman at the door said to Peter. "You are not also one of this Man's disciples, are you?" He said, "I am not." The servants and the guards had lit a fire and were standing round it to warm themselves because it was cold. Peter also stood there with them warming himself. The high priest questioned Jesus about His disciples and about His teaching. ... As Simon Peter stood warming himself, those standing there said to him, "You are not also one of His disciples, are you?" He denied it and said, "I am not." One of the high priest's servants, a relative of the man whose ear Peter had cut off, said to him, "Did I not see you with Him in the garden?" Again Peter denied it. At that moment a cock crowed. [2] Then Peter remembered the words Jesus had spoken, "Before a cock crows, you will deny me three times." He went outside and wept bitterly. [3]

After this [the death and resurrection of Jesus], He revealed Himself again to the disciples at the Sea of Tiberius. ... Jesus said to them, "Come and have some food." ... When they had eaten, Jesus said to Simon Peter, "Simon son of John, do you love me more than these?" He said to Him, "Yes, Lord, you know that I love you." Jesus said to him, "Feed my lambs." ... He said to him the third time, "Simon son of John, do you love me? ... Jesus said to him, "Feed my sheep". [4]

[1] Matthew 26:31-35 [2] John 18:15-19,25-27 [3] Matthew 26:75 [4] John 21:1,12.15-17

Day 309

The Jewish leaders did not have the power to condemn anyone to death and so Jesus was brought before the Roman authorities. To those who looked on, it was the Romans who were powerful and Jesus was weak. In reality, it was the other way round. God was working His purposes out in His way, and that included giving the Roman governor, Pilate, the power to condemn Jesus to death.

The crucifixion of Jesus: Jesus before Pilate

They [the Jewish leaders] brought Jesus from Caiaphas to the praetorium [judgment hall] of the Roman governor. ... Pilate went out to them and said, "What charges do you bring against this Man?" They replied, "If He were not a criminal, we would not have handed Him over to you." Pilate said to them, "Take Him yourselves and judge Him according to your own law." The Jews answered. "It is not lawful for us to put anyone to death." ...

Pilate went back again into the judgment hall and summoned Jesus and asked Him, "Are you the king of the Jews?" Jesus answered, "Is it your idea to ask me this, or have others told you about me?" Pilate answered, "Am I a Jew? It is your people and their chief priests who have handed you over to me. What have you done?" Jesus answered, "My kingdom is not of this world. If my kingdom were of this world, my servants would fight to prevent me being handed over to the Jews. But, as it is, my kingdom is not of this world." Pilate said to Him. "Then you are a king!" Jesus answered, "It is as you say for I am a king. Indeed, it is for this that I was born, and for this I came into the world, to bear witness to the truth. Everyone who is of the truth listens to my voice." Pilate said to Him, "What is truth?" When he had said this, he went out again to the Jews and said, "I find no fault in Him." [1]

"Pilate went into the judgment hall and said to Jesus, "Where do you come from?" Jesus did not answer him. Pilate said to Him, "Do you refuse to speak to me? Do you not know that I have power to release you and I have power to crucify you?" Jesus answered, "You would have no power over me if it were not given to you from above. For this reason the one who handed me over to you is the more guilty one" ... Then he handed Him over to them to be crucified." [2]

After they [the Apostles] were released, they returned to their own company ... they raised their voices together to God and said, "O Sovereign Lord, ... Indeed, in this city Herod and Pontius Pilate, with the Gentiles and the people of Israel, conspired together against your holy servant Jesus, whom you anointed, to do what your power and will had determined beforehand should happen." [3]

[1] John 18:28-38   [2] John 19:9-10,16   [3] Acts 4:23-24, 27-28.

Day 310

Jesus had every reason to protest at the injustice of what was done to Him, but He kept quiet. To speak out might have brought justice to Him, but it would have made impossible the making just of repentant sinners which His death would achieve. The cost to Jesus was great. It was part of the price He paid that we might be made fit for the kingdom of His Father.

The crucifixion of Jesus: Jesus is silent before his accusers

The chief priests and the whole Sanhedrin looked for false evidence against Jesus so that they could put Him to death. ... At last two came forward and said, "This fellow said, 'I am able to destroy the temple of God and build it again in three days,'" The high priest stood up and said, "Have you no answer? What about this that these men testify against you?" But Jesus remained silent. [1]

Jesus stood before the governor, and the governor asked Him, "Are you the king of the Jews?" Jesus answered, "Yes, it is as you say," But when He was accused by the chief priests and the elders, He did not answer. Then Pilate said to Him, "Do you not hear the serious accusations they are bringing against you?" But Jesus did not reply, not even to a single charge, so that the governor was amazed. [2]

When Pilate heard this he asked whether the Man was a Galilean. When He learned that Jesus was under Herod's jurisdiction, he sent Him to Herod, who was also in Jerusalem at that time. When Herod saw Jesus, he was very pleased, because he had been wanting to see Him for a long time. He had heard about Him and hoped to see Him perform some miracle. He asked Him many questions, but Jesus did not answer Him. The chief priests and the scribes also stood there accusing Him vehemently. Herod and his soldiers ridiculed and mocked Him, dressed Him in an elegant robe, and sent Him back to Pilate.[3]

[Isaiah:] He was oppressed and He was afflicted, yet He did not open His mouth; as a lamb is led to the slaughter, and as a sheep before her shearers is silent, so He did not open His mouth. By oppression and judgment He was taken away. Who can speak of His descendants? For He was cut off from the land of the living, He was stricken for the transgression of my people. [4]

[Peter:] He [Jesus] committed no sin, and no deceit was found in His mouth. When they hurled insults at Him, He did not retaliate; when He suffered, He made no threats. Instead, He entrusted Himself to Him who judges justly. He himself bore our sins in His body on the tree, so that we might die to sins and live for righteousness; by His wounds you have been healed. [5]

[1] Matthew 26:59-63   [2] Matthew 27:11-14   [3] Luke 23:6-12   [4] Isaiah 53:7-8   [5] 1 Peter 2:23-24

Day 311

Pilate, the governor of Palestine, could find no fault with Jesus, but he was afraid of the people because they could report Him to his superiors in Rome. In his fear he looked for a way out of the problem. To set Jesus free instead of Barabbas seemed a good idea. Not so to the Jewish leaders. Their choice of Barabbas rather than Jesus made them even more guilty of murdering an innocent man.

The crucifixion of Jesus: Barabbas or Jesus?

At the Feast [Passover], it was the custom of the Governor to set free for the people, a prisoner of their choice. At that time there was a notorious prisoner, named Barabbas. So when the crowd had assembled, Pilate asked them, "Whom do you want me to set free for you: Barabbas, or Jesus, who is called Christ?" He knew that it was out of envy that they had handed Jesus over to him.

While he [Pilate] was sitting on the judgment seat, his wife sent him a message: "Do not have anything to do with that innocent man, for today I have suffered a great deal in a dream because of Him." But the chief priests and the elders persuaded the crowd to ask for Barabbas and to have Jesus put to death. Again the governor said to them, "Which of the two do you want me to release for you?" And they said, "Barabbas!" Pilate said to them, "Then what shall I do with Jesus who is called Christ?" They all answered, "Let Him be crucified!" He said, "Why? What evil has He done?" But they shouted all the louder, "Let Him be crucified!" When Pilate saw that he could do nothing, and an uproar was about to break out, he took water and washed his hands before the crowd, saying, "I am innocent of this man's blood, see to it yourselves!" All the people answered, "Let His blood be on us and on our children!" So he released Barabbas to them and, after having Jesus flogged, handed Him over to be crucified.[1]

While he [the healed beggar] clung to Peter and John, all the people came running to them in utter amazement. ... When Peter saw this, he said to the people: "Men of Israel! ... The God of Abraham, the God of Isaac, the God of Jacob, and the God of our forefathers, has glorified His servant Jesus whom you handed over to be killed. You rejected Him before Pilate although He had decided to let Him go. You rejected the Holy and Righteous One and demanded that a murderer be released to you." [2]

He [Jesus] was in the world, and the world was made through Him, but the world did not know Him. He came to His own, but His own did not receive Him. But to all who received Him and believed in His name, He gave the right to become children of God, born, not of blood, nor of the will of the flesh, nor of the will of man, but of God.[3]

[1] Matthew 27:15-26   [2] Acts 3:11-14   [3] John 1:10-11

Day 312

Even before Jesus suffered the cruel death by crucifixion, He was mocked and terribly ill-treated. Not only had He done nothing to deserve such treatment, but He was the Creator of those who now mocked Him. Jesus could not have humbled Himself more completely to suffer such treatment at the hands of those whom He had created.

The crucifixion of Jesus: Jesus is mocked

The soldiers led Him [Jesus] away into the courtyard of the palace. ... They dressed Him in a purple robe and wove together a crown of thorns and they placed it on Him. They began to salute Him saying, "Hail, king of the Jews!" They struck Him on the head with a reed and spat on Him, fell on their knees and paid homage to Him. When they had finished making sport of Him, they took off the purple robe and put His own clothes on Him. Then they led Him out to crucify Him.[1]

Then Pilate took Jesus and had Him flogged. The soldiers twisted together a crown of thorns and put it on His head, and they dressed Him in a purple robe and went up to Him repeatedly, saying, "Hail, king of the Jews!" And they struck Him in the face.[2]

[Isaiah:] See, my servant will act wisely. He will be lifted up and highly exalted. As there were many who were appalled at Him because His appearance was marred more than that of any man and His form so disfigured that it appeared hardly human, so He will astonish many nations, and kings will be speechless before Him.[3]

Who has believed what has been made known to us, and to whom has the arm of the Eternal-God been revealed? He [the Servant of God] grew up before Him like a tender plant and like a root out of dry ground. He had no majesty or beauty that would make us look at Him, and nothing in His appearance that would make us desire Him. He was despised and rejected by men, a man of sorrows and acquainted with grief. Like one from whom people hide their faces, He was despised, and we took no account of Him. Surely He has borne our weakness and carried our sorrows, yet we considered Him stricken, smitten, and afflicted by God. But He was wounded for our transgressions, He was bruised for our iniquities; the punishment that brought us peace fell upon Him, and by His stripes we are healed. We, like sheep, have all gone astray, every one of us has turned to his own way; and the Eternal-God has laid on Him the iniquity of us all.[4]

Yet it was the will of the Eternal-God to crush Him with suffering, and when the Eternal-God makes His life an offering for sin, He will see His offspring and will prolong His days, and through Him the will of the Eternal-God will prosper.[5]

[1] Mark 15:16-20 [2] John 19:1-3 [3] Isaiah 52:13-15 [4] Isaiah 53:1-6 [5] Isaiah 53:10-11

Day 313

Judas betrayed Jesus into the hands of the soldiers who came to arrest Him. Soon Peter was going to deny that he ever knew Jesus. Both Judas and Peter behaved badly. The difference between them was that Peter repented of what he had done and Jesus forgave him and gave him a special work to do. Judas recognised that he had done a grievous wrong and he felt so guilty about it that he committed suicide. But he never repented of what he had done and ask Jesus to forgive him. God does not forgive sin where there is no repentance.

The crucifixion of Jesus: Judas commits suicide

When it was morning, all the chief priests and the elders of the people conferred together to put Jesus to death. They bound Him, led Him away and handed Him over to Pilate, the governor. When Judas, who had betrayed Him, saw that Jesus was condemned, He was filled with remorse and He took back the thirty silver coins to the chief priests and the elders saying, "I have sinned for I have betrayed innocent blood." They replied, "What is that to us? See to that yourself." Judas threw the pieces of silver down in the temple, then he went away and hanged himself. The chief priests picked up the pieces of silver and said, "It is not lawful to put this into the treasury for it is the price of blood." After discussing the matter, they used the money to buy the potter's field in which to bury strangers. That is why it has been called the Field of Blood to this day. Then the prophecy spoken by Jeremiah the prophet was fulfilled: "They took the thirty pieces of silver, the price of Him on whom a price had been set by the people of Israel, and they gave them to buy the potter's field, as the Eternal-God commanded me." [1]

On one of those days, Peter stood up ... and said, "Brothers and sisters, it was necessary that the Scripture be fulfilled which [God] the Holy Spirit foretold through the lips of David, about Judas. ... This man bought a field with the reward he gained for his wickedness and there he fell headlong, his body burst open and all his intestines poured out. All those who lived in Jerusalem heard about this, so they called that field in their language, Akeldama, that is, Field of Blood." [2]

[Paul:] It is impossible for those fall away from the faith, who have been enlightened, who have tasted the heavenly gift, who have become sharers in [God] the Holy Spirit, who have tasted the goodness of the word of God and the powers of the age to come, to be brought back to repentance, because they would be nailing the Son of God to the cross again and subjecting Him to public disgrace. ... Even though we speak like this, dear friends, for you, we are convinced of better things, things that accompany salvation. [3]

[1] Matthew 27:1-10   [2] Acts 1:18-19   [3] Hebrews 6:4-6, 9

Day 314

Jesus was sentenced to death by Pilate in the city of Jerusalem, but He was crucified outside the city. At first Jesus was made to carry the cross on which He was going to be crucified, but later they forced another man to do it. Even in those terrible circumstance, Jesus was able to speak words of encouragement to those who were weeping for Him. He knew that others would suffer as a result of the suffering He was enduring. Under the Old Covenant, the scapegoat was taken into the desert, outside the city of Jerusalem, symbolically carrying the sins of the people. Jesus did that for real.

The crucifixion of Jesus: Jesus is led to be crucified

They [the Roman soldiers] led Him [Jesus] out to crucify Him. They compelled a passer-by, Simon of Cyrene, the father of Alexander and Rufus, who was coming in from the country, to carry the cross. [1] They laid the cross on him and made him carry it behind Jesus. A large number of people followed them. Among them were women who mourned and lamented for Him. Jesus turned towards them and said, "Daughters of Jerusalem, do not weep for me, but weep for yourselves and for your children. The time will surely come when you will say, 'Blessed are the women who are barren, the wombs that never gave birth and the breasts that never nursed!' Then they will begin to say to the mountains, "Fall on us!" and to the hills "Cover us!"' For if people do these things when the wood is green, what will happen when it is dry?" [2]

The soldiers took Jesus and led Him away, carrying His own cross, to the place called 'The Skull' [Hebrew: Golgotha; Greek:Calvary]. There they crucified Him. [3]

Aaron is to offer the bull as a sin offering for himself. ... Then he shall take the two goats and present them before the Eternal-God at the entrance to the Tent of Meeting. Aaron shall cast lots for the two goats, one lot for the Eternal-God and the other for Azazel [the scapegoat]. Aaron shall bring the goat on which the lot fell for the Eternal-God and sacrifice it as a sin offering. But the goat on which the lot fell to be the scapegoat shall be presented alive before the Eternal-God, to make atonement over it, so that he may let it go in the wilderness as a scapegoat. ... Aaron shall lay both his hands upon the head of the live goat and confess over it all the sins of the Israelites ... and send it into the wilderness by a designated man. The goat will carry on itself all their iniquities to a barren place; and the man shall release it in the desert." [4]

When the blood of animals is brought into the Most Holy Place by the high priest as a sin offering, the bodies are burned outside the camp. And so Jesus also suffered outside the city to make the people holy through His own blood. So let us go to Him outside the camp, bearing the abuse He bore. ... Through Him, therefore, let us continually offer to God a sacrifice of praise, the fruit of lips that confess His name. [5]

[1] Mark 15:21 [2] Luke 23:27-31 [3] John 19:17-18 [4] Leviticus 16:6-10,21-22 [5] Hebrews 13:11-15

Day 315

The crucifixion of Jesus Christ was the greatest event of history. His death was not the death of an ordinary man. It was not just the end of a human life. During the time of crucifixion on the Cross, Jesus suffered, between Himself, 'God the Son', and 'God the Father', the spiritual consequences of all the sins of all those who would repent of their sin and trust in Him. The pain of that suffering, in His body and in His spirit, was greater than anyone can imagine. It was greater than any ordinary man or woman could bear.

The crucifixion of Jesus: Jesus is nailed to the cross

Finally Pilate handed Him over to them to be crucified. So the soldiers took Jesus, carrying His own cross, to the place called 'The Skull' [Golgotha or Calvary]. There they crucified Him with two others, one on either side and Jesus between them. Pilate had an inscription written and fastened to the cross. It read: "Jesus of Nazareth, The King of the Jews." Many of the Jews read this inscription, for the place where Jesus was crucified was near the city. The inscription was written in Aramaic, Latin and Greek. The chief priests of the Jews said to Pilate, "Do not write, 'The King of the Jews', but: 'He said I am the King of the Jews.'" Pilate answered, "What I have written, I have written." [1]

When they came to the place called 'The Skull', there they crucified Him with the criminals, one on His right and the other on His left. Jesus prayed, "Father, forgive them, for they do not know what they are doing." [2] There they offered Him wine mixed with gall to drink. When He had tasted it, He refused to drink it. [3]

At the sixth hour [noon] darkness came over the whole land until the ninth hour. [3 pm] At the ninth hour, Jesus cried in a loud voice, "Eloi, Eloi, lama sabachthani?" which means, My God, my God, why have you forsaken me? Some of those standing by heard this and said, "Listen! He is calling for Elijah." One man filled a sponge with sour wine, put it on a reed and gave it to Him to drink, saying, "Now leave Him alone. Let us see whether Elijah will come to take Him down." [4]

When Jesus had received the sour wine He said, "It is finished!" Then He bowed His head and gave up His spirit. [5]

[Peter:] He Himself bore our sins in His body on the tree, so that we might die to sin and live for righteousness. By His wounds you have been healed. [6]... For Christ died for sins once for all, the righteous for the unrighteous, that He might bring us to God [the Father]. In His human body He was put to death, but He was made alive in the spirit. [7]

[1] John 19:16-22 [2] Luke 23:33-34 [3] Matthew 27:34 [4] Mark 15:33-34,36 [5] John 19:30
[6] 1 Peter 2:24 [7] 1 Peter 3:18

Day 316

The soldiers sitting at the foot of the cross on which Jesus Christ, 'God the Son', was suffering the physical pain of death by crucifixion and the spiritual death of separation from 'God the Father' for their sins, represent something that God hates - apathy. They could not care less about what was happening. So they divided up the clothes of Jesus and gambled as to who should have the long seamless tunic. The attitude of those soldiers was not unexpected. God knew that it would be like that and prophesied so through a Psalm of David and in Lamentations.

The crucifixion of Jesus: The soldiers cast lots for Jesus' tunic

When the soldiers had crucified Jesus, they took His clothes and divided them into four shares, one for each soldier, with the tunic [long shirt-like undergarment] remaining. The garment was seamless, woven in one piece from top to bottom. So they said to one another, "Let us not tear it, but let us cast lots to decide who will get it." This was to fulfil the Scripture which said, "They divide my clothes among them and for my tunic they cast lots." That is what the soldiers did. [1] Then they sat down there and kept watch over Him. [2]

[David:] My God, my God, why have you forsaken me? Why are you so far from saving me and from the words of my groaning? ... I am poured out like water, and all my bones are out of joint. My heart is like wax; it has melted within me. My strength is dried up like a piece of pottery and my tongue sticks to my jaws. You lay me in the dust of death. Dogs are all around me; a band of evildoers has circled me and gloats over me. They have pierced my hands and my feet. I can count all my bones. They divide my clothes among them and cast lots for my tunic. [3]

[Jeremiah:] Is it nothing to you, all you who pass by? Look and see if there is any sorrow like my sorrow that is being inflicted on me, that the Eternal-God has inflicted on me in the day of His fierce anger. [4]

[John:] To the angel of the church in Laodicea write: These are the words of the Amen, the faithful and true witness, the author of God's creation. I know your works; you are neither cold nor hot. Would that you were cold or hot! So, because you are lukewarm, and neither hot nor cold, I will spit you out of my mouth. You say, 'I am rich, I have grown wealthy and in need of nothing'. You do not realise that you are wretched, pitiful, poor, blind and naked. ... So be earnest, and repent. Look! I stand at the door and knock. If anyone hears my voice and opens the door, I will come in to Him and will eat with Him and he with me. He who overcomes I will grant to sit beside me on my throne, as I overcame and sat down beside my Father on His throne. [5]

[1] John 19:23-24 [2] Matthew 27:36 [3] Psalm 22:1,14-18 [4] Lamentations 1:12 [5] Revelation 3:14-17,19-21

Day 317

How a person behaves while watching a moving event says something about that person. Some who watched Jesus dying hurled insults at Him. Others were shocked. The religious leaders of the Jews mocked Him and His claims to be King. They spoke truer words than they realised when they said that He saved others but He could not save Himself. He could not have saved others if He had saved Himself. A small group of women were there too, watching. Among them was the mother of Jesus. Only the soldiers who actually crucified Jesus appeared to have been unconcerned at what they were witnessing.

The crucifixion of Jesus: People watch Him dying

There [Golgotha or Calvary] they crucified Him. [1] Those who passed by jeered at him, wagging their heads and saying, "You who would destroy the temple and build it in three days, save yourself! If you are the Son of God, come down from the cross,!" In the same way the chief priests, the scribes and the elders mocked Him, saying, "He saved others, but He cannot save himself! If He is the King of Israel, let Him come down from the cross now, and we will believe in Him. He trusts in God; let God deliver Him now if He wants Him, for He said, 'I am the Son of God.'" The robbers who were crucified with Him also taunted Him in the same way. [2]

Now the centurion, seeing what had happened, praised God and said, 'Surely this was a righteous man." When all the people who had gathered to witness this spectacle saw what took place they went away beating their breasts. But all those who knew Him, including the women who had followed Him from Galilee, stood at a distance watching these things. [3]

Near the cross of Jesus stood His mother, His mother's sister, Mary the wife of Cleopas, and Mary Magdalene. When Jesus saw His mother there and the disciple whom He loved standing near her, He said to His mother, "Woman, here is your son," and to the disciple, "Here is your mother." From that hour the disciple took her into his home. [4]

[John:] We declare to you what was from the beginning, what we have heard, what we have seen with our eyes, what we have looked at and our hands have touched, concerning the Word of life which appeared to us, which we saw and to which we testify. We declare to you that the eternal life, which was with [God] the Father, has appeared to us. ... This is the message we have heard from Him and declare to you: God is light and in Him there is no darkness at all. ... But if we walk in the light, as He is in the light, we have fellowship with one another, and the blood of Jesus, His Son, makes us clean from all sin. [5]

[1] John 19:18   [2] Matthew 27:39-44   [3] Luke 23:47-49   [4] John 19:25-27   [5] 1 John 1:1-2, 5,7

Day 318

The two thieves who were crucified with Jesus faced the same fate—death, the end of their lives. There was a big difference, however, in their attitudes to Jesus, and that made the biggest difference of all—where they would spend eternity, with God or separated from Him. One thief repented of his sin and turned to Jesus to save him. The other did not repent and died mocking Jesus. As Samson in the Old Testament, so the thief turned to God in the last moments of his life. Both found that God was gracious in forgiving those who change their minds about their sin and trust in Him, even in their dying moments.

The crucifixion of Jesus: The prayer of the dying thief

Two robbers were crucified with Him, one on His right and one on His left. [1] One of the criminals who hung there railed at Him, saying, "Are you not the Christ? Save yourself and us!" The other rebuked Him, saying, "Do you not fear God seeing you are under the same sentence of condemnation? Indeed, we are punished justly, for we are receiving what our deeds deserve; but this Man has done nothing wrong." Then he said to Jesus, "Remember me when you come into your kingdom." Jesus answered him, "I tell you the truth, today you will be with me in paradise." [2]

[Isaiah:] He will see the outcome of the anguish of His soul and be satisfied. ... Therefore I will grant Him a portion with the great, and He will divide the spoils with the strong, because He poured out His life unto death, and was numbered with the transgressors. He bore the sin of many and interceded for the transgressors. [3]

[Before he was arrested, Jesus said to His disciples:] "I tell you, this Scripture must be fulfilled in me, 'And he was numbered with the transgressors', Indeed, what is written about me is being fulfilled." [4]

While their [the revellers'] hearts were merry, they shouted, "Call Samson to entertain us." So they called Samson out of the prison, and he performed for them. ... Then Samson prayed to the Lord, "O Sovereign Lord, remember me, I pray, and strengthen me only once more ..." Then he pushed with all his might, and the temple fell on the lords and all the people in it. [5]

The Eternal-God passed in front of him [Moses], and proclaimed, "The Eternal-God, the Eternal-God, God who is compassionate and gracious, slow to anger, abounding in love and faithfulness, keeping unfailing love for thousands, and forgiving iniquity, transgression and sin, yet who by no means clears the guilty but visits the iniquity of the parents upon the children, and the children's children, to the third and fourth generation." [6]

[1] Matthew 27:38   [2] Luke 23:39-43 22.;37   [3] Isaiah 53:11-12   [4] Luke 22:37
[5] Judges 16:25, 28,30   [6] Exodus 34:6-7

Day 319

The words which Jesus spoke while dying on the Cross expressed His deepest thoughts, and they were all for other people - those who were crucifying Him, for his own mother and for His disciples. His last words, "It is finished!" showed that He had completed what He had set out to do, to suffer in His body and spirit, the pain of His separation as 'God the Son' from 'God the Father'. He took on Himself the pain of the spiritual consequences of every sin of every repentant sinner who believed in Him.

The crucifixion of Jesus: His last words

When they came to the place called 'The Skull' [Golgotha or Calvary], there they [the Roman soldiers] crucified Him, along with the criminals, one on His right and the other on His left. And Jesus prayed, "Father, forgive them, for they do not know what they are doing." [1]

From the sixth hour [noon] until the ninth hour [3 pm], darkness came over all the land. About the ninth hour, Jesus cried out in a loud voice, "Eloi, Eloi, lama sabachthani?" which means, "My God! my God! Why have you forsaken me?" [2]

One of the criminals who hung there railed at Him: 'Are you not the Christ? Save yourself and us!" The other criminal rebuked him, saying, "Do not you fear God, since you are under the same sentence of condemnation? Indeed, we are receiving what our deeds deserve, but this Man has done nothing wrong. Then he said to Jesus, "Remember me when you come into your kingdom." Jesus said to him, "I tell you the truth, today you will be with me in paradise." [3]

Near the cross of Jesus stood His mother, His mother's sister, Mary the wife of Cleopas, and Mary Magdalene. Jesus, seeing His mother there, and the disciple whom He loved standing near by, said to His mother, "Woman, here is your son," and He said to the disciple, "Here is your mother." From that time on, this disciple took her into his home. [4]

Darkness came over the whole land and the sun was darkened until the ninth hour [3 pm] when the curtain of the temple was torn in two. Jesus called out with a loud voice, "Father, into your hands I commit my spirit." When He had said this, He breathed His last. [5]

Jesus, knowing that all was now finished, and to fulfil the Scripture, said, "I am thirsty." A jar of sour wine was there, so they soaked a sponge in it, put it on a reed of hyssop, and held it to His mouth. When He had received the sour wine, Jesus said, "It is finished." Then He bowed His head and gave up His spirit. [6]

[1] Matthew 27:45-46 [2] Luke 23:33-34 [3] Luke 23:42-43 [4] John 19:25-27 [5] Luke 23:45-46 [6] John 19:28-29

Day 320

The most important event which was happening while Jesus was being crucified was not that which was visible for all to see. The suffering for the sin of the world was being borne by Jesus as He 'God the Son' suffered the pain of separation from His Father, 'God the Father', in order to pay for the sin which separates us from Him. However, the natural world also felt the impact of what was happening. There was darkness over the land, an earthquake, graves being burst open. Most meaningful was the splitting of the curtain of the temple from top to bottom. That symbolic barrier to the Most Holy Place, the presence of God Himself, was broken down in reality by Jesus Christ.

The crucifixion of Jesus: Nature responds as Jesus dies

It was the third hour [9 am] when they crucified Him. ... At the sixth hour [noon] there was darkness over all the land until the ninth hour [3 pm]. ... At the ninth hour ... Jesus gave a loud cry and breathed His last breath. And the curtain of the temple was torn in two from top to bottom. [1]

At the moment the curtain of the temple was torn in two from top to bottom, the earth shook and the rocks were split. The tombs were opened and the bodies of many saints who had died were raised to life and, after His resurrection, they came out of the tombs and went into the holy city and appeared to many people. When the centurion and those with Him who were keeping watch over Jesus saw the earthquake and all that was happening, they were terrified, and exclaimed, "Truly this was the Son of God!" [2]

When God made His promise to Abraham, He swore by Himself since there was no one greater by whom to swear, saying, "I will surely bless you and I will multiply your descendants." ... Because God wanted to show the unchanging nature of His purpose very convincingly to those who would inherit the promise, He confirmed it with an oath. ... We have this hope as a firm and secure anchor for the soul which enters the inner sanctuary behind the curtain, where Jesus, our forerunner, has entered on our behalf. [3]

Therefore, brothers and sisters, since we have confidence to enter the Most Holy Place by the blood of Jesus, by this new and living way which He opened for us through the curtain, that is, His body, ... let us draw near to God with a true heart in full assurance of faith and with our hearts sprinkled clean from a guilty conscience and having our bodies washed with pure water. [4]

[1] Mark 15:25,33,37 [2] Matthew 27:51-54 [3] Hebrews 6:13,17,19-20 [4] Hebrews 10:19-22

Day 321

There was no doubt in the minds of the soldiers who crucified Jesus that He was dead. He might have survived His legs being broken, but He could not have survived a spear piercing His side and heart. On the cross, Jesus died a physical death in every sense of the word. He also died a spiritual death in the pain He suffered in His separation from 'God the Father'. The physical blood that flowed from the wound in His side spoke of greater things than confirming His physical death. That blood was a symbol of the greater spiritual meaning of 'the blood of Christ shed for the sins of world.'

The crucifixion of Jesus: The last moments on the Cross

Since it was the day of Preparation, and the following day was a special, solemn Sabbath, and because the Jews did not want the bodies left hanging on the crosses on the Sabbath, they asked Pilate to have the legs broken and the bodies removed. So the soldiers came and broke the legs of the first and of the other who had been crucified with Jesus. When they came to Jesus and saw that He was already dead, they did not break His legs. Instead, one of the soldiers pierced His side with a spear and blood and water flowed out.

The man who saw it has testified to it, and his testimony is true. Because he knows the truth, he has given his testimony so that you also may believe. These things happened so that the scripture might be fulfilled: "Not one of His bones will be broken," and also the scripture which says, "They will look on the One whom they have pierced." After this, Joseph of Arimathea, a disciple of Jesus, but secretly because he feared the Jews, asked Pilate to let him take away the body of Jesus. Pilate gave him permission, so he came and took away His body. [1]

Joseph of Arimathea, a respected member of the Council [Sanhedrin] who was himself waiting for the kingdom of God, went boldly to Pilate and asked for the body of Jesus. Pilate wondered whether He was already dead, so he summoned the Centurion and asked Him if Jesus was already dead. When he learned from the centurion that He was already dead, he gave the body to Joseph. [2]

Christ [the Messiah] died for sins once for all, the righteous for the unrighteous, that He might bring us to God. He was put to death in the body but He was made alive in the spirit. [3] ... Since Christ suffered in His body, arm yourselves with the same purpose, for whoever has suffered in his body has finished with sin, he no longer spends the rest of his earthly life for human desires but for the will of God. [4]

The love of Christ's compels us because we are convinced that One has died for all, therefore all have died. And He died for all, that those who live might live no longer for themselves but for Him who died and was raised again for them.[5]

[1] John 19:31-38 [2] Mark 15:43-45 [3] 1 Peter 3:18 [4] 1 Peter 4:1-2 [5] 2 Corinthians 5:14-15

Day 322

Jesus was buried in a tomb cut out of the rock for someone else - a rich man. The prophecy of Isaiah was fulfilled in great detail. The burial of Jesus also became a symbol. It marked the end of a life. In three days Jesus was going to be resurrected to new life. But He had to die and be buried first. That is, symbolically, what has to happen to every man and woman whom Jesus saves from sin to be one of the family of God. The kind of life which is self-centred and governed by Satan's standards has to be symbolically 'dead and buried' to enable the new life in Jesus to be lived out.

The crucifixion of Jesus: His burial

Joseph of Arimathea ... with the permission of Pilate, came and took the body away. Nicodemus, who had come to Jesus by night, also came bringing a mixture of myrrh and aloes. They took the body of Jesus' and wrapped it in linen cloths with the spice in preparation for burial, as was the Jewish custom. In the place where Jesus was crucified, there was a garden and in the garden there was a new tomb in which no one had ever been laid. Because it was the Jewish day of Preparation and the tomb was near by, they laid Jesus there. [1] Joseph took the body and wrapped it in a clean linen cloth and laid it in his own tomb, which he had hewn in the rock, and he rolled a big stone over the door of the tomb and went away. [2]

By oppression and judgement He was taken away. As for His generation, who among them considered that He was cut off from the land of the living. He was stricken for the transgression of my people, and in His death He was assigned a grave with the wicked and with the rich, although He had done no violence, nor was there any deceit in His mouth. [3]

As sin has reigned in bringing death, so grace may reign through righteousness which leads to eternal life through Jesus Christ our Lord. [4] What shall we say, then? Shall we continue in sin so that more grace may be given? Certainly not! How can we live in sin any longer since we have died to it? Do you not know that all of us who have been baptised into Christ Jesus have been baptised into His death? Therefore, we have been buried with Him by baptism into death, so that, as Christ was raised from the dead by the glory of the Father, we too might live in newness of life. For if we have become one with Him in His death, we will also be one with Him in His resurrection. [5]

If we have died with Christ, we believe that we will also live with Him. ... The death He died, He died to sin, once for all, but the life He lives, He lives to God [the Father] So count yourselves dead to sin but alive to God in Christ Jesus and do not let sin reign in your mortal bodies to yield to its evil passions.[6]

[1] John 19:38-42 [2] Matthew 27:59-60 [3] Isaiah 53:8-9 [4] Romans 5:21 [5] Romans 6:1-5 [6] Romans 6:8-12

Day 323

Women were not very highly regarded at the time when Jesus Christ lived on earth. Yet it was to women that Jesus appeared first early on that first Sunday morning. Jesus Christ was alive. The grave could contain Him no longer. However, He still did not appear to the world at large to announce His victory over death. It was to the few that He appeared, among whom were the women who came to the tomb early that morning.

The resurrection of Jesus: The women come to the sepulchre

When the Sabbath was over, at dawn on the first day of the week, Mary Magdalene and the other Mary went to look at the tomb. Suddenly there was a violent earthquake and an angel of the Lord descended from heaven, went to the tomb, rolled back the stone and sat on it. His appearance was like lightning, and His clothes were white as snow. The guards were so frightened of Him that they shook and became like dead men. The angel said to the women, "Do not be afraid. I know that you are looking for Jesus, who was crucified. He is not here, He has risen, as He said He would. Come, see the place where He lay, then go quickly and say to His disciples: 'He has risen from the dead and is going ahead of you into Galilee. There you will see Him as I have told you." So they left the tomb quickly, with fear and great joy, and ran to tell the disciples. Suddenly Jesus met them and said, "Hail!" They went to Him, clasped His feet and worshipped Him. Then Jesus said to them, "Do not be afraid. Go and tell my brothers and sisters to go to Galilee and there they will see me." [1]

Early on the first day of the week, while it was still dark, Mary Magdalene went to the tomb and saw that the stone had been removed from the entrance. So she came running to Simon Peter and the other disciple whom Jesus loved, and said to them, "They have taken away the Lord out of the tomb, and we do not know where they have laid Him!" So Peter and the other disciple [John] set out for the tomb. ... Then Simon Peter, who was behind him, came and went into the tomb. He saw the linen cloths lying there. The burial cloth that had been around Jesus' head was folded up by itself in a separate place. Then the other disciple, who had reached the tomb first, also went inside. He saw and believed, for they did not yet understand the Scripture which said that Jesus had to rise from the dead. [2]

[Paul:] God has saved us and called us to live holy lives. ... This grace was given us before the world began, but is now revealed through our Saviour Christ Jesus, who has abolished death and brought life and immortality to light through the gospel.[3]

God raised Him from the dead, freeing Him from the pangs of death, because it was impossible for death to continue to hold Him in its power. [4]

[1] Matthew 28:1-10   [2] John 20:1-9   [3] 2 Timothy 1:9-10   [4] Acts 2:24

Day 324

After His resurrection from the dead, Jesus did not appear to the crowds who had shouted for His death or who had condemned Him to die by crucifixion, but He did appear to over 500 people, many of whom had known Him before His death. This was a sufficient number to provide convincing evidence that He was, in truth, very much alive. This evidence was there for the followers of Jesus, then, and for generations to come.

The resurrection of Jesus: He appears to His disciples

The disciples went back [from the empty tomb] to their homes, but Mary stood outside the tomb weeping. As she wept, she bent down to look into the tomb and she saw two angels in white sitting there, one at the head and the other at the foot, where the body of Jesus had been. They said to her, "Woman, why are you weeping?" She said to them, "They have taken my Lord away, and I do not know where they have laid him." As she said this she turned round and saw Jesus standing there, but she did not know that it was Jesus. He said to her, "Woman, why are you weeping? Who are you looking for?" Supposing Him to be the gardener, she said, "Sir, if you have carried Him away, tell me where you have put Him, and I will take Him away." Jesus said to her, "Mary!" She turned round and said to Him in Aramaic, "Rabboni!" (which means Teacher). Jesus said, "Do not hold on to me, for I have not yet ascended to the Father. But go to my brothers and sisters and tell them, I am ascending to my Father and your Father, to my God and your God.'"

Mary Magdalene went to the disciples with the news that she had seen the Lord. Then on the first day of the week, when it was evening, the disciples were together with the doors locked for fear of the Jews, Jesus came and stood among them and said, "Peace be with you!" Then He showed them His hands and side and the disciples were overjoyed to see the Lord. [1]

[Paul:] Now, brethren, let me remind you of the gospel I preached to you, which you received and on which you stand. ... For I passed on to you as of first importance: that Christ died for our sins in accordance with the Scriptures, that He was buried, that He was raised on the third day ... and that He appeared to Peter, and then to the Twelve. Then He appeared to more than five hundred brothers and sisters at the same time, most of whom are still alive, though some have fallen asleep. He was seen by James, then by all the apostles, and last of all by me, as one born out of time. [2]

Later Jesus appeared to the Eleven as they were sitting at the table. He rebuked them for their lack of faith and their stubbornness because they refused to believe those who had seen Him after He had risen. [3]

[1] John 20:10-21   [2] 1 Corinthians 15:1-8   [3] Mark 16:14

Day 325

Two of Jesus followers, Cleopas and his companion—probably his wife—were sad as they talked about the death of Jesus. They thought His death meant that He could not be the Messiah they were so earnestly looking for. Little did they realise, at first, that the One who had joined them in their walk home was Jesus, that He was the Messiah, their Saviour, and He was very much alive. As He gave thanks for the meal they offered Him, possibly showing the scars of the nail marks in His hands, they not only recognised who He was, but they began to understand about His death and His resurrection.

The resurrection of Jesus: The disciples on the way to Emmaus

That same day [that Jesus was raised form the dead] two of them [His disciples] were going to a village called Emmaus, about seven miles from Jerusalem. They were talking with each other about all that had happened. While they were talking and discussed these things with each other, Jesus himself came up and walked with them, but their eyes were kept from recognising Him. He said to them, "What is it that you are talking about together as you walk along?" They stood still, their faces downcast. One of them, named Cleopas, said to Him, "Are you the only stranger in Jerusalem who does not know the things that have happened there in these days?" He said to them, "What things?" They said to Him, "About Jesus of Nazareth who was a prophet, mighty in word and deed before God and all the people, and how our chief priests and rulers handed Him over to be condemned to death, and crucified Him. We had hoped that He was the one who would redeem Israel. And besides all this, it is the third day since all this took place, and some of our women have astounded us. They were at the tomb early this morning but did not find His body. They came and told us that they had seen a vision of angels, who said that He was alive. Then some of those who were with us went to the tomb and found it just as the women had said, but they did not see Him." He said to them, "O how foolish you are and slow of heart to believe all that the prophets have spoken! Was it not necessary that the Christ should suffer these things and then enter His glory?" Then, beginning with Moses and all the prophets, He interpreted to them what was said in all the Scriptures concerning Himself. As they drew near to the village to which they were going, Jesus walked on as if He were going further. But they urged Him strongly, "Stay with us, for it is nearly evening and the day is nearly over." So He stayed with them.

When He was at the table with them, He took bread, gave thanks, broke it and was giving it to them when their eyes were opened and they recognised Him, and He vanished from their sight. They said to each other, "Were not our hearts burning within us while He talked with us on the road and opened to us the Scriptures?" [1]

[1] Luke 24:1-35

Day 326

When Jesus appeared to His disciples after His resurrection from the dead, He demonstrated that He had completed what He had set out to do by dying on the Cross. He was again very much alive. He also showed them that He was going to reach the world with His Good News through them They would be witnesses of His resurrection there in Jerusalem, throughout the then-known world, then to the ends of the earth.

The resurrection of Jesus: He appears - Thomas absent

While they were still talking about this [the appearance of Jesus to Cleopas], Jesus Himself stood among them and said to them, "Peace be with you." They were startled and terrified, thinking they were seeing a ghost. He said to them, "Why are you troubled, and why are there doubts in your minds? Look at my hands and my feet and see that it is I myself. Touch me and see, for a ghost does not have flesh and bones, as you see I have." When He had said this, He showed them His hands and His feet. While they still did not believe it for joy and amazement, He said them, "Have you anything here to eat?" They gave Him a piece of broiled fish, and He took it and ate it in their presence.

He said to them, "This is what I told you while I was still with you. Everything must be fulfilled that is written about me in the Law of Moses, the Prophets and the Psalms." Then He opened their minds to understand the Scriptures, and He said to them, "Thus it is written, that the Christ [Messiah] will suffer and, on the third day, rise from the dead, and repentance and forgiveness of sins will be preached in His name to all nations, beginning at Jerusalem. You are witnesses of these things." [1]

[Paul:] Moses writes concerning the righteousness which comes by obeying the Law [of Moses] "whoever does these things will live by them. But the righteousness that is by faith says: "Do not say in your heart, 'Who will ascend into heaven?' (that is, to bring Christ down) "or 'Who will descend into the abyss?'" (that is, to bring Christ up from the dead). But what does it say? "The word is near you; it is on your lips and in your heart," ... that if you confess with your mouth that Jesus is Lord, and believe in your heart that God raised Him from the dead, you will be saved. [2]

[Peter:] Brothers and sisters, I can tell you with confidence that the patriarch David died and was buried and his tomb is with us to this day. He was a prophet ... and prophesied of the resurrection of the Christ saying: He was not abandoned in Hades [the place of the dead] nor did His flesh see corruption. This Jesus, God [the Father] has raised up, and of that all of us are witnesses.[3]

[1] Luke 24:36-48 [2] Romans 10:6-10 [3] Acts 2:29-32

Day 327

Thomas, could not believe that Jesus was alive again. "Unless I see ... I will not believe," he said. Many people argue like that today. Jesus showed that thinking like that leaves out faith. You do not need faith if you can see with your physical eyes. Jesus showed His disciples the truth taught throughout the Bible, that without faith it is impossible to please God. God is spirit. He cannot be seen with our ordinary eyes. We can, however, know that He is there through faith which reasons from His word and from what we see in the world.

The resurrection of Jesus: He appears -Thomas present

Thomas (called Didymus [the Twin]), one of the Twelve, was not with the disciples when Jesus came. So the other disciples told him, "We have seen the Lord!" But he said to them, "Unless I see the nail marks in His hands and put my finger where the nails were, and put my hand into His side, I will not believe." A week later the disciples were in the house again, and Thomas was with them. Although the doors were locked, Jesus came and stood among them and said, "Peace be with you!" Then He said to Thomas, "Reach out your finger and touch my hands, put your hand into my side. Do not doubt but believe." Thomas said to Him, "My Lord and my God!" Jesus said to him, "Because you have seen me, do you now believe? Blessed are those who have not seen and yet have believed." [1]

By faith Enoch was taken so that he did not experience death; he was not found because God had taken him away. Before he was taken, it was testified of him that he pleased God. Without faith it is impossible to please God, for whoever comes to Him must believe that He exists and that He rewards those who earnestly seek Him. [2]

[Peter:] Although you have not seen Him [Jesus], you love Him. Though you do not see Him now, you believe in Him and rejoice with an inexpressible and glorious joy, for you are receiving the goal of your faith, the salvation of your souls. [3]

There are many other miraculous signs which Jesus did in the presence of His disciples, which are not written in this book. But these are written that you many believe that Jesus is the Christ, the Son of God, and that through believing you may have life in His name.[4] For it is by grace you have been saved, through faith, and this not your doing, it is the gift of God, not of works, so that no one can boast. [5]

[Jesus said:] "Indeed, as the Father raises the dead and gives them life, even so the Son also gives life to whom He is pleased to give it. ... I tell you the truth, whoever hears my word and believes Him who sent me has eternal life. He will not be condemned but has crossed over from death to life." [6]

[1] John 20:24-29 [2] Hebrews 11:5-6 [3] 1 Peter 1:8-9 [4] John 20:30-31 [5] Ephesians 2:8-9 [6] John 5:21,24

Day 328

Peter denied that he knew Jesus three times. Then he repented of what he had done with bitter tears. Jesus forgave him so completely that He was able to give him the special task of leading the new churches in Palestine, while to Paul was committed the churches of the non-Jews. Peter, the 'waverer', now became Peter the 'rock' on whose testimony—that 'Jesus is the Messiah'—God would build His world-wide church.

Jesus commissions Peter

Jesus appeared again to His disciples by the Sea of Tiberias. It happened like this: Simon Peter, Thomas (called Didymus), Nathanael from Cana in Galilee, the sons of Zebedee, and two other disciples were together when Simon Peter said, "I am going out to fish." They said, "We will go with you." They went out, got into the boat, but that night they caught nothing. As morning was breaking, Jesus stood on the shore, but the disciples did not know that it was Jesus. He called to them, "Children, you have not caught anything, have you? " They answered, "No!" He said to them, "Cast your net on the right side of the boat and you will find some." They did that and were not able to haul the net in because there were so many fish. ...

When they reached the shore, they saw a fire of coals burning there and fish on it, and bread. Jesus said to them, "Bring some of the fish you have just caught." So Simon Peter went aboard and hauled the net ashore full of fish, 153 of them. Even with this number of fish the net was not torn. Jesus said to them, "Come and have something to eat." None of the disciples dared to ask Him, "Who are you?" They knew it was the Lord.

Jesus came, took the bread and the fish and gave it to them. ... When they had finished eating, Jesus said to Simon Peter, "Simon son of John, do you love me more than these?" He said to Him, "Yes, Lord, you know that I love you." He said to him, "Feed my lambs." Again Jesus said, "Simon son of John, do you love me?" He answered, "Yes, Lord, you know that I love you." Jesus said, "Tend my sheep." The third time He said to him, "Simon son of John, do you love me?" Peter was hurt because Jesus said to him the third time, "Do you love me?" He said, "Lord, you know all things; you know that I love you." Jesus said, "Feed my sheep." [1]

When the day of Pentecost had come, ... Peter stood up with the Eleven, raised his voice and addressed the crowd. ... Men of Israel and all who live in Jerusalem, let this be known to you: ... Jesus of Nazareth was a man attested by God to you by miracles, wonders and signs which God worked among you through Him. ... God has made this Jesus, whom you crucified, both Lord and Christ." [2]

[1] John 21:1-6,9-17,24   [2] Acts 2:1,14,22,36

Day 329

In His physical body, Jesus could be in only one place at a time. He now tells His disciples that they would receive 'God the Holy Spirit', who would be with them wherever they were, and they were to be witnesses to Him all over the world. To them He gave the task of preaching and teaching all that He had taught them and of testifying to what He had done while He was with them. God was fulfilling the promise He gave to Abraham many years ago: He was going to bless the world through one of his descendents, that was Jesus, and the blessing was the saving from sin which Jesus achieved on the cross.

Jesus sends His disciples into the world

The eleven disciples went to Galilee, to the mountain where Jesus had instructed them to go. When they saw Him, they fell down and worshipped Him, but some doubted. Then Jesus came to them and said, "All authority in heaven and on earth has been given to me. Therefore, go and make disciples of all nations, baptising them in the name of [God] the Father and of [God] the Son and of [God] the Holy Spirit, and teach them to observe everything that I have commanded you. And be sure, I am with you always, to the end of the age." [1]

Later Jesus appeared to the Eleven. ... When He had rebuked them for their lack of faith and their stubbornness in refusing to believe those who had seen Him after He had risen, He said to them, "Go into all the world and preach the good news to the whole creation. Whoever believes and is baptised will be saved, but whoever does not believe will be condemned. These signs will be seen among those who believe: in my name they will cast out demons and they will speak in new tongues. They will pick up snakes in their hands and if they drink something which is poisonous, it will not hurt them. They will lay their hands on the sick and they will be healed. [2]

The Eternal-God appeared to Isaac and said, "Stay for the present in this land and I will be with you and bless you, for to you and to your descendants I will give all these lands and I will confirm the oath I swore to you father Abraham. I will make your descendants as numerous as the stars in the heavens and I will give them all these lands, and through your offspring all nations on earth will be blessed." [3]

When they [the disciples] had assembled, they asked Him [Jesus], "Lord, is this the time when you will restore the kingdom to Israel?" He said to them: "It is not for you to know the times or dates the Father has set by His own authority. But you will receive power when [God] the Holy Spirit comes on you, and you will be my witnesses in Jerusalem, in all Judea and Samaria, and to the ends of the earth. [4]

God [the Father] so loved the world that He gave His one and only [God the] Son, that whoever believes in Him shall not perish but have eternal life. [5]

[1] Matthew 28:16-20 [2] Mark 16:14-16 [3] Genesis 26:2-4 [4] Acts 1:6-8 [5] John 3:16

Day 330

When Jesus ascended into the clouds and out of sight of the disciples, that marked the end of the period of history which centred round the Jewish nation. It was also the beginning of another, that of the world-wide Christian church. That period is the one we are in now and it will not end until Jesus comes again as visibly as He disappeared into the clouds. It was also the beginning of the period in which 'God the Holy Spirit' is as clearly identified as was 'God the Father' and Jesus Christ, 'God the Son'.

The Ascension of Jesus into the clouds

After His suffering, He [Jesus] showed Himself to them [the Apostles] and gave many convincing demonstrations that He was alive. He appeared to them over a period of forty days and spoke about the kingdom of God. On one occasion, while He was sitting at table with them, He commanded them: "Do not leave Jerusalem, but wait for the promise of [God] the Father which you have heard me speak about. For John baptised with water, but not many days from now you will be baptised with [God] the Holy Spirit, ... and you will be my witnesses in Jerusalem, and in all Judea and Samaria, and to the ends of the earth." When He had said this, and as they were watching, He was taken up into a cloud which hid Him from their sight. Suddenly, as He was going up and they were looking intently into the sky, two men dressed in white stood beside them. They said, "Men of Galilee, why do you stand looking into the sky? This same Jesus, who has been taken from you into heaven, will come back in the same way that you have seen Him go into heaven." [1]

He had led them out as far as Bethany and, lifting up His hands, blessed them. While He was blessing them, He was parted from them and was taken up into heaven. Then they worshipped Him and returned to Jerusalem with great joy, and were continually in the temple, praising God. [2]

After He had spoken to them, the Lord Jesus was taken up into heaven where He sat at the right hand of God. Then they went out and preached everywhere, while the Lord worked with them and confirmed His word by the signs that accompanied it. [3]

[Paul:] To each one of us grace has been given according to the measure of Christ's gift. As it is written, "When He ascended on high He led captivity captive and bestowed gifts on people." What can this 'He ascended' mean except that He had first descended from the heights of heaven to the lower parts of earth. He who descended is the One who ascended above all the heavens that He might fill the whole universe.[4]

As man is destined to die once, and after that to face judgment, so Christ was sacrificed once to take away the sins of many people, and He will appear a second time, not to bear sin, but to bring salvation to those who are waiting for Him. [5]

[1] Acts 1:3-11 [2] Luke 24:50-53 [3] Mark 16:19-20 [4] Ephesians 4:7-10 [5] Hebrews 9:27-28

Day 331

Jesus had promised that, after He had gone, God the Holy Spirit would come to the disciples and live in them. That promise was fulfilled on the day of Pentecost. The disciples were changed from being sad, fearful, timid men and women, to being joyful, bold and vitally alive. The message they proclaimed was not their own idea. It was God's message of salvation to the world, and God the Holy Spirit confirmed it in the minds and hearts of those who were prepared to listen and respond.

God the Holy Spirit comes to the disciples at Pentecost

When the day of Pentecost came, they [the disciples] were all together in one place. Suddenly there came from heaven a sound like the rush of a violent wind and it filled the whole house where they were sitting. Divided tongues of fire appeared and rested on each of them and they were all filled with [God] the Holy Spirit and began to speak in other languages as the Spirit enabled them.

Now there were living in Jerusalem God-fearing Jews from every nation under heaven. When they heard this sound, a crowd gathered, bewildered because each one heard them [the disciples] speaking in his own language. They were beside themselves with amazement and said: "Are not all these who are speaking Galileans? Then how is it that we hear them, each one of us, in our own native language? ... All of us hear them speaking in our own native languages the mighty deeds of God!" In their amazement and bewilderment they asked one another, "What does this mean?" Some, however, mocked and said, "They have been drinking too much new wine!"

Then Peter, standing with the Eleven, raised his voice and addressed them: "You Jews and all of you who live in Jerusalem, let me make this clear, listen closely to what I say: These men are not drunk, as you suppose, for it is only the third hour [9 am] of the day. No, this is what was spoken by the prophet Joel: "It will come to pass in the last days, God says, that I will pour out my Spirit on all people. ... Therefore let all Israel know with certainty that God has made this Jesus, whom you crucified, both Lord and Christ." When the people heard this, they were cut to the heart and said to Peter and the other apostles, "Brothers, what shall we do?"

Peter answered them, "Repent and be baptised, every one of you, in the name of Jesus Christ for the forgiveness of your sins, and you will receive the gift of the Holy Spirit. For the promise is for you, for your children and for all who are far away, for everyone whom the Lord our God will call." And he witnessed with many other words, warning them and pleading with them, saying, "Save yourselves from this corrupt generation." [1]

[1] Acts 2:1-17, 36-40

Day 332

Jesus had promised that, when God the Holy Spirit came to live in the disciples, not only would they understand fully what He had been teaching them, but they would be able to do the kinds of things which He was doing, included performing miracles. This would confirm that they were then not only His disciples—learners of Him, but also His Apostles—sent by Him. The signs and wonders they would perform would, however, not be by their own power but by that of Jesus, who was reaching the world through them.

The healing of the crippled beggar

Peter and John were going up to the temple at the hour of prayer at the ninth hour [3 pm]. A man who was lame from birth was being carried to the gate of the Temple called Beautiful where he was laid every day to beg from those entering the temple. When he saw Peter and John about to enter, he asked them for alms. Peter looked at him, as did John, and said, "Look at us!" The man looked at them intently, expecting to receive something from them. Then Peter said, "Silver or gold, I have none, but what I have I give you. In the name of Jesus Christ of Nazareth, walk." He gripped him by the right hand and helped him to get up. Instantly the man's feet and ankles became strong. ... When all the people saw him walking and praising God, and recognised him as the man who used to sit begging at the temple gate called Beautiful, they were filled with wonder and amazement at what had happened to him.

While the beggar clung to Peter and John, all the people came running to them in Solomon's Colonnade, in utter astonishment. Peter, seeing this, said to the people, "Men of Israel, why are you surprised at this? Why do you stare at us as if by our own power or godliness we made this man walk? The God of Abraham, Isaac and Jacob, the God of our forefathers, has glorified His servant Jesus whom you handed over to be killed. You rejected Him before Pilate when He had decided to let Him go. You rejected the Holy and Righteous One and asked that a murderer be released to you. You killed the source of life, but God raised Him from the dead and to this we are witnesses. By faith in His name, this man whom you see and know, was made strong. It is faith in His name that has given this man complete healing, as you all see." [1]

Peter, filled with the Holy Spirit, said to them: "Know this, you and all the people of Israel, that it is in the name of Jesus Christ of Nazareth, whom you crucified but whom God raised from the dead, that this man stands before you perfectly healthy. ... There is salvation in no one else, for there is no other name under heaven given to men by which we must be saved." [2] There is one God [the Father] and one Mediator between God and people, the Man Christ Jesus [God the Son], who gave Himself as a ransom for everyone. [3]

[1] Acts 3:1-16   [2] Acts 4:8,10,12   [3] 1 Timothy 2:5-6

Day 333

Jesus had warned His disciples that they would face persecution and that they would be brought before civil authorities who would accuse them of acting against the law. The Apostles Peter and John were among the first to face this anti-Christ anger. The Jewish leaders thought they were defending their Jewish God-given faith as they put them in jail. The Apostles were, in fact, witnessing to their God-given Messiah. There are times when to obey God comes before obeying the authorities.

Peter and John before the Council

Peter and John were speaking to the people when the priests, the captain of the temple guard and the Sadducees came upon them. They were indignant because the apostles were teaching the people and proclaiming the resurrection of the dead in Jesus. They seized Peter and John, and because it was already evening, they put them in prison until the following day. ... On the next day, the rulers, elders and scribes, including Annas the high priest, Caiaphas, John and Alexander, and all who were of the high priest's family, met in Jerusalem. They made Peter and John stand in the middle of them and questioned them, saying, "By what power or by what name did you do this [miracle of healing the crippled beggar]?"

Peter, filled with the Holy Spirit, said to them: "Rulers of the people and elders of the council: If we are being examined today for a good deed done to a helpless cripple and we are asked how he was healed, then let it be known to you and all the people of Israel, that it is by the name of Jesus Christ of Nazareth, whom you crucified, but whom God raised from the dead, that this man stands before you in good health. He is 'the stone that was rejected by you builders, which has become the cornerstone.' There is salvation in no one else for there is no other name under heaven given to men by which we must be saved."

When they saw the courage of Peter and John and saw that they were unlearned, ordinary men, they were astonished and they recognized that they had been with Jesus. As they saw the man who had been healed standing there with them, they could not contradict them. ... They called them in again and ordered them not to speak or teach at all in the name of Jesus. But Peter and John replied, "Whether it is right in the sight of God to obey you rather than God, you must judge for yourselves. We cannot help speaking about what we have seen and heard." ...

When they were released, Peter and John went back to their own people. ... When they heard this, they raised their voices together in prayer to God. ... After they had prayed, the place where they were assembled was shaken. They were all filled with the Holy Spirit and spoke the word of God with boldness. [1]

[1] Acts 4:1-3, 5, 7-14,18-20, 23-24, 31

Day 334

When Christians realise that they all belong to Jesus Christ, the Saviour who died for each one of them, they also come to realise that they belong to each other. Some of those early Christians took this to the extent of sharing everything they had. They gave from what they possessed to others who were in need. There have been groups of people who have acted like that since then. Whether living together like that or separately in homes, the same principle applies. We are not our own. We belong to Jesus Christ and so does all that we possess, to be used responsibly to fulfil our personal, family and other responsibilities. And that includes the well-being of our neighbours—whoever they may be, and beyond them, others who are in need.

The believers share their possessions

All who believed were together and had everything in common. They sold their property and goods, and distributed the proceeds among themselves according to need. [1] All the believers were of one heart and mind. No one claimed that any of his possessions was his own, but everything they had they owned together. With great power the apostles testified to the resurrection of the Lord Jesus, and great grace was upon them all. There was not a needy person among them, for as many as were owners of land or houses sold them and, one by one, brought the money from the sales and laid it at the feet of the apostles. It was then distributed to each according to need. Joseph, a Levite from Cyprus, whom the apostles called Barnabas (which means 'Son of Encouragement'), sold a field he owned and brought the money and laid it at the feet of the Apostles. [2]

[James:] What good is it, my brothers and sisters, if a man claims to have faith but has no works? Can faith save him? ... If a brother or sister has no clothes nor daily food, and one of you says to him, "Go in peace. Keep warm and well fed," but does nothing about his bodily needs, what good is it? So faith, unless it is accompanied by deeds, is dead? [3]

[Moses:] There will be no poor among you, for in the land the Eternal-God, your God, is giving you to possess as your inheritance, He will richly bless you, if you obey fully the Eternal-God, your God, and are careful to keep all these commands which I command you this day. [4]

[John:] By this is we know what love is, that Jesus Christ laid down His life for us, and we ought to lay down our loves for one another. If anyone has this world's goods and sees his brother in need, but has no compassion on him, how can the love of God be in him? Dear children, let us not love in words or in speech but in actions and in truth. [5]

[1] Acts 2:44-45 [2] Acts 4:32-37 [3] James 2:14-17 [4] Deuteronomy 15:4-5 [5] 1 John 3:16-18

Day 335

It is no wonder that the deaths of Ananias and Sapphira caused great fear among the members of the church. At first sight it seems that the sin of these two Christians was to withhold some of their possessions from God. That was not, however, the worst sin. That was lying to God. It became very clear to everyone how serious it was to try to deceive God the Holy Spirit by asking Him to accept a lie. Jesus had warned the disciples about this great sin.

Ananias and Sapphira

A man named Ananias, with his wife Sapphira, also sold a piece of property. With his wife's knowledge he kept back part of the proceeds for himself, but brought the rest and laid it at the apostles' feet. Peter said to him, "Ananias, why has Satan so filled your heart that you should lie to the Holy Spirit and keep for yourself part of the money you received for the land? While it remained unsold, was it not your own? And after it was sold, was not the money at your disposal? How is it then, that you could think of doing this thing? You have not lied to men but to God."

When Ananias heard these words, he fell down and died. Great fear seized all who heard of what had happened. The young men came forward, wrapped up his body, and carried it out and buried it. About three hours later, his wife came in, not knowing what had happened. Peter said to her, "Tell me, did you sell the land for this price?" She said, "Yes, that is the price." Peter said to her, "How could you two agree to deceive the Spirit of the Lord? Look! The feet of those who buried your husband are at the door, and they will carry you out." Immediately she fell down at his feet and died. The young men came in, found her dead, carried her out and buried her beside her husband. Great fear seized the whole church and all who heard about these things. [1]

[Isaiah:] He [God] said: "Surely they are my people, sons who will not be false to me." So He became their Saviour, and in their distress He was distressed, the angel of His presence saved them, He lifted them up and carried them all the days of old. Yet they rebelled and grieved His Holy Spirit, and so He turned and became their enemy and He himself fought against them. [2]

[Jesus:] I tell you, every sin and blasphemy will be forgiven, but the blasphemy against [God] the [Holy] Spirit will not be forgiven. Whoever speaks a word against the Son of Man will be forgiven, but whoever speaks against the Holy Spirit will not be forgiven, either in this age or in the age to come. [3] He said this because they said, "He has an evil spirit." [4]

Let no evil talk come from your mouths. ... Do not grieve the Holy Spirit of God. [5]

---

[1] Acts 5:1-10 [2] Isaiah 63:8-10 [3] Matthew 12:31-32 [4] Mark 3:30 [5] Ephesians 4:29-30

Day 336

The early Christians soon discovered that there was a need for organisation in their growing numbers. Men and women were needed with particular gifts of administration to work together to ensure that the money given to help those in need was handled responsibly. Those taking these responsibilities needed to be as chosen of God as those who were in leading, preaching and teaching roles. As God called the twelve Apostles, so He called the seven administrators and helpers.

The choosing of the seven

At the time when the number of disciples was increasing, the Hellenists [Greek-speaking Jews] among them complained about the Jews because their widows were being overlooked in the daily distribution of food. So the Twelve [Apostles] gathered all the disciples together and said, "It is not be right that we should neglect the ministry of the word of God in order to serve at tables. Therefore, brethren, choose from among you seven men of good character who are known to be full of the [Holy] Spirit and wisdom to see to this task, but we will continue to devote ourselves to prayer and to the ministry of the word." This proposal pleased the whole assembly. They chose Stephen, a man full of faith and of the Holy Spirit, Philip, Procorus, Nicanor, Timon, Parmenas, and Nicolas from Antioch, a convert to Judaism. They presented these men to the Apostles who prayed and laid their hands on them. So the word of God spread and the number of disciples in Jerusalem increased greatly, and a large number of priests became obedient to the faith. [1]

[Paul:] In the church, God has appointed first of all apostles, second prophets, third teachers, then workers of deeds of power, those having gifts of healing, helpers, those with gifts of administration, and those speaking in different languages. [2] We have different gifts, according to the grace given us: if it is the gift of prophesy, use it in proportion to faith; if serving, give oneself to service; if teaching, then teach well; if encouragement, let him encourage; if contributing to the needs of others, give generously; if leadership, lead diligently; if showing mercy, do it cheerfully. Let love be sincere. Hate what is evil; hold fast to what is good. Love one another with brotherly affection. Never be lacking in zeal but be aglow with the Spirit, serving the Lord. [3]

Grace has been given to each of us according to the measure of Christ's gift. ... The gifts He gave were to some to be apostles, to some to be prophets, to some to be evangelists, and to some to be pastors and teachers, to equip God's people for works of service, and to build up the body of Christ, until we all come to unity in the faith and in the knowledge of the Son of God, and to maturity, to the measure of the full stature of Christ. [4]

[1] Acts 6:1-15 [2] 1 Corinthians 12:28 [3] Romans 12:6-8 [4] Ephesians 4:7,11-13

Day 337

Stephen was one of the first 'helpers'. In his role as an administrator of the finances of the growing church, God used him greatly. God enabled him to perform miraculous signs as well, but it was his wisdom that made Him stand out from the others. This wisdom was based on a knowledge of the Old Testament and the new light that God the Holy Spirit brought to it. Stephen was the first martyr for the name of Jesus Christ.

Stephen - the first martyr

Stephen, a man full of grace and power, did great wonders and miraculous signs among the people. Some of the synagogue of Freedmen [freed Jewish slaves] opposed Stephen and disputed with him, but they could not stand up against his wisdom or the spirit with which he spoke. They secretly instructed some men to say, "We have heard Stephen speak blasphemously against Moses and against God." The elders and the scribes arrested him and brought him before the council [Sanhedrin]. [1]

The high priest asked him, "Are these charges true?" He answered, "Brothers and fathers, listen to me! The God of glory appeared to our forefather Abraham while he was still in Mesopotamia ... and said to him, 'Leave your country and your people and go to the land I will show you.' ... God sent him to this land where you are now living, ... and God promised that He would give it to him and his descendants after him even though at that time Abraham had no child. ... You stiff-necked people! You are just like your forefathers. You have always resisted the Holy Spirit as they did! Which of the prophets did your forefathers not persecute? They killed those who predicted the coming of the Righteous One whom you have now betrayed and murdered, you who received the law through angels but have not obeyed it."

When they heard this, they were enraged and gnashed their teeth at him. But he, full of the Holy Spirit, gazed up to heaven and saw the glory of God and Jesus standing at the right hand of God. He said, "Look, I see the heavens opened and the Son of Man standing at the right hand of God." They put their hands over their ears and, with a loud shout, they rushed together at him, dragged him out of the city and began to stone him, while the witnesses laid their clothes at the feet of a young man named Saul. While they were stoning him, Stephen prayed, "Lord Jesus, receive my spirit." Then he fell on his knees and cried out loudly, "Lord, do not hold this sin against them." When he had said this, he fell asleep. [2]

[John saw in a vision of heaven:] They overcame him [Satan] by the blood of the Lamb and by the word of their testimony. They did not cling to their lives when faced with death. Therefore rejoice, O heavens and you who dwell in them. [3]

[1] Acts 6:8-10 [2] Acts 7:1-5,51-60 [3] Revelation 12:11-12

Day 338

In a remarkable way God sent His messenger, Philip, to a man of high rank in another country, who was not a Jew, to show to him and to the world, that the prophesies of the Old Testament belonged to the non-Jews as well as to the Jews. Philip could explain now that, where it is written "the Lord has laid on him the iniquity of us all" the 'Him' was Jesus, and 'us all' included the Ethiopian, a foreigner to the Jews. The Ethiopian believed God's word through Philip. There and then he became a member of God's family and was baptised as a testimony to that fact.

Philip and the Ethiopian official

An angel of the Lord said to Philip, "Get up and at midday go south to the desert road that runs from Jerusalem to Gaza." So he set off. There, an Ethiopian, a eunuch of high rank in charge of all the treasury of Candace, queen of the Ethiopians, who had gone to Jerusalem to worship, was on his way home. He was sitting in his chariot reading the book of the prophet Isaiah. The [Holy] Spirit told Philip, "Go and join that chariot." Philip ran up to the chariot and heard the man reading the prophet Isaiah and asked him, "Do you understand what you are reading?" He said, "How can I unless someone explains it to me?" So he invited Philip to come up and sit with him. The passage of Scripture which the eunuch was reading was this: "Like a sheep He was led to the slaughter, and as a lamb before its shearer is silent, so He did not open His mouth. In His humiliation He was denied justice. Who can speak of His generation? For His life was taken from the earth." The eunuch said to Philip, "Tell me, about whom is the prophet talking, about himself or about someone else?"

Then Philip, beginning with that passage of Scripture, told him the good news about Jesus. As they were going along the road, they came to some water and the eunuch said, "Look, here is water! What hinders me from being baptized? ... Then Philip and the eunuch went down into the water and Philip baptised him. When they came up out of the water, the Spirit of the Lord caught Philip away, and the eunuch saw him no more, but he went on his way rejoicing. Philip was found at Azotus and, as he passed through, he preached the gospel in all the towns to Caesarea. [1]

[Paul:] Remember that at one time you who are Gentiles by birth and called "uncircumcised" by those who call themselves the "circumcision", remember that, at that time, you were without Christ, aliens from the commonwealth of Israel and strangers to the covenants of the promise, without hope and without God in the world. But now in Christ Jesus you who once were far away have been brought near through the blood of Christ. [2]

[1] Acts 8:26-40 [2] Ephesians 2:11-13

Day 339

Paul was a very zealous man. As a highly educated Pharisee, he directed his zeal against those whom he saw as rebels against God. On the road to Damascus, he came into a living contact with Jesus Christ and his life was changed. He was still a zealous man, but from then on his zeal was directed in living out the life of the Jesus who had appeared to him and fulfilling the commission Jesus had given him at that moment.

The conversion of Paul

Saul was still breathing out murderous threats against the disciples of the Lord. ... As he was travelling and nearing Damascus, suddenly a light from heaven flashed around him and he fell to the ground. He heard a voice say to him, "Saul, Saul, why do you persecute me?" Saul said, "Who are you, Lord?" He replied, "I am Jesus, whom you are persecuting, now get up and go into the city, and you will be told what you must do." The men who were travelling with him stood there speechless; they could hear the voice but did not see anyone. Saul got up from the ground, but though his eyes were open he could see nothing, so they led him by the hand and brought him into Damascus. He was unable to see for three days and he neither ate nor drank.

There was a disciple in Damascus named Ananias. The Lord said to him in a vision, "Ananias!" He answered, "Here I am, Lord" The Lord said to him, "Get up and go to the street called Straight, and ask at the house of Judas for a man from Tarsus named Saul, for he is praying. He has seen in a vision a man named Ananias enter and place his hands on him to restore his sight." But Ananias answered, "Lord, I have heard from many people about this man and all the evil he has done to your saints in Jerusalem. Now he is here with authority from the chief priests to put in chains all who call on your name." The Lord said to him, "Go! for this man is my chosen instrument to bear my name to the Gentiles, to their kings and to the people of Israel. I will show him how much he must suffer for the sake of my name." Then Ananias went to the house, entered it and, placing his hands on Saul, he said, "Brother Saul, the Lord Jesus, who appeared to you on the road as you were coming here, has sent me so that you may recover your sight and be filled with the Holy Spirit." Immediately, something like scales fell from Saul's eyes, and he could see again. He got up and was baptised and, after taking some food, he regained his strength. [1]

Agrippa said to Paul, "You have permission to speak for yourself. Paul stretched out his hand and began his defence ... About noon, O King, I saw a light from heaven, brighter than the sun ... We all fell to the ground and I heard a voice saying to me in Hebrew, 'Saul, Saul, why do you persecute me? ... I am Jesus whom you are persecuting'... Whereupon, O King Agrippa, I was not disobedient to the vision from heaven.[2]

[1] Acts 9:1-19 [2] Acts 26:1,13-15, 19

Day 340

As Jesus had performed miracles as a sign of who He was, so He gave that same power to the Apostles. They were enabled to perform the kind of miracles that Jesus did, but only in His name. Peter must have known that it was the will of God to heal Aeneas and raise Dorcas to life again because this did not happen to everyone. The purpose of these signs was fulfilled as many came to know about Jesus through hearing about the miracles and then going on learn about Him and to believe in Him.

The Apostles perform miracles in the name of Jesus

Many miraculous signs and wonders were performed through the Apostles among the people. They all agreed to meet together in Solomon's Colonnade [in the Temple] Although they were highly regarded by the people, no one else dared join them. Nevertheless, more and more men and women believed in the Lord and were added to their number. They even brought the sick into the streets and laid them on mats so that at least the shadow of Peter might fall on some of them as he passed by. People gathered from the towns and villages around Jerusalem bringing the sick and those who were tormented by evil spirits, and they were all healed.

As Peter travelled up and down the country, he also went to visit the saints in Lydda. There he found a man named Aeneas, who had been paralysed and bedridden for eight years. Peter said to him, "Aeneas, Jesus Christ heals you. Get up and make your bed." Immediately Aeneas stood up. All those who lived in Lydda and Sharon saw what had happened to him and turned to the Lord. [1]

In Joppa there was a disciple named Tabitha. ... About that time she became ill and died. When they had washed her body they laid her in an upstairs room. Lydda was near Joppa, so when the disciples heard that Peter was there, they sent two men to him and begged him, "Please come to us at once!" ... Peter ... knelt and prayed. Turning towards the dead body, he said, "Tabitha, get up." She opened her eyes and when she saw Peter she sat up. He took her by the hand and helped her up. Then he called in the believers and the widows and presented her to them alive. This became known in Joppa, and many people believed in the Lord. [2]

Since, in the wisdom of God, the world did not know Him through wisdom, He was pleased to save those who believe by the foolishness of what was preached. Jews demand miracles and Greeks look for wisdom, but we preach the crucified Christ, who is, to the Jews, a stumblingblock, and to the Greeks, foolishness, but for those who are called, both Jews and Greeks, He is Christ the power of God and the wisdom of God. For the foolishness of God is wiser than man's wisdom, and the weakness of God is stronger than man's strength. [3]

[1] Acts 5:12-16   [2] Acts 9:32-43   [3] 1 Corinthians 1:21

Day 341

Many Jews thought that the 'God of the Jews' was exclusive to them. They were His chosen people and everyone else was 'unclean'. God showed the early church through the dramatic way that He worked in Cornelius, that He was the God of all who were made clean by Him, through the 'Blood of Christ'.

Peter at the house of Cornelius

At Caesarea there was a man named Cornelius, a centurion in what was known as the Italian Regiment. He was a devout and God-fearing man, as was his household. ... One day at about the ninth hour [3 pm], he had a vision in which he saw clearly an angel of God, who came to him and said, "Cornelius!" He stared at him in terror and said, "What is it, Lord?" The angel said to him, "Your prayers and gifts to the poor have come up as a memorial before God. Now send men to Joppa and bring back a man named Simon, who is called Peter. He is lodging with Simon the tanner, whose house is by the sea." When the angel who spoke to him had left, he called two of his servants and a God-fearing soldier who was one of his attendants. He told them everything that had happened and sent them to Joppa.

About noon the following day, as they were on their way and approaching the city, Peter went up on the roof to pray. He became hungry and wanted something to eat. While the meal was being prepared, he fell into a trance. He saw the heavens opened and something like a large sheet was lowered to earth by its four corners. It contained all kinds of four-footed animals, as well as reptiles of the earth and birds of the air. Then he heard a voice which said, "Get up, Peter, kill and eat." Peter said, "No, by no means, Lord! I have never eaten anything impure or unclean." The voice spoke to him a second time, "What God has made clean, do not call unclean. " ...

While Peter was perplexed about the meaning of the vision, the men sent by Cornelius had found where Simon's house was and had stopped at the gate. ... As Peter arrived, Cornelius met him and fell at his feet and worshipped him. But Peter made him get up and said to him, "Stand up, I myself am only a man." As he talked with him, Peter went inside and found a large group of people assembled. He said to them: "You yourselves know that it is against our law for a Jew to associate with a Gentile or visit him, but God has shown me that I should not call any man impure or unclean. ... I understand now that God is no respecter of persons, but in every nation whoever fears Him and does what is right is acceptable to Him.[1]

[Paul:] Through faith in Christ Jesus you are all children of God. ... There is neither Jew nor Greek, slave nor free, male nor female; you are all one in Christ Jesus. [2]

[1] Acts 10:1-6, 9-17, 25-28,34-35 [2] Galatians 3:28

Day 342

Many Jews who became Christians in the early church found it hard to believe that faith in Jesus Christ set them free from the rites and ceremonies of their old beliefs. They thought that Gentiles who became Christians should follow the same rules as the Jews. The experience of Peter and Cornelius helped the leaders who met in Jerusalem to decide on this issue with the assurance that it was God's will working through them.

Peter convinces the Christian Jews in Jerusalem

The apostles and the believers throughout Judea heard that the Gentiles also had received the word of God. When Peter went up to Jerusalem, the 'circumcised [Jewish] believers' criticised him and said, "Why do you go into the houses of uncircumcised [non-Jewish] men and eat with them." Peter explained all that had happened to them [with Cornelius]. He said, "I was in the city of Joppa praying, and in a trance I saw in a vision something like a large sheet lowered from heaven by its four corners. I looked into it and saw unclean animals and birds of the air. ... The voice said, "What God has made clean do not call 'unclean'." ... At that moment, three men arrived, sent to me [by Cornelius] from Caesaria. The Holy Spirit instructed me to accompany them. ... As I began to speak, the Holy Spirit came on them as He had come on us at the beginning. Then I remembered that the Lord had said: 'John baptised with water, but you will be baptised with the Holy Spirit.' If God gave to them the same gift as He gave to us who believed in the Lord Jesus Christ, who was I that I could oppose God?" When they heard this, they made no further objections and praised God, saying, "God has granted even to the Gentiles repentance unto life." [1]

When Peter came to Antioch, I [Paul] opposed him to his face because he was clearly in the wrong. Until certain men came from James, he used to eat with the Gentiles, but when they came he drew back from the Gentiles and kept apart from them because he was afraid of those who belonged to the 'circumcision party'. Other Jews also joined him in their hypocrisy and even Barnabas was led astray. When I saw that they were not acting in accordance with the truth, I said to Peter in front of them all, "If you, though a Jew, live like a Gentile, and not like a Jew, how can you force the Gentiles to live like the Jews? We who are Jews by birth and not Gentile sinners, know that a man is not justified by works of the law, but by faith in Jesus Christ. We have put our faith in Christ Jesus that we may be justified by faith in Him, and not by observing the law, because no one will be justified by works of the law." ...

I have been crucified with Christ. It is no longer I who live, but Christ who lives in me, and the life I live in the body, I live by faith in the Son of God who loved me and gave Himself for me. [2]

[1] Acts 11:1-18   [2] Galatians 2:11-16,20

Day 343

Jesus appeared to Paul on the road to Damascus and gave him his special commission. Later, in another unusual experience, God revealed to Him details of the Gospel he was to preach. He checked this first with Peter, then later the other Apostles, and found that what Jesus had taught them corresponded exactly with what God had revealed to him. Truth that is shared adds to the conviction with which it is held and preached.

Paul is given a special revelation of the Gospel

[Paul:] You have heard of my former way of life in Judaism, how violently I persecuted the church of God and tried to destroy it. I advanced in Judaism and in zeal for the traditions of my fathers, beyond many men of my own race and age. But when God, who set me apart before I was born and called me by His grace, was pleased to reveal His Son in me, so that I might preach him among the Gentiles, I did not confer with any man, nor did I go up to Jerusalem to those who were apostles before I was, but I went immediately into Arabia and afterwards returned to Damascus.

After three years, I went up to Jerusalem to meet Peter and I stayed with him for fifteen days. I did not see any of the other apostles, except James, the brother of the Lord. ... Then I went into the regions of Syria and Cilicia. I was unknown by sight to the churches of Judea that are in Christ. They only heard it said that 'He who formerly persecuted us is now preaching the faith he once tried to destroy.' And they praised God because of me. [1]

Fourteen years later I went up again to Jerusalem with Barnabas and Titus. I went because it was revealed to me that I should go. I laid before them the gospel which I preach among the Gentiles. I did this in private to those who were recognised leaders, to make sure that I was not running or had not run my race in vain. ... For God, who worked through Peter as an apostle to the Jews, was also at work in me as an apostle to the Gentiles. When James, Peter and John, who were reputed to be pillars of the church in Jerusalem, recognised the grace given to me, they gave me and Barnabas the right hand of fellowship. [2]

I know a man in Christ who, fourteen years ago, whether in the body or out of the body, I do no know, was caught up to the third heaven, and he heard things which cannot be put into words. [3]

Surely you have heard about the stewardship of God's grace that was entrusted to me for you, the mystery which was made known to me by revelation, ... that through the gospel, the Gentiles are now fellow-heirs [with Israel] of the same promise in Christ, and members together of the same body. [4]

[1] Galatians 1:13-24 [2] Galatians 2:1-2, 10 [3] 2 Corinthians 12:2-4, 7 [4] Ephesians 3:2,6

Day 344

God did not help every Apostle to escape from prison every time, but He did open the prison doors for Peter on one occasion. It was God's will to save him from public trial on the following day. It was also His will to answer those who earnestly prayed for Peter's safety. Their earnestness in prayer was greater than their faith, and they could not, at first, believe, that God had answered their prayers in such an amazing way.

Peter's miraculous escape from prison

About this time King Herod persecuted the church and arrested some who belonged to it. He put James, the brother of John, to death with the sword. When he saw that this pleased the Jews, he proceeded to arrest Peter also. This happened during the Feast of Unleavened Bread. When he had seized him, he put him in prison and handed him over to a guard of four squads of four soldiers each, with the intention of bringing him out for trial before the people after the Passover.

Peter was kept in prison, but the church prayed fervently to God for him. The night before he was due to be brought to trial, Peter was sleeping between two soldiers, bound with two chains and guarded by sentries at the entrance, when suddenly an angel of the Lord appeared and a light shone in the cell. The angel struck Peter on the side and woke him up, saying, "Quick, get up!" and the chains fell from Peter's wrists. Then the angel said to him, "Wrap your cloak around you, put on your sandals and follow me." Peter followed him out of the prison, but he did not realize that what the angel was doing was real; he thought he was seeing a vision. When they had passed the first and second guards and came to the iron gate leading to the city, it opened of its own accord and they went out into the street where the angel left him. ...

Then Peter came to himself and said, "Now I know without any doubt that the Lord sent His angel and rescued me from the hand of Herod and from all that the Jewish people were expecting." When he realised this he went to the house of Mary, the mother of John, also called Mark, where many had gathered and were praying. Peter knocked at the outer gate and a servant girl named Rhoda came to answer. When she recognised Peter's voice, she was so overjoyed that she ran back without opening it and said to the people, "Peter is at the door!" They said to her. "You are out of your mind." She persisted in saying that it was so. They said, "It must be his angel." But Peter kept on knocking. When they opened the door and saw him, they were amazed. [1]

[Jesus said:] "So I say to you: Ask and it will given to you; seek and you will find; knock and the door will be opened to you." [2]

[1] Acts 12:1-16   [2] Luke 11:9

Day 345

It was in Antioch that the followers of Jesus were first called 'Christians'. It was the Christians there who invited Paul to be their teacher. It is not surprising therefore, that a church which had so much spiritual life should send out two of its most gifted workers to take the Gospel to the countries where it was not known. Jesus first said, "Come ... learn of me," then, to the same people, "God into all the world and preach the Gospel."

The Christians at Antioch commission Paul and Barnabas

Barnabas went to Tarsus to look for Saul, and when he found him, he brought him to Antioch. For a whole year Barnabas and Saul met together with the church and taught a great number of people. The disciples were first called Christians at Antioch.[1]

In the church at Antioch there were prophets and teachers: Barnabas, Simeon called Niger, Lucius of Cyrene, Manaen (a member of the court of Herod the Tetrarch) and Saul. While they were worshipping the Lord and fasting, the Holy Spirit said, "Set apart for me Barnabas and Saul for the work to which I have called them." After fasting and praying, they laid their hands on them and sent them off.

So the two of them, being sent on their way by the Holy Spirit, went down to Seleucia and from there sailed to Cyprus. When they arrived at Salamis, they preached the word of God in the Jewish synagogues. John (Mark) was with them to help them. They travelled through the whole island until they came to Paphos.[2]

Paul and his companions sailed from Paphos, to Perga in Pamphylia. ... From Perga they went on to Antioch in Pisidia. On the Sabbath they went into the synagogue and sat down. After the reading from the Law and the Prophets, the leaders of the Synagogue sent word to them, saying, "Brothers, if your have a message of encouragement for the people, speak."

Paul stood up, motioned with his hand and said: "Men of Israel and you [Gentiles] who worship God, listen! ... We are bringing you the good news that what God promised our forefathers, He has fulfilled in us, their children, by raising Jesus from the dead. ... Let it be known to you, therefore, my brothers and sisters, that through this Man, Jesus, the forgiveness of sins is proclaimed to you, and through Him everyone who believes is set free from every sin from which you could not be set free by the Law of Moses."[3]

From Attalia they sailed back to Antioch, where they had been commended to the grace of God for the work which they had now completed. On arriving there, they gathered the church together and told all that God had done through them and how He had opened the door of faith to the Gentiles.[4]

[1] Acts 11:25-26 [2] Acts 13:1-6 [3] Acts 13:13-16, 32, 38 [4] Acts 14:26-27

Day 346

Miracles demand someone to perform them. Where the power working the miracle is not recognised as God, then superstition and false gods are the most common ways of explaining them. There are also many counterfeit miracles performed in the world by Satanic powers. It did not take very long for the crowds that wanted to worship Paul and Barnabas as gods, to change their minds and stone them. Many people are easily deceived and give false explanations for what comes from God.

Paul at Lystra

In Lystra there sat a man who could not use his feet; he was lame from birth and had never walked. He listened to Paul as he was speaking. Paul looked straight at him, saw that he had faith to be healed and said in a loud voice, "Stand up on your feet!" The man jumped up and began to walk.

When the crowd saw what Paul had done, they shouted in the Lycaonian language, "The gods have come down to us in human form!" Barnabas they called Zeus, and Paul they called Hermes, because he was the chief speaker. The priest of Zeus, whose temple was just outside the city, brought bulls and garlands to the city gates where he and the crowd wanted to offer sacrifices to them.

When the apostles Barnabas and Paul heard of this, they tore their clothes and rushed out into the crowd, shouting: "Men, why are you doing this? We too are men, just like you. We are bringing you the good news that you should turn from these worthless things to the living God, who made heaven and earth and sea and everything in them. In past generations, He let the nations go their own ways. Yet He did not leave himself without testimony, for He has shown kindness by giving you rain from heaven and crops in their seasons, and satisfying you with food and filling your hearts with joy."

Even with these words, they found it difficult to keep the crowd from sacrificing to them. Then some Jews who had come there from Antioch and Iconium won over the crowd and they stoned Paul and dragged him outside the city, thinking he was dead. But the disciples formed a circle round him. He got up and went into the town. The next day he and Barnabas went on to Derbe. [1]

Paul stood in the centre of the Areopagus [debating hall] and said: "Men of Athens! I can see how very religious you are in every way. As I walked around and looked carefully at the objects of your worship, I came across an altar with this inscription: TO AN UNKNOWN GOD. Now what you worship as unknown, that I proclaim to you. The God who made the world and everything in it, as He is Lord of heaven and earth, does not live in shrines made by human hands. [2]

[1] Acts 14:8-19   [2] Acts 17:22-23

Day 347

Several times in the history of the Christian church, its leaders have had to meet to face some heresy which threatened the truth of the Gospel. The Council at Jerusalem met to face a false teaching. Some Christian teachers were insisting that, as the Christian Gospel came out of the Jewish religion, you could not be saved by faith in Jesus alone; the rite of circumcision, which was a sign of membership of the Jewish faith, was also necessary. The unanimous decision revealed that God gave all those in the Council one mind about a very important matter.

The Council at Jerusalem

Some men came from Judea to Antioch and taught the brothers and sisters: "Unless you are circumcised according to the custom of Moses, you cannot be saved." Paul and Barnabas disagreed very strongly. This led to such a sharp dispute and debate that Paul and Barnabas were appointed to go to Jerusalem with some other believers, to confer with the apostles and elders there about this question. They were sent on their way by the church. As they travelled through Phoenicia and Samaria, they told of the conversion of the Gentiles. This caused great rejoicing among the brothers and sisters.

When they came to Jerusalem, they were welcomed by the church and the apostles and elders, to whom they recounted all that God had done through them. ... The apostles and elders assembled to consider the question, and, after much discussion, Peter got up and said to them: "Brothers and sisters, you know that some time ago God made the choice among you that by me the Gentiles should hear the message of the gospel and believe. God, who knows the heart, bore witness of this to them by giving them the Holy Spirit, as He did to us. He made no distinction between us and them, for He cleansed their hearts by faith. Now then, why do you provoke God by putting on the necks of the disciples, a yoke which neither we nor our fathers have been able to bear? We believe that we are saved through the grace of our Lord Jesus, just as they are." ... When they finished talking, James spoke: "Brothers and sisters, listen to me. ... It is my judgment that we should not put obstacles in the way of the Gentiles who are turning to God. Instead we should write to them, telling them to abstain from food polluted by being offered to idols, from sexual immorality, from the meat of animals that have been strangled and from blood." [1]

[Jesus prayed:] My prayer is not for these alone. I pray also for those who will believe in me through their word, that all of them may be one, just as you, Father, are in me and I am in you. ... that they may be completely one so that the world may know that you sent me and that you have loved them even as you have loved me. [2]

---

[1] Acts 15:1-4,6-13,19-20, [2] John 17:20-23

Day 348

The loving heart of God reaches our to people all over the world. It was for all of them that Jesus died. When He lives in Christians, it is natural that He would give them a desire to reach out themselves to those who are not Christians to tell them of the Good News which has changed their lives. God calls some Christians to go to a particular place, as He did with Paul, and serve Him and witness to Him there. It is through the obedience of those who hear that call that the Gospel is reaching the world today.

Paul's vision of the Macedonian

As they [Paul and Silas] went from town to town, they passed on to them the decisions made by the apostles and elders in Jerusalem. So the churches were strengthened in their faith and they increased in numbers daily. They went through the region of Phrygia and Galatia, and, having been forbidden by the Holy Spirit to preach the word in Asia, they reached the border of Mysia and tried to go into Bithynia, but the Spirit of Jesus prevented them. So, passing by Mysia, they went down to Troas. That night, Paul had a vision. A man of Macedonia stood and pleaded with him, "Come over to Macedonia and help us." When Paul had seen the vision, we at once prepared to leave for Macedonia, convinced that God had called us to preach the gospel to them. [1]

[Jesus said:] "I am the good shepherd. I know my sheep and my sheep know me, as [God] the Father knows me and I know the Father. I lay down my life for the sheep. I have other sheep that are not of this fold. I must bring them in also, they will listen to my voice, and there will be one flock and one shepherd." [2]

Outside the city gate there were four men who suffered from leprosy. They said to one another, "Why are we sitting here until we die? ... Let us go to the army of the Syrians. ... The Syrians rose and fled in the twilight and left the camp. ... When they [the four men] reached the edge of the camp, they entered one of the tents, ate and drank, and carried away and hid silver, gold and clothes. They returned and entered another tent and took things from it and hid them too. Then they said to each other, "We are not doing right. This is a day of good news, and we are keeping it to ourselves. Let us go and tell the king's household. [3]

[John:] Then I saw another angel flying in mid-air. He had the eternal gospel to proclaim to those who live on the earth, to every nation, tribe, language and people. [4]

[Paul:] I am not ashamed of the gospel, for it is the power of God for salvation for everyone who believes: for the Jew first, then for the Gentile. For in the gospel a righteousness from God is revealed, which comes by faith and leads to faith, as it is written: "He who is righteous will live by faith." [5]

[1] Acts 16:8-10   [2] John 10:14-16   [3] 2 Kings 7:8-9   [4] Revelation 14:6   [5] Romans 1:16

Day 349

The evil spirit which controlled the slave girl recognised the God who was working through Paul and Silas. The Roman authorities who put them into prison did not. Both the evil spirit and the Roman authorities were subject to the power of God. Both the slave girl and the prison jailor found that the power of Jesus was sufficient to release them from the powers of evil. It was the God of the prisoners who triumphed.

Paul and Silas in prison

As we [Paul, Silas and Luke] were going to the place of prayer, we were met by a slave girl who had a spirit of divination [claiming to predict the future]. ... She persisted in following Paul and the rest of us, shouting, "These men are servants of the Most High God, who announce to you the way of salvation." ... Finally Paul became very troubled. He turned and said to the spirit, "In the name of Jesus Christ I command you to come out of her!" and it came out of her at that moment. When her owners realised that their hope of making money had gone, they seized Paul and Silas and dragged them before the authorities in the market-place. When they had brought them before the magistrates, they said, "These men are Jews, and are throwing our city into an uproar by encouraging customs unlawful for us Romans to adopt or practise." ... After they had flogged them severely, they threw them into prison, and the jailer was given strict orders to guard them carefully.

On receiving such strict orders, he put them into the inner prison and fastened their feet in the stocks. About midnight Paul and Silas were praying and singing hymns to God, and the other prisoners were listening to them. Suddenly there was a violent earthquake and the foundations of the prison were shaken. At once all the doors flew open, and everybody's chains became unfastened. The jailer woke up, and when he saw that the prison doors were open, he drew his sword and was about to kill himself because he supposed that the prisoners had escaped. But Paul shouted, "Do not harm yourself! We are all here!" The jailer called for lights, rushed in and fell down trembling before Paul and Silas. Then he brought them out and said, "Sirs, what must I do to be saved?" They answered, "Believe on the Lord Jesus, and you will be saved, you and your household." Then they spoke the word of the Lord to him and to all who were in his house. At that same hour of the night, the jailer took them and washed their wounds, and immediately he and all his family were baptised. ... He was filled with joy because he and his household had come to believe in God." [1]

[Paul:] We know that in all things God works for the good of those who love Him, who are called according to His purpose. [2]

[1] Acts 16:16-40   [2] Romans 8:28

Day 350

Wherever Paul went in his missionary tours, he visited the Jewish Synagogues first. This happened at Athens. Among the 'God fearing Greeks' were some philosophers and it was through them that he was invited to speak to a group of debaters at the Areopagus. This was one of the most important speeches that Paul ever made. It gives a clear picture of what God intended when He created the universe and the people in it, and why He hid Himself in it so that people would have to seek for Him and reach out for him and some of them find Him.

Paul at Athens

While Paul was waiting in Athens, he was greatly distressed to see that the city was full of idols. So he reasoned in the synagogue with the Jews and the God-fearing Greeks, as well as in the market-place day after day with those who happened to be there. Some of the Epicurean and Stoic philosophers began to argue with him. Some said, "What is this babbler saying?" Because he preached Jesus and the resurrection, others said, "He seems to be advocating foreign gods!" Then they took him and brought him to the Areopagus [a Greek debating forum], where they said to him, "May we know what this new teaching is that you are presenting? You are bringing strange ideas to our ears, and we would like to know what they mean." ...

Paul stood up in the meeting of the Areopagus and said: "Men of Athens! I see that in every way you are very religious. For as I walked around and noted carefully the objects of your worship, I came across an altar with this inscription: TO AN UNKNOWN GOD. Now what you worship as unknown, I am making known to you. The God who made the world and everything in it, as He is Lord of heaven and earth, does not live in shrines made by human hands, neither is He served by human hands, as if He needed anything, for it is He who Himself gives all men life and breath and everything else. From one He made every nation of men to inhabit the whole earth. He determined the times when they should live, and the exact places which they should inhabit. God did this so that men would have to seek for Him and reach out for Him and perhaps find Him, though He is not far from each one of us. 'For in Him we live and move and have our being.' ... Since we are God's offspring, we should not think that God is like gold or silver or stone, an image made by man's art and skill."

"In the past God allowed such ignorance, but now He commands all people everywhere to repent. For He has set a day when the world will be judged with justice by the Man [Jesus] whom He has appointed. He has given assurance of this to everyone by raising Him from the dead." When they heard about the resurrection of the dead, some of them scoffed. ... A few joined Him and became believers. [1]

[1] Acts 17:16-34

Day 351

Jesus warned His disciples that their message would not be well received by everyone. There would be opposition and persecution. Paul found this to be very true. However, in the midst of the violent opposition, not only were some men and women becoming Christians in response to his preaching, but God Himself encouraged him by a special vision. That encouragement comes to us today through His Word, the Bible, which include two letters which Paul wrote to the church which grew in Corinth.

Paul in Corinth

Paul left Athens and went to Corinth. There he met a Jew named Aquila, a native of Pontus, who had recently come from Italy with his wife Priscilla because Claudius had issued a decree ordering all the Jews to leave Rome. Paul went to see them, and because they were a tentmakers as Paul was, he stayed and worked with them. Every Sabbath he reasoned in the synagogue, seeking to convince Jews and Greeks. When Silas and Timothy arrived from Macedonia, Paul devoted himself wholly to preaching and testifying to the Jews that Jesus was the Christ. As some of the Jews opposed Paul and became abusive, he shook the dust from his clothes and said to them, "Your blood be on your own heads! I am innocent. From now on I will go to the Gentiles."

Paul left the synagogue and went next door to the house of a man named Titius Justus, a worshipper of God. Crispus, the leader of the synagogue, with all his household believed in the Lord, and many of the Corinthians who heard him believed and were baptised. One night the Lord said to Paul in a vision: "Do not be afraid but speak and do not be silent. I am with you, and no one is going to attack you or harm you, for I have many people in this city." Paul stayed there for a year and a half, teaching them the word of God.

When Gallio was proconsul of Achaia, the Jews made a united attack on Paul and brought him before the judge, saying, "This man is persuading the people to worship God in ways which are contrary to the law." As Paul was about to speak, Gallio said to the Jews, "If you were bringing a complaint about some misdemeanour or serious crime, I would have cause to listen to you. But since it is a matter of questions about words and names and your own law, see to it yourselves. I am not going to be a judge of such things." So he dismissed them from the court. Then they all turned on Sosthenes, the leader of the synagogue, and beat him in front of the court. But Gallio paid no attention to any of this. [1]

[Moses:] Be strong and courageous. Do not be afraid or terrified because of them, for it is the Eternal-God, your God, who goes with you. He will never fail you nor forsake you. [2]

---

[1] Acts 18:1-17 [2] Deuteronomy 31:6

Day 352

Preachers and teachers need encouragement and help as well as everyone else. Priscilla and Aquila were a couple whom God used to guide the eloquent Apollos. Although able to teach the Scriptures powerfully, he had not grasped the full truth as Paul taught it. It was the gift that Priscilla and Aquila were given to invite people, like Apollos, into their home, give them hospitality, and then chat over the great truths which could then be taught with all the skill of a great preacher, which Apollos was.

Priscilla, Aquila and Apollos

Paul stayed in Corinth for a considerable time. Then he said farewell to the brothers and sisters there and sailed for Syria, accompanied by Priscilla and Aquila. At Cenchrea, he cut his hair for had made a vow. They arrived at Ephesus, and there he left the others while he went into the synagogue and talked with the Jews. When they asked him to stay longer with them, he would not do so but, as he left, he said, "I will come back if it is God's will." Then he set sail from Ephesus. When he landed at Caesarea, he went up and greeted the church [at Jerusalem] and then went to Antioch. After spending some time in Antioch, Paul set out from there and went from place to place throughout the region of Galatia and Phrygia, strengthening the disciples.

Meanwhile, a Jew named Apollos, a native of Alexandria, came to Ephesus. He was an eloquent man, well versed in the Scriptures. He had been instructed in the way of the Lord, and he spoke with great zeal and taught accurately that which concerned Jesus, though he knew only the baptism of John. He began to speak boldly in the synagogue. When Priscilla and Aquila heard him, they invited him to their home and explained to him the way of God more accurately. When Apollos wanted to cross over to Achaia, the brothers and sisters encouraged him and wrote to the disciples there to welcome him. On arriving, he was a great help to those who through grace had believed, for he vigorously refuted the Jews in public, showing from the Scriptures that Jesus was the Christ. [1]

[Paul to Timothy:] Study and do your best to present yourself to God as one who is approved by Him, a worker who has no cause to feel ashamed and who rightly explains the word of truth. [2] In the presence of God and of Christ Jesus, I charge you to preach the word, be prepared, in season and out of season, to correct, rebuke and encourage with utmost patience and careful instruction. [3]

[Paul:] Let us hold fast to the hope we profess, for He who has promised is faithful. Let us consider how we may encourage one another to love and good deeds, not neglecting to meet together, as some are in the habit of doing, but encouraging one another, and all the more as you the Day approaching. [4]

[1] Acts 18:18-28 [2] 2 Timothy 2:15 [3] 2 Timothy 4:2 [4] Hebrews 10:23-24

Day 353

John the Baptist taught that people should repent of their sins and be baptised as a sign of their repentance. He did not know then that Jesus was going to teach the further important truth that, when God the Father forgives sin, God the Holy Spirit enters the forgiven sinner and lives His life in him or her. That is the great truth that some followers of Jesus learned at Ephesus. Some began to twist that truth and acted as if they could use God the Holy Spirit for their own ends. They learned a bitter lesson.

Paul in Ephesus

While Apollos was at Corinth, Paul took the road through the inland regions and arrived at Ephesus where he found some disciples. He asked them, "Did you receive the Holy Spirit when you believed?" They answered, "No, we have not even heard that there is a Holy Spirit." Then he said, "Into what were you baptised?" They said, "Into John's baptism." Paul said, "John baptised with the baptism of repentance and told the people that they should believe in the One coming after him, that is, in Jesus." On hearing this, they were baptised into the name of the Lord Jesus. As Paul laid his hands on them, [God] the Holy Spirit came on them, and they spoke in other languages and prophesied. There were about twelve of them.

Paul went into the synagogue and spoke boldly there for three months and argued persuasively about the kingdom of God. When some of them stubbornly refused to believe and publicly spoke evil of the Way, Paul left them and, taking the disciples with him, went on holding discussions daily in the lecture hall of Tyrannus. ...

God did extraordinary miracles through Paul so that when handkerchiefs or aprons which had touched him were brought to the sick, they were healed and evil spirits came out of them. Some Jews, who were travelling exorcists, tried to use the name of the Lord Jesus over those who had evil spirits, saying, "In the name of Jesus, whom Paul preaches, I command you to come out." Seven sons of Sceva, a Jewish chief priest, were doing this and one evil spirit answered them, "Jesus I know, and Paul I know, but who are you?" Then the man with the evil spirit jumped on them and overpowered them all. He treated them so violently that they ran out of the house naked and bleeding. This became known to the Jews and Greeks living in Ephesus. They were all seized with fear, and the name of the Lord Jesus was highly praised. [1]

[Paul:] The coming of the lawless one will be through the activity of Satan and will be displayed in all kinds of counterfeit miracles, signs and lying wonders, and in every kind of wicked deception for those who are perishing, because they refused to love the truth and so be saved. [2]

[1] Acts 19:1-9,11-17 [2] 2 Thessalonians 2:9-10

Day 354

Paul was nearing the end of his life and he knew it. When he said good bye to the elders at Ephesus, he expressed the most important concerns of his life—a clear conscience. He had lived as God would have him live, and he had preached the truth God had revealed to him faithfully everywhere he went. His final advice was how to face error and enemies in the church. It was a parting marked by deep sadness and also deep joy.

Paul's farewell to elders at Ephesus

From Miletus, he [Paul] sent to Ephesus to summon the elders of the church. When they arrived, he said to them: "You yourselves know how I lived among you all the time I was with you. I served the Lord with humility and with tears although I suffered severely from the plots of the Jews. You know that I did not shrink from telling you anything that was for your benefit, teaching you both publicly and from house to house. I have testified to both Jews and Greeks urging them to turn to God in repentance and to have faith in our Lord Jesus.

"And now, compelled by the [Holy] Spirit, I am going to Jerusalem, not knowing what will happen to me there, except that, in every city, the Holy Spirit testifies to me that prison and suffering await me. But I do not consider my life as dear to me, if only I may finish the course and complete the ministry the Lord Jesus has given me, that of testifying to the gospel of God's grace.

"Now I know that none of you among whom I have gone about preaching the kingdom will ever see my face again. Therefore, I declare to you this day that I am innocent of the blood of any of you. For I have never shrunk from proclaiming to you the whole purpose of God. Keep watch over yourselves and over all the flock of which the Holy Spirit has made you guardians, to be shepherds of the church of God, which He bought with His own blood. I know that after I have gone, savage wolves will come in among you and will not spare the flock. Even from your own number some will arise and distort the truth in order to draw away disciples after them. Therefore, always be alert! And now I commit you to God and to the word of His grace, which is able to build you up and give you an inheritance among all those who are sanctified." ... When he had said this, he knelt down with them all and prayed. They all wept as they threw their arms round his neck and kissed him. [1]

[Jude] Now to Him who is able to keep you from falling and to present you in the presence of His glory without fault and with great joy, to the only God, our Saviour, be glory, majesty, power and authority, through Jesus Christ our Lord, before all time, now and for ever. Amen. [2]

[1] Acts 20:17-32, 38   [2] Jude 24-25

Day 355

Paul knew that his preaching would bring opposition. He had been brought before the governing authorities many times. However, he kept within the law, even if that was not properly enforced. His arrest, like that of Jesus Christ, His Master, was unlawful, but that did not prevent God working out His purposes through those who arrested Him. This was the first step on the road that God had planned for Paul to take the Gospel to Rome, the capital and commercial centre of the Roman empire.

Paul is arrested in Jerusalem

When we [Paul, Luke and companions] arrived at Jerusalem, the brothers and sisters received us warmly. The next day Paul went with us to see James. All the elders of the church were present. Paul greeted them and gave them a detailed account of what God had done among the Gentiles through his ministry. When they heard this, they praised God. Then they said to Paul: "You see, brother, how many thousands of Jews are believers, and all of them are zealous for the law [of Moses]. They have been informed that you teach all the Jews who live among the Gentiles to forsake Moses and not to circumcise their children or live according to our customs. What then is to be done? They will certainly hear that you have come, so do what we tell you. There are four men with us here who have made a vow. Join these men in their purification rites and pay their expenses, so that they may have their heads shaved. Then everybody will know there is no truth in what they have been told about you, but that you yourself live in obedience to the law. ...

When the seven days [of purification] were nearly completed, some Jews from the province of Asia saw Paul in the temple. They stirred up the crowd and seized him, shouting, "Men of Israel, help us! This is the man who teaches all men everywhere against our people, our law and this place. He has even brought Greeks into the temple and defiled this holy place." They had previously seen Trophimus, the Ephesian, in the city with Paul and supposed that he had brought him into the temple. The whole city was aroused, and people came running from all directions. They seized Paul and dragged him from the temple, and immediately the gates were closed. While they were trying to kill him, word reached the Tribune of the Roman garrison that the whole city of Jerusalem was in an uproar. So he took soldiers and centurions and ... he approached and arrested Paul and ordered that he be bound with two chains.[1]

Then Joseph said to his brothers, "Come near to me. ... I am Joseph, your brother, whom you sold into Egypt! And now, do not be distressed and do not be angry with yourselves for selling me here, because it was God who sent me ahead of you to save lives. ... So then, it was not you who sent me here, but God." [2]

[1] Acts 21:17-24, 27-40   [2] Genesis 45:4-8

Day 356

Paul had stood before the civil authorities in different countries many times. This time it was in his own country and before his fellow Jews, the Pharisees and the Sadducees who formed the Sanhedrin. That made it more difficult and more dangerous for him.

Paul before the Sanhedrin

The next day, he [the Roman Tribune] released him [Paul] and ordered the chief priests and all the Sanhedrin to assemble because he wanted to find out why Paul was being accused by the Jews. He brought Paul and made him stand before them. [1]

Paul looked straight at the Sanhedrin and said, "My brothers, I have lived with a clear conscience before God and doing my duty to this day." At this the high priest Ananias ordered those who were standing near Paul to strike him on the mouth. Paul said to him, "God will strike you, you whitewashed wall! Do you sit there to judge me according to the law, yet you yourself violate the law by ordering that I be struck!" Those who were standing near said, "Do you dare to insult the high priest of God?" Paul said, "Brothers, I did not realise that he was the high priest; for it is written: 'Do not speak evil of the ruler of your people.'"

Paul, seeing that some of them were Sadducees and the others Pharisees, cried out in the Sanhedrin, "My brothers, I am a Pharisee, the son of Pharisees. I am on trial because of the hope in the resurrection of the dead." When he had said this, a dispute arose between the Pharisees and the Sadducees, and the assembly was divided. ... There was a great uproar, and some of the scribes who were Pharisees stood up and argued strongly, saying, "We find nothing wrong with this man. What if a spirit or an angel has spoken to him?"

The dispute became so violent that the Tribune was afraid that Paul would be torn to pieces by them and he ordered the troops to go down and take him away from them by force and bring him into the barracks. The following night the Lord stood near Paul and said, "Take courage! As you have borne witness to me in Jerusalem, so you must also bear witness to me in Rome." [2]

(Jesus said:) They will lay hands on you and persecute you. They will hand you over to synagogues and prisons, and you will be brought before kings and governors for the sake of my name. This will be your time to bear witnesses to them. So make up you mind not to work out beforehand how you will defend yourselves, for I will give you words and wisdom that none of your adversaries will be able to resist or contradict. You will be betrayed even by parents, brothers, relatives and friends, and they will put some of you to death. You will be hated by everyone because of my name, but not a hair of your head will perish. Stand firm and you will gain life. [3]

[1] Acts 22:30   [2] Acts 23:1-11   [3] Luke 21:12-15

Day 357

As in the trial of Jesus, there was a difference of opinion between the Jewish religious leaders and the Roman authorities. Paul was caught between the two. As with Jesus, it was the Jewish leaders who hated him and wanted to put him to death, but they did not have the legal power to do so. Their scheming took Paul a stage nearer Rome.

The plot to kill Paul

The next morning, the Jews formed a conspiracy and bound themselves with an oath not to eat or drink until they had killed Paul. More than forty men joined in this conspiracy. They went to the chief priests and elders and said, "We have bound ourselves by a solemn oath not to eat anything until we have killed Paul. Now, you and the Sanhedrin request the commander to bring him before you on the pretext that you want more accurate information about his case. We are ready to kill him before he arrives." The son of Paul's sister heard of this plot and he went into the barracks and told Paul. Then Paul called one of the centurions and said, "Take this young man to the commander, for he has something to tell him." So he took him to the commander. ... The commander took the young man by the hand, drew him aside and asked him privately, "What is it that you have to tell me?" He replied, "The Jews have agreed to ask you to bring Paul to the council tomorrow as if they wanted to examine him more carefully. Do not be persuaded by them, for more than forty men are lying in ambush for him." The commander dismissed the young man, saying, "Do not tell anyone that you have said this to me."

Then he summoned two of his centurions and ordered them, "Get ready two hundred soldiers, seventy horsemen and two hundred spearmen to go to Caesarea by the third hour tonight [9 pm]. Provide mounts for Paul to ride and take him safely to Felix, the governor." ... The soldiers carried out their orders and took Paul with them during the night and brought him to Antipatris. The next day they let the cavalry go on with him, while they returned to the barracks. When they arrived in Caesarea, they delivered the letter to the governor and handed Paul over to him. The governor read the letter and asked to what province he belonged. When he learned that he was from Cilicia, he said, "I will hear your case when your accusers are here. Then he ordered that Paul be kept under guard in Herod's palace. [1]

What, then, shall we say to this? If God is for us, who can be against us? ... Who shall ever separate us from the love of Christ? Shall suffering or hardship or persecution or famine or nakedness or peril or sword? ... As it is written: "For your sake we are put to death all day long; we are considered as sheep for the slaughter." In all these things we are more than conquerors through Him who loved us. [2]

[1] Acts 23:12-24,31-35   [2] Romans 8:31,35,37

Day 358

Paul was forced to face false charges before three governors. On each occasion he not only protested his innocence, but he testified to the truth of the Gospel and to the reality of Jesus, His Master. He always defended himself with a graciousness which was unlike the Saul he was before his conversion. God spoke to Paul's accusers not only through the truth of what he said, but through the way he said and did things. The governors were very deeply disturbed by the power of Paul's defence. Throughout all this, Paul remained calm in the confidence that God was with him.

Paul before Felix and Festus

Five days later the high priest Ananias went down to Caesarea with some of the elders and a lawyer named Tertullus. ... When Paul was called in, Tertullus presented his case before Felix: ... "We have found this man to be a troublemaker, an agitator causing riots among the Jews all over the world. He is a ringleader of the sect of the Nazarenes. He even tried to desecrate the temple, so we seized him. ..."

Paul replied: "After several years, I came to Jerusalem to bring alms for my people and to make offerings. I was doing this and following the rites of purification when they found me in the temple. There was no crowd with me, nor was there any disturbance ... " Then Felix ... adjourned the proceedings. ... He ordered the centurion to keep Paul under guard, allow him some liberty and not to prevent his friends from taking care of his needs.

Several days later Felix came with his wife Drusilla, who was a Jewess. He sent for Paul and listened to him speaking about faith in Christ Jesus. As Paul continued to argue about righteousness, self-control and the judgment to come, Felix was alarmed and said, "Go away for now! You may leave. When I have a convenient opportunity I will send for you."

After two years had passed, Felix was succeeded by Porcius Festus, and wanting to gain favour with the Jews, Felix left Paul in prison. [1]

Three days after arriving in the province, Festus went up from Caesarea to Jerusalem, where the chief priests and Jewish leaders laid charges against Paul. ... Then Paul said in his defence: "I have not offended against the law of the Jews or against the temple or against Caesar. ... But if there are no grounds for their charges against me, no one can hand me over to them. I appeal to Caesar!" After Festus had conferred with his council, he said: "You have appealed to Caesar; to Caesar you will go!" [2]

[Isaiah:] This is what the Sovereign Lord, the Holy One of Israel, says: "In returning to me and in rest is your salvation, in quietness and trust is your strength." [3]

---

[1] Acts 24:1-6,17-18,22-25 [2] Acts 25:1-2,8-12 [3] Isaiah 30:15

Day 359

Paul was a prisoner before King Agrippa. In reality, it was Paul who was free. The King was facing a man in whom God lived and who knew freedom in his spirit. The King had to face himself and how he stood before God. He had either to accept or reject the truth, not only Paul's evidence about himself, but also God's truth for him. As with Pilate when faced with Jesus, King Agrippa acted knowing the truth but unwilling to accept it.

Paul before King Agrippa

The next day, [King] Agrippa and [Queen] Bernice came with great pomp and went into the audience hall accompanied by the commander and prominent citizens of the city. Festus gave the order and Paul was brought in. [1] ... Then Agrippa said to Paul, "You have permission to speak for yourself." Paul motioned with his hand and began his defence: "I consider myself fortunate, King Agrippa, to stand before you today. ... All the Jews know the way I have lived since I was a child in my own country, and also in Jerusalem. ... I was myself convinced that I ought to do many things against the name of Jesus of Nazareth. And that is just what I did in Jerusalem. With the authority of the chief priests I put many of the saints in prison, and when they were condemned to death, I cast my vote against them. I punished them in all the synagogues, and I tried to force them to blaspheme. In my fury against them, I pursued them even to foreign lands.

"On one such journey, I was travelling to Damascus with the authority and orders of the chief priests. About noon, O King, as I was on the road, I saw a light from heaven, brighter than the sun, shining around me and those who were with me. We all fell to the ground, and I heard a voice saying to me in Hebrew, 'Saul! Saul! Why are you persecuting me? It is hard for you to kick against the goads.' Then I said, 'Who are you, Lord?' The Lord replied, 'I am Jesus, whom you are persecuting. Now get up and stand on your feet. I have appeared to you for this purpose, to appoint you as a servant and as a witness to what you have seen of me and to what I will show you. I will rescue you from your own people and from the Gentiles to whom I am sending you to open their eyes, so that they turn from darkness to light, and from the power of Satan to God, and receive forgiveness of sins and a place among those who are sanctified by faith in me.' After that, O King Agrippa, I was not disobedient to the heavenly vision."

Agrippa said to Paul, "Do you think that you can so quickly persuade me to be a Christian?" Paul replied, "Quickly or not, I pray God that not only you but all who are listening to me today may become what I am, except for these chains." [2]

[1] Acts 25:23   [2] Acts 26:1-4,9-19,28-29

Day 360

God had told Paul that he must appear before Caesar, the Emperor of Rome. He was not, therefore, going to be drowned at sea. His Master was Jesus, and Jesus had proved that He was master of the wind and waves on the sea of Galilee. His concern in this shipwreck was not for himself, but for the crew and passengers. If they obeyed God's orders, they too would be safe, as he knew he was going to be. Paul was the only person who could be calm in that storm-tossed boat.

Paul's ship is shipwrecked on the way to Rome

When it was decided that we [Paul, Luke and companions] would sail for Italy, Paul and some other prisoners were handed over to a centurion of the Imperial Regiment, named Julius. We boarded a ship from Adramyttium. ... The following day we landed at Sidon. ... From there we put out to sea and passed to the lee of Cyprus because the winds were against us. ... Much time had been lost, and sailing had become dangerous because by now it was after the Fast [the Day of Atonement, about the middle of September]. So Paul warned them, saying, "Men, I can see that our voyage is going to bring disaster and great loss to ship and cargo, and also to our own lives." But the centurion followed the advice of the pilot and of the owner of the ship rather than pay attention to Paul. The harbour was unsuitable to pass the winter in, so the majority decided that we should sail on, hoping to reach Phoenix and winter there. ...

When a gentle south wind blew, they thought that they had what they were looking for, so they weighed anchor and sailed along the coast of Crete. Before long, a violent wind, called the "north-easter", blew down from the island. The ship was caught by the storm and was unable to head into the wind. So we gave way to it and were driven along. ...

After the men had eaten nothing for a long time, Paul stood up among them and said: "Men, you should have listened to me and not sailed from Crete and you would have avoided this damage and loss. Now I urge you to keep up your courage, because there will be no loss of life, only the ship will be lost. Last night an angel of God, whose I am and whom I serve, stood by me and said, 'Do not be afraid, Paul. You must stand before Caesar, and God has given you the lives of all who sail with you.' So keep up your courage, men, for I have faith in God that it will happen just as I was told. Nevertheless, we will run aground on some island." ... So it was that everyone reached land in safety. [1]

Trust in the Lord with all your heart and do not rely on your understanding. In all your ways acknowledge Him, and He will make your paths straight. [2]

[1] Acts 27:1-4,9-15,21-44   [2] Proverbs 3:5-6

Day 361

In Rome, Paul had reached the last place of which we have any record, where God wanted him to preach the Gospel. While in chains he talked to those who came to see him and he wrote letters to Christians in places he had visited in the past. Paul faced death with great confidence, witnessing to His Master to the very end.

Paul arrives in Rome

After three months [in Malta] we put out to sea in a ship that had wintered in the island. ... We put in at Syracuse and stayed there three days. From there we followed the coast to Rhegium. One day later, a south wind sprang up, and the next day we reached Puteoli. There we found some brothers and sisters who invited us to stay with them for seven days. And so we came to Rome.

When we got to Rome, the centurion handed the prisoners over to the captain of the guard, and Paul was allowed to live by himself, with a soldier to guard him. Three days later he called together the local leaders of the Jews. When they had assembled, Paul said to them: "My brothers, although I have done nothing against our people or against the customs of our forefathers, I was arrested in Jerusalem and handed over to the Romans. After they had examined me, they wanted to release me, because I was not guilty of any crime deserving death, but the Jews objected and I was compelled to appeal to Caesar, though I had no charge to bring against my own people. For this reason I asked to see you and talk with you. It is because of the 'Hope of Israel' [the Messiah] that I am bound with this chain." They answered him, "We have not received any letters from Judea concerning you, and none of the brothers who have come from there has reported or said anything bad about you. But we want to hear what your views are, for people everywhere are denouncing this sect." ... From morning till evening he explained and testified to them about the kingdom of God and tried to convince them concerning Jesus from the Law of Moses and from the Prophets. Some were convinced by what he said, and believed, but others did not. ... For two whole years Paul stayed there at his own expense in his own rented house. He welcomed all who came to see him and preached the kingdom of God and taught about the Lord Jesus Christ boldly and without hindrance.[1]

[Paul:] As for me, I am already being poured out like a drink offering, and the time for my departure has come. I have fought the good fight, I have finished the race, I have kept the faith. Henceforth there is laid up for me the crown of righteousness, which the Lord, the righteous Judge, will award to me on that day, and not only to me, but also to all who have longed for His appearing. [2]

[1] Acts 28:11-14,16-24,30-31   [2] 2 Timothy 4:6-8

Day 362

The imprisonment of the Apostle John on the Island of Patmos is probably the last recorded historical event of the Bible. It was there that God revealed to John some of the events which were to happen in the future. John was not told when they would happen, but he was given very vivid pictures of the final stages of this age in which we live. We still do not know exactly how some of the prophecies will be fulfilled, but the message of hope and triumph they convey is unmistakeable.

The Apostle John on the island of Patmos

I, John, your brother and companion in the suffering, reign and patient endurance of Jesus, was on the island of Patmos because of the word of God and the testimony of Jesus. I was in the Spirit on the Lord's Day, and I heard behind me a loud voice like a trumpet, saying, "I am the Alpha and the Omega, the First and the Last. Write on a scroll what you see and send it to the seven churches in Asia: to Ephesus, to Smyrna, to Pergamum, to Thyatira, to Sardis, to Philadelphia and to Laodicea."

I turned to see the voice that was speaking to me and I saw seven golden lampstands, and in the midst of the lampstands was someone like a 'Son of Man'', dressed in a robe reaching down to His feet and with a golden sash across His chest. His head and hair were white like wool, as white as snow, and His eyes were like flames of fire. His feet were like fine brass glowing in a furnace, and His voice was like the sound of many waters. In His right hand He held seven stars, and out of His mouth came a sharp double-edged sword, and His face shone like the midday sun. When I saw Him, I fell at His feet as though dead. Then He laid His right hand on me and said: "Do not be afraid. I am the First and the Last. I am the Ever-living One. I was dead, but see, I am alive for ever and ever, and I hold the keys of death and Hades. Write, therefore, the things you see, what they are now and what will take place in the future." [1]

"He who has is able to hear, let him hear what [God] the [Holy] Spirit says to the churches. To him who overcomes, I will give the right to eat from the tree of life, which is in the paradise of God.[2] He who overcomes will not be harmed by the second death.[3] ... To him who overcomes, I will give to eat some of the hidden manna. I will also give him a white stone with a new name engraved on it, known only to him who receives it, [4] ...

To him who overcomes, I will grant him to sit with me on my throne, as I overcame and sat down with [God] my Father on His throne. He who has an ear, let Him hear what [God] the [Holy] Spirit says to the churches. [5]

[1] Revelation 1:9-19   [2] Revelation 2:7   [3] Revelation 2:11   [4] Revelation 2:17   [5] Revelation 3:21

Day 363

The throne of God is the seat of the highest authority of all authorities. God the Father sits there. It was from there that the world was created. It will be from there that God, in final triumph, will show His complete justice and mercy. The picture language of the rainbow, flashes of lightning, dazzling jewels and crystal glass give only a glimpse of the glory of that throne which everyone will see one day.

John is given a vision of the Throne of God

After this I looked, and there before me a door stood open in heaven. And the first voice which I had heard speaking to me like a trumpet, said, "Come up here, and I will show you what must take place in the future." Immediately I was in the Spirit, and there before me in heaven was a throne with One sitting on it. The One who sat there appeared like jasper and carnelian. Around the throne there was a halo that looked like an emerald. Surrounding the throne were twenty-four other thrones, and seated on them were twenty-four elders dressed in white and with crowns of gold on their heads. ... Also in front of the throne there was what looked like a transparent sea of glass, as if made of crystal. Around the throne, and on each side were four living creatures. ... Each of the four living creatures had six wings. ... Day and night they never stop saying: "Holy, holy, holy is the Lord God Almighty, who was, and who is, and who is to come." Whenever the living creatures give glory, honour and thanks to Him who sits on the throne and who lives for ever and ever, the twenty-four elders fall down before Him who sits on the throne, and worship Him who lives for ever and ever. They lay down their crowns before the throne and sing: "You are worthy, our Lord and God, to receive the glory and the honour and the dominion, for you created all things. It was by your will that they were created and are now." [1]

"Then I heard every creature in heaven and on earth and under the earth and on the sea, and all that is in them, singing: "To Him who sits on the throne and to the Lamb be praise and honour and glory and power, for ever and ever!" [2]

Then I saw a great white throne and the One who was seated on it. From His presence the earth and the heavens fled and no place was found for them. I saw the dead, great and small, standing before the throne. And books were opened. And another book was opened which is the 'book of life'. The dead were judged by what they had done as recorded in the books. The sea gave up the dead who were in it, and death and Hades [the place of the dead] gave up the dead who were in them, and each one was judged according to what he had done. Then death and Hades were thrown into the lake of fire, which is the second death. If anyone's name was not found written in the Book of Life, he was thrown into the lake of fire. [3]

[1] Revelation 4:1-11 [2] Revelation 5:13 [3] Revelation 20:11-15

Day 364

When John the Baptist first saw Jesus, he was the first person to say: "Look, the Lamb of God, who takes away the sin of the world." Now the Apostle John sees, in a vision, Jesus, 'God the Son', as the Lamb of God sitting with 'God the Father' on the great throne in heaven. Millions of people will praise God for the Lamb and for the Blood He shed to make them fit for His kingdom.

John is given a vision of the Lamb of God

[John:] Then I saw in the right hand of Him who sat on the throne a scroll written on both sides and sealed with seven seals. I saw a mighty angel proclaiming in a loud voice, "Who is worthy to open the scroll and break its seals?" There was no one in heaven, on earth or under the earth who was able open the scroll or look into it. I wept bitterly because no one was found who was worthy to open the scroll or look into it. Then one of the elders said to me, "Do not weep! See, the Lion of the tribe of Judah, the Root of David, has triumphed! He can open the scroll and its seven seals."

Then I saw in the midst of the throne, the four living creatures and the elders, a Lamb standing as if it had been slain. ... He came and took the scroll from the right hand of Him who sat on the throne. And when He had taken it, the four living creatures and the twenty-four elders fell down before the Lamb. ... And they sang a new song: "You are worthy to take the scroll and to open its seals, because you were slain, and with your blood you purchased men for God from every tribe and language and people and nation. You have made them a kingdom and priests to serve our God, and they will reign on the earth." Then I looked and I heard the voice of many angels, living creatures and the elders around the throne, numbering thousands upon thousands, and ten thousand times ten thousand. In a loud voice they sang: "Worthy is the Lamb, who was slain, to receive power and wealth and wisdom and might and honour and glory and blessing!" [1]

After this I looked and there before me was a great multitude which no one could count, from every nation, tribe, people and language, standing before the throne and before the Lamb, wearing white robes and holding palm branches in their hands and crying in a loud voice: "Salvation belongs to our God who sits on the throne, and to the Lamb." [2]

I saw no temple in the city, for the Lord God Almighty and the Lamb are its temple. The city had no need of sun or moon to shine on it, for the glory of God is its light. ... Its gates will never be closed by day and there will be no night there. ... But nothing unclean will enter it, nor anyone who does what is shameful, but only those whose names are written in the Lamb's 'book of life'. [3]

---

[1] Revelation 5:1-14　　[2] Revelation 7:9　　[3] Revelation 21:22

Day 365

As "in the beginning, God created the heavens and the earth," so it will be at the end of the present age, God will create 'the new heaven and the new earth'. Although sufficiently similar for the same names—heaven and earth—to be used of both, there will also be great differences. The new heavens and earth will be everlasting, there will be no pain or death there and nothing and no one in it who is not pure and holy.

John is given a vision of the new heaven and the new earth

Then I saw a new heaven and a new earth, for the first heaven and the first earth had passed away, and there was no longer any sea. I saw the Holy City, the new Jerusalem, coming down out of heaven from God, prepared as a bride beautifully adorned for her husband. And I heard a loud voice from the throne saying, "See, the dwelling of God is now with men, and He will live with them. They will be His people, and He Himself will be with them and be their God. He will wipe every tear from their eyes. There will be no more death, nor mourning, nor crying, nor pain, for the former order of things has passed away." He who was seated on the throne said, "See! I am making all things new!"

Then he said to me, "It is done! I am the Alpha and the Omega, the Beginning and the End. To the thirsty I will give water without price from the fountain of the water of life. Those who conquer will inherit these things and I will be God to them and they will be my children. [1]

Then the angel showed me the river of the water of life, as clear as crystal, flowing from the throne of God and of the Lamb, through the middle of the broad street of the city. On either side of the river, the 'tree of life' yielded fruit each month. The leaves of the tree were for the healing of the nations. No longer will there be anything there that is cursed, but the throne of God and of the Lamb will be in it. His servants will worship Him, they will see His face and His name will be in their foreheads. And there will be no more night. They will need no light from lamp or sun, for the Lord God will be their light and they will reign for ever and ever. He said to me, "These words are trustworthy and true, for the Lord, the God of the spirits of the prophets, has sent His angel to make known to His servants what must soon take place." [2]

"I [Jesus] am coming soon and my rewards will be with me to give to everyone according to what they have done. I am the Alpha and the Omega, the First and the last, the Beginning and the End. Blessed are those who wash their robes so that they have the right to the tree of life and may enter through the gates into the city. ... He who testifies to these things says: Yes! I am coming soon. Amen. Come, Lord Jesus. [3]

[1] Revelation 21:1-7   [2] Revelation 22:1-6   [3] Revelation 22:12-14,21

Special Occasions 1

On Christmas Day, God's people celebrate the birth of Jesus Christ as a human baby. As such He was wholly 'one of us'. He was also 'God the Son', the second member of the God-Family. His name 'Emmanuel', meaning 'God with us', indicates the great purpose of his coming among people. He shows us what all the God-Family—Father, Son and Holy Spirit—is like, and He came to suffer for the sins of all those who repent of their sin and trust in Him. He came to be, and is still for all who receive Him, the Saviour of the world.

Christmas Day

While they [Joseph and Mary] were there [in Bethlehem], the time came for the baby to be born, and she gave birth to a Son, her first-born. She wrapped Him in swaddling cloths and laid Him in a manger, because there was no room for them in the inn.

Nearby there were shepherds keeping watch over their flocks in the fields at night. An angel of the Lord appeared before them, and the glory of the Lord shone around them, and they were terrified. The angel said to them, "Do not be afraid. I am bringing you good news of great joy for all the people. Today, in the town of David, a Saviour has been born to you. He is Christ the Lord. And this will be a sign for you: You will find a baby wrapped in swaddling clothes and lying in a manger. Suddenly there appeared with the angel a great company of angels, praising God and saying, "Glory to God in the highest, and on earth peace to men and women of good will who please Him." When the angels had left them ... they set off in haste and found Mary and Joseph, and the baby who was laying in a manger. ... All who heard what the shepherds said were amazed, but Mary treasured up these things and pondered over them in her heart. The shepherds returned, glorifying and praising God for all the things they had heard and seen.[1]

All this took place to fulfil the word of the Eternal-God through the prophet [Isaiah]: "See! The virgin will conceive and give birth to a son, and they will call Him Emmanuel," which means "God with us." [2] For to us a Child is born, to us a Son is given, and the government will be on His shoulders, and His name will be Wonderful Counsellor, Mighty God, Everlasting Father, Prince of Peace. Of the increase of His authority and peace there will be no end. [3] "She [Mary] will bear a Son and you will call Him Jesus, for He will save His people from their sins." [4]

He [Jesus] came into the world, and though the world was made through Him, the world did not recognise Him. He came to His own, but His own did not receive Him. But to all who did receive Him, that is, to those who believed in His name, He gave the right to become children of God." [5]

[1] Luke 2:6-20 [2] Matthew 1:22-23 [3] Isaiah 9:6-7 [4] Matthew 1:22-23 [5] John 1:10-12

Special Occasions 2

The day on which Jesus Christ was put to death by crucifixion was the most important day in the whole of human history. What happened then affected the relationship of God with the evil world of Satan, over whom Jesus triumphed, and with every man and woman on earth. When Jesus died, physically and spiritually, He bore in Himself the terrible spiritual consequences of the sins of all those who repent of their sin and trust in Him. The pain He suffered in His spirit and in His body is beyond human understanding, as He, 'God the Son' took on Himself the sin of the world in His painful separation from 'God the Father'. He suffered in our place, so that we might be forgiven; so that we might be saved from the family of Satan and be 'born again' into His family, to be there for ever. On this day Jesus, the sinless One, died that we, sinful ones, might live.

Good Friday

They [the guards] brought Jesus into the judgment all. And it was early. [1]... Finally, Pilate handed Him over to them to be crucified. So the soldiers took Jesus and they led Him away carrying His own cross, to the place of the Skull [in Aramaic: Golgotha; in Greek: Calvary]. There they crucified Him, and with Him two others, one on each side of Him.[2] They offered Jesus wine mixed with gall to drink; but after tasting it, He refused to drink it. [3]

One of the criminals who were hanging there railed at Him: "Are you not the Christ, [the Messiah]? Save yourself and us!" But the other criminal rebuked him, saying, "Do you not fear God seeing that you are under the same sentence? We indeed suffer justly, for we are receiving what our deeds deserve, but this Man has done nothing wrong." [4] At the sixth hour [noon] there was darkness over the whole land until the ninth hour [3 pm]. And at the ninth hour Jesus cried out in a loud voice, "Eloi, Eloi, lama sabachthani?" which means: 'My God, my God, why have you forsaken me?' ... With a loud cry, Jesus breathed His last breath.[5]

Now He [Jesus] has appeared once for all at the end of the age to put away sin by the sacrifice of Himself. Just as it is appointed for men to die once, and after that to face judgment, so Christ was sacrificed once to take away the sins of many people. [6]

[Isaiah:] He has borne our infirmities and carried our sorrows, yet we considered Him stricken and afflicted by God. He was wounded for our transgressions, He was bruised for our iniquities; the punishment that brought us peace was upon Him, and by His stripes we are healed. All of us have gone astray like sheep, each of us has turned to His own way, and the Eternal-God has laid on Him the iniquity of us all. [7]

He [Jesus] Himself bore our sins in His body on the cross, so that we might die to sins and live for righteousness. By His wounds we have been healed. [8]

[1] John 18:28   [2] John 19:16-22   [3] Matthew 27:34   [4] Luke 23:39-41   [5] Mark 15:33-34,37
[6] Hebrews 9:26-28   [7] Isaiah 53:4-6   [8] 1 Peter 2:24

Special Occasions 3

This is a day of triumph, a reminder of the greatest victory the world has ever known, the triumph of Jesus Christ, 'God the Son', over the powers of sin and evil. Because of the sin of Adam and Eve, all their descendants, including us, are born into the family of Satan, and once we have sinned, there would be no hope of escape. But Jesus died to free repentant sinners from that slavery and to give them 'new birth' into the family of God. 'God the Holy Spirit' raised Jesus Christ, 'God the Son', from the death of spiritual separation from 'God the Father' in order to demonstrate that Jesus had finished what He came to do. He rose from the dead, triumphing over death, and is alive for evermore. We, who share in that risen life, rejoice that, in Him, we too have eternal life.

Easter Sunday

At dawn, on the first day of the week after the Sabbath, Mary Magdalene and the other Mary went to look at the tomb. There was a violent earthquake and an angel of God came down from heaven, went to the tomb, rolled back the stone and sat on it. His appearance was like lightning and his clothes were as white as snow. On seeing him, the guards were so frightened that they shook and became like dead men. The angel said to the women, "Do not be afraid, for I know that you are looking for Jesus who was crucified. He is not here. He has risen, as He said He would. Come, see the place where He lay, then go quickly and tell His disciples: 'He has risen from the dead and is going ahead of you into Galilee. There you will see Him, as I have told you." So the women left the tomb hurriedly, afraid yet filled with joy, and ran to tell His disciples. Suddenly Jesus met them and said, "Greetings!" They came to Him, clasped his feet and worshipped Him. Then Jesus said to them, "Do not be afraid. Go and tell my brothers and sisters to go to Galilee and there they will see me." [1]

Early on the first day of the week, while it was still dark, Mary Magdalene came to the tomb and saw that the stone had been moved from the entrance. She came running to Simon Peter and the other disciple, the one Jesus loved, and said, "They have taken away the Lord out of the tomb, and we do not know where they have put Him!" ... Then Simon Peter ... arrived and went into the tomb. He saw the linen cloths lying there and the burial cloth that had been around Jesus' head folded up by itself. ... Finally the other disciple, who had reached the tomb first, also went inside. He saw and believed. [2] God raised Him from the dead, setting Him free from the agony of death, because it was impossible for Him to be held in death's power. [3]

But Christ has indeed been raised form the dead, the firstfruits of those who have fallen asleep. For since death came through a man, the resurrection of the dead comes also though a Man. For, as in Adam all die, so in Christ all will be made alive.[4]

[1] Matthew 28:1-10   [2] John 20:1-9   [3] Acts 2:24   [4] 1 Corinthians 15:20-22, 53-55

Special Occasions 4

Jesus ascended into the clouds as His disciples watched. As Jesus Christ, God the Son, His work on earth was complete. He was going to continue His work in heaven, seated at the right hand of God the Father. His work on earth was to be continued by God the Holy Spirit until He comes again.

Ascension Day

After His suffering, He [Jesus] showed Himself to them [His disciples] with many convincing proofs that He was alive. He appeared to them over the course of forty days and spoke of the kingdom of God. While He was eating with them on one occasion, He said, "Do not leave Jerusalem, but wait for the gift which my Father promised and about which you have heard me speak. For John baptised with water, but in a few days you will be baptised with [God] the Holy Spirit."

So when they were assembled together they asked Him, "Lord, is this the time when you are going to restore the kingdom to Israel?" He said to them: "It is not for you to know the times or dates that [God] the Father has set by His own authority. But you will receive power when [God] the Holy Spirit has come upon you, and you will be my witnesses in Jerusalem, in all Judea, in Samaria, and to the ends of the earth." When He had said this, and as they were looking at Him, He was taken up and a cloud hid Him from their sight.

They were looking intently into the sky as He was going, when suddenly two men dressed in white robes stood beside them and said, "Men of Galilee, why do you stand here gazing into the sky? This same Jesus, who has been taken from you into heaven, will return in the same way that you have seen Him go into heaven." [1]

He [Jesus] lifted up His hands and blessed them. While He was blessing them, He left them and was taken up into heaven. Then they worshipped Him and returned to Jerusalem with great joy. [2] After the Lord Jesus had spoken to them, He was taken up into heaven and He sat down at the right hand of God. The disciples went out and preached everywhere. [3]

[Peter:] In the days of Noah, eight people were saved through water. This is a figure of baptism which saves you by the resurrection of Jesus Christ, who has gone into heaven and is at the right hand of [God] the Father, with angels, authorities and powers made subject to Him. [4]

[Paul:] To each one of us grace has been given according to the measure of Christ's gift. This is why it is written, "When He ascended on high, He led captivity captive ... He ascended high above all the heavens that He might fill all things." [5]

[1] Acts 1:3-11   [2] Luke 24:50-53   [3] Mark 16:19-20   [4] 1 Peter 3:21-22   [5] Ephesians 4:7-10

Special Occasions 5

On the Day of Pentecost, ten days after the ascension of Jesus into heaven, 'God the Holy Spirit' came into Jesus' disciples. The church of Jesus Christ was born. For the first time, 'God, the Holy Spirit' was fully revealed as the third member of the God-Family. As Jesus Christ, 'God the Son' was Emmanuel, *God with us*, so 'God the Holy Spirit', is the 'Paraclete', *God in us*, the 'one alongside us', our comforter, advocate, counsellor and enabler. The Holy Spirit is *in* everyone who is born into the Family of God.

The Day of Pentecost

When the day of Pentecost came, they [the disciples] were all together in one place. Suddenly there came from heaven a sound like the rush of a violent wind and it filled the whole house where they were sitting. Divided tongues of fire appeared and rested on each of them and they were all filled with [God] the Holy Spirit and began to speak in other languages as the Holy Spirit enabled them.

Now there were living in Jerusalem God-fearing Jews from every nation under heaven. When they heard this sound, a crowd gathered, bewildered because each one heard them [the disciples] speaking in his own language. They were beside themselves with amazement and said: "Are not all these who are speaking Galileans? Then how is it that we hear them, each one of us, in our own native language? ... we all hear them speaking in our own native languages the mighty deeds of God!" In their amazement and bewilderment they asked one another, "What does this mean?" Some, however, mocked and said, "They have been drinking too much new wine!"

Then Peter, standing with the Eleven, raised his voice and addressed them: "You Jews and all of you who live in Jerusalem, let this be known to you and listen closely to what I say. These men are not drunk, as you suppose, for it is only the third hour [9 am] of the day. No, this is what was spoken by the prophet Joel: "It will come to pass in the last days, God says, that I will pour out my Spirit on all people. Your sons and your daughters will prophecy. Your young men will see visions and your old men will dream dreams. On my servants, both men and women, I will pour out my Spirit in those days and they will prophecy. ... Therefore let all Israel know with certainty that God has made this Jesus, whom you crucified, both Lord and Christ." When the people heard this, they were cut to the heart and said to Peter and the other apostles, "Brothers, what shall we do?" [1] With great power the Apostles testified to the resurrection of Jesus Christ and great grace was upon them all. [2]

[Jesus:] I will ask [God] the Father and He will give you another Comforter to be with you for ever. ... You know Him because He lives with you and will be in you. [3]

[1] Acts 2:1-18, 36-40   [2] Acts 4:33   [3] John 14:16-17

Special Occasions 6

When God created the world, He set the seasons to give the sun, wind and rain needed to grow food. Each harvest is a sign of God fulfilling His covenant. The world can produce enough food for everyone's need, but not enough for everyone's greed. In thanking God for harvest we acknowledge His faithfulness to us and recognise our responsibility to use what He plentifully gives us. That includes providing for those who do not have enough food for whatever reason: poverty, drought, war or civil strife.

Harvest Thanksgiving

[Moses:] You shall celebrate the Feast of Harvest [Pentecost] with the firstfruits of your hard work. Celebrate the Feast of Ingathering [Booths or Tabernacles] at the end of the year, when you gather in your harvest from your fields. [1] When you reap the harvest of your land, do not reap to the very edges of your field, or gather the fallen ears of your harvest. ... Leave them for the poor and the stranger. I am the Eternal-God, your God. [2]

[After the Flood:] Noah built an altar to the Eternal-God, took some of all the clean animals and birds, and sacrificed them as burnt offerings on it. The Eternal-God smelled the pleasing aroma and said in His heart: "Never again will I curse the ground because of mankind, for every inclination and imagination of people's hearts is evil from childhood. And never again will I destroy every living creature, as I have done. As long as the earth endures, seed time and harvest, cold and heat, summer and winter, day and night will not cease." [3]

In the past, He [God] has allowed all nations go their own way. Nevertheless, He did not leave them without any witness to Himself. He has shown kindness to you by giving you rain from heaven and fruitful seasons, giving you plenty of food and filling your hearts with joy. [4]

Praise is due to you, O God, in Zion. ... You visit the earth and water it. You enrich it with abundance. The river of God is filled with water to provide the people with corn, for so you have ordered it. [5] He makes grass grow for the cattle, plants for man to use to bring forth food from the earth, wine that gladdens the heart of man, oil to make his face shine, and bread to sustain his heart. [6]

[Paul:] Whoever sows grudgingly will reap sparingly, and whoever sows generously will reap bountifully. ... Now He [God] who provides seed for the sower and bread for food, will also supply and increase your seed for sowing and will increase the harvest of your righteousness. You will be made rich in every way so that you can be generous, and that will bring thanksgiving to God. [7]

[1] Exodus 23:16   [2] Leviticus 19:9-10   [3] Genesis 8:20-22   [4] Acts 14:16-17   [5] Psalm 65:9
[6] Psalm 104:14-15   [7] 2 Corinthians 9:6,10-11

Special Occasions 7

Times of crisis, caused either by internal political problems or by relations with other countries, are occasions for Christians to look to God. Individuals can feel very weak on their own and unable to do anything to influence things. God has promised that, as He works through governments as well as through individuals, He can overrule in the affairs of governments to bring about His greater glory.

A time of national political crisis

Let everyone be subject to the governing authorities, for there is no authority except that which God permits, and those which exist are by His appointment.[1] Submit yourselves to every authority instituted among men for the sake of the Lord.[2] Where there is no vision, the people perish.[3] This is what the Sovereign Eternal-God, the Holy One of Israel, says: "In repentance and rest shall be your salvation, in quietness and trust shall be your strength."[4]

[Paul:] I urge, then, first of all, that requests, prayers, intercessions and thanksgiving be made for everyone, for kings and all who are in positions of authority. ... This is good and pleasing to God our Saviour, who desires all men to be saved and to come to a knowledge of the truth.[5]

[Solomon prayed to God:] "When your people Israel are defeated by an enemy because they have sinned against you and then they turn back and confess your name, praying and making supplication before you in this temple, then hear from heaven and forgive the sin of your people Israel, and bring them back to the land you gave to them and their forefathers."[6]

God is our refuge and strength, a very present help in time of trouble. Therefore we will not fear, though the earth should change and the mountains be shaken. ... He makes wars to cease to the ends of the earth. ... 'Be still and know that I am God.'[7]

He who dwells in the shelter of the Most High and rests in the shadow of the Almighty, will say of the Eternal-God, "He is my refuge and my fortress, my God in whom I trust. He will surely save you from the snare of the fowler and from the deadly pestilence. He will cover you with His feathers, and under His wings you will find refuge. His faithfulness will be your shield and buckler. You will not be afraid of the terror of the night nor of the arrow that flies by day, nor of the pestilence that stalks in the darkness, nor the destruction that lays waste at noonday. ... Because you have made the Eternal-God your refuge, and the Most High, your dwelling-place, no disaster will overtake you nor plague come near your tent, for He will command His angels concerning you, to guard you in all yours ways."[8]

[1] Romans 13:1,4   [2] 1 Peter 2:13   [3] Proverbs 29:18   [4] Isaiah 30:15   [5] 1 Timothy 2:1-4
[6] 2 Chronicles 6:24-25   [7] Psalm 46:1-2,10   [8] Psalm 91:1-11

Special Occasions 8

Natural disasters—earthquakes, droughts, floods, lightning strikes, hurricanes, storms at sea—are not normally caused by human activity, although this can sometimes bring about disasters. Natural disasters occur because this world has been spoilt by the entry of sin into the world in the rebellion against God as Creator by the first man and woman, Adam and Eve. However, God is still sovereign in His world and He is able to bring good even from the worst disaster, the greatest good being that people turn to Him in their hour of need, and let Him make right their relationship to Him.

A time of natural disaster

There was a man in the land of Uz, named Job, who was blameless, upright and feared God. ... A messenger came to Job and said, "The oxen were ploughing and the donkeys feeding near them when the Sabeans fell on them, carried them off and killed all the servants. ... Another messenger said, "Your sons and daughters were feasting and drinking wine in the house of the oldest brother, when suddenly a strong wind swept in from the desert and struck the four corners of the house. It fell on them and they are dead. ... " Job rose, tore his robe, shaved his head, and fell to the ground in worship, saying, "Naked I came from my mother's womb, and naked I shall depart. The Lord gave and the Lord has taken away. Blessed be the name of the Lord."[1]

Then he [Solomon] said: ... "When the heavens are shut up and there is no rain because your people have sinned against you, if they pray towards this place and confess your name and turn from their sin because you have afflicted them; ... When there is famine or plague, or blight or mildew, locusts or grasshoppers in the land or when an enemy besieges them in any of their cities, or whatever disaster or disease may come, if a prayer or plea is made by any of your people Israel; ... Then hear in heaven and forgive, and act, dealing with each man according to his ways, since you know his heart, for you alone know what is in the hearts of all men. [2]

There were some present at that time who told Jesus about the Galileans whose blood Pilate had mixed with their sacrifices. Jesus answered them, "Do you think that those Galileans were worse sinners than all the other Galileans because they suffered in this way? ... Or those eighteen who were killed when the tower in Siloam fell on them, do you think they were worse offenders than all the others who were living in Jerusalem? I tell you, no! But unless you repent, you too will perish." [3]

I lift my eyes to the hills, but from where does my help come? My help comes from the Eternal-God, who made heaven and earth. ... The Eternal-God will keep you from all evil. He will keep your life. He will keep watch over your going out and your coming in from now and for ever more. [4]

[1] Job 1:1,14,18-21 [2] 1 Kings 8:35-39 [3] Luke 13:1-5 [4] Psalm 121:1-4,7-8

Special Occasions 9

All Christians are called to serve God in the fellowship of the church and in the world. He has ordained that some forms of service should be confirmed by being recognised by the church fellowship, and those so called be commissioned for their task. This commissioning expresses an identification of the fellowship with the aims and activities of the service, a recognition of God's call in the workers, and a commitment to support them in prayer, encouragement and every other possible way.

The call and commissioning a worker

In the year that King Uzziah died, I saw the Eternal-God seated on a high and lofty throne. ... Above Him were the seraphim [angels]. ... They called to one another, saying, " Holy, holy, holy is the Eternal-God, the Almighty. The whole earth is full of His glory. The foundations of the doorposts shook at the sound of their voices. ... Then I cried, "Woe to me! I am ruined, for I am a man of unclean lips, and I live among a people of unclean lips, and my eyes have seen the King, the Eternal-God, the Almighty. Then one of the seraphim flew to me with a live coal in his hand which he had taken with tongs from the altar. With it he touched my mouth and said, "See, this has touched your lips, your guilt is taken away and your sin blotted out." Then I heard the voice of the Eternal-God saying, "Whom shall I send, and who will go for us?" I said, "Here am I, send me!" He said, "Go ..." [1]

The Lord appointed seventy others and sent them in pairs ahead of Him to every town and place where He was about to go. He said to them, "The harvest is plentiful, but the workers are few, therefore pray the Lord of the harvest to send out workers into His harvest. Go! I am sending you out like lambs among wolves." [2]

[Paul:] I said, "Who are you Lord?" The Lord said, "I am Jesus, whom you are persecuting. Now get up and stand on your feet, for I have appeared to you to appoint you to serve and to witness to what you have seen of me and to what I will show you. ... I am sending you to open their eyes so that they turn from darkness to light" [3]

In the church at Antioch there were prophets and teachers. ... While they were worshipping the Lord and fasting, [God] the Holy Spirit said, "Set apart for me Barnabas and Saul for the work to which I have called them" After they had fasted and prayed, they laid their hands on them and sent them off. [4]

[Jesus said:] "All authority in heaven and on earth has been given to me. Go, therefore, and make disciples of all nations. Baptize them in the name of [God] the Father, [God] the Son and [God] the Holy Spirit, and teach them to obey everything I have commanded, and I will be with you always, to the end of the age." [5]

[1] Isaiah 6:1-9   [2] Luke 10:1-3   [3] Acts 26:15-18   [4] Acts 13:1-3   [5] Matthew 28:18-20

Special Occasions 10

On the evening before Jesus was crucified, He shared with His disciples a traditional Passover meal which reminded Jews of their deliverance from the slavery of Egypt. Jesus made that meal special, by showing that it was no ordinary Passover supper. He, Jesus, the Messiah, was the deliverer from another slavery, that of sin. The 'bread' represented His 'sinless body' which was about to be broken by crucifixion. The 'wine' represented the 'blood He shed' in His dying, which was the Bible way of referring to the spiritual pain He was to suffer when He bore the spiritual consequences of the sin of every man and woman who would repent of their sin and trust in Him. Whenever God the Father looked at such a person, He would see, not the person's sin, but the 'blood of Christ' and He would 'pass over' him or her with nothing to condemn. Whenever the symbols were used in the future, He would be there in spirit to make their meanings real.

A service of Holy Communion

The Eternal-God said to Moses and Aaron in Egypt, "This month will be for you the first month ... each man is to take a lamb for his family. ... Take some of the blood and put it on the sideposts and the lintels of the door-frames of the houses where they eat. ... The blood will be a sign for you on the houses where you live, and when I see the blood, I will pass over you. No destructive plague will touch you when I strike the land of Egypt. ... In all your houses, you will not eat unleavened bread." [1]

Then came the day of Unleavened Bread on which the Passover lamb had to be sacrificed. ... When the hour came, Jesus and His disciples sat at the table. He said to them, "I have eagerly desired to eat this Passover with you before I suffer, for I tell you, I will not eat it again until it is fulfilled in the kingdom of God." [2]

[Paul:] The Lord Jesus, on the night He was betrayed, took bread, and when He had given thanks, He broke it and said, "This is my body, which is for you. Do this in remembrance of me." In the same way, after supper He took the cup, saying, "This cup is the new covenant in my blood. Do this, as often as you drink it, in remembrance of me." Whenever you eat this bread and drink this cup, you proclaim the Lord's death until He comes. Whoever eats the bread or drinks the cup of the Lord in a way that is unworthy, will be treating unworthily the body and blood of the Lord. Let every one examine himself before he eats of the bread and drinks of the cup. For anyone who eats and drinks without recognising that it represents Christ's body, eats and drink judgment on himself. [3]

The cup of blessing on which we ask God's blessing, is it not a sharing in the blood of Christ, and the bread that we break, is it not a sharing in the body of Christ, for as we eat of the one bread, we, who are many, are one body. [4]

[1] Exodus 12:1,2,7,13,20 [2] Luke 22:7,14-16 [3] 1 Corinthians 11:23-29 [4] 1 Corinthians 10:16-17

Special Occasions 11

'Prayer' is the name given to both listening to God and speaking to Him. It includes confession of sin—any sin that comes between those who are praying and God, accepting God's forgiveness, praise for who He is and what He has done, and requests for every kind of need to which the answer is 'according to His will'. Prayer is directed to 'God the Father', requests are made in the name of Jesus, 'God the Son', who pleads His sin-cleansing blood on behalf of repentant sinners. Prayer is in 'God the Holy Spirit' as He guides in what to pray for and how to pray, especially when it is difficult to put requests into words. Prayer is against Satan and all his devises to oppose the will of God.

A meeting for prayer

O you who hear prayer, to you all mankind will come.[1] [Jesus:] Wherever two or three come together in my name, there am I in the midst of them.[2] The Eternal-God says: "Before they call I will answer, and while they are still speaking I will hear." [3]

Elijah was a man like us. He prayed earnestly that it would not rain, and no rain fell on the earth for three and a half years. He prayed again, and the heavens gave rain, and the earth yielded its crops.[4]

Jesus was praying in a certain place, and when he finished, one of His disciples said to him, "Lord, teach us to pray, as John taught his disciples." He said to them, "When you pray, say, "'Father, may your name be hallowed. Your kingdom come. Give us each day our daily bread. Forgive us our sins, for we also forgive everyone who sins against us. And lead us not into temptation.'" [5] "So I say to you, ask and it will be given to you, seek and you will find, knock and the door will be opened to you. For every one who asks receives, he who seeks finds, and to him who knocks, the door will be opened." [6]

For the present you are sorrowful, but I will see you again and you will rejoice, and no one will take your joy from you. When that time comes, you will not need to ask me for anything. I tell you the truth, [God] my Father will give you whatever you ask in my name. Until now you have not asked for anything in my name. Ask and you will receive so that your joy will be complete. [7]

[God] the [Holy] Spirit helps us in our weakness, for we do not know what we should pray for, but the [Holy] Spirit Himself intercedes for us with yearnings that words cannot express. And He who searches the hearts of people knows the mind of the Spirit, because the Spirit intercedes for the saints according to the will of God. [8]

Jesus said, "If you live in me and my words live in you, ask whatever you will, and it will be done for you." [9]

---

[1] Psalm 65:2   [2] Matthew 18:20   [3] Isaiah 65:13,24   [4] James 5:17-18   [5] Luke 11:1-4   [6] Luke 11:9-10
[7] John 16:22-24   [8] Romans 8:26-27   [9] John 15:7

Special Occasions 12

Giving of what one has to God is a way of giving oneself. Dedicating offerings to God is (a) a thanksgiving for what one has received, (b) a dedication to Him of those who give, (c) a request that God will use the gifts for His purposes, and (d) a pledge to support, especially in prayer, the objects of the giving - those in need, God's work and workers.

Dedication of offerings

The Eternal-God said to Moses, "Say to the Israelites that they may make an offering to me, and you are to receive the offering to me from everyone whose heart prompts them to give. [1] Three times a year all your males are to appear before the Eternal-God. ... They shall not appear before Him empty-handed. Every one shall give as he is able and according to the way the Eternal-God, your God, has blessed him. [2]

The people rejoiced because their leaders had given willingly, for they had given freely and wholeheartedly to the Eternal-God. ... David praised the Eternal-God in the presence of the whole assembly, saying, "Praise be to you, O Eternal-God, the God of Israel, our forefather. Yours, O Eternal-God, is the greatness, the power, the glory, the victory and the majesty, for all that is in the heavens and on earth is yours. ... All things comes from you and of your own have we given you." [3]

Honour the Lord with all that you have and with the firstfruits of all your harvest; then your barns will be filled, and your vats will overflow with new wine.[4]

[Paul:] I am not looking for a gift, but I am looking for fruit to be credited to your account. ... I have enough and more, now that I have received from Epaphroditus the gifts you sent. They are a fragrant offering, a sacrifice which is pleasing to God. My God will meet your every need according to His riches in glory in Christ Jesus.[5]

Through Jesus Christ, let us continually offer to God a sacrifice of praise which is the fruit of lips that confess His name. Do not neglect to do good and to share what you have with others, for such sacrifices please God. [6]

[Paul:] Entirely on their own, they [the Macedonian churches] pleaded with us for the privilege of sharing in the ministry to the saints. ... They gave themselves first to the Lord and then to us. ... If the willingness to give is there, the gift is acceptable according to what a person has, not according to what he does not have. [7]

Whoever sows grudgingly will reap sparingly, and whoever sows generously will reap bountifully. Let each one give as he has decided in his heart to give, not reluctantly or under compulsion, for God loves a cheerful giver. And God is able to make all grace yours abundantly, so that, in all things, at all times, and having all that you need, you will be able to contribute bountifully to every good work. [8]

---

[1] Exodus 25:1-2   [2] Deuteronomy 16:16-17   [3] 1 Chronicles 29:9-11,14   [4] Proverbs 3:9-10
[5] Philippians 4:17-19   [6] Hebrews 13:15   [7] 2 Corinthians 8:4-5,12   [8] 2 Corinthians 9:6-8

Becoming a Christian is a change that God works in a person who responds to Him in repentance and faith. Repentance means a 'change of mind' from the way a person thinks naturally to the way God thinks about things—acknowledgement of Him as God and Creator, accepting that sin, such as lying, deceiving, thieving, hating, is sin against Him, as well as against others. Faith is trusting that Jesus Christ suffered in Himself the consequences of all sin confessed to Him, and accepting God's forgiveness.

Becoming a Christian

Jesus came into Galilee preaching the good news of God and saying, "The time has now come, and the kingdom of God is near. Repent and believe the good news." [1]

He [Nicodemus] came to Jesus by night. ... Jesus said to him, "I tell you the truth, unless a person is born again, he cannot enter the kingdom of God." Nicodemus said to Him, "How can anyone be born when he is old? Can he again enter his mother's womb and be born?" Jesus answered him, "I assure you this is the truth: unless a person is born of water and of the Spirit, he cannot enter the kingdom of God. What is born of the flesh is flesh and what is born of [God] the [Holy] Spirit is spirit. [2]

If we say that we have no sin, we deceive ourselves and the truth is not in us. If we confess our sins, He [God] is faithful and just and will forgive our sins and cleanse us from all unrighteousness. [3]

When the people heard this [the words of Peter on the Day of Pentecost], they were cut to the heart and said to Peter and the other apostles, "Brothers, what are we to do?" Peter answered them, "Repent and be baptised, every one of you, in the name of Jesus Christ for the forgiveness of your sins, and you will receive the gift of [God] the Holy Spirit. The promise is for you and your children, for all who are far away, for all whom the Lord our God calls to himself." [4]

[Jesus said:] "See! Here I am standing at the door and knocking. If anyone hears my voice and opens the door, I will come in and eat with him, and he with me." [5]

The jailor ... fell trembling before Paul and Silas. He brought them out and said, "Sirs, what must I do to be saved?" They replied, "Believe on the Lord Jesus, and you will be saved, you and your household." [6]

The word [of God] is near you, on your lips and in your heart, that is the word of faith which we proclaim: If you confess with your lips that Jesus is Lord, and believe in your heart that God raised Him from the dead, you will be saved. For it is with your heart that you believe and are made righteous, and it is with your mouth that you confess and your salvation is confirmed." [7]

[1] Mark 1:15 [2] John 3:2-6 [3] 1 John 1:8-9 [4] Acts 2:37-39 [5] Revelation 3:20
[6] Acts 16:29-31 [7] Romans 10:8-10

The outward physical ceremony of baptism is a picture of an inner spiritual experience. Those who are baptised by being immersed in, or sprinkled with water, in the presence of other people, testify to the world by an outward ceremony, that they have been spiritually 'buried with Christ' to sin, and have risen from 'spiritual death' to 'spiritual life' in Christ Jesus. They are now spiritually 'buried with Christ', as far as their old lives in the family of Satan are concerned, and they have now 'risen with Christ' into new life in the family of God. Baptism is a public declaration that the baptised person is a Christian who is dead to life in the family of Satan, and alive in the family of God.

Baptism

Jesus came to them [His disciples] and said, "All authority in heaven and on earth has been given to me. Go, therefore, and make disciples of all nations. Baptize them in the name of [God] the Father, [God] the Son and [God] the Holy Spirit, and teach them to obey everything I have commanded you, and I will be with you always, to the end of the age." [1] "Go into all the world and preach the Good News to all creation. Whoever believes and is baptised will be saved, but whoever does not believe will be condemned." [2] [Peter:] "Repent and be baptised every one of you in the name of Jesus Christ for the forgiveness of your sins. [3]

[Paul:] Do you not know that all of us who have been baptised into Christ Jesus were baptised into His death? We were, therefore, buried with Him by baptism into death in order that, as Christ was raised from the dead through the glory of the Father, so we too may live in newness of life. [4] You are all sons of God through faith in Christ Jesus, for those of you who were baptised into [the death of] Christ have put on [the life of] Christ. There is now neither Jew nor Greek, slave nor free, male nor female, for you are all one in [the life of] Christ Jesus. [5]

[Peter:] The ark, in which a few people, eight in number, were saved through water, is a picture of the baptism which saves you, not by the removal of dirt from the body by water, but by giving a guilt-free conscience towards God, through the resurrection of Jesus Christ, who has entered into heaven and is at the right hand of God. [6]

[Paul:] There is one body and one [God the Holy] Spirit, as there is also one hope to the calling you have received, one Lord [Jesus Christ], one faith, one baptism, and one God the Father of us all, who is over all, through all and in all. [7]

In Christ, all the fullness of God lives bodily. ... You have been buried with Him in baptism and raised with Him through faith in the power of God, who raised Him from the dead. When you were dead in your sins and in your slavery to your sinful nature, God made you alive with Christ. [8]

[1] Matthew 28:18-20 [2] Mark 16:15-16 [3] Acts 2:38 [4] Romans 6:3-4 [5] Galatians 3:26-28
[6] 1 Peter 3:20-22 [7] Ephesians 4:4-6 [8] Colossians 2:9,12-13

A wedding represents the fulfilment of one of God's purposes in creation: that people should increase in numbers and live in families. God created the first man and woman to live in a faithful, loving marriage relationship while they were both alive. He saw what He had created and was very pleased with it. Jesus Himself blessed marriage by confirming its original purposes and by accepting an invitation to a wedding Himself.

A Wedding

God said, "Let us make man in our image, to be like us. ... So God created man in His own image, in the image of God He created him: male and female He created them. God blessed them and said to them, "Be fruitful and increase in numbers. Fill the earth and subdue it." [1]

Jesus said, "Have you not read that He [God] who made them [husband and wife] at the beginning made them male and female, and said, 'for this reason a man will leave his father and mother and be joined to his wife and the two will become one flesh'? So they are not longer two, but one. Therefore what God has joined together, let no one separate. [2]

On the third day there was a wedding at Cana in Galilee and the mother of Jesus was there. Jesus and His disciples had also been invited to the wedding. [3]

[Paul:] Submit to one another out of reverence for Christ. Wives submit to your husbands as you do to the Lord. For the husband is the head of the wife as Christ is the head of the church, His body, of which He is the Saviour. ... Husbands, love your wives as Christ loved the church and gave Himself up for her in order to make her holy. ... No one ever hates his own body, but he nourishes and cares for it, as Christ does the church. ... For this reason a man will leave his father and mother and be joined to his wife and the two will become one flesh. [4]

[Peter:] Husbands, be considerate to your wives as you live together. Treat them with respect as the [physically] weaker partner and as joint heirs with you of the gracious gift of life, so that nothing hinders your prayers. [5]

[Paul:] I bow my knees before [God] the Father, from whose Fatherhood every family in heaven and on earth derives its name. [6]

Love is patient; love is kind; love never envies or boasts; love is not proud or rude or insists on its rights; love is not irritable or resentful; love does not take pleasure in wrong-doing but rejoices when truth prevails; love endures all things, believes all things and hopes all things; love never fails. [7]

[1] Genesis 1:26-28   [2] Matthew 19:4-6   [3] John 2:1-2   [4] Ephesians 5:21-26,29-31   [5] 1 Peter 3:7
[6] Ephesians 3:14-17   [7] 1 Corinthians 13:4-8

Special Occasions 16

God created men and women, not only that they would be able to bring children into the world, but that they would provide a secure and loving home for them. The birth of a baby is a time of rejoicing for the beginning of a new life, a gift from God. God gives most, however, to those parents who give their children back to Him in recognition that they are a gift from Him, in dedicating themselves to bringing up their children in God's ways and in declaring to the world that their children, although unable yet to understand what it means, belong, in faith, to the family of God and not to whatever other religions there may be around them.

The birth and dedication of a baby

God created man in His own image, in the image of God He created him; male and female He created them. God blessed them and said to them, "Be fruitful and increase in numbers. Fill the earth and subdue it." [1]

Esau looked up and saw the women and children, and said, "Who are these with you?" Jacob answered, "They are the children God has graciously given your servant." [2]

Hannah conceived and in due time gave birth to a son. She named him Samuel because, she said, "I asked the Eternal-God for him." ... When she had weaned him, she took him, together with a bull, an ephah of flour and a skin of wine, to the house of the Eternal-God at Shiloh. They sacrificed the bull and brought the boy to Eli. Hannah said to him, "O my Lord, as surely as you live, I am the woman who stood here beside you praying to the Eternal-God. It was for this child that I prayed, and the Eternal-God has given me what I asked of Him. Now I give him to the Eternal-God. For as long as he lives he is given to the Eternal-God." [3]

While they [Joseph and Mary] were there, the time came for the baby to be born, and she gave birth to her first-born Son. She wrapped Him in swaddling cloths and laid Him in a manger, because there was no room for them in the inn. [4]

Then little children were brought to Jesus that He might put His hands on them and pray for them. But the disciples rebuked those who brought them. Jesus said, "Leave the children alone. Let them come to me and do not hinder them, for it is to such as these that the kingdom of heaven belongs. He placed His hands on them and then went on His way. [5]

[Isaiah:] Comfort! comfort my people, says your God, speak tenderly to Jerusalem. ... See, the Sovereign Eternal-God comes with great might. ... His reward is with Him and His recompense before Him. He tends His flock like a shepherd. He gathers the lambs in His arms and carries them close to His heart." [6]

[1] Genesis 1:27-28 [2] Genesis 33:5-6 [3] 1 Samuel 1:20, 24-28 [4] Luke 2:6-7 [5] Matthew 19:13-15 [6] Isaiah 40:1,10-11

Special Occasions 17

Wherever a person—man or woman, single or married—lives, that is 'home'. When a man and a woman are married, wherever they begin their new life together is 'home'. When children are born, the home becomes larger. When a person or a family moves from one place to another, where they move to becomes a 'new home'. Homes, houses and families are meant to be centres of peace to those who live in them and light to the people around. God blesses the homes of those who honour Him in their individual lives, family relationships and witness to their neighbours and visitors.

A new home

Joshua gathered all the tribes of Israel ... and said to them: "This is what God says, 'I have given you a land for which you did not work and cities you did not build, ... you eat of vineyards and olive groves which you did not plant. Now, therefore, fear the Eternal-God and serve him faithfully. ... But if to serve the Eternal-God is not what you want, then choose for yourselves this day whom you will serve, ... as for me and my household, we will serve the Eternal-God. [1]

[Moses:] If a man has just married, he must not be sent to war or be charged with any other duty. For one year he is to be free to stay at home and enjoy happiness with the wife he has just married. [2]

[David:] I will sing of your mercy and justice. To you, O Eternal-God, I will sing. I will take care to live a blameless life. O when will you come to me? In my house I will live with integrity of heart. I will set before my eyes nothing that is base.[3]

[Jesus:] Whoever hears these words of mine and acts on them is like a wise man who built his house on the rock. ... And whoever does not act on them is like a fool who built his house on the sand. [4] No foundation can anyone lay other than that which is already laid, that is Jesus Christ. [5] So do not worry, saying, 'What shall we eat?' or 'What shall we drink?' or 'What shall we wear?' It is godless people who run after all these things. [God] your heavenly Father knows that you need them. So seek first His kingdom and His righteousness and all these things will be given to you as well. [6]

All the believers were together and had everything in common. They sold their possessions and gave to all according to their needs. Every day they met together in the temple courts, and in their homes they broke bread, ate together with glad and generous hearts, praised God and enjoyed the favour of the people. [7]

May God be gracious to us and bless us and make His face to shine upon us, that your ways may be known on earth, your saving power among all nations. [8]

[1] Joshua 24:1,13-15 [2] Deuteronomy 24:5 [3] Psalm 101:1-3 [4] Matthew 7:24-25 [5] 1 Corinthians 3:11 [6] Matthew 6:31-33 [7] Acts 2:44-47 [8] Psalm 67:1-2

Special Occasions 18

An anniversary is a time to look back with thankfulness to God and to look forward with faith in Him. The feasts of the Passover and Pentecost celebrated anniversaries of past events, and they also held promise for the future. Remembrance with gratitude leads to a determined consecration to live in the light of past events and with renewed faith in God who keeps all his promises.

An anniversary

The Eternal-God gave Israel all the land He had sworn to their forefathers to give them. ... Not one of all the good things which the Eternal-God had promised to the house of Israel failed; every one came to pass. [1]

[Solomon:] Blessed be the Eternal-God, who has given rest to His people Israel according to all His promises. Not one word has failed of all the good things He promised through His servant Moses. May the Eternal-God, our God, be with us as He was with our forefathers. May He never leave us nor forsake us, and may He turn our hearts to Him, to walk in all His ways, and to keep His commandments. [2]

As Samuel was offering up the burnt offering, the Philistines approached to attack Israel, but that day the Eternal-God thundered loudly against the Philistines and they were thrown into confusion and were defeated. ... Then Samuel took a stone and set it up between Mizpah and Jeshanah and named it 'Ebenezer', saying, "Thus far has the Eternal-God helped us. [3]

O give thanks to the Eternal-God, call on His name and make His deeds known among the people. Sing praises to Him and tell of all His wonderful works. Seek the Eternal-God and His strength, seek His presence continually. Remember the wonderful deeds He has done. [4]

Know that the Eternal-God is God indeed. It is He who made us and we are His. We are His people and the sheep of His pasture. Enter His gates with thanksgiving and His courts with praise. Give thanks to Him and praise His name. [5] For the Eternal-God is a sun and shield. He bestows favour and honour, and no good thing does He withhold from those whose lives are blameless. [6]

Remember your leaders who brought to you the word of God, and consider what has happened as a result. Jesus Christ is the same, yesterday, today and for ever. [7]

[Moses:] Lord, you have been our dwelling-place throughout all generations. Before the mountains came to be, and earth and the world were formed, from everlasting to everlasting you are God. ... Teach us to number our days, that we may gain a heart of wisdom. [8]

[1] Joshua 21:43,45   [2] 1 Kings 8:56-57   [3] 1 Samuel 7:12   [4] 1 Chronicles 16:8,11-12   [5] Psalm 100:3-4
[6] Psalm 84:11   [7] Hebrews 13:8   [8] Psalm 90:1-2,12

Special Occasions 19

Abraham was the first person whom God called to go to another place and change his work. Whenever God calls people to new tasks, He gives them the unfailing promise that He will be with them and will guide them. For some, new tasks mean great changes; for others, they may make little difference. God called David from being a shepherd to being a king. For Stephen, it was to use his administrative skills in a new way.

Beginning a new career

The Eternal-God said to Abram, "Go from your country, your people and your father's house and go to the land I will show you." [1]

The Eternal-God said to Moses, "I have seen the misery of my people in Egypt. ... Now go, I am sending you to Pharaoh so that you may bring my people out of Egypt. Moses said to God, "Who am I, that I should go to Pharoah and bring the Israelites out of Egypt." God said, "I will be with you." [2]

The angel of the Eternal-God turned to him [Gideon] and said, "Go in the strength that you have and save Israel from the hand of Midian. Have I not sent you?" Gideon said to him, "How can I deliver Israel? My clan is the weakest in Manasseh, and I am the least in my family. The angel said to him, "I will be with you." [3]

[God spoke through Isaiah:] When you turn to the right or when you turn to the left, your ears will hear a voice behind you, saying, "This is the way; walk in it." [4]

As Jesus was walking by the Sea of Galilee, He saw two brothers, Simon called Peter and his brother Andrew who were casting a net into the lake. ... Jesus said to them, "Come follow me and I will make you fishers of men." [5]

At that time, when the number of disciples was increasing rapidly, the Hellenists [Greek-speaking Jews] among them complained against the ordinary Jews because their widows were being overlooked in the daily distribution of food. The twelve called together all the disciples and said to them, "Choose seven men of good repute among you, who are known to be full of [God the Holy] Spirit and wisdom to whom we may give this responsibility. ... They presented these men to the apostles, and they prayed and laid their hands on them. [6]

While they [the church leaders] were worshipping the Lord and fasting, the Holy Spirit said, "Set apart for me Barnabas and Saul for the work to which I have called them. After they had fasted and prayed they placed their hands on them and sent them on their way. [7]

[Paul] Whether you eat or drink or whatever you do, do it all for the glory of God. [8]

[1] Genesis 12:1   [2] Exodus 3:11-12   [3] Judges 6:14-16   [4] Isaiah 30:21   [5] Matthew 4:18-20
[6] Acts 6:1-3,6   [7] Acts 13:2-3   [8] 1 Corinthians 10:31

Special Occasions 20

To doubt can be a necessary exercise which leads to a fuller understanding and a stronger conviction of truth. It can also be a rejection of truth because it is not acceptable. God has made people so that they have to search for Him in His universe in order to find Him. God has promised to give certainty about the most important facts of our lives - that He is there, forgiveness of sins and security in His family. Doubts are cleared as the person seeks genuinely to know the truth and acts honestly with what is known to be true.

A time of spiritual doubt

Eliphaz the Temanite answered him [Job], "Can a man be of any value to God? Can even the wise be of service to Him? Does it give the Almighty any pleasure that you are righteous.?" [1] Job answered, "If only I knew where to find him [God]; if only I could go to where He dwells! I would lay my case before Him and fill my mouth with arguments. ... If I go east, He is not there; if I go west, I cannot find Him. ... but He knows the way that I take; when He has tested me, I shall come forth as gold." [2] The secret of the Eternal-God is with those who fear Him. He will make His covenant known to them. [3]

Peter climbed out of the boat, walked on the water and came towards Jesus. But when he saw the strong wind, he was frightened. As he began to sink, he cried out, "Lord, save me!" Immediately Jesus reached out His hand and caught him, saying, "O you of little faith, why did you doubt?" [4]

A week later His disciples were in the house again and Thomas was with them. Although the doors were closed, Jesus came and stood among them and said, "Peace be with you!" Then He said to Thomas, "Put your finger here and see my hands; reach out your hand and put it into my side. Do not doubt but believe." Thomas said to him, "My Lord and my God!" Jesus said to him, "Because you have seen me, you believe; blessed are those who have not seen me and yet believe." [5]

[Paul:] We have not received the spirit of the world but the Spirit who is from God so that we may understand what God has given us. ... The unspiritual person does not accept the things which come from the Spirit of God for they are foolishness to him, and he is unable to understand them for they are spiritually discerned.[6]

Half way through the Feast [of Tabernacles] Jesus went into the temple and began to teach. The Jews were astonished and said, "How is it that this man has such learning when He has never been taught. Jesus answered them, "My teaching is not my own but is from Him who sent me. If anyone desires to do God's will, He will know whether the teaching comes from God or whether I speak on my own." [7]

---

[1] Job 22:.1-3   [2] Job 23:1-5,8,10   [3] Psalm 25:14   [4] Matthew 14:29-31   [5] John 20:26-29
[6] 1 Corinthians 2:12-14   [7] John 7:16-17

Special Occasions 21

There is a point at which care and concern for someone or some situation becomes anxiety. It is there that we are reminded that our lives are in God's hands and He cares for us. There are times when we can do nothing to affect the situation or help a person in need or danger; but we can commit everything into the hands of God who works for the good of everyone in every situation.

A time of anxiety

"Comfort, O comfort my people, says your God. ... Why do you say, O Jacob, and declare, O Israel, 'my way is hidden from the Eternal-God and my right is ignored by God.' Do you not know? Have you not heard? The Eternal-God, the Creator of the ends of the earth, does not faint or grow weary and His understanding is beyond measure." [1] "Do not fear, for I am with you; do not be afraid, for I am your God. I will strengthen you and help you and I will support you with my right hand. [2]

[Jesus said:] "Stop worrying! Do not say, 'What shall we eat?' or 'What shall we drink? or 'What shall we wear?' For the ungodly seek after all these things, and your heavenly Father knows what you need. Seek first His kingdom and His righteousness and all these things will be given to you as well. Do not worry about tomorrow for tomorrow will have its own worries." [3] "Come to me, all you who are weary and burdened, and I will give you rest. Take my yoke upon you and learn from me, for I am gentle and humble in heart, and you will find rest for your souls, for my yoke is easy and my burden is light." [4]

[Paul:] Do not be anxious about anything, but in everything, by prayer and supplication, with thanksgiving, make your requests to God. And the peace of God, which surpasses all understanding, will guard your hearts and your minds in Christ Jesus. [5]

Keep your lives free from the love of money and be content with what you have, because God has said, "I will never leave you nor forsake you. So we say with confidence, "The Lord is my helper, I will not be afraid. What can any one do to me?" [6]

[James:] Is any one of you suffering? He should pray. Is any one joyful? Let him sing praise to God. Is any one of you sick? He should call the elders of the church to pray over him and anoint him with oil in the name of the Lord, and the prayer offered in faith will restore him. If he has sinned, he will be forgiven. Confess your sins to each other and pray for each other so that you may be restored. [7]

[Peter:] Cast all your anxiety on Him because He cares for you. ... And after you have suffered a little while, the God of all grace, who has called you to His eternal glory in Christ, will Himself restore you and settle you. [8]

[1] Isaiah 40:1,27-28 [2] Isaiah 41:10 [3] Matthew 6:31-34 [4] Matthew 11:28-30 [5] Philippians 4:6-7 [6] Hebrews 13:5-6 [7] James 5:13-16 [8] 1 Peter 5:7,10

Special Occasions 22

Temptation to sin comes in many different ways and often when the Christian feels least able to withstand it. Jesus was also tempted and His example is a guide. The most powerful means of resisting temptation comes from a deep understanding of what God has done in saving from sin and giving an inheritance which far surpasses anything that this world can offer. When the gains of the sin to which one is being tempted are seen relative to what God gives, it is possible so to consider oneself 'dead to sin' that temptation loses its power. Jesus resisted temptation because of the 'joy that was set before Him'. God enables us to resist as we allow Him to show us what we lose by sinning compared to what we gain by resisting.

A time of temptation

Jesus [God the Son] was led by [God] the [Holy] Spirit into the wilderness to be tempted by the devil [Satan]. ... The devil said to Him, "If you are the Son of God, command these stones to become bread. ... All the kingdoms of the world I will give you if you will bow down and worship me. ... Throw yourself down, for it is written: 'He will command His angels ... so that you will not dash your foot against a stone.'" ... Jesus answered, "It is written: 'Man does not live by bread alone. ... Worship the Eternal-God, your God, and serve Him only. ... Do not put God to the test." [1]

We do not have a high priest who is unable to understand out weaknesses, but we have One who has been tempted in every respect just as we are, yet without sin. Let us then approach the 'throne of grace' with confidence, so that we may receive mercy and find grace to help us when we need it. [2] He himself suffered temptation and He is, therefore, able to help those who are being tempted. [3]

[Peter:] If He [God] rescued Lot, a righteous man, who was distressed by the immoral lives of lawless men, ... then the Lord knows how to rescue godly people from temptation and keep the unrighteous for the day of judgment. [4]

[James:] When tempted, no one should say, "I am being tempted by God." For God cannot be tempted by evil, and He himself tempts no one. Every person is tempted when He is drawn away and enticed by His own evil desire. When desire has conceived, it gives birth to sin; and sin, when it is fully grown, gives birth to death.[5]

[Paul:] Flee from the lusts of youth. [6] Do not conform to the ways of this world but be transformed by the renewing of your mind. [7] [James:] Submit yourselves to God. Resist the devil and He will flee from you.[8]

[Paul:] No temptation has overtaken you which is not common to everyone. God is faithful and He will not let you be tempted beyond what you can endure, but will, as you are being tempted, provide a way to enable you to resist it. [9]

---

[1] Matthew 4:1-10 [2] Hebrews 4:15-16 [3] Hebrews 2:18 [4] 2 Peter 2:7-9 [5] James 1:13-15
[6] 2 Timothy 2:22 [7] Romans 12:2 [8] James 4:7 [9] 1 Corinthians 10:13

Special Occasions 23

When we say Goodbye to each other, we do not say Goodbye to God. Parting is a painful experience, especially when those leaving each other love each other in either a human or in God's family. We were designed to enjoy each others' company and so to leave this can be difficult. As children of God, Goodbye becomes the prayer: "God be with you."

A parting of loved ones

Jacob dreamed that there was a ladder set up on the earth with its top reaching to heaven. Angels of God were ascending and descending on it. The Eternal-God stood beside him and said, "I am the Eternal-God. ... I am with you and I will watch over you wherever you go, and I will bring you back to this land. I will not leave you until I have done all that I have promised you" [1]

[Samuel:] As for me, far be it from me that I should sin against the Eternal-God by failing to pray for you, ... only fear the Eternal-God and serve Him faithfully with all your heart. Think of how great are the things He has done for you. [2]

My help comes from the Eternal-God who made heaven and earth. He will not let your foot slip, He who keeps you will not slumber. ... The Eternal-God is your keeper. ... The Eternal-God will keep you from evil; He will keep your life; He will watch over your coming and your going, now and for evermore. [3]

[David] Where can I go from your Spirit? Where can I flee from your presence? If I ascend into heaven, you are there; if I make my bed in Sheol [the place of the dead], you are there. If I take the wings of the morning and settle on the farthest limits of the sea, even there your hand will guide me and your right hand will hold me fast. If I say, "Surely the darkness will hide me and the light around me become night," even the darkness is not dark to you, and the night is as bright as the day, for darkness is as light to you. ... All the days ordained for me were written in your book when there was as yet none of them. [4]

[Paul:] Who shall separate us from the love of Christ? Shall suffering or distress or persecution or famine or nakedness or danger or sword? ... No, in all these things we are more than conquerors through Him who loved us. For I am convinced that neither death, nor life, nor angels, nor demons, nor the present, nor the future, nor any powers, nor height, nor depth, nor anything else in all creation, will be able to separate us from the love of God that is in Christ Jesus our Lord. [5]

May the grace of [God the Son] the Lord Jesus Christ, and the love of God [the Father], and the fellowship of [God] the Holy Spirit be with you all. [6]

---

[1] Genesis 28:15　[2] 1 Samuel 12:23　[3] Psalm 121:2-4,7　[4] Psalm 139:7-12,16
[5] Romans 8:35-39　[6] 2 Corinthians 13:14

Special Occasions 24

When a person is dying, he or she is nearing the end of their human life, but not the end of their spiritual life. Those whose names are written in the 'Lamb's book of life' have nothing to fear: great joy awaits them. Those who have never repented of their sin and trusted in Christ have much to fear. Some people are confident of their place in heaven. Others are not. It is impossible for those looking on to be sure and so, as death approaches, there is a combination of warning and of joyous anticipation.

Approaching death

By faith Jacob, when he was dying, blessed each of Joseph's sons, and bowed in prayer as he leaned on the top of his staff. [1]

If we deliberately persist in sinning after we have received the knowledge of the truth, there is no sacrifice for sins left, but only a fearful prospect of judgment and of fire that will consume the enemies of God. [2]

One of the criminals who hung there hurled insults at Him [Jesus]. ... But the other criminal rebuked him, saying, "Do you not fear God? We are suffering justly, for we are receiving what our deeds deserve. But this Man has done nothing wrong." Then he said, "Jesus, remember me when you come into your kingdom." Jesus answered him, "I tell you the truth, today you will be with me in paradise." [3]

[David:] The Eternal-God is my shepherd, I shall not be in want. He makes me lie down in green pastures. He leads me beside quiet waters. He restores my soul. He leads me in the paths of righteousness for His name's sake. Even though I walk through the valley of the shadow of death, I will fear no evil, for you are with me, your rod and your staff comfort me. ... Surely goodness and unfailing love will follow me all the days of my life, and I will dwell in the house of the Eternal-God for ever. [4]

[Paul:] For me, to live is Christ and to die is gain. ... I am torn between the two: My desire is to depart and be with Christ, which is far better, but to remain in my body is more necessary for you. [5] I am already being poured out as a libation [ceremonial drink-offering], and the time for my departure is near. I have fought the good fight, I have finished the race, I have kept the faith. There is reserved for me the crown of righteousness, which the Lord, the righteous Judge, will award me on that day, and not only to me, but also to all who have longed for His appearing. [6]

[Job:] I know that my Redeemer lives, and that, at the last, He will stand upon the earth. And after my skin has been destroyed, then in my flesh I will see God. I shall see Him with my own eyes, and He will not be as a stranger! [7]

[1] Hebrews 11:21 [2] Hebrews 10:26-27 [3] Luke 23:39-43 [4] Psalm 23:1-4,6 [5] Philippians 1:21-24
[6] 2 Timothy 4:6-8 [7] Job 19:25-27

The death of a loved one is a sad event, but it is not without hope. There is sorrow, and that is natural and right. God appears to be particularly concerned to comfort those who mourn. God's comfort is not just sympathy; it is rather the giving of a sure hope that death is not the end. He has conquered death and in heaven there will be no more parting and no more tears.

Bereavement

Jesus said to her [Martha]: "I am the resurrection and the life. He who believes in me, even though he dies, yet he will live, and whoever lives and believes in me will never die. Do you believe this?" [1]

[Paul:] Brothers and sisters, we do not want you to be ignorant about those who fall asleep, so that you do not grieve like those who have no hope. As we believe that Jesus died and rose again, so we believe that God will bring with Jesus those who have fallen asleep in Him. [2]

The fact is that Christ has indeed been raised from the dead, the first-fruits of those who have fallen asleep. For since through a man, death came into the world, so also through a Man has come the resurrection from the dead. For as in Adam all die, so in Christ all will be made alive. ... When the perishable has put on the imperishable, and the mortal has put immortality, then will be fulfilled the Scripture which says, "Death has been swallowed up in victory. Where, O death, is your victory? Where, O death, is your sting? [3]

[John:] Then I heard a voice from heaven say, "Write this: Blessed are the dead who die in the Lord from now on. "Yes," says [God] the [Holy] Spirit, "they will rest from their labours, for their deeds will follow them." [4]

[Paul:] The Lord himself will descend from heaven, with a loud cry of command, ... and the dead in Christ will rise first. Then we who are still alive and are left will be caught up in the clouds together with them to meet the Lord in the air. And so we will be with the Lord for ever. [5]

[John:] Then I saw [in a vision] a new heaven and a new earth, for the first heaven and the first earth had passed away. ... And I heard a loud voice from the throne saying: "See! The home of God is with men, and He will live with them. They will be His people, and He Himself will be with them and will be their God. He will wipe every tear from their eyes, and there will be no more death, nor mourning, nor crying, nor pain, for the old order of things has passed away. He who is seated on the throne said, "See! I am making all things new." [6]

[1] John 11:25   [2] 1 Thessalonians 4:13-14   [3] 1 Corinthians 15:20-22,54-55   [4] Revelation 14:13
[5] 1 Thessalonians 4:16-17   [6] Revelation 21:1,3-5

Special Occasions 26

Jesus warned His disciples that they would be persecuted for His sake. He also promised that He would be with them in their suffering for Him. There would be those who would be killed because of their testimony to Jesus. Since then there have been many martyrs, and there are still today, those die for their faith in Jesus. Persecution for Jesus' sake is painful, but there is also joy in following Him and the promise of a 'crown of life' in the life to come.

A time of persecution

[Jesus to His disciples:] See, I am sending you out as sheep among wolves, so be wise as serpents and as guileless as doves. Be on your guard against men, for they will hand you over to councils and flog you in their synagogues. You will be brought before governors and kings on my account to bear witness to them and to the Gentiles. When they arrest you, do not be anxious about what you will say or how you will say it. What you are to say will be given you at that moment, for it will not be you speaking, but the Spirit of your Father speaking through you. [1] Then they will hand you over to be tortured and put to death. You will be hated by all nations because of my name. [2] I have told you all these things so that you will not be taken by surprise. They will put you out of the synagogues. A time is coming when whoever kills you will think he is offering a service to God. They will do these things because they have not known [God] the Father nor me [God the Son].[3]

[Paul] Indeed, all who want to live a godly life in Christ Jesus will be persecuted, while evil men and imposters will go from bad to worse. [4]

When the Lamb opened the fifth seal, I saw under the altar the souls of those who had been slain for the word of God and for their testimony. ... Then each of them was given a white robe, and they were told to wait a little while longer until the number was completed of their fellow-servants and brothers and sisters who were to be killed as they had been. [5] Now the salvation, the power and the kingdom of our God have come, for the accuser of our brothers and sisters [Satan], who accuses them before our God day and night, has been thrown down. They overcame him by the blood of the Lamb and by the word of their testimony, for they did not cling to their lives even when faced with death. [6]

[Paul:] Who shall separate us from the love of Christ? Shall suffering or hardship or persecution or famine or nakedness or danger or sword? As it is written, "For your sake we are put to death all day long. We are regarded as sheep for the slaughter." Yet, in all these things we are more than conquerors through Him who loved us. [7]

[1] Matthew 10:16-20 [2] Matthew 24:9 [3] John 16:1-3 [4] 2 Timothy 3:12-13 [5] Revelation 6:9-11
[6] Revelation 12:10-11 [7] Romans 8:35-37

The greatest story ever told

Adam to Joseph

1	God created the heavens and the earth	Genesis 1:1,3,11,16,20,24,31
2	God created Man in His own image	Genesis 1:26-27
3	God created man - male and female	Genesis 2:20-23
4	God planned for marriage	Genesis 2:18,21-24
5	Satan, the accuser	Genesis 3:1
6	Sin enters through Adam and Eve	Genesis 2:8-9,15-17
7	Sin separates people from God	Genesis 3:6-13,16-19,23
8	God planned for the wearing of clothes	Genesis 2:22,25
9	Cain murders Abel	Genesis 4:3-16
10	God shows Cain and Abel how to worship Him	Genesis 4:3-5
11	The great cities of the world	Genesis 4:16-17
12	Nomads and pilgrims	Genesis 4:19-20
13	The father of musicians	Genesis 4:20-21
14	The father of metal craftsmen	Genesis 4:19,22
15	God's judgment on a wicked people	Genesis 6:11,5-7,13,17-19,22
16	God's covenant with Noah	Genesis 7:1,11-12,23
17	The Tower of Babel	Genesis 11:1-9
18	Job is tested	Job 1:8-22
19	Job prays for his friends	Job 42:1-13
20	God calls Abram and changes his name him to Abraham	Genesis 12:1-4
21	Lot makes his choice	Genesis 13:5-13
22	The birth of Ishmael	Genesis 16:1,3-11,15
23	God fulfils His promise to give Abraham a son	Genesis 18:1-5,8-10,13-14
24	Abraham pleads for Lot	Genesis 18:16,18-27,30-32
25	Sodom and Gomorrah are destroyed	Genesis 19:1-10,15-16,24-25
26	Circumcision - the sign of the covenant	Genesis 17:1-2,10-11
27	Abraham is tested	Genesis 21:1-3
28	God finds a wife for Isaac	Genesis 24:1-8,9-16,50-51
29	Esau sells his birthright	Genesis 25:21,24-27,29-34
30	Jacob dreams of a ladder	Genesis 28:10-19
31	Joseph's dreams	Genesis 37:3-14,17-20,23-24,26-28,34
32	Joseph is tested at work and in prison	Genesis 39:1-12,19-21
33	Joseph and Pharaoh's dreams	Genesis 41:1-16,25,28-30,39-40
34	Joseph meets his brothers again	Genesis 42:1-2,6-8,18-22

Egypt to Canaan

35	Israel becomes a nation of slaves in Egypt	Exodus 1:7-13
36	God's chosen people	Deuteronomy 6:4
37	The birth of Moses	Exodus 1:8,15
38	The call of Moses	Exodus 3:1-10

Jesus Christ, the Messiah

The Apostles and the Church

Special Occasions